The **Rough Guide** to

Florida

written and researched by

Stephen Keeling, Rebecca Strauss, and Ross Velton

ROUGH GUIDES

www.roughguides.com

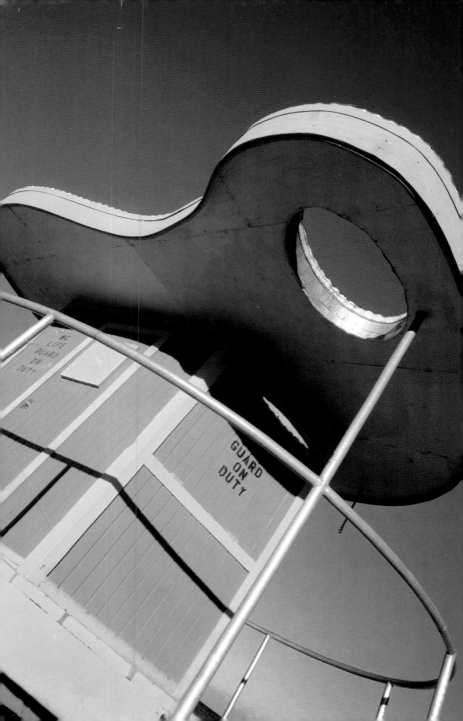

Contents

Color section   1

Introduction 04
Where to go 06
When to go 09
Things not to miss 11

Basics   17

Getting there........................... 19
Getting around......................... 23
Accommodation...................... 27
Food and drink 29
The media............................... 33
Festivals.................................. 34
Sports..................................... 34
  Watersports and outdoor
  activities 36
Traveling with children 38
Travel essentials 39

Guide   51

1 Miami 53
2 The Florida Keys 119
3 The Everglades 167
4 The Southeast................... 183
5 Sarasota and the
  Southwest.....................…..231

6 Orlando and Disney
  World. 271
7 The Northeast 319
8 Tampa Bay and the
  Northwest ....…361
9 The Panhandle................. 413

Contexts   455

The historical framework........ 457
Natural Florida 472
Florida on film 480
Books 487

Travel store   495

Small print & Index   499

Coastal Florida
colour section following
p.144

Unexpected Florida
colour section following
p.304

◄◄ Causeway above Biscayne Bay ◄ Lifeguard tower, Miami

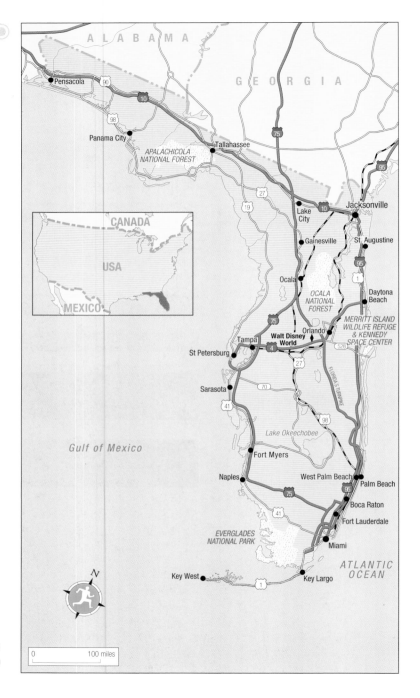

Introduction to
Florida

The cut-rate package trips and photos of tanning flesh and Mickey Mouse that fill the pages of glossy vacation brochures ensure that everyone has an image of Florida – but seldom one that's either accurate or complete. Pulling in over eighty million visitors a year to its beaches and theme parks, the aptly nicknamed "Sunshine State" is devoted to the tourist trade, yet it's also among the least understood parts of the US, with a history, character, and diversity of landscape unmatched by any other region. Beyond the palm-fringed sands, hiking and canoeing trails wind through little-known forests and rivers, and the famed beaches themselves can vary wildly over a short distance – hordes of copper-toned partiers are often just a Frisbee's throw from a deserted, pristine strand coveted by wildlife-watchers. Variations continue inland, where busy, modern cities are rarely more than a few miles away from steamy, primeval swamps.

With an average of a thousand people a day moving to Florida, the state's demographics have gradually been changing, challenging the common notion that Florida is dominated by retirees (though, coincidentally, the state song is a venerable spiritual entitled "Old Folks at Home") or is part of the conservative Deep South – even if similarities do abound. The new Floridians tend to be a younger breed, taking advantage of the economic development along the Interstate Highway 4 corridor in the center of the state – and Florida's lack of a state income tax. Immigration from outside the country has also been on the increase, with Spanish- and French-Creole-speaking enclaves providing a reminder of geographic and economic ties to Latin America and the Caribbean. These links proved almost as influential in raising the state's material

5

Fact file

- Spanish explorers named this territory after Pascua Florida, the "feast of flowers" celebrated at Easter; it was during this festival in 1513 that Ponce de León and crew landed on Florida's shores.

- Florida's 447-mile-long peninsula stretches between the Gulf of Mexico and the Atlantic Ocean and features 663 miles of beaches and about 4500 individual islands of ten acres or more.

- Five flags have been flown here: the French (1564), Spanish (1565–1763 and 1783–1821), British (1763–83), Confederate (1861–65), and US (1821–61 and 1865 to the present). It was admitted as the 27th state in the Union in 1845; the capital is Tallahassee.

- Though 22nd in total area with 58,560 square miles, Florida is the fourth most populous state in the US, with more than eighteen million people.

- The two major industries are tourism and agriculture; in fact, Florida produces more citrus, tomatoes, green peppers, watermelon, sweet corn, and sugar than any other state.

- There are more golf courses in Florida than any other US state (nearly 1500), with the greatest concentration found in Palm Beach, which has more courses than any other county.

◀ Hawksbill sea turtle

wealth in the 1990s as the arrival of huge domestic and international businesses. However, with the bursting of Florida's real estate bubble and the economic crisis that rocked the US in 2008, the growth of both the state's economy and population looks like slowing down for the first time in decades.

> **Hordes of copper-toned partiers are often just a Frisbee's throw from a deserted, pristine strand coveted by wildlife-watchers**

Not everyone has benefited from the state's growth; levels of poverty in the rural areas can be severe, and in an increasingly multi-ethnic society, racial tensions frequently surface. Another hot issue is how towns should be expanded to accommodate the burgeoning population without jeopardizing the environment; uncontrolled development is posing serious ecological problems – not least to the Everglades. Nevertheless, large

Florida sun

Any visitor with sensitive skin should remember Florida shares a latitude with the Sahara Desert; the power of the **sun** in the state should never be underestimated – no matter where you are.

Time spent outdoors should be planned carefully at first, especially between 11am and 2pm, when the sun is at its strongest. A powerful **sunscreen** is essential; anything with an SPF of less than 25 is unlikely to offer the necessary protection. Make sure to apply sunscreen liberally about thirty minutes before venturing outdoors (so that your skin has a chance to absorb it) and re-apply every two hours or if you've been in the water, regardless of whether the sunscreen is labeled "waterproof." Light-colored, loose-fitting, lightweight clothes should protect any parts of your body not accustomed to direct sunlight. Wear a hat with a wide brim as well as sunglasses with UV protection, and keep to the shaded side of the street. Drink plenty of **fluids** (but not alcohol) to prevent dehydration – public drinking-water fountains are provided for this purpose.

amounts of land are under state or federal protection, and there are signs that the conservation lobby is gaining the upper hand. For the most part, however, these factors will remain unfelt by visitors to Florida, who are likely to find its relentlessly sunny disposition and natural splendor difficult to resist.

Where to go

Florida is compact enough to be toured easily and quickly. The essential stop is **Miami**, whose addictive, cosmopolitan vibe is enriched by its large Hispanic population, and where the much-photographed Art Deco district of **South Beach** provides an unmistakeable backdrop for the state's best nightlife.

From Miami, a simple journey south brings you to the **Florida Keys**: a hundred-mile

▼ Key West

Cuban heritage

Nowhere is evidence of Florida's **Cuban heritage** stronger than in **Miami**. Cubans began fleeing the Batista and Castro regimes in the 1950s and 1960s, heading for the closest major city on US shores; many more were boatlifted there a few decades later. The influx has gradually reshaped the city, making it in essence a bilingual one; Hispanics, mostly of Cuban descent, now account for the majority of Miami's population, and their influence is felt in everything from the *nuevo cubano* cuisine in haute South Beach restaurants to local politics. Dominating the latter, the expatriate Cuban community here is largely composed of middle-class professionals, a staunchly conservative group that funds powerful lobbying at both state and federal levels.

Key West and **Tampa**, meanwhile, benefited enormously from the presence of the Cuban cigar industry. Merchants regularly commuted between factories in Key West and plantations in Havana; when Key West's fortunes failed in the 1880s, the Cuban workers decamped to Tampa further up the coast – then a small, nondescript settlement – and helped turn it into "The Cigar Capital of the World," a title the city would enjoy for forty years. With the mass arrival of the workers – as well as the railroad – Tampa was transformed into the commercial hub it remains today.

string of islands, each with its own special draw, be it sport fishing, coral-reef diving, or a unique species of dwarf deer. The single road spanning the Keys comes to a halt at **Key West**, a blob of land that's legendary for its sunsets and anything-goes attitude. North from Miami, much of the **southeast coast** is a disappointingly urbanized commuter strip. Alongside the busy towns, however, beaches flow for many unbroken miles and finally escape the

> **The Art Deco district of South Beach provides an unmistakeable backdrop for the state's best nightclubs**

residential stranglehold along the **northeast coast**, where communities are often subservient to the sands that flank them.

When you tire of beach life and ocean views, make a short hop inland, where the verdant terrain features cattle farms, grassy hillsides, and isolated villages beside expansive lakes. The sole but rather dramatic disruption to this rural idyll are the theme parks around Orlando, notably **Walt Disney**

World, which practices tourism on the scale of the infinite. If you're not in the mood to indulge in this ingenious fix of escapist fun, skip north to the deep forests of the **Panhandle** – Florida's link with the Deep South – or to the artsy towns and sunset-kissed beaches of the **northwest and southwest coasts**. Explore these at your leisure as you progress steadily south to **the Everglades**, a massive, alligator-filled swathe of sawgrass plain, mangrove islands, and cypress swamp, which provides a definitive statement of Florida's natural beauty.

When to go

You'll have to take into account Florida's climate – and, of course, what your goals are – when deciding on the best time for a visit. Florida is split into **two climatic zones**: subtropical in the south and warm temperate – like the rest of the southeastern US – in the north. These two zones determine the state's tourist seasons and can affect costs accordingly.

Anywhere **south of Orlando** experiences very mild winters (Nov–April), with pleasantly warm temperatures and a low level of humidity. This is the peak period for tourist activity, with prices at their highest and crowds at their largest. It also marks the best time to visit the inland parks and

Theme parks

Florida's most trumpeted attractions, its grandiose **theme parks**, offer prefabricated entertainment to millions of visitors – and locals – annually. When Walt Disney began secretly purchasing nearly thirty thousand acres of land in central Florida during the late 1960s, few could have

guessed the impending seismic shift in the state's fortunes. The vast and lucrative vacation complex that resulted opened the floodgates to a number of imitators, including nearby Universal Orlando and SeaWorld Orlando, as well as Busch Gardens in Tampa. Notwithstanding the unabashed commercialism that pervades them all, each park has its own appeal and they can be great fun for adults and kids alike if approached with buckets of enthusiasm.

swamps. The southern summer (May–Oct) seems hotter than it really is (New York is often warmer) because of the extremely high humidity, relieved only by afternoon thunderstorms and sometimes even hurricanes (though the chances of being there during one are remote). Lower prices and fewer tourists are the rewards for braving the mugginess, though mosquitoes can render the natural areas off-limits.

Winter is the off-peak period **north of Orlando**; in all probability, the only chill you'll detect is a slight nip in the evening air, though it's worth bearing in mind that at this time of year the sea is really too cold for swimming,

▼ John Pennekamp Coral Reef State Park

and snow has been known to fall in the Panhandle. The northern Florida summer is when the crowds arrive, and when the days – and the nights – can be almost as hot and sticky as southern Florida.

Average temperatures

	Jan	Feb	Mar	Apr	May	Jun	Jul	Aug	Sept	Oct	Nov	Dec
Jacksonville												
°F	53	55	62	68	74	80	82	82	78	70	62	56
°C	12	13	17	20	23	27	28	28	26	21	17	13
Key West												
°F	70	70	74	77	81	83	85	84	83	80	76	72
°C	21	21	23	25	27	28	29	29	28	27	24	22
Miami												
°F	67	68	72	75	79	81	83	83	82	78	73	69
°C	19	20	22	24	26	27	28	28	28	26	23	21
Orlando												
°F	61	61	67	73	78	81	83	83	81	75	67	62
°C	16	16	19	23	26	27	28	28	27	24	19	17
Pensacola												
°F	51	54	60	67	75	80	82	82	78	69	61	54
°C	11	12	16	19	24	27	28	28	26	21	16	12
Tallahassee												
°F	51	53	60	66	74	80	81	81	78	68	60	53
°C	11	12	16	19	23	27	27	27	26	20	16	12
Tampa												
°F	60	61	67	71	77	81	82	82	81	75	68	63
°C	16	16	19	22	25	27	28	28	27	24	20	17

things not to miss

It's not possible to see everything that Florida has to offer in one trip — and we don't suggest you try. What follows is a selective taste of the state's highlights: great beaches, outstanding national parks, spectacular wildlife — even good things to eat and drink. It's arranged in five color-coded categories, which you can browse through to find the very best things to see, do, and experience. All highlights have a page reference to take you straight into the Guide, where you can find out more.

01 Kennedy Space Center Page **323** • Everything you ever wanted to know about the history of the US space program, and within sight of the launchpads on nearby Merritt Island.

03 Captain Tony's Saloon Page **160** • Relax in this rustic hangout, which Ernest Hemingway made his own during ten raucous yet productive years in Key West.

02 Miami Art Deco Page **72** • The pastel-shaded architecture of South Beach is the reason many visitors make a beeline for the area.

04 Alligator encounters Page **173** • The "keepers of the Everglades," alligators are visible throughout the national park, particularly along the Anhinga Trail.

05 **Swimming with manatees** Page **397** • Take a dip with these gentle, endangered creatures in Crystal River, north of Tampa.

06 **Cedar Key** Page **399** • This remote island off Florida's northwest coast makes an enchanting getaway, with tumble-down shacks lending an atmospheric touch.

07 **Sunshine Skyway Bridge** Page **383** • This impressive four-mile span almost seems to soar across Tampa Bay south of St Petersburg and offers fantastic views; the collapsed remnants of an earlier version of the bridge are now the longest fishing piers in the world.

09 **Miami Art Museum** Page **78** • Engaging displays of art from the 1940s to the present make this Miami institution the state's top attraction for art lovers.

08 **Cuisine** Page **29** • Sample the wide variety of excellent food the state has to offer – including the Caribbean-influenced "Floribbean" cuisine, the ever-present Cuban sandwiches, and, of course, the huge range of fresh seafood.

10 **The Amazing Adventures of Spider-Man, Islands of Adventure** Page **304** • The thrill rides at Universal Orlando's Islands of Adventure trump those of the other Orlando theme parks, perhaps none more so than this high-tech adventure.

12 Expedition Everest Mountain

Page **296** • The newest ride at Disney's Animal Kingdom features a train that careers (both forwards and backwards) around a replica of a Himalayan mountain, building up to a memorable encounter with a yeti.

11 Canoeing in the Everglades

Page **174** • Florida has innumerable creeks and swamps for canoeing, the most impressive of which are in the Everglades.

13 Sanibel Island

Page **257** • Stroll the island's sun-washed beaches in search of colorful shells.

14 **St Augustine's Old Town** Page **343** • Explore the narrow streets, preserved houses, and centuries-old fortress of America's oldest city.

15 **Apalachicola Trail** Page **429** • One of Florida's largest and most pristine national forests, Apalachicola offers endless opportunities for outdoor enthusiasts, like the thirty-mile Apalachicola Trail.

Basics

Basics

Getting there 19

Getting around 23

Accommodation.. 27

Food and drink.. 29

The media 33

Festivals 34

Sports 34

Watersports and outdoor activities 36

Traveling with children 38

Travel essentials... 39

Getting there

Florida has never been as easily accessible as it is now. Both Miami and Orlando have major international airports, and all the state's other cities and large towns – particularly Fort Lauderdale and Tampa – have good links from other US cities.

Remember airfares depend on the **season**, and Florida is split into two climatic zones (see Introduction, p.9). Flying on weekends is typically more expensive; price ranges quoted below assume midweek travel. For some of the more popular destinations, you may even find it cheaper to pick up a bargain **package deal** from one of the tour operators listed below and then find your own accommodation when you get there.

Flights from the US and Canada

Of the **major US carriers**, Delta and American Airlines have the best links with the state's many smaller regional airports. Flying in to any of the three main airports, you can expect to pay in the region of $150 for a single from either one way from either **New York** or **Chicago**; from **LA**, the lowest fare will be around $300. You'll find a few excellent, low-cost airlines serving multiple Florida locations: try JetBlue, which is especially good for one-way flights to Orlando, Fort Lauderdale, Fort Myers, Jacksonville, Tampa, Sarasota, and West Palm Beach. Carriers often run web-only specials, so be sure to check their sites before making a final purchase. Also try Air Tran Airways, based in Atlanta, which has flights to Fort Lauderdale, Fort Myers, Miami, Orlando, West Palm Beach, Jacksonville, Pensacola, Sarasota, and Tampa from a number of southern, Midwestern, and East Coast cities; or Allegiant Air, which serves Fort Lauderdale, Tampa, and Orlando's second airport at Sanford.

From **Toronto**, Air Canada flies direct to Miami, Orlando, Tampa, and Fort Lauderdale, as well as Fort Myers in winter only; from **Montréal** the company has direct flights to Orlando, Fort Lauderdale, and Miami; and from **Vancouver**, they offer direct flights to Miami. Westjet flys direct to Fort Myers, Fort Lauderdale, Tampa, and Orlando from Toronto, and does seasonal direct flights to the latter three cities (check the website for details). From Toronto and Montréal, expect to pay around Can$200 for a one-way flight to Miami; Can$300 from Vancouver. American Airlines often has competitive fares, with direct flights from Toronto and Montreal to Miami. They also fly to Miami from Vancouver (with a connection).

Flights from the UK and Ireland

Although you can fly to the US from many of Britain's regional airports, the only nonstop scheduled flights to Florida are from London, and all of these land either at Miami or, less often, Orlando. The flight time is around eight hours, leaving London (Heathrow for Miami, Gatwick for Orlando, with British Airways) around midday and arriving during the afternoon (local time). The return journey is slightly shorter, leaving in the early evening and flying through the night to arrive around breakfast time. A basic round-trip economy-class ticket will cost £250–350 for a midweek flight in low season and £600–700 for a weekend flight in high season.

Travel agents can offer cut-price seats on direct **charter flights**. These are particularly good value if you're traveling from a British city other than London, though they tend to be limited to the summer season, be restricted to so-called "holiday destinations" (such as Orlando), and have fixed departure and return dates. Brochures are available in most high-street travel agents, or contact the specialists direct.

Many more routings use direct **one-stop** flights to Florida. Obviously, these take a few hours longer than nonstop flights but can be more convenient (and sometimes cheaper) if

Six steps to a better kind of travel

At Rough Guides we are passionately committed to travel. We feel strongly that only through traveling do we truly come to understand the world we live in and the people we share it with – plus tourism has brought a great deal of benefit to developing economies around the world over the last few decades. But the extraordinary growth in tourism has also damaged some places irreparably, and of course climate change is exacerbated by most forms of transport, especially flying. This means that now, more than ever, it's important, to travel thoughtfully and responsibly, with respect for the cultures you're visiting – not only to derive the most benefit from your trip but also in order to preserve the best bits of the planet for everyone to enjoy. At Rough Guides we feel there are six main areas in which you can make a difference:

• Consider what you're contributing to the local economy, and indeed how much the services you use do the same, whether it's through employing local workers and guides or sourcing locally grown produce and local services.

• Consider the environment on holiday as well as at home. Water is scarce in many developing destinations, and the biodiversity of local flora and fauna can be adversely affected by tourism. Patronise businesses that take account of this rather than those that trash the local environment for short-term gain.

• Give thought to how often you fly and what you can do to redress any harm that your trips create. Reduce the amount you travel by air; avoid short hops and more harmful night flights.

• Consider alternatives to flying, traveling instead by bus, train, boat and even by bike or on foot where possible. Take time to enjoy the journey itself as well as your final destination.

• Think about making all the trips you take "climate neutral" via a reputable carbon offset scheme. All Rough Guide flights are offset, and every year we donate money to a variety of charities devoted to combating the effects of climate change.

• Travel with a purpose, not just to tick off experiences. Consider spending longer in a place, and really getting to know it and its people – you'll find it much more rewarding than dashing from place to place.

---

you're not aiming specifically for Miami or Orlando. Alternatively, you could take a flight to New York or **another city** on the northern East Coast and travel on from there – this won't save any money overall but is an option if you want to see more of the country before reaching Florida. Travel agents will have the cheapest offers.

Flights from Australia, New Zealand and South Africa

There are **no direct flights** to Florida from Australia or New Zealand. Travelers should fly to Los Angeles or San Francisco – the main points of entry to the US – and make their way from there.

A basic round-trip **economy-class ticket** out of Sydney or Melbourne will cost around Aus$2000 during the low season, Aus$2800 high season, while from Auckland (to Los Angeles) it will be around NZ$2300; add NZ$100 for departures from Christchurch or Wellington. Once in the States, you'll be looking at another US$350 or so to get to Miami. Various coupon deals, valid within the continental US, are available with your main ticket.

Getting to Florida from South Africa will also involve flying to a major US port of entry and continuing on to Florida from there. South African Airways fly from Johannesburg direct to New York and Washington; a return ticket to either of these cities costs from around R8000 during the low season or R10,000 high season.

Round-the-world flights

If you intend to take in Florida as part of a world trip, a **round-the-world** (RTW) ticket offers the greatest flexibility. Qantas and Air New Zealand have allied themselves with one of three globe-spanning networks: the "Star Alliance," "One World," and "Skyteam". Fares depend on the number of segments required and the continents visited, but start at around Aus$3499 (low season) for a US–Europe–Asia and home itinerary. If this is more flexibility than you need, you can save Aus$200–300 by going with an individual airline (in concert with code-share partners) and accepting fewer stops.

Car

Easily reachable by **car** for those living in the immediate region, Florida lies at the end of three major Interstate highways: I-95, which runs up the East Coast to Maine; I-75, which winds through the south on the way to Ohio and Michigan; and I-10, which stretches west across Texas and finally halts at Los Angeles.

How feasible it is to drive to Florida depends, of course, on exactly where you live (or arrive) and how much time you have. If you're aiming for the bustling, tourist hot spots like Orlando and Miami, you may enjoy the option of being able to spend a few days driving around the relaxing scenery of the southeast during your trip. From both New York City and Chicago, reckon on around 20 hours of actual driving to get to Miami; from Los Angeles you'll probably need around 45 hours behind the wheel.

If you live in the region, **renting a car** is the usual story of phoning your local branch of one of the major rental agencies (Avis, Hertz, Budget, Thrifty, etc – listed on p.24), of which Thrifty tends to be the cheapest. Most have offices at destination airports, and addresses and phone numbers are in the Yellow Pages. For more specific information on car rental, see "Getting around," p.23.

Also worth considering are **fly-drive deals**, which give cut-rate (and sometimes free) car rental when buying your air ticket. They usually work out cheaper than renting on the spot and are especially good value if you intend to do a lot of driving.

Trains

A few years ago, the deregulation of the airline industry helped make domestic air travel as cheap as train travel. In an effort to win back business, **Amtrak** (☎1-800/872-7245,

ⓦwww.amtrak.com) has made improvements in all areas: raising comfort levels, offering better food, and introducing "Thruway" buses to link with its trains (notably between Orlando and the Tampa Bay area). Consequently, traveling to Florida by train can be enjoyable and relaxing, if not particularly inexpensive.

From **New York**, the *Silver Meteor* and the *Silver Star* traverse the eastern seaboard daily to Miami via Orlando. The return fare is $230, or half that for a one-way ticket, and the journey from New York takes between 27 and 30 hours.

If you really can't bear to be parted from your car and you live within driving distance of Lorton, Virginia (just south of Washington, DC), the *Auto Train* will carry you and your vehicle to Sanford, near Orlando. The journey time is 16 to 17 hours and passenger fares range from around $90 to $225 each way depending on the time of year; the additional charge for a regular-sized car starts at around $300 each way.

All the above involve overnight travel. To spare yourself a restless night, Amtrak offers various types of **sleeping accommodation**, which includes meals, en-suite cabins, and will set you back over $300 per night.

Buses

Long-distance travel on **Greyhound** buses (☎1-800/231-2222, ⓦwww.greyhound.com) can be an endurance test but is usually the cheapest form of public transport to the Sunshine State. Scan your local newspaper or call the local Greyhound station for special fares, which are offered periodically, and remember that midweek travel is marginally cheaper than traveling on weekends.

Otherwise, the approximate regular round-trip fare from New York to Miami is $270; Chicago to Miami is $290; and LA to Miami is $400. The regular ticket allows an 80 percent refund; non-refundable tickets and non-refundable, 7-day advance purchase tickets are also available at reduced prices.

Online booking

ⓦ **www.ebookers.com**
ⓦ **www.expedia.com**
ⓦ **www.lastminute.com**
ⓦ **www.opodo.com**
ⓦ **www.orbitz.com**

Air, rail, and bus passes

Air passes

The three global airline networks – Star Alliance, One World, and Skyteam – all sell their own North America **air passes** in conjunction with an international round-trip ticket. You must purchase at least three **coupons** (and up to a maximum of ten), each valid for a one-way flight in the US. Prices depend on factors such as the total number of coupons bought, the time of year, and the duration of each flight, but generally range from $100 to $350 per coupon.

Amtrak rail pass

Although rail travel can't get you around all of Florida, you might consider buying an Amtrak rail pass should you be planning on seeing more of the US than just the Sunshine State. The **US Rail Pass** entitles you to travel throughout the US, for fifteen, thirty, or forty days, for a price of $389, $579, and $749 respectively. Children under 15 receive a fifty percent reduction. Passes can be bought online at ⓦwww .amtrak.com and be collected at any Amtrak station. You must pre-reserve trains – ideally as far in advance as possible (call ☏1-800/872-7245 from the US or ☏+1 215/856-7953 from abroad). On production of a passport and one of these passes, your tickets will be issued.

Greyhound Discovery Pass

Those intending to travel virtually every day by bus, or to venture further around the US, can buy a **Greyhound Discovery Pass**, offering unlimited travel within a set time limit: order online at ⓦwww.greyhound.com. Prices are $329 for a 7-day pass, $483 for a 15-day pass, $607 for a 30-day pass, and $750 for a 60-day pass. Children under 12 receive a forty percent discount; seniors five percent. The first time you use your pass, the ticket clerk will date it (this becomes the commencement date of the ticket), and write your destination on a page the driver will tear out and keep as you board the bus. Repeat this procedure for every subsequent journey.

ⓦwww.travelocity.com
ⓦwww.travelonline.co.za
ⓦwww.zuji.com.au

Airlines

Air Canada ⓦwww.aircanada.com
Air New Zealand ⓦwww.airnz.co.nz
Air Tran Airways ⓦwww.airtran.com
Allegiant Air ⓦwww.allegiantair.com
American Airlines ⓦwww.aa.com
British Airways ⓦwww.ba.com
Continental Airlines ⓦwww.continental.com
Delta Air Lines ⓦwww.delta.com
Frontier Airlines ⓦwww.flyfrontier.com
Japan Airlines (JAL) ⓦwww.jal.com
JetBlue ⓦwww.jetblue.com
Northwest ⓦwww.nwa.com
Qantas ⓦwww.qantas.com
Southwest Airlines ⓦwww.southwest.com
United Airlines ⓦwww.united.com
US Airways ⓦwww.usair.com
Virgin Atlantic Airways ⓦwww.virgin-atlantic.com
Westjet ⓦwww.westjet.com

Agents and operators

British Airways Holidays UK ☏0844/493 0787, ⓦwww.baholidays.com. Packages, city breaks, tours, and tailor-mades to Florida destinations such as Miami, Orlando, Tampa, and Key West.
Contiki Tours ☏1-800/268-1835, ⓦwww .contiki.com. Trips for the 18- to 35-year-old crowd, including the "Eastern Discovery," which runs between New York and New Orleans, taking in St Augustine, Orlando, and Pensacola.
Creative Holidays Australia ☏1300/747 400, ⓦwww.creativeholidays.com.au. Packages to Disney World.
Delta Vacations ☏1-800/654-6559, ⓦwww .deltavacations.com. Good for package tours to Orlando, Miami, Daytona Beach, and much more.
Monarch Holidays UK ☏0871/423 8568, ⓦwww.holidays.monarch.co.uk. Operated by Cosmos Holidays (the UKs largest tour operator) and offering fly-drives, packages, and flights to different parts of Florida.
North South Travel UK ☏01245/608 291, ⓦwww.northsouthtravel.co.uk. Friendly, competitive

travel agency, offering discounted fares worldwide. Profits are used to support projects in the developing world, especially the promotion of sustainable tourism. **STA Travel** US ☎1-800/781-4040, UK ☎0871/2300 040, Australia ☎134 782, New Zealand ☎0800/474 400, South Africa ☎0861/781 781; ⓦwww.statravel.com. Worldwide specialists in independent travel; also student IDs, travel insurance, car rental, rail passes, and more. Good discounts for students and under-26s.

Suntrek ☎1-800/SUN-TREK, ⓦwww.suntrek.com. Group travel tours, including the "Florida Sunshine" trip ($600–775), which takes in the sights from Orlando down through the Keys.

Thomas Cook UK ☎0871/895 0055, ⓦwww.thomascook.com. Long-established one-stop travel agency for package holidays – including some good deals for Disney World – or scheduled flights, with bureaux de change issuing Thomas Cook traveler's checks, and providing travel insurance and car rental.

Trailfinders UK ☎0845/058 5858, Republic of Ireland ☎01/677 7888, Australia ☎1300/780 212; ⓦwww.trailfinders.com. One of the best-informed and most efficient agents for independent travellers.

Trek America ☎0845/330-6095, ⓦwww.trekamerica.com. Small-group camping adventure trips throughout the US, including a few long-distance tours which include Florida.

Virgin Holidays ☎0871/222 5825, ⓦwww.virginholidays.co.uk. Flights, fly-drive deals, tailor-mades, and packages to almost anywhere in Florida.

Getting around

Travel in surprisingly compact Florida is rarely difficult or time-consuming. Crossing between the east and west coasts, for example, takes only a couple of hours. With a car you'll have no problems, but traveling by public transport requires adroit planning: cities and larger towns have bus links – and, in some cases, an infrequent train service – but many rural areas and some of the most enjoyable coastal sections are much harder to reach.

By car

As a major vacation destination, Florida is one of the cheapest places in the US in which to **rent a car**, thanks to a very competitive market. Drivers are supposed to have held their licenses for at least one year (though this is rarely checked), and people under 25 may very well encounter problems or restrictions when renting, usually having to pay an extra $10–25 a day. If you're under 25, always call ahead. If you're under 21, you will not be able to rent a car at all.

Car rental companies will also expect you to have a **credit card**; if you don't have one, they may let you leave a hefty deposit (at least $300–500) but it's highly unlikely. Fly-drive deals are good value, though you can save up to sixty percent simply by booking in advance with a major firm (call their toll-free numbers for the best rates – most will try to beat the offers of their competitors, so it's worth haggling). Remember standard rental cars have automatic transmissions.

Many airport car rental branches also levy additional charges of up to ten percent onto the rental price – Miami doesn't, but most other Florida airports do. Always be sure to get free unlimited mileage and be aware leaving the car in a different city than the one in which you rent it may incur a drop-off charge of as much as $200 – though most firms do not charge drop-off fees within Florida.

Loss Damage Waiver (LDW) is a form of insurance that often isn't included in the initial rental charge, and without it you're liable for every scratch to the rental car – even those that aren't your fault (you are in any case insured for damage to other vehicles). LDW costs $20–27 a day, although some credit card companies offer

Driving for foreign visitors

UK, Canadian, Australian, and New Zealand nationals can **drive** in the US provided they have a full driving license from their home country (International Driving Permits are not always regarded as sufficient).

Roads

The best roads for covering long distances quickly are the wide, straight, and fast interstate highways, usually at least six lanes wide and always prefixed by "I" (for example I-95) – marked on maps by a red, white, and blue shield bearing the number. Even-numbered interstates usually run east–west and those with odd numbers north–south.

A grade down are the **state highways** (eg Hwy-1) and the **US highways** (eg US-1), sometimes divided into scenic off-shoots such as Hwy-A1A, which runs parallel to US-1 along Florida's east coast. There are a number of toll roads, by far the longest being the 318-mile Florida's Turnpike; tolls range from 25¢ to $6 and are usually graded according to length of journey – you're given a distance marker when you enter the toll road and pay the appropriate amount when you leave. You'll also come across toll bridges, charging sometimes as much as $3 to cross. Some major roads in cities are technically state or US highways but are better known by their local names. Part of US-1 in Miami, for instance, is more familiarly known as Biscayne Boulevard. Rural areas also have much smaller **county roads**, which are known as routes (eg Rte-78 near Lake Okeechobee); their number is preceded by a letter denoting their county.

Rules of the road

Although the law says drivers must keep up with the flow of traffic, which is often hurtling along at 80mph, the official speed limit in Florida is 55mph (70mph on some interstate stretches), with lower signposted limits – usually around 30–35mph – in built-up areas. A minimum speed limit of 40mph also applies on many interstates and highways.

automatic LDW coverage to anyone using their card to pay in full for the rental. You'll also be charged a Florida surcharge of $2.03 per day.

Standard third-party liability (or supplemental liability) policies only cover you for the first $10,000 of the third party's liability claim against you (plus an additional $10,000 for property damage), a paltry sum in litigation-conscious America. Supplemental liability insurance will cost a further $10–16 a day, but indemnifies the driver for up to $1,000,000.

If you **break down** in a rented car, call the emergency number pinned to the dashboard or on your keychain. If there isn't one, you should sit tight and wait for the Highway Patrol or State Police, who cruise by regularly. If in your own vehicle, call the American Automobile Associiation (**AAA**) (☎1-800/222-4357, ⊛www.aaa.com). Note that if you're not an AAA member or affiliate, you'll have to become one to get service.

Raising the hood of your car is recognized as a call for assistance, though women traveling alone should, obviously, be wary of doing this.

Taxi service is available in most cities and towns; detailed information is provided throughout the Guide.

Major car rental agencies

In North America

Alamo ⊛www.alamo.com
Avis ⊛www.avis.com
Budget ⊛www.budget.com
Dollar ⊛www.dollar.com
Enterprise Rent-a-Car ⊛www.enterprise.com
Hertz ⊛www.hertz.com
National ⊛www.nationalcar.com
Thrifty ⊛www.thrifty.com

Renting an RV

Recreational Vehicles (or **RVs**) – those huge juggernauts that rumble down the

Apart from the obvious fact Americans drive on the **right**, various rules may be unfamiliar to foreign drivers. US law requires any **alcohol** be carried unopened in the trunk of the car; it's illegal to make a U-turn on an interstate or anywhere where a single unbroken line runs along the middle of the road; it's also illegal to park on a highway, and for front-seat passengers to ride without fastened seatbelts. At intersections, you can **turn right on a red light** if there is no traffic approaching from the left; and some junctions are four-way stops: a crossroads where all traffic must stop before proceeding in order of arrival.

It can't be stressed too strongly that **driving under the influence** (DUI) is a very serious offence. In some parts of the state the police are empowered to suspend your driving license immediately. The minimum fine for a first offence is $500 along with 50 hours' community service and, in extreme cases, the possibility of a prison term of up to six months.

Parking

You'll find, in cities at least, that **parking meters** are commonplace. Charges for an hour range from 25¢ to $1. **Car parks** (US "parking lots") generally charge $2–3 an hour, $6–12 per day. If you park in the wrong place (such as within ten feet of a fire hydrant) your car is likely to be towed away, or **wheel-clamped** – a sticker on the windscreen will tell you where to pay the fine ($30–45). Watch out for signs indicating the **street cleaning** schedule, as you mustn't park overnight before an early-morning clean. **Validated parking**, where your fee for parking in, say, a shopping mall's lot is waived if one of the stores has stamped your parking stub (just ask), is common, as is **valet parking** at even quite modest restaurants, for which a small tip is expected.

Whenever possible, park in the **shade**; if you don't, you might find the car too hot to touch when you return to it – temperatures inside cars parked in the full force of the Florida sun can reach 140°F (60°C).

highway complete with multiple bedrooms, bathrooms, and kitchens – can be rented from around $525 per week for a basic camper on the back of a pick-up truck. These are good for groups or families traveling together, but they can be quite unwieldy on the road.

Rental outlets are not as common as you might expect, as people tend to own their own RVs. On top of the rental fees you have to take into account mileage charges, the cost of gas (some RVs do twelve miles to the gallon or less), and any drop-off charges. In addition, it is rarely legal simply to pull up in an RV and spend the night at the roadside; you are expected to stay in designated RV parks – some of which charge $35–50 per night.

The Recreational Vehicle Rental Association (☎703/591-7130, ⓦ www.rvra .org) publishes a newsletter and a directory of rental firms. One of the larger companies offering RV rentals is Cruise

America (☎800/671-8042, ⓦ www.cruise america.com).

By bus

Buses are normally the cheapest way to travel. The only long-distance service is **Greyhound**, which links all major cities and some smaller towns. In isolated areas buses are fairly scarce, sometimes only appearing once a day, if at all – so plot your route with care. Between the big cities, buses run around the clock to a fairly full timetable, stopping only for meal breaks (almost always fast-food dives) and driver change-overs. Any sizeable community will have a Greyhound station; in smaller places the local post office or gas station doubles as the stop and ticket office.

Fares are relatively inexpensive – for example $51 one way between Miami and Orlando – and can often be reduced by twenty percent if you buy your ticket at least one week in advance. Student, child, and senior discounts are also available – for more information, visit ⓦwww.greyhound.com, which also has an easy-to-use timetable and fare information; otherwise, contact the local terminals. The phone numbers for the larger Greyhound stations are given in the Guide.

If you plan on doing a lot of traveling, Greyhound's **Discovery Pass** is a good choice (for more details, see box, p.22).

By train

The Amtrak rail network in Florida is of limited scope, which makes the train a less viable way of getting around. Florida's railroads were built to service the boom towns of the 1920s and, consequently, some rural nooks have rail links as good as the modern cities. The actual trains are clean and comfortable, with most routes in the state offering two services a day. In some areas, Amtrak services are extended by buses, usable only in conjunction with the train.

Fares can sometimes be cheaper than the bus – $35 one way between Miami and Orlando, for example. Again, student, child, and senior discounts are available.

The Tri-Rail

Designed to reduce road traffic along the congested southeast coast, the elevated **Tri-Rail** system came into operation in 1989, ferrying commuters between Miami and West Palm Beach, stopping at places such as Fort Lauderdale and Boca Raton on the way. The single-journey fare is calculated on a zone basis, and ranges from $2 to $5.50; the majority of services tend to run around rush hours – meaning a very early start or an early-evening departure. There are fewer services (eight each way) on Saturdays and Sundays. All-day tickets, available on weekends and holidays, are only $4. Tickets must be bought at the station (not on the train), and those riding without them may be subject to hefty fines. Tri-Rail information: ☎1-800/874 7245, ⓦwww.tri-rail.com.

By air

Provided your plans are flexible and you take advantage of the special cut-rate fares regularly offered by airlines, off-peak plane travel within Florida can work out to be only slightly more expensive than taking a bus or train – and will also, on the longer journeys at least, save you some time. Typical cut-rate one-way fares are around $90 for Miami–Orlando and $270 for Miami–Tallahassee; full fares are much higher.

By bicycle

Cycling is seldom a good way to get around the major cities (with the exception of some sections of Miami), but many smaller towns are quiet enough to be pleasurably explored by bicycle. In addition, there are many miles of marked cycle paths along the coast, and long-distance bike trails crisscross the state's interior.

Bikes can be **rented** for $15–30 a day, $40–80 a week, from many beach shops and college campuses, some state parks, and virtually any place where cycling is a good idea; outlets are listed in the Guide.

The best cycling areas are in north central Florida, the Panhandle, and in parts of the northeast coast. By contrast, the southeast coastal strip is heavily congested and many south-Florida inland roads are narrow and dangerous. Wherever you cycle, avoid the heaviest traffic – and the midday heat – by doing most of your pedaling before noon.

For free biking **information** and detailed **maps** ($2–15) of cycling routes, write to the Florida Pedestrian and Bicycle Program, Florida Department of Transportation, 605 Suwannee St, Tallahassee, FL 32399-0450 (☎850/245-1500, ⓦwww.dot.state.fl.us). You can get many of the maps online or from most youth hostels.

Hitching

Hitching is **illegal** in Miami and on the outskirts of many other cities and in whole counties. We advise you don't do it anywhere or at any time.

Accommodation

Accommodation options in Florida range from the chain hotels and motels lining almost every highway to the resorts found at the main tourist destinations. Some towns and cities have more intimate bed and breakfasts, while camping is possible at Florida's many state parks.

Hotels and motels

While motels and hotels essentially offer the same things – double rooms with bathroom, TV, and phone – motels are often one-off affairs run by their owners and tend to be cheaper (typically $45–55) than hotels ($65–90), which are likely to be part of a nationwide chain. Dependable **budget-priced chain hotels**, which, depending on location, can cost the same as a privately run motel, include *Days Inn*, *Econo Lodge*, and *Super 8*. Higher up the scale are mid-range chains like *Best Western*, *Howard Johnson's*, and *La Quinta*. Prices quoted by hotels and motels are almost always for the actual room rather than for each person using it – "singles" are typically double rooms at a slightly reduced rate – and most establishments will usually set up a third single bed for around $5–10 on top of the regular price, reducing costs for three people sharing. **Reservations** are only held until 5pm or 6pm unless you've told the hotel you'll be arriving late.

All but the cheapest motels and hotels have pools for guests' use and many offer cable TV, free local phone calls, and, increasingly, wireless internet access. Under $60, rooms tend to be similar in quality and features; spend $60–70 in rural areas or $80–100 in the cities and you get more luxury – a larger room and often additional facilities such as a tennis court, gym, and golf course. Paying over $150 brings all the above, plus likely an ocean view and some upmarket trappings.

Resorts

On your travels you'll also come across **resorts**, which are motels or hotels equipped with a restaurant, bar, and private beach – on average these cost $90–150, with some establishments adding a "resort fee" of as much as $25 a day on top of the room rate; and **efficiencies**, which are motel rooms adapted to offer cooking facilities – ranging from a stove squeezed into a corner to a fully

Accommodation price codes

It's a fact of Florida resort life that the plain and simple hotel room, which costs $50 on a weekday in low season, is liable to cost two or three times that amount on a weekend in high season. To further complicate matters, high and low season vary depending on whether you're in north or south Florida, and some establishments that depend on business travelers for their trade (such as those in downtown areas, distanced from the nearest beach) will actually be cheaper on weekends than on weekdays. Local events – such as a Space Shuttle launch on the Space Coast, or Spring Break in Panama City Beach – can also cause prices to increase dramatically.

Throughout the book, we've graded accommodation prices according to the cost of the least expensive double room in high season – but do allow for the fluctuations outlined above.

❶ $40 and under	❹ $81–100	❼ $176–250
❷ $41–60	❺ $101–130	❽ $251 and over
❸ $61–80	❻ $131–175	

equipped kitchen – usually for $10–15 above the basic room rate.

There are of course – especially in cities – plenty of **high-end establishments**, which can cost just about any amount of money, depending on the luxury – we've pointed out which ones are worthwhile in the Guide. Bear in mind that the most upmarket establishments have all manner of services that may appear to be free but for which you'll be expected to **tip** in a style commensurate with the hotel's status.

Discount options

During **off-peak periods** many motels and hotels struggle to fill their rooms, and it's worth **haggling** to get a few dollars off the asking price. Staying in the same place for more than one night may bring further reductions. In addition, pick up the many discount coupons that fill tourist information offices and Welcome Centers (see p.48), and look out for the free *Traveler Discount Guide*. Read the small print, though: what appears to be an amazingly cheap room rate sometimes turns out to be a per-person charge for two people sharing and limited to midweek.

Bed and breakfasts

Bed and breakfast inns, or "**B&Bs**," are often restored buildings or homes in the smaller cities and more rural areas, and we've listed several throughout the Guide. B&Bs can offer a more personal experience than staying in a large and anonymous chain hotel – some enjoy the close interaction with one's hosts; others may find it a little overbearing.

While always including a huge and wholesome breakfast (five courses are not unheard of), prices vary greatly: anything from $50 to $200 depending on location and season; most cost between $80 and $120 per night for a double. Bear in mind most are booked well in advance, making it sensible to contact the inn directly at least a month ahead – longer in high season.

Hostels

At around $15–30 per night per person for a bed in a dormitory, hostels are clearly the cheapest accommodation option other than camping. There are three main kinds

of hostel-like accommodation in the US: YMCA/YWCA hostels (known as "Ys"), offering accommodation for both sexes or, in a few cases, women only; the internationally affiliated HI-AYH hostels; and a growing number of independent hostels. There are none of the first two kinds in Florida, leaving just a smattering of independent hostels in tourist centers such as Miami, St Augustine, and the Everglades. You can book a dorm bed or a private room ($35–60) at most of these establishments via their websites. Few hostels provide meals, but most have cooking facilities. Other amenities include communal areas, lockers, washing machines, and wi-fi access. Visit ⓦwww .hostels.com/us.fl.html for a current listing of Florida hostels.

Camping

Florida **campgrounds** range from the primitive (a flat piece of ground that may or may not have a water tap) to others that are more like open-air hotels with shops, restaurants, and washing facilities. Naturally, prices vary according to amenities, ranging from nothing at all for the most basic plots to around $30 a night for something comparatively luxurious. There are plenty of campgrounds but often plenty of people intending to use them: take special care over plotting your route if you're camping during public holidays or weekends, when many sites will be either full or very crowded. For camping in the wilderness, there's usually a nightly charge of $3 or so payable at the area's administrative office.

Privately run campgrounds are everywhere, their prices ranging from $8 to $35, and the best are listed throughout the Guide. For a fuller list, check out the free *Florida Camping Directory*, published by the Florida Association of RV Parks and Campgrounds, 1340 Vickers Drive, Tallahassee, FL 32303 (ⓣ850/562-7151, ⓦwww .floridacamping.com); you can order it online for a $5 postage fee.

State and national parks

State parks – there are over 150 in Florida – can be excellent places to camp and some of the more basic campgrounds in these parks will often be completely empty midweek. Sites cost $12–38 for up to four people sharing; visitors must make reservations a minimum of two days in advance. Bear in mind that some park gates close at sunset; you won't be able to camp there if you arrive later. Most state parks have information lines, listed in the guide, but all reservations are made through ReserveAmerica, (☎800/326-3521, ⓦwww .reserveamerica.com). If you're doing a lot of camping in state parks, get the free booklet, the *Florida State Parks Guide* from any state park office. Similarly priced campgrounds exist in **national parks and national forests** – see the details throughout

the Guide. You may contact the Southeast Archeological Center, a National Park Service affiliate, 2035 E. Paul Dirac Drive, Johnson Building, Suite 120, Tallahassee, FL 32310 (☎850/580-3011, ⓦwww.cr.nps .gov/seac), or for the Apalachicola, Ocala, or Osceola National Forests, the US Forest Service (Forest Supervisors Office), 325 John Knox Rd, Suite F-100, Tallahassee, FL 32303 (☎850/523-8500, ⓦwww.fs.fed .us/r8/florida).

However desolate it may look, much of undeveloped Florida is, in fact, private land, so rough camping is illegal. For **permitted rough camping**, see "Outdoor activities," p.37.

Food and drink

Florida has a mass of restaurants, fast-food outlets, and cafés on every main street, all trying to outdo one another with their cut-price daily specials.

Fresh fish and **seafood** are abundant all over Florida, as is the high-quality produce of the state's cattle farms – served as ribs, steaks, and burgers – and junkfood is as common as anywhere else in the country. But the choice of what to eat is influenced by where you are. In the northern half of the state, the accent is on hearty cooking – traditional Southern dishes such as grits (a hot cereal), cornbread, and fried chicken. As you head south through Florida, this gives way to the most diverse and inexpensive gathering of Latin American and Caribbean cuisines to be found anywhere in the US – you can feast on anything from curried goat to mashed plantains and yucca.

As for service and **tipping**, foreign visitors should note to top up the bill in restaurants by 15–20 percent; a little less perhaps at a bar.

Breakfast

For the price (on average $5–10) **breakfast** makes a good-value, very filling start to the day. Go to a diner or café, both of which are

very similar and usually serve breakfast until at least 11am (some continue all day) – though there are special deals at earlier times, say 6am to 8am, when the price may be even less.

Lunches and snacks

Between 11.30am and 1.30pm, look for excellent-value **set menus** and **all-you-can-eat specials**. Most Cuban restaurants and fishcamps (see "Fish and seafood," p.30) are exceptionally well priced all the time and you can get a good-sized lunch at either for $4–5. **Buffet restaurants** – most of which also serve breakfast and dinner – are found in most cities and towns; $8–10 lets you pig out as much as you can from a wide variety of hot dishes.

If it's a warm day and you can't face hot food, delis usually serve a broad range of salads for about $3 a pound. Frozen yogurt or ice cream may be all you feel like eating in the midday heat: look for exotic versions made with mango and guava sold by Cuban vendors.

Snacks

For **quick snacks**, many **supermarket deli** counters do ready-cooked meals for $4–6, as well as a range of salads and sandwiches. **Street stands** sell hot dogs, burgers, or a slice of pizza for around $1–2; in Miami, Cuban fast-food stands serve crispy pork sandwiches and other spicy snacks for $2–3. Bags of fresh oranges, grapefruit, and watermelons are often sold from the roadside in rural areas, as are boiled peanuts – a dollar buys a steaming bagful. Southern fast-food chains like *Popeye's Famous Fried Chicken* and *Sonny's Real Pit Bar-B-Q* will satisfy your hunger for around $5, but are only marginally better than the inevitable burger chains.

Dinner

Even if it sometimes seems swamped by the more fashionable regional and ethnic cuisines, traditional **American cooking** is found all over Florida. Portions are big and you start with salad, eaten before the main course arrives; look out for heart of palm salad, based around the delicious vegetable at the heart of the sabal palm tree (unfortunately for the tree, once the heart is extracted, the plant dies). Enormous steaks, burgers, piles of ribs, or half a chicken tend to dominate main dishes, and often come with a vegetable and/or some form of potato.

Throughout the northern half of the state, vegetables such as okra, collard greens, black-eyed peas, fried green tomatoes, and fried eggplant are added to staples including fried chicken, roast beef, and **hogjaw** – meat from the mouth of a pig. Meat dishes are usually accompanied by cornbread to soak up the thick gravy poured over everything;

with fried fish, you'll get **hush puppies** – fried corn balls with tiny bits of chopped onion. Okra is also used in gumbo soups, a feature of **Cajun** cooking, which originated in nearby Louisiana as a way of using up leftovers. A few (usually expensive) Florida restaurants specialize in Cajun food but many others offer a few Cajun items (such as red beans and rice, and hot and spicy shrimp and steak dishes).

Alligator is on many menus: most of the meat comes from alligator farms, which process a certain number each year. The tails are deep-fried and served in a variety of styles – none of which makes much of a mark on the bland, chicken-like taste. **Frogs' legs** also crop up occasionally.

Regional **nouvelle cuisine** is largely too pretentious and expensive for the typical Floridian palate, although some restaurants in the larger cities do create extraordinary and inspired dishes with local fish and the produce of the citrus farms, creating small but beautifully presented affairs for around $40–50 a head.

Almost wherever you eat you'll be offered **Key lime pie** as a dessert, a dish that began life in the Florida Keys, made from the small limes that grow there. The pie is similar to lemon meringue but with a sharper taste. Quality varies greatly; take local advice to find a good outlet and your taste buds will tell you why many swear by it.

Fish and seafood

Florida excels at **fish and seafood** – which is great news for non-meat-eaters. Even the shabbiest restaurant is likely to have an excellent selection, though fish comes freshest and cheapest at **fishcamps**: rustic places right beside a river or a lake where

Free food

Some **bars** are used as much by diners as drinkers, who fill up on the free **hors d'oeuvres** laid out by a lot of city bars between 5pm and 7pm Monday to Friday – an attempt to nab the commuting classes before they head off to the suburbs – and sometimes by beachside bars to grab beach-goers before they head elsewhere for the evening. For the price of a drink you can stuff yourself on chili, seafood, or pasta. Similarly, you may find your **hotel** lays on some sort of complimentary evening cocktail reception at around 6pm, featuring food, wine, beer, and soft drinks.

Latin American food terms

Ajiaco criollo Meat and root vegetable stew
Arroz Rice
Arroz con leche Rice pudding
Bocadillo Sandwich
Chicarones de pollo Fried chicken crackling
Frijoles Beans
Frijoles negros Black beans
Maduros Fried plantains
Masitoas de puerca Fried spiced pork
Morros y Christianos Literally "Moors and Christians," black beans and white rice
Pan Bread
Pan con lechon Crispy pork sandwich
Piccadillo Minced meat, usually beef, served with peppers and olives
Pollo Chicken
Puerca Pork
Sopa de mariscos Shellfish soup
Sopa de plantanos Meaty, plantain soup
Tostones Fried mashed plantains
Vaca Beef

your meal was swimming just a few hours earlier; a fishcamp lunch or dinner will cost around $5–10. Grouper tends to top the bill, but you'll also find catfish, dolphin (the fish, not the mammal – sometimes known by its Hawaiian name, mahi–mahi), mullet, tuna, and swordfish, any of which (except catfish, which is nearly always fried) may be boiled, grilled, fried, or "blackened" (rubbed with zesty spices and charcoal-grilled). Of **shellfish**, the tender claws of stone crabs, eaten dipped in butter, raise local passions during the mid-October to mid-May season; spiny (or "Florida") lobster is smaller and more succulent than its more famous Maine rival; oysters can be extremely fresh (the best come from Apalachicola) and are usually eaten raw (though are best avoided during summer, when they carry a risk of food poisoning) – many restaurants have special "raw bars," where you can also consume meaty shrimp, in regular and jumbo sizes. Another popular crustacean is the very chewy **conch** (pronounced "konk"); abundant throughout the Florida Keys, they usually come deep-fried as fritters served up with various sauces, or as a chowder-like soup.

Ethnic cuisine

Florida's **ethnic cuisines** become increasingly exotic the further south you go. You'll find plenty of **Cuban food** in Miami. Most Cuban dishes are meat-based: frequently pork, less often beef or chicken, always fried (including the skin, which becomes a crispy crackling) and usually heavily spiced, served with a varying combination of yellow or white rice, black beans, plantains (a sweet, banana-like vegetable), and yucca (cassava) – a potato-like vegetable completely devoid of taste. Seafood crops up less often, most deliciously in thick soups, such as *sopa de mariscos* (shellfish soup). Unpretentious Cuban diners serve a filling lunch or dinner for under $6, though a growing number of upmarket restaurants will charge three times as much for identical food. In busy areas, many Cuban cafés have street windows where you buy a thimble-sized cup of sweet and rich *café Cubano* (Cuban coffee) strong enough to make your hair stand on end; also available is *café con leche* (coffee with warm milk or cream), though it's strictly for the unadventurous and regarded by Cubans as a children's drink. If you want a cool drink in Miami, look out for roadside stands offering *coco frio* – coconut milk sucked through a straw directly from the coconut – for $1.

Although nowhere near as prevalent as Cuban cooking, foods from other parts of the **Caribbean** and **Latin America** are easily found around Miami: Haitian, Argentinian,

Colombian, Nicaraguan, Peruvian, Jamaican, and Salvadoran restaurants also serve the city's diverse migrant populations – at very affordable prices.

Other ethnic cuisines can be found all around the state. **Chinese** food is everywhere and often very cheap, as is **Mexican** – though many Mexican restaurants are more popular as places to knock back margaritas than to eat in; **Japanese** is more expensive; **Italian** food is popular but can be expensive once you leave the simple pastas and explore the more gourmet-inclined Italian regional cooking in the major cities. **French** food, too, is widely available, though pricey. **Thai**, **Korean**, and **Indonesian** cuisine is similarly city-based, though usually cheaper. More plentiful are well-priced, family-run **Greek** restaurants; and a smattering of **Minorcan** places are evidence of one of Florida's earliest groups of European settlers.

Drinking

Much **drinking** in Florida is done in restaurant or hotel lounges, at fishcamps (see p.30), or in "tiki bars" – open-sided straw-roofed huts beside a beach or hotel pool. Some beachside bars, especially in Panama City Beach, are split-level, multi-purpose affairs with discos and stages for live bands – and take great pride in being the birthplace of the infamous wet T-shirt contest (nowadays sometimes joined by G-string and "best legs" shows), an exercise in unrestrained sexism that shows no signs of declining in popularity among a predominantly late-teen and twenty-something clientele.

To buy and consume alcohol you need **to be 21 or over** and could well be asked for ID even if you look much older; this is particularly common at family-orientated places such as Walt Disney World. Even elsewhere, recent clampdowns have resulted in bars "carding" anyone who looks 30 and under. Licensing laws and drinking hours vary from area to area, but generally alcohol can be bought and drunk in a bar, nightclub, or restaurant any time between 10am and 2am. More cheaply, you can usually buy beer, wine, or spirits in supermarkets and, of course, liquor stores, from 9am to 11pm Monday to Saturday and from 1pm to 11pm on Sundays. It is illegal to consume alcohol in a car, on most beaches, and in all state parks, with a possible fine of $100 or more.

Beer

A small band of Florida **microbreweries** create interesting beers, though these are rarely sold beyond their own bar or restaurant. It's more common for discerning beer drinkers to stick to imported brews, the most widely available of which are the Mexican brands Bohemia, Corona, and Dos Equis. Don't forget that in all but the more pretentious bars, you can save money by buying a quart or half-gallon pitcher of beer. If bar prices are a problem, you can stock up with six-packs from a supermarket at $5–7 for domestic, $8–12 for imported brews.

Wine and cocktails

If **wine** is more to your taste, try to visit one of the state's fast-improving wineries: several can be toured and their products sampled for free. One of the most successful is Chautauqua Vineyards, in "De Funiak Springs" in the Panhandle (see p.432). In a bar or restaurant, however, beside a usually threadbare stock of European wines, you'll find a selection from Chile and California. A decent glass of wine in a bar or restaurant costs around $5–8, a bottle $15–30. Meanwhile, buying a bottle from a supermarket can cost as little as $7.

Cocktails are extremely popular, especially rich fruity ones consumed while gazing over the ocean or into the sunset. Varieties are innumerable, sometimes specific to a single bar or cocktail lounge, and most will cost $5–10. Cocktails and all other drinks come cheapest during **happy hours** (usually 5–7pm; sometimes much longer) when many are half price.

The media

Florida ranks among the country's more media-savvy regions, with the range of media outlets the best in the southeastern US.

Newspapers

The best-read of Florida's **newspapers** is the *Miami Herald*, providing in-depth coverage of state, national, and world events; the *Orlando Sentinel* and *St Petersburg Times* are not far behind and, naturally enough, excel at reporting their own areas. Overseas newspapers are often a preserve of specialist bookshops, though you will find them widely available in major tourist areas.

Every community of any size has at least a few **free newspapers**, found in street distribution bins or just lying around in piles. It's a good idea to pick up a full assortment: some simply cover local goings-on; others provide specialist coverage of interests ranging from long-distance cycling to getting ahead in business. Many of them are also excellent sources for bar, restaurant, and nightlife information, and we've mentioned the most useful titles in the Guide.

TV and radio

Florida **TV** is pretty much the standard network sitcom and talk-show barrage you get all over the country, with frequent interruptions for hard-sell commercials. Slightly better are the cable networks, to which you'll have access in most hotels. Especially in the south, Spanish-language stations provide services for the Hispanic communities.

Most of Florida's **radio stations** stick to the usual commercial format of retro-rock, classic pop, country, or easy-listening. In general, except for news and chat, the occasional fire-and-brimstone preacher, and Latin and Haitian music, stations on the AM band are best avoided in favor of the FM band, in particular the public and college stations on the air in Tallahassee, Gainesville, Orlando, Tampa, and Miami, found on the left of the dial (88–92FM). These invariably provide diverse and listenable programming, whether it be bizarre underground rock or abstruse literary discussions, and they're also good sources for local nightlife news.

Festivals

Someone somewhere is always celebrating something in Florida, though few festivities are shared throughout the region. Instead, there is a disparate multitude of local annual events: art and craft shows, county fairs, ethnic celebrations, music festivals, rodeos, sandcastle-building competitions, and many others of every description. The most interesting of these are listed throughout the Guide and you can phone the visitor center in a particular region ahead of your arrival to ask what's coming up. For the main festivities in Miami and Miami Beach see the box on pp.112–113 and in Key West p.161.

The biggest annual event to hit Florida is **Spring Break**: a six-week invasion (late Feb to early April) of tens of thousands of students seeking fun in the sun before knuckling down to their final exams. Times are changing, however: one traditional Spring Break venue, Fort Lauderdale, persuaded the students to go elsewhere; another, Daytona Beach, has had less success. Panama City Beach, though, welcomes the carousing collegiates with open arms, and Key West – despite its lack of beach – is fast becoming a favorite Spring Break location. If you are in Florida during this time, it will be hard to avoid some signs of Spring Break – a mob of scantily clad drunken students is a tell-tale sign – and at the busier coastal areas you may well find accommodation costing three times the normal price; be sure to plan ahead.

Sports

Florida is as fanatical about sports as the rest of the US, but what's more surprising is that collegiate sports are often, especially among lifelong Floridians, more popular than their professional counterparts. This is because Florida's professional teams are comparatively recent additions to the sporting scene and have none of the traditions and bedrock support the state's college sides enjoy. In fact, it's common to find seventy thousand people attending a college football match. Other sports less in evidence include soccer, volleyball, greyhound racing, and Jai Alai – the last two chiefly excuses for betting. Hiking and other outdoor pursuits, like canoeing, are also plentiful in the state's undeveloped regions.

Baseball

Until April 1993 Florida had no professional baseball team of its own – now, the state has two. In 1997, the first Florida team to come along, the **Florida Marlins**, became the youngest expansion team in history to win the World Series, shelling out millions of dollars to attract star-quality players. The team later slashed its budget, lost most of its marquee names, and is now a young, developing squad. The Marlins play at **Dolphin Stadium**, sixteen miles northwest of downtown Miami. The team are due to move to a new stadium in 2011 (on the site of the former Orange Bowl, 1400 NW 4th St, Little Havana), when they will be officially known as the Miami Marlins. Tickets are available direct from the box office (☎1-877/MARLINS, ⓦwww.florida.marlins.mlb.com); seats cost $9–103.

Florida's other baseball team, the **Tampa Bay Rays**, were long considered to be one of the worst in the country. However, in the 2008 season they reached the World Series, losing eventually to the Philadelphia Phillies. The Rays play at Tropicana Field (☎727/825-3137, ⓦwww.tampabay.devilrays.mlb.com), which is actually located in St Petersburg; seats are generally $9–117.

The major league **baseball season** runs from April to early October, with the league championships and the World Series, the final best-of-seven playoff, lasting through the end of that month.

Spring training

Even if the local pro team is slumping, Florida has long been the home of **spring training** (Feb and March) for a multitude of professional ball clubs – and thousands of fans plan vacations so they can watch their sporting heroes going through practice routines and playing in the friendly matches of the Grapefruit League (the Cactus League plays in Arizona). Much prestige is attached to being a spring training venue and the local community identifies strongly with the team it hosts – in some cases the link goes back fifty years. Turn up at 10am to join the crowds watching the training (free); the twenty-odd sides who come to train in Florida include: the Atlanta Braves, Champion Stadium, Disney's Wide World of Sports, Orlando (☎407/839-3900); the Boston Red Sox, City of Palms Park, Fort Myers (☎1-617/482-4SOX); the Detroit Tigers, Joker Marchant Stadium, Lakeland (☎866/66-TIGER); the NY Mets, Tradition Field, Port St Lucie (☎772/871-2115); and the NY Yankees, Steinbrenner Field, Tampa (☎813/287-8844). For the training locations of other teams, visit ⓦwww.springtrainingonline.com.

Football

Of the state's three **professional football teams**, the **Miami Dolphins** have been the most successful, appearing five times in the Super Bowl and, in 1972, enjoying the only undefeated season in NFL history. They, like the Marlins, play at Dolphin Stadium (ⓦwww.miamidolphins.com; most tickets around $40–105). The **Jacksonville Jaguars**, who entered the league in 1995, have stolen a bit of the Dolphins' thunder; they've already been in the playoffs six times, twice coming within one game of the Super Bowl. They play at Jacksonville Municipal Stadium (☎877/4-JAGS-TIX, ⓦwww.jaguars.com; most tickets $50–100). The **Tampa Bay Buccaneers** have also had recent success; after years of losing seasons, they won the Super Bowl in 2003. The Bucs play at Raymond James Stadium (☎813/879-BUCS or 1-800/795-2827, ⓦwww.tampabaybucs.com; home tickets usually sold out to season ticket holders).

Even greater fervor is whipped up by both the **University of Florida Gators** (in Gainesville), the **Florida State University Seminoles** (in Tallahassee), and the **University of Miami Hurricanes.** All play around eleven games a season. Tickets to college games run upwards of $40 and can be difficult to come by for the more competitive games. Further details are given in the Guide.

The **football season** for both the professional and collegiate levels begins in late summer and lasts through January.

Basketball

The state's two **professional basketball teams** have enjoyed intermittent success in the NBA. The **Miami Heat** play at the American Airlines Arena (☎786/777-1502, ⓦwww.nba.com/heat), while the **Orlando Magic** play at the Amway Arena (☎407/89-MAGIC, ⓦwww.nba.com/magic). Tickets for both teams are in the $10–115 range.

Top among the **college teams** are the **Florida University Gators** (☎1-800/34-GATOR or 352/375-4683, ⓦwww.gatorzone.com) and the **Miami University Hurricanes** (☎1-800/GO-CANES, ⓦwww.hurricanesports.cstv.com).

Ice hockey

Florida boasts two teams in the NHL: the **Florida Panthers** (☏954/835-PUCK, Ⓦwww.panthers.nhl.com), who play at the BankAtlantic Center in Sunrise near Fort Lauderdale, and the **Tampa Bay Lightning** (☏813/301-6600, Ⓦwww.tampabaylightning .com), who play at the St Pete Times Forum. The NHL **season** runs between October and June, and most tickets for both teams are $15–110.

Watersports and outdoor activities

Even nonswimmers can quickly learn to **snorkel**, which is the best way to see one of the state's finest natural assets: the living coral reef curling around its southeastern corner and along the Florida Keys. Many guided snorkeling trips run to the reef, costing $30–50 – further details are given throughout the Guide. More adventurous than snorkeling is loading up with air tanks to go **scuba diving**. You'll need a diving license to do this; if you don't already have one you'll be required to take the three-day Open Water Certification course, involving both water time and reading, and costing from around $350 and up. Get details from diving shops, always plentiful near good diving areas, which can also provide equipment, maps, and general information.

The same reefs that make snorkeling and diving so much fun cause **surfing** to be less common than you might expect, limiting it to a few sections of the east coast. Florida's biggest waves strike land between Sebastian Inlet and Cocoa Beach, and surfing tournaments are held in the area during April and May. Lesser breakers are found at Miami Beach's First Street Beach, Boca Raton's South Beach Park, and around the Jacksonville beaches. Surfboards can be rented from local beach shops for $10–15 a day.

If you prefer to cut a (usually) more gentle passage through water, many of the state's rivers can be effortlessly navigated by **canoe**; see p.37, for more details.

Fishing

Few things excite higher passions in Florida than **fishing**: the numerous rivers and lakes and the various breeds of catfish, bass, carp, and perch inhabiting them bring eager fishermen from all over the US and beyond. Saltwater fishing is equally popular, with barely a coastal jetty in the state not creaking under the strain of weekend anglers. The most sociable way to fish, however, is from a "party boat" – a boatload of people putting to sea for a day of rod-casting and boozing; these generally cost $25–30 per person and are easily found in good fishing areas. Sportsfishing – heading out to deep water to do battle with marlin, tuna, and the odd shark – is much more expensive. In the prime sportsfishing areas, off the Florida Keys and off the Panhandle around Destin, you'll need at least $500 a day for a boat and a guide. To protect fish stocks, a highly complex set of rules and regulations governs where you can fish and what you can catch. For the latest facts, get the free *Florida Fishing Handbook* from the Florida Fish and Wildlife Conservation Commission, Farris Bryant Building, 620 S Meridian St, Tallahassee, FL 32399-1600 (☏850/488-4676, Ⓦmyfwc.com).

Hiking

Almost all state parks have undemanding nature trails intended for a pleasant hour's ramble; anything called a **hiking** or **backpacking trail** – plentiful in state and national parks, national forests, and threading some unprotected land as part of the Florida National Scenic Trail – requires more thought and planning.

Many hiking trails can easily be completed in a day, the longer ones have rough camping sites at regular intervals (see "Camping," p.28), and most periodically pass through fully equipped camping areas – giving the option of sleeping in comparative comfort. The best time to hike is from late fall to early spring: this avoids the exhausting heat of the summer and the worst of the mosquitoes and reveals a greater variety of animals.

In some areas you'll need a **wilderness permit** (free or $2) from the local park ranger's or wilderness area administration office, where you should call anyway for maps, general information on the hike, and a weather forecast – sudden rains can flood trails in swampy areas. Many state parks run organized hiking trips, details of which are given throughout the Guide.

The 1300-mile **Florida National Scenic Trail**, stretching the length of the state, is about 85 percent completed. The loosely connected footpath extends from the Gulf Islands National Seashore in the northwest down to Big Cypress National Preserve in the Everglades. Those wanting to hike the trail end to end ("through-hike") must join the Florida Trail Association (see below), which arranges permissions and permits on hikers' behalf as some trail sections fall on private property.

While hiking, be extremely wary of the **poisonwood tree** (ask a park ranger how to identify it); any contact between your skin and its bark can leave you needing hospital treatment – and avoid being splashed by rainwater dripping from its branches. Besides food, carry plenty of drinking water, a first-aid kit, insect repellent, and sunscreen.

For general hiking information, write to or check the website of the Florida Department of Environmental Protection, Office of Greenways and Trails, 3900 Commonwealth Blvd, MS 795, Tallahassee, FL 32399–3000 (☎850/245-2052, ⓦwww.dep.state.fl.us) or the Florida Trail Association (FTA), 5415 SW 13th St, Gainesville, FL 32608 (☎1-877/ HIKE-FLA or 352/378-8823, ⓦwww.florida -trail.org). The website of the FTA gives details of most trails and is constantly

updated. Two useful online hiking resources are ⓦwww.trailmonkey.com, which focuses on trails near the national parks and seashores, and ⓦwww.trails.com, a subscription service ($49.95 per year) that lets members download topographic maps and full trail descriptions.

Camping

All hiking trails have areas designated for **rough camping**, with either very limited facilities (a handpump for water, sometimes a primitive toilet) or none at all. Traveling by canoe, you'll often pass sandbars, which can make excellent overnight stops. It's preferable to cook by stove, but otherwise start fires only in permitted areas – indicated by signs – and use deadwood. Where there are no toilets, bury human waste at least four inches in the ground and a hundred feet from the nearest water supply and campground. Burn rubbish carefully, and what you can't burn, carry away. Never drink from rivers and streams, however clear and inviting they may look (you never know what unspeakable acts people – or animals – further upstream have performed in them), or from the state's many natural springs; water that isn't from taps should be boiled for at least five minutes or cleansed with an iodine-based purifier before you drink it. Always get advice, maps, and a weather forecast from the park ranger's or wilderness area administration office – often you'll need to fill in a wilderness permit, too, and pay a small nightly camping fee.

Canoeing

One way to enjoy natural Florida without getting blisters on your feet is by **canoeing**. You can rent canoes for around $20–30 a day wherever conditions are right: the best of Florida's rivers and streams are found in north central Florida and the Panhandle. Many state and national parks have canoe runs, too; the **Florida Canoe Trails System** comprises 36 marked routes along rivers and creeks, covering a combined distance of nearly a thousand miles – for more information, pick up the free *Florida Paddling Trails* brochure (available from the **Department of Environmental Protection**, address above), or go to ⓦwww.dep.state.fl.us/gwt.

Before setting off, get a canoeing **map** (you'll need to know the locations of access points and any rough camping sites) and check **weather conditions** and the river's **water level**: a low level can expose logs, rocks, and other obstacles; a flooded river is dangerous and should not be canoed; coastal rivers are affected by tides. Don't leave the canoe to walk on the bank, as this will cause damage and is likely to be trespassing. When a **motorboat** approaches, keep to the right and turn your bow into the wake. If you're **camping**, do so on a sandbar unless there are designated rough camping areas beside the river. As with any hike you might do (see p.36), make sure you carry the usual outdoor essentials.

Several small companies run canoe trips ranging from half a day to a week; they supply the canoe and take you from the end of the route back to where you started. Details are given throughout the Guide.

Birdwatching

Florida's location on the north–south bird migration route means opportunities for birdwatching here are very good, and visitors are likely to spot many unfamiliar species in greater numbers than they would elsewhere. Commonly sighted birds include the **snowy egret** (entirely white, with bright yellow feet), the **brown pelican** (grayish-brown body with a white head and neck), and the **cormorant** and **anhinga** (both sleek, black fish-catchers), and though you stand a better chance of seeing them in the winter months, some species are present year-round.

Casual and experienced birders alike can take advantage of the **Great Florida Birding Trail** (☎850/488-9478, ⓦwww .floridabirdingtrail.com), which links clusters of existing birding sites (such as parks, conservation areas, and sanctuaries) via highways throughout the state using special highway signs and detailed maps. Overseen by the state's Fish and Wildlife Conservation Commission, the trail covers most of the state, from the east coast (Jacksonville area south to Ft Pierce) to the Panhandle and on the west coast as far south as Naples.

Traveling with children

Much of Florida is geared toward child-friendly travel, what with the theme parks, water parks, beaches, and so on, so you're unlikely to encounter too many problems with children in tow.

Hotels and **motels** usually welcome children; those in major tourist areas such as Orlando often have a games room and/or a play area, and allow children below a certain age (usually 14, sometimes 18) to stay free in their parents' room.

In all but the most formal restaurants, young diners are likely to be presented with a **kids' menu**, plus crayons, drawing pads, and assorted toys.

Activities

Most large towns have at least one child-orientated **museum** with plenty of interactive educational exhibits – often sophisticated enough to keep even some adults amused for hours. Virtually all museums and other tourist attractions have reduced rates for children under a certain age.

Florida's **theme parks** may seem the ultimate in kids' entertainment, but in fact are much more geared toward entertaining adults than most people expect. Only Walt Disney World's Magic Kingdom is tailor-made for young kids (though even here, parents are warned some rides may frighten the very young); adolescents (and adults) are likely to prefer Disney's Hollywood Studios or the two parks at Universal Orlando.

Away from the major tourist stops, **natural Florida** has much to stimulate the young. In the many state parks and in Everglades National Park, park rangers specialize in tuning formative minds in to the wonders of nature – aided by an abundance of alligators, turtles, and all manner of brightly colored birds. A boat trip in dolphin-inhabited waters – several of these are recommended in the Guide – is another likely way to pique curiosity in the natural world.

On a more cautious note, adults should take great care not to allow young skin to be exposed to the Florida sun for too long: even

a few minutes' unprotected exposure can cause serious **sunburn**.

A good idea in a major theme park is to show your child how to find (or how to recognize and ask uniformed staff to take them to) the "**Lost Kids Area**." This designated space not only makes lost kids easy to locate but also provides supervision plus toys and games to keep them amused until you show up.

Getting around

Children under 2 years old **fly** for free – though that doesn't mean they get a seat – and when aged from 2 to 12 they are usually entitled to half-price tickets.

If you're doing a fly-drive vacation, car rental companies can usually provide kids' car seats for around $5 a day. You would, however, be advised to take your own, as they are not always available.

Travel essentials

Costs

If you're coming from elsewhere in the US, you'll likely not find Florida any more or less expensive, save in the resorts and big cities. For foreign visitors, even when the **exchange rate** is at its least advantageous, you'll find virtually everything – accommodation, food, gas, cameras, clothes, and more – to be better value in the US than it is at home.

Accommodation is likely to be your biggest single expense. Few hotel or motel rooms in cities cost under $40 – around $75 is more usual for a halfway decent room – while rates in rural areas are a little cheaper. Although hostels offering dorm beds – generally for $15–25 – exist, they are not widespread and in any case represent only a very small saving for two or more people traveling together. Camping, of course, is cheap (anywhere from free to perhaps $30 per night), but is rarely practical in or around the big cities.

As for **food**, $15 a day is enough to get you an adequate life-support diet, while for a daily budget of around $30 you can dine pretty well. Beyond this, everything hinges on how much sightseeing, taxi-taking, drinking, and socializing you do. Much of any of these – especially in the major cities – and you're likely to go through upward of $70 a day, excluding the other expenses mentioned above.

The rates for **traveling around** on buses, trains, and even planes, may look cheap on paper, but the distances involved mean costs soon mount. For a group of two or more, **renting a car** can be a very good investment (see "Getting around," p.23), not least because it enables you to stay in the ubiquitous budget motels along the highways instead of relying on expensive downtown hotels.

A **sales tax** of 6 percent is added to virtually everything you buy in shops,

Tipping

You shouldn't depart a bar or restaurant without leaving a **tip** of at least 15–20 percent (unless the service is utterly disgusting). About the same amount should be added to taxi fares – and round them up to the nearest 50¢ or dollar. Tip hotel porters roughly $1 per item for carrying your baggage to your room. When paying by credit or charge card, you're expected to add the tip to the total bill before filling in the amount and signing.

except for groceries, but it isn't part of the marked price.

Crime and personal safety

No one could pretend Florida is trouble-free, though outside the urban centers crime rates are relatively low. Even the lawless reputation of Miami is in excess of the truth, though several clearly defined areas are strictly off limits. At night you should always be cautious – though not unduly so – wherever you are. All the major tourist and nightlife areas in cities are invariably brightly lit and well policed. By being careful, planning ahead, and taking good care of your possessions, you should, generally speaking, have few real problems.

Car crime

Given that many visitors get around by car in Florida, car crime is arguably the main danger to one's personal safety. When **driving**, under no circumstances stop in any unlit or seemingly deserted urban area – and especially not if someone is waving you down, suggesting there is something wrong with your car. Similarly, if you are "accidentally" rammed by the driver behind, do not stop immediately but drive on to the nearest well-lit, busy, and secure area (such as a hotel, toll booth, or gas station) and phone the emergency number (☏**911**) for assistance. Keep your doors locked and windows never more than slightly open (as you'll probably be using air conditioning, you'll want to keep them fully closed anyway).

Always take care when planning your route, particularly through urban areas, and be sure to use a **reliable map** such as the ones we've recommended on p.45. Particularly in Miami, local authorities are making

efforts to add directions to tourist sights and attractions to road signs, thereby reducing the possibility of visitors unwittingly driving into dangerous areas. Aside from these problem areas, however, there is an easy-going and essentially safe atmosphere on roads throughout the state.

Street crime and hotel burglaries

After car crime, the biggest problem for most travelers in Florida is the threat of **mugging**. It's impossible to give hard-and-fast rules about what to do if you're confronted by a mugger. Whether to run, scream, or fight depends on the situation – the most common advice would be to offer no resistance and just hand over the money.

There are a few **basic rules** worth remembering: don't flash money around; don't peer at your map (or this book) at every street corner, thereby announcing you're a lost stranger; avoid dark streets and never start to walk down one you can't see the end of; and in the early hours stick to the roadside edge of the sidewalk so it's easier to run into the road to attract attention.

If the worst happens, try to find a phone and dial ☏**911**, or head to the nearest police station. If you're in a big city, ring the local Travelers Aid (their numbers are listed in the phone book) for sympathy and practical advice.

Another potential source of trouble is having your hotel room burglarized. Some Orlando area hotels are notorious for this and many such break-ins appear to be inside jobs. Always store valuables in the hotel safe when you go out; when inside, keep your door locked and don't open it to anyone you don't trust; if they claim to be hotel staff and you don't believe them, call reception to check.

Stolen traveler's checks and credit cards

Keep a record of the numbers of your **traveler's checks** separately from the actual checks; if you lose them, call the issuing company on the toll-free number below. You should get the missing checks reissued within a couple of days – and perhaps an emergency advance to tide you over.

Electricity

In the US the **electrical** current is 110V AC and all plugs are two-pronged. British-made equipment won't work unless it has a voltage-switching provision.

Entry requirements

Citizens of Australia, the UK, Ireland, New Zealand, and most European countries do not require visas for trips to the US of less than ninety days. Instead they need a machine-readable passport (MRP) and a visa waiver form, which is provided either by a travel agent or by the airline during check-in or on the plane, and must be presented to immigration on arrival. The MRP includes a few lines of digital information about you at the bottom of the passport; each country is in varying stages of compliance. If you don't have an MRP, you'll be required to obtain a nonimmigrant visitor's visa (see below). The visa waiver form covers entry across the land borders with Canada and Mexico as well as by air. Those eligible for the scheme must apply for a visa if they intend to work, study, or stay in the country for more than ninety days.

Prospective visitors from parts of the world not mentioned above must have a valid passport and a nonimmigrant visitor's visa. How you'll obtain a visa depends on what country you're in and your status when you apply, so call the nearest US embassy or consulate (see below). More information can be found at ⓦhttp://travel.state.gov/visa/visa_1750.html. Whatever your nationality, visas are not issued to convicted felons.

US embassies and consulates abroad

Australia MLC Centre, Level 59, 19–29 Martin Place, Sydney ☏02/9373 9200, ⓦusembassy-australia.state.gov
Ireland 42 Elgin Rd, Ballsbridge, Dublin ☏01/668 8777, ⓦdublin.usembassy.gov
New Zealand 29 Fitzherbert Terrace, Thorndon, Wellington ☏04/462 6000, ⓦnewzealand.usembassy.gov
South Africa 877 Pretorius St, Arcadia, Pretoria ☏12/431-4000, ⓦsouthafrica.usembassy.gov
UK 24 Grosvenor Square, London W1A 1AE ☏020/7499 9000, ⓦwww.usembassy.org.uk; 3 Regent Terrace, Edinburgh EH7 5BW ☏0131/556 8315, ⓦwww.usembassy.org.uk/scotland; Danesfort House, 223 Stranmillis Rd, Belfast BT9 5GR ☏028/9038 6100, ⓦwww.usembassy.org.uk/nireland

Immigration controls and customs

During the flight, you'll be handed an **immigration form** (and a customs declaration), which must be filled out and, after landing, given up at immigration control. Part of the form will be attached to your passport, where it must stay until you leave, when an immigration or airline official will detach it.

On the form you must cite your proposed length of stay and list a verifiable address, at least for your first night. If you have no accommodation arranged for your first night, pick a plausible-sounding hotel from the appropriate section of the Guide and list that.

You should also be able to prove you have a return air ticket (if flying in) and enough

---

To report stolen traveler's checks and credit cards, call:

American Express checks ☏1-800/221-7282
American Express cards ☏1-800/528-4800
MasterCard ☏1-800/627-8372
Thomas Cook ☏1-800/223-7373
Visa checks ☏1-800/227-6811
Visa cards ☏1-800/847-2911

money to support yourself while in the US; around $300–400 a week is usually considered sufficient – waving a credit card or two may do the trick. Anyone revealing the slightest intention of working while in the country is likely to be refused admission. You may also experience difficulties if you admit to being HIV-positive or having TB. For details on customs, check the US Customs and Border Protection website at ⓦwww .cbp.gov/xp/cgov/travel.

Extensions and leaving

The date stamped on the form in your passport is the latest you're legally entitled to stay. Leaving a few days after may not matter, especially if you're heading home, but more than a week or so can result in a protracted – and generally unpleasant – interrogation from officials, which may cause you to miss your flight and be denied entry to the US in the future. Your American hosts and/or employer may also face legal proceedings.

Alternatively, you can do things the official way and get an **extension** before your time is up. The process can take a while, so it should be started as early as possible, but in no case later than your "leave by" date. This can be done by mailing form I-539 (and the $300 filing fee) to the nearest **US Citizenship and Immigration Services (USCIS)** service center (for Florida, the address is: USCIS Vermont Service Center, ATTN: I-539, 75 Lower Welden St, St Albans, VT 05479; info at ⓦuscis.gov). You may need to provide evidence of sufficient finances and, if possible, an upstanding American citizen to vouch for your worthiness. You'll also have to explain why you didn't plan for the extra time initially.

Gay and lesbian travelers

The biggest gay and lesbian scene in Florida is in Key West, at the very tip of the Florida Keys. The island town's live-and-let-live tradition has made it a vacation destination favored by American gays and lesbians for decades, and many arrivals simply never went home: instead, they've taken up permanent residence and opened guesthouses, restaurants, and other businesses – such as running gay and lesbian snorkeling and diving trips.

In **Miami** and **Fort Lauderdale** the networks of gay and lesbian resources, clubs, and bars are quite extensive – within certain areas – and it's not hard to pick up on the scene. There are smaller levels of activity in the other cities, and along developed sections of the coast a number of motels and hotels are specifically aimed at gay travelers – Fort Lauderdale, for example, has over thirty gay hotels. Predictably, attitudes to gay and lesbian visitors get progressively worse the further you go from the populous areas. Being open about your sexuality in the rural regions is likely to provoke an uneasy response if not open hostility. There are also active and relaxed gay scenes in **Pensacola** and, to a lesser extent, **Tallahassee**.

For a complete rundown on local resources, bars, and clubs, see the relevant headings within accounts of individual cities. On the internet, ⓦwww.gay-guide.com and ⓦwww.funmaps.com provide a wide range of useful information about gay and lesbian travel in Florida.

Contacts and resources

In the US & Canada

Damron Company ☎1-800/462-6654 or 415/255-0404, ⓦwww.damron.com. Publishes pocket-sized listings of hotels, bars, clubs, accommodation and resources for gay men and women.
Gayellow Pages ☎646/213-0263, ⓦwww .gayellowpages.com. Directory of businesses in the US and Canada.
International Gay/Lesbian Travel Association ☎954/630-1637, ⓦwww.iglta.org. Provides a list of gay- and lesbian-owned or friendly travel agents, accommodation, and other travel businesses.

In the UK

www.gaytravel.co.uk Online gay and lesbian travel guides – including Miami and Key West.
Madison Travel ☎01273/202 532 or 020/7183 0253, ⓦwww.madisontravel.co.uk. Gay-orientated travel agent offering trips to Miami and Key West for women and men.

Health

For the average traveler, a case of sunburn is as about as serious an injury that can be sustained while in Florida. If you do have a serious accident though, emergency medical services will get to you quickly and charge you later. For emergencies or ambulances, dial ☏911 (or whatever variant may be on the information plate of the pay phone). If you have an accident but don't require an ambulance, most hospitals will have a walk-in emergency room (ER). For the nearest hospital, check with your hotel or dial information at ☏411. We've also listed a couple of ERs in the Guide.

Should you need to see a doctor, you can find lists in the *Yellow Pages* under "Clinics" or "Physicians and Surgeons." A basic consultation fee is about $100, payable in advance. Medication isn't cheap either – keep receipts for all you spend and claim it back on your insurance policy when you return (see "Insurance," below, for more).

To avoid painful – and potentially dangerous – **sunburn**, apply liberal amounts of sunscreen whenever outside. Those with fair skin should wear a wide-brimmed hat and consider staying out of the sun entirely during its brightest period (11am–3pm).

From mid-May to November, **mosquitoes – known as "no see'ums"** – are a tremendous nuisance and virtually unavoidable in any area close to fresh water. During these months, insect repellent is essential, as is wearing long-sleeved shirts and long pants. It's rare for mosquitoes to carry diseases here, though during 2001 and 2002 Florida was hit by an outbreak of West Nile virus, a mosquito-borne flu-like disease that can cause death, the elderly being especially vulnerable. As each generation of mosquitoes dies out during the winter, it's unlikely this will be repeated – at least not for many years.

Dangerous animals

Florida's **snakes** don't go looking for trouble, but several species will retaliate if provoked – which you're most likely to do by standing on one. Two species are potentially deadly: the coral snake, which has a black nose and bright yellow and red rings covering its body, and usually spends the daylight hours under piles of rotting vegetation; and the cotton-mouth moccasin (sometimes called the water moccasin), dark-colored with a small head, which lives around rivers and lakes. Less harmful, but still to be avoided, are two types of rattlesnake: the easily identified diamond-back, whose thick body is covered in a diamond pattern, and which turns up in dry, sandy areas and hammocks; and the gray-colored pygmy, so small it's almost impossible to spot until it's too late. You're unlikely to see a snake in the wild and snake attacks are even more rare, but if bitten you should contact a ranger or a doctor immediately. It's a wise precaution to carry a snakebite kit, available for a couple of dollars from most camping shops.

The biggest surprises among Florida's wildlife may be the apparent docility of **alligators** – almost always they will back away if approached by a human (though this is not something you should put to the test) The only truly dangerous type of alligator is a mother guarding her nest or tending her young. Even then, she'll give you plenty of warning, by showing her teeth and hissing, before attacking.

For more on Florida's wildlife and its habitats, see "Natural Florida" in Contexts, p.472.

Medical resources for travelers

CDC ☏1-800/311-3435, 🌐 wwwn.cdc.gov/travel. Official US government travel health site.
International Society for Travel Medicine ☏1-770/736-7060, 🌐 www.istm.org. Has a full list of international travel health clinics, including an extensive list for Florida.

Insurance

Getting travel insurance is highly recommended, especially if you're coming from abroad and are at all concerned about your health – prices for medical attention in the US can be exorbitant.

A typical travel insurance policy usually provides cover for the loss of baggage, tickets, and – up to a certain limit – cash or checks, as well as cancellation or curtailment of your journey. Most of them exclude so-called **high-risk activities** unless an extra premium is paid: in Florida, this could mean scuba diving and windsurfing. If you need to make a claim, you should keep receipts for medicines and medical treatment, and in the event you have anything stolen, you must obtain an official theft report from the police.

Internet

You'll find **internet cafés** in most of Florida's cities and many towns. You'll generally pay $7–10 an hour. If you're toting along a laptop and want to get connected, browse ⓦwww.wififreespot.com or www.jiwire.com, which list locations offering free wireless access throughout Florida and the rest of the US.

Laundry

All but the most basic hotels will wash **laundry** for you, but you can also do a wash (about $1.50–2) and tumble dry ($1–1.50) in the laundromats found all over; take plenty of quarters. Some hotels also have machines available for guests – ask when you check in.

Living in Florida

Far from being the land of the "newly wed and the nearly dead" as many comedians have described the state, Florida's immaculate climate has persuaded people from all over the US and the rest of the world to arrive in search of a subtropical paradise. The following suggestions for finding work are basic and, if you're not a US citizen, represent the limits of what you can do without the all-important Social Security number (without which, legally, you can't work at all).

Finding work

Since the federal government introduced **fines** of up to $10,000 for illegal employees, employers have become understandably choosy about whom they hire. Even the usual **casual jobs** – catering, restaurant, and bar work – have tightened up for those without a **Social Security number**. If you do find work it's likely to be of the less visible, poorly paid kind – as washer-up rather than waiter. **Agricultural work** is always available on central Florida farms during the October to May citrus harvest; check with the nearest university or college, where noticeboards detail what's available. There are usually no problems with papers in this kind of work, though it often entails working miles from major centers and is wearying "stoop" (continually bending over) labor in blistering heat. If you can stick it out, the pay is often good and comes with basic board and accommodation. House-cleaning and baby-sitting are also feasible, if not very well-paid options.

Publications and websites

Another pre-planning strategy for working abroad is to check websites such as ⓦwww.overseasjobs.com, part of a network of sites with worldwide job listings. Vacation Work (an imprint of Crimson Publishing, ⓦwww.crimsonpublishing.co.uk) also publishes books on summer jobs abroad and how to work your way around the world. Travel magazines like the reliable *Wanderlust* (ⓦwww.wanderlust.co.uk) have a Job Shop section that often advertises job opportunities with tour companies.

Study and work programs

From the UK & Ireland

BUNAC (British Universities' North America Club) ☏020/7251 3472, ⊛www.bunac.co.uk. Organizes working holidays in the US for students, typically at summer camps or training placements with companies.

From Australia & New Zealand

Australians Studying Abroad ☏1800/645 755 or 03/9822 6899, ⊛www.asatravinfo.com.au. Study tours focusing on art and culture.
International Exchange Programs (IEP) ☏1300/300 912, ⊛www.iep.org.au. BUNAC's sister organization, arranging working holidays for Australian and New Zealand students.

Mail

Ordinary mail within the US costs 42¢ for a letter weighing up to an ounce; addresses must include the zip code (a five-digit postal code), as well as the sender's address on the envelope. **Air mail** between Florida and Europe generally takes about four days to a week to arrive. Postcards, aerograms, and letters weighing up to an ounce (a single sheet) cost 94¢.

Letters can be sent c/o **General Delivery** (what's known elsewhere as **poste restante**) to any post office in the state, but must include the post office's zip code and will only be held for thirty days before being returned to the sender – so make sure there's a return address on the envelope.

Rules on sending **parcels** are very rigid: packages must be sealed according to the postal service's instructions, which are given at the start of the *Yellow Pages* and at the post office. To send anything out of the country, you'll need a **customs declaration form**, available from the post office. **Sending** a parcel weighing 1lb to Europe or Australia by airmail will cost $10.30, to New Zealand the rate is $9.85; by land prices are about two-thirds less expensive, but it can take six times as long for the parcel to arrive. The post office website (⊛www.usps.com) has a useful tool for calculating postal rates to anywhere in the world.

Maps

The excellent *Florida Official Transportation Map*, available for free at tourist offices, covers the state's roads in detail and also has plans of the principal cities and tourist areas. Otherwise, general-purpose road maps from publishers like the American Automobile Association (AAA), Rand McNally, and Universal Map concentrate on providing information for drivers, although they may also include some tourist information or street plans. The detailed **Rough Guides' Florida map**, on waterproof, tearproof paper, highlights the main sights of interest. Some publishers (ITMB, Rand McNally, MapEasy) also do sectional maps just for the Gold Coast, Florida Keys, Central Florida, and so on.

You can pick up local **hiking maps** at ranger stations in state and national parks, and some camping shops carry a supply.

Members of the AAA and its overseas affiliates (such as the AA and the RAC in Britain) can also benefit from this organization's maps and general assistance. The AAA is based at 1000 AAA Drive, Heathrow, FL 32746-5063 ☏407/444-4240, ⊛www.aaasouth.com); further offices all across the state are listed in local phone books or on the association's website.

Opportunities for foreign students

Foreign students wishing to **study in Florida** can either try the long shot of arranging a year abroad through their own university, or apply directly to a Florida university (be prepared to stump up the painfully expensive fees). The Student and Exchange Visitor Program, for which participants are given a J-1 visa enabling them to take a job arranged in advance through the program, is not much use since almost all the jobs are at American summer camps – of which the state has none. If you're interested anyway, organizations to contact in the UK include BUNAC; see above for details.

Money

US currency comes in notes worth $1, $5, $10, $20, $50, and $100, plus various larger (and rarer) denominations. Confusingly, all are the same size and same green color, making it necessary to check each note carefully. More recent $5, $10, $20, and $50 bills do have some added color. The dollar is made up of 100 cents (¢) in coins of 1 cent (known as a penny), 5 cents (a nickel), 10 cents (a dime), and 25 cents (a quarter). Change (quarters are the most useful) is needed for buses, vending machines, and telephones, so always carry plenty.

With an **ATM card**, you can withdraw cash from just about anywhere in Florida; transaction fees vary, but are usually under $5. Foreign cash-dispensing cards linked to international networks, such as Plus or Cirrus, are also widely accepted. Check with your bank for details before leaving home.

Credit cards

If you don't already have a **credit card**, you should think seriously about getting one before you set off. For many services, it's simply taken for granted that you'll be paying with plastic. When renting a car (or even a bike) or checking in to a hotel, you may well be asked to show a credit card to establish your credit-worthiness – even if you intend to settle the bill in cash – or as security, or both; and hotels will often require you to leave a cash deposit of around $100 to cover incidental room charges should you not have a credit card.

Traveler's checks and cash

US dollar traveler's checks are a safe way for foreign visitors to carry money; they offer the great security of knowing that lost or stolen ones will be replaced. The **usual fee** is one or two percent, though this may be waived if you purchase them through a bank where you have an account. You should have no problem using the better-known checks, such as American Express and Visa, in shops, restaurants, and gas stations in just the same way as you would use cash. Be sure to have plenty of the $10 and $20 denominations for everyday transactions.

Major Florida **banks** – such as Bank of America, SunTrust, and Wachovia – will (with considerable fuss) change traveler's checks in other currencies and foreign currency. Commission rates tend to be lower at **exchange bureaux** such as Thomas Cook and American Express; airport exchange offices can also be reasonable. Rarely, if ever, do hotels change foreign currency.

Youth and student discounts

Full-time students are eligible for the **International Student ID Card** (ISIC, Ⓦ www.isiccard.com in the UK, or go to www.istc.org for more information), which entitles the bearer to special air, rail, and bus fares, and discounts at museums, theaters, and other attractions. The card costs $22 for Americans; Can$16 for Canadians; Aus$18 for Australians; NZ$20 for New Zealanders; £9 in the UK; and €13 in the Republic of Ireland.

For non-students, two other cards are available at the same prices as the ISIC card and offering the same benefits: you only have to be 26 or younger to qualify for the **International Youth Travel Card**, while teachers are eligible for the **International Teacher Card**. All these cards are available from student-oriented travel agents in North America, Europe, Australia, and New Zealand. Several other organizations and accommodation groups also sell their own cards, good for various discounts.

A university photo ID might open some doors, but is not as easily recognizable as the ISIC card; note that the latter is often not accepted as valid proof of age – in bars or liquor stores, for example. To prove your age, carry some form of government ID, such as a passport or driving license.

Opening hours and public holidays

Banking hours in Florida are generally 10am until 3pm Monday to Thursday and 10am to 5pm on Fridays, while **post offices** are usually open Monday to Friday 9am to 5pm and Saturday 9am to noon.

The biggest and most all-American of all the **public holidays** is **Independence Day**

National Public holidays

New Year's Day Jan 1
Martin Luther King, Jr's Birthday
Third Mon in Jan
Presidents' Day Third Mon in Feb
Memorial Day Last Mon in May
Independence Day July 4
Labor Day First Mon in Sept
Columbus Day Second Mon in Oct
Veterans' Day Nov 11
Thanksgiving Day Fourth Thurs
in Nov
Christmas Day Dec 25

on July 4, when most of Florida grinds to a standstill as people salute the flag and take part in firework displays, marches, beauty pageants, and more. The large amusement parks, particularly Disney World, are completely swamped during this time. More sedate is **Thanksgiving Day**, on the fourth Thursday in November, which is essentially a domestic affair, when relatives return to the familial nest to stuff themselves with roast turkey.

On the national public holidays listed below, banks and offices are liable to be closed all day, and shops may reduce their hours.

Phones

Local calls cost a minimum of 50¢ from coin-operated public phones. More expensive are **non-local calls** ("zone calls") to numbers within the same area code (commonly, vast areas are covered by a single code) and **long-distance calls** (to a different area code), for which you'll need plenty of change. Non-local calls and long-distance calls are far cheaper if made between 6pm and 8am. Detailed rates are listed at the front of the telephone directory (the *White Pages*). Note that some budget hotels offer free local calls from rooms (ask when you check in) and that rates are generally much cheaper using prepaid **phone cards** sold at convenience stores in denominations of $5, $10, and $20.

Another option is using a **calling card** or **telephone charge card** from your phone

company back home. Using a PIN, you can make calls that will be charged to your home account, but bear in mind that rates may well be more expensive than calling from a public phone.

Many government agencies, car rental firms, hotels, and other services have **toll-free numbers**, which have the prefix 1-800, 1-866, 1-877, or 1-888. Within the US, you can dial any number starting with those digits free of charge (even from a public phone), though some numbers only operate inside Florida (this won't be apparent until you try the number).

Phone numbers throughout this book are given with the area code followed by the local number: for local calls just dial the seven-digit local number; for calls to a different area code, dial 1 followed by the area code and local number. For international calls dial the country's access code, then 1 and the area and local numbers (see p.48).

Useful phone numbers and codes

Emergencies & information

Emergencies ☏911; ask for the appropriate emergency service: fire, police, or ambulance
Local directory information ☏411
Long-distance directory information
☏1- (area code)/555-1212
Directory enquiries for toll-free numbers
☏1-800/555-1212
Operator ☏0

Cell phones

US and Canadian cell phone users will likely find that their phones work fine throughout most of Florida. But before leaving home, be sure to check with your service provider to make sure costly roaming charges don't apply. Quite often, you can change your service plan to fit your traveling needs if necessary.

If you're coming from abroad and want to use your mobile phone in Florida, you'll need to check with your phone provider whether it will work abroad, and what the call charges are. Unless you have a tri-band or a 4-band phone, a cell phone bought for use outside the US may not work inside the States (and vice versa).

Calling home from abroad

Note that the initial zero is omitted from the area code when dialling the UK, Ireland, Australia and New Zealand from abroad.

Australia international access code + 61.

New Zealand international access code + 64.

UK international access code + 44.

US & Canada international access code + 1.

Republic of Ireland international access code + 353

South Africa international access code + 27.

In the UK, you may need to inform your phone provider before going abroad to get international access switched on. You may be charged extra for this depending on your existing package and where you are traveling to. You are also likely to be charged extra for incoming calls when abroad, as the people calling you will be paying the usual rate. If you want to retrieve messages while you're away, you also may have to ask your provider for a new access code, as your home one might not work abroad.

Senior travelers

Along with being a popular place to retire to, people over the age of 62 can enjoy a tremendous variety of discounts when traveling in Florida. Both Amtrak and Greyhound, for example, and many US airlines, offer modest reductions on fares to older passengers. Museums, art galleries, and even hotels offer small discounts as well, and since the definition of "senior" can drop as low as 55, it is always worth asking.

Any US citizen or permanent resident aged 62 or over is entitled to free admission for life to all national parks, monuments, and historic sites using an **America the Beautiful – National Parks and Federal Recreational Lands Pass – Senior Pass**, for which a one-time $10 fee is charged; it can be issued at any such site. This free entry also applies to any accompanying passengers in the car or, where a per person rather than a per vehicle fee is demanded, the passport-holder can bring in up to three additional adults free of charge. It also gives a fifty percent reduction on fees for camping, parking, and boat launching.

Contacts and resources

In the US

American Association of Retired Persons (AARP) 601 E Street NW, Washington, DC 20049 ☎ 1-888/687-2277 ⓦ www.aarp.org. Can provide discounts on accommodation and vehicle rental. Membership open to anyone aged 50 or over for an annual fee of $12.50 (US residents), $17 (Canadian residents), or $28 (everyone else).
Elderhostel 11 Avenue de Layfayette, Boston, MA 02111 ☎ 1-877/454-5768, ⓦ www.elderhostel .org. Runs an extensive worldwide network of educational and activity programs, cruises, and homestays for people over 55 (companions may be younger). Programs generally last a week or more and all-inclusive costs are around $115 per day. Florida destinations include St Augustine, Sarasota, and the Everglades.

In the UK

Saga Holidays The Saga Building, Enbrook Park, Folkestone, Kent CT20 3SE ☎ 0800/096 0089, ⓦ www.saga.co.uk/travel. The country's biggest and most established specialist in tours and holidays aimed at older people. Offers several Florida packages.

Time

Most of Florida follows Eastern Standard Time, which is five hours behind Greenwhich Mean Time. However, as you travel west through the Panhandle you'll eventually cross into the Central Time zone (at a point about 45 miles west of Tallahassee), which is an hour behind Eastern Time.

Tourist information

Florida's official tourism website (ⓦ www .visitflorida.com) is a reasonable starting point for advance information. Once you've arrived in the state, you'll find that most large towns have at least a Convention and Visitors Bureau ("CVB," usually open Mon–Fri 9am–5pm, Sat 9am–1pm), offering detailed information on the local area and discount coupons for food and accommodation; but they are unable to book accommodation.

In addition you'll find **chamber of commerce offices** almost everywhere; these are designed to promote local business interests, but are more than happy to provide travelers with local maps and information. Most communities have local free newspapers carrying news of events and entertainment – the most useful of which we've detailed in the Guide.

Drivers entering Florida will find **Welcome Centers**, fully stocked with information leaflets and discount booklets, at four points: on Hwy-231 at Campbellton, near the Florida–Alabama border; off I-75 near Jennings, just south of the Florida–Georgia line; on I-10 16 miles west of Pensacola; and for I-95 drivers, there's one just north of Yulee. There's another in the Capitol building in Tallahassee (detailed in the Guide).

Travelers with disabilities

The US has one of the best infrastructures in the world for disabled people, and travelers with mobility problems or other physical disabilities are likely to find Florida to be in tune with their needs. All public buildings must be wheelchair-accessible and have suitable toilets, many city street corners have dropped curbs, and most city buses are able to "kneel" to make access easier and are built with space and handgrips for wheelchair users.

When organizing your holiday, read your **travel insurance** small print carefully to make sure that people with a pre-existing medical condition are not excluded. A **medical certificate** of your fitness to travel, provided by your doctor, is also extremely useful; some airlines or insurance companies may insist on it. Carry spares of any clothing or equipment that might be hard to find; if there's an association representing people with your disability, contact them early in the planning process.

On the ground, the **major car rental firms** can, given sufficient notice, provide vehicles with hand controls (though these are usually only available on the more expensive makes of vehicle); **Amtrak** will provide wheelchair assistance at its train stations and adapted seating on board, provided they have 72 hours' notice – and will give a fifteen percent discount on the regular fare; **Greyhound** buses, despite the fact that they lack designated wheelchair space, will allow a necessary helper to travel at a fifty percent discount.

Many of Florida's **hotels and motels** have been built recently, and disabled access has been a major consideration in their construction. Rarely will any part of the property be difficult for a disabled person to reach, and often several rooms are specifically designed to meet the requirements of disabled guests.

The state's major **theme parks** are also built with disabled access in mind, and attendants are always on hand to ensure a disabled person gets all the necessary assistance and derives maximum enjoyment from their visit. Even in the Florida wilds, facilities are good: most **state parks** arrange programs for disabled visitors; in Everglades National Park, all the walking trails are wheelchair-accessible, as is one of the backcountry camping sites.

In the US

Access-Able ⓦ www.access-able.com. Online resource for travelers with disabilities.
Mobility International USA 132 E Broadway, Suite 343, Eugene, OR 97401 ☎ 541/343-1284 (voice and TDD), ⓦ www.miusa.org. Information and exchange programs for students with disabilities studying in the US.
Society for Accessible Travel & Hospitality (SATH) 347 Fifth Ave, Suite 605, New York, NY 10016 ☎ 212/447-7284, ⓦ www.sath.org. Nonprofit educational organization that has actively represented travelers with disabilities since 1976.

Guide

Guide

1 Miami...53

2 The Florida Keys 119

3 The Everglades...167

4 The Southeast...183

5 Sarasota and the Southwest 231

6 Orlando and Disney World....................................271

7 The Northeast 319

8 Tampa Bay and the Northwest 361

9 The Panhandle 413

1

Miami

ALABAMA

GEORGIA

ATLANTIC OCEAN

Gulf of Mexico

N

0   100 miles

CHAPTER 1 # Highlights

* **South Beach** Enjoy the beach and the nightlife, but don't miss the fabulous array of Art Deco buildings, mostly hotels, from the 1930s and 1940s. See p.67

* **Boat and kayak tours of Biscayne Bay** Take a boat tour around the celebrity mansions of Biscayne Bay, or soak up the stellar views from a kayak. See p.80

* **Art walks** Miami is one of the most dynamic art centers in the world, best experienced on a monthly art walk around the galleries of Wynwood. See p.83

* **Venetian Pool, Coral Gables** Coral Gables' civic amenities don't come better than this – a converted quarry that's both inviting and historic. See p.91

* **Key Biscayne** Just minutes from downtown, this upmarket island boasts pristine beaches, giant iguanas and tranquil bike trails. See p.96

* **Yambo, Little Havana** Forget the ersatz Cuban restaurants on the beach and step into this café for a true taste of Latin America. See p.105

▲ Sunday lunch crowd at Yambo in Little Havana

1

Miami

By far the best-known city in Florida, **MIAMI** is a gorgeous gaudy city, part tropical paradise, part throbbing urban hub. It lives up to every cliché of the holiday brochures: the bodies on the beach are as buff and tanned as you'd imagine, the nightlife raucous and raunchy, and the Art Deco hotels stylish. There are palm trees everywhere, and the temperature rarely dips below balmy. And though the climate and landscape may be near-perfect, it's the people that give Miami its depth and diversity. Two-thirds of the city's over two million population is of Hispanic origin, of which the most visible – and powerful – ethnic group are Cubans. Spanish is the main language in most areas, and news from Havana, Caracas, or Bogotá frequently gets more attention than the latest word from Washington.

Miami has cleaned itself up considerably since the 1980s, when it was plagued by the highest murder rate in America. The city has grown rich as a key gateway for US–Latin American trade, to which the glut of expensively designed banks and financial institutions bears witness. Strangely enough, another factor in Miami's revival was the mid-1980s cop show *Miami Vice*, which was less about crime than designer clothes and subtropical scenery, a tradition continued since 2002 by the ever-popular TV show **CSI: Miami**. Miami is also a major hub for Spanish-language TV studios, and a gaggle of Mexican and Colombian *telenovela* stars. Away from the beaches, Miami is gaining a reputation as one of the foremost centers for **contemporary art** in the US, with areas like the Wynwood district studded with galleries and studios.

Some history

Little has been recorded of the area's indigenous inhabitants: the **Tequesta** people were virtually wiped out by the **Spanish** conquistadores led by Juan Ponce de León, who arrived in 1513. The new invaders had no interest in developing southern Florida, being far more concerned with Cuba, and built only a few small settlements along the Miami River and around Biscayne Bay. The whole of the region was finally sold by Spain to the British in 1763, and until a century ago Miami was a swampy outpost where some one thousand mosquito-tormented settlers commuted by boat between a trading post and a couple of coconut plantations. The first mention of the "**Village of Miami**" comes after the Second Seminole War in 1842, when a William English re-established a plantation once owned by his uncle and started selling plots of land. Cleveland natives **William Brickell** (who set up a trading post on the Miami River in 1871) and **Julia Tuttle** (the "mother of Miami") are credited with founding the modern city; much of today's downtown area was a citrus

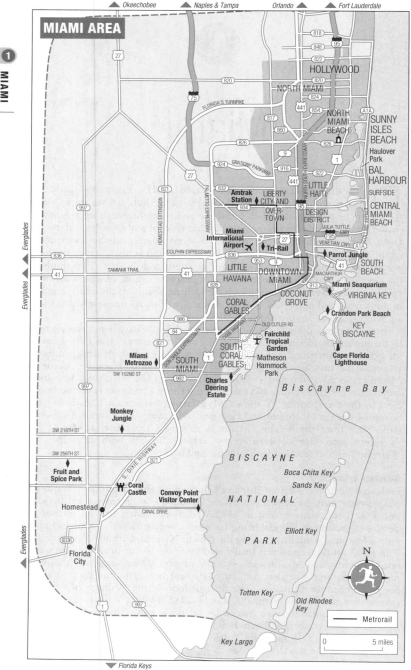

MIAMI AREA

▲ Okeechobee   ▲ Naples & Tampa   Orlando ▲   ▲ Fort Lauderdale

HOLLYWOOD

NORTH MIAMI

NORTH MIAMI BEACH

SUNNY ISLES BEACH

Haulover Park

BAL HARBOUR

SURFSIDE

CENTRAL MIAMI BEACH

LITTLE HAITI

DESIGN DISTRICT

GRATIGNY PARKWAY

FLORIDA'S TURNPIKE

HOMESTEAD EXTENSION

PALMETTO EXPRESSWAY

Amtrak Station

LIBERTY CITY AND OVER-TOWN

Miami International Airport

Tri-Rail

DOLPHIN EXPRESSWAY

TAMIAMI TRAIL

LITTLE HAVANA

DOWNTOWN MIAMI

JULIA TUTTLE CWY

VENETIAN CWY

Parrot Jungle

SOUTH BEACH

MACARTHUR CWY

Miami Seaquarium

VIRGINIA KEY

Crandon Park Beach

KEY BISCAYNE

CORAL GABLES

COCONUT GROVE

OLD CUTLER RD

Fairchild Tropical Garden

Matheson Hammock Park

Cape Florida Lighthouse

DON SHULA EXPRESSWAY

Miami Metrozoo

SOUTH MIAMI

SOUTH CORAL GABLES

SW 152ND ST

Charles Deering Estate

S. DIXIE HIGHWAY

Biscayne Bay

Monkey Jungle

SW 216TH ST

SW 256TH ST

BISCAYNE

Boca Chita Key

Sands Key

NATIONAL

Fruit and Spice Park

Coral Castle

Convoy Point Visitor Center

Homestead

CANAL DRIVE

Elliott Key

PARK

Florida City

N

Totten Key

Old Rhodes Key

——— Metrorail

0   5 miles

Key Largo

Everglades

▼ Florida Keys

farm owned by Tuttle in the 1890s, and it was thanks to her efforts that oil tycoon **Henry Flagler** was persuaded to extend his railroad south (though only after he'd been given vast swathes of land in return).

The completion of the railroad in 1896 gave Miami its first fixed land link with the rest of the country, and literally cleared the way for the 1920s property boom. Entire communities, such as George Merrick's **Coral Gables**, sprang up almost overnight and formed the basis of the city that stands today; the land here was relentlessly hawked to sun-seeking northerners who swarmed down to enjoy Florida's climate.

The most popular part of the city remains **Miami Beach**. Three miles offshore, sheltering Biscayne Bay from the Atlantic Ocean, Miami Beach was an ailing fruit farm in the 1910s when its Quaker owner, John Collins, formed an unlikely partnership with a flashy entrepreneur named Carl Fisher. With Fisher's money, Biscayne Bay was dredged, and the muck raised from its murky bed provided the landfill that transformed it into the sculptured landscape of palm trees, hotels, and tennis courts that – by and large – it is today.

During the 1950s, Miami Beach established itself as a celebrity-filled resort, while at the same time – and with much less fanfare – thousands of Cubans fleeing the successive Batista and Castro regimes began arriving in mainland Miami. The 1960s and 1970s brought decline, as Miami Beach's celebrity cachet waned and it became a haven for retirees. The city's tourist industry was damaged still further by the Liberty City Riot of 1980, which marked a lowpoint in Miami's black–white relations.

Since then, with the strengthening of Latin American economic links and a younger, more cosmopolitan breed of visitor energizing Miami Beach – notably the fashionable district of **South Beach** – the city is enjoying a surge of affluence and optimism. This surge is best symbolized by its skyline, now a forest of cranes tapped to construct dozens of luxury high-rises along the waterfront by 2010.

Arrival and information

However and whenever you arrive in Miami, you will not have difficulty getting your bearings. All points of entry are within a few miles of the center, and public transportation links are generally reliable. Note that by 2012, all trains and buses (including Amtrak and Greyhound services), will arrive at the new **Miami Intermodal Center** (ⓦwww.micdot.com) next to the airport.

By air

All passenger **flights** land at Miami International Airport (ⓣ305/876-7000, ⓦwww.miami-airport.com), a chaotic complex six miles west of downtown Miami. Once through the gate, it's a simple matter to get across the city.

Some of the main **car rental firms** (see "Driving and car rental," p.59) have desks close to the baggage claim area and provide free transport to collect a vehicle. Otherwise, you have to grab your luggage, leave the terminal, and flag down a bus belonging to your rental company. **Local buses** (ⓣ305/770-3131) depart from the bus station on the ground level of concourse E; take #7

($2 exact change only; every 30min; Mon–Fri 5.16am–8.51pm, Sat & Sun 6.20am–6.52pm) to downtown Miami (40–50min), or the #J bus ($2; every 20–40min; Mon–Fri 4.37am–11.38pm, Sat & Sun 5am–midnight) for the slightly longer journey to Miami Beach (50min–1hr at peak times). Shuttle buses also leave from the airport bus station to the nearby **Tri-Rail** station, with onward services to Palm Beach. A short taxi ride ($10) from the airport will deliver you to the Miami Greyhound station (see below), which has links to other parts of Miami and beyond.

Quicker, if more expensive, than public transportation, the blue and yellow **SuperShuttle** minivans (☎305/871-2000, ⓦwww.supershuttle.com) run around the clock and will deliver you to any address in or around Miami, with per-person rates ranging from $15 for downtown and Coconut Grove to $20 for South Beach. Their representatives are easy to spot as you leave the baggage claim area. **Taxis** are in plentiful supply outside the airport building and there are flat rates from the airport: $24 to the cruise terminals, $32 to South Beach, and $37-52 to areas in northern Miami Beach. Downtown and Coconut Grove should be around $22 (for full fare information, see ⓦwww.miami-airport .com/html/taxi_and_shuttle_service.html).

By bus

Of several **Greyhound** (☎305/871-1810 or 24hr info line ☎1-800/231-2222, ⓦwww.greyhound.com) terminals in the city, the busiest is **Miami**, which is actually farther out near the airport, at 4111 NW 27th St. Most Greyhound buses, however, including those to and from Key West, also stop at the **Downtown** terminal, 1012 NW 1st Ave (☎305/374-6160) in Overtown. This is the nearest stop to downtown Miami and South Beach, though onward transportation is annoyingly inconvenient: you'll have to walk one block east to N Miami Avenue to catch bus #6 into downtown. It's worth noting Overtown is not a pleasant place to arrive in during the day, let alone after dark. Local bus services are detailed on p.61.

By train and Tri-Rail

The Amtrak **train** station, 8303 NW 37th Ave (☎305/835-1221, ⓦwww .amtrak.com), is seven miles northwest of downtown Miami, with plenty of taxis waiting outside; you can also take bus #L from here to Central Miami Beach. Three blocks south lies the **Tri-Rail Metrorail Station** at 1125 E 25 St (coming from Amtrak take a taxi, as this area can be unsafe), where Tri-Rail (☎1-800/TRIRAIL), the cheap commuter service running between Miami and West Palm Beach (see Basics, p.26), connects with Metrorail services to downtown Miami ($2; see p.60). Bus #L also makes a stop here.

By car

Most of the major **roads** into Miami take the form of elevated expressways that – accidents and rush hours permitting – make getting into the city simple and quick. From the north, **I-95** (also called the **North–South Expressway**) streaks over the downtown streets before joining **US-1** (also called **South Dixie 1**), an ordinary road that continues on through South Miami. Unless you're taking the slower, scenic coastal route from Hollywood and Fort Lauderdale (**Hwy-A1A**), the fastest way to **South Beach** is to take **I-395** east off I-95, which merges with **US-41** at the MacArthur Causeway. Crossing the Everglades from the west coast on **US-41** (also called the **Tamiami Trail**), you'll save time by turning off north along Florida's Turnpike then heading east along **Hwy-836**, which rejoins US-41 (via I-395) at the MacArthur Causeway.

Information

Miami airport operates a **tourist information center** on concourse E, level 2 (daily 5am–10pm; ☏305/876-7000). The downtown office of the Miami Convention & Visitors Bureau, Suite 2700, inside the Bank of America building at 701 Brickell Ave (Mon–Fri 8.30am–6pm; ☏305/539-3000, ⓦwww.miamiandbeaches.com), is more of an adminstration office and not geared to handle drop-ins, so you're better off visiting the information stand at the entrance to Bayside Marketplace, or the **Downtown Welcome Center** in the lobby of the Olympia Theater, 174 E Flagler St (Mon noon–5pm, Tues–Sat 10–5pm; ☏305/379-7070, ⓦwww.downtownmiami.com).

In Miami Beach, try the **Chamber of Commerce**, 1920 Meridian Ave (Mon–Fri 9am–6pm, Sat & Sun 10am–4pm; ☏305/672-1270, ⓦwww.miamibeach chamber.com), which is crammed with leaflets and staffed by helpful locals. In South Beach, the **Art Deco Welcome Center**, 1001 Ocean Drive, is undergoing a major renovation which should be complete by early 2010. Until then the **Miami Design Preservation League** (☏305/672-2014, ⓦwww.mdpl.org) tours will run from the gift shop on 12th Street, just off Ocean Drive.

Getting around

While designed for the car, Miami is an easily navigable city boasting a comprehensive public transit system that provides a sound alternative for daytime travel.

Driving and car rental

Driving around Miami is practical and reasonably easy. Traffic in and out of Miami can be heavy, but the city's **expressways** (see "Arrival and information") will carry you swiftly from one area to another. Driving between Miami and Miami Beach is straightforward using one of six causeways; each is well marked and quickly accessed from the main arteries.

There is plenty of provision for street **parking** in Miami, though actually finding an empty space can prove difficult, particularly at night in Coconut Grove and South Beach. Parking meters are everywhere and range 25–50¢ per twenty minutes; save every quarter you get as you'll need vast quantities. Parking at public **parks and beaches** normally costs $4–5 per day; **parking lots** are pricier – the most convenient on South Beach is the municipal garage on 13th Street between Ocean Drive and Collins Avenue, which costs $1 per hour for the first four hours, and a flat $15 thereafter for up to 24 hours. For

> ## Miami addresses and orientation
>
> Miami's **street naming and numbering system** may seem confusing at first but won't take long to get used to. On the mainland, the city splits into quadrants (northeast, southeast, northwest, and southwest), divided by Flagler Street and Miami Avenue, which intersect downtown; numbers rise as you move away from this intersection in any direction. Meanwhile, within each quadrant, Roads, Avenues, Courts, and Places run north–south, while everything else runs east–west.
>
> In some areas the pattern varies, most obviously in Coral Gables, where streets have names instead of numbers and avenues are numbered in sequence from Douglas Road. In Miami Beach, most avenues run north–south and streets run east–west.

downtown and Bayside Marketplace the best option is the parking garage on NE Second Avenue between NE 2nd and 3rd streets, which costs a maximum of $12 (24hr) Monday through Friday and just $6 Saturday and Sunday. Note that parking in a marked residential area will incur a ticket.

Most of the major **car rental** companies have booking desks at the airport and provide free transportation from the terminals to their offices, where your car will be waiting. Many companies also have offices along Collins Avenue in South Beach (see Listings p.117). Charges – including taxes – are around $35–50 a day or $150–300 a week for an economy car, with an insurance premium of $25–40 per day depending on the type of cover.

Public transportation

An integrated **public transportation** network of buses, trains, and a monorail run by Metro-Dade Transit covers Miami (☎305/770-3131, ⓦ www.miamidade .gov/transit), making the city easy – if time-consuming – to get around by day. Night travel is much harder, especially away from South Beach.

Bus routes cover the entire city, most emanating from downtown Miami, and run from 4am to 2.30am daily. The flat-rate one-way **bus fare** is $2, payable on board by dropping the exact amount in change or notes into a machine beside the driver. If you need to transfer to another bus, say so when you get on; for an additional 50¢, the driver will give you a **transfer** ticket, which you hand over to the driver of the next bus. Transfer tickets are route- and time-stamped to prevent you lingering too long between connections or taking scenic detours (if you do so, you'll be charged the full fare again). One way to get around South Beach is via the **South Beach Local** – an air-conditioned shuttle that runs solely on electricity. The route runs along almost the entire length of Washington Avenue before cutting up Meridian Avenue (past the visitor center and Holocaust Memorial) before looping back down West Avenue and Alton Road (every 10–15min; Mon–Sat 7.45am–1am, Sun 10am–1am; 25¢, exact change only; ☎305/770-3131).

On the mainland there are two further options: the first, **Metrorail**, is an elevated railway that links the northern suburbs with South Miami. Trains run every five to twenty minutes between 5am and midnight. Useful stops are Government Center (for downtown), Vizcaya, Coconut Grove, and Douglas Road or University (for Coral Gables). Stations do, however, tend to be awkwardly situated, and you'll often need to use Metrorail services in conjunction with a bus. One-way **Metrorail fares** are $2, while transfers between buses and Metrorail cost 50¢ from the bus driver or a Metrorail station transfer machine.

Downtown Miami is ringed by the **Metromover** (sometimes called the "People Mover"), a monorail loop that is fast and clean, if a little limited – but a great way to get your bearings on arrival (daily 5.30am–midnight, later during major events at American Airlines arena; free; ☏305/770-3131).

For **free route maps and timetables**, go to the Transit Service Center inside the Metro-Dade Center in downtown, 101 NW 1st St (Mon–Fri 8am–6pm).

Taxis

Taxis are abundant and often the only way to get around at night without a car. **Fares** are $2.50 for the first sixth of a mile and 40¢ for each additional sixth of a mile. In case of complaints, call ☏305/375-2460. An empty cab will stop if the driver sees you waving, but if you want to prebook, try one of the following: Central Cab (☏305/532-5555) and Metro Taxi (☏305/888-8888) are fairly reliable.

Cycling

If you're keen to **cycle** around, it's best to steer clear of downtown – there are few cycle lanes and the traffic can be terrifying. Instead, follow the fourteen-mile path down to South Miami from Coconut Grove; or opt for a jaunt round the leafy parks of Key Biscayne. South Beach, where car parking's pricey, is also bike-friendly: try an oceanfront cycle at dawn along Ocean Drive. If you'd rather join an organized trip, note that Dr Paul George (see below) often leads cycle tours to and around historical points of interest. See Listings (p.117) for **bike rental** companies.

Tours

For an informative and entertaining stroll, take one of **Dr Paul George's Walking Tours** (no tours July & Aug; $20 and up; ☏305/375-1621, ⓦwww.hmsf.org), which are offered in conjunction with the Historical Museum of Southern Florida and take in a number of areas, including downtown Miami, Coconut Grove, Coral Gables, Little Havana and South Beach. There are numerous other itineraries, each lasting around 2–3 hours, though he tends to organize just four to six tours per month (usually at the weekends).

Major Miami bus routes

Metro-Dade Transit, from downtown Miami to:
Biscayne Corridor #3
Coconut Grove #48
Coral Gables #24
Key Biscayne #B
Little Havana #8
Miami Beach #C, #S or #K (along Washington Ave)
Miami International Airport #7

Miami media

Miami's one daily **newspaper**, the *Miami Herald* (35¢ weekdays, $1 Sunday), is disappointingly bland, but provides coverage of state, national and world events. The best day to pick up a copy is Friday when a free and informative entertainment supplement is included. Otherwise, try the *South Florida Sun-Sentinel* (50¢ weekdays, $1.50 Sunday) – less good on local news, but with more in-depth national reporting.

The following are the best sources of up-to-date entertainment and arts listings; most can be picked up free around town and at hotels.

GADA (Go Anywhere, Do Anything) ⓦwww.gadamag.com. This elusive freesheet (published six times a year), is the most insidery of all – pick it up at record stores or trendy bars, and trust the listings to be locals-aimed and refreshingly hype-free.

Miami New Times ☏305/372-0004, ⓦwww.miaminewtimes.com. The best weekly listings paper in Miami covers food, drink, entertainment, and, to a lesser extent, the arts. Published Thursdays (free).

Ocean Drive ☏305/532-2544, ⓦwww.oceandrive.com. Glossy magazine available in every hotel that follows the Beautiful People on the local scene; otherwise for sale at bookshops and newsstands ($5.99).

Scene in the Tropics ⓦhttp://blogs.herald.com/scene_in_the_tropics. Local gossip maven, nightlife connoisseur, and all-round connected chick, Lesley Abravanel, writes this amusing, spot-on blog for the *Miami Herald*.

For less-visited parts of the city, try **David Brown**, who specializes in Miami's black neighborhoods, including Liberty City and Little Haiti (☏305/663-4455, ⓦwww.miamiculturaltours.com).

In South Beach, don't miss the ninety-minute **Art Deco Walking Tour**. A perfect introduction to the area's phenomenal architecture, the tour ($20; ☏305/672-2014) will run Tuesday, Wednesday, Friday, Saturday, and Sunday at 10.30am and Thursday at 6.30pm from the Art Deco gift shop on 12th Street, just off Ocean Drive, until the Art Deco Welcome Center reopens in 2010 (see p.59). The shop also offers a self-guided audio walking tour of the district (available daily 9.30am–5pm; 90min; $15).

Wildlife enthusiasts should contact **Eco Adventures** (☏305/365-3018, ⓦwww.miamiecoadventures.org), a Miami-Dade Parks initiative to provide a variety of guided excursions to Biscayne Bay (kayaking and snorkeling), Key Biscayne (by boat), and further afield into the Everglades. For general **boat tours**, see p.80.

Accommodation

Finding a place to stay in Miami is only a problem over New Year's and important holiday weekends such as Memorial Day and Labor Day. The lion's share of **hotels** and **motels** are in **South Beach**, an ideal base for nightlife, beachlife, and seeing the city. Prices vary from $35 to $500, but you can anticipate spending at least $75 during the summer and $120-150 during the winter (or upwards of $250 per night in the increasing number of ultra-luxe South Beach hotels).

For most visitors, the draw of staying on or near the beach is strong, though we've provided picks for the best of the rest. While there are pleasant enough places in Coconut Grove or Coral Gables, there's no compelling reason to stay in either place for the casual visitor. Otherwise, downtown is clogged with expensive business chains, and Key Biscayne's luxury pads are out of most people's budgets; conversely, the cheap motels that line Biscayne Boulevard close to Little Haiti and the Design District are mostly flophouses or worse. The **airport** area hotels should only be considered if you're catching a plane at an unearthly hour or arriving late and want to avoid driving into Miami after dark.

During the winter you'd be well advised to **reserve ahead**, either directly or through an agent, especially during peak times like the Winter Music Conference (see box, p.113). Between May and November, however, you'll save by going for the best deals on the spot (though you may want to arrange your first night in advance). Don't be afraid to **bargain**, as this can result in more than a few dollars being lopped off the advertised rate – especially if you're staying for more than a few days, though **single** rooms are rarely cheaper than **doubles**.

Prices below are for low season – in other words, summer; expect higher rates December to April, especially at weekends.

South Beach

Albion Hotel 1650 James Ave ☎305/913-1000 or 1-877/RUBELLS, ⊛www.rubellhotels.com. A sensitive conversion of a classic Nautical Deco building, this is one of the best-value hotels on the beach. Rooms are stylishly simple, while the raised pool – with portholes cut into its sides – is also a big draw. ❸

Cadet Hotel 1701 James Ave ☎305/672-6688, ⊛www.cadethotel.com. Tranquil boutique hotel, with a fresh, clean look enhanced with bamboo floors and a patio-garden where you can enjoy a glass of wine; the fresh strawberries and chocolate in the rooms upon arrival are nice touches. ❺

Catalina 1732 Collins Ave ☎305/674-1160, ⊛www.catalinahotel.com. Newish mid-range hotel on the hot upper Collins strip. Simple white rooms are filled with luxe touches like flatscreen TVs and marble bathrooms, plus outdoor pool, sundeck and a bamboo-filled zen courtyard for reading or meditating. ❹

Clay Hotel Hostel-Miami Beach International Youth Hostel 406 Española Way ☎305/534-2988 or 1-800/379-CLAY, ⊛www.clayhotel.com. The location's great, and this hotel-hostel hybrid is a terrific place to meet other travelers – just see a room before you commit, since some are cleaner and more welcoming than others. Private rooms with bath from $75, without bath from $60; dorm rooms $25 IYH members, $26 others including linens, with rates dropping to $20 for all guests in the summer.

Delano 1685 Collins Ave ☎305/672-2000, ⊛www.delano-hotel.com. One of South Beach's chicest (and most expensive) lodgings mixes Art Deco with minimalist modernism (eg, lots of white) and all-round luxury. Gauzy white curtains billow in the lobby and the stunning pool features underwater music. ❽

De Soleil South Beach 1458 Ocean Drive ☎305/672-4554 or 877/688-4232, ⊛www .desoleilsouthbeach.com. One of the few newly built hotels in South Beach, this all-suite spot was designed by Arquitectonica (see p.82) and surrounds an outdoor courtyard with pool and hot tub; many of the large, subtly decorated rooms also have private hot tubs as well as patios. ❼

The Hotel 801 Collins Ave ☎305/531-2222 or 1-877/843-4683, ⊛www.thehotelof southbeach.com. Designer Todd Oldham oversaw every element in the renovation of this hotel, and his colorful yet thoughtful makeover makes it one of the best luxury options on the beach. Don't miss the rooftop pool, shaped like a gemstone in honor of the hotel's original name, preserved in the "Tiffany" sign on the turret. ❻

Miami Beach International Travelers Hostel 236 9th St ☎305/534-0268, ⊛www.hostel miamibeach.com. Friendly hostel with beds in four-person dorms starting at $25, as well as private singles (from $89) and doubles ($49 per person) centrally positioned in South Beach. Offers free breakfast, internet facilities, kitchen, laundry, a comfortable movie-lounge, and also books tours.

Park Central 640 Ocean Drive ☎ 305/538-1611 or 1-800/727-5266, 🖰 www.theparkcentral.com. One of the first hotels to be reborn during the South Beach renaissance of the early 1990s. Its colonial safari-style wicker-crammed rooms feature major soundproofing on the windows to keep out the throb of nearby clubs, and the surprisingly reasonable prices make it even more attractive. ❺

Pelican 826 Ocean Drive ☎ 305/673-3373 or 1-800/773-5422, 🖰 www.pelicanhotel.com. Irreverent Italian jeanswear company Diesel owns this hotel, so the quirky, campy decor of the rooms should come as no surprise. Each is individually themed and named – try the lush red bordello known as the "Best Little Whorehouse" room. ❻

The Ritz-Carlton South Beach 1 Lincoln Rd ☎ 786/276-4000 or 1-800/241-3333, 🖰 www .ritzcarlton.com. The new owners of the vintage *DiLido* have sensitively spruced the place up: the design of the lobby is exactly as it was in its 1950s heyday, though with more durable materials, such as walls made of cherry wood, while the rooms themselves are large but bland. It's popular with the hordes of hip-hop artists who visit Miami to use the city's recording studios. ❽

Sagamore 1671 Collins Ave ☎ 305/535-8088 or 1-877/242-6673, 🖰 www.sagamorehotel.com. A low-key luxury hotel, with enormous rooms decorated in muted shades of chocolate and taupe. There's a beachfront pool, where you can swim a few laps then climb out straight onto the sands. Don't miss the exuberant art dotted around the public areas. ❽

The Setai 2001 Collins Ave ☎ 305/520-6000, 🖰 www.setai.com. Condo tower-cum-hotel that's known for its celeb-heavy clientele (Lenny Kravitz bought a penthouse complete with recording studio in the building) as much as for its pricey, vaguely Asian-themed rooms. Splurge for the snob appeal and the best views on the beach. ❽

The Standard Miami 40 Island Ave ☎ 305/673-1717, 🖰 www.standardhotels.com/miami/. The Miami outpost of hip hotelier Andre Balazs' *Standard* chain has transformed a forlorn hotel on Belle Isle into a spa accommodation that serves as a sanctuary from the craziness on the beach, with onsite Turkish baths and a yoga center. ❻

🏃 **The Tides** 1200 Ocean Drive ☎ 1-800/439-4095 or 305/604-5070, 🖰 www .thetideshotel.com. Spectacularly situated on Ocean Drive, with enormous floor-through rooms featuring ocean and city views; Kelly Wearstler is behind the glamorous new design unveiled in 2007, with comfier beds and plush linens enhanced with iPod docking stations and espresso machines; sea view rooms come with telescopes. ❽

🏃 **Townhouse** 150 20th St ☎ 305/534-3800 or 1-877/534-3800, 🖰 www.townhouse hotel.com. From the small but beautifully designed white rooms to the chatty, cheerful staff and the relaxing roofdeck filled with squishy waterbeds, this boutique hotel aims to please – and the prices are surprisingly low, too. ❺

The Tropics Hotel and Hostel 1550 Collins Ave ☎ 305/531-0361, 🖰 www.tropicshotel.com. Housed in a stylish Art Deco building, this is more of a hotel than a hostel and more genteel than both. Spotless, comfortable four-person dorms start at $25 per person, with doubles for $60–70. A clean kitchen, swimming pool, laundry facilities, and airport shuttle are all available. Attracts a more mature crowd.

Hotel Victor 1144 Ocean Drive ☎ 305/428-1234, 🖰 www.hotelvictorsouthbeach.com. The latest lavish South Beach hotel is designed by hotelier Jacques Garcia, and is in the style of a clubby, Ibiza-style spot, complete with in-residence DJs spinning daily throughout the hotel until midnight. The rooms all have deep soak tubs and LCD TVs but they're surprisingly small. ❽

Central Miami Beach and north

Circa 39 3900 Collins Ave ☎ 305/538-4900 or 1-877/8-CIRCA39, 🖰 www.circa39.com. Another mid-range Miami Beach hotel given the boutique makeover: the rooms here are, predictably, all white with pale blue accents, and feature CD players and flatscreen TVs. The common areas are more playful, with mismatched Modernist furniture scattered through the lobby as well as a handy, well-priced onsite café; incredibly cheap rates in the off season. ❹

Eden Roc Renaissance Resort & Spa 4525 Collins Ave, Miami Beach ☎ 1-786/276-0526, 🖰 www.boldnewedenroc.com. A Miami Beach landmark since the 1950s, *Eden Roc* was given a huge makeover in 2008 – expect infinity pools, tropical fountains, a stunning 1950s lobby and rooms equipped with iPod docks, HDTV and marble bathrooms. ❽

Fontainebleau 4441 Collins Ave, Miami Beach ☎ 305/538-2000 or 1-800/548-8886, 🖰 www .fontainebleau.com. Once the last word in glamour, this Miami icon reopened in 2008 after a lavish renovation which sees the addition of two new, luxury all-suite towers with kitchenettes and spacious balconies overlooking the Atlantic; even the stunning pool has been remodeled, and you now have 11 restaurants and lounges and a giant spa to enjoy. ❽

Trump International Resort 18001 Collins Ave, Sunny Isles Beach ☎ 305/692-5600, 🖰 www .trumpmiami.com. Trump's signature gaudy opulence is ignored here in favor of luxurious and elegant rooms, all featuring balconies, microwaves and marble baths. The adjacent beach is gorgeous and fairly quiet, but a long way from the South Beach action. 8

Downtown Miami

Holiday Inn Marina Park – Port of Miami 340 Biscayne Blvd ⓣ305/371-4400 or 1-800/344-7128, ⓦwww.holiday-inn.com/portofmiami. A bland exterior shields a much warmer, more welcoming interior, with standard but comfy rooms and views across the Port of Miami and neighboring parks. 4

Mandarin Oriental 500 Brickell Key Drive, Brickell Key ⓣ305/913-8383, ⓦwww.mandarinoriental.com/miami/. The pick of the luxury chains downtown for its jaw-dropping views across Biscayne Bay. The modern Asian-themed rooms come with marble bathrooms and cherry-wood furnishings, and the spa, private beach and restaurants are all world-class. Excellent service. 8

Miami River Inn 118 SW S River Drive ⓣ305/325-0045 or 1-800/468-3589, ⓦwww.miamiriverinn.com. Most of the buildings making up the inn date to 1908 and provide basic accommodation clustered around a tree-shaded pool. There's free breakfast and friendly staff – but it's off the beaten track and only really an option if you have a car. 4

Coral Gables and Coconut Grove

Biltmore 1200 Anastasia Ave, Coral Gables ⓣ305/445-1926 or 1-800/727-1926, ⓦwww.biltmorehotel.com. A landmark, Mediterranean-style hotel that has been pampering the rich and famous since 1926. The rooms, furnished in peach and cream tones, are reminiscent of a Spanish villa, but it's the massive chevron-shaped pool that proves to be the main draw. 7

Gables Inn 730 S Dixie Hwy, Coral Gables ⓣ305/661-7999, ⓦwww.thegablesinn.net. Coral Gables' version of a motel – so it's slightly fancier than most, with its Mediterranean Revival architecture. Note that it's located right on the S Dixie Highway, so it can be noisy, and the rooms are showing their age. 4

Hampton Inn 2800 SW 28th Terrace, Coconut Grove ⓣ305/448-2800 or 1-800/HAMPTON, ⓦwww.hamptoninncoconutgrove.com. Basic but bright accommodation, geared to the business traveler – the free local calls, free breakfast, pool, and onsite coin laundry make this an attractive option for those on a budget. 4

Mayfair Hotel & Spa 3000 Florida Ave, Coconut Grove ⓣ305/441-0000 or 1-800/433-4555, ⓦwww.mayfairhotelandspa.com. Groovy spa hotel in the heart of the Grove, with two-person tubs on the balconies of every room and quirky touches like a free mojito on check-in and iPods on loan by the rooftop pool; note that the brilliant white color scheme is starting to show some wear and tear. 5

Hotel St Michel 162 Alcazar Ave, Coral Gables ⓣ305/444-1666, ⓦwww.hotelstmichel.com. A small, romantic hotel just off the Miracle Mile, with modernized rooms, Laura Ashley decor, and copious European antiques. Rates include continental breakfast. 6

Key Biscayne

Ritz Carlton Key Biscayne 455 Grand Bay Drive ⓣ305/365-4500 or 1-800/241-3333, ⓦwww.ritzcarlton.com. This enormous family-friendly hotel – decked out in the usual chintzy *Ritz* décor – has its own beach, several onsite bars and restaurants (including the outstanding *Cioppino* – see p.106) and tennis club. There's also an adults-only, oceanview lagoon pool. All rooms were refurbished in 2008. 8

Silver Sands Beach Resort 301 Ocean Drive ⓣ305/361-5441, ⓦwww.key-biscayne.com/accom/silversands. Fairly standard and aging rooms, but this hotel is very laid-back; marine iguanas occasionally swim in the pool. Popular base for families who get to enjoy Key Biscayne for a bargain price. 5

South of Miami

Florida City Travelodge 409 SE 1st Ave, Florida City ⓣ305/248-9777 or 1800/758-0618, ⓦwww.tlflcity.com. One of the most comfortable places to stay hereabouts, and usefully located between the Keys, Miami, and the Everglades. Decent free breakfast and wi-fi. 3

Grove Inn Country Guesthouse 22540 SW Krome Ave, Redland ⓣ305/247-6572, ⓦwww.groveinn.com. A former fruit farm, this comfortable B&B is a secluded getaway, made ever more attractive by its friendly, helpful owners. 3

Redland Hotel 5 S Flagler Ave, Homestead ⓣ305/246-1904 or 1-800/595-1904, ⓦwww.redlandhotel.com. An historic inn, where each room is named for a local pioneer family. The rooms are floral and chintzy, but comfortable. 4

At the airport

Airways Inn & Suites 5001 NW 36th St ⓣ305/883-4700 or 1-800/824-9910. Basic rooms decked out with floral bedspreads and wood furniture; worth considering as one of the cheapest deals in the area, but expect a fairly barebones experience. 4

Hampton Inn Miami Airport-Blue Lagoon 777 NW 57th Ave ☎ 305/262-5400 or 1-800/HAMPTON, F 305/262-5488, Ⓦ www.hamptoninnmiamiairport .com. Good-value branch of this hotel chain two miles from the airport, offering some of the best rates in the area. 24hr courtesy bus available to airport. **⑥**

Miami International Airport Hotel ☎ 305/871-4100 or 1-800/327-1276, Ⓕ 305/871-0800,

Ⓦ www.miahotel.com. There's no excuse for missing your plane if you stay here; this fully equipped, if bland, hotel is located inside the airport (concourse E), but you'll pay for the convenience. There's also a day rate (10am–6pm) for rooms if you have a long layover and want to shower and relax between flights ($105). **⑦**

The City

Miami is a city of wildly diverse districts, jigsawed into a vast urban corridor from two technically separate cities (though most amenities are shared): mainland **Miami** and the huge sandbar known as **Miami Beach**. Distances between its neighborhoods can be large, so if you're planning on exploring the whole city, it's worth renting a car. If you're sticking to the most popular areas downtown and on Miami Beach, though, you can zip around easily by bus and on foot. Either way, it pays to remember that, though the crime-spattered Miami of the 1980s is a distant memory, there are still some rough areas where visitors should exercise caution – we've noted them in the text.

Most people spend their time in **South Beach**, a fairly small area at the southern end of the sand bar, where you'll find many of Florida's leading art galleries, trendsetting restaurants, and much of its boisterous club scene. Heading north, **Central Miami Beach** was where 1950s screen stars had fun in the sun and helped cement Miami's international reputation as a glamorous vacation spot.

Surprisingly few tourists venture beyond Miami Beach, and so miss out on some of the most enticing parts of the city. To see these, a good place to start is **downtown Miami**, where an astonishing construction boom has seen the waterfront crammed with ostentatious skyscrapers. Tucked away in the **Metro–Dade Cultural Center** are the city's excellent history and art museums, while Bayside Marketplace is the staging post for **boat tours** of Miami's most exclusive offshore keys.

To the north sits the city's buzziest neighborhood, the strip of land along and around Biscayne Boulevard, known as the **Biscayne Corridor**; it includes the dazzling Performing Arts Center, the art galleries and showrooms of **Wynwood** and the **Design District**, and even the grubby but thrilling immigrant neighborhood known as **Little Haiti**.

The first of Miami's Cubans settled southwest of downtown, just across the Miami River, in **Little Havana**. This is still one of the more intriguing parts of the city, rich with Latin American looks and sounds, though it's less solidly Cuban than it used to be. Immediately south, Little Havana's grid gives way to the spacious boulevards of **Coral Gables**. This ersatz-European fantasy of broad lawns, massive houses, and ornate public buildings was the brainchild of one man, George Merrick, who decided to replicate a chunk of Spain in southern Florida. South of the downtown area is **Coconut Grove**, the oldest settlement in the area and once an arty, bohemian place, but nowadays known for its malls and cafés. The large island visible off the coast of Coconut Grove is **Key Biscayne**, linked to the mainland via the massive Rickenbacker Causeway. This classy, secluded island community offers exquisite beaches and bike trails, only five miles from downtown.

Beyond Coconut Grove and Coral Gables, lackluster **South Miami** fades into farming territory toward **Homestead**, where the Coral Castle and Biscayne National Park make entertaining diversions en route to the Everglades or Florida Keys.

South Beach

Undoubtedly, Miami's most exciting area is **SOUTH BEACH**, which occupies the southernmost three miles of Miami Beach. Filled with pastel-colored Art Deco buildings, up-and-coming art galleries, modish diners, and suntanned beach addicts, it's been celebrated as one of the hippest places in the world. Socially, South Beach has an unbeatable buzz. Here, Latin, black, and white cultures happily collide, gay and straight tourists soak up the sun together, and Cuban cafés and chic boutiques sit side by side. Though elsewhere Miami's cultural schizophrenia may cause friction, here it's at its riotous, cocktail-clinking best.

Although South Beach suffered through tough economic times in the 1980s, there's little remaining of that edgy, dangerous period. More than anywhere else in the city, you can wander safely in South Beach day or night. The only time the streets are empty is early morning, when most of Miami Beach is still sleeping off the excesses of the night before. This is also the perfect time to grasp South Beach's allure for photographers and see the sheer beauty of its Art Deco buildings; make sure to turn in early one night and wake at dawn for an early morning stroll – the lucid white light and wave-lapped tranquility are striking.

Ocean Drive

Much of South Beach falls within the **Art Deco District**, an area of around 1,200 protected Art Deco gems recognized by the National Register and bounded roughly by 5th and 23rd streets and Ocean Drive and Lenox Avenue. The best place to start exploring this rich architectural legacy is **Ocean Drive**,

Miami beaches

Miami Beach boasts gorgeous Art Deco buildings and a glittering nightlife, but the core of its appeal remains its fabulous **strip of clean, bone-white sands**. With twelve miles of calm waters, swaying palms, and the famous candy-colored **lifeguard towers**, you can't go wrong picking a spot (restrooms and showers line the beach at regular intervals). To the south, **First Street Beach** and **South Pointe** are favored by families, and are especially convivial at weekends. The young and the beautiful soak up the rays between 5th and 21st streets, a convenient hop from the bars and cafés of South Beach. From 6th to 14th streets, **Lummus Park** – much of whose sand was shipped in from the Bahamas – is the heart of the scene; there's an unofficial gay section at 12th Street (rainbow flags mark the spot). North of 21st, things are more family-oriented, with a **boardwalk** running between the shore and the posh hotels up to 46th. For good **swimming**, head up to **North Shore State Recreation Area** around 85th, a quiet stretch just south of Surfside.

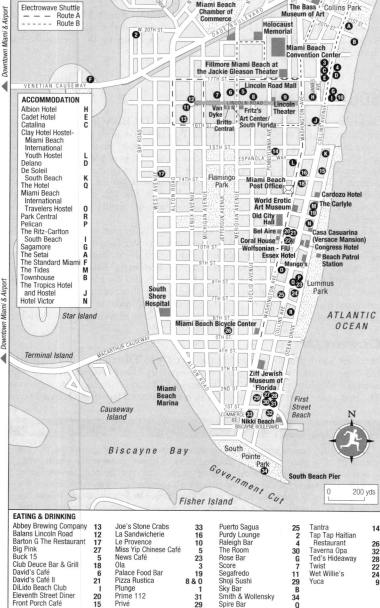

Downtown Miami & Airport

SOUTH BEACH

Central Miami Beach ▲

Electrowave Shuttle
— — — Route A
- - - - - Route B

Miami Beach
Chamber of
Commerce

The Bass
Museum of Art

Collins Park

Holocaust
Memorial

Miami Beach
Convention Center

Fillmore Miami Beach at
the Jackie Gleason Theater

Lincoln Road Mall

Lincoln
Theater

Van
Dyke

Fritz's
Art Center/
South Florida

Britto
Central

Flamingo
Park

Miami Beach
Post Office

Cardozo Hotel
The Carlyle

World Erotic
Art Museum
Old City
Hall

Bel Aire
Coral House
Wolfsonian - FIU
Essex Hotel

Casa Casuarina
(Versace Mansion)
Congress Hotel
Beach Patrol
Station

Mango's

Lummus
Park

South
Shore
Hospital

ATLANTIC
OCEAN

Miami Beach Bicycle Center

Star Island

MACARTHUR CAUSEWAY

Terminal Island

Ziff Jewish
Museum of
Florida

First
Street
Beach

Miami
Beach
Marina

Causeway
Island

Nikki Beach
BISCAYNE BOULEVARD

South
Pointe
Park

South Beach Pier

Biscayne Bay

Government Cut

Fisher Island

0   200 yds

N

ACCOMMODATION

Albion Hotel	H
Cadet Hotel	E
Catalina	C
Clay Hotel Hostel-Miami Beach International Youth Hostel	L
Delano	D
De Soleil South Beach	K
The Hotel	Q
Miami Beach International Travelers Hostel	O
Park Central	R
Pelican	P
The Ritz-Carlton South Beach	I
Sagamore	G
The Setai	A
The Standard Miami	F
The Tides	M
Townhouse	B
The Tropics Hotel and Hostel	J
Hotel Victor	N

EATING & DRINKING

Abbey Brewing Company	13	Joe's Stone Crabs	33	Puerto Sagua	25	Tantra	14
Balans Lincoln Road	12	La Sandwicherie	16	Purdy Lounge	2	Tap Tap Haitian	
Barton G The Restaurant	17	Le Provence	10	Raleigh Bar	4	Restaurant	26
Big Pink	27	Miss Yip Chinese Café	5	The Room	30	Taverna Opa	32
Buck 15	5	News Café	23	Rose Bar	G	Ted's Hideaway	28
Club Deuce Bar & Grill	18	Ola	3	Score	7	Twist	22
David's Café	6	Palace Food Bar	19	Segafredo	11	Wet Willie's	24
David's Café II	21	Pizza Rustica	8 & 0	Shoji Sushi	29	Yuca	9
DiLido Beach Club	I	Plunge	1	Sky Bar	B		
Eleventh Street Diner	20	Prime 112	31	Smith & Wollensky	34		
Front Porch Café	15	Privé	29	Spire Bar	Q		

the main drag that hugs the gloriously wide beach. You can admire the exquisite Art Deco on display by simply wandering the streets around here, and though few buildings are open to the public, all the **hotels** listed below are generally tolerant of small groups of tourists taking a quick peek at the lobby, and you can always stop for a drink or something to eat – worth considering, as the interiors are often even more exuberant than the outsides. You can also take a **walking tour** (see p.61), a fun way to see the key buildings and hear the colorful stories behind their construction and preservation.

One of the earliest renovations was **Park Central**, at 640 Ocean Drive: completed in 1937 by **Henry Hohauser** (one of Miami's most lauded architects), it's a geometric tour de force, with octagonal windows, terrazzo floors and sharp vertical columns in the facade, part of the signature Art Deco "rule of three"; a strong central section supported by two complementary side sections.

A few blocks north in Lummus Park (the grassy patch that separates Ocean Drive from the beach), stands the boat-shaped **Beach Patrol Station** unmistakeable for its vintage oversized date and temperature sign, and still the base of the local lifeguards. Nearby back on Ocean Drive, the **Congress Hotel** at no. 1036 is one of the purest examples of Miami Art Deco (today it's just a shop). Notice the "frozen fountains" framing the entrance, another popular Art Deco feature, based on fanciful Mayan imagery.

Casa Casuarina

Undeniably one of the most popular tourist sights on the beach, **Casa Casuarina** (☎305/672-6604, ⓦwww.casacasuarina.com), at 1116 Ocean Drive, is the former home of murdered designer Gianni Versace. It was completed in 1930 as a replica of the Alcázar de Colón in Santo Domingo, built by Christopher Columbus' son in 1510, which is claimed to be the oldest house in the Western Hemisphere. After a time as a run-down apartment complex, the space was rescued by Versace, who bought the place in 1992 and lived here until his murder on the front steps five years later. After Versace's untimely demise, his opulent pad was snapped up by developer Peter Loftin, who's said to have paid around $19m. After four years of dithering, Loftin finally transformed the house into a jet-set members-only club, with initiation fees today running to $50,000. In 2008, the club opened its doors to the public for the first time: daily **tours** (9am–6pm, call for exact times) of the lavish interior cost an appropriately extortionate $65 (you do get a free mimosa). An additional fee will buy you lunch ($35) or breakfast ($25) inside. Check the website for the latest situation.

North along Ocean Drive

Those less flush with cash can check out the **Hotel Victor**, next door to Casa Casuarina at 1144 Ocean Drive, where the entrance to the *Vix Restaurant* features a hypnotic fish tank full of live **jellyfish**. You have to walk through the stunning lobby to get there, touched up with modern designer sofas but otherwise looking remarkably similar to the 1937 original; note the fancy hanging lamps, lavish mosaics and flamingo mural by artist Earl LePan, featuring a typical South Florida landscape.

Further up Ocean Drive, **The Tides** at no. 1220 was designed by master architect L. Murray Dixon, its tall and imposing facade completed in 1936 from limestone and blocks of bleached coral excavated from the ocean floor. Take a look inside the lobby, one of the most mesmerizing spaces on South Beach. The luxurious interior looks like a giant piece of installation art, a sophisticated blend of earthy browns and beiges with rattan, wood and leather furnishings. The fancy hotel restaurant is decorated with giant tortoise shells, and is separated from the lobby by an arrangement of bleached white driftwood.

The facade of **The Carlyle** at no. 1250 featured in the movie *Birdcage* (1996), and today the former hotel has been converted into 19 condos going for $1 million and above. Nearby at no. 1300, the **Cardozo Hotel** is another Hohauser masterpiece, finished in 1939 and now owned by Gloria and Emilio Estefan. Featuring a rounder, softer style, the *Cardozo* housed the original offices of Barbara Capitman (see p.72) and appeared in the movie *Something About Mary* (1998).

Collins Avenue

The Art Deco theme continues on Collins Avenue, one block west of Ocean Drive, lined with mid-range hotels and a swanky shopping strip between 5th and 7th streets; it runs along the coast all the way to Fort Lauderdale.

The pick of several architectural highlights here is the former **Tiffany Hotel** at no. 801, now just *The Hotel*. Also designed by L. Murray Dixon, its 1939-terrazzo floors and mosaic mirrors have been faithfully restored, but its most iconic feature is the futuristic spire on top; head up to the funky *Spire Bar* (see p.108) on the roof for a closer look and stupendous views of the Atlantic. Further along at no. 1001, the **Essex House Hotel** is a real treat; built by Hohauser in 1938, the lobby features another mural by LePan, this time featuring a Seminole Indian hunting in the Everglades. Look for the arrows set into the terrazzo floor, a not-so-subtle legacy of illegal gambling in the 1940s – gamblers would follow the arrows and place their bets at the back.

Washington Avenue

Washington Avenue is the area's main commercial artery, where small, Cuban-run supermarkets stand alongside local boutiques and nightclubs. Its grubbiness is pleasantly refreshing after the plucked-and-tweezed perfection

▲ South Beach from the Setai Hotel

closer to the beach. Take a peek inside the **Astor Hotel** at no. 956, designed by T. Hunter Henderson in 1936. The original exterior facade of cut coral has been beautifully maintained, while the lobby features the original Vitrolite wall panels. Grab a drink at *Joley* (from 3pm daily), the handsome onsite restaurant.

Just across the street from the *Astor* sits the imposing **Wolfsonian–Florida International University art gallery**, 1001 Washington Ave (Mon, Tues, Sat & Sun noon–6pm; Thurs & Fri noon–9pm; $7, free admission Fri 6–9pm; ☎305/531-1001, ⓦwww.wolfsonian.fiu.edu). Some 70,000 decorative arts and crafts from Europe and the Americas dating from 1885 to 1945 have been assembled in this florid Mediterranean-Revival building by Mitchell Wolfson Jr, a local businessman. Anyone with a passing interest in decorative, architectural, or politically inspired art will find something of interest in the galleries, though it's confusingly curated and many of the exhibits blur into one another. The highlights here are often the high-profile, traveling exhibitions.

Walk north on Washington Avenue and you should see the **Coral House** on the left in between 10th and 11th streets, built around 1922 and one of the oldest buildings on Miami Beach; it looks a bit like a tiny stone cottage and utterly out of place here. The house has been threatened with demolition many times; signs have been advertising its imminent opening as a restaurant for years (without progress), but at least the facade now seems safe from developers. The Coral House forms part of the sprawling and rather forlorn **Bel Aire**, a faded motel complex. The main lobby is at no. 1050, boasting some rare examples of original neon lighting and streamlined steel railings on the stairs.

Further north, you'll find one of the more quirky sights in South Beach, the **World Erotic Art Museum**, 1205 Washington Ave (daily 11am–midnight; $15; ☎305/532-9336, ⓦwww.weam.com). It's home to the $10-million collection of erotic ephemera amassed by a filthy minded rich widow – Miami's philanthropic answer to Dr Ruth – who's put on show everything from cheeky bottom-baring Victorian figurines to *The Pillow Book*, Japan's calligraphic version of the Kama Sutra.

On the corner of 13th Street is the strikingly simple **Miami Beach Post Office**, 1300 Washington Ave (lobby Mon–Fri 6am–5pm, Sat 6am–4pm; ☎305/672-2447, ⓦwww.usps.com), a squat dome built in the Depression Moderne style. Duck into the rotunda to see its flashy **geometric murals** of Spanish conquistadors Ponce de León and De Soto, and a depiction of a treaty being signed between the US army and the Seminoles – a sadly fictional event.

Española Way

At the northern end of Washington Avenue, sandwiched between 14th Place and 15th Street stands **Española Way**, a pedestrian strip built by Carl Fisher, who disliked the prevalent Art Deco style and made this Mediterranean-Revival development his pet project. Completed in 1925, it was grandly envisaged as an artists' colony – today it's lined with commercial art galleries, trinket stores, and a haphazard market. Though the architecture is certainly novel and there are a couple of enticing places to eat here, you won't miss much by skipping it.

Lincoln Road Mall and around

A short walk further north, between 16th and 17th streets, the pedestrianized **Lincoln Road Mall** was considered the flashiest shopping precinct outside of New York during the 1950s, its jewelry and clothes stores earning it the label

Decoding Art Deco

Miami became a haven for **Art Deco** in large part due to the wrecking power of South Florida's hurricanes. In 1926, the city was leveled by a devastating storm, and its wooden buildings were replaced with concrete structures in the newly modish Art Deco style.

Art Deco in the city can be split into three sub-styles, which are easily identifiable by their signature features. The earliest phase, **Tropical** or **Miami Deco** (most popular in the 1920s and 1930s), is the base style from which all the other Deco types spring: look for "eyebrows" above the windows that provided shade as well as decoration, elements in groups of three, porthole windows, stepped rooflines and reliefs featuring palm trees and flamingoes. This style gave way to **Streamline Moderne** (1930s–1940s), most prevalent in Miami Beach today, which bridges the simplicity of early Deco and the playfulness of Miami Modern or MiMo (1945–69). As with many MiMo structures (see p.75), all elements of Streamline buildings are designed to give a feeling of movement, and the hard edges are rounded off. The simpler **Depression Moderne** was a sub-style of Streamline, often used for governmental buildings, such as the Post Office (see p.71); it was less ostentatious and ornamental than Miami Deco, and money was spent subtly on interior spaces, like murals and ironwork. Though Deco dominated building in Miami for more than twenty years, there was a contemporary alternative, known as **Mediterranean Revival**, whose asymmetry and ramshackle design were intended to give the impression of age. Many at the time sniffed that this was how gangsters and movie stars – ie, those with more money than taste – liked to commission houses; even so, almost one-third of the structures in the so-called Art Deco District are classified under this style.

It's a sobering thought that Miami Beach almost lost all of these significant structures. In the mid-1970s, the **Miami Design Preservation League** – whose first meeting drew just six people – was born with the aim of saving the buildings and raising awareness of their architectural and historical importance. The league's success has been dramatic – a major turning point was convincing the buck-hungry developers of the earning potential of such a unique area. The driving force of the movement was the late Barbara Capitman, but it was her preservation partner, interior designer Leonard Horowitz, who came up with the now-trademark palette of sherbet yellows, pinks, and blues – "a palette of Post Modern cake-icing pastels now associated with *Miami Vice*," in the words of disgruntled Florida architecture chronicler Hap Hatton. Originally, most Deco buildings were painted white with their features picked out in navy or dark brown – a rare surviving example of this color scheme is the City Hall in Coconut Grove.

"Fifth Avenue of the South." Store dresser-turned-architect Morris Lapidus (see p.75) was the genius behind its pedestrianization – then a revolutionary idea – and also designed the space-age structures that serve as sunshades. Though its fortunes plummeted alongside the rest of South Beach in the 1970s and 1980s, now it's a sparkling shopping strip lined with groovy brand-name stores and dozens of sidewalk cafés; the Sunday afternoon stroll here is a ritual not to be missed. It's worth stopping by the Richard Shack Gallery at the **ArtCenter/South Florida** at no. 800 (Mon–Wed 11am–10pm, Thurs–Sun 11am–11pm; free; T305/674-8278, Wwww.artcentersf.org), an artists' collective that has been here since 1984, to see the work of more than fifty local painters, sculptors, and photographers through revolving exhibitions. Art lovers should also check out **Britto Central** (daily 11am–11pm; T305/531-8831, Wwww.britto.com) at no. 818, showcasing the flamboyant pop art of Brazilian Romero Britto.

Back on **Collins Avenue** just east of Lincoln Road Mall, it's worth rounding off a tour of Art Deco South Beach with a look at some of the most opulent hotels on the strip. The **Delano** at no. 1685 was the tallest building in Miami Beach when it opened in 1947; check out Philippe Starck's recently added drape-lined lobby, and the fabulous pool at the back (see p.108 for bar review). Pop into the **Sagamore** at no. 1671 to admire the vivid contemporary art displayed in the lobby and immaculate all-white bar areas, while one block to the north at no. 1775, the **Raleigh Hotel** is the place to end your stroll with a cocktail by its gorgeous palm-fringed Modernist pool. Another jewel designed by L. Murray Dixon in 1940, the hotel is now part of the André Balazs stable.

The Jackie Gleason Theater

Immediately north of Lincoln Road Mall, the 2600-seat **Fillmore Miami Beach at the Jackie Gleason Theater** at 1700 Washington Ave is worth a visit for Pop artist Roy Lichtenstein's expressive *Mermaid* sculpture at the front, and for its classical concerts (see p.112). However, it is best known to middle-aged Americans as the home of entertainer Jackie Gleason's immensely popular TV show, *The Honeymooners*, which began in the 1950s and ran for twenty years.

The Holocaust Memorial

It's impossible not to be moved by Kenneth Treister's **Holocaust Memorial**, 1933 Meridian Ave (daily 9am–9pm; free; $2 donation for brochure; T 305/538-1663, W www.holocaustmmb.org), just northwest of the Jackie Gleason Theater. Completed in 1990 and dedicated to Elie Wiesel, the monument depicts a 42-foot-high bronze arm tattooed with an Auschwitz number reaching toward the sky. Life-sized figures of emaciated, tormented people attempt to climb this wrenching sculpture. The black marble walls around it are etched with the names of the dead as well as some shockingly graphic photographs of Nazi atrocities.

The Bass Museum of Art

A little further north stands the **Bass Museum of Art**, 2121 Park Ave (Tues–Sat 10am–5pm, Sun 11–5pm; $8; T 305/673-7530, W www.bassmuseum.org). The only fine-art museum on Miami Beach, the Bass is housed in a squat, white 1930s building designed by Russell Pancoast, the architect son-in-law of beach pioneer John Collins. What began as the local public library became a museum to house the private collection of local socialites John and Johanna Bass, which was donated to the city in 1963. The museum unveiled a showy expansion by Japanese architect Arata Isozaki in 2002 – the white box he grafted onto the original building along Park Avenue tripled its exhibition space. It's a shame, then, that the holdings are so hit and miss: there are some gems in the collection, notably the stunning Flemish tapestry known as *The Tournament*, but many of the big names here, such as Rubens and Botticelli, are represented by minor works.

South of 5th Street

The last chunk of South Beach to undergo gentrification lies south of 5th Street, where bars and restaurants are slowly spreading downward and bringing the tourist crowds with them. This area was originally the Jewish ghetto on the beach, since 5th Street marked the northernmost point where Jews could buy housing. By the 1980s, though, the area had collapsed into a shabby, crime-ridden, no-go area, spurred by the arrival of undesirables in the wake of the Mariel boatlift (see "the Cuba Question," p.87). The most obvious sign of the current upswing is an influx of new residents, drawn to what local realtors have taken to calling "SoFi" (South of Fifth), especially at the southern tip known as South Pointe. The high-rises here – like the luxury 26-story **South Pointe Towers** that leap skyward from South Pointe Park (see below) – dwarf the area and give it a rather soulless feel, and it's fairly pointless just wandering around. Come for the Ziff Museum or some of South Beach's hottest, swankiest hotels and restaurants instead, such as the *Bentley Beach Hotel* and *Prime 112* (see p.103 for details).

Ziff Jewish Museum of Florida

During the 1920s and 1930s, South Beach became a major destination for Jewish tourists escaping the harsh northeastern winters. In response, many of the hotels placed "Gentiles Only" notices at their reception desks, and the slogan "Always a view, never a Jew" appeared in many a hotel brochure. Despite this, by the 1940s South Beach had a largely Jewish population and for a time it was home to the second largest community of Holocaust survivors in the country. The **Ziff Jewish Museum of Florida**, 301 Washington Ave (Tues–Sun 10am–5pm; $6, free Sat; ☎305/672-5044, ⓦwww.jewishmuseum .com), bears testimony to Jewish life not only in Miami Beach, but in all of Florida, since the earliest days of European settlement. The permanent collection is exhaustive, and there are visiting exhibitions on Jewish life in general – make sure to chat with one of the volunteers when wandering around as they're enthusiastic and knowledgeable. The museum itself is housed in an elegant 1936 Art Deco building – now lavishly restored – that served as an Orthodox synagogue for Miami Beach's first Jewish congregation.

South Pointe

The best route to **South Pointe** is the mile-long shorefront boardwalk, beginning near the southern end of Lummus Park and finishing by the 300-foot-long jetty lined with people fishing off First Street Beach, the only **surfing** beach in Miami and packed with tanned, athletic bodies even when the waves are calm. You can swim and snorkel here, too, but bear in mind that the big cruise ships frequently pass close by and stir up the current.

On its inland side, the boardwalk skirts **South Pointe Park** (daily 8am–sunset), whose lawns and tree-shaded picnic tables were given a handsome refurbishment in 2008. The park is a good place to be on Friday evenings when its open-air stage is the venue for enjoyable free **music events** (details are posted around South Beach), while you can admire the sea views and cruise ships over a cold beer at *Smith & Wollensky* (see p.103).

Central Miami Beach

Art Deco gives way to massive tower blocks as South Beach settles into the more sedate area known as **CENTRAL MIAMI BEACH**. Collins Avenue charts a five-mile course through the area, between Indian Creek and the once-swanky **hotels** around which the Miami Beach high life revolved during the glamorous 1950s. The good times were short-lived however, and by the 1970s, many of the hotels looked like what they really were: monsters from another age. The 1980s saw Miami's social star re-emerge, and many of the polished-up hotels are now occupied by well-heeled Latin American tourists – along with gray-haired swingers from the US for whom Miami Beach never lost its cachet.

These often madly ostentatious establishments are the main attraction here with little in the way of traditional sights; the strand itself is largely the preserve of families and older folk, and is backed by a long and lovely boardwalk that stretches over a mile from 21st Street.

Before Central Miami Beach became a celebrities' playground, the nation's rich and powerful built rambling shorefront mansions here. One of them, the winter home of tire-baron Harvey Firestone, was demolished in 1953 to make room for the **Fontainebleau**, 4441 Collins Ave (℡305/538-2000, Ⓦwww .fontainebleau.com), a dreamland of kitsch and consumerism cooked up by architect Morris Lapidus that defined the Miami Beach of the late 1950s and 1960s. Gossip-column perennials, such as Joan Crawford, Joe DiMaggio, Lana Turner, and Bing Crosby, were Fontainebleau regulars, as was crooner Frank Sinatra who, besides starting a scrambled-egg fight in the coffee shop, shot many scenes here as the private-eye hero of the 1960s film *Tony Rome*. The interior has been brutally remodeled several times since Lapidus first designed it, but its 2008 restoration returned many of his elegant touches, including ripping up carpet so that the bowties (Lapidus' trademark) embedded in the lobby's terrazzo floor can once again be seen.

North Miami Beach

Collins Avenue continues up through **North Beach** between 63rd Street and 87th Terrace, the latest beachfront enclave to be eyed by preservationists, thanks to its heavy concentration of playful mid-century **MiMo** buildings. The Fontainebleau's Morris Lapidus was one of the best known proponents of this style, which emphasizes swooping movement and speedy touches like rooftop fins, as well as decorative, non-functioning elements like cheesehole (holes bored through concrete like bubbles in Swiss cheese). Eight blocks of the eastern side of Collins Avenue, from 63rd to 71st streets, were designated the North Beach Resort Historic District in 2004: this area includes masterpieces like the **Sherry Frontenac** hotel at 65th and Collins, with its jazzy neon signs, and the stone grill-fronted **Golden Sands** at 69th and Collins – though neither is particularly noteworthy for its rooms, both are ideal photo ops. For more MiMo buildings, head west along 71st Street onto **Normandy Isle**, which is rapidly becoming a trendy hub for hipsters priced out of South Beach as well as a cluster of expat Argentinians who've earned the area its nickname of Little Buenos Aires (for more on eating here, see p.103).

The low-rise buildings of the next neighborhood, **Surfside**, retain a rather appealing old-fashioned ambience; the **beach**, between 91st and 95th streets, is the main reason most people spend an afternoon here. Directly north, **Bal Harbour** – its aspirations of "Olde Worlde" elegance reflected in its anglicized name – is similar in size to Surfside but entirely different in character: an upmarket area filled with the carefully guarded homes of some of the nation's wealthiest people. The exclusive Bal Harbour Shops, 9700 Collins Ave (Mon-Sat 10am–9pm, Sun noon–6pm; ℡305/886–0311, Ⓦwww.balharbourshops.com), packed with outrageously expensive designer stores, sets the tone for the area; ironically, given its upmarket aspirations, the town's origins lie in a soldiers' training camp that once stood here during World War II.

The most notorious local attraction, though, is further north, in **Haulover Beach Park** (℡305/947-3525, Ⓦwww.miamidade.gov/parks/parks/haulover _park.asp). This is Miami's only nude beach, but the furore over the clothing-free bathing eclipses its other upsides – the sands are wide enough to never feel crowded, there are ample picnic tables, showers, and bathrooms, and it's only a twenty-minute drive from South Beach. To get there take buses #H, #K, or #S up Collins Avenue and get off at the coastguard station, where there are also parking facilities ($5). From here turn right for the regular beach or left for the "clothing optional" one, which starts at beach watch-station 24 and ends at watch-station 29, predominantly a gay area.

Beyond Haulover Park, the resort of **Sunny Isles Beach** has long been clogged with mainly European package tourists and the condo-hotels and chain restaurants that cater to them; today the area is increasingly dominated by expat Russians, and also known as Little Moscow. The main draw here is the still-sumptuous beaches; to combat erosion, they're regularly replenished by sand dredged from the ocean floor. By the time you reach **Golden Beach**, the northernmost community of Miami Beach, much of the traffic pounding Collins Avenue has turned inland on the Lehman Causeway (192nd Street), and the anachronistic hotels have given way to quiet shorefront homes. Collins Avenue, as Hwy-A1A, continues north to Hollywood and Fort Lauderdale (see p.188).

Downtown Miami and around

For years **DOWNTOWN MIAMI** was the chaotic, Latin heart of the city, but while a few Cuban coffee counters remain, those days are largely gone. The whole area, from Brickell in the south to the Omni mall north of I-395, is being transformed by one of the largest construction booms in the United States. Vast, shimmering towers of glass and steel now line the waterfront, far taller than anything on Miami Beach, a mixture of offices, hotels and above all, pricey condos. The latter focus means that downtown, while retaining its commercial

---

Watson Island

Traveling between Miami Beach and downtown it's worth stopping at **Watson Island**, midway along the MacArthur Causeway as you cross Biscayne Bay. For many years, it was a seaplane landing area and haven for local vagrants, which was an embarrassing eyesore for the city's government. That's all changed since the arrival of **Jungle Island** (daily 10am–6pm; $29.95, parking $7 per vehicle; ☎305-2-JUNGLE, ⓦwww.jungleisland.com), a wildlife park that features a flamingo lake, serpentariam, parrot bowl and even tiger compound, all hidden within a lushly landscaped jungle habitat. One of the best areas is the Manu Encounter, modeled on a Peruvian mountaintop, where you can wander among free-flying macaws. Next door, the renovated **Ichimura Miami-Japan Garden** (daily; free) was established in the 1950s, but given a spiffy makeover in 2006, making for a delightful, if tiny, place to stroll.

Opposite the garden and Jungle Island sits the **Miami Children's Museum** (daily 10am–6pm; $12; ☎305/373-5437, ⓦwww.miamichildrensmuseum.org), housed in a jagged building designed by Arquitectonica (see p.82). It's a quirky place, ideal to amuse restive youngish children for an afternoon or so: among other interactive exhibits, there's a mini supermarket and television studio and even a bank where you can design your own currency. The Castle of Dreams interior playground is terrific for any tykes who need to burn off excess energy.

There's plentiful parking on the island if you're coming by car (the lot near the museum is $3 for up to 3hr Mon–Fri, $5 per day Sat–Sun); otherwise, you can catch bus #S, #K, or #C from either downtown or South Beach.

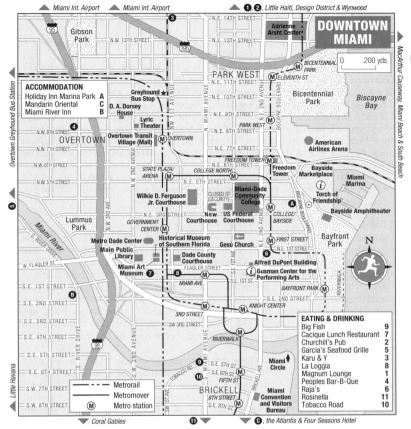

DOWNTOWN MIAMI

0   200 yds

MacArthur Causeway, Miami Beach & South Beach

Overtown Greyhound Bus Station

Little Havana

Coral Gables

ACCOMMODATION
Holiday Inn Marina Park A
Mandarin Oriental C
Miami River Inn B

N.E. 14TH STREET
N.E. 13TH STREET
Adrienne Arsht Center
Gibson Park
N.W. 13TH STREET
N.E. 11TH STREET
PARK WEST
ELEVENTH ST
BICENTENNIAL PARK
Bicentennial Park
Biscayne Bay
Greyhound Bus Stop
D. A. Dorsey House
Lyric Theater
Overtown Transit Village (Mall)
OVERTOWN
N.W. 8TH STREET
N.W. 7TH STREET
N.W. 6TH STREET
N.W. 5TH STREET
PARK WEST
N.E. 8TH STREET
N.E. 7TH STREET
American Airlines Arena
FREEDOM TOWER
Freedom Tower
Bayside Marketplace
Miami Marina
Torch of Friendship
Bayside Amphitheater
STATE PLAZA/ ARENA
COLLEGE NORTH
N.E. 5TH STREET
Miami-Dade Community College
CLOSED ST (SECURITY)
COLLEGE/ BAYSIDE
Wilkie D. Ferguson Jr. Courthouse
New Courthouse
US Federal Courthouse
Lummus Park
GOVERNMENT CENTER
Metro Dade Center
Main Public Library
Historical Museum of Southern Florida
Gesú Church
FIRST STREET
N.E. 1ST STREET
Bayfront Park
Miami Art Museum
Dade County Courthouse
Alfred DuPont Building
Gusman Center for the Performing Arts
FLAGLER STREET
S.E. 1ST ST.
Miami River
S. RIVER DRIVE
W. FLAGLER ST.
S.E. 1ST STREET
S.E. 2ND STREET
MIAMI AVE.
S.E. 2ND STREET
BAYFRONT PARK
RIVERWALK
S.E. 3RD STREET
3RD STREET
SW 3RD STREET
KNIGHT CENTER
S.E. 4TH STREET
S.W. RIVER DRIVE
RIVERWALK
S.E. 5TH STREET
S.E. 5TH ST.
S.E. 6TH STREET
FIFTH ST
S.W. 7TH STREET
BRICKELL
8TH STREET
S.W. 8TH STREET
S.E. 8TH ST.
Miami Circle
Miami Convention and Visitors Bureau
TOBACCO RD.

N

Metrorail
Metromover
Metro station

EATING & DRINKING
Big Fish 9
Cacique Lunch Restaurant 7
Churchill's Pub 2
Garcia's Seafood Grille 5
Karu & Y 3
La Loggia 8
Magnum Lounge 1
Peoples Bar-B-Que 4
Raja's 6
Rosinella 11
Tobacco Road 10

core, is set to become primarily an upmarket residential area in the next few years, though just how successful this metamorphosis will be is not yet clear – most apartments remain unsold and the area quickly empties of people after 6pm. Until things take off, there's little to keep you here for long; vestiges of the center's bustling heyday can be found on **Flagler Street**, now largely given over to cut-price electronics, clothes, and jewelry stores. The main attractions are the **Historical Museum of Southern Florida** and the absorbing modern art round-up at the **Miami Art Museum**, but you should also make time for a boat tour of **Biscayne Bay** from **Bayside Marketplace**. Most of the new development lies along the bay, and a few blocks inland change is proceeding far more slowly, where older neighborhoods – and roughness – remain. Wandering downtown on foot is manageable and safe enough during the day, though the Metromover (see p.61) is a handy way to jump between the main sights.

Flagler Street

Despite the proximity of so much opulent development, **Flagler Street,** the traditional heart of downtown Miami, seems yet to benefit. For now the once bustling thoroughfare is a down-at-heel mix of discount stores and cheap cafés, livened somewhat by students from the Miami-Dade Community College campus nearby.

A few remnants of the street's golden age survive, notably the 1939 **Alfred I. DuPont Building** at no. 169 (at the eastern end), one of Miami's only Moderne skyscrapers (260ft) and currently a fancy events venue. Opposite, the **Gusman Center for the Performing Arts**, no. 174 (☎305/374-2444, ⓦwww.gusmancenter.org) began life in 1926 as the vaudeville **Olympia Theater**, and also hosts the Downtown Welcome Center (see p.59). It's worth a look at the lobby for a taster of the exquisitely kitsch trappings inside, though to experience the Moorish-inspired auditorium you'll have to see a performance. Further along the street, at 73 West Flagler, four forbidding Doric columns mark the entrance to the **Dade County Courthouse**. Completed in 1928 on the site of an earlier courthouse – where public hangings used to take place – this was Miami's tallest building (360ft) for 44 years, and its night lights showed off a distinctive stepped pyramid peak that beamed out a symbolic warning to wrongdoers all over the city.

The Metro-Dade Cultural Center

Little inside the courthouse is worth passing the security check for. Instead, you should cross SW First Avenue toward the giant, air-raid shelter-like building of the **Metro-Dade Cultural Center** at 101 W Flagler St, entered via a ramp off Flagler. This was an ambitious attempt by renowned architect Philip Johnson to create a postmodern Mediterranean-style piazza, a congenial gathering place where Miami could display its cultural side. The theory almost worked: a superb art gallery, historical museum, and a major library frame the courtyard, but Johnson forgot the power of the south Florida sun. Rather than pausing to rest and gossip, most people scamper across the open space toward the nearest shade.

In addition to temporary exhibitions on topics as diverse as Florida cartoons and Miami's African Diaspora, the **Historical Museum of Southern Florida** (Mon–Sat 10am–5pm, Sun noon–5pm, every third Thurs open till 9pm; $8; ☎305/375-1492, ⓦwww.hmsf.org) houses a permanent "Tropical Dreams" section upstairs, a well chronicled account of the region's history. Beginning with displays on early Native American inhabitants and the **Miami Circle** (see p.81), the exhibition covers early European colonization and the rivalry between Spain and England. Also well charted are the Seminole wars, the fluctuating fortunes of Key West and its "wrecking," sponge and cigar industries, and Miami Beach, from its early days as a celebrity vacation spot – with amusing photos of 1920s Hollywood greats – through to the renovation of the Art Deco district. The exhibition ends with a look at the arrival of Cuban and Haitian immigrants, including two genuine refugee rafts, shockingly small given their passenger load.

A few yards away at the plaza's eastern edge, the **Miami Art Museum** (Tues–Fri 10am–5pm, Sat & Sun noon–5pm, third Thur of each month 10am–9pm; $8; free every second Sat; ☎305/375-1700, ⓦwww.miamiart museum.org) has a stunning and intelligently curated permanent collection. Its display is refreshed four times yearly, though highlights are likely to include brightly colored canvases by Damien Hirst, photographs of Ku Klux Klansmen by Andres Serrano, and sketches by Christo. Don't miss the gorgeous works by the late Cuban-American conceptual artist Felix Gonzalez-Torres: the museum has several of his organic pieces, designed to change through viewing – for example a pile of candy stacked in a stark white corner that dwindles as passersby help themselves to it. The museum is planning to decamp from the cultural center to a new, waterfront space at Bicentennial Park, north of Bayside Marketplace. This so-called **Museum Park** will be shared with Coconut Grove's Museum of Science (see p.95) and is expected to open in early 2012; call or check the art museum website for details.

Adjoining the Cultural Center to the north, the **Government Center** chiefly comprises county government offices, notable as the place where, on November 22, 2000, young Republicans stormed the Stephen P. Clark Center to stop the **recount** of votes in the disputed presidential election (see p.470).

North of Flagler Street

The little commercial activity there is falls away completely as you head **north of Flagler Street**. Look out for the 1925 Catholic **Gesú Church**, 118 NE Second St (☎305/379-1424), its painted exterior the color of peach sherbet with foamy lemon meringue touches. The interior, worth a quick peek, is a stout, darkish sanctum that usually hums with private prayers and is brightened by lavish stained glass windows and imposing marble *retablo* (altarpiece) – it's designed without pillars so the Jesuits would have uninterrupted sightlines for their fiery sermons. Continue north along First Avenue and you'll reach Miami's now heavily policed court house district. The old **US Federal Courthouse**, no. 300 (now the David W. Dyer Federal Building; ☎305/523-5100), with its Neoclassical design and Corinthian columns, was finished in 1931. Sadly, in 2008 the deterioration of the building (mold in the basement is said to be a serious health hazard), forced its closure. A block away at 400 N Miami Ave the new $163 million boat-shaped **Wilkie D. Ferguson Jr. Federal Courthouse** was designed by Arquitectonica. Check out the surrounding park (with grassy mounds symbolizing sand dunes), designed by Maya Lin, who shot to fame as the designer of the Vietnam War Memorial in Washington, DC.

Bayside Marketplace and Biscayne Bay

Typical Miamian consumerism is on display at the **Bayside Marketplace**, 401 N Biscayne Blvd (Mon–Thurs 10am–10pm, Fri & Sat 10am–11pm, Sun 11am–9pm; ☎305/577-3344, ⓦwww.baysidemarketplace.com), a large, pink shopping mall providing pleasant waterfront views from its terraces. The views – and the handy unofficial tourist information stand at its western entrance by NE 5th Street – are reasons enough to stop by, though you'd be remiss not to take one of the **boat tours** around **Biscayne Bay** that leave from the dock here (see box, p.80).

Bayside Marketplace caps the northern end of Bayfront Park, a pleasant enough greenspace that is home to the John F. Kennedy Memorial **Torch of Friendship** (though its perpetual flame has long been extinguished). It was designed in 1960 to symbolize good relations between the US and its southern neighbors, with a pointed space left for the Cuban national emblem among the alphabetically sorted crests of each country.

North of downtown

The once impoverished area of waterfront north of downtown Miami is gradually being transformed by a spate of new condos, hotels and cultural projects, notably **Museum Park** (see above), the revitalization of the Omni shopping mall on Biscayne Boulevard between 15th and 17th streets, and the astonishing Cesar Pelli-designed Performing Arts Center, a sprawling modernist masterpiece (see p.80). Before you get there, however, there's one notable

Biscayne Bay's million-dollar mansions

America's rich and famous have been coming to Miami for years, hiding away within ostentatious palm-smothered mansions on the keys that lie between the city and Miami Beach. With the exception of Fisher Island, all of these can be reached by road (from the causeways that cross Biscayne Bay), but the only way to get a good look at the houses is to take a boat tour from Bayside Marketplace. These are unashamedly touristy, but provide fabulous views of the city, and include a narrated jaunt around some of the most exclusive keys (which must seriously irritate their affluent inhabitants). Guides will point out the opulent mansions of Shaquille O'Neal, Sean Combs (aka Diddy), and Gloria Estefan on Star Island, Oprah Winfrey's palace on Fisher Island and Al Capone's former abode on Palm Island, among numerous others.

Operators include **Island Queen Cruises** (ⓣ305/379-5119, ⓦwww.islandqueencruises.com), which runs daily 90-minute tours (11am–7pm, on the hour) for $22, and **Thriller Speed Boat** (ⓣ305/373-7001, ⓦwww.thrillermiami.com), which runs 45-minute powerboat tours for $32. For a more sedate voyage around the bay, try *Heritage Of Miami II*, an elegant schooner that makes two, 2-hour circuits daily (1.30pm & 4pm) for $20, and 1 hour trips at 6.30pm and 8pm for $15 (ⓣ305/442-9697, ⓦwww.heritageschooner.com).

You can also tour the same islands by **kayak**, though it pays to take the boat tour first so you know which celebrity backyard you're paddling past. Be sure to stop at **Flagler Memorial Island**, which is topped with a 110-foot obelisk honoring oil baron and Miami pioneer Henry Flagler, and has picnic tables and a short strip of sand, though it can get mobbed at the weekends.

Try **South Beach Kayak** (Wed-Sat 10.30am–sunset, Sun & Mon 11am–sunset; $25 per 2hr, $80 per day; ⓣ305/332-2853, ⓦwww.southbeachkayak.com), 1771 Purdy Ave, Miami Beach, near the Venetian Causeway; lessons are an additional $25.

attraction on Biscayne Boulevard, across from Bayside Marketplace: the 225-foot **Freedom Tower**, originally home to the now defunct *Miami News*. It earned its current name by housing the Cuban Refugee Center, which began operations in 1962. Most of those who left Cuba on the "freedom flights" got their first taste of US bureaucracy here: between 1965 and 1972, ten empty planes left Miami each week to collect Cubans allowed to leave the island by Fidel Castro. The 1925 building isn't the only one in Miami that was modeled on the Giralda bell tower in Seville, Spain; so was the Biltmore Hotel in Coral Gables (see p.92). Today the tower is owned by Miami-Dade College and is occasionally used as an art exhibition space – call ⓣ305/237-7186 to see if it's open.

Beyond the Freedom Tower lies **Park West**, a warehouse district that the city has cannily designated a nightlife zone, granting 24-hour liquor licenses to a cluster of clubs along 11th street with the idea that it will draw traffic away from South Beach's choked bars. For reviews of its nightclubs, see p.110.

Adrienne Arsht Center for the Performing Arts

Masterminded by architect Cesar Pelli, the enormous **Adrienne Arsht Center for the Performing Arts** (ⓣ305/372-7611, ⓦwww.arshtcenter.org), on Biscayne Boulevard between 13th and 14th streets, opened in 2006 as the second-largest performing arts center in the US, after New York's Lincoln Center. The one historic landmark on the site, the octagonal, medieval fortress-like Art Deco tower next to the opera house, was once part of the now-demolished 1929 Sears flagship building, and may open as a restaurant in 2009.

The best way to appreciate Pelli's grand vision is to take a **free one-hour tour** (Mon & Sat noon; ☏305/949-6722) from the Ziff Ballet Opera House, which includes all the theaters, as well as a peek into star dressing rooms, private rooms and lounges not open to the public. It's also worth taking in a performance at one of the three main venues; the **John S. and James L. Knight Concert Hall** is a 2200-seat shoebox-design space intended to maximize acoustics; the slightly larger **Ziff Ballet Opera House** is devoted to opera, dance, and Broadway-style shows; and the tiny **Carnival Studio Theater**, with a flexible 200-seat auditorium, is available to local arts groups.

The center has four resident companies: the Florida Grand Opera, Miami City Ballet, New World Symphony, and Concert Association of Florida. The superb Cleveland Orchestra has also signed on for a ten-year annual residency where it will stage a three-week season in South Florida every winter. For ticket information, see box, p.111.

Overtown

From the earliest days, Coloredtown, as **OVERTOWN** was previously known, was divided by train tracks from the white folks of downtown Miami: safely cordoned off from the rest of the population, the black community here thrived – during the 1930s, jazz clubs crammed NW 2nd Avenue between 6th and 10th streets (then variously known as Little Broadway, The Strip or even The Great Black Way), thrilling multiracial audiences. By World War II, though, the area was in decline, accelerated rapidly in the 1960s by the construction of the I-95 freeway through the neighborhood, which displaced some 20,000 residents and isolated it from local amenities. Overtown came to be synonymous with Miami's every ill, from drugs to violence, and though today it's clawing its way back to economic health, it can still be a dangerous place for visitors even during the day. If you're curious to visit this historic part of Miami, make sure to do so on an organized tour (see p.61) – preferably one that includes the **Overtown Historic District**. Though it's now dirty and rubbish-strewn, there are a few remnants of Overtown's glory days still standing here, notably the **D.A. Dorsey House** at 250 NW 9th St. This white, two-story clapboard home is an exact replica of the one built in 1914 by the first African-American millionaire in Miami (fittingly, given today's construction boom, Dana Albert Dorsey made his money in real estate). The house is a private home so you can't go inside. Close by, on a deserted strip, is the regal **Lyric Theater**, 819 NW 2nd Ave, where the likes of Nat King Cole and Lena Horne were once regular performers. Now run by a local non-profit, it was beautifully renovated in 2007, with the addition of a glass atrium to its northern side to expand the theater's capacity. The theater anchors one of several ambitious projects to regenerate the district, given the umbrella title **Overtown Folklife Village**.

The Miami Circle

Fifteen minutes' walk south along SE Second Avenue from Flagler Street, the **Miami River** marks the southern limit of downtown, now totally hemmed in by skyscrapers. As you cross the Brickell Bridge, glance across to the tip of the southern bank; you should be able to make out the mysterious ring of 24 holes cut into the limestone bedrock known as the **Miami Circle**. The developer who bought this land for a condo complex was shocked when in 1998 the archaeologists hired to clear the area unearthed the circle, along with prehistoric remains such as shell-tools and burnt wood, carbon-dated to be 1700 to 2000 years old; after a heated legal contest and local protests, the developer agreed to sell the site to the state (for a tidy profit of just over $18 million), and today it remains conspicuously condo-free. No one knows much about the circle's true purpose, though it seems reasonable to assume that it was constructed by the ancestors of the Tequesta people. The **Historical Museum of Southern Florida** (which has a permanent exhibit on the circle, see p.78) took over management of the site in 2008, and should be offering tours in 2009.

Brickell

In the 1870s, "father of Miami" William Brickell established a trading post on the south side of the Miami River, in an area now known as **BRICKELL** (rhymes with pickle). Beginning immediately across the Brickell Bridge and running to Coconut Grove (see p.93), its main thoroughfare, **Brickell Avenue**, was *the* address in 1910s Miami, easily justifying its "millionaires row" nickname. While the original grand homes have largely disappeared, money is still Brickell Avenue's most obvious asset: over the bridge begins a half-mile parade of **condominiums** and **banks**, whose imposing forms are softened by forecourts filled with sculptures, fountains, and palm trees. Far from being places to change travelers checks, these institutions are bastions of international high finance. From the late 1970s, Miami emerged as a corporate banking center, cashing in on political instability in South and Central America by offering a secure home for Latin American money, some of which needed laundering.

Until 2011 (when one of several new skyscrapers should top out), the 70-story **Four Seasons Hotel** at 1435 Brickell Ave will remain the city's loftiest building at 789ft. The posh bars and restaurants inside (enhanced by a modern sculpture collection worth over $3.5 million) make for a luxurious if expensive pit-stop, though you won't get higher than the seventh floor (the upper levels are private condos). Highlights include the massive **Fernando Botero** bronze sculpture in the lobby, *Seated Woman, 2002*. Don't miss the sparkling glass tower of **Espírito Santo Plaza** at no. 1395, a local favorite for its scintillating 36-story curving facade.

Further south (and best seen from a car or bus window), astronomically priced condo towers now overshadow the building that most defined Miami in the 1980s: the **Atlantis**, at no. 2025. Finished in 1983, the Atlantis crowned several years of innovative construction by a small architectural firm called Arquitectonica, whose style – variously termed "beach-blanket Bauhaus" and "ecstatic modernism" – fused postmodern thought with a strong sense of Miami's eclectic architectural heritage. The building's focal point is a gaping square hole through its middle where a palm tree, a jacuzzi, and a red-painted spiral staircase tease the eye.

The Biscayne Corridor

On Miami's run-down north side lie chunks of the city that have only recently appeared on visitor itineraries, in an area known as the **Biscayne Corridor**, after its main artery, Biscayne Boulevard. The most noteworthy example of its rebirth is in the southernmost area, where neighborhoods are being transformed by the migration of **contemporary art galleries**. The **Wynwood Art District** has become a haven for artists driven out of the funky if somewhat artificial **Design District** further north, while **Little Haiti** is a great place to try cheap, tasty Caribbean food. Art fans should also make the trek up to North Miami for the overlooked **Museum of Contemporary Art**, the city's beguiling showcase for the avant-garde.

Wynwood Art District

North of 20th Street, sandwiched between I-95 and N Miami Avenue, the **Wynwood Art District** is home to one of the largest and most dynamic concentrations of **art galleries** in the city. Most of the seventy or so exhibition spaces occupy a ramshackle area of warehouses, wholesale clothing stores and overgrown lots that can seem deserted even during the day; though it's relatively safe to explore, the area remains sketchy at night and galleries are spread out, so this part of the Biscayne Corridor is best experienced by car. Work here ranges from the seriously engaging to dismally child-like, but you may stumble on the next big thing – just park your car outside and have a look. Every second Saturday of each month an **Art Walk** is held from 7pm to 11pm, when all galleries and studios open their doors to the public for art, music and refreshments – you can get details from any of the galleries listed here (the "walk" is really an open evening rather than an organized guided tour).

Highlights include **Twenty Twenty** at 2020 NW Miami Court, 2/F, near NW 20th Street (Mon–Sat, call ahead; ☎786/217-7683, Ⓦwww.twentytwentyprojects .com), a high-quality showcase for up-and-coming talent, and **Locust Projects**, 105 NW 23rd St (Thurs–Sat noon–5pm; ☎305/576-8570, Ⓦwww.locustprojects .org), a warehouse crammed with tantalizing multimedia installations. Call ahead to see if **MOCA at Goldman Warehouse**, 404 NW 26th St, a satellite of the Museum of Contemporary Art (see p.86) is open, and visit the **Margulies Collection at the Warehouse**, 591 NW 27th St (Wed–Sat 11am–4pm; $10; ☎305/576-1051, Ⓦwww.margulieswarehouse.com), a beautifully presented ensemble of video, sculpture and a particularly fine collection of twentieth-century photography, with work by Walker Evans and Cindy Sherman. The

▲ Rubell Collection exhibits

Rubell Collection, 95 NW 29th St (Wed–Sat 10am–6pm, second Sat of each month 10am–10pm; $5; ☎305/573-6090, ⓦwww.rubellfamilycollection.com), is a massive modern art collection housed in an old warehouse once used by the Drug Enforcement Agency for storing evidence. An exhaustive survey of the last thirty years in modern art, the collection sets acknowledged masterpieces alongside lesser-known, more experimental work, including early photography from Cindy Sherman, postmodern sculpture from Jeff Koons, and even graffiti canvases by the late Keith Haring.

You can also check out the contemporary art cooked up by residents of the **Bakehouse Art Complex**, 561 NW 32nd St (daily noon–5pm; free; ☎305/576-2828, ⓦwww.bacfl.org), which comprises two galleries, a jewelry studio, ceramic kiln, woodworking and welding areas, and seventy individual artist studios.

The Design District

Miami's flourishing **Design District** (ⓦwww.miamidesigndistrict.net), hemmed in by 36th Street and 41st Street between Miami Avenue and Biscayne Boulevard, was originally a pineapple plantation owned by Theodore Moore, the "Pineapple King of Florida." On a whim, he opened a furniture showroom on NE 40th Street, and had soon created what became known as **Decorators' Row**. During Miami's Art Deco building boom of the 1920s and 1930s, this was the center of the city's design scene, filled with wholesale interiors stores selling furniture and flooring: look for the Designers' Walk of Fame along 40th Street, where stars embedded into the sidewalk honor design luminaries of that time.

By the early 1990s, though, the factory-filled district was deserted and crime-ridden. Savvy developer Craig Robins, one of the masterminds behind the gentrification of South Beach, spotted the potential here and started buying buildings, enticing high-end showrooms like Knoll and Kartell. He's overseen the regeneration of the area, including an emphasis on public art and sculpture: one of his best-known projects is the whimsical **Living Room Building**, 4000 N Miami Ave, at NE 40th Street. The entranceway to this squat office block has been turned inside out, and features a giant pink concrete sofa and standard lamp, as well as bright orange walls – in other words, a witty, irresistible photo opportunity (though it's been marred slightly by graffiti). Robins' initial plans have been revamped somewhat, and now the district's fifteen art galleries and around forty design showrooms have been joined by trendy restaurants (see p.104), boutiques and jazzy, mid-rise condo towers.

The Design District can be an intriguing area for a stroll, though note that the main emphasis (obviously) is on designer furniture and art galleries with little else to see (shops tend to open Mon–Sat 11am–5pm). Most of the action takes place on 39th and 40th streets between NE 2nd Avenue and N Miami Avenue; **bus** #9 and #10 zip up and down NE 2nd Avenue from downtown, and if you drive, metered parking is available everywhere ($1 per hr). Make sure you see the **Moore Space** (Wed–Sat 10am–5pm; ☎305/438-1163, ⓦwww.themoorespace.org), inside the Moore Building at 4040 NE 2nd Ave, at 40th Street, host to exhibits by acclaimed artists such as Tracey Emin and Hernan Bas. Take a break next door in the **Rainforest Garden Lounge**, a bamboo garden designed by Enzo Enea and embellished with sofas and lily ponds. The **Haitian Heritage Museum**, 3940 N Miami Ave, at NE 40th Street (Tues–Fri 10am–5pm; ☎305/371-5988, ⓦwww.haitianheritagemuseum.org; free) showcases Haitian visual arts and Haitian literary works, but call ahead to confirm opening times.

Little Haiti

About 200,000 Haitians live in Miami, forming one of the city's major ethnic groups – albeit it far smaller than the Cuban population – and roughly a third of them live in **LITTLE HAITI**, a district running along the bay from 40th to 85th streets. There are few specific sights in Little Haiti, so it's best to wander along the main drag, NE 2nd Avenue (known here as "Avenue Felix Moisseau Leroy"), and enjoy the Caribbean colors, music, and smells; coming from the Design District you can take the Little Haiti Connector (bus #202). Almost all Miami's Haitians speak English as a third language after Creole and French, so you'll see trilingual signage throughout. It's easy enough to spot one of the area's landmarks, the **Caribbean Marketplace** at 5927 NE 2nd Ave, with its brightly colored ironwork modeled after the Iron Market in Port-au-Prince, Haiti. After years of neglect, the market is being completely renovated as part of the spanking new **Little Haiti Cultural Complex** behind it at 250 NE 59th Terrace; this will serve as a theater/auditorium, a dance facility, a community meeting room and gallery space. Both should be up and running in 2009, but call ☎305/960-4660 for an update.

A short walk north, at the southeast corner of NE 2nd Avenue and 62nd Street, sits one of the oldest buildings in the area. Built in 1902 in what was once the heart of Lemon City, the now-derelict **Dupuis Building** served as a pharmacy and a post office before being abandoned several decades ago. A few blocks west, at N Miami Avenue and 62nd Street, you'll see the striking 13.5-foot bronze statue of the father of Haitian independence, **Toussaint L'Ouverture**, erected in 2005. For a taste of Caribbean music, head north to **Les Cousins Books and**

Santería: saints and sacrifices

Estimated numbers of those practicing the Caribbean religion of **Santería** worldwide vary wildly, anywhere from 60,000 up to 5 million; regardless, it has a hidden but influential role in Miami society, as many people are at least part-time believers. A secretive religion with an oral tradition, Santería was one of the many spiritual hybrids created under colonial rule. Slaves, many of them Yoruba from West Africa, were forcibly baptized and converted to Christianity, but this conversion proved to be largely cosmetic: to preserve their own religions, gods or *orishas* in the African pantheon were "translated" into Christian saints, so that they could be worshipped without fear of being caught. In fact, the name Santería itself began as slang, when colonial Spaniards noticed how greatly their African slaves venerated the saints rather than Christ.

Much like the gods in Ancient Greece, *orishas* have flaws and favorites: each is identified with a given color, food, and number, and requires animal sacrifices and human praise for nourishment. Altars in Santería temples are covered with offerings of cigarettes or designer perfume – the *orishas* are all too human in their vulnerability to flattery and expensive gifts. Religious services, conducted in secret by a priest or priestess, involve channeling the gods through dance and trance. Its practitioners can get *orishas* to give magical aid and guidance through plant, food, or animal sacrifices offered during chants and dancing initiations.

Wandering around Miami, you'll see signs of Santería activity if you look hard enough – streetside offerings, usually nailed to holy kapok trees, are common in Little Havana and Haiti. There is also much sensationalist reporting when Santería offerings are discovered near local courthouses, supposedly attempts by family members to invoke the *orishas'* help during trials. Despite opposition to the religion – much of it from animal-rights activists – a court case in Miami's Hialeah district in 1993 confirmed the constitutional rights of adherents to practice their religion.

Records, 7858 NE 2nd Ave, Little Haiti's first book and record store founded by Viter Juste, popularly known as the "Father of Little Haiti."

If you're in the area, be sure to make a detour down **54th Street**, the heart of Miami's *voudou* and Santería culture, which is lined with several **botanicas**, stores where believers can purchase ritual potions, candles, and statuettes. Almost all will permit a casual visitor to browse their merchandise but it goes without saying that photographing the racks of gaudy statuary and glass jars packed with herbs is both rude and foolish.

The Museum of Contemporary Art

Ten miles north of downtown, Biscayne Boulevard leads into **North Miami**, another neighborhood noted for its Haitian community. Despite some signs of regeneration, this area remains a fairly depressed suburb, and is not a place to linger unless you're visiting the small but absorbing **Museum of Contemporary Art**, 770 NE 125th St (Tues–Sat 11am–5pm, Sun noon–5pm; $5; ☎305/893-6211, ⓦ www.mocanomi.org). Temporary exhibits here and at its Goldman Warehouse site in the Wynwood Art District (see p.83) feature young and emerging local and international talent – expect extremely innovative multimedia work blending film and installations with traditional art forms. You may also see pieces from the museum's permanent collection, which includes art by Yoko Ono, John Baldessari, Dan Flavin, Louise Nevelson and Gabriel Orozco. To **get here** by bus, take nos. 16, 10, or G to the corner of NE 125th Street and NE 8th Avenue, or nos. 75 and 9 to the corner of NE 125th Street and NE 6th Avenue.

Little Havana

The impact of **Cubans** – unquestionably the largest ethnic group in Miami – on the city over the last four decades has been incalculable. Unlike most Latino immigrants to the US, who trade one form of poverty for another, Miami's first Cuban arrivals in the late 1950s had already tasted affluence in their home country. They rose quickly through the social strata and nowadays wield considerable clout in the running of the city, and indeed the state.

Cubans first settled a few miles west of downtown Miami in what became known as **LITTLE HAVANA**, a quiet district of sherbet-colored houses where you're more likely to see newspaper boxes selling *El Nuevo Herald* than the English-language *Miami Herald*, and statues of Cuba's patron saint, the Virgin Mary, in front gardens. Only the neighborhood's main strip, SW 8th Street, or **Calle Ocho**, offers more than houses: street-side counters serve up tiny cups of sweet Cuban coffee; the odors of baking bread and cigars being rolled waft across the sidewalk; shops sell Santería (see box, p.85) ephemera beside six-foot-high models of Catholic saints; and you'll spot the only branch of *Dunkin' Donuts* with guava-filled doughnuts. Though there are few official sights, most people come here to gorge themselves on the delicious, gut-busting Cuban food in one of the local restaurants and to wander around the monuments on Memorial Boulevard (see opposite). For all the reminders of the area's fierce connection to Cuba, Little Havana is increasingly a misnomer: as the successful Cuban community decamps to wealthier neighborhoods like Coral Gables, they're gradually replaced by Latin American immigrants from Honduras, Colombia, and Nicaragua (the eastern portion of Little Havana is often referred to as Little Managua.)

The Cuban question

Proximity to Cuba has long made Florida a refuge for its activists and economic migrants. A raft from Cuba's northern shore can take four days to arrive in South Florida. However, until comparatively recent times, New York, not Miami, was the center of Cuban émigré life in the US.

During the mid-1950s, when opposition to the Batista dictatorship began to assert itself, a trickle of Cubans started arriving in the predominantly Jewish section of Miami called Riverside. The trickle became a flood when **Fidel Castro** came to power, and as Cuban businesses sprang up on SW 8th Street and Cubans began making their mark on Miami life, the area began to be known as **Little Havana**.

These Cubans were derived largely from the affluent middle classes and stood to lose the most under communism. Many regarded themselves as the entrepreneurial sophisticates of the Caribbean. Stories are plentiful of formerly high-flying Cuban capitalists who arrived penniless and, over the course of two decades – and aided by a network of old expats – toiled, wheeled, and dealed their way to positions of power and influence.

The second great Cuban influx into Miami was of a quite different social nature and racial composition: the **Mariel boatlift** in May 1980 brought 125,000 predominantly black islanders from the Cuban port of Mariel to Miami. These arrivals were largely poor and uneducated; a fifth of them were fresh from Cuban jails – incarcerated for criminal rather than political crimes. Most "Marielitos" settled in South Beach, where they proceeded to terrorize the local community, becoming a source of embarrassment for Miami's longer-established, determinedly respectable – and white – Cubans.

Local division gives way to fervent agreement when discussing Castro: he's universally detested. But despite failing to depose the Cuban leader, Cuban-Americans (which have a 70 percent turn-out rate at elections) have been far more successful at influencing the US government. Ronald Reagan gained immense popularity among Miami Cubans for his support of the Nicaraguan Contras – and for his conservative policies in general – in the 1980s. Cubans have been vociferous supporters of the **Republican Party** ever since, though things are changing; in the landmark 2008 presidential election, 55 percent of Miami Cuban-Americans aged 29 or younger voted for Barack Obama. And with **Raúl Castro** formally replacing his ailing brother as Cuban president in 2008, the US Cuban community is planning for the post-Fidel era and the eventual end of the **US embargo of Cuba** (imposed in 1962).

Be sure to check out the **Calle Ocho Festival** in March (see p.113), and at other times of year the **Viernes Culturales** (Cultural Fridays), an arts, music and culture fair held every last Friday night of the month (6.30–11pm) along Calle Ocho between 14th and 17th Avenues (Ⓦwww.viernesculturales.org).

Along Calle Ocho

The defining events and heroes of the Cuban-American community are honored along **Cuban Memorial Boulevard**, the stretch of SW 13th Avenue just south of Calle Ocho. You'll find a cluster of monuments here, of which the **Brigade 2506 Memorial** is the best known. Inscribed with the brigade crest and topped by the Cuban flag, this simple stone remembers those who died at the Bay of Pigs on April 17, 1961, during the attempt by a group of US-trained Cuban exiles to invade the island and wrest control from Castro. Depending on who tells the story, the outcome was the result of either ill-conceived plans, or the US's lack of commitment to Cuba (JFK withheld air support that may have changed the battle's outcome) – to this day, sections of the Cuban community hate Kennedy only slightly less than Fidel Castro. Every anniversary, veterans clad in combat fatigues and carrying assault rifles gather here to make pledges of patriotism throughout the night.

Close by lies a simple bust of Cuban independence fighter **Antonio Maceo**, and a statue of the Virgin Mary holding a decapitated (by vandals) baby Jesus, whose state of disrepair underscores the brooding isolation of the monuments. Further along is a 16-foot raised map of Cuba bearing a worn inscription by independence hero José Martí: *La patria es agonia y deber*, ("The homeland is agony and duty"). The massive tree looming over the monuments is a kapok, sacred to the santería religion (see box, p.85). Back on the corner of Calle Ocho and the memorial boulevard is one of the oldest and best open-air coffee counters in the area, *Los Pinareños Frutería*, at 1334 SW 8th St. Order a potent *cafecito*, *batido de níspero* (loquat smoothie), sugar cane juice or *coco frio* (coconut water), served straight out of the shell. The place doubles as a small tropical fruit stall.

Music fans should head east along Calle Ocho from here to check out **Lily's Records** at 1260 SW 8th St, which has a vast selection of Latin music from Cuba, Venezuela and Mexico among others. Keep walking for one of the area's treasures, **El Titan de Bronze Cigars** (Mon–Sat 9am–5pm) at 1071 SW 8th St near SW 11th Avenue, the home of hand-crafted Cuban style cigars. For general souvenirs try **Little Havana To Go** at 1442 SW 8th St, west of the memorial boulevard, a store that sells Cuban flags, paintings, music, dolls, T-shirts and other paraphernalia. Beyond here lies the **Máximo Gómez Domino Park** (daily 8am–6pm), on the corner of 14th Avenue; access to its open-air tables is (quite illegally) restricted to men over 55, and this is one place where you really will see old men playing dominoes. Be aware that the men don't take kindly to snapshot-happy tourists.

Further west, the peaceful greenery of **Woodlawn Cemetery**, 3260 SW 8th St (daily sunrise–dusk), belies the scheming and skulduggery that some of its occupants indulged in during their lifetimes. Two former Cuban heads of state are buried here: Gerardo Machado, ousted from office in 1933, is in the mausoleum, while one of the protagonists in his downfall, Carlos Prío Socarras, president from 1948 to 1952, lies just outside. Also interred in the mausoleum (and marked only by his initials) is **Anastasio Somoza**, dictator of Nicaragua until overthrown by the Sandinistas in 1979, and later killed in Paraguay. George Merrick, founder of Coral Gables (see below), is also buried here.

Coral Gables

Though all of Miami's constituent cities are quick to assert their individuality, none has a greater case than **CORAL GABLES**, south of Little Havana. Encompassing twelve square miles of broad boulevards and leafy streets lined by elaborate Spanish- and Italian-style architecture, the city was the pet project of one man, **George Merrick**. Taking Mediterranean Europe as his inspiration, he envisaged a lavish Venetian settlement (albeit with Spanish street names) steeped in old-world grandeur to inspire civic pride among its residents. He enlisted his artist uncle, Denman Fink, and architect Phineas Paist to plan the plazas, fountains, and carefully aged stucco-fronted buildings that would sit on the 3000 acres of citrus groves and pineland he inherited from his father.

Merrick's true flair, however, was in publicity, and he staged countless stunts to attract attention and residents – including sending fleets of coral-colored

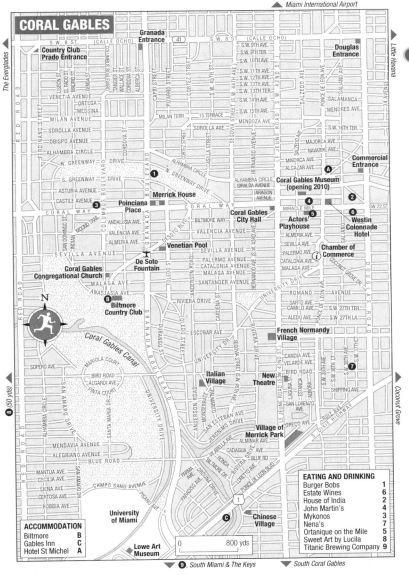

CORAL GABLES

▲ Miami International Airport

The Everglades

Little Havana

Granada Entrance 41

S.W. 8 ST. (CALLE OCHO)
S.W. 8 ST. (CALLE OCHO)

Country Club Prado Entrance

Douglas Entrance

S.W. 9TH AVE.
S.W. 9TH TER.
S.W. 10TH AVE.
S.W. 11TH AVE.
S.W. 12TH TER.
S.W. 13TH AVE.
S.W. 13TH TER.
S.W. 14TH AVE.

VENETIA AVENUE
ORTEGA
MESSINA
MILAN AVENUE

MILAN TERR.

S.W. 15TH AVE.

SALZEDO AVENUE
PONCE DE LEON RD.

SALAMANCA
MENORES AVE.

MENDOZA AVE.

S.W. 16TH TER.

SOROLLA AVENUE
OBISPO AVENUE
ALHAMBRA CIRCLE

N. GREENWAY DRIVE

MAJORCA AVE.
NAVARRE AVE.

MINORCA AVE.
ALCAZAR AVE.

Commercial Entrance

S. GREENWAY DRIVE
ASTURIA AVENUE
CASTILE AVENUE

ALHAMBRA CIRCLE
N. GREENWAY DRIVE

ALHAMBRA CIRCLE /
GIRALDA AVENUE

ARAGON AVENUE

Coral Gables Museum (opening 2010) Ⓐ

❸ Poinciana Place

Merrick House

CORAL WAY

Coral Gables City Hall

MIRACLE MILE

SW 22 ST.

ANDALUSIA AVE.
VALENCIA AVE.
ALMERIA AVE.

BILTMORE WAY

VALENCIA AVENUE

ALMERIA AVE.
SEVILLA AVE.

❹
❺

Actors' Playhouse

❻ **Westin Colonnade Hotel**

SEVILLA AVENUE

Venetian Pool

PALERMO AVENUE
CATALONIA AVENUE
MALAGA AVENUE
SANTANDER AVENUE

PALERMO AVE.
CATALONIA AVE.
MALAGA AVE.

ⓘ **Chamber of Commerce**

De Soto Fountain

Coral Gables Congregational Church

MALAGA AVE.
ANASTASIA AVE.

RIVIERA DRIVE

ROMANO AVENUE
SARTO AVE.
CAMILO AVE.
ALEDO AVE.

S.W. 27TH TER.
S.W. 27TH LA.

❸ **Biltmore Country Club**

Coral Gables Canal

French Normandy Village

CANDIA AVE.
VELARDE AVE.
BIRD ROAD

S.W. 38TH CT.
S.W. 37TH CT.

MARIOLA COURT
BIRD ROAD
ALGARDI AVE.
PINTA COURT

Italian Village

New Theatre

LAGUNA ST.
ESTANCIA ST.
ALBERCA ST.

SHIPPING AVE.

Coconut Grove

SOPERO AVE.

❼

SAN LORENZO AVE.

Village of Merrick Park

MENDAVIA AVENUE
ALEGRIANO AVENUE
BLUE ROAD

ALMINAR AVE.

S. DIXIE HIGHWAY

MANTUA AVE.
CECILIA AVE.
SIENA AVE.
CERTOSA AVE.
ROBBIA AVE.

CAMPO SANO AVENUE

EATING AND DRINKING
Burger Bobs 1
Estate Wines 6
House of India 2
John Martin's 4
Mykonos 3
Nena's 7
Ortanique on the Mile 5
Sweet Art by Lucila 8
Titanic Brewing Company 9

University of Miami

Ⓒ **Chinese Village**

0   800 yds

ACCOMMODATION
Biltmore   B
Gables Inn   C
Hotel St Michel   A

Lowe Art Museum

❾ , South Miami & The Keys

▼ South Coral Gables

buses across Florida to ferry potential customers down to the site. Of the $150 million he made in the five years following the first sale in 1921, he funneled one third into publicity and advertising. The layout and buildings of Coral Gables quickly took shape, but the sudden end of Florida's property boom in 1926 (see Contexts, p.467) wiped Merrick out. He ran a fishing camp in the Florida Keys until that was destroyed by a hurricane, and wound up as Miami's postmaster until his death in 1942.

Coral Gables, however, was built with longevity as well as beauty in mind. Despite successive economic crises, it has never lost its good looks, and these days, boosted equally by a host of multinational companies working out of renovated office buildings and its very image-conscious residents, Coral Gables is as well-to-do and well kept as ever. **Ponce de León Boulevard** is serviced frequently by the Coral Gables trolley bus, which terminates at Douglas Road Metrorail and Metrobus station, but to really tour the whole area you'll need a car. Collect info from the **Chamber of Commerce**, 224 Catalonia Ave (Mon–Thurs 8.30–5pm, Fri 8.30–4pm; ⊤305/446-1657, Ⓦ www.coralgableschamber.org).

The liveliest time to be here is on the first Friday of every month, when the Coral Gables Gallery Association (⊤305/444-4493) organizes **Gables Gallery night** (7–10pm), and free shuttle buses link the area's fine art galleries and studios.

The Miracle Mile and around

Coral Gables' main commercial drag is SW 22nd Street, which is known downtown as the **Miracle Mile** (though only half a mile long). Until recently, this strip was rather forlorn, filled with cobwebby ladies' boutiques and bridal emporia, yet it's now recharged its retail batteries with an aggressive redevelopment plan that has lured casual cafés and shops back to the main street. Notice the ornate arcades and balconies along its course and the spirals and peaks of the **Westin Colonnade Hotel** at 180 Aragon Ave, one block north. The building was completed in 1926 – just a few months before the property crash – to accommodate Merrick's land sales office and served as a soundstage for Miami's nascent film industry before its latest incarnation as a corporate hotel. Further along, the Gables' original police and fire station at 285 Aragon Ave is expected to open as the **Coral Gables Museum** sometime in 2010 – check Ⓦ www.coralgablesmuseum.org for updates.

If you head west back on the Miracle Mile, you'll reach the grandly pillared **Coral Gables City Hall**, 405 Biltmore Way (Mon–Fri 8am–5pm; ⊤305/460-5217, Ⓦ www.coralgables.com), whose corridors are adorned with posters from the 1920s advertising the "City Beautiful" and with newspaper clippings bearing witness to the property mania of the time. From the third-floor landing you can view Denman Fink's impressive blue and gold mural of the four seasons, which decorates the interior of the bell tower (not to be confused with the dreadful mural nearby spotlighting Coral Gables' key attractions).

About half a mile further west, at no. 907 on Coral Way – a typically peaceful and tree-lined Coral Gables residential street – is Merrick's childhood home, the **Coral Gables Merrick House** (by 45min tour only; Sun & Wed 1pm, 2pm, 3pm; $5; ⊤305/460-5361). In keeping with its restrictive hours, the museum offers one of the pithiest overviews of the area's past, via its focus on Merrick's family. In 1899, when George was 12, his family arrived here from New England to run a 160-acre fruit and vegetable farm – and, in the case of George's father, to deliver sermons at the local Plymouth Congregational Church in Coconut Grove. The farm was so successful that the house quickly grew from a wooden shack into a modestly elegant dwelling of coral rock and gabled windows (the inspiration behind the name of the city that later grew up around the family farm). The dual blows of the property crash and a citrus blight led to the gradual deterioration of the house, until restoration began in the 1970s. The place now showcases several of Denman Fink's chocolate box-like canvases as well as quirky Merrick memorabilia. A few houses west at the corner

Coral Gables: entrances and villages

To make a strong first impression on visitors to Coral Gables, founder George Merrick planned eight grand **entrances** on the main access roads, of which only four were completed before he went bust. The three most impressive are along a two-and-a-half-mile stretch of SW 8th Street and well worth seeking out.

The million-dollar **Douglas Entrance** (junction with Douglas Rd) was the most ambitious, consisting of a gateway and tower with two expansive wings of shops, offices, and artists' studios. During the 1960s it was almost bulldozed to make room for a supermarket, but survived to become a well-scrubbed business area, still upholding Merrick's Mediterranean themes in its architecture. Further west, the sixty-foot-high vine-covered **Granada Entrance** (junction with Granada Blvd) is based on the entrance to the city of Granada in Spain. An even better appetizer for Coral Gables is the **Country Club Prado Entrance** (junction with Country Club Prado), the expensive re-creation of a formal Italian garden bordered by freestanding stucco-and-brick pillars topped by ornamental urns and lamps with wrought-iron brackets.

To revive the flagging housing market, which began to soften in the 1920s, Merrick hit on another architectural gimmick: the so-called **International Villages**, which were clusters of houses around town each built in a different style. Though fourteen were planned, only seven were built before Merrick ran out of money. The most eye-popping of these is the **Chinese Village**, just south of US-1 on Riviera Drive: its red and yellow chinoiserie, complete with carved balconies and dragons, is gaudy and irresistible. There's also the brown and white timber-beamed cottages of the **French Normandy Village**, on the 400 block Vizcaya Avenue at Le Jeune Road, and the **French City Village**, on the 1000 block Hardee Road, where the front gardens of the neat town houses are boxed in by high walls.

of Granada Boulevard, at 937 Coral Way, stands **Poinciana Place**, one of the earliest structures in the city; Merrick built this ranch-style home, with its low-slung terracotta tiling, close to his family's base when he married Eunice Peacock in 1916.

De Soto Boulevard and south

From Poinciana Place, turn left down Granada Boulevard and head toward the opulent **De Soto Fountain**, named for conquistador Hernando de Soto, who led an expedition to Florida from Cuba in 1539. Just north of here, along De Soto Boulevard, lies one of Merrick's grand achievements. While his property-developing contemporaries left ugly scars across the city after digging up the local limestone, Merrick had the foresight − and the help of Denman Fink − to turn his biggest quarry into a sumptuous swimming pool. **The Venetian Pool**, 2701 De Soto Blvd (June–Aug Mon–Fri 11am–7pm; Sept & Oct and April & May Tues–Fri 11am–5.30pm; Nov–March Tue–Fri 10am–4.30pm; year-round Sat & Sun 10am–4.30pm; April–Oct $10, Nov–March $6.75; ☎305/460-5356, ⓦwww.venetianpool.com), an elaborate conglomeration of palm-studded paths, Venetian-style bridges, and coral-rock caves, was open in 1924. Despite its ornamentation, the pool was never designed with the society in mind; admission was cheap and open to all, and even today local residents special discount.

Follow De Soto Blvd south of the fountain for a few minutes and you come to the **Coral Gables Congregational Church**, 3010 De Soto Blvd (☎305/448-7421, ⓦwww.coralgablescongregational.org), a Spanish Revival flurry topped by a barrel-tiled roof and capped by Baroque features, built on land donated by Merrick. Though somewhat dark inside, the building has excellent interior acoustics that make it a popular venue for jazz and classical **concerts**; ask for details at the church office, just inside the entrance.

The Biltmore Hotel

Merrick's crowning achievement — aesthetically if not financially — was the **Biltmore Hotel**, 1200 Anastasia Ave (T 305/445-1926 or 1-800/727-1926, W www.biltmorehotel.com). The hotel's 26-tory tower can be seen across much of low-lying Miami: if it seems similar to the Freedom Tower (see p.80), it's because they're both modeled on the Girda bell tower of Seville Cathedral in Spain. The Biltmore was hawked as "te last word in the evolution of civilization," and everything about it was utrageous: 25-foot-high frescoed walls, vaulted ceilings, a wealth of imported arble and tiles, immense fireplaces, and custom-loomed rugs.

Although high-profile celebrities, such Bing Crosby, Judy Garland, and Ginger Rogers, kept the Biltmore on the itineraries, the end of the Florida land boom and the start of the Depressiomeant that the hotel was never the success it might have been. After decades decline the hotel reopened in 1993 after a multimillion dollar refit. Now oncagain it is functioning as a hotel; you can step inside to admire the elaborate hitecture or take **afternoon tea** in the lobby for $17 (Mon–Fri 3pm & 30pm sittings). There are also free historical tours beginning at 1.30pm, 2.?m, and 3.30pm every Sunday in the main hall, but these tend to be hit and s — the best way to absorb the hotel's grandeur is just to amble through its spous common areas.

The neighboring **Biltmore Countrylub**, also open to the public, has fared better. You can poke your head insidor a closer look at its painstakingly renovated Beaux Arts features, but mpeople turn up to knock a ball along the lush fairways of the **Biltmore lf Course**, a par-71 course that was designed in 1925 and which, in the g days of the hotel, hosted the highest-paying golf tournament in the worlt's now home to an upmarket Golf Academy which offers various lessonkages — call or check the hotel website for details (T 305/460-5364, W wwvtmorehotel.com/golf/instruction.asp).

▲ Biltmore Hotel

The Lowe Art Museum

One of the few parts of Coral Gables where Mediterranean-style architecture doesn't prevail is on the campus of the **University of Miami**, about two miles south of the Biltmore, with dismal, box-like buildings that are disappointingly bland. The campus' star attraction is the rather overrated **Lowe Art Museum**, 1301 Stanford Drive (Tues & Wed, Fri & Sat 10am–5pm, Thurs noon–7pm, Sun noon–5pm; $10; ☎305/284-3535, ⓦwww.miami.edu/lowe). Established in 1950, the Lowe underwent major renovation and extension work in 1995 and is now one of the largest museums in Florida. Its holdings zigzag from Old Master paintings to pre-Columbian, African, and East Asian artifacts; it also absorbed the collection of the controversial Cuban Museum of the Americas, which was finally shuttered in 1999 after one too many firebomb attacks. Sadly, the European pictures are mostly shabby small canvases and the non-Western artifacts are largely ephemera; the few standouts are in the museum's modern art collection, including the freakishly life-like football player sculpted in fiberglass by Duane Hanson.

Coconut Grove

A stomping ground of down-at-heel artists, writers, and lefties throughout the 1960s and 1970s, **COCONUT GROVE** is better known these days for two large malls and a slew of expensive condo towers with stunning waterfront views. Though it may have lost its counter-culture edge, Coconut Grove has retained its ornery character: many locals still treat it as distinct from the rest of Miami, which annexed it in the late nineteenth century. It owes its character in part to the strange mix of settlers who first called it home: Bahamian immigrant laborers lived alongside New England intellectuals who came here searching for spiritual fulfillment, and together created a fiercely independent community. The distance between Coconut Grove and the rest of Miami is still very much apparent: cleaner and richer than ever, but continuing to fan the flames of liberalism – indeed, the local populace has tried several times to secede from the city, to no avail. The **Coconut Grove Chamber of Commerce**, 2820 MacFarlane Rd (Mon–Fri 9am–5pm; ☎305/444-7270, ⓦcgcc.coconutgrove.com), on a corner of the Peacock Park south of CocoWalk, has copious selections of free leaflets and maps of the area.

Central Coconut Grove and around

Central Coconut Grove is compact and walkable, filled with shops and restaurants – including two of the city's best-known malls – and plentiful parking. In recent years retail business has suffered from competition elsewhere in the city, and it's not as busy or as appealing as it once was. Open-air **CocoWalk** at 3000 Grand Ave was a major revitalizing force when it was first built in the 1990s, and is still loaded with restaurants, bars, and a movie theater (see "Film", p.112). The more upmarket **Streets of Mayfair**, further along Grand Avenue, was less successful; its meandering walkways – decorated by fountains, copper sculptures, climbing vines, and Romanesque concrete doodles – are almost always empty, and there are dozens of vacant store spaces, making it an oddly lifeless place to browse, especially now that much of the failed space has been occupied by offices.

The Barnacle Historic State Park

Heading south down Main Highway from CocoWalk, a short, tree-shaded track on the left leads to the tranquil bayside **Barnacle Historic State Park**. The

Barnacle is the park's most striking feature, a house (Fri–Mon 9am–5pm; tours depart at 10am, 11.30am, 1pm, and 2.30pm from the porch; $1; ☏305/442-6866, ⓦwww.floridastateparks.org/TheBarnacle), built by "Commodore" Ralph Middleton Munroe in 1891, the sailor and brilliant yacht-designer. The pagoda-like structure was ingeniously put together with local materials and tricks learned from nautical design. Raising the structure eight feet off the ground in 1908 improved air circulation and prevented flooding, a covered veranda enabled windows to be opened during rainstorms, and a skylight allowed air to be drawn through the house – all major innovations that alleviated some of the discomforts of living all year in the heat and humidity of south Florida. More inventive still, when Munroe needed additional space for his family he simply jacked up the single-story structure and added a new floor underneath. Only with the **guided tour** can you see inside the house, where many original furnishings remain alongside some of Munroe's intriguing photos of pioneering Coconut Growers. You are free to explore the park, however, on your own. The lawn extends to the shore of Biscayne Bay, while behind the house are the last remnants of the tropical hardwood hammock that extended throughout the Miami area.

The Kampong

One of the city's best undiscovered sights is the 11-acre **Kampong Garden** (Mon–Fri 9am–2pm, reservations required; $10; ☏305/442-7169, ⓦntbg.org/gardens/kampong.php) at 4013 Douglas Rd. It's a mile or so southwest of downtown Coconut Grove and can be a little hard to find – look for the semicircular entrance and tiny street number sign along a stretch of residential mansions – but the Kampong holds an exuberant collection of more than 5000 tropical flowers, fruit trees and plants. They were collected by a local heiress, who picked up interesting specimens on her travels and then sent them back to be planted at her Florida home. The result is an eclectic, far-reaching display with an emphasis on Asia: look for the wide-leafed philodendra, whose enormous, waxy fronds are used as impromptu umbrellas.

South Miami Avenue

In 1914, farm-machinery mogul James Deering followed his brother, Charles (of Charles Deering Estate fame; see "South Miami," p.98), to south Florida and blew $15 million re-creating a sixteenth-century Italian villa within the belt of vegetation between Miami and Coconut Grove, now preserved as part of the **Vizcaya Museum and Gardens**, 3251 S Miami Ave (daily 9.30am–4.30pm; $12; ☏305/250-9133, ⓦwww.vizcayamuseum.com). Taken individually, the rooms here are dazzling, but en masse they can get overwhelming – you can wander on your own, but the tours (every 15–30min; free) provide a more structured introduction. The lasting impression of the grandiose structure is that both Deering and his designer (the crazed Paul Chalfin, who was hell-bent on becoming an architectural legend) were driven more by the need to acquire than any sense of taste. Deering's madly eclectic art collection and his belief that the villa should appear to have been inhabited for 400 years, resulted in a thunderous clash of Baroque, Renaissance, Rococo, and Neoclassical fixtures and furnishings, and even the landscaped **gardens**, with their fountains and sculptures, weren't spared his grand pretensions. Even so, Villa Vizcaya is one of Miami's unmissable sights, showcasing yet again Miami's obsession with the watery old world grandeur of Venice, especially in its waterfront plaza and stone barge. The house is a short walk from the Vizcaya Metrorail station (or bus #12 and #48), but most people drive – it's too far to walk comfortably from downtown Coconut Grove.

Miami Science Museum

Straight across S Miami Avenue from Villa Vizcaya is the family-friendly **Miami Science Museum**, at no. 3280 (daily 10am–6pm; $20; ☎305/646-4200, ⓦwww.miamisci.org). Its interactive exhibits provide a good two-hour diversion, though a stronger reason to visit is the collection of **wildlife** at the museum's rear. Vultures and owls are among a number of injured birds seeing out their days here, a variety of snakes can be viewed at disturbingly close quarters, and the resident tarantula is happy to be handled. The adjoining **planetarium** has the usual trips-around-the-cosmos shows; details are available by phone, website or from the ticket office inside the museum. The museum is scheduled to relocate downtown in 2012, as part of the Museum Park project (see p.79).

Ermita de la Caridad

Five minutes' walk south of the museum along S Miami Avenue, look for signs down a winding side road (at the "3601 Block") to the **Ermita de la Caridad**, 3609 S Miami Ave (daily 8am–9pm; ☎305/854-2404), perched on the water-front in the shadows of the massive Mercy Hospital. Looking like a large, angular meringue half-dipped in chocolate, the modernist church was built on 10¢ donations from Miami Cubans and dedicated to Our Lady of Charity, an incarnation of the Virgin Mary dating back to seventeenth-century Cuba; the statue inside is a replica of the revered original from the shrine in El Cobre, Cuba, smuggled into the US in 1961. The church is the religious heart of expat Cuban life and its architecture and design are highly symbolic: the six columns represent the six traditional provinces of Cuba, while beneath the altar there's Cuban soil, sand, and rock salvaged from a refugee boat. There's also a large sepia mural behind the altar tracing the island's history.

Key Biscayne and Virginia Key

A compact, immaculately manicured community just five miles off the Miami shore, **Key Biscayne** is a different world to downtown Miami and South Beach. Seeking relaxation and creature comforts away from life in the fast lane, the moneyed of Miami fill the island's upmarket homes and condos: even Richard Nixon had his presidential winter house here. This elite enclave got its start in the decades after World War I, when the Matheson family – who made millions supplying mustard gas to the government – moved in to manage a huge coconut plantation, but it wasn't until the opening of Rickenbacker Causeway in 1947 that large-scale development began. In the 1960s the island came to be known as a place where the rich could live undisturbed. More recently, many wealthy Europeans and Latin Americans have bought second homes here, and it's estimated two-thirds of Key Biscayne's population is Hispanic. For visitors Key Biscayne and the smaller island to the north, **Virginia Key**, offer a couple of inviting beaches, a third inside a state park, a chance to see some wildlife without leaving the city, and a fabulous cycling path running the full length of the island. **Rent bikes** from Mangrove Cycles in Key Biscayne village (see p.117) or at the parking lot in Baggs Cape Florida State Recreation Area (daily 10am–sunset; $8 per 1hr, $15 per day).

Virginia Key

Without a private yacht, the only way onto Key Biscayne is via **Rickenbacker Causeway**, a four-mile-long continuation of SW 26th Road just south of downtown Miami; it soars above Biscayne Bay, allowing shipping to glide underneath, and provides a scintillating view of the Brickell Avenue skyline. Drivers have to pay a $1.50 toll (no charge coming back); otherwise you can cross the causeway by bus (#B), bike, or even on foot.

The first land you'll hit is the unexceptional and sparsely populated **VIRGINIA KEY**. Its main point of interest is **Virginia Key Beach Park** (daily 8am–sunset; cars $3; ☏305/960-4600, ⓦwww.virginiakeybeachpark.net), reached by a two-mile lane that winds through a cluster of woodland. During the years of segregation, this was set aside for Miami's black community (chosen, cynics might say, for its proximity to a large sewage works), but in 2008 it reopened after a major renovation, with a toy train for kids, new facilities, and nature trails; a museum of black history is also in the works.

In contrast, on the right side of the main road, the **Miami Seaquarium** marine park (daily 9.30am–6pm; box office closes 4.30pm; adults $35.95, kids ages 3 to 9 $26.95; parking $8 per car; ☏305/361-5705, ⓦwww.miamiseaquarium.com) is a bustling place where you can while away three or four hours watching the usual roster of performing seals and dolphins. Be sure not to miss Lolita, the 8000-pound star of the spectacular **killer whale** show; show times vary, but are most frequent between 9.30am and noon. You can also swim with **dolphins** as part of the Dolphin Encounter program, but you need to call in advance (☏305/365-2501). The park's most important work – undertaking breeding programs to preserve Florida's endangered sea life and serving as a halfway house for injured manatees and other sea creatures – goes on behind the scenes.

Key Biscayne

Not content with living in one of the best natural settings in Miami, the people of **KEY BISCAYNE** also possess one of the finest landscaped beaches in the city – **Crandon Park Beach** (8am–sunset; lifeguards on duty Nov–March 9.15am–4.45pm; April–Oct 9.15am–6.45pm; parking $5 per car; ☏305/361-5421), a mile along Crandon Boulevard (the main road that continues beyond the causeway from Virginia Key). Three miles of golden beach fringe the park, and you can wade out in knee-deep water to a sandbar far from the shore. Filled by the sounds of boisterous kids and sizzling barbecues on weekends, the park at any other time is disturbed only by the occasional jogger or holiday-maker straying from the expensive hotels nearby. Other than the beach, the main attraction here is the **Biscayne Nature Center** (daily 10–4pm; free; ☏305/361-6767, ⓦwww.biscaynenaturecenter.org) at the park's northern end, which is especially fun for kids. Exhibit rooms, videos and mini-aquariums provide an insight into the marine and wildlife found on the island, and the center also organizes special programs featuring kayaking, snorkeling and guided hikes – check the website for details.

Besides its very green, manicured looks and some excellent places to eat, the **residential section** of Key Biscayne (known simply to locals as the "village"), beginning with an abrupt wall of apartment buildings at the southern edge of Crandon Park Beach, has little to offer visitors. You'll need to pass through, however, on the way to the much more rewarding Bill Baggs Cape Florida State Recreation Area (see opposite), and while doing so should pick up information

Key Biscayne wildlife

The most notorious inhabitants of Key Biscayne are its fast-multiplying **iguanas** - descendants of pets released into the wild – from bright green sprinters to lumbering eight-foot pink and brown giants. Most environmentalists want to control the population, though locals remain divided; some find them cute (the golf club promotes them as a unique obstacle), while others find the swimming pool-spoiling creatures unbearable. You should see plenty basking on the sides of roads or on the bike paths; look for them in the trees near *Boater's Grill* (see p.106). In cooler weather, you might see them literally falling from the trees (they actually seize up). Another exotic yet common island native is the curve-beaked **ibis** – the birds tend to congregate at the junction of East Enid St and Crandon Blvd, but you'll see them all over the place. The beaches are also rich in marine life; **spotted eagle rays** and **dolphins** are particularly common offshore. In the summer months **leatherback turtles** lay eggs on the Atlantic beaches, and nests are marked off with yellow tape – ask at the Biscayne Nature Center for special tours and volunteer programs.

on the area at the **Chamber of Commerce** inside the Village Hall at 88 West McIntyre St (Mon–Fri 9am–5pm; ℡305/361-5207, ⓦwww.keybiscayne chamber.org). They have an excellent information room stocked with leaflets and maps open 24hr.

Crandon Boulevard terminates at the entrance to the 400-acre **Bill Baggs Cape Florida State Recreation Area** (daily 8am–sunset; cars $5, pedestrians and cyclists $1; ℡305/361-5811, ⓦwww.floridastateparks.org /capeflorida), which covers the southern extremity of Key Biscayne. An excellent swimming **beach** lines the Atlantic-facing side of the park, and a boardwalk cuts around the wind-bitten sand dunes toward the **Cape Florida Lighthouse** (Thurs–Tues 9am–5pm; free) built in 1825 and one of the oldest structures in south Florida. The lighthouse was severely damaged in 1836 (during the Second Seminole War), but rebuilt and extended in 1855. Climb the 95-foot-high structure (109 steps) for mesmerizing views of the whole island, downtown Miami, and the last few remaining huts of Stilts-ville (see below). For more detailed information, take a ranger-led tour (Thurs–Tues 10am & 1pm; free) and check out the exhibits and video in the **lighthouse keeper's cottage**, a 1967 replica of the nineteenth-century original. The lighthouse remained in use until 1878, and now serves as a navigation beacon. Grab a drink or light lunch at the *Lighthouse Café* nearby (℡305/361-8487), overlooking the beach.

Stiltsville

Looking out from Bill Baggs park across the bay, you'll spy the grouping of fragile-looking houses known as **Stiltsville**. Held above water by stilts, these wooden dwellings were built and occupied by fishermen in the 1930s, becoming a haven for illegal alcohol joints and gambling in the 1950s. Stilts-ville's demise was compounded by the destruction wrought by Hurricane Andrew in 1992; only seven of the houses are still standing. Thanks to aggressive local attempts to secure funding for preservation – charted online at the S.O.S. (Save Our Stiltsville) site ⓦwww.stiltsville.org – the buildings are now overseen and being restored by **Biscayne National Park** (see p.101). Until restoration is complete they remain sadly off-limits; whether the rickety structures can survive many more of Florida's increasingly fierce hurricane seasons remains to be seen.

South Miami

South of Coral Gables and Coconut Grove, monotonous middle-class suburbs consume almost all of **SOUTH MIAMI**, an expanse of cozy family homes reaching to the edge of the Everglades, interrupted only by golf courses, minimalls and a few contrived tourist attractions along US-1. You can't avoid this route entirely, but from South Coral Gables a better course is **Old Cutler Road**, which makes a pleasing meander from Coconut Grove through a thick belt of woodland between Biscayne Bay and the suburban sprawl.

Fairchild Tropical Garden

Dividing Coconut Grove and South Miami, the **Fairchild Tropical Garden**, 10901 Old Cutler Rd (daily 9.30am–4.30pm; $20; ☎305/667-1651, ⓦwww .fairchildgarden.org), turns otherwise rugged terrain into lawns, flowerbeds, and gardens decorated by artificial lakes. A good way to begin exploring the 83-acre site – the largest tropical botanical garden in the continental United States – is to hitch a ride on the free tram (departing hourly, on the hour from 10am, from inside the garden's entrance) for a forty-minute trip along the trails, with a live commentary on the various plants.

As a research institution, Fairchild works with scientists all over the world to preserve ecological diversity; many of the plant species here, such as Cape Sable Whiteweed and Alvaradoa, are extinct in their original environments, and efforts have been made to re-establish them in their places of origin. Don't miss the "Windows to the Tropics," a hothouse filled with the most delicate, exotic plants, as well as the *amorphophallus titanum*, nicknamed "Mr Stinky," whose rare blooms are renowned for their rotting-flesh smell. Given the garden's steep admission fee though, the less well-known, cheaper and equally enchanting Kampong (see p.94) might be a better choice for green-fingered tourists.

You can bring food into the gardens but it can only be consumed in a special picnic area; you'll need to stock up before entry as there are no grocery shops within or nearby. Otherwise, you'll find only a small **café** (winter 9.30am–4.30pm, summer 10am–3pm) serving overpriced sandwiches and snacks.

The Charles Deering Estate

Long before modern highways scythed through the city, Old Cutler Road was the sole road between Coconut Grove and Cutler, a small town that went into terminal decline in the 1910s after being bypassed by the new Flagler railroad. A wealthy industrialist and amateur botanist, Charles Deering (brother of James, the owner of Villa Vizcaya; see p.94), was so taken with the natural beauty of the area that he purchased all of Cutler and, with one exception, razed its buildings to make way for the **Charles Deering Estate**, 16701 SW 72nd Ave (10am–5pm, last ticket sold at 4pm; $10; ☎305/235-1668, ⓦwww.deeringestate.com), completed in 1922. The one building that Deering preserved was Richmond

---

Visitor information

While in this vicinity, you should take advantage of the excellent **Tropical Everglades Visitor Information Center** (Mon–Sat 8am–5pm, Sun 10am–2pm; ☎305/245-9180 or 1-800/388-9669, ⓦwww.tropicaleverglades.com), located at 160 US-1, close to the junction with Hwy-9336 (344th Street); it offers a wealth of information on attractions around South Miami, but is particularly strong on the Everglades.

▲ Deering Estate grounds

Cottage, Cutler's only hotel, which he turned into his own living and dining quarters. Its pleasant wooden form now stands in marked contrast to the limestone mansion he erected alongside, whose interior – echoing halls, dusty chandeliers, and checker-board-tile floors – is Mediterranean in style but carries a Gothic spookiness. Though Deering's daughters sold off much of the opulent furnishings after his death, the estate has gradually been clawing back some of his key works of art (many donated by the family), including 340 historic books and several vigorous paintings by Ramon Casas Carbo. Make time to amble around the tranquil, 420-acre grounds; signs of human habitation dating back 10,000 years have been found amid the pine woods, mangrove forests, and tropical hardwood hammocks. The ticket price includes a free one-hour historical tour of the interior (daily 10.30am & 3pm) and various tours of the grounds, led by extremely knowledgeable rangers – make sure not to miss out.

Metrozoo

An extensive display of wildlife is on view at the **Metrozoo**, 12400 SW 152nd St (daily 9.30am–5.30pm, last admission 4pm; adults $15.95, children $11.95; ☏305/251-0401, ⓦwww.miamimetrozoo.com). This vast compound organizes animals by continent, and mixes in unusual creatures like anoa (which resemble small buffalo) alongside the giraffes and lions. The zoo uses moats and other natural barriers rather than cages, and the educational plaques flagging each species are highly informative. Come early in the day, as the baking noonday sun makes most of the animals sluggish.

Fruit and Spice Park and Monkey Jungle

The subtle fragrances wafting out of the **Fruit and Spice Park**, 24801 SW 187th Ave (daily 9am–5pm, tours daily at 11am, 1.30pm, & 3pm; $6; ☏305/247-5727, ⓦwww.fruitandspicepark.org), tickle your nostrils as soon as you enter. Star fruit and the aptly named Panama candle tree are the highlights of a host of tropical curiosities, grouped together by species or by theme (look for the bizarre banana plantation where dozens of misshapen varieties are grown together). Labeling at the park is spotty at best, however, so unless you're an avid gardener or prepared to traipse around with a tour, you're unlikely to be able to identify or learn about much here (again, the Kampong is a more appealing and accessible alternative – see p.94).

Continuing south toward Homestead, at 14805 SW 216th St, **Monkey Jungle** (daily 9.30am–5pm; last admission 4pm; adults $25.95, children 3–9 $19.95; ⓣ305/235-1611, ⓦwww.monkeyjungle.com) is one of the few preserves in the US for endangered primates. Covered walkways keep visitors in closer confinement than the monkeys and lead through a steamy hammock where baboons, orangutans, gorillas, and 35 species of monkeys move through the vegetation. Despite initial impressions, plenty of the monkeys are in cages and signage is infrequent, making it far from the eco-utopia its owners claim. However, it's a fun place to visit – make sure to bring plenty of quarters to buy nuts to feed the monkeys, who've devised ingenious ways of accessing food dishes.

Homestead and around

Suburbia yields to agriculture as you leave South Miami along US-1, where broad, fertile fields grow fruit and vegetables for the nation's northern states. Aside from offering as good a taste of Florida farm life – the region produces the bulk of America's winter tomatoes – as you're likely to find so close to its major city, the district can be a money-saving stop (see "Accommodation," p.65) on route to the Florida Keys or the Everglades National Park.

HOMESTEAD is the agricultural area's main town and the least galvanizing section of Miami. Krome Avenue, just west of US-1, slices through the center, but besides admiring a few restored 1910s–1930s buildings, time is better spent around Homestead than actually in it.

The Coral Castle

The one essential stop in these parts is the **Coral Castle**, 28655 S Dixie Hwy (Sun–Thurs 8am–6pm, Fri & Sat 8am–9pm; adults $9.75, children 7–12 $5; ⓣ305/248-6345, ⓦwww.coralcastle.com), whose bulky coral-rock sculptures can be found about six miles northeast of Homestead, beside US-1, at the junction with 286th Street. Remarkably, these fantastic creations, whose delicate finish belies their imposing size, are the work of just one man – the enigmatic **Edward Leedskalnin**. Jilted in 1913 by his 16-year-old fiancée in Latvia, Leedskalnin spent seven years working his way across Europe, Canada, and the US before buying an acre of land just south of Homestead. Using a profound – and self-taught – knowledge of weights and balances, he raised enormous hunks of coral rock from the ground, then used a workbench made from car running boards and handmade tools fashioned from scrap to refine the blocks into chairs, tables, and beds. It is thought the castle was intended as a love nest to woo back his errant sweetheart. Leedskalnin died here in 1951.

You can wander around the slabs (listening to the 30min audio tour), sit on the hard but surprisingly comfortable chairs, swivel a nine-ton gate with your pinkie, and admire the numerous coral representations of the moon and planets that reflect Leedskalnin's interest in astronomy and astrology; also on display is his twenty-foot-high telescope. But you won't be able to explain how the sculptures were made. No one ever saw the secretive Leedskalnin at work, or knows how, alone, he could have loaded 1100 tons of rock onto the rail-mounted truck that brought the pieces here in 1936.

Biscayne National Park

If you're not going to the Florida Keys, make a point of visiting **Biscayne National Park**, at the end of Canal Drive (328th St), east of US-1 (underwater section open 24hr; visitor center daily 9am–5pm; ☎305/230-7275, Ⓦwww.nps.gov/bisc). The bulk of the park lies beneath the clear ocean waters, where stunning formations of living coral provide a habitat for shoals of brightly colored fish and numerous other creatures too delicate to survive on their own. For a full description of the wondrous world of the living coral reef, see John Pennekamp Coral Reef State Park, in "The Florida Keys," p.125.

The visitors' center at Convoy Point lies at the end of a featureless road, Canal Drive (or 328th St), 9 miles from the US-1 turn-off. If you want to see the whole park without breaking a sweat, opt for the daily glass-bottomed boat trip (2hr 30min–3hr; $45) from the Biscayne National Underwater Park concession (☎305/230-1100, Ⓦwww.biscayneunderwater.com) at Convoy Point, but for a fuller encounter you should embark on one of their one-hour snorkel tours ($40) or two-tank scuba diving trips ($99). The concession also rents out kayaks (90min $16) and canoes (90min $12). Maps and information about the park are available at the visitor center next door. For tours and dives, phone at least a day ahead to make reservations; the schedules are subject to change, so make sure to confirm departure times.

Another option is to visit the Park's **barrier islands**, seven miles out. The concessionaire runs three-hour tours to **Boca Chita Key** ($35), where you can climb the pretty little lighthouse built in the 1930s and nearby **Elliott Key**, a seven-mile, forested island with a decent beach; check the concession for the latest schedule and prices. You can **camp** on both islands ($15), though only Elliott Key has freshwater showers, drinking water and restrooms; the ferry will drop you off and pick you up at a pre-arranged time for $50 (usually Fri–Sun).

Eating

Miami's cosmopolitan character is best displayed in its **food**, a realm in which the city's cobbled-together history fuses the flavors and traditions of Haiti, Cuba, the US, and elsewhere. The 1990s saw the development of a hybrid style of cooking known as **New Floridian** (also **Floribbean**), which successfully combines nouvelle cuisine methods and presentation with Caribbean ingredients, such as tropical fruit and fish. In the last few years this has been complemented by a wider **fusion cuisine** movement, which blends these styles with just about anything; Chinese, Indian, Italian and South American. **Seafood**, every bit as plentiful and good as you would expect so close to fish-laden tropical waters, is a common feature on every menu. Much of what is out there is fairly affordable, at least by American big-city standards, so you'll rarely need an expense account to dine out on a giant mess of **stone-crab claws** – a regional specialty – or fresh **lobsters**.

Miami offers ethnic cuisines from every continent, though of course **Cuban** food is a staple. The price of a sizeable lunch or dinner in one of the innumerable small, family-run Cuban diners will normally be less than $10. **Haitian** cooking is also popular in Miami, and the restaurants in Little Haiti, just north of downtown, are the most authentic places in which to sample it. **Argentine**, **Jamaican**, and **Peruvian** restaurants bear witness to the city's strong Caribbean and Latin American elements, though aside from Cuban food, for sheer quality and value for money it's hard to better the many **Japanese** outlets, most north of downtown and a few in South Miami. Chinese and Thai places are abundant, too, as are **Italian**. By contrast, **Mexican** food is far less common than in most other parts of the US. All of the restaurants listed below are open for lunch and dinner unless otherwise noted, while most Cuban restaurants also have a limited breakfast service (including coffee and snacks). Always check your bill when you get it, especially around the South Beach tourist drags – and remember they'll often automatically add a fifteen percent gratuity you can cross off if you're not happy with the service.

South Beach

Balans Lincoln Road 1022 Lincoln Rd ☎ 305/534-9191. Serves stylish brunches to visitors and locals alike – don't expect warm service, but it's a great place to see and be seen on Lincoln Rd. Good weekday breakfast specials (budget around $12 a head), and do try the chunky, crunchy *Balans* potatoes ($3).

Barton G The Restaurant 1427 West Ave ☎ 305/672-8881, Ⓦ www.bartong.com. Quirky mid-priced food from flamboyant local caterer Barton G. Gimmicks like "disco" crab (chilled and served with a trio of dips) or lobster pop tarts (sandwiched between flaky pastry) may seem off-putting at first, but the food is top-notch, as is the friendly vibe. It's especially popular with an older singles crowd.

Big Pink 157 Collins Ave ☎ 305/532-4700, Ⓦ www.bigpinkrestaurant.com. Futuristic diner decked out in pink Lucite and aluminum that serves massive portions of all-American favorites – try the novel TV dinners presented on old-fashioned trays or the lush red-velvet cake. The long tables are good for getting to know your fellow diners.

David's Café 1058 Collins Ave ☎ 305/534-8736, Ⓦ www.davidscafe.com. Locals will tell you that this is *the* Cuban restaurant on the beach. Eat deep-fried delicacies and daily specials like chicken with rice and beans ($6) on the tables outside, or grab a *café Cubano* (95¢) at the take-out window. There's dining room-style seating at the second branch, 1654 Meridian Ave, just off Lincoln Rd: browse the unfussy, bilingual menu for staples like Cuban sandwiches ($7.95) and pork chops ($12.45). Both locations open 24hr.

Eleventh Street Diner 1065 Washington Ave ☎ 305/534-6373. All-American diner chow – biscuits and gravy, fried chicken and mac & cheese – served in a converted silver railroad car, shipped in from Pennsylvania. Service can be spotty, though, and it can be swamped with tourists. Open 24hr.

Front Porch Café 1418 Ocean Drive ☎ 305/531-8300, Ⓦ www.frontporchcafe .com. This local hangout is refreshingly low-key given its touristy location: the delicious, dinner-plate-sized pancakes will double as both breakfast and lunch, as will the chunky sandwiches. Entrées hover around $10 for lunch (daily happy hour 4–7pm).

Joe's Stone Crabs 11 Washington Ave ☎ 305/673-0365, Ⓦ www.joesstonecrab.com. Open from Oct–May when Florida stone crabs are in season (and June & July Wed–Sun dinner only); expect long lines of tourists waiting (usually a couple of hours) to pay $20 or more for a succulent plateful.

La Sandwicherie 229 W 14th St ☎ 305/532-8934, Ⓦ www.lasandwicherie.com. Open until 5am, this outdoor café serves sandwiches stuffed with gourmet ingredients – prosciutto, cornichons, imported cheeses, and the like – that make others look miniature in comparison – from $5.30 to $8.95.

Le Provence 1629 Collins Ave ☎ 305/538-2406, Ⓦ www.laprovencemiami.com. This French bakery close to the beach is a terrific place to stock up on baguettes and brioches before a day on the sands. The croissants are outstanding. Daily 7am–8pm.

Miss Yip Chinese Café 1661 Meridian Ave ☎ 305/534-5488, Ⓦ www.missyipchinesecafe.com. Trendy Chinese spot with a vibe like a swanky café in Shanghai's decadent 1930s heyday and an old world, mostly Cantonese menu: dim sum at lunchtime (around $4–5), sweet and sour pork at night ($14.95).

News Café 800 Ocean Drive ☎ 305/538-NEWS, Ⓦ www.newscafe.com. Sidewalk café/brasserie with an extensive mid-price breakfast, lunch, and dinner menu, and front-row seating for the South Beach promenade. Not the scene it once was, but still a local favorite. Open 24hr.

Ola *Sanctuary Hotel*, 1745 James Ave ☎ 305/695-9125, Ⓦ www.olamiami.com. Helmed by superstar chef Douglas Rodriguez, this hot spot recently decamped to this prime South Beach hotel. Highlights of the pricey pan-Latin menu include a vast range of ceviches (try the oyster or Ecuadorian shrimp) as well as some knockout mojitos. Open from 6pm daily.

Pizza Rustica 863 Washington Ave ☎ 305/674-8244, also 667 Lincoln Rd ☎ 305/672-2334, www.pizza-rustica.com. Mouthwatering gourmet pizza, with slab-like slices costing around $5. Try the signature "rustica" which comes with lashings of artichoke, prosciutto, sun-dried tomato, and olives. You'll also find a branch on 667 Lincoln Rd (☎305/672-2334).

Prime 112 112 Ocean Drive ☎305/532-8112, www.prime112.com. Housed in a converted 1915 hotel, this trendy spot features a dining room plastered with vintage press cuttings and waiters decked out in butcher aprons. The steak-heavy menu is pricey but tasty – and the $20 Kobe beef hot dog is more than splurge-worthy. Lunch Mon–Fri, dinner daily.

Puerto Sagua 700 Collins Ave ☎305/673-1115. Where local Cubans meet gringos over espresso coffee, beans, and rice. Cheap, filling breakfasts, lunches, and dinners – the *ropa vieja* (shredded beef) is $10.25 and sandwiches range $6–7.

Segafredo 1040 Lincoln Rd ☎305/673-0047, www.segafredocafe.com. Pleasant Italian café with ample outdoor seating at Lincoln Rd's western end: curl up on one of the comfy crushed velvet sofas and try specialty salads (from $8.50), panini (from $7.95), and cakes – try the *crostata di bosco* (wild berry tart) for $6.50.

Shoji Sushi 100 Collins Ave ☎305/532-4245, www.shojisushi.com. Best place for sushi in South Beach, with delectable fresh sashimi ($1–8) and sushi rolls ($6–12.50) prepared by skillful Japanese master chef Shingo "Shin" Inoue. Sit outside in the garden or drink like a salaryman at the sake bar, which seats just five. Lunch Mon–Fri only, dinner daily.

Smith & Wollensky 1 Washington Ave (at South Pointe Park) ☎305/673-2800, www.smithandwollensky.com. This steakhouse chain deserves a mention for its superb location; sit overlooking the mouth of the Miami River and watch cruise ships plough into the harbor. The signature steaks start at around $39, but you can order cheaper grills and burgers for lunch.

Tantra 1445 Pennsylvania Ave ☎305/672-4765, www.tantrarestaurant.com. The sensual French/Mediterranean flavors offered up here are no mistake – the restaurant's theme, enhanced by muted lighting, is based on Tantric philosophies and aphrodisiac ingredients (the Tantra plate includes lust-powering oysters, calamari, and eel). Fun, if a little hokey, the restaurant even has belly dancers during dinner. Budget at least $80–90 a head, especially if you want to try one of the restaurant's tasty but sweet martinis.

Tap Tap Haitian Restaurant 819 5th St ☎305/672-2898, www.taptaprestaurant .com. The tastiest and most attractively presented Haitian food in Miami – the goat in a peppery tomato broth is a knockout – at very reasonable prices, most under $10. Wander around the restaurant to admire the Haitian murals. Dinner only.

Taverna Opa 36–40 Ocean Drive ☎305/673-6730, www.tavernaoparestaurant.com. This massive Greek restaurant – with its frantic table-dancing, loud music, and Mediterranean-themed decor – might at first seem like a tourist trap, but it's an absolute gem. Skip the forced bonhomie inside and grab a table on the patio out back; the food is delicious, authentic, and well priced – the tapas-style *meze* dishes run $5–10.

Yuca 501 Lincoln Rd ☎305/532-9822, www.yuca.com. Serving some of Miami's best Nuevo Cubano cuisine, this gourmet restaurant is a high-priced, high-style experience, even if it's no longer the white-hot place it once was; try the guava BBQ back ribs ($17.95) or tuna Chino-Latino, marinated in soy and then yucca-crusted and seared (most entrées around $25).

Central Miami Beach and north

Buenos Aires Bakery 7134 Collins Ave ☎305/861-7887. Gourmet bakery in the Argentinean expat hub that serves glistening handmade tarts, breads and empanadas, as well as coffee and a small selection of ice creams by the cone.

Chef Allen's 19088 NE 29th Ave, Aventura ☎305/935-2900, www.chefallens.com. It may be a long drive north, but this outstanding "New Floridian" restaurant is worth the trek for cuisine like yellowtail smothered in a coconut-milk-and-curry sauce, and Caribbean antipasto. The ever-changing menu is created by Allen Susser, widely rated as one of America's greatest chefs. Most mains cost $30–40, but the special tasting menus are usually better value; summer rates can be as low as $36 per person for an entrée and appetizer.

The Forge 432 41st St ☎305/538-8533, www.theforge.com. Dining at this Miami Beach institution is an unmissable experience, not for the staggeringly huge wine cellar, the hearty and traditional steaks and chops ($25–50 per entrée), or the kitschy 1930s gilt decor, but rather for the vibrant scene, where you'll find hip locals eating alongside 60-something old school Miami Beachers.

Roasters' n Toasters 525 41st St (Arthur Godfrey Rd) ☎305/531-7691, www.roastersntoasters.com. This chain does a reasonable job of re-creating a NY-style deli, right in the middle of the main Jewish drag at the beach. Stock up on smoked fish platters, salads, grills, bagels, and gut-busting corned beef or turkey sandwiches for $10.25. Daily 6.30am–3.30pm.

Timo 17624 Collins Ave, Sunny Isles Beach ☎ 305/936-1008, ⊛ www.timorestaurant.com. It might not seem like much from the outside, but this is one of most enticing restaurants at the northern end of Miami Beach, with friendly service and a tasty menu of Italian classics; pizza and pasta ($14–21), excellent seafood ($20–30) and a superb tasting menu ($58 per person). Lunch Mon–Fri, dinner daily.

Downtown

Big Fish 55 SW Miami Ave ☎ 305/373-1770, ⊛ www.thebigfishmiami.com. Lively spot on the Miami River, with folding chairs, benches, and picnic tables. Menu includes home-cooked fish dishes and vegetarian options – try the delicious signature crab cakes ($9.50). The main fish dishes go for around $20, but the grilled meats are pricey ($27–32).

Cacique Lunch Restaurant 112 W Flagler St ☎ 305/372-3323. No frills Cuban diner, convenient for lunch or snacks near the historical museum. Take-out the cheap empanadas, or sit down for the bargain breakfast plates (from $2), hearty sandwiches ($3.75–5.25) and Cuban classics, all under $10. Closes 3pm.

Garcia's Seafood Grille 398 NW N River Drive ☎ 305/375-0765. Charming waterfront café where Spanish is the *lingua franca*, with ramshackle wooden benches and superb, fresh fish dishes for around $15; there's also an onsite fish market. Tends to fill up fast for lunch; open daily 11am–9.30pm.

La Loggia 68 W Flagler St ☎ 305/373-4800, ⊛ www.laloggiaristorante.com. Somewhat upmarket Italian wine bar–restaurant serving simple pasta dishes for $15–18 or pizzas for $13 or so. One of the few restaurants that's open for dinner in central downtown.

🏃 Peoples Bar-B-Que 360 NW 8th St ☎ 305/373-8080. This friendly BBQ joint has been serving Overtown since 1962, its roster of Southern-style dishes including sumptuous barbecue chicken, cubed steak with collard and turnip greens, fresh cornbread and ribs, all under $10.

Raja's 33 NE 2nd Ave ☎ 305/539-9551. This no-nonsense restaurant serves South Indian staples like *masala dosa* (potato pancake) accompanied by tangy *sambhar* (hot and sour soup). Combo plates (rice, a main and a side) are $6.95, and the portions are generous. Closes 6pm weekdays, 4.30pm Sat & Sun.

Rosinella 1040 S Miami Ave ☎ 305/372-5756, ⊛ www.rosinella.net. Outstanding family-run restaurant where you can tuck into classic Italian comfort food at reasonable prices. All the bread and pasta is made onsite but Mama Rosinella is best known for her soft, floury gnocchi ($11.95).

The Biscayne Corridor

Chez Le Bebe 114 NE 54th St, Little Haiti ☎ 305/751-7639. Cheap and authentic Haitian food, with a short, basic menu of classics; try the tender *griot* (fried pork) and aromatic stewed goat. Every main meat dish comes with rice, beans, plantains, and salad. Portions are massive but you'll rarely pay more than $10.

🏃 Dogma 7030 Biscayne Blvd ☎ 305/759-3433, ⊛ www.dogmagrill.com. Hipsters make pilgrimages to this stylish hot dog stand on a sketchy part of Biscayne Blvd. Sit at red and white tables and munch on crinkle-cut fries and cheap, filling dogs – try the traditional LA chili dog ($3.95) or more exotic inventions like the Athens, topped with feta, oregano, and cucumbers ($4.15).

Domo Japones 4000 NE 2nd Ave, Design District ☎ 305/573-5474, ⊛ www.domojapones.com. Ultra fashionable cocktail lounge, doubling as Japanese restaurant specializing in sushi, sashimi and Chef Timon Balloo's "Japanese bistro fare"; try the zesty tofu or luscious pork ramen ($15–20). Dinner only, closed Sun.

Fratelli Lyon 4141 NE 2nd Ave, Design District ☎ 305/572-2901, ⊛ www.fratellilyon.com. One of the most authentic Italian restaurants in Miami, with wonderfully fresh pasta, sausage and seafood, and an exceptional selection of antipasti. The super-hip interior features items from the adjacent Driade Italian furnishings store.

🏃 Michael's Genuine Food 130 NE 40th St, Design District ☎ 305/573-5550, ⊛ www .michaelsgenuine.com. One of the hottest restaurants in the Design District, with seasonal, local ingredients whipped into eclectic creations by lauded chef Michael Schwartz; expect pizza and steaks along with wood-roasted onion stuffed with lamb and crispy beef cheek, in sizes that range small to extra large (medium and large entrées $10–27).

Soyka 5582 NE 4th Court, Little Haiti ☎ 305/759-3117, ⊛ www.soykacafe.com. This upmarket restaurant, among the first of its kind to open in the area, serves tasty, Italian-inflected dishes (including fantastic crispy, wafer-thin pizzas) in a raw, spacious concrete hall. Lunch is much more reasonable ($11–16 per dish) than dinner.

Little Havana

Ayestarán 720 SW 27th Ave ☎ 305/649-4982. Long a favorite Cuban restaurant among those in the know, open for breakfast, lunch, and dinner, and especially good value for its $6–9 daily specials like roast pork. Otherwise, try the killer pressed Cuban sandwich.

Casa Panza 1620 SW 8th St ☏305/643-5343. Less formal and more Iberian than many of the other Spanish restaurants hereabouts, with authentic tapas, *raciones*, and main dishes prepared in a mainly *madrileño* (Madrid) style. On the downside, it's a little overpriced (minimum $20 charge per person), and the free flamenco on Tues, Thurs and Sat evenings can be hit-and-miss (call ahead to check times). Morphs into a yuppie-packed club until 4am most nights.

Exquisito 1510 SW 8 St ☏305/643-0227. Authentic Cuban diner run by émigrés since the 1970s, and the most convenient spot for lunch if you're touring the main Little Havana drag, Calle Ocho. Hearty roast meats and sandwiches range $6–10.

El Palacio de los Jugos 5721 W Flagler St ☏305/264-4557. A handful of tables at the back of a Cuban produce market, where the pork sandwiches and shellfish soup from the takeout stand are the tastiest for miles. Be sure to try one of the namesake *jugos* (juices) for $2–3; orange-carrot and *guanabana* are both outstanding.

El Rey de las Fritas 1821 SW 8th St ☏305/644-6054. Regulars come here for one thing, the tangy *frita*, or Cuban hamburger (less than $3), smothered with home-made shoestring fries, though the *batidos* (shakes) are also good.

Los Pinareños Fruteria 1334 SW 8th St ☏305/285-1135. Enormous *fruteria* sprawling along the southern side of Little Havana's main drag: for $2 you'll snag a flagon of juice squeezed to order. Even better, you'll rub elbows with the old timers from the neighborhood who hang out here during the day. Breakfast and lunch only.

Sergio's Cafeteria 3252 Coral Way ☏305/529-0047. Noisy and fun, *Sergio's* is a Cuban diner with plenty of attitude, welcoming late-night eaters with a wide menu at fair prices. A great place to finish up a long Friday night and chow down on one of the best Cuban sandwiches in town. Open 24hr.

Versailles 3555 SW 8th St ☏305/444-0240, ⓦwww.versaillescuban.com. Gorge on inexpensive, authentic Cuban food amid a kitschy decor of chandeliers and mirrored walls (hence the name) and a buzzing neighborhood atmosphere (expect to see politicians doing deals over plates of rice and beans) – the takeout coffee window is said to serve over a thousand *cafécitos* daily.

Yambo 1643 SW 1st St ☏305/642-6616. For less than $5 a plate you can gorge on Nicaraguan specialties like *puerca asada* (grilled pork), but the real draw is the atmosphere: a slice of Central America, with mosaic-encrusted tables, Spanish-language radio blaring from the kitchen, and passersby peddling CDs at your table.

Coral Gables

Burger Bobs 2001 Granada Blvd ☏305/567-3100. Tucked away in the clubhouse of the public Granada Golf Course, this homey café, with its green Formica chairs, white plastic tables, and yellow mustard bottles, is a grimy but tasty hideaway: try the cheeseburger, a steal at $4. Closure was narrowly averted in 2008 – call ahead to see if it remains open. Breakfast and lunch only.

Estate Wines 92 Miracle Mile ☏305/442-9915. The tastiest eat-in café in downtown Coral Gables with hot ($7–8) and cold (from $7) sandwiches on offer – try the gooey hot ham and cheese on a roll – as well as house-baked pastries like the German owner's recipe for a flaky, spicy apple strudel. Closed Sun.

House of India 22 Merrick Way ☏305/444-2348. Catch-all Indian diner famous for two things: excellently priced, tasty lunch buffets (Mon–Thurs $10.95, Fri $11.95, Sat & Sun $12.95), and exceptionally poor service – leave a less than generous tip if you dare. Last buffet serving 2.45pm.

Mykonos 1201 Coral Way ☏305/856-3140, ⓦwww.mykonosmiami.com. Greek food in an unassuming atmosphere, popular with students from the nearby university. *Spanakopita*, lemon chicken soup, *gyros*, *souvlaki*, and huge Greek salads are among the offerings, along with good vegetarian options.

Ortanique on the Mile 278 Miracle Mile ☏305/446-7710, ⓦwww.cindyhutsoncuisine.com. Expect innovative (though pricey) tropical fusion eats in a lush terrace garden setting, part of the Cindy Hutson group; look for the painted flamingo on the sidewalk which marks its entrance. Try the coconut-infused West Indian bouillabaisse (market price) or jerk pork chop ($32). Lunch Mon–Fri, dinner daily.

Sweet Art by Lucila 5734 Bird Rd ☏305/668-0060, ⓦwww.sweetartbylucila.com. This venerable cake shop is worth a visit for the finest vanilla rum cake in the state, a moist, tangy delight that's almost as good as the chocolate cake. Closed Sun.

Coconut Grove

A.C.'s Icees Kennedy Park parking lot, 2600 S Bayshore Drive. A.C. has been knocking out delicious frozen lemonade from his white van since 1978, becoming something of a Coconut Grove institution; the frosted drinks range $2.50–5, and he also serves hot dogs.

Bizcaya Grill *Ritz Carlton Coconut Grove*, 3300 SW 27th Ave ☎ 305/644-4670. Sure, it's inside a hotel on the mainland but this is a buzzy spot – and its excellent reputation is well deserved. You can put it all down to the fantastic food, best described as simple but flavor-packed – try the home-made frittata ($9) or rock shrimp risotto ($25). Dinner Tues–Sat, lunch daily.

Daily Bread Marketplace 2400 SW 27th St ☎ 305/856-0363, ⓦ www.dailybreadmarketplace .com. Middle Eastern grocery store where you can pick up salads, falafel and pita sandwiches filled with aromatic ingredients. Also delicious are the spinach pie and the sticky pistachio baklava.

Dolce Vita Gelato Café 3462 Main Hwy ☎ 305/461-1322. Part of a local *gelateria* chain that serves up glorious sorbets and ice creams topped with fresh fruit. Look out for branches downtown at 22 E Flagler St (☎ 305/577-2423) and Miami Beach, 1655 Collins Ave (☎ 305/5604-0104).

Greenstreet Café 3468 Main Hwy ☎ 305/444-0244, ⓦ www.greenstreetcafe.net. Quaint sidewalk café with an eclectic assortment of low- to mid-priced cuisine ranging from Middle Eastern to Italian, including lamb burgers with goats cheese ($12) or taboule salad ($8). The terrific, hearty egg breakfasts make this spot a real scene at weekends.

Las Culebrinas 2890 SW 27th Ave ☎ 305/448-4090. Family favorite, knocking out some of the best Cuban food in the city. Start with the superb *tostones rellenos*, before sampling one of the large main plates of sumptuous pork, yuca and beans. Service is always good here, and entrées average $15. Live music Thurs–Sat.

Nena's 3791 Bird Rd, no phone. The lunchtime hub of Miami's power Cuban scene: within a derelict-looking building are two lunch counters and a couple of tables, with whiteboards on the wall listing the day's offerings – try the juicy *croqueta preparada* (Cuban sandwich). Also great for breakfast. Closes 3pm; closed Sun.

Scotty's Landing 3381 Pan American Dr ☎ 305/854-2626, ⓦ www.sailmiami.com/scottys .htm. Tasty, inexpensive seafood and fish 'n' chips

served at marina-side picnic tables in a simple setting. You'll find it hard to spend more than $10 a head on food. Somewhat hard to find as it's tucked away on the water by City Hall – ask for directions.

Key Biscayne and Virginia Key

Boater's Grill 1200 S Crandon Blvd (Bill Bags Cape Florida State Park) ☎ 305/361-0080. This Cuban-style restaurant sits on stilts overlooking No Name Harbor (the park entry fee is waived for diners at night); the soothing bay views, Cuban dishes (divine home-made flan) and top-notch seafood (try the conch fritters or grilled fresh fish) make for a relaxing meal weekdays, though you may have a long wait at weekends (reservations for dinner only).

Cioppino in the *Ritz-Carlton Key Biscayne*, 455 Grand Bay Drive ☎ 305/365-4286, ⓦ www .ritzcarlton.com. Upmarket Italian eatery that makes almost every major restaurant critic's US Top 10, this hushed spot has an ever-changing menu of seasonal staples, though the namesake *cioppino* – a feisty, mussels-dominated stew – is usually on offer. Bank-breaking, but worth it.

Donut Gallery 83 Harbor Drive ☎ 305/361-9985. With its red vinyl stools and faded formica tables, this old-time diner (open at 5.30am for breakfast) is a great place to indulge a craving for sugar-dusted donuts. Closes 2pm.

Rusty Pelican 3201 Rickenbacker Causeway, Virginia Key ☎ 305/361-3818, ⓦ www.miami .therustypelican.com. The American, Italian, and seafood dishes are only OK, but you'll mainly want to come here to enjoy the absolutely breathtaking views of the bay as you dine.

Tango Grill 328 Crandon Blvd, Suite 112 ☎ 305/361-1133. A small Argentine grill in one of the Key Biscayne Village strip malls, *Tango Grill* serves superb *bife de chorizo* (sirloin steak) and other South American specialties to a heavily Latin crowd.

South Miami

Akashi 5830 S Dixie Hwy, South Miami ☎ 305/665-6261. Generous sushi boats make this

Best budget eats

Burger Bobs 2001 Granada Ave, Coral Gables ☎ 305/567-3100
David's Café 1058 Collins Ave, South Beach ☎ 305/534-8736
Dogma 7030 Biscayne Blvd, Biscayne Corridor ☎ 305/759-3433
El Palacio de los Jugos, Little Havana 5721 W Flagler Ave ☎ 305/264-1503
Garcia's Seafood Grille 398 NW N River Drive, downtown ☎ 305/375-0765

restaurant trip worthwhile. The cooked food isn't bad either – try the tender chicken *teriyaki* or the *ton katsu* (Japanese fried pork chop), but make reservations.

🏃 **Robert Is Here** 19200 SW 344th St, Homestead ☎ 305/246-1592, ⓦ www .robertishere.com. Legendary local fruit stand, serving creamy smoothies blended with whatever fruits are in season, though it's hard to beat the Key Lime milkshakes. Close to the eastern entrance to the Everglades National Park (see p.169). Closed Sept & Oct.

Rosita's Restaurante 199 W Palm Drive, Florida City ☎ 305/246-3114. Delicious Mexican dishes each accompanied by creamy refried beans and tongue-lashing salsa. The decor's nothing fancy, but the real atmosphere comes from the radio blaring Spanish-language news and music.

Sango Jamaican and Chinese Restaurant 9485 SW 160th St, South Miami ☎ 305/252-0279. Somewhat of an offbeat combination, and the Caribbean food is far better than the Chinese confections, but it's still a worthwhile stop, especially given its low prices. Try the curried goat and jerk chicken. Mainly a takeout joint, but there are a few tables if you want to linger. Closed Sun.

Shorty's Bar-B-Q 9200 S Dixie Hwy, South Miami ☎ 305/670-7732, ⓦ www.shortys.com. Sit at a picnic table, tuck a napkin in your shirt, and graze on barbecued ribs (a full rack including slaw and garlic bread is $17.49), chicken (wings with blue cheese dip are a steal at $7.29), and corn on the cob – pausing only to gaze at the cowboy memorabilia on the walls.

🏃 **Whip 'n Dip Ice Cream Shoppe** 1407 Sunset Drive ☎ 305/665-2565, ⓦ www .whipndipicecream.com. This is the best ice cream in the city, with a roster of constantly changing flavors and plenty of extra sweet treats: chocolate-covered bananas, ice cream cannoli, and frozen cakes. It's a short drive off US-5, in the southern section of Coral Gables.

Drinking

For a city renowned for its nightlife, Miami is not a hard **drinking** town. Its upmarket lounges and louche bars are places where you can linger all evening over a cocktail or two; most restaurants will also have a small bar area, as will the hipper hotels (in fact, the hotel bars here are often the trendiest pit stops). There are also a few old-time dive bars left where anyone determined to drink to oblivion can happily – and more cheaply – do so.

South Beach has the largest selection of drinking spots, though you'll find a few places worth a detour scattered around the city: the burgeoning **Biscayne Corridor** enclave on the mainland is increasingly lively in the evenings, and there's a locals-heavy scene in **Coconut Grove** and in **Brickell**.

Most places where you can drink don't really get going until about 10pm – before then, there's little atmosphere anywhere – and they keep serving until at least 2am. It's also worth remembering that most bars will be buzzing every night of the week, and it's often best to avoid the hippest places at weekends, when they'll be choked with suburbanites, sniffily nicknamed the Causeway Crowds by South Beach locals.

Bear in mind that the dividing lines between bars, restaurants, and clubs can be blurry, so check the "Nightlife" listings on pp.109–111 for additional suggestions.

South Beach

The Abbey Brewing Company 1115 16th St ☎ 305/538-8110. Small, unpretentious, pub-like microbrewery serving the best beers on SoBe, acclaimed for its creamy Oatmeal Stout. Open daily 1pm–5am.

Buck 15 707 Lincoln Lane ☎ 305/534-5488. Artsy lounge-bar-gallery above *Miss Yip's* (see p.102) with a thrift-store chic interior (look for the bar salvaged from a 1970s high-rise condo) and most of the graffiti-spattered street art comes from Jenny Yip's own collection. The rotating roster of guest DJs is always impressive and eclectic. Tues–Sat 10pm–5am.

Club Deuce Bar & Grill 222 14th St ☎ 305/531-6200. Raucous neighborhood dive bar open until 5am, with a CD jukebox, pool table, and a clientele that includes cops, transvestites, artists, and models. Its low prices are a major plus.

DiLido Beach Club *Ritz Carlton South Beach*, 1 Lincoln Rd ☏786/276-4000. Dreamy beachfront club, with a large blue-tiled bar and day beds scattered throughout the gardens. It's worth trying the refreshing house special, frozen mojitos, though just one costs over $20 when tax and gratuity are factored in.

🏃 **Plunge** *Gansevoort South Hotel*, 2377 Collins Ave ☏305/604-1000. Mesmerizing roof-top bar and pool which morphs into a fashionable lounge with palm trees and comfy sofas overlooking the ocean.

Privé 136 Collins Ave ☏305/674-8630, 305-531-5535. This hidden lounge, attached to the *Opium Garden* nightclub, is tucked away in a back alley. The door policy is one of the tightest around, especially on Friday nights, so make sure to sashay like a VIP if you want to sip with the A-list behind the silk curtains. Usually open Thurs–Sun 11pm-5am, but call ahead.

🏃 **Purdy Lounge** 1811 Purdy Ave ☏305/531-4622, 🌐www.purdylounge.com. A little-known beachside gem, this large neighborhood bar open until 5am sees a mixed crowd of Beautiful People and locals, all enjoying cheap drinks in a vaguely Arabian setting.

The Raleigh Bar *Raleigh Hotel*, 1775 Collins Ave ☏305/534-6300. Settle in for an evening of elegant drinking at this classic 1940s hotel bar with lushly restored wood paneling.

The Room 100 Collins Ave at 1st St ☏305/531-6061. Miami outpost of the minimalist New York bar, with raw concrete floors, industrial metal tables, and low lighting.

Rose Bar *Delano Hotel*, 1685 Collins Ave ☏305/672-2000. Spilling onto the hotel's white gauze-draped lobby, this appropriately pinkish spot features ornate chandeliers and a long, candlelit bar.

Sky Bar *Shore Club*, 1901 Collins Ave ☏786/276-6771. Sprawling outdoor bar arranged around the hotel pool, with giant overstuffed square seats. Check out the smaller *Sandbar* attached to it, with fine views of the beach and ocean, and the *Rumbar*, with 75 types of rum on offer.

🏃 **Spire Bar** *The Hotel*, 801 Collins Ave, South Beach ☏305/531-2222. Nestling in the shadow of the famous Tiffany neon-lit sign, this colorful rooftop bar has bright red cushions and candy-striped floorboards. Make sure to order the bartender's special, a Champagne mojito ($15). Open Thurs–Sat only, from 6pm.

Ted's Hideaway 124 Second St ☏305/532-9869. Laid-back local sports bar with an extended happy hour (noon–7pm); beers are $4.50. Daily noon–5am.

Wet Willie's 760 Ocean Drive ☏305/532-5650. There's something irresistibly uncool about this fratboy-packed bar: chug one of the frozen drinks, served from washing-machine-sized mixers, on its upstairs terrace. Open until 3am nightly.

Downtown and north

Churchill's Pub 5501 NE 2nd Ave, Little Haiti ☏305/757-1807. A British enclave, with big-screen live soccer matches and UK beers on tap. Look out for the enormous Union Jack emblazoned on the side of the building. See also "Live music," p.111.

Karu & Y 71 NW 14th St ☏305/403-7850, 🌐www.karu-y.com. Ultra-hip lounge bar, with outdoor seating, gardens and a soothing "reflection pool." It also has a smart restaurant, notable for its Dale Chihuly blue icicle chandelier more than the food, and a popular nightclub on site.

Magnum Lounge 709 NE 79th St, Biscayne Corridor ☏305/757-3368. This out-of-the-way restaurant-bar feels more like a bordello or a speakeasy, with its lush red banquettes and hidden entrance. The food's so-so, but the campy sing-alongs around the piano and stiff cocktails make it a fun detour for a drink or two. Closed Mon.

🏃 **Tobacco Road** 626 S Miami Ave, downtown ☏305/374-1198. Gloriously gritty dive bar, which snagged the city's first liquor license in 1912 and has been pouring drinks ever since; it's also a venue for lively R&B (see "Live music," p.111).

Coral Gables

John Martin's 253 Miracle Mile ☏305/445-3777. Irish pub and restaurant with occasional folk singers and harpists accompanying a good batch of imported brews. See "Live music," p.111.

Titanic Brewing Company 5813 Ponce de León Blvd ☏305/668-1742. Excellent microbrewery, serving draft stouts and ales brewed on the premises (pints $4); the boiler room nut brown ale is magnificent. Very popular with students and features live rock music at the weekends.

Coconut Grove

Monty's Raw Bar 2550 S Bayshore Drive ☏305/856-3992. Drinkers often outnumber diners at this tiki-style bar, drawn here by the gregarious mood and the views across the bay. The reggae music can be overpoweringly loud though, and it's become quite touristy – try to come at happy hour (Mon–Fri 4–8pm), when drinks are half-price. There's a branch at 300 Alton Rd, South Beach (☏305/672-1148).

Tavern in the Grove 3416 Main Hwy ☏305/447-3884. Down-to-earth student-heavy locals' haunt with a bouncy jukebox and easy-going mood. The real draw, however, is the rock-bottom drink prices.

Key Biscayne and Virginia Key

Jimbo's inside the park at Virginia Key Beach, Virginia Key ☎ 305/361-7026. Renowned ramshackle bar established by octogenarian Jimbo Luznar in the 1950s, where you can help yourself to a beer from a wheelbarrow filled with ice and chat with the old-timers. Also known for its smoked fish.

Joe's Tiki Bar 3301 Rickenbacker Causeway, Virginia Key ☎ 305/361-0788. This friendly pub has become the favorite drinking hole of local charter boat captains (especially on Sun), and the views of Miami's skyline are superb: you can also eat here.

Nightlife

Miami is a city with a flexible concept of what makes a club or a restaurant or a bar: you could end up dancing almost anywhere, since aside from a few megaplexes (listed below) almost every dancefloor is attached to a bar or restaurant. And while Miami's **nightlife** scene may have sobered up slightly since its debauched and celebrity-studded heyday of the early 1990s, there's still plenty of choice and – especially away from the beach – some intriguing options. Many of the major clubs (like *Space*) are located in **Park West**, a warehouse district just north of downtown, though there's little to do here other than dance. Earlier in the evening, you're better off sticking to South Beach and one of the better bars for dancing like **Mynt**. Otherwise, if you're feeling adventurous, skip the hard house and techno beats, and check out one of the city's **salsa** or **merengue** clubs, hosted by Spanish-speaking DJs.

Most places open at 10pm, but don't even think of turning up before midnight as they only hit a peak between then and 2am – although some continue until 7am or 8am. However, Miami Beach's liquor laws prohibit drinks from being served after 5am – past this you'll need to head to the mainland, where there's no such proscription on partying.

Expect a **cover charge** of around $20, and a **minimum age of 21** (it's normal for ID to be checked). In a city as VIP-conscious as Miami, it also pays to remember that the downright scruffy will be turned away at almost every door. Note also that clubs open and close with alarming regularity in Miami, so call ahead before you jump in a taxi.

Many of the clubs below present gay nights during the week; for gay-and-lesbian-specific clubs, see p.115. As ever, the best place for up-to-date listings is the freesheet *New Times* or the website ⓦ www.cooljunkie.com.

Miami Beach

B.E.D. 929 Washington Ave ☎ 305/532-9070, ⓦ www.bedmiami.com. This restaurant-cum-lounge is best known for its sexy club nights, from Pillowtalk Wednesdays to Sheets and Pillows Saturdays – most try to grab one of the beds that ring the dance floor rather than a table. Ladies usually free before 12.30am.

Café Nostalgia inside the *Versailles Hotel*, 3425 Collins Ave ☎ 305/531-6092, ⓦ www .cafenostalgia.com. This itinerant and legendary Cuban club has found yet another new home: these days it's a ritzy, sultry spot ensconced in Miami Beach. In the evening, the older crowd listens to live music from established bands, but come 1am it morphs into a Latin hip-hop spot for 20-something locals. Wed–Sun 8pm–5am.

Cameo 1445 Washington Ave, South Beach ☎ 305/532-2667, ⓦ www.cameomiami.com. The hardest partying club on the beach, with heavy-hitting house DJs most nights and a hip-hop room upstairs. Thurs–Mon 10pm–5am.

Mansion 1235 Washington Ave ☎ 305/532-1525, ⓦ www.mansionmiami .com. A nightclub complex, with six VIP areas, nine bars, and five different dancefloors, each usually showcasing a different style of music. Fiercest and most fun is We Rock Hip Hop on Fridays, anchored by DJ Ideal and one of the best hip-hop parties in the city. Tues–Sun 11pm–5am.

Mokaï 235 23rd St ☎ 305/531-4166, ⊛ www
.mokaimiami.com. This enormous, moody lounge
fills with a glossy, dressy crowd who don't mind
paying for bottle service. The incomprehensible
name's a nod to its inspiration, a vast canyon in
New Zealand used to film *Lord of the Rings*. If
you're peckish, there's a snack menu including
grilled cheese served until 5am.

Mynt Ultra Lounge 1921 Collins Ave ☎ 786/276-
6132, ⊛ www.myntlounge.com. Lounge/danceclub
washed in green light, with an vast bar, large, black
leather sofas and backlight perspex tables for
bottle service. It's becoming more mainstream after
several years as the hottest night spot in town, but
expect wall-to-wall models and a tough door policy
any night of the week. Wed–Sat 11pm–5am.

🏃 **Nikki Beach Club** 1 Ocean Drive
☎ 305/538-1111, ⊛ www.nikkibeach.com
/miami. Located right on the beach, this popular
club features loungers, beds and palm trees,
offering a real iconic South Beach experience. The
restaurant is open daily, but the dancing gets going
Fri, Sat and Sun with international and local DJs
spinning till dawn.

Rok Bar 1905 Collins Ave ☎ 305/674-4397,
⊛ www.rokbarmiami.com. This upmarket dive bar
co-owned by Tommy Lee re-opened as a hip club in
2007, with DJs spinning an eclectic mix of house,
rock and indie music, artily decorated walls and a
door policy that favors VIPs Fri & Sat. Open Tues–Sat.

Mainland

Metropolis 950 NE 2nd Ave, Park West
☎ 305/415-0088, ⊛ www.metropolisdowntown
.com. Sprawling across 35,000 square feet, a night
at this venue is a five-for-one deal, with distinct
clubs and music styles in each of its different
rooms, from the Egypt-themed *Allure* to Asian-
themed *Discotekka*. Even better, you can stay out
until dawn, thanks to the club's 24hr liquor license.
Thurs–Sat 10pm–11am.

🏃 **Nocturnal** 50 NE 11th St, Park West
☎ 305/576-6996, ⊛ www.nocturnalmiami
.com. This sprawling club is as much high tech as
hard house: the rooftop terrace has a 360 degree
IMAX-style screen where trippy images can be
projected all night, while staff are equipped with
wireless PDAs so they can not only summon a
bottle to your table in around 5min, but also send
for your car via valet without a wait.

Park West 30 NE 11th St, Park West, ☎ 305/350-
7444, ⊛ www.stereomiami.com. Cavernous
warehouse club best known for its Stereo Fridays
(ladies free before 12:30am), tripped out with the
video screens, an LED video wall, and an Asian-
inspired decor.

Space 34 NE 11th St, Park West, ☎ 305/375-0001,
⊛ www.clubspace.com. This downtown warehouse
pioneer has a rough decor and highly regarded
resident DJs, spinning a mix of house and hip-hop.
Most people migrate here when the other venues
shut down – the Rooftop Terrace hosts "Sunrise
Sessions" into the afternoon. Fri 10pm–10am, Sat
10pm through to Sun 4pm.

Vagabond 30 NE 14th St, Park West ☎ 305/358-
8007, ⊛ www.thevagabondmiami.com. This hip
venue (with $1 beers on Fri) seems to attract an
unpretentious, eclectic crowd, from sandals to
suits, and the outdoor patio is always packed. One
room usually features alternative, soul and rock,
with another playing dance and electronica. Cover
normally $5.

Live music

Live music can be a bit hit-and-miss in Miami, though it's not hard to find
rock, jazz, reggae and Latin bands playing somewhere in the city. If you're
hoping to catch some good **Cuban music**, forget it. None of the musicians
from Cuba can come here, and local talent is rather thin on the ground. In
contrast, Miami's **hip-hop** scene has experienced a small renaissance since 2006
with local stars such as Rick Ross and DJ Khaled. Though several radio stations
and websites (see ⊛ www.miamihiphop.net) cater to the genre, the best places
to see a live performance are night clubs (see *Sobe Live* opposite).

Other than for megastar performers (who charge at least $50 a ticket), to see
a band you've heard of, expect to pay $25 upwards; for a local act, admission
will be $5–10 or free. Check the *New Times* for weekly gig listings.

Latin

Café Mystique 7250 NW 11th St, Miami (near the airport) ☎305/262-9500, ⓦwww.cafemystique.net. Don't be put off by the out-of-the-way location – this is one of the premier salsa clubs in the city. Catch big-name performers at the weekends or take free lessons every Thursday from in-house teachers. Friendly, funky and fun. Thurs & Sun 9pm–4am, Fri 5pm–5am, Sat 9pm–5am. Cover $20 on Sat (usually free other nights).

Hoy Como Ayer 2212 SW 8th St, Little Havana ☎305/541-2631, ⓦwww.hoycomoayer.net. About the only place to hear decent Cuban music in Miami, this dark, smoky joint is plastered with black and white photos of Cuban crooners past. A superb place to discover funky, emerging Latin talent. Wed–Sat 9am–3am; cover varies, ranging $7–35.

Mango's 900 Ocean Drive, South Beach ☎305/673-4422, ⓦwww.mangoscafe.com. Shamelessly tacky and gloriously over-the-top, with mainstream, Latin-inflected music spilling out onto the sidewalk. Best on weekdays when the crowd's more local. Free–$20.

Rock, jazz, reggae and hip-hop

Churchill's Pub 5501 NE 2nd Ave, Little Haiti ☎305/757-1807, ⓦwww.churchillspub.com. Good place to hear local hopeful rock and indie bands. Cover usually ranges $8–15. See "Drinking," p.108.

Jazid 1432 Washington Ave, South Beach ☎305/673-9372, ⓦwww.jazid.net. An alternative to the relentless house music heard on South Beach's main clubbing drag, *Jazid* showcases a blend of Latin reggae, hip-hop and jazzy funk – live bands backed up by DJs most nights. Also hosts rock nights on Thursdays and a popular reggae night on Sunday from 9pm (free). Daily 9pm–3am. Cover $5 Thurs, $10 after 11pm Fri & Sat, free other nights.

John Martin's 253 Miracle Mile, Coral Gables ☎305/445-3777, ⓦwww.johnmartins.com. Spacious Irish bar (see "Drinking," p.108) and restaurant with Irish folk music several evenings a week. No cover.

Luna Star Café 775 NE 125th St, North Miami ☎305/892-8522, ⓦlunastarcafe.com. This largely vegetarian café hosts an eclectic range of live bands and folk concerts, usually from 8pm on, but phone before you go. Closed Sun & Mon. There is a $7 minimum per person charge (for drinks/food) on live nights, and sometimes a small cover ($5).

Sobe Live 1203 Washington Ave ☎305/725-3353, ⓦwww.sobelivesouthbeach.com. Established in 2002, *Sobe Live* is the only performance venue in Miami dedicated to hip-hop. Expect a mix of hip-hop, R&B, and reggae from both mainstream and underground artists, and DJs filling in between acts. Cover varies.

Tobacco Road 626 S Miami Ave, downtown Miami ☎305/374-1198, ⓦwww.tobacco-road.com. This rather grotty downtown bar is known for its two stages, where nightly live acts perform. Mon–Fri 11am–5am, Sat & Sun noon–5am. Cover is usually $5.

The Van Dyke Café 846 Lincoln Rd, South Beach ☎305/534-3600, ⓦwww.thevandykecafe.com. For serious jazz fans only – don't expect to chatter during the nightly performance on the second floor, or you'll get glowers from other patrons. Usually free; live acts 9pm–1am.

Classical music, dance, and opera

The classical scene was transformed thanks to an infusion of both cash and connections at the Adrienne Arsht Center for the Performing Arts downtown (see p.80 and below). It's home to almost every major performing arts company in the city including the **Florida Grand Opera** (ⓦwww.fgo.org), which brings impressive names to the area to perform a varied repertoire, and the **Miami City Ballet** (ⓦwww.miamicityballet.org). The **New World Symphony Orchestra** (ⓦwww.nws.org) is primarily based at the Lincoln Theater in South Beach, offering concert experience to some of the finest graduate **classical** musicians in the US, so the quality of performances is usually high. Tickets generally cost $20–150, with opera tickets at the upper range. Alternative options include the **Ballet Flamenco La Rosa** (☎305/899-7729, ⓦwww.panmiami.org/bflr.cfm), devoted to exploring new and avant-garde styles based on traditional Flamenco and Latin dance; call for schedules and prices. To find out **what's on**, the best source is to read the listings in the free *New Times* (published on Thurs).

1

Adrienne Arsht Center for the Performing Arts 1300 Biscayne Blvd, downtown Miami ☎305/372-7611, ⓦwww.arshtcenter.org. Premier arts venue in Miami, with three main performance spaces (see p.80).

The Fillmore Miami Beach at the Jackie Gleason Theater 1700 Washington Ave, South Beach ☎305/673-7300, ⓦwww.livenation.com. Biggest venue in Miami Beach, with acts tending more towards pop and rock music, but with occasional dance and classical concerts.

Gusman Center for the Performing Arts 174 E Flagler St, downtown Miami ☎305/372-0925, ⓦwww.gusmancenter.org. Historic and atmospheric venue (see p.78), with an eclectic line-up of ballet, folk and classical music.

Gusman Concert Hall, Frost School of Music 1314 Miller Drive, University of Miami ☎305/284-6477, ⓦwww.music.miami.edu. The Frost School puts on concerts year-round by guest artists as well as university ensembles (which are usually free).

Lincoln Theater 541 Lincoln Rd, South Beach ☎305/673-3330 ⓦwww.nws.org. Home of the New World Symphony Orchestra.

Miami-Dade County Auditorium 2901 W Flagler St, downtown Miami ☎305/547-5414 ⓦwww.miamidade.gov/parks. Huge county-owned venue hosting opera, symphony orchestras, theater, concerts and ballets.

Theater

Miami's **theater** scene is lively, if mainstream, though Spanish speakers should make a point of visiting one of the city's **Spanish-language theaters**, whose programs are listed in *El Nuevo Herald* (the Spanish-language version of the *Miami Herald* newspaper): try Teatro de Bellas Artes, 2173 SW 8th St (☎305/325-0515) for plays and musicals, and Teatro Trail, 3713 SW 8th St (☎305/448-0592) for comedies.

Actors Playhouse 280 Miracle Mile, Coral Gables ☎305/444-9293, ⓦwww.actorsplayhouse.org. There are three stages here – a 100-seat black box raw space for experimental work, the 300-seat Balcony Theater, and the main stage, which is twice the size. Often part of the Off-Broadway tryout circuit for major new shows like the recent revival of *1776*, as well as showy local stagings of favorites like *Grease* or *Les Misérables*. Tickets $35–48.

The New Theatre 4120 Laguna St, Coral Gables ☎305/443-5909, ⓦwww.new-theatre.org.

Sitting neatly between mainstream and alternative, this intimate, 100-seat space often produces the best theater in the city; the Pulitzer-winning *Anna in the Tropics* was commissioned here. Tickets $35–40.

Olympia Theater at the Gusman Center 174 E Flagler St ☎305/372-0925, ⓦwww.gusmancenter.org. Classical and contemporary plays, music, and dance are staged here from October to June. The only way to check out the elaborate interior is by taking in a show. Tickets vary dramatically according to performances, from $8 to $150.

Film

The choice of movies in Miami is vibrant and wide-ranging. For one, there's the **Miami Film Festival** (☎305/237-FILM, ⓦwww.miamifilmfestival.com), ten days and nights of new films from far and wide in February held at various locations across the city. There's also a strong **Gay & Lesbian Film Festival** in April (see opposite). In fact, at one point in American history, Florida might have rivaled Hollywood as the film capital of the world (see the *Colonnade Hotel* in Coral Gables, p.90, and "Contexts," p.480). There are plenty of multi-screen **cinemas** inside shopping malls showing first-run American features: check the "Weekend" section of the Friday *Miami Herald* for complete listings, or call the Movie Hotline (☎305/888-FILM).

AMC CocoWalk 16 3015 Grand Ave, Coconut Grove ☎305/466-0450. Another slightly aging multi-screen cinema, best option for downtown, Key Biscayne and Coconut Grove ($9.50).
AMC Sunset Place 24 5701 Sunset Drive, South Miami, in the Sunset Place mall ☎305/466-0450. Vast multiplex cinema sporting the latest in technology – but a bit of a drive from the main tourist areas, and very busy at weekends. Tickets $10.
Cosford Cinema University of Miami campus, Memorial Building, Coral Gables ☎305/284-4861,

ⓦwww.miami.edu/cosford. Shows classic and new indie and academic movies, Fri–Sun. Tickets $8.
Miami Beach Cinematique 512 Espanola Way, South Beach ☎305/673-4567, ⓦwww.mbcinema .com. Excellent line-up of arthouse films – tickets usually $10.
Regal South Beach 18 1120 Lincoln Rd, South Beach ☎305/673-6766. Only multiplex in South Beach, showing all the main Hollywood block-busters (tickets $10).

Miami festivals

Miami likes to party, and the city celebrates a wide variety of **festivals** year-round. Art festivals have become increasingly in vogue in recent years, with major events like Art Basel (see p.114) complemented by monthly Art Walks in the Wynwood District (see p.83) and Coral Gables (see p.88).

The precise dates of the festivals listed below vary from year to year; check the details at any tourist information office or Chamber of Commerce, or online at ⓦwww.festivalsmiami.com.

January

Art Deco Weekend ☎305/672-2014, ⓦwww .mdpl.org. Talks and free events along Ocean Drive, focusing on South Beach architecture.
Taste of the Grove ☎305/444-7270, ⓦwww .coconutgrove.com. Pig out on food and free music in Coconut Grove's Peacock Park.

February

Homestead Championship Rodeo ☎305/247-3515, ⓦwww.homesteadrodeo.com. Professional rodeo cowboys compete in steer-wrestling, bull-riding, calf-roping, and bareback riding.
Coconut Grove Arts Festival ☎305/447-0401, ⓦwww.coconutgroveartsfest.com. Hundreds of (mostly) talented unknowns display their works along S Bayshore Drive in Coconut Grove and on nearby streets.
Miami Film Festival ☎305/237-3456, ⓦwww .miamifilmfestival.com. Arthouse and mainstream films from the US and overseas are shown across the city at six venues including the Regal Theater and Wolfsonian Museum on South Beach and the Gusman Center in downtown Miami.

March

Carnaval Miami/Calle Ocho Festival ☎305/644-8888, ⓦwww.carnavalmiami.com. A nine-day celebration of Latin culture, with Hispanic-themed events across the city culminating in the huge Calle Ocho street party in Little Havana, with food kiosks and live music.

Sony Ericsson Open ☎305/446-2200 for information; ☎305/442-3367 for tickets, ⓦwww .sonyericssonopen.com. Men and women compete in the world's largest tennis tournament held at the Crandon Park Tennis Center in Key Biscayne.
Winter Music Conference ☎954/563-4444, ⓦwww.wmcon.com. This convention brings together music promoters, producers and managers, as well as well-known DJs who perform at local clubs.

April

Miami Gay and Lesbian Film Festival ☎305/534-9924, ⓦwww.mglff.com. Amateur and professional submissions are shown at four different venues, including the Regal Theater in South Beach.

May

The Great Sunrise Balloon Race & Festival ☎305/273-3063, ⓦwww.sunriseballoonrace.org. Held at Kendall-Tamiami airport.

June

Goombay Festival ☎1-800/891-7811, ⓦwww .goombayfestivalcoconutgrove.com. A spirited bash in honor of Bahamian culture, in and around Coconut Grove's Peacock Park.

July 4

America's Birthday Bash ☎305/358-7550, ⓦwww.bayfrontparkmiami.com. Music, fireworks, and a laser-light show celebrate the occasion at

Bayfront Park in downtown Miami. The annual *Miami Beach Fourth of July Celebration* also ends with spectacular fireworks (☎ 305/673-7400).

August

Miami Reggae Festival ☎ 305/891-2944. Celebration on the first Sunday of the month of Jamaican Independence Day with dozens of top Jamaican bands playing around the city.

October

Festival Miami ☎ 305/284-4940, ⓦ www.festival miami.com. Four weeks of performing and visual arts events organized by the University of Miami, mostly taking place at the Adrienne Arsht Center for the Performing Arts and the university.

Columbus Day Regatta ⓦ www.columbusday regatta.net. Florida's largest watersports event is a race commemorating Columbus's historic voyage. At Key Biscayne.

November

Miami Book Fair International ☎ 305/237-3258, ⓦ www.miamibookfair.com. A wealth of volumes from across the world spread across the campus of Miami-Dade Community College in downtown Miami.

Harvest Festival ☎ 305/375-1492, ⓦ www .fairexpo.com. A celebration of southern Florida's agricultural traditions, including home-made crafts, music, and pioneer re-enactments at the Fair Expo Center on Coral Way.

The White Party ⓦ www.whiteparty.net. Huge HIV/AIDS fundraiser held over the Thanksgiving weekend, with parties held across the city culminating in the outrageous White Party costumed ball at Villa Vizcaya.

December

Art Basel Miami Beach ⓦ www.artbasel miamibeach.com. One of the most important art festivals in the US, combining top galleries with a program of special exhibitions, parties and events featuring music, film, architecture and design. Exhibition sites are located throughout South Beach and the Wynwood district.

King Mango Strut ☎ 305/401-1171, ⓦ www .kingmangostrut.org. A very alternative New Year's Eve celebration, with part-time cross-dressers and clowns parading through Coconut Grove.

Gay and lesbian Miami

Miami has long been viewed as a prime destination by **gay and lesbian** tourists – a welcoming place with an "anything goes" Caribbean vibe that only grew stronger during South Beach's glory days of the early 1990s. Now, though, the pace has slowed somewhat as mainstream tourism has taken over the beach – the number of gay-targeted bars and clubs has rapidly dwindled as gay or lesbian locals have migrated further up the coast to Fort Lauderdale (see p.188). Even as the population shifts, there's little evidence of discrimination or discomfort with gay and lesbian tourists anywhere in the city, though it's only in South Beach that same-sex couples are likely to stroll hand-in-hand - it's here you'll also find the "**gay beach**", opposite 12th Street, marked by rainbow flags. Gay culture utterly subsumes straight culture twice a year; during the **White Party** at Thanksgiving (see "Miami festivals," p.113), and at the **Winter Party** (ⓦ www.winterparty .com) in March, the biggest gay beach party in North America.

Resources

Gay South Beach ⓦ www.sobegayinfo.com. Useful website with advice, shopping tips and plenty of listings.

Hot Spots Magazine ⓦ www.hotspotsmagazine .com. Covers the whole of the state, with a heavy focus on the party scene; better for men's information than for women's.

Miami Dade Gay & Lesbian Chamber of Commerce 3510 Biscayne Blvd, Suite 202, Biscayne Corridor ☎ 305/573-4000,

ⓦ www.gogaymiami.com. This gay chamber of commerce can advise on accommodation, amenities, and all aspects of local gay life.

Out in Miami ⓦ www.outinmiami.com. Smart, informative web-only resource, with an emphasis on personal ads, apartment listings and gay news.

Wire Magazine South Beach-centric weekly freesheet available in bars, record stores and clubs that's good for clubs and other nightlife listings. Published every Thurs.

Bars, clubs, and discos

Boy Bar 1220 Normandy Dr, Central Miami Beach ☏ 305/864-2697. Prime cruising pub, with a back room for men only and outdoor patio. Daily 5pm–5am.

Click Sundays at *Aero Bar*, 247 23rd St, South Beach ☏ 305/674-1110, ⓦ www.aerobarmiami.com. Sunday's gay mecca, replacing the now defunct *Anthem*; venues have jumped around in the past, so call ahead to make sure. 10pm–5am, cover usually $10.

Club Boi 726 NW 79th St, Biscayne Corridor ☏ 305/836-8995, ⓦ www.clubboi.com. A refreshing change from the circuit boy scene on South Beach, this largely black club plays hip-hop, house, and old-school R&B every Fri and Sat night.

Martini Tuesdays Gay promoter Edison Farrow runs this roaming party, which shuttles between different venues each Tues, 9pm–1am; the crowd's youngish and friendly, making most of the parties great fun. Call ☏ 305/535-6696 or check ⓦ www.sobesocialclub.com for up-to-date listings. No cover.

O'zone 6620 SW 57th St, South Miami ☏ 305/667-2888. Thurs, Sat and Sun cater to a predominantly Latino gay crowd at this popular club, while Friday's Cherry Pie is dedicated to the lesbian scene. Open from 9pm to 5am.

Palace Food Bar 1200 Ocean Drive, South Beach ☏ 305/531-7234. Friendly, welcoming bar-café opposite the gay beach, with a diverse clientele – old and young, buff and less so. The circular bar that looks overlooks the sidewalk is a pleasant place for a cocktail or two – look for the $6 mojitos on Mondays – but their burgers and wraps are pricey ($15–20).

Score 727 Lincoln Rd, South Beach ☏ 305/535-1111, ⓦ www.scorebar.net. This video bar on the Lincoln Rd main drag attracts a dressed-up, mostly male crowd. The half-price happy hour is a terrific deal (Mon–Fri 3–9pm). Cover for club nights ranges $7–20. Upstairs, the swishy, dressier *Crème Lounge* (ⓦ www.cremelounge.net) is especially popular on Thurs (no cover) and has an all-women party, Siren, on Sat ($8).

Twist 1057 Washington Ave ☏ 305/538-9478, ⓦ www.twistsobe.com. Longest-running gay bar on SoBe and a bit of an institution. Now featuring six different environments with comfy lounges, an outdoor terrace and two packed techno dancefloors. Go-go boys perform nightly. Daily two-for-one happy hour 1–9pm.

Shopping

Shopping for the sake of it isn't the big deal in Miami that it can be in other American cities, though there's plenty of opportunity for eager consumers to exercise their credit cards. The big disappointment in Miami's retail landscape is the dearth of bookstores. There are, however, plenty of options for music buffs, especially anyone interested in club or Cuban culture, and Miami has a growing reputation for young **fashion** designers, showcased along with the best Latin American talent at the annual **Miami Fashion Week** (usually held in March in South Beach). For couture designed by local star **Esteban Cortazar** – often described as Flamenco meets Hollywood – try Neiman Marcus in the Village of Merrick Park (see p.116). Most stores in the city stay open late, so you can browse well into the evening, often until 9pm or 10pm, especially in South Beach.

The most eclectic collection of shops is in South Beach, along Collins and Washington avenues, and Lincoln Road. Away from the beach, you're better off sticking to the **malls** – sterile, perhaps, but they do have the widest selection. Coral Gables has spruced up the offerings along its Miracle Mile, although there aren't many shops especially worth seeking out, aside from a huge outpost of Barnes & Noble. Supermarkets are plentiful and usually open until 10pm: alcohol is sold there, too, as well as in the many **liquor stores**.

Books

Barnes & Noble 152 Miracle Mile, Coral Gables ☏ 305/446-4152. The only centrally located branch of this mega-chain within reach of downtown Miami or Miami Beach, stocking the usual wide mix of books and records. Daily 9am–11pm.

Books & Books 296 Aragon Ave, Coral Gables ☏ 305/442-4408, Ⓦ www.booksandbooks.com. Excellent stock of general titles but especially strong on Floridian art and design, travel, and new fiction; also has author signings and talks. Call ☏ 305/444-9044 for the latest events. Daily 9am–11pm. Branches: 933 Lincoln Rd, South Beach (☏ 305/532-3222) and 9700 Collins Ave, Bal Harbour (☏ 305/864-4241).

Eutopia Books 1627 Jefferson Ave, Miami Beach ☏ 305/532-8680. Fabulous antiquarian bookstore in the heart of South Beach, with rare books as well as regular secondhand gems and new publications.

Fifteenth Street Books 296 Aragon Ave, Coral Gables ☏ 305/442-2344, Ⓦ www.fifteenthstreet books.com. Run by the original founder of Books & Books, this highly browsable secondhand store is strong on art books and old hardcovers in prime condition.

Kafka's Kafe 1464 Washington Ave, South Beach ☏ 305/673-9669, Ⓦ www.kafkaskafe.com. Rather ratty selection of used books – only good for budget-priced beach reading. Daily 8am–midnight.

Clothes and thrift stores

Banana Republic 1100 Lincoln Rd, South Beach ☏ 305/534-4706. There are branches of this chain everywhere, but whether you like the clothes it's worth stopping in to see how they converted an old bank, where the vaults are now changing rooms.

Base 939 Lincoln Rd, South Beach ☏ 305/531-4982, Ⓦ www.baseworld.com. Funky urban clothes for men and women, designed by choreographer-turned-fashion designer Stephen Giles, plus a tiny collection of homewares.

Consign of the Times 1635 Jefferson Ave, South Beach ☏ 305/535-0811. Miami's obsession with designer labels pays off here – locals offer their Gucci cast-offs for sale, splitting the profits with the store.

Douglas Gardens Thrift Store 5713 NW 27th St, Liberty City ☏ 305/638-1900. One of several vast warehouses of secondhand clothes clustered together, where you'll find outrageous bargains, but be sure to drive here as it's a sketchy area (park next to the police station opposite).

Recycled Blues 1507 Washington Ave, South Beach ☏ 305/538-0656. Largest selection of vintagewear (especially denim) on South Beach: a great choice, but not cheap.

Tomas Maier 1800 West Ave ☏ 1-888/373-0707, Ⓦ www.tomasmaier.com. Formerly the creative head of Italian label Bottega Veneta, Maier now has a namesake concept store, an ultracool spot where he stocks everything from clothes to CDs, books and homewares.

Department stores and malls

Bal Harbour Shops 9700 Collins Ave, Miami Beach ☏ 305/866-0311, Ⓦ www.balharbourshops .com. Packed with designer names like Gucci and Prada, this upmarket mall is always crowded, but great fun to browse in.

CocoWalk 3015 Grand Ave, Coconut Grove ☏ 305/444-0777, Ⓦ www.cocowalk.net. In the heart of Coconut Grove, this open-air complex has a relatively small range of stores, some good places to eat, and a decent sixteen-screen multiplex cinema.

The Falls US-1 and SW 136th St, South Miami ☏ 305/255-4570, Ⓦ www.shopthefalls.com. Sit inside a gazebo and contemplate the waterfalls and the rainforest that prettify suburban Miami's classiest set of shops.

Mary Brickell Village 901 S Miami Ave, ☏ 305/381-6130, Ⓦ www.marybrickellvillage.com. Located in the heart of Miami's financial district, this fancy mall offers plenty of bars and restaurants as well as shops: Village Humidor, Sowinski Jewelers, Vertigo, Studio LX and Marco Serussi among them.

Prime Outlets 250 E Palm Drive, Florida City ☏ 305/248-4727 or 1-888/545-7198, Ⓦ www .primeoutlets.com. On the Florida Turnpike and US-1, conveniently located for people traveling to the Keys or Everglades. Dedicated shoppers will find huge savings on name brands.

Village of Merrick Park Ponce de León Blvd and US-1, Coral Gables ☏ 305/529-0200, Ⓦ www .villageofmerrickpark.com. Recent upmarket rival to long-established Bal Harbour Shops: amid the open-air walkways, you'll find a branch of the sumptuous Elemis Spa, as well as fashions from Burberry, Diane von Furstenberg, and Jimmy Choo.

Music

Grooveman Music 1543 Washington Ave, South Beach ☏ 305/535-6257, Ⓦ www.chopinhaguen .com. A DJ's dream, stocking an ample selection of house and trance.

Les Cousins 7858 NE 2nd Ave, Little Haiti, no phone. Smallish store specializing in Caribbean music, terrific if you're looking for authentic sounds.

Lily's Records 1419 SW 8th St, Little Havana ☏ 305/856-0536. Unsurpassed stock of salsa, merengue, and other Latin sounds.

Spec's Music 501 Collins Ave, South Beach ☏ 305/534-3667. Mainstream record store with an adequate selection of well-known music of all genres. The place to pick up another CD to listen to on the beach – just don't go looking for anything too obscure.

Specialty goods

El Credito Cigar Factory 1106 SW 8th St, Little Havana ☏ 305/858-4162. One of the best-known smokeshops in the city, with rows of *tabaqueros* (cigar rollers) working here.

Halouba Botanica 101 NE 54th St, Little Haiti ☏ 305/751-7485. One of many *botanicas* on the *voudou* strip, this store is spacious and a little less daunting than some of the others, selling trinkets, religious candles and bead necklaces.

La Casa de las Guyaberas 5840 SW 8th St, Little Havana ☏ 305/266-9683. Pick up one of the billowy Cuban shirts known as *guyaberas* here; the cheapest cost around $20, while a custom-made design starts at $250.

Listings

American Express Main hotline (Bal Harbour) ☏ 1-800/325-1218. Offices around the city: in downtown Miami, 100 N Biscayne Blvd ☏ 305/358-7350; in Coral Gables, 32 Miracle Mile ☏ 305/446-3381; in Miami Beach, at Bal Harbour Shops, 9700 Collins Ave ☏ 305/865-5959.

Bike rental You can rent a bike from several outlets including: Mangrove Cycles, The Square Mall, 260 Crandon Blvd in Key Biscayne (Tues–Sat 10am–6pm, Sun 10am–5pm; $15 a day, $30 for 3 days; ☏ 305/361-5555); and the Miami Beach Bicycle Center, 601 5th St, South Beach (Mon–Sat 10am–7pm, Sun 10am–5pm; $8 per hr, $24 for 24hr; ☏ 305/674-0150, ⓦ www .bikemiamibeach.com). Helmets are usually included in the price, though you may have to pay an extra $1 per day for the lock.

Boat rental Club Nautico (☏ 305/673-2502, ⓦ www.clubnauticousa.com) at Miami Beach Marina, 300 Alton Rd and 4000 Crandon Blvd, Key Biscayne (☏ 305/361-9217) rents power boats from $329 for a half-day.

Car rental Alamo, 2401 Collins Ave (☏ 1-800/327-9633); Avis, 99 SE 2nd St, 8330 S Dixie Highway & 2318 Collins Ave (☏ 1-800/831-2847); Budget, 6742 Collins Ave & 665 SW 8th St (☏ 305/871-2722); Hertz, 354 SE 1st St & 1619 Alton Rd (☏ 305/871-0300); Thrifty, 1520 Collins Ave (☏ 1-800/367-2277).

Consulates Canada, 200 S Biscayne Blvd, Suite 1600, downtown Miami ☏ 305/579-1600; Denmark, PH 1D, 2655 Le Jeune Rd, Coral Gables ☏ 305/446-0020; France, 1395 Brickell Ave Suite 1050, downtown Miami ☏ 305/403-4150; Germany, Suite 2200, 100 N Biscayne Blvd, downtown Miami ☏ 305/358-0290; Netherlands, 701 Brickell Ave, 5th floor, downtown Miami ☏ 786/866-0480; UK, 1001 Brickell Bay Drive, Suite 2800, downtown Miami ☏ 305/374-1522.

Hospitals with emergency rooms. In Miami: Jackson Memorial Hospital, 1611 NW 12th Ave ☏ 305/585-1111, ⓦ www.um-jmh.org; Mercy Hospital, 3663 S Miami Ave ☏ 305/854-4400, ⓦ www.mercymiami.com. In Miami Beach: Mt Sinai Medical Center, 4300 Alton Rd ☏ 305/674-2121, ⓦ www.msmc.com.

Internet cafés Available all over Miami and South Beach in particular. Prices are generally $4 per hr, or $1 for 15min, and most branches of *Starbucks* have free wi-fi. The best places to surf are at the public libraries, which offer 15–45min free. Otherwise try these South Beach locations: *Kafka's Kafe*, 1464 Washington Ave (daily 8am–midnight; ☏ 305/673-9669), or *Cybr Caffe*, 1574 Washington Ave (daily 9am–1am; ☏ 305/534-0057).

Lost and found For items lost on Metro-Dade Transit, call ☏ 786/469-5564 (Mon–Fri 8am–noon & 1–5pm). Otherwise contact the Miami Beach police (☏ 305/673-7900).

Money exchange Using your bank/credit card at an ATM is the easiest and safest way. Alternatively, bring US dollar traveler's checks or cash, but if you need to change money, facilities are available at the airport, at American Express offices, and the following locations in downtown Miami: Bank of America, 5350 W Flagler St (Mon–Thurs 9am–4pm, Fri 9am–6pm, Sat 9am–1pm; ☏ 305/445-1025); SunTrust Bank, 1 SE 3rd Ave (Mon–Thurs 8.30am–5pm, Fri 8.30am–6pm ☏ 305/789-7289) & 777 Brickell Ave (Mon–Thurs 9am–4pm, Fri 9am–6pm; ☏ 305/577-5210).

Police Non-emergency: ☏ 305/673-7900 (Miami Beach Police); emergency: ☏ 911. If you are robbed anywhere on Miami Beach, report it at the station at 1100 Washington Ave and the report (for insurance purposes) can usually be collected within 3 – 5 days (records office Tues–Fri 8am–3pm; ☏ 305/673-7100).

Post offices In Miami Beach, 1300 Washington Ave (☏305/538-2708); in downtown Miami, 500 NW 2nd Ave (☏305/373-7562); in Coral Gables, 20 Miracle Mile & 251 Valencia Ave (☏305/443-2532); in Coconut Grove, 3191 Grand Ave (☏305/529-6700); in Homestead, 739 Washington Ave (☏305/247-1556). All open Mon–Fri 8.30am–5pm, Sat 8.30am–2pm, or longer hours.

Rollerblading Still popular in Miami, especially in South Beach. Fritz's Skate, Bike, & Surf Shop, at 730 Lincoln Rd (daily 10am–10pm;

☏305/532-1954), both sells and rents out rollerblades and safety gear. Rentals costs $10 per hr, $24 per day; bike rentals are also available at the same rates.

Sports See Basics p.34

Windsurfing Visit Sailboards Miami on the Rickenbacker Causeway (☏305/361-7245, ⓦwww.sailboardsmiami.com), which guarantees to teach you to windsurf in just 2hr ($69). They also rent kayaks ($15 per hr, $40 for 3hr) and windsurf boards ($30 per hr).

Travel details

Trains

Amtrak

Miami to: New York (2 daily; 26hr 54min–31hr 40min); Ocala (via Lakeland, 1 daily; 7hr 4min); Orlando (2 daily; 5hr 3min–7hr 18min); Sebring (2 daily; 3hr 9min); Tampa (1 daily at 11.50am; 5hr 15min); Washington DC (2 daily; 23hr 6min–27hr 24min); Winter Haven (2 daily; 3hr 50min).

Tri-Rail (Mon–Fri 25 daily; Sat & Sun 8 daily)

Miami to: Boca Raton (1hr); Delray Beach (1hr 10min); Fort Lauderdale (40min); Hollywood (26min); West Palm Beach (1hr 34min).

Buses

Miami to: Daytona Beach (2 direct daily; 8hr; 3 daily via Orlando; 7hr 25min–9hr 30min); Fort Lauderdale (12 daily; 45min); Fort Myers (3 daily; 4hr); Fort Pierce (9 daily; 3hr–3hr 50min); Jacksonville (3 daily; 8hr 40min–9hr 55min); Key West (2 daily; 4hr 30min); Orlando (9 daily; 5hr 20min–6hr 20min); Sarasota (3 daily; 6hr 10min–6hr 40min); St Petersburg (3 daily; 7hr 20min–7hr 50min); Tampa (3 daily; 8–9hr); West Palm Beach (9 daily; 1hr 50min–2hr 35min).

2

The Florida Keys

CHAPTER 2 # Highlights

* **John Pennekamp State Park** Dive or snorkel this rich undersea preserve, with a long stretch of the Florida Reef teeming with tropical fish, barracuda and the occasional shark. See p.125

* **Indian Key** The ruins of the settlement that once thrived here are spooky and evocative, overrun by untamed greenery. See p.131

* **No Name Pub** This oddball gem encapsulates the cranky charm of the Keys better than almost anywhere else. See p.139

* **Key West** Soak up the Caribbean vibes in America's southernmost town, with weathered conch cottages, absorbing museums and famously raucous nightlife. See p.142

* **Key lime pie and conch fritters** Every restaurant in the Keys has a take on these fine local specialties, with the best-loved cooked up in Key West. See p.159

* **Dry Tortugas** Spend a day or two at this cluster of islands at the western end of the Keys. The coral reef is stunning, and there's a bird sanctuary and an old fort to explore on land. See p.164

▲ Seven Mile Bridge

The Florida Keys

Trailing from Florida's southern tip, the **FLORIDA KEYS** are a string of over ten thousand small islands of which fewer than fifty are inhabited. The hundred-mile long arc peters out to within ninety miles of Cuba. The Keys (so named from the Spanish word "cayo," meaning small islet or coral bank) are most known for the **Florida Reef**, a great band of living coral just a few miles offshore whose range of color and dazzling array of ocean life – including dolphins and loggerhead turtles – are exceptional sights. Throughout the Keys, and especially for the first sixty-odd miles, fishing, snorkeling, and diving dominate, and if you're not planning to indulge in watersports, you'll be hard-pressed to find much else to fill your time. Here and there, houses built around the turn of the nineteenth century by Bahamian settlers and seedy waterside bars run by refugees from points north hint at the islands' history. And while there are some stunning natural areas and worthwhile ecology tours, the whole stretch is primarily a build-up to **Key West**, the real pearl on this island strand.

Heading down the chain from the mainland, the first place to visit on the reef is the **John Pennekamp State Park**, one of the few interesting features of **Key Largo** on the **Upper Keys**. Like **Islamorada**, further south, Key Largo is rapidly being populated by suburban Miamians, drawn by the sailing and fishing but unable to survive without shopping malls. Islamorada is the best base for fishing, and also has some natural and historical points of note – as does the next major settlement, **Marathon**, which is at the center of the **Middle Keys** and thus makes a useful short-term base. Thirty miles on, the **Lower Keys** get fewer visitors and less publicity than their neighbors, but in many ways they're the most unusual and appealing of the chain. Covered with scrubby forest, they are home to a tiny and endangered species of Key deer, and, at **Looe Key**, offer a tremendous departure point for trips to the Florida Reef. **Key West** is the end of the road in every sense: shot through with an intoxicating aura of abandonment, but also an immensely vibrant place. The only part of the Keys with a real sense of history, Key West was once – unbelievably – the richest town in the US and the largest settlement in Florida. There are old homes and museums to explore and plenty of bars in which to while away the hours.

Beaches are rarely found in the Keys owing to the reef, though the sands at **Bahia Honda State Park** are pretty good. What the islands offer in abundance are spectacular **sunsets**; as the nineteenth-century ornithologist John James Audubon once rhapsodized: "a blaze of refulgent glory streams through the portals of the west, and the masses of vapor assume the semblance of mountains of molten gold."

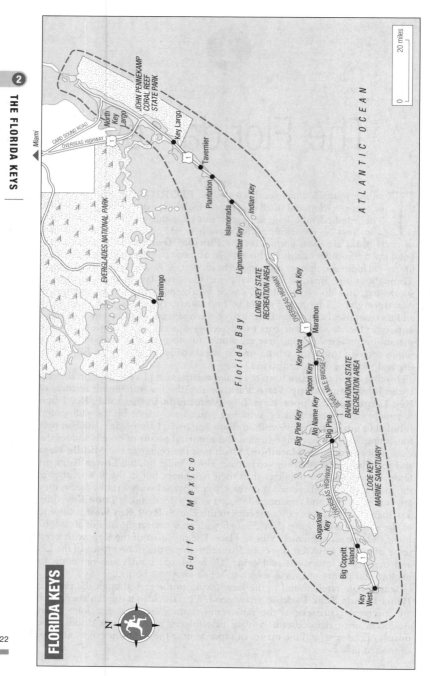

Practicalities

Traveling through the Keys could hardly be easier as there's just one route all the way through to Key West: the **Overseas Highway (US-1)**, which follows the path of Henry Flagler's old railway (destroyed in a 1935 hurricane; see p.136). This is punctuated by **mile markers (MM)** – posts on which mileage is marked, starting with MM127, just south of Homestead, and finishing with MM0, in Key West at the junction of Fleming and Whitehead streets. Almost all places of business use mile markers as an address, and throughout this chapter they are tagged with an "MM" (for example, "the *Holiday Inn*, at MM100"). We've also followed the local convention of indicating whether buildings sit on the Bayside (Key West-bound) or Oceanside (Miami-bound) side of the freeway.

To keep up with closures and potential problems on US-1, tune to US-1 Radio (104.1FM; ⓦ www.us1radio.com) or Conch FM (WCNK 98.7FM); call the local sheriff's office on ☏ 305/293-7300 or 305/293-7311, or check ⓦ www.monroecounty-fl.gov for updates.

Public transportation is skimpy: it consists of two daily Greyhound **buses** between Miami and Key West (see "Travel details" at the end of the chapter) and a local bus service between Key West and Marathon (12 buses daily 5.30am–10pm; $3). Keys Shuttle (☏ 305/289-9997, ⓦ www.keysshuttle.com) runs a door-to-door minibus service from Miami and Fort Lauderdale airports to anywhere in the Keys six times a day; Miami rates are $60 to Key Largo and $90 to Key West.

Accommodation is abundant but more expensive than on the mainland. Though there are a few cheap exceptions (noted below), during high season (Nov to April), budget for *at least* $100 a night, and $60–75 the rest of the year; in many hotels rooms can double in price in high season. Prices are always much cheaper in the wetter summer months, but remember that underwater visibility is often poor at this time, and hurricanes are a possibility. As always,

Swimming with dolphins

Dolphins are a common sight around the Florida Keys and are the star attraction of the state's many marine parks – though watching them perform somersaults in response to human commands gives just an inkling of their potential. However, there is some attempt at preservation, and the **Dolphin Research Center**, MM59-Bayside in Marathon (daily 9am–4.30pm; ☏ 305/289-1121, ⓦ www.dolphins.org), rescues and rehabilitates sick or wounded dolphins and other sea mammals found around the Keys. At the center, dolphins participate in therapy programs for cancer sufferers and mentally disabled children; the exceptional patience and gentleness displayed by the dolphins (all of which are free to swim out to sea whenever they want) in this work suggest their sonar system may allow them to make an X-ray-like scan of a body to detect abnormalities and perhaps even to "see" emotions. Take a **tour** (daily 9am–4pm every half hour; $19.50, age 4–12 $13.50) of the research center to become better informed on these remarkable – and still barely understood – mammals. The Dolphin Research Center is also one of four places in the Florida Keys where you can **swim with dolphins** ($180 for around 20min); call at least a month ahead (six weeks in high season, ☏ 305/289-0002) to book a session. Averaging seven feet in length, dolphins look disconcertingly large at close quarters – and will lose interest in you long before you tire of their company – but if you do get the opportunity to join them, it's an unforgettable experience. You can also visit **Dolphins Plus** and **Dolphin Cove** in Key Largo (see p.127), and **Theater of the Sea** in Islamorada (see p.131).

price codes in the guide reflect the price of the cheapest double in high season. **Camping** is considerably less expensive year-round, and is well catered for throughout the Keys.

Official visitor centers are listed at the beginning of the relevant section. Be aware these will be signposted by a blue sign with white writing at the roadside – all others you'll pass, however smart-looking, are privately run concerns that are not guaranteed to provide the best impartial advice.

The Upper Keys

The northernmost portion of the Florida Keys, the **UPPER KEYS** are roughly made up of three major communities – Key Largo, Tavernier, and Islamorada – between which lies a scattering of small islands, most accessible only by boat. **Key Largo** is the biggest, though not the prettiest, of the Keys and boasts the **John Pennekamp Coral Reef State Park**. Lower down the island, the little town of **Tavernier** is really a place to pass through on the way to bigger and livelier **Islamorada**, which comprises a string of state parks.

Key Largo

Thanks to the 1948 film in which Humphrey Bogart and Lauren Bacall grappled with what were then Florida's best-known features – crime and hurricanes – almost everybody has heard of **KEY LARGO**. Yet the main section of the island can be a disappointing introduction to the Keys, since most of its beauty is underwater; on land, it's largely gas stations, dive shops with gaudily painted signs, and chain restaurants. Ironically, the film's title was chosen for no other reason than it suggested somewhere warm and exotic, and, though set here, *Key Largo* was almost entirely shot in Hollywood – hoodwinking countless millions into thinking paradise was a town in the Florida Keys. Tenuous links with Hollywood (and Bogart) are maintained today by the steam-powered boat *The African Queen*, used in the 1951 movie of the same name and displayed at the marina of the *Holiday Inn*, MM100-Oceanside (it's no longer taken out on tours).

There are some good restaurants in town, but it's **John Pennekamp Coral Reef State Park** and the offshore islands that are the best reasons to stay for a night or two; while the touristy designation "diving capital of the world" is pushing things a bit, the magnificent scuba and fishing opportunities the Keys are known for begin here in earnest. Stop in at the **Key Largo Visitor Center**, MM106-Bayside (daily 9am–6pm; ☎305/451-1414 or 1-800/822-1088), for information on these activities and other general information.

Accommodation

You'll usually have no problem finding reasonably priced accommodation in Key Largo – it has some of the widest range of choices in the Keys, albeit in the least prepossessing setting.

Coconut Palm Inn MM92-Bayside ☎305/852-3017 or 1-800/765-5397 ⓦwww.coconutpalminn.com. This simple but stylish waterfront hotel is great value, with twenty rooms and suites beautifully decked out with modern wooden beds and tiled floors. Amenities include a small but attractive pool, white-sand beach with hammocks and free wi-fi. ❼

Ed & Ellen's Economy Efficiency MM103.5-Oceanside ☎305/451-9949 or 1-888/333-5536, ⓦwww.ed-ellens-lodgings.com. On the corner of Snapper Avenue, this seven-room motel is hidden from the main road by a leafy sea grape grove. It's a terrific low-cost option: rooms are basic but clean, and each has a small kitchenette and private bathroom; Ed & Ellen were looking to sell the place in 2009, so call ahead. ❸

John Pennekamp Coral Reef State Park MM 102.5-Oceanside ☎305/451-1202 or 1-800/326-3521. The cleanest and cheapest of the many campgrounds in and around Key Largo has sites for RVs or tents for $20.50. Book several months ahead for high season.

Jules' Undersea Lodge 51 Shoreland Drive ☎305/451-2353 or 1-800/858-7119, ⓦwww.jul .com. This tiny hotel, thirty feet below the ocean's surface, is always booked well in advance; the two-bedroom accommodations are perfectly safe and are linked to land by an intercom system. Just remember your diver's certificate – otherwise you'll have to take the hotel's 3hr crash course ($120) before you'll be allowed to unpack. Very costly, but

one of a kind: those on a budget can still experience it via a 3hr visit to watch a movie or eat lunch for ($125 per person). ❽

The Key Largo Kampground MM101.5-Oceanside ☎305/451-1431 or 1-800/526-7688, ⓦwww.key largokampground.com. This campground is a reasonable alternative for both RVs (from $57 per hook up per day) and tents (from $33.50 per pitch per day).

Kona Kai Resort MM97.8-Bayside ☎305/852-4629 or 1-800/365-7829, ⓦwww.konakairesort .com. The chalets here are huge and stylish, a dozen strains of banana grow in the garden, and the hotel has its own art gallery, private beach, tennis court, and pool. No children. ❽

Largo Lodge MM101.5-Bayside ☎305/451-0424 or 1-800/468-4378, ⓦwww.largolodge.com. Gloriously quirky and old fashioned, this sprawling motel offers six large cottages and one basic motel room; interiors resemble late 1980s bachelor pads with overstuffed sofas and glass-topped tables, though the best feature is the tiled screen porches where you can spy racoons and iguanas in the garden. No children. ❻

Seafarer Resort MM97.8-Bayside ☎305/852-5349 or 1-800/599/7112, ⓦwww.seafarerresort .com. Spotless but functional cottages with kitchens, as well as some simpler motel-style rooms, very popular with divers. Some rooms are showing their age, but the private beach and lush grounds are pleasant extras, and the dive shop can arrange trips to the local marine sanctuaries. Rooms ❹, apartments ❻.

John Pennekamp Coral Reef State Park

The one essential stop as you approach the center of Key Largo is the **John Pennekamp Coral Reef State Park**, at MM102.5-Oceanside (daily 8am–sunset; $3.50 per car and driver, plus $2.50 for first passenger, 50¢ for each additional passenger, pedestrians and cyclists $1.50; ☎305/451-1202, ⓦwww .pennekamppark.com). At its heart is a protected 78-square-mile section of living coral reef three to eight miles off Key Largo, part of a chain running from here to the Dry Tortugas (see p.164). Just a few decades ago, great sections of the reef were dynamited or hauled up by crane to be broken up and sold as souvenirs. These days, collecting Florida coral is illegal, and any samples displayed in tourist shops have most likely been imported from the Philippines. Despite the damage wrought by ecologically unsound tourism, experts still rate this as one of the most beautiful reef systems in the world. Whether you opt to visit the reef here or elsewhere in the Keys (such as Looe Key, see p.140), make sure you do visit it – the eulogistic descriptions you'll hear are rarely exaggerations.

Seeing the reef: practicalities

Since most of the park lies underwater, the best way to see it is with a tour arranged by onsite concessionaire Coral Reef Park Company. Take a **snorkeling tour** (9am, noon, & 3pm; 1hr 30min; adults $29.95, plus $9 for equipment;

305/451-6300, ⓦ www.pennekamppark.com) or, if you're qualified, a two-tank **guided scuba dive** (9.30am & 1.30pm; 2hr; $60, plus $29 for full equipment; diver's certificate required; ⓣ 305/451-6322). If you prefer to stay dry, a remarkable amount of the reef can be enjoyed on the park's two-and-a-half-hour **glass-bottomed boat tour** (9.15am, 12.15pm, & 3pm; $24; ⓣ 305/451-6300).

You can also **rent a boat** – canoes cost $12 per hour, double kayaks $17 per hour, and power boats from $182 for 4 hours (ⓣ 305/451-6325). To be sure of a space on a dive or tour, make a **reservation**; if there's no room, try one of the numerous local dive outfits along US-1 (see box opposite).

At the reef

The reef shelters a multitude of crazy-colored fish and exotic marine life, and even from the glass-bottomed boat you're virtually guaranteed to spot lobsters, angelfish, eels, and wispy jellyfish shimmering through the current, as well as shoals of minnows stalked by angry-faced barracudas, and many more less easily identified aquatic curiosities.

Despite looking like a big lump of rock, the **reef** itself is a delicate living thing, composed of millions of minute coral polyps that extract calcium from the seawater and grow from one to sixteen feet every 1000 years. Coral takes many shapes and forms, resembling anything from staghorns to a bucket, and comes in a paint-box variety of colors due to the plants, zooxanthellae, living within the coral tissues. Sadly, it's far easier to spot signs of death than life on the reef: white patches show where a carelessly dropped anchor or a diver's hand have scraped away the protective mucus layer and left the coral susceptible to lethal disease.

This destruction got so bad at the horseshoe-shaped **Molasses Reef**, about seven miles out, the authorities sank two obsolete coastguard cutters nearby to create an alternative attraction for divers. In as much as the destruction has slowed, this plan worked and today you'll enjoy some great snorkeling around the reef and the cutters. If you prefer diving amid older wrecks, head for **the Elbow**, a section of the reef a few miles northeast of Molasses, where a number

▲ Christ of the Deep, John Pennekamp Coral Reef State Park

of intriguing, barnacle-encrusted nineteenth-century specimens lie; like most of the Keys' diveable wrecks, these were deliberately brought here to bolster tourism in the 1970s.

By far the strangest thing at the reef is the **Christ of the Deep**, a nine-foot bronze statue of Christ intended as a memorial to perished sailors. The algae-coated creation, twenty feet down at Key Largo Dry Rocks, is a replica of Guido Galletti's *Christ of the Abyss*, similarly submerged off the coast of Genoa, Italy – and is surely the final word in Florida's long-time fixation with Mediterranean art and architecture. Glass-bottomed boat trips, by the way, don't visit the Elbow or the statue.

Back on land

Provided you visit the reef early, there'll be plenty of time left to enjoy the terrestrial portion of the park. The ecological displays at the **visitor center** (daily 8am–5pm) provide an inspiring introduction to the flora and fauna of the Keys, especially its **aquarium**, replete with pristine corals, moray eels and nurse sharks. It will also give you a practical insight into the region's transitional zones: the vegetation changes dramatically within an elevation of a few feet.

Short **hiking trails** cut through the park's fine tropical **hardwood hammock** – a pocket of woodland able to flourish where the ground elevation rises a few feet above the surrounding wetlands – and meander through red mangroves, pepper trees, and graceful frangipani. Raccoon, heron, and fiddler crab tracks are everywhere, and hairy-legged, golden orb spiders dangle from many a branch. The park also boasts some small but fine artificial **beaches** (you'll find very few others – artificial or not – until Bahia Honda), but note the coral is very unforgiving to bare feet. Another option for exploring the park is to rent a canoe or kayak (see opposite) and glide around the mangrove-fringed inner waterways.

Dolphins Plus and Dolphin Cove

You'll find two spots on Key Largo where you can swim with **dolphins**. The first is **Dolphins Plus**, 31 Corrine Place (daily 9am–5pm; ☎305/451-1993 or 1-866/860-7946, ⓦwww.dolphinsplus.com), a dolphin education and research

---

Fishing and snorkeling trips off Key Largo

The reef and tiny, uninhabited **islands** off Key Largo make glorious forays for snorkeling and fishing, and if you can't make the official boat trips in the state park (see p.125), there's no shortage of alternatives along US-1. The most reliable **snorkeling** options are Keys Diver at MM100-Oceanside (☎305/451-1177, ⓦwww.keysdiver.com) and Sundiver III at MM102.8-Bayside (☎305/451-2220, ⓦwww.snorkelingisfun.com). Sailors Choice (☎305/451-1802, ⓦwww.sailorschoice.com), also at *Holiday Inn Marina* at MM100-Oceanside, runs family-friendly **fishing** trips ($40), though serious fishing aficionados should get in touch with Key Largo Fishing Adventures at MM103.9-Bayside (☎305/923-9293, ⓦwww.keyssportfishing.com; full day trips from $800). To explore on your own, make for Boat Rental Florida Keys at *Snapper's*, 147 Seaside Ave, MM95-Oceanside (☎305/852-7300, ⓦwww.boatrental411.com), which rents powerboats from $170 a day.

If a **glass-bottomed boat tour** is more up your alley, head to the **Holiday Inn** docks at MM100-Oceanside, where the **Key Largo Princess** makes two-hour cruises around the John Pennekamp Coral Reef State Park at 10am, 1pm, and 4pm ($25; ☎305/451-4655, ⓦwww.keylargoprincess.com).

facility where you can indulge in a "dolphin encounter" with one of twelve friendly creatures. To find it, head south on Ocean Bay Drive off US-1, just beyond the *Holiday Inn* (MM100-Oceanside). The price of a "structured" half-hour swim with the dolphins is $185 in peak season and $165 non-peak (8.30am, 12.45pm, & 3pm; to observe only $10, kids 7–17 $5), and there is also a "natural" swim with wild dolphins for $125 – though with the latter, contact is not guaranteed (9.30am & 1.30pm).

The other venue is **Dolphin Cove**, a five-acre marine environment research center at MM102-Bayside (℡ 305/451-4060, ⊛ www.dolphinscove.com). Structured swims (9am, 1pm, & 3.30pm; $165–185) begin with a 30–45 minute educational talk, and end with participants taking turns to interact with dolphins in a small lagoon opening directly onto the sea. There's also a natural swim (9.45am), where you snorkel alongside the dolphins but aren't guaranteed contact, for $125. If you can't afford a close encounter, $20 (under-16s $15) gets you in as a non-swimming observer. Dolphin Cove is also the departure point for **Captain Sterling's Eco-Tours** (daily 11am, 1.30pm, & 4pm; $49, children $29; ℡ 1-305/853-5161 or 888/224-6044, ⊛ www.captainsterling.com; reservation required), one of the more knowledgeable backcountry tours in the area.

Eating and drinking

Far enough south for fine Caribbean cuisine, but close enough to the Everglades for a taste of 'gator, Key Largo is a fine place for **eating**. Some of the restaurants also double as down-home drinking dens. For home-made Key lime pies to take-out, visit roadside *Key Lime Tree* (℡ 305/853-0378, ⊛ www.keylimeproducts .com) at MM95-Oceanside, which sells thick, piquant pies for $12.50.

Alabama Jack's 58000 Card Sound Rd ℡ 305/248-8741, ⊛ www.alabamajacks .com. If you'd like to relax with some good conch fritters and a beer while a jam band plays in the background, stop off here, just north of the toll booth on the Card Sound Road (Hwy-905A) before you enter the Keys proper. It's a local tradition and a perfect introduction.

Ballyhoo's MM97.8 in the median ℡ 305/852-0822, ⊛ www.ballyhoosrestaurant.com. Opened 25 years ago by a couple of fishermen, this small shack-like diner features a wide selection of grilled food and drinks, with a Friday night fish fry and all-you-can eat stone crab, in season (Oct–May). Lunch specials from $6.99. Opposite *Kona Kai* and near *Seafarers*.

The Caribbean Club MM104-Bayside ℡ 305/451-4466. The place for a lively drink, providing you're not daunted by the sight of bikers in leather jackets and tropical shorts. They serve basic pub food and also offer cheap jet-ski rentals during the day. Carl Fisher, of Miami Beach fame, built the club in 1938, though the claim that *Key Largo* was shot here is highly dubious.

The Fish House MM102.4-Oceanside ℡ 305/451-4665, ⊛ www.fishhouse.com. For a splash-out seafood meal, as dressy a spot as you'll find in Key Largo. Fish of the day is offered in various styles,

from traditional blackened or broiled to more adventurous options like Matecumbe (with capers, tomatoes and shallots) or Jamaican Jerk (from $19.95).

Harriette's MM95.7-Bayside ℡ 305/852-8689. Best place for a filling, diner-style breakfast, set in a modest but cozy shack just off the highway. Try the massive Key lime muffin, and order the tasty biscuit instead of toast. Open till 2pm.

Mrs Mac's Kitchen MM99.5-Bayside ℡ 305/451-3722, ⊛ www .mrsmacskitchen.com Consistently fabulous home-style food at reasonable prices, set in a no-frills diner festooned with license plates. The fresh fish and home-made chili are highlights, but the crab cakes, Key lime pie and conch fritters are must-try; look out for all-you-can-eat fish nights on Thur.

Snapper's 139 Seaside Ave, at the end of Ocean View Ave off US-1 at MM94.5-Oceanside ℡ 305/852-5956, ⊛ www.snapperskeylargo.com. Enjoy the waterside setting – one of the most romantic around – or swing by for the Sunday Champagne jazz brunch (10am–2pm). The menu features Keys staples like coconut-crusted shrimp ($13) and the house special, chunks of alligator served like chicken nuggets with blue cheese dipping sauce ($9).

Tavernier

Huddled at the southern end of Key Largo is **TAVERNIER** (Tav-uh-NEE-uh), a small, homely town that was once the first stop on the Flagler railway. There's not a whole lot here, but the Cuban food in the *Sunshine Restaurant* is worth a pit stop.

Just before crossing into Tavernier, at MM93.6-Bayside, is the **Florida Keys Wild Bird Center** (daily 8.30am–5.30pm; free; ℡305/852-4486, Ⓦwww.fkwbc.org), an inspirational place where volunteers rescue and rehabilitate birds that have been orphaned or have met with other common catastrophes like colliding with cars or power lines. A wooden walkway is lined with huge enclosures, and signs detail the birds' histories – watch out for the brown booby dubbed "Byron", who was discovered wrapped in fishing line and now makes his permanent home at the center because he can no longer fly.

If you drop into **Harry Harris Park**, MM 93.5-Oceanside at the end of long, snaking Burton Drive (7.30am–sunset; nonresidents $5 per car at weekends and on public holidays; ℡305/852-7161), on a weekend, you could well find an impromptu party and live music – locals sometimes drop by with instruments and station themselves on picnic tables for jam sessions. Otherwise, during the week, it's a fine place to lounge since there's a wide, sandy beach.

Practicalities

If you're in the mood for a delicious, dark *café cubano* for just 85¢, stop by ⚐ *Sunshine Restaurant*, MM91.8-Oceanside (no phone), a top-notch, low-key café sitting next to a supermarket. You can also dig in to a piled-high plate of Cuban food: a juicy sandwich is just $4.50, while grilled fresh fish meals cost under $10. There's little English spoken, so non-Spanish speakers should be prepared to get by with smiles and gestures. Next door, the *Tavernier Hotel*, MM91.8-Oceanside (℡305/852-4131 or 1-800/515-4131, Ⓦwww.tavernierhotel.com; ❹) is a charmingly old-fashioned hotel, painted pale pink, which began life as an open-air theater; the homey rooms have fridges and there's an onsite coin laundry.

Islamorada

Fishing is headline news in **ISLAMORADA** (meaning "purple island" and pronounced "eye-lah-more-RAH-da"). Tales of monstrous tarpon and blue marlin captured off the coast are legendary, and there's no end to the smaller prey routinely hooked by total novices. You reach Islamorada by crossing Tavernier Creek: the "town" is actually a twenty-mile strip of separate islands, including Plantation, Windley, and Upper and Lower Matecumbe, collectively dubbed Islamorada. For **information**, visit the Islamorada Visitors Center, MM83.2-Bayside (Mon–Fri 9am–5pm, Sat 9am–4pm, Sun 9am–3pm; ℡305/664-4503, Ⓦwww.islamoradachamber.com).

Accommodation

In general, you're unlikely to find **accommodation** in Islamorada for under $100 a night, although there are a handful of bargain motels listed below. For **camping**, aim for the Long Key State Park (see p.132).

Sportfishing, snorkeling, and diving

Islamorada claims to be the sportfishing capital of the world, so as you'd expect it's easy to charter **fishing** boats ($550 per day), or, for much less, join a fishing party boat from any of the local marinas (around $60). The biggest docks are at the Holiday Isle, MM84.5-Oceanside (to book a fishing charter call 1-800/327-7070, or to rent a boat call ☎305/664-9425, www.holidayisle.com) and Bud 'n' Mary's Fishing Marina, MM79.8-Oceanside (☎1-800/742-7945, ⓦwww.budnmarys.com).

There's notable **snorkeling** and **diving** in the area, too. Crocker and Alligator reefs, a few miles offshore, both have near-vertical sides, whose cracks and crevices provide homes for a lively variety of crabs, shrimp, and other small creatures that in turn attract bigger fish looking for a meal. Nearby, the wrecks of the *Eagle* and the *Cannabis Cruiser* provide a home for families of gargantuan amberjack and grouper. Get full snorkeling and diving details from the marinas (see above) or any dive shop on the Overseas Highway – expect to pay $35–40 for a half-day of snorkeling.

Cheeca Lodge & Spa MM82-Oceanside ☎305/664-4651 or 1-800/327-2888, ⓦwww .cheeca.com. This lavish lodge was built on a historic spot – the onetime hunting grounds of Herbert Hoover – and has been refurbished to reflect its swanky beginnings. There's a private beach, kayaks, bikes, onsite spa, Jack Nicklaus-designed golf course, and simple, country-club-style rooms – be prepared for the hefty $39 per day resort fee, though. **❼**

Drop Anchor MM85-Oceanside ☎305/664-4863 or 1-888/664-4863, ⓦwww.dropanchorresort.com. A little out of town, this upmarket, zen-like motel has a pool and manicured private beach with loungers, picnic tables and swaying palm trees; the spacious plantation-style rooms have ceiling fans, verandas and wooden shutters. **❺**

Islander Resort MM82.1-Oceanside ☎305/664-2031 or 1-800/753-6002, ⓦwww.islander floridakeys.com. Hands down, the best pool around – in fact, two: one huge freshwater spot and another saltwater dipping pool. It's also family friendly, with bungalow rooms sprawling across a large campus; the best of them have screened-in verandas where you can lounge, mosquito-free, in the evenings. Other nifty touches include the onsite tiki bar, free book loan from reception, and the fact the local strip of restaurants is just a short walk away. **❻**

Key Lantern/Blue Fin Inn MM82.1-Bayside ☎305/664-4572 and 305/664-8709, ⓦwww.keylantern.com. These twinned motels are true budget gems in the Keys. The *Blue Fin* has 14 basic rooms; the 10 spots at the *Key Lantern*, though, are better. With naturally cooling coral rock walls and terrazzo floors, plus pastel-colored period bathrooms, they're pristine examples of a mid-century motel (rooms 2 and 7 are the largest). The same woman owns the equally well-priced *Sunset Inn* nearby (MM-82.2, ☎305/664-3454, ⓦwww .sunsetinnkeys.com; **❷**) so ask about availability there if these two are full. **❷**

Pines & Palms MM80.4-Oceanside ☎1-800/624-0964, ⓦwww.pinesandpalms.com. This old-style Keys throwback (floral sofas and wicker furniture) has 25 bright, plush rooms, each with a kitchenette. Groups can snag a bargain at the two-bedroom condo complete with dining room, jacuzzi, and washer dryer – it sleeps 6 people, starting at $399 per night. The views from the oceanfront pool are spectacular. **❺**

Ragged Edge Resort MM86.5-Oceanside, 243 Treasure Harbor Rd, Plantation Key ☎305/852-5389 or 1-800/436-2023, ⓦwww.ragged-edge .com. Rooms right on the ocean, offering cozy cottages or efficiencies with kitchenettes and new bathrooms; furnishings are a bit dated, but all rooms are spotless. Friendly owners, great service and decent fishing off the pier, plus bike rentals and free wi-fi. **❹**

Upper Matecumbe Key and around

Long considered Islamorada's "downtown", **Upper Matecumbe Key** is a built-up island with a couple of mildly interesting diversions along its relatively busy commercial strip. The **Florida Keys History of Diving Museum** at MM83-Bayside (daily 10am–5pm; $12; ☎305/664-9737, ⓦwww .divingmuseum.com) boasts an odd but absorbing collection of rare diving helmets and suits, as well as exhibits highlighting the three-thousand year history of diving and the role of undersea treasure-seekers in South Florida.

A short drive south at MM81.6-Oceanside, the Art Deco **Hurricane Monument** marks the grave of the 1935 Labor Day hurricane's 425 victims, many killed when a tidal wave hit the train attempting to evacuate them. It's estimated many more people died in the storm, but exact numbers will never be known.

You could also pass a couple of hours at the **Theater of the Sea**, at MM84.5-Oceanside back on Windley Key (daily 9.30am–4pm; adults $25.95, kids 3–10 $18.95; ☎305/664-2431, ⓦwww.theaterofthesea.com), but only if you're not planning to visit any of the other marine parks in Florida, such as SeaWorld, most of which are better. Here, you'll find the usual dolphin and sea lion shows and marine exhibits, and kids will enjoy swimming with dolphins ($175), stingrays ($55) and sea lions ($135), though considering the prices, parents may not be so keen.

Indian Key and Lignumvitae Key

Indian Key and **Lignumvitae Key** – two state parks at the southern end of Islamorada (☎305/664-2540, ⓦwww.floridastateparks.org) – offer a broader perspective of the area than just fishing and diving. The former reveals a near-forgotten chapter of the Florida Keys' history, the latter an enchanting virgin forest. Ranger-led one-hour **tours** of Lignumvitae Key run Friday to Sunday at 10am and 2pm ($1); they need at least four people to run boats ($20 including tour) over from Robbie's Marina, MM77.5-Bayside (☎305/664-9814, ⓦwww.robbies.com). At the time of writing there were no tours to Indian Key, and the only way to visit either island was by renting kayaks or boats: Robbie's rents powerboats from $135 per half-day, and you can get kayaks from Florida Keys Kayak ($20 per hr, $50 per day; ☎305/664-4878, ⓦwww .floridakeyskayakandski.com), also at the marina.

At Robbie's you can also feed the monstrous **tarpons** (entry $1): buy a bucket of herring for $2 and toss chunks from the pier to get the fish leaping out of the shallow waters.

Indian Key Historic State Park

You'd never guess from the highway that **Indian Key Historic State Park** (daily 8am–sunset), one of many small, mangrove-skirted islands off Lower Matecumbe Key, was once a busy trading center, given short-lived prosperity – and notoriety – by a nineteenth-century New Yorker named Jacob Housman. After stealing one of his father's ships, Houseman sailed to Key West looking for a piece of the lucrative wrecking (or salvaging) business. Ostracized by the close-knit Key West community, he retreated to Indian Key, which he bought as a base for his own wrecking operation in 1831. In the first year, Housman made $30,000 and furnished the eleven-acre island with streets, a store, warehouses, a hotel, more than two dozen homes and a population of around fifty. However, much of his income was not honestly gained; he was frequently accused of deliberately running ships aground on the reef using misleading lanterns on the island's shore, and eventually lost his license for salvaging in 1838. That same year, Housman sold Indian Key to plant-mad doctor Henry Perrine, who had been cultivating species in the Keys with an eye to their commercial potential (one of his abortive schemes centered on growing mulberry trees to kick-start a silk industry). Perrine's plans were thwarted after the Seminoles launched a midnight attack in August 1840, burning every building to the ground and ending the island's habitation. Eighteen people died in the raid; Housman was lucky, surviving by hiding in the water behind his cottage, but Perrine was discovered in the cupola of his house, hacked to death. The doctor's plants still thrive today, though, and the island is now choked with agave cacti, as well as sisal, coffee, tea, and mango plants. The trip here is well worth it for the **ruins**, which are an evocative, if crumbling, reminder of early settler life in the Keys – especially the grassy paddock that was once the town square – and the observation tower's spectacular views across the island's lush and jumbled foliage. Look, too, for **Housman's grave** – his body was brought here after he died working on a wreck off Key West.

Lignumvitae Key Botanical State Park

By the time you finish the one-hour tour (see p.131) of **Lignumvitae Key Botanical State Park** (Thurs–Mon 9am–5pm) you'll know a strangler fig from a gumbo limbo and be able to recognize many more of the hundred or so species of tropical trees in this two-hundred-acre hammock. The key is named after the lignumvitae tree (Latin for "wood of life") that's common here and whose extraordinary wood has been prized for centuries – denser and tougher than iron, it's almost impossible to wear out and has been used for everything from ship hulls to false teeth. The trail through the forest was laid out by wealthy Miamian **W.J. Matheson**, who made millions supplying mustard gas to the government during World War I, and purchased the island for only $1 in 1919. The **limestone house** he built that year is the island's only sign of habitation and shows the deprivations of early island living, even for the well-off; the house actually blew away in the 1935 hurricane, but was found and brought back.

Lignumvitae Key is considered the best remaining example of Florida Keys tropical hammock (oddly, thanks to its location in the Gulf of Mexico and thick forest of trees, the temperature here is usually at least 10 degrees cooler than on the main islands). The island is ravaged by mosquitoes, so make sure to bring long-sleeved shirts, long pants, plus plenty of repellent.

Long Key State Park

You can spot many of the tree species found on Lignumvitae Key at **Long Key State Park**, MM67.5-Oceanside (daily 8am–sunset; $3.50 per car and driver, plus $2.50 for first passenger, 50¢ for each additional passenger, pedestrians and cyclists $1.50; ☎305/664-4815, ⓦwww.floridastateparks.org). There's a nature trail that takes you along the beach and on a boardwalk over a mangrove-lined lagoon or, better still, you can rent a canoe ($5 per hr, $10 per day) and follow the simple **canoe trail** through the tidal lagoons in the company of mildly curious wading birds. **Camping** in the park costs $31.49 for sites with showers and electricity (☎1-800/326-3521, ⓦwww.reserveamerica.com), or $6 (one person) and $11 (2 people) for primitive sites (☎305/664-4815).

Eating and drinking

Provided you avoid the obvious tourist traps, you can **eat** well and fairly cheaply in Islamorada. When it comes to **nightlife**, many people get no further than the huge *Tiki Bar* at *Holiday Isle Beach Resort* (MM84.5-Oceanside), which throbs most nights to the sound of insipid rock and pop bands; it also claims to have invented the rumrunner, a mind-bending concoction of Bacardi, banana, black-berry brandy and lime juice.

Hungry Tarpon MM77.5-Bayside ☏305/664-0535, ⓦ www.hungrytarpon .com. This converted 1940s bait shop is tucked away in Robbie's Marina – watch for it by the bridge at the north end of the key. Open daily 6.30am–3pm, it serves killer breakfasts like burritos (from $7), French toast ($6), and huge pancakes ($6), all dished up with piles of crispy hash browns. Ask for a table out back on the wooden jetty. Sometimes closes late Aug to early Oct.

Islamorada Fish Company MM81.5-Bayside ☏305/664-9271 or 1-800/258-2559, ⓦ www .islamoradafishcompany.com. An excellent-value seafood dinner spot which exports its fresh local catch all over the world. Despite a constant full house (try to get here before 6pm), the staff is particularly friendly. Try the coconut fried shrimp ($8.95) or Islamorada fish sandwich ($12.95). You can also sip a whisky and suck on a stogie upstairs at the Zane Grey cigar lounge. The adjacent fresh fish market is open Mon–Thurs 9am–7pm, and Fri & Sat 9am–8pm.

Islamorada Restaurant & Bakery MM81.6-Bayside ☏305/664-8363, ⓦ www .bobsbunz.com. Known locally as *Bob's Bunz* and famous for its gooey cinnamon buns, this homey bakery opens at 6am for early risers (it closes at 2pm) and usually fills with families; there are some plastic tables inside if you want to linger, as well as a few picnic tables outside on shaded porch.

Little Italy Restaurant MM68.5-Bayside ☏305/664-4472. One of the few places open for breakfast, lunch, and dinner, this Italian–American joint wouldn't be out of place on Mulberry St. Most of the hearty mains hover under $17: try the veal *piccata* or the hefty serving of sausage and peppers.

Lorelei MM81.9-Bayside ☏305/664-4656, ⓦ www.loreleifloridakeys.com. Investigate the nightly drink specials at this popular waterfront bar, where sunset celebrations reel in the crowds. They also have a large beachside eating area, where you can eat breakfast, lunch, and dinner; try the cracked conch sandwich ($10.95) or yellowtail snapper ($21.95).

Morada Bay Beach Café MM81.6-Bayside ☏305/664-0604, ⓦ www.moradabay -restaurant.com. Perfect choice for a splurge or romantic dinner on the beach, with fire-lit tiki huts and mesmerizing sunsets. Everything on the seafood-heavy menu is top-notch, but the grouper cerviche ($12) and chunky home-made coconut sorbet ($7) are standouts. Entrées $24–33.

Whale Harbor MM83.5-Oceanside ☏305/664-4959, ⓦ www.wahoosbarandgrill.com. No-nonsense café, just before the bridge to Windley Key, that draws crowds of devil-may-care gluttons to its massive seafood buffets, Mon–Fri after 4pm, Sat after 2pm and Sun after noon ($25.95–28.95). Grab a sunset cocktail at next door *Wahoo's Bar & Grill*, overlooking the marina.

Woody's MM82-Bayside ☏305/664-4335. For raunchy blues and boozing, visit this much less touristy bar-cum-strip joint, right on the side of US-1, which picks up steam after 11pm. Comedians occasionally sub for the strippers. Closed Sun–Mon.

The Middle Keys

The Long Key Bridge (alongside the old Long Key Viaduct) points south from Long Key and leads to the **Middle Keys**, which stretch from Duck Key to Pigeon Key. The largest of these islands is Key Vaca – once a shantytown of railway workers – which holds the area's major settlement, **MARATHON**, an appealingly blue-collar town said to be named for the back-breaking shifts that workers endured as they raced to finish the Seven Mile Bridge (see p.136).

Middle Keys information

For information on the Middle Keys area and accommodation, head to the **Marathon Chamber of Commerce** at MM53.5-Bayside (daily 9am–5pm; ☏305/743-5417 or 1-800/262-7284, ⓦ www.floridakeysmarathon.com).

Marathon

If you didn't get your fill of tropical trees at Lignumvitae Key (see p.132), turn right at MM50.5-Bayside (opposite the K-Mart), for the 63 steamy acres of subtropical forest at **Crane Point** (Mon–Sat 9am–5pm, Sun noon–5pm; $8; ⊤305/743-9100, ⑩www.cranepoint.net).

At the entrance, the park's excellent **Museum of Natural History of the Florida Keys** offers a thought-provoking rundown of the area's history – starting with the Calusa Indians (who had a settlement on this site until they were wiped out by disease brought by European settlers in the 1700s) and continuing with the story of early Bahamian and American settlers. A large section of the museum features interactive displays designed to introduce kids to the wonders of the Keys' subtropical ecosystems, including the hardwood hammocks and reefs. Much the same ground is covered at the adjoining **Children's Activity Center**, which houses touch tanks crammed with marine life and a small replica of a seventeenth-century galleon.

A free booklet gives details of the hardwood trees you'll find along the 1.5-mile **nature trail from here**; half way along you'll pass **Adderley House**, built in 1903 by Bahamian immigrants and giving a vivid impression of what life was like for them, with its simple construction and bare-bones amenities. Towards the end of the trail, near the coast, the **Wild Bird Center** rehabilitates injured birds – you may see terns, gulls and even ospreys here.

If you have more leisurely activities in mind, spend the day at **Sombrero Beach** (daily 7.30am–dusk; free parking). Follow the signs for Sombrero Beach Road or Marathon High School, turning off the Overseas Highway near

---

Snorkeling, diving, and fishing

The choice locale for the pursuits of **snorkeling** and **scuba diving** is around **Sombrero Reef**, marked by a 142-foot-high nineteenth-century lighthouse, whose nooks and crannies provide a safe haven for thousands of darting, brightly colored tropical fish. The best time to go out is early evening when the reef is most active, since the majority of its creatures are nocturnal. The pick of local dive shops is Hall's Diving and Snorkeling Center (⊤305/743-5929 or 1-800/331-4255, ⑩www.hallsdiving.com), at MM48.5-Bayside. Day-long introductory diving courses cost $175 (minimum 2 people), while night diving, wreck diving, and instructor's certificate courses are available to the experienced. Once certified, you can rent equipment and join a dive trip ($105 for two 1hr dives, including equipment). Spirit Snorkeling at MM47.5-Bayside (⊤305/289-0614, ⑩www.spiritsnorkeling.net) runs a modern catamaran out to the reef for its popular daily snorkeling trips (9am & 1pm; $30).

Around Marathon, **spearfishing** is permitted a mile offshore (there's a three-mile limit elsewhere), and the town hosts four major **fishing tournaments** each year: tarpon (May), dolphin fish (May/June), bonefish (Oct) and sailfish (Dec–Jan). Entering costs several hundred dollars and only the very top anglers participate, but if you feel inspired to put to sea yourself, wander along one of the marinas and ask about chartering a boat. Boats take up to six people and charge between $600 and $1000 for a full day's fishing (7am–4pm), including bait and equipment. If you can't get a group together, join one of the countless group boats for about $60 per person for a full day – remember, though, it's easier to catch fish with fewer people aboard. Reliable options for **fishing charters** include Tina Brown (⊤305/942-3806, ⑥tina824us@yahoo.com), who is a good choice for novices, and Captain Pip's Marina at MM47.5-Bayside (⊤305/743-4403, ⑩www.captainpips.com), home to several highly experienced fishing captains and guides ($875–925 per day).

K Mart Plaza, MM50-Oceanside (opposite Crane Point): a couple of miles along Sombrero Beach Road there's a slender, well-kept strip of sand, with full facilities including showers, a kids' playground, volleyball net, and picnic tables, plus a bit of shade from lush palms.

Not far from Crane Point, the **Turtle Hospital** at MM48.5-Bayside (tours daily 10am, 1pm, & 4pm; $15; ☎305/743-2552, ⓦwww.turtlehospital.org) mounts often heart-breaking efforts to save injured or sick turtles picked up all over the Caribbean; boat hits, oil spills and a virus that causes crippling tumors are typical problems. The guided tour includes a look at the turtle rehabilitation area, a short slide show, and a chance to feed some of the loveable permanent residents.

Just east of Marathon is the **Dolphin Research Center**, MM59-Bayside (daily 9am–5pm; ☎305/289-1121, ⓦwww.dolphins.org), which offers dolphin encounters – for details, see box, p.123.

Accommodation

Anchor Inn MM51.3-Oceanside ☎305/743-2213, ⓦwww.anchorinnkeys.com. The seven blue and white rooms at this delightful nautically themed budget motel vary in size and amenities: if you want to cook, ask for rooms 3, 6 or 7, each of which has a full kitchenette (the others have just microwaves and fridges). There's a BBQ grill for guests, as well as an onsite laundry. **❸**

Banana Bay MM49.5-Bayside ☎305/743-3500 or 1-800/226-2621, ⓦwww.bananabay.com. This beachside resort is set back from the road amid a dense forest of tropical greenery. The rooms may be a little forlorn (old but clean bedspread, rather rickety furniture) but the fantastic facilities more than make up: there's a private beach, onsite boat rentals, freshwater swimming pool with the requisite tiki spot plus another bar on the ocean where you can catch the sunsets over a cocktail or two. **❻**

Curry Hammock State Park MM56-Oceanside ☎305/289-2690, ⓦwww.floridastateparks.org. This campground is made up of a group of small islands centering on Little Crawl Key and has picnic tables, grills, and showers. Pitches are $13.49 (ⓦwww.reserveamerica.com for pitch reservations).

Flamingo Inn MM59.3-Bayside ☎305/289-1478 or 1-800/439-1478, ⓦwww.theflamingoinn.com.

Brightly painted in greens and pinks, this lovingly maintained retro motel is a terrific value for the location: the big beds are very comfortable and all the spotless rooms come with free wi-fi, while the two-room suites have kitchenettes. Rates are a steal Sept–Dec. **❹**

The Hammocks at Marathon MM48-Bayside ☎305/743-9009, ⓦwww.bluegreenrentals.com. This upmarket, family-friendly resort is set within lush, landscaped gardens with palm trees, hammocks and tiki torches right on the water. Rooms range from cozy studios to spacious two-room suites with kitchens and sea views. **❼**

Knights Key Campground MM47-Oceanside ☎305/743-4343 or 1-800/348-2267, ⓦwww.keysdirectory.com/knightskeycampground. This campground permits you to pitch a tent (many around Marathon are designed for RVs and trailers only) for $35–65.

🏃 **Sea Dell** MM49.8-Bayside ☎305/743-5161 or 1-800/648-3854, ⓦwww.seadellmotel.com. The bright white and turquoise rooms are simply furnished but spotlessly clean, making this one of the best budget options in the Keys. It's also well located for local nightlife and has a freshwater heated pool. **❺**

Eating

Marathon will definitely be your base for **eating** in this stretch of the Middle Keys. It does go to sleep early, though; for nightlife, you're best joining the standard locals' pub crawl starting at the *Hurricane Grille* (see p.136). All the places below can be found on Key Vaca.

🏃 **Castaway** 1406 Oceanview Ave, off 15th St, at MM47.5-Oceanside ☎305/743-6247. No-nonsense local restaurant with several different dining areas: a screened-in porch overlooking the water, a cozy lounge, and a casual café facing the jetty that doubles as a buzzy bar in the evenings.

The restaurant is best known for its plates of peel-it-yourself beer-steamed shrimp ($19.95, second plate free); every dinner includes a visit to the huge salad bar and a basket of hot, honey-drenched donut-style buns. Closes Sun & Mon in the off season.

ChikiTiki Bar & Grille 1200 Oceanview Ave, at MM47.5-Oceanside ⓣ305/743-9204. Large, thatched-roof bar-restaurant on the waterfront (part of Burdines Marina), with terrific views from the outdoor lounge on the second floor. To reach it, turn towards the ocean down 15th St from US-1 (you'll pass *Castaway*). The food is Mex-inflected American, like a green chili cheeseburger and taco salad, but they also do fried Key lime pie (seriously); most dishes are under $10.

The Hurricane Grille MM49.5-Bayside ⓣ305/743-2220, ⓦwww.thehurricanegrille.com. Classic roadside American bar with nightly live music on a small stage in the back. This is an early stop on the nightly pub crawl that concludes around 4am in the *Brass Monkey*, MM50-Oceanside in nearby K-Mart Plaza (ⓣ305/743-4028).

Leigh Ann's Coffee House MM51-Oceanside ⓣ305/743-2001, ⓦwww.leighannscoffeehouse.com. Look for the weatherbeaten pink tea cup sign to spot this café, housed in an old pioneer house. You'll find gourmet cakes and coffee (by the cup, or take-home beans by the pound) as well as classic breakfast food like biscuit and sausage gravy ($6.95), sandwiches like a BLT ($7.95) and chicken pot pie ($8.95). You can even order a few wines by the glass, mostly $6.95. Closed Sun.

Porky's Bayside MM47.5-Bayside ⓣ305/289-2065. This thatched shack by the marina serves inexpensive if average food – the BBQ baskets ($9–15) are among the better options. Notable for being one of the few cheap options in the area; the all-you-can-eat ribs (Tues and Wed; $16.75) and catfish nights (Thurs; $15.25) are especially good value, and you should also try the fried Key lime pie ($5.75).

The Seven Mile Grill MM47.5-Bayside ⓣ305/743-4481. It may not look like much – the decoration's limited to some old beer cans and pictures of fans in Seven Mile Grill T-shirts in front of world landmarks – but locals flock here for fine conch chowders ($6.95) and shrimp steamed in beer ($13.50), not to mention the silky Key lime pie, said to be the best outside Key West ($4.75). The home-made peanut butter pie is nearly as addictive. Open from 7am, closes 9pm winter, 7pm summer.

Taino's MM53-Oceanside, at 114th St ⓣ305/743-5247. Good Cuban food at reasonable prices. Though the decor's nothing to rave over, the food's cheap, filling, and authentic; try any of the fresh fish dishes, or a quick cubano sandwich for $6.95. Lunch and dinner only, closed Sun.

The Seven Mile Bridge and Pigeon Key

In 1905, Henry Flagler, whose railway opened up Florida's east coast (see Contexts, p.465), undertook the extension of its tracks to Key West. The Overseas Railroad, as it became known (though many called it "Flagler's folly"), was a monumental task that took seven years to complete and was marked by the appalling treatment of the railworkers.

Bridging the Middle Keys gave Flagler's engineers some of their biggest headaches. North of Marathon, the two-mile-long Long Key Viaduct, a still-elegant structure of nearly two hundred individually cast arches, was Flagler's personal favorite and was widely pictured in advertising campaigns. Yet a greater technical accomplishment was the **Seven Mile Bridge** (built from 1908 to 1912) to the south, linking Marathon to the Lower Keys. At one point, every US-flagged freighter on the Atlantic was hired to bring in materials – including German concrete impervious to salt water seepage – while floating cranes, dredges, and scores of other craft set about a job that eventually cost the lives of 700 laborers. When the trains eventually started rolling, passengers were treated to an incredible panorama: a broad sweep of sea and sky, sometimes streaked by luscious red sunsets or darkened by storm clouds.

The Flagler bridges were strong enough to withstand everything the Keys' volatile weather could throw at them, except for the calamitous 1935 Labor Day hurricane, which tore up the railway. The bridges were subsequently adapted to accommodate a road: the original Overseas Highway. Tales of hair-raising bridge crossings (the road was only 22 feet wide), endless tailbacks as the drawbridges jammed – and the roadside parties that ensued – are part of

Keys folklore. The later bridges, such as the $45-million new **Seven Mile Bridge** between Key Vaca and Bahia Honda Key that opened in the early 1980s, certainly improved traffic flow but also ended the mystique of traveling the old road.

The old bridge, intact but for the mid-sectional cuts to prevent access, now makes extraordinarily long fishing piers and jogging strips. A section of the former Seven Mile Bridge also provides the only land access to **Pigeon Key**, which served as a railway work camp from 1908 to 1912, and later as home to a small village of workers maintaining the bridges till 1982. Today its primary function is to host school science trips, but its seven original wooden buildings have been restored and opened to visitors as **Historic Pigeon Key** (daily 9am–5pm, last ferry at 4pm; $11; ☎305/743-5999, ⓦwww.pigeonkey.net), whose small **museum** reveals the hardships routinely suffered by the workers. It's also one of the few places you can study the original bridge up close; the rail bridge was unnervingly slim, before being widened slightly in 1938 to allow cars to pass.

Private cars are banned from Pigeon Key, and in any case the bridge to the island will be closed to all vehicles (for renovation) till at least the end of 2010; until then it's safe to walk or cycle the 2.2 miles to the island. Visitors can also take a **ferry**, which is included in the entry price. Ferries are met by enthusiastic volunteers who give illuminating tours of the island (up to 1hr). Afterwards, you're welcome to hang out all day on the island (**snorkeling** around the piers is good in winter and spring). You might also consider walking back; giant stingrays and sharks are often easy to spot from the bridge.

Ferries depart at 10am, 11.30am, 1pm, and 2.30pm from the **visitor center** (daily 9.30am–2.30pm) on Knight's Key at MM47-Oceanside, a converted 1915 dining car that once plied the railway to Key West. Ferries usually make the return trip thirty minutes later, with a final departure at 4pm. Note that even if you walk or cycle both ways, you must still pay the entrance fee at the visitor center before heading out. If you like the idea of **spending the night** on the island, the Pigeon Key Foundation (☎305/289-0025) rents one of the buildings – bedding included – for $1000 a night (it can sleep up to 12 people).

The Lower Keys

Starkly different from their northerly neighbors, the **LOWER KEYS** are quiet, heavily wooded, and predominantly residential. Unlike the Upper and Middle Keys, they are aligned north–south rather than east–west, and rest on a base of limestone, not coral reef. These islands have flora and fauna that are very much their own; species like the Key deer, the Lower Keys cotton rat, and the Cudjoe Key rice rat – all of which are endangered – live here, though mainly tucked away miles from the Overseas Highway. Most visitors speed through the area on the way to Key West, just forty miles further on, but the area's lack of rampant tourism and easily found seclusion make this a good place to linger for a day or two.

Bahia Honda State Park

While not officially part of the Lower Keys, the first place of consequence you'll hit after crossing the Seven Mile Bridge is the 300-acre **Bahia Honda State Park**, MM37-Oceanside (daily 8am–sunset; $3.50 per car and driver, plus $2.50 for first passenger, 50¢ for each additional passenger, pedestrians and cyclists $1.50; ☎305/872-2353, ⓦwww.bahiahondapark.com), boasting the Keys' best **beaches** and inviting, two-tone ocean waters. Turn left after the park entrance for delightful **Sandspur Beach**, which has scattered plants growing in the sand and all the usual amenities; while here, take a ramble on the **nature trail**, which loops from the shoreline through a hammock of silver palms, geiger, and yellow satinwood trees, passing rare plants, such as dwarf morning glory and spiny catesbaea. Keep a lookout for white-crowned pigeons, great white herons, roseate spoonbills, and giant ospreys (whose bulky nests are plentiful throughout the Lower Keys, often atop telegraph poles). Of the ranger-run programs offered every day, the nature **walk** every Tuesday at 11am is by far the best, but it's all pleasant enough without a guide.

Calusa Beach at the park's western tip, near the marina and concession, is more family friendly, with plenty of shady pavilions, though the ripe ocean smells and sea grass debris may be off-putting to some. Far more appealing (but with little shade), **Loggerhead Beach** faces the ocean on the other side of the concession, a gloriously isolated strip of golden sand. The waters here are good for swimming, as well as for snorkeling, diving, and especially windsurfing – rent equipment from the marina concession. You'll see small spotted eagle rays frolicking in the thick seagrass beds here, large jackfish and the occasional nurse shark.

Near the beach a path leads from the road through the undergrowth toward the two-story **Old Bahia Honda Bridge**, where you can gaze down on huge stingrays gliding through the channel. The unusually deep waters here (Bahia Honda is Spanish for "deep bay") made this the toughest of the old railway bridges to construct, and widening it for the road proved impossible; the solution was to put the highway on a higher tier. Nearby, the tiny **Sun and Sea Nature Center** at the end of the main parking lot (Thurs–Mon 9am–5pm) has displays on the local flora and fauna.

Facilities in the park include a campground and cabins, a snack bar, and a concession offering **snorkeling** trips (daily 9.30am and 1.30pm; $29.95, full equipment rental $12; ☎305/872-3210) twelve miles out to the **Looe Key Marine Sanctuary** (see p.140), and **kayak** rental ($10 per hr, $30 per half day).

Big Pine Key and around

The eponymous trees on **Big Pine Key** are less of a draw than its **Key deer**, delightfully tame creatures that enjoy the freedom of the island; don't feed them (it's illegal and will cost you $250 in fines), and be cautious when driving – signs alongside the road state the number of road-kills to date during the year. The

▲ No Name Pub

animals are a relatively small species related to white-tailed deer and arrived long ago when the Keys were still joined to the mainland. For many years, sailors and Key West residents hunted them but this and the destruction of their natural habitat led to near extinction by the late 1940s. The **National Key Deer Refuge**, set up here in 1957 to safeguard the animals and their population, has now grown to around 800, thanks to rigorous preservation tactics including specially excavated tunnels beneath the roads so that the deer can cross in safety.

Pick up information on the deer (and maps showing where to see them) from the **refuge headquarters** (Mon–Fri 8am–5pm, park open daily sunrise–sunset; ☎305/872-2239, Ⓦnationalkeydeer.fws.gov), tucked away in the Big Pine Key Shopping Plaza off Key Deer Boulevard, just north of US-1 at MM30 (call ahead, as lack of volunteers can mean shorter hours). To see the creatures, drive to the end of Key Deer Boulevard or turn east onto No Name Key. You should spot a few; the best time is at sunrise or sunset, when the deer come out to forage. Also on Key Deer Boulevard, the **Blue Hole** is a freshwater lake with a healthy population of soft-shelled turtles and several alligators, which now and then emerge from the cool depths to sunbathe – parts of the lakeside path may be closed if they have staked out a patch for the day. Should the alligators get your adrenalin pumping, take a calming stroll along two **nature trails** a quarter of a mile to the north: The Watson Trail (0.6 miles) cuts through the tropical hardwood hammock, while the Mannillo Trail (800ft) is wheelchair accessible and takes in pine rocklands and a freshwater wetland slough.

Further east, the rollicking **No Name Pub** (☎305/872-9115, Ⓦwww .nonamepub.com) is well worth the circuitous detour for a sight of the rather unusual wallpaper: dollar bills covering every inch of wall and ceiling inside, worth some $60,000 by the owners' account. If you fancy adding a bill or two, just ask the staff for the house staple gun. Built in 1936, the premises served time as a general store, brothel and fishing shop before opening as a restaurant and pub in the 1950s (see p.142 for review). To find the pub, head north along Key

Deer Boulevard to Watson Boulevard and turn right; follow this curving road for two miles through a residential neighborhood until the pub appears on the left. The pub lies just before the bridge leading to **No Name Key**, home to a few settlers living off solar power and septic tanks, but better known as the staging ground for the Bay of Pigs invasion (see p.87).

The rest of the Lower Keys

An even more peaceful atmosphere prevails on the Lower Keys south of Big Pine Key, despite the efforts of property developers. **The Torch Keys**, so-named for their forests of torchwood – used for kindling by early settlers, since it burns even when green – can be swiftly bypassed on the way to **Ramrod Key**, where you can access Looe Key Marine Sanctuary and the offshore coral reef (see below).

Looe Key Marine Sanctuary

Keen underwater explorers should head for **Looe Key Marine Sanctuary**, named after HMS *Looe*, a British frigate that sank here in 1744. This five-square-mile area of protected crystal-clear waters and reef formations creates an unforgettable spectacle: showy elkhorn and star coral, as well as rays, octopus, and a multitude of gaily colored fish flit between tall coral pillars. The water, which ranges 8 to 35 feet deep, will appeal to novice and experienced snorkelers alike, but anyone wanting to catch sight of the HMS *Looe* will be disappointed as it has long since disintegrated.

The **Florida Keys National Marine Sanctuary office** in Key West (33 East Quay Rd, Mon–Fri 8am–5pm; ☎305/809-4700, ⓦwww.fknms.nos.noaa .gov) offers basic information (you should also pop in to the Florida Keys Eco-Discovery Center, p.154), but you can only visit the reef on a trip organized by one of the many diving shops throughout the Keys; the nearest to the reef is the **Looe Key Dive Center** (☎305/872-2215 or 1-800/942-5397, ⓦwww .diveflakeys.com), MM27.5-Oceanside (on **Ramrod Key**), which offers daily five-hour trips (10am–3pm) for snorkeling ($40) and diving (three dives; $80). You can also visit the sanctuary from the Bahia Honda State Park (see p.138).

If you're here around the second Saturday in July, you may want to don your flippers and check out the annual **Lower Keys Underwater Music Festival**. The music is broadcast via special speakers suspended beneath boats positioned above the reef, and there's quite a carnival atmosphere, with most of the divers dressing up before they go down. There's no actual charge, though you'll have to pay for the boat and diving equipment at the sanctuary office. For more info call ☎305/872-9100 or check ⓦwww.us1radio.com.

Perky's Bat Tower

On Sugarloaf Key, eleven miles west of Ramrod Key, the 35-foot **Perky's Bat Tower** stands as testimony to one man's misguided belief in the mosquito- killing powers of bats. A get-rich-quick book of the 1920s, *Bats, Mosquitoes, and Dollars*, led Richter C. Perky, a property speculator who had recently purchased the island, into thinking bats would be the solution to the Keys' mosquito problem. With much hullabaloo, he erected this brown cypress lath tower in 1929 and dutifully sent away for the costly "bat bait," which he was told would lure an army of bats to the tower. It didn't work:

no bat ever showed up, the mosquitoes stayed healthy, and Perky went bust soon after (in fact, if he'd imported the bats himself, it might have worked as a single bat will eat its own weight in insects each night). The background story is far more interesting than the actual tower, but if the tale tickles your fancy, drive down the narrow road between the air strip and the sprawling *Sugarloaf Lodge*, at MM17-Bayside.

Accommodation

Accommodation options here are more limited than further north in the Keys, and many of the motels are pricey for the few amenities they offer; below are some smart exceptions.

The Barnacle 1557 Long Beach Drive, Big Pine Key, MM33-Oceanside ☎305/872-3298 or 1-800/465-9100, ⓦwww.thebarnacle.net. This B&B is one of the standout spots in the Keys. At the end of Long Beach Drive you'll find a glorious modernist house featuring four bright blue, waterfront rooms with fridges, queen beds, TVs and private bathrooms. ❻

Big Pine Key Fishing Lodge MM33-Oceanside ☎305/872-2351. One of the best choices for budget camping, with sites from $39–55. Offers full hook-ups, heated pool, convenience store, and great access for fishing and diving.

Little Palm Island MM28.5-Oceanside, off Little Torch Key ☎305/872-2524 or 1-800/343-8567, ⓦwww.littlepalmisland.com. The thirty thatched cottages – each with its own outdoor bamboo shower – are the ultimate splurge, set in lush gardens a few feet from the beach on an idyllic private islet. It also has a fantastic – though expensive – fish restaurant, often rated by critics as the best in the Keys. No children allowed. ❾

Looe Key Reef Resort MM27.5-Oceanside, Ramrod Key ☎305/872-2215 or 1-800/942-5397,

ⓦwww.diveflakeys.com. Especially convenient for visiting the marine sanctuary: the rooms smell rather strongly of air freshener and the decor is early 1980s but this super clean, two-story motel offers terrific value for its location. Guests also have access to free kayak and snorkel gear. ❹

Parmer's Resort 565 Barry Ave, Little Torch Key, off US-1 at MM28.5-Bayside ☎305/872-2157, ⓦwww.parmersplace.com. This friendly resort offers a range of good-value options, from standard motel rooms (❻) to one- or two-bedroom apartments with kitchens (from ❼). Made up of a complex of buildings set in lush, green gardens, it has an old Keys vibe, thanks to its tropical bedspreads and the flock of tame parrots living and squawking here all day. There's an onsite coin-operated laundry and free breakfast – it's worth paying extra for a room with a veranda.

Sugar Loaf Key KOA MM20-Oceanside ☎305/745-3549 or 1-800/562-7731, ⓦwww.koa.com. This leafy campground is tucked away down a long winding road and has ample facilities including plenty of picnic tables for eating alfresco. Tent sites are $60 in high season, without hook-ups.

Eating and drinking

You'll find a few good **eating** options here, especially around the settlement on Big Pine Key. But as the Lower Keys increasingly serve as a bedroom community for Key West, the liveliness is waning and people prefer to drive into the town for dinner. It's the same with nightlife; locals who want to live it up head for Key West. Otherwise, try the *No Name Pub* or the *Looe Key Reef Resort* (see above) for weekend **drinking**.

Baby's Coffee MM15-Oceanside ☎1-800/523-2326, ⓦwww.babyscoffee.com. Unbeatable, warehouse-like coffee shop, serving six delicious home-roasted blends ($1 a cup) as well as gourmet cakes, Key lime pie and chocolates; they also sell T-shirts, and even wine by the bottle and you can buy house blends by the pound to take home (a great Keys souvenir). Mon–Fri 7am–6pm, Sat 7am–5pm, Sun 8am–5pm.

Big Pine Restaurant & Coffee Shop MM30-Bayside ☎305/872-2790. A dark locals' joint where you can sit at wooden tables with Lalique-style chandeliers and gorge on specials like crab salad crammed into a pitta bread ($9.95) or peppery shrimp ($15.95) and fried scallops ($16.95); despite the hype, the ribs are also genuinely good (from $13.95). Closed Mon.

Bobalu's Southern Café MM10-Bayside ☎ 305/296-1664. A brightly painted café that makes for a terrific pre-Key West pit stop for hearty soul food at lunch or dinner, though it also does some of the best pizzas (from $13) in the Keys – New Haven style (with a thin, bitter crust), thanks to the Connecticut owners. Otherwise sample specials like a fried conch sandwich ($10) or fried green tomatoes ($3.95) along with belly-busting sides like sweet potato casserole ($1.50). Closed Sun & Mon. Cash only.

The Cracked Egg Café MM31-Bayside ☎ 305/872-7030. Head to the small, yellow, homey café in the parking lot of the *Big Pine Motel* for its bargain breakfasts; a hefty ham and eggs for $5.95, slabs of French toast or waffles for $4.50, and even chocolate chip pancakes for $2.95. Daily 6am–2pm.

Mangrove Mama's MM20-Bayside ☎ 305/745-3030. Stop here for the rustic, ramshackle atmosphere, great seafood (try the catch of the day baked with almonds or the conch fritters), and home-baked bread. Go for the fish or conch sandwiches at lunch ($9.50). Usually closed Sept.

No Name Pub N Watson Blvd, Big Pine Key ☎ 305/872-9115, ⓦ www.nonamepub .com. In addition to its oddball dollar-bill "wallpaper", it's also worth ducking in to the oldest pub in the Keys for their knockout thin-crust "gourmet" pizzas for $17–20, like the delicate, spicy Caribbean Chicken or the Mexican, loaded down with chili, cheddar cheese, sour cream, and salsa. Beer drinkers should enjoy the No Name Pub Amber ($2.50).

Key West

Closer to Cuba than mainland Florida, **KEY WEST** often seems very far removed from the rest of the US. Famed for their tolerant attitudes and laid-back lifestyles, its 30,000 islanders seem adrift in a great expanse of sea and sky. Despite the million tourists who arrive each year, the place resonates with an anarchic and individualist spirit that hits you the instant you arrive. Long-term residents here are known as Conchs (pronounced "konk"), named after the giant sea snails eaten by early settlers, and ride bicycles, shoot the breeze on street corners, and smile at complete strangers.

Yet as wild as it may at first appear, Key West today is far from being the misfits' paradise it once was. Much of the sleaziness has been brushed away through rather cutesy restoration and revitalization – it takes a lot of money to buy a house here now – paving the way for a sizeable vacation industry that at times seems to revolve around party boats and heavy drinking. Not that Key West is near to losing its special identity. The liberal attitudes have attracted a large influx of gay people, estimated at two in five of the population, who take an essential role in running the place and sink thousands of dollars into its future.

For many tourists a trip to Key West boils down to just two things: **fishing**, and its notoriously bacchanalian **nightlife**. There's much more to the town than that; while Key West's knack for tourism can be gaudy, it's quite easy to bypass the commercial traps and discover an island as unique for its present-day society as for its remarkable past.

The tourist epicenter is on **Duval Street**, whose northern end is marked by **Mallory Square**, a historic landmark now home to a brash chain of bars that entirely ignores the whimsical, freethinking spirit of the island. But just a few steps east of here is the historic section, a network of streets teeming with rich foliage and brilliant blooms draped over curious architecture. This area boasts many of the best guesthouses and lots of restaurants and wacky galleries, while to the west lies **Bahama Village**, a neighborhood of dusty lanes where cockerels wander and birds screech into the night.

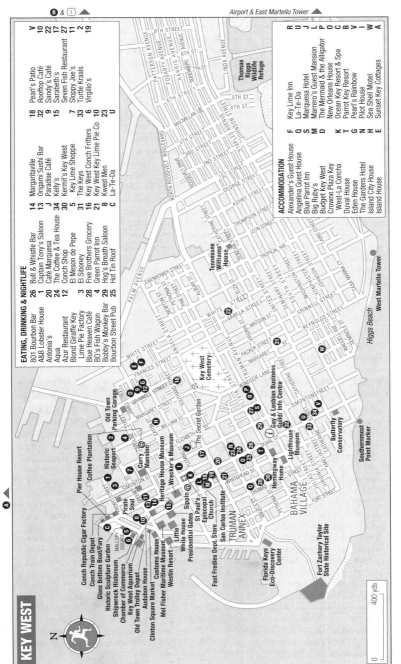

Some history

Piracy was the main activity around Key West (known in Spanish as Cayo Hueso), before Florida joined the US and the navy established a base here in 1823. This cleared the way for a substantial **wrecking industry**. Millions of dollars were earned by lifting people and cargo off shipwrecks along the Florida reef, and by the 1850s Key West was the wealthiest (per capita) city in the US. Key West also played a crucial role in the Civil War, as, along with Fort Jefferson (see p.164), it was a Union port while the rest of Florida hewed to the Confederacy. Its decision to side with the North wasn't wholly voluntary – Key West port was being blockaded into submission, since the Union wanted to be able to liquidate the Confederate ships it captured at Key West's lucrative wreckers' auctions.

The building of reef lighthouses sounded the death knell for the wrecking business by the end of the nineteenth century, but Key West continued to prosper even so. Many **Cubans** arrived bringing **cigar-making** skills, and migrant **Greeks** established a lucrative **sponge** enterprise. Industrial unrest and a sponge-blight drove these businesses north to Tampa and Tarpon Springs and left Key West ill-prepared to face the **Depression**. Diehard Conchs, living on fish and coconuts, defied any suggestion they move to the mainland, but by the summer of 1934 they were finally driven into bankruptcy. Under Franklin Roosevelt's New Deal, Key West was tidied up and readied for tourism, yet the 1935 Labor Day hurricane blew away the Flagler railway – Key West's only land link to the outside world. Luckily, the bridges were used for the construction of the Overseas Highway, which opened in 1938.

An injection of naval dollars during World War II eventually saved Key West by providing the backbone for its economy, while **tourists** started arriving in force during the 1980s, just as a taste for independence was rising among the locals and a strange chain of events led to the formation of the "**Conch Republic**".

The Conch Republic

The story behind Key West's nickname, the "**Conch Republic**," offers a telling example of the town's political savvy and its sense of humor. In April 1982, the US Border Patrol set up a roadblock on US Highway 1 at the **Last Chance Saloon** in Florida City, ostensibly to prevent illegal aliens from entering the US mainland; while local residents were suspected of smuggling Cuban refugees, drugs were also thought to be a target. The roadblock effectively cut off the Florida Keys at the confluence of the only two roads out to the mainland, leading to seventeen-mile tailbacks and a sudden, sharp decline in tourist numbers – as well as causing massive disruption to basic services. The mayor of Key West (with the backing of other community leaders), after failing to remove the checkpoint through legal means, formed the "Conch Republic" and **seceded from the US** in Mallory Square on April 23 – and declared war on Washington for good measure. The first "shots" fired were of stale Cuban bread broken over the head of a man dressed in an admiral's uniform – though some claim there were more concrete targets in the form of federal spies who had quickly descended on the town. The mayor-turned-prime minister then surrendered to the US navy – and demanded US foreign aid and war reparations of one billion dollars. Washington didn't respond directly (at least with an aid package), though it did quietly remove the offending checkpoint. A publicity stunt for sure, but one that worked, and the event is now celebrated annually at the **Conch Republic Independence Celebration** (see box, p.161), a great excuse for having a week-long party. There's a small brass plaque commemorating the event outside the Visitors' Center in Mallory Square.

Coastal Florida

As far as the tourist is concerned, Florida's 1300 miles of coastline easily surpasses that of any state in the continental US. The beaches that run along it range from rugged, windswept dunes to sun-washed sugary sands, and the climate allows for a beach vacation nearly any time of year. But the shoreline offers far more than just fun in the sun: wildlife abounds in the verdant parklands, waterways, and refuges that dot the coast, where you might spot sea turtles and manatees, birds of all stripes, and dolphins frolicking in the waves.

Beaches

The Sunshine State takes great pride in its roughly 660 miles of clean, tidy, and safe beaches. Some of the most popular are around **Miami** on the Atlantic coast, although there are also some excellent beaches on the **Gulf of Mexico** coast, where warm breezes and spectacular sunsets are big draws. The **Tampa Bay** area on the Gulf rivals Miami in visitor numbers, with a similar – and ever growing – beachside jungle of high-rise condos and hotels, but more of a family-oriented atmosphere and a generally older clientele. Head just north or south of Tampa and you'll have idyllic, near-deserted barrier-island beaches all to yourself.

Despite overdevelopment in some areas, the **Panhandle** features pockets of wonderfully rugged and windswept coastal scenery – all made more tempting by spectacular sunsets. The **Gulf Islands National Seashore**, stretching for

Sombrero Beach, the Florida Keys ▲

Caladesi Island beach, Tampa Bay area ▼

Nightlife on Ocean Drive, South Beach ▼

Beach bashes

For beachside **partying**, nowhere in the state is more famous than Miami's **South Beach**, a three-mile stretch that oozes self-indulgent delight. Revelers relax on the sands by day before heading to **Ocean Drive's** pastel-hued Art Deco café terraces and packed nightclubs when the sun goes down.

Bikers from all over North America gather in bustling **Daytona Beach** every March to swill beer and take advantage of local laws permitting **driving on the beach**, while at roughly the same time thousands of college students choose **Panama City Beach**, in the heart of the Panhandle's "Redneck Riviera," to spend their **Spring Break** as decadently as possible.

Five beaches to visit

▶▶ **Bahia Honda State Park** The Keys' best sandy strips, all imbued with a distinctly tropical feel. See p.138

▶▶ **Dog Island** Perfect for windswept walks among some of Florida's tallest sand dunes. See p.436

▶▶ **Fort de Soto Park** Excellent beaches combined with lush walking trails, camping facilities, and a nineteenth-century fort. See p.387

▶▶ **Haulover Beach** This open-minded nude beach – one of the most famous in the US – is the ultimate melting pot. See p.75

▶▶ **Sanibel Island** Shell-hunting reaches its ultimate expression on Sanibel, where 400-plus varieties wash ashore and an annual three-day festival draws hundreds of shell-seekers. See p.257

▲ Bahia Honda beach, the Florida Keys

▼ Siesta Key

150 miles from near Pensacola to Mississippi, is known for its craggy coast strewn with sand dunes. The **South Walton** beaches – and also **Siesta Key** in Sarasota to the south – are blanketed in the finest sand imaginable, derived from quartz rather than the more usual ground coral.

On the **northeast coast**, once you get north of occasionally frenzied Daytona Beach, the communities become more low-key, providing a refreshing change of pace. Come here out of season and the sands are blessedly free from the crowds – and commercialization – that blight some of the more popular resorts.

Although the beaches in the rest of the state might be better known, the Florida Keys – best known for sport fishing, diving, and Key West – offers stunning sandy strips too, including those at Bahia Honda State Park, in the Lower Keys, and Sombrero Beach, on Marathon Key.

Bottlenose dolphins, Panama City ▲

Elkhorn coral, the Upper Keys ▼

Wildlife

Think in terms of the "Big Three" when it comes to viewing Florida wildlife. **Alligators** inhabit the wetlands, lakes, and rivers, are ubiquitous enough, and quite easy to spot. More effort is required to see **manatees**, the endangered herbivorous mammals that live in the rivers, bays, and shallow coastal waters. **Dolphins**, meanwhile, are commonly seen cavorting in the waters around the Keys and Panama City. The Florida coastline is dotted with state parks and wildlife refuges that protect birds, animals, and vegetation. The most incongruous of these parklands is the **Merritt Island National Wildlife Refuge**, which shares an island with the Kennedy Space Center in a stretch known as the Space Coast. Merritt Island is rich in **birdlife** – keep your eyes peeled for snail kites, reddish egrets, and cinnamon teals. The Space Coast is also the second largest **turtle nesting** site in the world; in June and July turtle walks are a popular pastime. Some of the most interesting parts of the **Everglades National Park** are its brackish coastal sections, where **mangrove islands** protect the complex ecosystem from surge tides while supporting a great variety of wildlife including **otters**, **raccoons**, and **pelicans**.

The coral reef

The Florida Keys are surrounded by the only **living coral reef** in the continental US, which, despite the inevitable degradation caused by tourism, is still replete with exotic and colorful underwater life, from bright angelfish to menacing barracuda. You'll find plenty of opportunities to explore the aquatic world at **John Pennekamp Coral Reef State Park** in the Upper Keys and the **Looe Key Marine Sanctuary** in the Lower Keys.

Arrival and information

Four miles east of the old town along S Roosevelt Blvd is the Key West International Airport (☎305/296-5439), whose name belies its services – it only handles flights from Miami and other Florida cities. Most of Key West's car rental firms have offices at the airport, and city buses ($2) make the journey into town from the east end of the terminal. **Taxis** charge $7.50 per person for trips to and from the airport, though solo travelers have to pay by the meter (around $16 into town). Heading back to the airport try Florida Keys Taxi (☎305/296-6666) or Friendly Cab (☎305/292-0000).

The terminus for Greyhound buses in Key West is also at the airport. Driving into the Old Town on US-1 is straightforward enough, and most hotels have parking arrangements. Metered parking ($1.50 per hr) on the street is available but hard to find in the Old Town and non-residents will be towed if they use spaces marked "Residential Parking", so it's best to aim for the Old Town Parking Garage at the corner of Caroline and Grinnell streets (daily 7am–midnight; $2 per hr, $13 per day; ☎305/293-6426) – your parking ticket can be used by one person to claim free rides on all city buses throughout the day.

The **Greater Key West Chamber of Commerce**, behind Mallory Square at 402 Wall St (Mon–Fri 8.30am–6.30pm, Sat & Sun 9am–6pm; ☎305/294-2587 or 1-800/527-8539, ⓦwww.keywestchamber.org), offers plenty of tourist pamphlets and discount vouchers. A number of easily found **free publications** list current events: *Solares Hill* (weekly; ⓦhttp://pdf.keysnews.com/weeklys /SolaresHill.pdf is the most informative. The local newspaper is the *Key West Citizen* (50¢; ⓦwww.keysnews.com) whose comprehensive entertainment supplement, *Paradise*, is bundled with the main paper on Thursdays.

Getting around

For **getting around** the narrow, pedestrian-filled streets of the Old Town, you're far better off walking or cycling than driving. If street signs appear curiously absent, you'll find them painted vertically on the base of each junction lamppost, though many are peeling off. To venture further afield, **rent a bike** ($15 per day) or scooter (single from $55 per day, double from $80 per day) from one of the Adventure Scooter & Bicycle Rentals locations: handiest are 617 Front St (☎305/293-9955) or 1 Duval St next to the Pier House (☎305/293-0441). Remarkably, there is a **bus service** ($2; ☎305/292-8164, ⓦwww.keywestcity .com) in Key West: two routes, clockwise and counterclockwise, loop around the tiny island roughly every ninety minutes between 6am and midnight.

You'll also notice the **cycle-rickshaws** that are pedaled around (in their highest gear) and charge $15 for ten minutes – that's about $25 from one end of Duval Street to the other. Otherwise, if you're feeling flush or lazy, try one of the nifty mini **electric cars** that can be rented from Key West Cruisers, 500 Truman Ave at Duval Street (two-seaters from $58 for 2hr, four-seaters from $78 for 2hr; ☎305/294-4724 or 1-888/800-8802, ⓦwww.keywestcruisers.com).

Tours

The oft-plugged, ninety-minute guided tours of the island's main sights might seem a tourist-ready rip-off, but the best known, the **Conch Tour Train** (hop on at Mallory Square; every 20–30min, 9am–4.30pm; $29; ☎305/294-5161,

@www.conchtourtrain.com), is astonishingly informative and its drivers' commentary far from rote or robotic. A similar alternative is the **Old Town Trolley** (board at any of the marked stops around the Old Town; every 30min, 9am–4.30pm; $29; ☎305/296-6688, @www.oldtowntrolley.com).

For some kitschy fun, take one of the ninety-minute **Ghost Tours** (daily 8pm and 9pm; $15; ☎305/294-9255, @www.hauntedtours.com), a guided walking tour that starts at the *Crowne Plaza* on Duval St, and takes in some of the numerous haunted homes and ghost legends of Key West.

Accommodation

Accommodation costs in Key West are always high – particularly from January to April when the simplest motel room will be in excess of $125 per night. Prices drop considerably at other times, but expect to pay at least $75 wherever you stay. Genuine **budget options** are limited to the seaside (but out of town) *Boyd's Campground*, 6401 Maloney Ave (☎305/294-1465, @www.boydscampground.com; tent sites $55–75), or the *Key West International Hostel*, 718 South St (☎305/296-5719, @www.keywesthostel.com; members $34, nonmembers $39), with grubby dorms. You'll find cheaper **motels** along US-1 at the northern end of the island, but any savings on the room will be eaten up by the cost of parking in town. You're better off checking into one of the centrally located hotels or guesthouses we've listed here. Wherever you stay, a **reservation** is essential from November to April, and would be a sensible precaution for weekends at any other time. If you arrive in October during Fantasy Fest, expect a hike in room cost and a multi-night minimum stay. For longer stays and larger groups, **renting an apartment** can be an economic alternative; @www.rentkeywest.com is a good place to start, with weekly rates starting at $950 for studios and $1200 for two bedrooms.

Many of the restored villas operating as guesthouses in the historic district are gay- and lesbian-run, and while most welcome all adults, few accept young children. A handful (we've noted which ones) are exclusively gay male, while only one is for lesbians only.

Hotels and motels

Budget Key West 1031 Eaton St ☎305/294-3333 or 1-800/403-2866, @www.historickeywestinns .com. Tucked away north of the Old Town near the seaport, this is a rare find in Key West, offering low prices and seventeen rooms equipped with private bathroom, cable TV, microwave, and fridge – check them first, as some can be cleaner than others. **❺**

Crowne Plaza Key West-La Concha 430 Duval St ☎305/296-2991 or 1-800/745-2191, @www .laconchakeywest.com. Now a link in the *Crown Plaza* chain, this colorful hotel, the tallest building in Key West, first opened in 1925 and has retained some of its 1920s-style decor. Big pluses are the large swimming pool and bar overlooking the town, but it's the fabulous central location that proves the biggest draw. **❺**

Ocean Key Resort & Spa Zero Duval St ☎305/296-7701 or 1-800/328-9815,

@www.oceankey.com. Perched by the ocean at the tip of Duval St, this is one of the plushest hotels in the city, though you'll pay for the convenience and views. The lavish rooms are brightly furnished in tropical prints, and many have balconies. **❼**

Parrot Key Resort 2801 N Roosevelt Blvd ☎305/809-2200, @www.parrotkeyresort .com. One of the most luxurious resorts in town, with tranquil conch-style houses (one, two and three bedroom) with back porches, whimsical furniture, full kitchens and plasma TVs. Set in lush gardens on Florida Bay (with a narrow white-sand beach), a short taxi ride from the Old Town. **❽**

Sea Shell Motel 718 South St ☎305/296-5719, @www.keywesthostel.com. If the adjoining youth hostel is full or doesn't appeal, this very basic place offers standard motel rooms at the lowest rates in the neighborhood. **❺**

Sunset Key Cottages 245 Front St ☎305/292-5300 or 1-888/477-7786, ⓦwww.sunsetkeyisland.com. A 10min ferry ride from the *Westin Key Resort*, where you check-in (guests share facilities), this luxurious, car-free, manmade island – just 40 years old – features 37 elegant standalone cottages, that are like private homes with maid service. Try to nab one of the cottages on the northwest side for the best views of sunset. ❽

Guesthouses

🏃 **Angelina Guest House** 302 Angela St ☎305/294-4480 or 1-888/303-4480, ⓦwww.angelinaguesthouse.com. A charming guesthouse, with a cool, Caribbean feel, tucked away in the back streets of the Bahama Village. One of the best deals in town (even the shared bathrooms are lovely), with fourteen simple rooms (no phones or TVs) decorated in pastel yellow or blue. The small pool is a great place to enjoy the owners' cinnamon rolls at breakfast. No children. Shared bath ❹, private bath ❺.

Blue Parrot Inn 916 Elizabeth St ☎305/296-0033 or 1-800/231-2473, ⓦwww.blueparrotinn.com. The friendly owners of this comfy 1884 house in the heart of the historic district serve excellent breakfasts in a lush, courtyard garden. Rooms have standard tropical decor, with fridges and ceiling fans. No children. ❻

Duval House 814 Duval St ☎305/294-1666 or 1-800/223-8825, ⓦwww.duvalhousekeywest.com. The lower-priced rooms are relatively good value, and paying a bit more gets you a four-poster bed and a balcony overlooking the grounds, a collection of seven historic Key West houses. One of the few places with ample parking. ❻

🏃 **Eden House** 1015 Fleming St ☎305/296-6868, ⓦwww.edenhouse.com. Don't let the rather grotty reception put you off this place – it's a gem, run by the Eden family for over thirty years. Rooms (some with private bath) are decorated in the usual pastels and pale woods, though many have large, claw-foot tubs and most overlook the pool. Best of all, there's free off-street parking and a complimentary happy hour every night 4–5pm (plus a beer at check-in). Shared baths ❻; private baths from ❼.

🏃 **The Gardens Hotel** 526 Angela St ☎1-800/526-2664 or 305/294-2661, ⓦwww.gardenshotel.com. One of the swishest hotels in town, this graceful inn has only 17 rooms, decked out in an airy Bahamian plantation style with flat-screen TVs, fresh flowers, and enormous beds. The honeymoon-worthy luxury is ramped up by the namesake groves of greenery and orchids enveloping the building, swathing it from prying eyes. ❼

Island City House 411 William St ☎305/294-5702 or 1-800/634-8230, ⓦwww.islandcityhouse.com. This massive mansion, built in the 1880s for a Charleston merchant family, claims to be the oldest in town (it's been welcoming paying guests since 1912). The luxurious studios and one- or two-bedroom apartments overlook the pool and tropical gardens, and are accessed by a shady tunnel from the main street; choose from suites in the main house (Victorian; ❼), Cigar House (old Florida plantation; ❼), and Arch House (modernized antique; ❻).

Key Lime Inn 725 Truman Ave ☎305/294-5229 or 1-800/549-4430, ⓦwww.historickeywestinns.com. A cluster of cottages (the oldest built in 1854), near the center of the Old Town, with a variety of rooms done in Key West tropical style. A good buffet breakfast is served by the pool, and ample onsite parking is a major plus. Splash out on one of the bungalows for their seclusion and verandas. ❺

La-Te-Da 1125 Duval St ☎305/296-6706 or 1-877/528-3320, ⓦwww.lateda.com. An 1890s house (where José Martí addressed cigar workers in 1892), with fifteen spacious rooms with comfortable wicker furniture, small fridges, and ceiling fans with in-wall a/c, and vaguely heraldic decor; many overlook the cozy sunken pool area which also adjoins a couple of friendly mixed/gay bars plus the *Crystal Room* cabaret, which features popular drag shows (see p.163). ❻

Marquesa Hotel 600 Fleming St ☎305/292-1919 or 1-800/869-4631, ⓦwww.marquesa.com. A grand guesthouse built in 1884 with a formal clientele and lush green surroundings including its own onsite waterfall and swimming pools. The spotless rooms are smart and modern, with marble bathrooms and tranquil patios. ❼

Marrero's Guest Mansion 410 Fleming St ☎305/294-6977 or 1-800/459-6212, ⓦwww.marreros.com. Reputedly haunted, this antique-crammed old mansion is an opulent place to stay – ghost-hunters should ask for room 18, where most paranormal activity has been reported. Rooms ❺, room 18 ❻.

The Mermaid & the Alligator 729 Truman Ave ☎305/294-1894 or 1-800/773-1894, ⓦwww.kwmermaid.com. This 1904 mansion has a stunning interior, pool deck and individually decked out rooms. The fabulous gardens, TV-free rooms, lush breakfasts (try the banana pancakes), and wine served each evening make for a deeply relaxing stay. No children under 16. ❼

Pilot House 414 Simonton St ☎305/293-6600 or 1-800/648-3780, ⓦwww.pilothousekeywest.com. Large suites all have kitchenettes, big bathrooms, and wicker furniture; the poolside rooms are airy and modern, but the antique-filled suites in the main house are more appealing, so ask for a room there. Clothing is optional around the smallish pool, and the crowd a mix of gay and straight; children are not permitted. The house was once owned by Joseph Otto, a prominent Prussian surgeon, who has one of the oddest graves in Key West cemetery (see p.155). **⑤**

Exclusively gay guesthouses

Alexander's Guest House 1118 Fleming St ☎ 305/294-9919, ⓦ www.alexanders keywest.com. The antithesis of most antique-filled B&Bs, this sleek, all-male spot has white modernist furniture in its large lobby, a big onsite bar (where happy hour is held daily 5.30–7.30pm so guests can mingle), and roomy suites, most with king-size beds, decked out in stark white style. No kids, pets, or smoking. **⑦**

Big Ruby's 409 Appelrouth Lane ☎ 305/296-2323 or 1-800/477-7829, ⓦ www.bigrubys.com. Part of a mini-chain of gay guesthouses, this hotel consists of a cluster of buildings, all dotted round a lagoon pool and patio where you can lounge and listen to piped-in Motown. There are lots of extras, including splendid Sunday brunches (try the eggs Benedict), and free drinks 6–8pm. **⑤**

Island House 1129 Fleming St ☎ 305/294-6284 or 1-800/890-6284, ⓦ www.islandhousekeywest .com. Men-only clothing optional resort that's one of the few remaining cruisey accommodation options in town: there's a sauna, video room, and large pool-cum-sundeck (in fact, guests need only wear clothes when using the exercise equipment in the gym). The surprisingly appealing rooms have overstuffed leather chairs, VCR, and crisp white linens; the largest suites are poolside. Even if you're not staying here, you can buy a pass to use the hotel's amenities ($25 per day, $80 per week). Private bath **⑦**, shared bath **⑤**.

New Orleans House 724 Duval St ☎ 305/293-9800 or 1-888/293-9873, ⓦ www.neworleans housekw.com. Huge, very clean rooms come with full kitchens at this centrally located guesthouse – it's a pity the common areas are so tatty. Ask for a room at the back if you want to sleep before 3am, as the guesthouse is attached to the popular *Bourbon Street Pub*. **⑥**

Pearl's Rainbow 525 United St ☎ 305/292-1450 or 1-800/749-6696, ⓦ www.pearlsrainbow.com. The lone women-only guesthouse on the island, this attractive former cigar factory – owned by *Marrero's* – serves breakfast and has two pools and two jacuzzis. There's also *Pearl's Patio*, a bar also open to non-guests (Sun–Thurs noon–10pm, Fri & Sat noon–midnight). **⑥**

The Town

The square mile of the **Old Town** contains most of what you'll want to see and is certainly the best place to absorb Key West's easygoing atmosphere, despite the throngs of tourists. Though visitors choke the main streets, only blocks away the casually hedonistic mood infects everyone, whether you've been here twenty years or twenty minutes. All of the Old Town can be seen on foot in a couple of days, but you should allow at least three – dashing through won't do the place justice.

Along Duval Street

Anyone who saw Key West two decades ago would now barely recognize the main promenade, **Duval Street**, which cuts a mile-long swathe right through the Old Town. Teetering precariously on the safe side of seedy for many years, much of the street has been transformed into a well-manicured strip of boutiques, beachwear stores, coffee shops, and chain restaurants – all catering to the vacationing middle-aged of Middle America. Yet its colorful "local characters" and round-the-clock action mean Duval Street is still an interesting place to hang out – just try to avoid cruise ship arrivals, when the street becomes depressingly overwhelmed with shoppers.

Other than shops and bars, few places on Duval Street provide a break from tramping the pavement. One, however, is the **Oldest House Museum**, also

Beaches and watersports

Key West is not a **beach** resort, but if you're really desperate, the beach at **Fort Zachary Taylor** (see p.155) is OK for a few hours of lounging, while tiny **Higgs Beach** at the end of Reynolds Street has a decent strip of sand (though the water isn't that enticing), with a cheap café and bar nearby. Further east, along South Roosevelt Boulevard, **Smathers Beach** is the weekend parade ground of Key West's most toned physiques and a haunt of windsurfers and parasailors – this one-mile stretch of fine sand usually has plenty of beach chairs, windsurfers, jet skis and kayaks to rent.

Key West is far better known as a **watersports** and **fishing** center. You'll find most charters in the Historic Seaport district (see p.153).

Andy Griffiths Charters 40 Key Haven Rd ℡305/292-2277, ⓦwww.fishandy.com. Experienced local fisherman arranges 2-to 3-day fishing excursions out to the Dry Tortugas (from $2500). Check the website for the more affordable five-hour trips for parties of six anglers for $95 per person.

Fury Glass Bottom Boat Pier House Resort dock, end of Duval Street ℡305/296-6293, ⓦwww.furycat.com. Modern glass-hulled catamaran that makes two-hour trips over the reef for those unwilling to get wet ($40). The same outfit also offers snorkeling and watersports rentals.

Jolly II Rover Foot of Greene and Elizabeth streets ℡305/304-2235, ⓦwww.schoonerjollyrover.com. Live out your pirate fantasies on this square-rigged schooner; daily trips for $35.

Sebago Watersports William Street, Historic Seaport ℡305/294-5687, ⓦwww.keywestsebago.com. Offers sunset cruises ($39), dolphin charters ($79), snorkeling ($49), parasailing ($49), jet ski tours ($150) and cheap dive trips ($45 plus $35 equipment).

Southpoint Divers Divers should contact this highly acclaimed outfit, 610 Front St (℡1-800/891-3483, ⓦwww.southpointdivers.com). The shop runs two trips daily (8.30am for wreck and reef, 1.30pm for two reefs); snorkelers pay $45, divers $85–108.

Sunny Days Foot of Greene and Elizabeth streets ℡305/296-5556, ⓦwww.sunnydayskeywest.com. Snorkel trips (3.5hr) on a sleek 78ft catamaran from $38. Sangria sunset sails (2hr) from $35, with unlimited booze. Also runs special 3-hour dolphin trips (℡305/293-5144; $55).

known as the **Wrecker's Museum** (daily 10am–4pm, last entry 3.45pm; free; ℡305/294-9502, ⓦwww.oirf.org), at no. 322. Built in 1829, it's the oldest house on the street but originally stood a few blocks away at the junction of Whitehead and Caroline streets. The exhibits here give some background to the **wrecker industry** – the salvaging of cargo and passengers from foundering vessels – on which Key West's earliest good times were based. Judging by the choice furniture filling the museum, Captain Watlington, the wrecker who lived here during the 1830s, did pretty well. Three-quarters of the pieces are original – look for the courting lamp in the parlor, which provided amorous couples the chance to chat as long as the oil lasted, and the wonky cookhouse in the back garden, built separately from the main house to reduce risks of fire.

One block south, **St Paul's Episcopal Church**, at no. 401 (daily 9am–5.30pm; ℡05/296-5142), dates from 1912 and is worth entering briefly for its richly colored stained-glass windows. Further along, at no. 500, is **Fast Buck Freddies**, the campy department store with its extraordinary window displays that's been a Key West fixture for decades. Just beyond here, at no. 516, stands the imposing **San Carlos Institute** (Fri–Sun noon–6pm; free, $3 suggested donation; ℡305/294-3887, ⓦwww.institutosancarlos.org), which has played a leading role in Cuban exile life since it opened on nearby Anne Street in 1871. It was here in 1892 that Cuban Revolution hero José Martí welded the exiles into a force that would achieve the island's independence ten years later. The current building, which dates from 1924, was financed by a $100,000 grant from the Cuban government after a hurricane wrecked the original wooden shack. Cuban architect Francisco Centurion designed the two-story structure in the **Cuban Baroque** style of the period, noticeable in the wrought-iron balconies and creamy facade. The soil on its grounds is from Cuba's six provinces, and a cornerstone was taken from Martí's tomb (he was killed in Cuba in 1895). Today it contains a passable permanent exhibition focusing on Martí and his men, mostly old newspaper clippings and letters, exhibits on Cuban presidents 1902 to 1958, and a section on Cuban immigrants; you can also watch absorbing DVDs, on demand, on Martí's life and a host of other subjects including Cuban music.

A worthy diversion on the lower Duval drag is the surprisingly charming **Butterfly Conservatory**, 1316 Duval St (daily 9am–5pm, last ticket sold at 4.30pm; $10; ☎305/296-2988 or 1-800/839-4647, Ⓦwww.keywestbutterfly .com). Race through the entrance hall – a junk-filled gift shop and sparse waiting room – and head straight for the enormous conservatory. It's a dazzling experience to be surrounded by flocks of tame butterflies that dive bomb or land on you without hesitation – an odd, almost creepy sensation. Butterflies here have double the lifespan they would in the wild (the blue morphos live up to 45 days). It's essential they don't breed – caterpillars consume such huge volumes of greenery they'd devastate the foliage within days – so there are no plants here that are used by any species' caterpillar as their sole source of food. Instead, the fertilized pupae are shipped in and hatched onsite in a special standalone nursery – you can see rows of the pods dangling in its glass windows like an alien hatchery. The best time to visit is early in the morning just after the insects have been woken by their keepers.

You'll know when you get near the southern end of Duval Street because, whether it's a motel, filling station, or a pharmacy, everything sprouts a "southernmost" epithet. The true **southernmost point** in Key West, and consequently in the continental US, is at the intersection of Whitehead and South streets: it's only 90 miles from Cuba and flagged by a squat red, black, and white marker.

Mallory Square and around

In the early 1800s, thousands of dollars' worth of marine salvage was landed at the piers, stored in the warehouses, and sold at the auction houses on **Mallory Square**, just west of the northern end of Duval Street. Nowadays the spacious waterfront section contrasts with the hubbub of the area behind it (alongside Wall St), as thousands of cruise ship passengers and other tourists flock here by day for the souvenir market selling overpriced ice cream, trinkets, and T-shirts; it's a constant jam of shuttles, trolleys and tour buses. Come evening, it's still just as busy, thanks to the touristy **sunset celebration** (Ⓦwww .sunsetcelebration.org), started in the 1960s by local hippies but now stage-managed by the Key West Cultural Preservation Society. Jugglers and fire-eaters are on hand to create a merry backdrop for the sinking of the sun, and though the event's charms are rather overrated, it's worth experiencing at least once – some of the entertainers are real characters, and their performances are certainly enhanced by the plastic cups of beers and $7 cocktails sold at the stands nearby.

In between Wall Street and Mallory Square (in front of the waterfront Playhouse Theater) is the **Historic Sculpture Garden** (free; ☎305/294-2587), anchored by the heroic *Wreckers*, a striking monument symbolizing the spirit of Key West. The rest of this tiny, offbeat walled garden houses cast-iron busts of a random selection of local heroes, most of whom look as if they'd be more at home in a waxwork chamber of horrors than this supposedly stirring tribute. Aside from heavyweights like Hemingway, Truman, and Henry Flagler, look for the scions of several local families whose names – like Whitehead and Mallory – now grace streets and squares round town.

Key West Aquarium

More entertaining than the square's daytime scene is the small gathering of sea life inside the adjacent Art Deco **Key West Aquarium**, 1 Whitehead St (daily 10am–6pm; $12; ☎305/296-2051 or 1-800/868-7482, ⓦwww.keywestaquarium.com). Built in 1934 as an open-air attraction it's been enclosed and enlarged since then without compromising its superb design. These days the aquarium is home to fascinatingly ugly creatures such as porcupine fish and longspine squirrel fish who leer from behind glass, and sharks (the smaller kinds such as lemon, blacktip, and bonnethead) are known to jump out of their open tanks out back during the half-hour **guided tours and feedings** (11am, 1pm, 3pm, & 4.30pm). If you intend to eat conch you might change your mind after seeing the live ones here – they're not the world's prettiest crustaceans.

Shipwreck Historeum

Housed in a towering wooden plank structure opposite the aquarium is the kitschy **Shipwreck Historeum** (daily 9.40am–6pm; shows run every 20min till 5pm; $12; ☎305/292-8990, ⓦwww.shipwreckhistoreum.com). Enthusiastic guides throw out dozens of creaky gags while introducing an informative, if careworn, movie on the wrecking industry. On the two upper floors are several exhibits of cargo from the *Isaac Allerton*, which sank in 1856 and remained untraced until 1985: the most arresting items are feathery lace gloves, still intact after more than a century in the sea, and pots ornamented with crusty coral. Better still is the panoramic view of Key West seen from the top of the rickety tower.

Mel Fisher Maritime Museum and the Customs House

Not all the ships that foundered off Key West were salvaged when they sank – some early galleons, which plied the trade route between Spain and its New World colonies during the sixteenth and seventeenth centuries, held onto their treasure until only a few decades ago when advanced technology enabled treasure hunters to locate them. You can see a lavish selection of such rescued cargo at the **Mel Fisher Maritime Heritage Society Museum**, 200 Greene St (Mon–Fri 8.30am–5pm, Sat–Sun 9.30am–5pm; $12; ☎305/294-2633, ⓦwww.melfisher.org), among them a chunky emerald cross, a gold bar you're allowed to actually lift, and a "poison cup" said to neutralize toxins, all salvaged from two seventeenth-century wrecks.

In 1980, after years of searching, Fisher discovered the *Santa Margarita*, and five years later, the *Nuestra Señora de Atocha,* both sunk during a hurricane in 1622, forty miles southeast of Key West – they yielded a haul said to be worth at least $200 million. Though it's easy to get sidetracked by the monetary value of such finds – the *Atocha* yielded 1041 silver bars and 77 gold bricks – the collection has immense historic importance, offering a window into the early years of Spanish colonization of America. Inca symbols as well as European technology and an incredibly eclectic range of items from jewelry, cookware, ceramics and pots to weaponry, medicinal items and even rat bones were discovered – there's also a sobering display dedicated to the slave ship *Henrietta Marie* (which sunk in 1700), replete with evil-looking leg and neck-irons. Upstairs, the La Plata del Mar exhibit also includes silver from fleets sunk in 1715 and 1733.

The final section of the museum highlights Fisher himself, a real American rags-to-riches story. Although he died in 1998, he's still the high priest of Florida's many treasure-seekers, and ran a surf shop in California before arriving in Florida armed with several old Spanish sea charts and unbending optimism (his motto: "Today's the day!"). Briefly touched on is the raging dispute between Fisher and the state and federal governments over who owns what, resolved after years of legal wrangling in 1982 (Fisher agreed to give the state 25 percent of everything he found in Florida waters), though the ecological disturbance that uncontrolled treasure-seeking has wrought upon the Keys (reason for a name change from the original "Treasure Exhibit" to the current "Heritage Museum") is discreetly ignored.

Across the road at Greene and Front streets, the imposing, rust-brown Romanesque **Customs House** (daily 9am–5pm; $10; ☎305/295-6616, ⓦwww.kwahs.com) was built in 1891 and used as a post office, customs office, and federal courthouse. It was long derelict, but is now used to house the Key West Museum of Art & History – exhibits are hit and miss, and much of the museum can be taken up with temporary displays of local art, but it's worth dawdling here for an hour or so. Permanent exhibits usually include an absorbing display dedicated to Hemingway (which treats long-suffering wife Pauline a tad more fairly than the guides at his house), and sections on Key West's nineteenth-century history, with an impressive seven-foot diorama of the town in its bustling 1850s heyday. Above all, don't miss the craggy portraits of Conchs by local artist Paul Collins that line the upstairs corridor, especially Lee Neil, the so-called Queen of Key Lime Pies, with her veiny arms, seemingly exhausted after hours of lime squeezing.

Audubon House and Tropical Gardens

Just across Whitehead Street from Mel Fisher's, the **Audubon House and Tropical Gardens** (daily 9.30am–5pm, last tour 4.15pm; $11, $6.50 for gardens only; ☎305/294-2116, ⓦwww.audubonhouse.com) was the first of Key West's elegant Victorian-style properties to get a thorough renovation in 1958. The wealthy Wolfson family, who purchased the place to prevent its demolition, set about restoring the house to its original grandeur, using the family collection of furniture and decorative arts. Their success encouraged a host of others to follow suit and sent housing prices soaring.

The house takes its name from famed ornithologist John James Audubon, who actually had nothing to do with the place. Audubon spent a few weeks in Key West in 1832, scrambling around the mangrove swamps looking for the birdlife he later portrayed in his highly regarded *Birds of America* portfolio. His link to the house goes no further than the lithographs decorating the walls and staircase. The man who actually owned the property was a wrecker named John Geiger. In addition to twelve children of their own, Geiger and his wife took in many others from shipwrecks and broken marriages. Guided tours of the first floor (continuously throughout the day) provide an introduction to the house's fine nineteenth-century European furniture and antiques, after which you're free to explore the gardens and second and third floors.

Heritage House Museum

You can easily spend a delightful hour or two at the charming **Heritage House Museum**, one block south of Audubon House on Whitehead St, at 410 Caroline St (Mon–Sat 10am–4pm, tours begin every half hour; Aug & Sept self-guided only; $5, $7 guided tour; ☎305/296-3573, ⓦwww.heritagehouse museum.org). This double-veranda, Colonial-style home dating from 1834 has been owned by the same family for seven generations. The current owner is the granddaughter of Jessie Porter, who died in 1979; she in turn was the great-granddaughter of William Curry (see below). Miss Jessie, as she was known, was renowned as a lavish society hostess, and she used her connections to preserve the historic section of town. Among the luminaries she counted as friends were Tallulah Bankhead, who visited with Tennessee Williams, Gloria Swanson, and Thornton Wilder; their photographs are mounted in the hallway. **Robert Frost** also came and lived in a specially built cottage in the garden in 1940. While you can dawdle in the orchid-packed garden and listen to recordings of Frost reading his poetry, the cottage itself is off-limits.

Other highlights include an enticing music room where you can play the 1865 French piano, a library of rare books, and an exotic room filled with Oriental *objets d'art* Miss Jessie collected on her extensive travels. Don't miss the chance to chat with the knowledgeable volunteers, whose enthusiastic stories do much to illuminate the house and its history.

Caroline and Greene streets

Keep walking along **Caroline Street** or **Greene Street**, and you'll come across numerous examples of late-1800s "**conch houses**," built in a mix-and-match style fusing elements of Victorian, Colonial, and Tropical architecture. The houses were raised on coral slabs and rounded off with playful "gingerbread" wood trimming. Erected quickly and cheaply, conch houses were seldom painted, but many here are bright and colorful, evincing their recent transformation in the last fifteen years from ordinary dwellings to hundred-thousand-dollar winter homes. The reason such houses have lasted so long is many were put up by shipwrights using boat-building techniques, so they sway in high winds and weather extremes of climate well.

In marked contrast to the tiny conch houses, the grand three-story **Curry Mansion**, 511 Caroline St (daily 9am–5pm; $5; ☎305/294-5349 or 1-800/253-3466, ⓦwww.currymansion.com), was first built in 1855 as the abode of William Curry, Florida's first millionaire (who made his loot by selling salvaged goods in the 1830s). The current structure dates from 1899, when Curry's son Milton rebuilt the mansion after a major fire. Exhaustively restored, the house is an awkward hybrid of museum and hotel; inside, amid a riot of antiques and oddities, is a stash of strange and stylish fittings such as Henry James's piano and a lamp designed by Frank Lloyd Wright. The real reason to stop by, however, is the **Widow's Walk** (a tiny lookout on the roof where sailors' wives watched for their husbands' return), which affords an impressive view across the Old Town.

Historic Seaport

The standout site of the **Historic Seaport** area, a few blocks east of Duval Street on Front and Greene streets, is **Pirate Soul**, 524 Front St (daily 9am–7pm; $13.95; ☎305/292-1113, ⓦwww.piratesoul.com) opened by Pat Croce, the former president of the Philadelphia 76ers basketball team. The museum is as sassy and spirited as the movie *Pirates of the Caribbean*, bringing the swashbuckling past to life better than any other spot in town. It's crammed with Croce's own collection of more than 500 pirate-related artifacts, including the sole authenticated pirate chest in the world (owned by pirate Thomas Tew – look for the hidden lock on this 400-year-old gem); Captain Kidd's actual journal (you can read virtual versions via a touch-screen); and even one of only two existing Jolly Roger flags. Don't miss the evocative "below decks" room, a pitch-black spot where you sit in darkness wearing headphones as Black Beard whispers in your ear and tells the story of how he died; the three-minute audio is thrilling and vivid, but not suitable for young children.

Otherwise, starting at the end of Front Street, the Harbor Walk follows the marina to Margaret Street, where the **Historic Seaport** has been spruced up into a shopping and eating strip known as **Lands End Village** (see "Nightlife," p.160). Here you'll find numerous **fishing charters**, plus the ferries to the **Dry Tortugas** (see p.140). One of the highlights is the restaurant-bar *Turtle Kraals*, in business as a turtle cannery until 1971, when harvesting turtles became illegal. Just along the short pier opposite, the **Historic Turtle Cannery & Maritime Museum** has a grim gathering of the gory machines used to slice and mince green turtles that were captured off the Nicaraguan coast. The museum is just an old shack on the pier; hours can be erratic (and the restaurant is no longer involved), but it's more likely to be open in the afternoon.

The Truman Annex and Little White House

The old naval storehouse containing the Fisher trove (see p.151) was once part of the **Truman Annex** (daily 8am–6pm; free), a decommissioned naval base established in 1822. Some of the buildings subsequently erected on the base, which spans a hundred acres between Whitehead Street and the sea, were – and still are – among Key West's most distinctive. In 1986, the Annex passed into the hands of a property developer who encouraged redevelopment by opening up the **Presidential Gates** on Caroline Street to the public (previously it was only accessible to heads of state); this smart move defused much local suspicion and anxiety. The complex is now the site of some of the most luxurious private homes in Key West – pick up a **free map** from one of the boxes located at the complex entrances. The buildings' interiors, unfortunately, are closed to the public.

The most famous among them, however, is the comparatively plain **Harry S. Truman Little White House Museum** (daily 9am–4.30pm; $15, admission by guided tour only; ☏305/294-9911, ⓦwww.trumanlittlewhitehouse.com), 111 Front St at Caroline Street, inside the complex. Built in 1890, this house earned its name by being the favorite holiday spot of President Harry S. Truman (for whom the Annex was named), who first visited in 1946 and allegedly spent his vacations playing poker, cruising Key West for doughnuts, and swimming. Primitive plumbing meant no one in the house was allowed to flush the toilet during his visits. The house is now a museum chronicling the Truman years with an immense array of memorabilia; there's nothing especially compelling about the trinkets here, but the affable tour guides' encyclopedic knowledge enlivens the visit considerably.

Florida Keys Eco-Discovery Center and Fort Zachary Taylor

The Truman Annex also provides access, via Southard Street, to the waterfront **Florida Keys Eco-Discovery Center** (Tues–Sat 9am–4pm; free; ☏305/809-4750, ⓦwww.floridakeys.noaa.gov), which provides a comprehensive introduction to the fauna and flora of the Keys. Among the hands-on exhibits inside is a mock-up of Aquarius, the world's only underwater ocean laboratory (currently located near the reef off Key Largo), an interactive weather kiosk, a movie theater, a vivid living reef exhibit and a special display on the Dry Tortugas (see p.164).

Beyond the center lies the **Fort Zachary Taylor Historic State Park** (daily 8am–sunset; $3.50 per car and driver, plus $2.50 for first passenger, 50¢ for each additional passenger, pedestrians and cyclists $1.50; ℗305/295-0037, ⓦwww .fortzacharytaylor.com), built in 1845 and later used in the blockade of Confederate shipping during the Civil War. Yet within fifty years, the fort was made obsolete, thanks to the invention of the powerful rifled cannon, and over ensuing decades the structure simply disappeared under sand and weeds. Recent excavation work has gradually revealed much of historical worth, though it's hard to comprehend the full importance without joining the free 45-minute **guided tour** (daily at noon & 2pm). Most locals pass by the fort on the way to the best **beach** in Key West – a place yet to be discovered by tourists, just a few yards beyond, with picnic tables, public grills, and plenty of trees for shade. Be aware the beach is a mix of crushed coral, sand and pebbles, and the craggy sea bottom can be tough on your feet, so bring waterproof sandals.

Key West Cemetery

Leaving the waterfront and heading a mile inland along Angela Street will take you to the **Key West Cemetery** (daily: winter sunrise–6pm, summer 7am–7pm; free), which dates back to 1847, and whose residents are buried in vaults above ground. (Solid coral rock – and the quick-rotting conditions below ground because of a high water table – prevents the traditional six-feet-under interment.) There may be a lack of celebrity stiffs here, but by wandering through this massive graveyard you'll notice the impact of immigration on Key West – the cemetery is filled with people from across the country and abroad. Most visitors amble about without guides (you can usually grab a **free map** at the entrance, under the historic marker), but a far better plan is to join one of the chatty, low-key one hour tours run by the Historic Florida Keys Foundation (Tues & Thurs 9.30am; $15, reservations essential; ℗305/292-6718, ⓦwww.historicfloridakeys.org). If you decide to explore on your own, start at the plot dedicated to the **USS Maine** near the entrance, usually marked by US flags (though two British sailors are also buried here); survivors of the *Maine*'s mysterious destruction – which started the Spanish American War in 1898 – were brought back to Key West from Havana, and many died here from their injuries.

Several individual plots are worth seeking out, including those of Edwina Lariz, whose stone reads "devoted fan of singer Julio Iglesias"; B.P. Roberts, who continues to carp from beyond the grave "I told you I was sick"; and Thomas Romer, a Bahamian born in 1789 who died 108 years later and was "a good citizen for 65 of them." Look out also for the fenced grave of Dr Joseph Otto, whose family home is now the *Pilot House* guesthouse (see p.147). Included on the plot is the grave of his pet Key deer, Elphina and three of his Yorkshire terriers, one of whom is described as being "a challenge to love."

A fifteen-minute walk from the cemetery, at 1431 Duncan St, is the modest two-story clapboard **house** kept by **Tennessee Williams**, who arrived in 1941 and died in 1983. Unlike his more flamboyant counterparts, Williams – Key West's longest residing literary figure, made famous by his steamy evocations of Deep South life in plays such as *A Streetcar Named Desire*, which he wrote while living in town – kept a low profile during his thirty odd years here. In fact, this house was originally situated downtown on Bahama Street but Williams was so keen for seclusion he had it moved here, which at the time was a swampy backwater outside town. The building itself, which unfortunately isn't open to the public, is still a fine example of a Bahamian-style home, though it's only worth a pilgrimage if you're a devoted fan – nothing marks the famous association.

The Secret Garden

Heading back to Duval Street from the cemetery, make time for Nancy Forrester's **Secret Garden,** entrance on Free-School Lane, just off Simonton Street, between Southard and Fleming streets (daily 10am–5pm; $6; ☎305/294-0015, ⓦ www.nfsgarden.com), a tranquil spot with a typically unconventional Key West background. Local artist Nancy Forrester and friends began working on the garden in the 1970s, transforming a one acre group of lots behind her home on Elizabeth Street into a leafy, tropical escape that "nourishes the spirit and soul," opening it to the public in 1994 (city dwellers will be amused to note Forrester considers modern Key West a "concrete jungle"). Her efforts have produced a truly magnificent botanical garden, with numerous orchids, bromeliads, aroids, ferns and over 150 different species of palms. You can even stay the night in the romantic cottage on the grounds (❼).

The Ernest Hemingway Home and Museum

Home to one of America's literary giants for almost ten years, the **Ernest Hemingway Home and Museum**, 907 Whitehead St (daily 9am–5pm; $12, tours leave every 10–30min and last approximately 30min; ☎305/294-1136, ⓦ www.hemingwayhome.com) is Key West's top tourist draw, though tours of the house tend to exaggerate the importance of the contents inside. The authenticity of the furnishings for example – a motley bunch of tables, chairs, and beds – was hotly disputed by Hemingway's former secretary. Hemingway bought the house in 1931, not with his own money but with an $8000 gift from the rich uncle of his then wife, Pauline. Originally one of the grander (and hurricane-resistant) Key West homes, built in 1851 for a wealthy merchant, the dwelling was seriously run-down by the time the Hemingways arrived. It soon acquired such luxuries as an indoor bathroom and a swimming pool.

Hemingway produced some of his most acclaimed work in the deer-head-dominated **study**, located in an outhouse, which the author entered by way of a home-made rope bridge (now long gone). Here he penned the short stories "The Short Happy Life of Francis Macomber" and "The Snows of Kilimanjaro"; the novella *The Old Man and the Sea* and the novels *A Farewell to Arms* and *To Have and Have Not*, the latter describing Key West life during the Depression.

To see inside the house you usually have to join the half-hour **guided tour**, though at quiet times you'll be allowed to wander around unattended. Tours provide a brief introduction to the author, enhanced by numerous old photos of him and his four wives, as well as a closer look at all that disputed furniture, some of which comes from medieval Spain. In the garden, a water trough for the cats is supposedly a urinal from *Sloppy Joe's* (see "Nightlife," p.161), where the big man downed many a drink. When Hemingway divorced Pauline in 1940, he boxed up his manuscripts and moved them to a back room at *Sloppy Joe's* before heading off to a house in Cuba with his new wife, journalist Martha Gellhorn.

▲ Entrance to Hemingway Home and Museum

After the tour, you're free to roam at leisure and play with some of the fifty-odd **cats**, several of which have paws with extra toes. The story that these are descendants from a feline family that lived in Hemingway's day is yet another dubious claim: the large colony of inbred cats once described by Hemingway was at his home in Cuba.

The Lighthouse Museum and the Bahama Village

From the Hemingway House, you'll easily catch sight of the 86-foot **Lighthouse Museum**, 938 Whitehead St (daily 9.30am–5pm; $10; ☎305/294-0012, ⓦ www.kwahs.com) – one of Florida's first, raised in 1847, and still functioning. Start at the **keeper's quarters**, a simple white house in the gardens, with furnishings and other bits and pieces dating to the 1910s, as well as a more absorbing DVD about the lighthouse and some of the people that served here – including the remarkable women that took over from their temporarily injured husbands for prolonged periods. After that it's possible (if tedious) to climb the 88 steps to the top of the tower, though the views of Key West are actually better from the top-floor bar of the Shipwreck Historeum (see p.151) or the Curry Mansion (see p.153). Most of the pictures taken here are not of the lighthouse but of the massive Chinese banyan tree at the base. You can ogle the lighthouse's huge lens – a twelve-foot-high, headache-inducing honeycomb of glass, from the ground floor.

The narrow streets around the lighthouse and to the west of Whitehead Street constitute **Bahama Village**, one of the few places that still has the feel of old Key West (and the highest point in town, so it never floods during hurricanes). Many of the small buildings – some of them former cigar factories – are a little run-down, in refreshing contrast to much of the over-elegant restoration found elsewhere in the Old Town. The Caribbean vibe here is authentic, dating back to the many Bahamians working in the salvage trade who eventually settled in Key West, and noticeable in the lilting music playing in cafés and the laid-back attitude of locals. For now, the place is still relatively untouched. Though you may see chickens on the street everywhere in Key West, you're likely to see the largest number here. The descendants of Cuban fighting cocks, they are protected from harm by law, especially as their appetite for scorpions helps keeps the population down.

The rest of Key West

There's not much more to Key West beyond its compact Old Town. Most of the **eastern section** of the island – encircled by the north and south sections of Roosevelt Boulevard – is residential, but Key West's longest **beach** is located here (see p.149), and there are several minor points of botanical, natural, and historical interest.

The most worthwhile, just beyond the airport at 3501 S Roosevelt Blvd, is the **Fort East Martello Museum and Gardens** (daily 9am–4.30pm; $6; ☎305/296-3913, ⓦwww.kwahs.com) the second of two Civil War lookout posts that complemented Fort Zachary Taylor. The solid, vaulted casements now store a fascinating assemblage on local history, plus the wild junk-sculptures of legendary Key Largo scrap dealer Stanley Papio and the Key West scenes created in wood by a Cuban-primitive artist named Mario Sanchez. There are also displays on local writers and **Robert the Doll**, a creepy looking sailor-suited doll said to be haunted; owned by Key West artist Robert Eugene Otto in the late nineteenth century, it was so scary it was locked in an attic until the 1970s. Today Robert is said to ruin photographs and cause unexplained events – typically, he's become something of a Key West mascot.

Eating

While you'll find some excellent **restaurants** and **snack stands** along the main streets, it's difficult to eat cheaply in Key West. There's no shortage of chic venues for fine French, Italian, and Asian cuisine, but if you want really good, inexpensive food and don't want to resort to fast-food chains, your best bet is to head for the **Cuban sandwich shops**, which offer filling, tasty meals at a fraction of the price of a main-street pizza. Those same cafés also serve up thimble-sized shots of sweetened espresso, known as a *cafecito* elsewhere but nicknamed a *buchi* in Key West. Most menus, not surprisingly, feature fresh **seafood**, and you should sample **Key lime pie** and **conch fritters** – Key West specialties – at least once.

Cafés, bakeries, and sandwich shops

The Coffee & Tea House 1211 Duval St ☎305/295-0788. Surprisingly cozy hangout given its location on the main drag, and popular with locals – this is where cops come for coffee and donuts (plus there's sandwiches and cakes). If you want to linger, kick back on one of the comfy chairs dotted around the veranda and front porch.
Conch Shop 308 Petronia St, opposite *Blue Heaven Café* ☎305/294-4140. Formica tables and a staff sweating over bubbling oil makes this down-to-earth "soul & seafood" restaurant appear

kind of gritty, but the conch fritters ($6 for six), served with potato salad and iced tea or jungle punch, are excellent. Erratic opening hours, especially on the weekend.
Five Brothers Grocery 930 Southard St ☎305/296-5205 or 1-888/646-6423, ⓦwww.5brothersgrocery.tripod.com. Expect long lines at this age-old grocery store, a real locals' favorite for its strong Cuban coffee and cheap Cuban sandwiches ($4.50). It's also crammed with provisions, plus pots and pans dangling from the ceiling. There are a few benches out front if you want to hang out. Opens at 6am; closes at 2pm on

Key lime pie

Hands down, Key West's best known foodie export is **Key lime pie**, a tangy, sweet-crusted slab made from the tiny, yellow citrus fruits every local seems to grow in their backyard. Almost every restaurant in town turns out its own tweak on the traditional pie, but there are a few specialists:

Blond Giraffe Key Lime Pie Factory (107 Simonton St ☏305/296-9174 ⓦwww .blondgiraffe.com). Renowned pie sold in several chain stores throughout town, but best experienced at the factory store where the pies are made. The custardy filling is topped with a thick layer of fluffy meringue (whole pie $25); they also do whipped cream toppings ($23). Slices $4.95. Daily 9am–6pm.

Kermit's Key West Key Lime Shoppe (200 Elizabeth St ☏305/296-0806, ⓦwww .keylimeshop.com) serves a pie with a consistency somewhere between gelatin and cake, and a perfect blend of sugary and tart. Slices are $3.95, whole pies $14.95. Daily 9am–9pm.

Key West Key Lime Pie Co (available at Circle K store, 1075 Duval St; Five Brothers Cuban Market, 930 Southard St ☏877/882-7437, ⓦwww.keywestkeylimepieco .com). Another popular pie, made on Big Pine Key but available all over the Keys – these are the most convenient Key West locations. Served frozen giving thick, custard-like consistency, with a crusty graham cracker base. Pies are $13.99, slices $3; they do all sorts of fancy versions, including mango, pineapple and coconut.

🏃 **Rooftop Café** (310 Front St ☏305/294-2042) The insider's choice. The secret of this addictive recipe is two-fold: a top layer of fluffy meringue and the gooey graham cracker crust which oozes with a tangy syrup made with lime juice and traces of melted butter. Slices are $7.

Sunday. Look out for *Five Brothers Grocery Two* on Ramrod Key (MM27 ☏305/872-0702).

🏃 **Key West Conch Fritters** Mallory Square (no phone). This salmon and white shack, immediately in front of the Aquarium, is the best place in town to try conch fritters. A dozen fritters cost $11 (six for $6.25), and the coconut shrimp is also worth a try. Daily 10.30am–6pm.

Paradise Café 1000 Eaton St ☏305/296-5001 Bustling made-to-order sandwich spot, with a ramshackle interior. The superb, doorstop-sized sandwiches ($7–8) are piled with fresh-cut onions and layers of meat with lashings of mustard. Mon–Sat 6am–4pm; closed Sun.

Sandy's Café inside the M&M Laundry, 1026 White St ☏305/295-0159. A basic counter serving terrific cheap Cuban sandwiches. Try the Cuban-mix sandwich ($6.50) or shots of potent *cortado* ($1.75), settle onto a stool at the counter outside, and watch the locals milling round you.

Restaurants

A&B Lobster House 700 Front St ☏305/294-5880, ⓦwww.aandblobsterhouse.com. There could hardly be a more scenic setting than this harborside restaurant, which is actually two separate restaurants originally opened by a pair of fisherman in 1947. Upstairs, *Berlin's* is an upmarket spot for a

luxury seafood dinner including seared Key West shrimp pasta ($29.50) or a saffron-heavy bouillabaise ($32.50). If you find the prices too rich (or are here during lunch), head downstairs to *Alonzo's Oyster Bar* where the simpler dishes cost about half the price.

Antonia's 615 Duval St ☏305/294-6565, ⓦwww .antoniaskeywest.com. This inviting, upmarket spot has two very different dining rooms; ask for a table in the old front room rather than the anodyne modern extension out back. Once you've settled in, pick from a menu of northern Italian specials like spinach and ricotta dumplings, linguine with clams, or duck leg confit. Entrées $20–30.

🏃 **Azur Restaurant** 425 Grinnell St ☏305/292-2987, ⓦwww.azurkeywest .com. Arguably the best restaurant in town, and certainly the best service; the superb Mediterranean-influenced food (think braised lamb ribs with Moroccan chick peas or daily fish *carpaccio*) is served up in a cool blue dining room with a soothing waterfall. If nothing else, come for the Key lime pie-stuffed French toast for breakfast ($9). Dinner entrées average $25.

🏃 **Blue Heaven Café** 729 Thomas St at Petronia St ☏305/296-0867, ⓦblueheavenkw.homestead.com. Sit in this dirt yard in Bahama Village where Hemingway once refereed boxing matches and enjoy the superb food while chickens wander aimlessly around your feet. For breakfast, try the mouthwatering banana bread or the lobster Benedict; for dinner, the pork tenderloin with sweet potato is a standout. Dinner entrées start at $20.

BO's Fish Wagon 801 Caroline St ☎ 305/294-9272. Quirky local institution that looks like a cross between a junkyard and a seafood shack – napkins are a self-serve roll of paper towel, and most of the interior has been salvaged from dumpsters (the showstopper's an entire wrecked truck). The simple food is tasty but not as interesting as the surroundings: best bets are the fried fish sandwich of the day for $8.75 (add $1 for grilled) or the soft-shell crab sandwich for $10. Beers are just $4.50 and every Friday evening there's an impromptu gathering of local musicians who jam and booze together.

Café Marquesa 600 Fleming St ☎ 305/292-1244, ⓦ www.marquesa.com. Chichi, hushed café inside the *Marquesa Hotel* that's the best fine-dining spot in the city. They offer an imaginative New American menu – expect great seafood like macadamia crusted yellowtail snapper ($30) and Key West seafood dumplings in saké miso broth ($10.50).

El Siboney 900 Catherine St ☎ 305/296-4184, ⓦ www.elsiboneyrestaurant.com. A little out of the way, but well worth the effort for some of the best – and best-value – Cuban food on the island. Sit at canteen-style tables with red and white checkered table cloths and ask the wait staff for recommendations; specials might include red snapper and mahi-mahi ($13.95), cubano sandwiches and punchy home-made sangria.

Hot Tin Roof inside the *Ocean Key Resort*, Zero Duval St ☎ 305/295-7057, ⓦ www.oceankey.com. The food's rich and Caribbean-inflected (they call it "Conch Fusion") at this upmarket restaurant – try the conch ceviche ($10) or the hearty Hot Tin paella ($34) – the best tables are outside on the patio overlooking the water.

Origami Sushi Bar Duval Square shopping center, 1075 Duval St ☎ 305/294-0092. The sushi served at this tiny restaurant is tasty, fresh, and a bargain compared to many restaurant nearby: most rolls are around $5, while sushi is $1.50–3 per piece. Also does Japanese hot staples such as chicken teriyaki ($16.50) and mahi-mahi katsu ($11.50). Dinner only.

🏃 **Sarabeth's** 530 Simonton St ☎ 305/293-8181, ⓦ www.sarabethskeywest.com. New outpost of the New York restaurant, stashed in an old wooden clapboard house with whirring ceiling fans and a light jazz soundtrack, all of which give the place a welcoming, homey vibe. The food's equally homestyle, from the herby, moist roast chicken served with crisp green beans ($17.50) to a turkey club with maple mustard mayo ($13.25). It's especially buzzy during brunch – try the almond-crusted cinnamon French Toast ($9.50). Closed Mon & Tues.

Seven Fish Restaurant 632 Olivia St ☎ 305/296-2777, ⓦ www.7fish.com. This little-known bistro, easy to miss in its tiny white corner building, serves some of the tastiest food in Key West – there are just over a dozen tables, so it's worth making a reservation. The food is simple and delicious – shrimp scampi for $19 and meatloaf for $16. Save room for the sweet potato pie ($7.50).

Nightlife

The carefully cultivated "anything goes" nature of Key West is exemplified by the **bars** that make up the bulk of the island's **nightlife**. These gregarious, rough-and-ready affairs are often open until 4am and offer a cocktail of yarn-spinning locals, revved-up tourists, and (often) live blues, funk, country, folk, or rock music. The mainstream bars are grouped around the northern end of Duval Street, no more than a few minutes' stagger apart. Much of Key West's best nightlife, though, revolves around its restaurants, and the best are far from Mallory Square's well-beaten path.

Bars, clubs, and live music venues

The Bull & Whistle Bar 224 Duval St ☎ 305/296-4565. Sanitized rock venue with the best of local musicians each night, mainly playing blues and R&B. Check the list on the door to see who's on – or just turn up to drink. It's jammed with tourists,

though, so don't expect to rub elbows with slumming conchs. Open till 4am nightly.

🏃 **Captain Tony's Saloon** 428 Greene St ☎ 305/294-1838, ⓦ www.capttonyssaloon .com. This rustic saloon was the original *Sloppy Joe's* between 1933 and 1937 until its owner, rumrunner Joe Russell, decamped to the current

location in protest at a $1 rise in rent. It's renowned as a hangout of Ernest Hemingway – he met his third wife, Martha Gellhorn, here. One of the better choices for live music as well as a busy pool table, and a must-stop for Hemingway fans.
El Meson de Pepe next to Mallory Square at 410 Wall St ☎305/295-2620. Cuban-style restaurant-bar in a converted warehouse, decked out with brightly colored murals and the obligatory black and white photos of 1950s Havana. The faux Cuban shtick can be a little cloying, but the pleasant tiki bar in the garden makes for a fair refuge from Mallory Square at sunset and the food's much tastier than its location might suggest.
Green Parrot Inn 601 Whitehead St ☎305/294-6133, ⊛www.greenparrot.com. Grubby old-time pub that's been a landmark for more than 100 years. Drinks are cheap, the place is full of locals, and there are antique bar games alongside the pool tables. Often hosts live music at weekends on its small stage.
Hog's Breath Saloon 400 Front St ☎305/292-2032, ⊛www.hogsbreath.com. Despite its central location, and the boozed-up patrons staggering out of the front door whatever the time of day, this bar's one of the best spots in town to catch live music, mostly for a nominal cover. Lots of bottled beers and cocktails, but only Bud and Amber Ale on draft. Also does juicy burgers for $6.95.
Kelly's 301 Whitehead St ☎305/293-8484. Key West's very own microbrewery, with tasty beers like Havana Red Ale and Southern Clipper served in the original PanAm ticket office from 1927 – the tropical gardens and an outdoor deck make a

pleasant place to while away the afternoon, and they also do decent pastas and seafood.
Margaritaville 500 Duval St ☎305/292-1435, ⊛www.margaritaville.com. Owner Jimmy Buffett – a Florida legend for his rock ballads extolling a laid-back life in the sun – occasionally pops in to join the live country bands that play here nightly. Enjoy the music, but skip the below-average bar food.
Sloppy Joe's 201 Duval St ☎305/294-5717. Despite the memorabilia on the walls, this bar – with live rock or blues nightly from 10pm – is not the one made famous by Ernest Hemingway's patronage (that's *Captain Tony's Saloon* round the corner – see opposite). The constant stream of cruise ship passengers and karaoke-sounding rock acts can be offputting, but brave the hordes for one of the frozen drinks, slopped in a foam cup and dressed with a cherry: for $7.50, the *piña coladas* are some of the stiffest, tastiest cocktails around.
Turtle Kraals Land's End Village, 231 Margaret St ☎305/294-2640. A locals' hangout, offering fine views over the marina and mellow blues on Friday and Saturday nights from the second-story *Tower Bar*. Also does breakfast, and classics like fish and chips for $10–13.
Virgilio's On Appelrouth Lane, adjoining *La Trattoria* at 524 Duval St ☎305/296-1075, ⊛www.virgilioskeywest.com. This glitterball-crowned martini bar has an outdoor patio, as well as small indoor bar and stage, for live music nightly from 10.30pm until 1am (expect loud, zesty Cuban bands). Drinks are served with a flourish, as each cocktail's overflow is presented alongside your glass in a mini carafe on ice (martinis are $5 on Mon).

Key West festivals

Key West celebrates everything from Hemingway's birthday to the "independ-ence" of the Conch Republic through a line-up of famously boisterous festivals throughout the year. Get precise dates on all of these from the Chamber of Commerce or check online at the sites listed below.

January

Key West Literary Seminar ☎1-888/293-9291, ⊛www.kwls.org. Four-day celebration of the island's famous four – Tennessee Williams, Ernest Hemingway, Robert Frost, and Thornton Wilder. Includes seminars, discussions, and readings with well-known living authors as well as special tours, headquartered in and around the San Carlos Institute.

March

Conch Shell Blowing Contest ☎305/294-9501, ⊛www.oirf.org. Also called the "Conch Honk",

usually held at the *Ocean Key Resort & Spa*'s sunset pier, Duval St. Anyone can enter (free), and you can buy a conch shell onsite if you don't have your own. Entrants are judged on the quality, duration, loudness, and novelty of the sound they produce.

April

Conch Republic Independence Celebration ☎305/294-2298, ⊛www.conchrepublic.com. A week of raucous celebrations starting with a symbolic raising of the Conch Republic flag at Fort

Taylor, and including a drag race, parades, mock battles and lots of serious partying. Commemorates the declaration of the Keys' independence from the US in 1982 (see box, p.144).

June
Cuban-American Heritage Festival ☎305/295-9665, ⓦ www.cubanfest.com. A celebration of all things Cuban-American, including a street fiesta as well as more serious discussions at a symposium. **Goombay Summerfest** ☎305/294-9024, ⓦ www.goombay-keywest.org. Caribbean street party in Bahama Village.

July
Hemingway Days ☎305/294-5717, ⓦ www.sloppyjoes.com. Literary seminars, writers' workshops, daft trivia competitions, a wacky "Running of the Bulls", and look-alike contests commemorate Ernest Hemingway, Key West's best-known writer. Held around his birthday on July 21.

October
Fantasy Fest ☎305/296-1817, ⓦ www.fantasy fest.net. A gay-dominated version of Mardi Gras that elects its own King & Queen in a sequin-spangled parody of a high school prom. There are outrageous costumes paraded throughout the night along Duval Street and it's a raunchy, adults-only good time. If you want a room at this time you'll need to book well in advance and expect significant rate hikes.

December
Lighted Boat Parade ☎305/292-3373, ⓦ www.schoonerwharf.com. Lighted boats sail in and around Key West Harbor.
New Year's Eve Key West's party town reputation serves it well for this huge, boisterous night along Duval St with its twin markers of midnight: a conch that drops on the roof of *Sloppy Joe's* and a giant falling slipper (complete with drag queens) outside the Bourbon St Complex. There's also much Mardi Gras bead throwing.

Gay and lesbian Key West

Gay life in Key West is always vibrant and attracts frolicking hordes from North America and Europe. The party atmosphere is laid-back, sometimes outrageous, and there's an exceptional level of integration between the straight and gay communities.

The tragedy of AIDS has hit Key West hard since the mid-1980s. A somber but important trip to the ocean at the end of White Street reveals a striking **AIDS memorial** (ⓦ www.keywestaids.org), where blocks of black granite embedded in the walkway are engraved with a roll call of the more than 1000 people in Key West, including mayor Richard Herman, who the disease has killed.

Just about all the gay bars and hotels – from Duval Street's 800 block southwards – are male-orientated, though most are welcoming to women. Stop in at the gay and lesbian chamber of commerce, the **Key West Business Guild**, 513 Truman Ave (daily 9am–5pm; ☎305/294-4603 or 1-800/535-7797, ⓦ www.gaykeywestfl.com); the team here is chatty and so informed that it's a better information source for any traveler than the mainstream Chamber office. The Guild runs a terrific weekly gay-themed, 75-minute historic trolley tour which leaves at 11am every Saturday from the parking lot behind City Hall on Simonton St (between Southard and Angela).

The unofficial gay beach is **Higgs Beach**, at the southern end of Reynolds Street; to cruise on water rather than land, take one of the day or evening **boat trips** departing from the old port – one of the best is Blu Q (☎305/923-7245, ⓦ www.bluqkeywest.com). You can head on regular gay or lesbian two-hour sunset trips ($45 per person including drinks) or opt for daytime sailing and snorkeling jaunts ($85 including lunch). For information on what's happening pick up a copy of the free *Gay Rag* monthly guide (ⓦ www.keywestgayrag.com) from hotels and restaurants, or check the business guild website.

Bars

801 Bourbon Bar 801 Duval St ☎ 305/294-4737, ⓦ www.801bourbon.com. Free drag shows upstairs every night at 9 and 11pm, while downstairs you'll find a nondescript bar with a mixed, slightly older crowd that opens onto Duval St, so you can watch passersby.

Aqua 711 Duval St ☎ 305/294-0555, ⓦ www.aquakeywest.com. Large, pumping club with a massive dancefloor; the music's usually mainstream house and Hi-NRG other than on Monday (karaoke from 8.30pm) and Friday (campy disco). Drag shows throughout the week (Tues–Sun 9pm) with a $12 cover Tues–Thurs, and $15 Fri–Sun.

🕺 **Bobby's Monkey Bar** 900 Simonton St ☎ 305/294-2655. A great place for a quiet drink, this mixed gay/straight bar is a welcoming pub-style joint, best known as the headquarters for the No Name Drag Players, a troupe whose claim to fame is that it's the only one whose members include a real woman.

🕺 **Bourbon Street Pub** 724 Duval St ☎ 305/296-1992, ⓦ www.bourbonstpub .com. A huge pub complex with five bars, seven TV screens, and a pleasant garden, lit by tiki torches out back, complete with large hot tub. There are go-go boys every night, underwear-clad bartenders, and good happy hour (buy one, get one free till 8pm daily). The crowd's youngish and a diverse blend of locals and tourists.

The Keys 1114 Duval St ☎ 305/294-8859, ⓦ www.akeywestpianobar.com. Key West's newest gay venue opened in 2008, a New York-style piano bar with food and daily live shows at 4pm – there's also an open-mic segment for wannabe performers. No cover, but two drink minimum. Open from 5pm daily.

Kwen Men 705 Duval St ☎ 305/292-8500. Small, cruisey bar on the main drag where there's a daily happy hour 3–9pm with drinks specials. From 10pm onwards, there are go-go boys dancing to the pumping house music and the place becomes a real pick-up joint.

La-Te-Da 1125 Duval St ☎ 305/296-6706 or 1-877/528-3320, ⓦ www.lateda.com. The various bars and discos of this hotel complex have long been a favorite haunt of locals and visitors. The *Pearl Bar* hosts a popular tea dance every Sunday from 4pm, while the upstairs *Crystal Room* is one of the best-known showcases for drag divas in town – during season (usually Dec–April) there are usually shows Wed–Sat at 8pm or 9pm ($24.50–28.50).

Pearl's Patio 525 United St ☎ 305/292-1450. The sole women-only bar in town is attached to *Pearl's Rainbow* guesthouse but female non-residents can stop by poolside for cocktails and snacks whenever it's open (Sun–Thurs noon–10pm, Fri & Sat noon– midnight) It's especially lively during the happy hour (Mon–Sat 5–7pm).

Listings

Airport See p.145.

Bike rental See p.145.

Bookstores Best local outlet is the Key West Island Bookstore, 513 Fleming St (daily 10am– 9pm; ☎ 305/294-2904), which is packed with the works of Key West authors and Keys-related literature, and has an excellent selection of rare and secondhand books.

Buses Local information ☎ 305/809-3910 (Mon–Fri 8am–5pm) or 305/293-6426 other times, ⓦ www.keywestcity.com.

Car rental Only worth it if you're heading off to see the other Keys or driving back to the mainland after a one-way flight. All companies are based at the airport: Alamo (☎ 305/294-6675); Avis (☎ 305/296-8744); Budget (☎ 305/294-8868); Dollar (☎ 305/296-9921); Hertz (☎ 305/294-1039); Thrifty (☎ 305/294-8644).

Cigars Key West used to be a major producer of cigars, but now the traditional industry survives in only a few workshops. The best places to pick up

cigar souvenirs are Conch Republic Cigar Factory, 512 Greene St (☎ 1-800/317-2167, ⓦ www .conch-cigars.com), Sunset Cigar Co of Key West, 306 Front St (☎ 305/295-0600), and Tropical Republic, 112 Fitzpatrick St (☎ 305/292-9595).

Greyhound Office at airport (☎ 305/296-9072).

Hospitals 24hr ER (casualty department) at Lower Keys Medical Center, 5900 College Rd, Stock Island (☎ 305/294-5531).

Internet cafés Getting connected to the internet is not cheap in Key West, and the majority of cyber- cafés charge at least $10 for an hour's access. However, if you do need to get online, the best options are the coffee shop *Sippin' at Java Joe's*, 424 Eaton St (daily 7am-11pm; ☎ 305/293-0555), which has terminals (20¢ per min) and wireless access (10¢ per min), or the free terminals at Monroe County Library, 700 Fleming St (1hr max per person; Wed 9.30am–8pm, Tues, Thurs–Fri 9.30am–6pm, Sat 10am–6pm; ☎ 305/292-3595). For those with laptops, many cafés, such as the

Coffee Plantation, 713 Caroline St (☏305/295-9808), offer free wi-fi.
Laundry Try Old Town Laundry, 517 Truman Ave (daily 8am–10pm; $2.25 per load, or $10 to leave it).

Police Emergency ☏911, nonemergency ☏305/809-1111.
Post office 400 Whitehead St (Mon–Fri 8.30am–5pm, Sat 9.30am–noon; ☏305/294-9539). Zip code 33040.

Dry Tortugas National Park

Though getting to the **Dry Tortugas National Park** (open 24hr; $5, valid for 7 days; ☏305/242-7700, ⊛www.nps.gov/drto), some seventy miles west of Key West, takes some time and a fair amount of cash, it's worth the effort; approaching the weathered stone walls of Fort Jefferson by sea is a magical experience, a fortified rock set deep into the Gulf of Mexico. Its curious military history, pristine, fish-filled waters, and a real sense of isolation and tranquility make the Tortugas a beguiling destination. It's also a paradise for bird lovers, home to significant colonies of sooty terns, frigate birds and brown noddies.

Spanish conquistador Juan Ponce de León named the islands for the large numbers of turtles (*tortugas* in Spanish) he found there in 1513 – the "dry" was added later to warn mariners of the islands' lack of fresh water. Comprising Garden Key and seven neighboring reef islands, the park was created primarily to protect the nesting grounds of the **sooty tern** – a black-bodied, white-hooded bird unusual among terns for choosing to lay its eggs in scrubby vegetation and bushes. From early January, these and a number of other winged rarities show up on Bush Key, and they are easily spied with binoculars from Fort Jefferson on Garden Key.

You can fly or take a fast ferry to Garden Key, but you can only access the other islands with your own boat (most of which are off limits).

Fort Jefferson and Garden Key

Garden Key is the last place you'd expect to find the US's largest nineteenth-century coastal fortification, but **Fort Jefferson** (daily during daylight hours), which rises mirage-like in the distance as you approach, is exactly that. Started in 1846 and intended to protect US interests on the Gulf, the fort was never completed, despite thirty years of building. Instead it served as a prison, until intense heat, lack of fresh water, outbreaks of disease, and savage weather made the fort as unpopular with its guards as its inmates; in 1874, after a hurricane and the latest yellow fever outbreak, it was abandoned. Look for the change in colors of the bricks: the shift marks the outbreak of the Civil War, when the Union-loyal fort here was no longer able to buy supplies from Key West. Of course, the bricks shipped down from the north at the top of the walls have weathered the hot, humid weather less well than the local materials at the base. Most ferry trips include a 45-minute tour of the fort, but otherwise following the signposted **walk** and viewing the odds and ends in the small **visitor center** at the entrance won't take more than an hour.

Most trips include at least another couple of hours to explore the enticing beaches and waters ringing the fort. Visibility is normally excellent and you'll see plenty of fish (and occasionally turtles) lazing in the moat and right off the beach and pier; note, though, there isn't much coral close to Garden Key itself. Barracuda are common, as are multicolored clown parrotfish, and you'll spy great flocks of frigate birds on nearby Long Key and sooty terns (Feb–Sept) on Bush Key.

▲ Fort Jefferson

Practicalities

You can **get to Garden Key** by air in half an hour with Seaplane of Key West from the Key West airport ($229 half-day, $405 full day; ℡305/294-0709, ⓦwww.seaplanesofkeywest.com) – a beautiful if pricey trip that takes you low over the turquoise water. Less expensive and more relaxed is taking one of two high-speed ferries from the Historic Seaport (both daily 8am): *Yankee Freedom II*, (end of Margaret St; $159; ℡305/294-7009 or 1-800/322-0013, ⓦwww.yankeefreedom.com) and *Sunny Days* (end of William St; $135; ℡305/292-6100, ⓦwww.drytortugasferry.com). The price includes breakfast, lunch, guided tour, and snorkel gear. After a few leisurely hours at the fort, the ferries return by 5pm.

Avid birdwatchers can **camp** ($3 per person) at Fort Jefferson for up to fourteen days, though given its lack of amenities you have to come well prepared with your own supplies of water and food; only in an emergency can you count on help from the park rangers (who live here in surprisingly comfortable quarters 365 days a year).

Travel details

Buses

Two Greyhound buses (℡1-800/410-5397 or 1-800/231-2222) a day run between Miami (departing 12.35pm, 6.50pm for Key West) and Key West (departing 8.55am and 5.45pm for Miami).

Scheduled stops are listed below, though the bus can unofficially be waved down at other stops – stand by the side of the Overseas Highway and jump about like a maniac when you see the bus coming. **Scheduled stops:** Key Largo (Central Plaza, 103200 Overseas Highway; ℡305/451-6280);

Islamorada (*Burger King*, MM82; ☎305/296-9072); Marathon (MA Inc, 12222 Overseas Highway; ☎305/296-9073); Big Pine Key (*Big Pine Motel*, MM30.2; ☎305/296-9072); Key West (Key West International Airport ☎305/296-9072).
From Miami to: Big Pine Key (3hr 35min); Islamorada (2hr 5min); Key West (4hr 30min); Marathon (3hr 10min); Key Largo (1hr 30min).

Ferries

A passenger-only ferry service operated by Key West Express (☎1-888/539-2628, ⓦwww .seakeywestexpress.com) runs from Key West across to Fort Myers or Marco Island on the Gulf of Mexico side of mainland Florida (see "Sarasota and the Southwest" chapter). The ferry leaves from the terminal in the Historic Seaport at 100 Grinnell St, and is a good way of getting to Florida's west coast without zigzagging back across the Keys and through the Everglades. The ferry runs daily to Fort Myers – weather permitting – at 6pm ($85.50 single; $129 round-trip; 3hr 45min), and daily in season (usually Dec–April) at 5pm to Marco Island ($85.50 single; $130 round-trip; 3hr 30min).

Flights

Cape Air ☎1-800/352-0714 flies to Fort Myers from Key West six times daily from around $140 each way, while American Airlines (see p.22) flies to Miami for around $150.

The Everglades

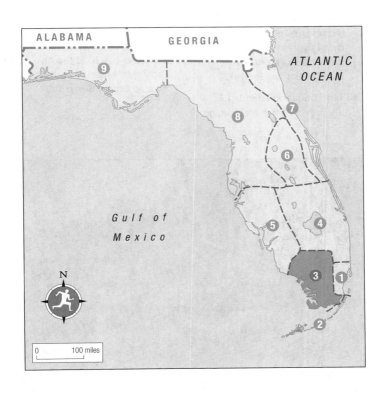

CHAPTER 3 # Highlights

✳ **The Anhinga Trail** In season, this popular hiking path is teeming with birds and plenty of alligators. See p.173

✳ **Shark Valley** Cycle or join the entertaining – and educational – tram tour into the heart of the "River of Grass". See p.175

✳ **Fakahatchee Strand** Roam through this alluring swamp of dwarf cypress trees and royal palms, domain of the rare Florida panther. See p.178

✳ **Ten Thousand Islands** Ply the waters of this archipelago of dense mangrove cays by boat or by canoe, home to pelicans, dolphins and sea turtles. See p.179

✳ **Manatee tours** Take a boat tour specializing in lumbering but loveable manatees, the endangered sea mammals that graze the Florida coast. See p.180

✳ **Big Cypress Seminole Reservation** Soak up Seminole culture at the Ah-Tah-Thi-Ki Museum and Billie Swamp Safari. See p.180

▲ Big Cypress National Preserve

3

The Everglades

One of the country's most celebrated natural areas, **the EVERGLADES** is a vast watery wilderness with a raw but subtle appeal that makes a stark contrast to America's more rugged national parks. The most dramatic sights are small pockets of trees poking above a completely flat sawgrass plain, yet these wide-open spaces resonate with life, forming part of an ever-changing ecosystem, evolved through a unique combination of climate, vegetation, and wildlife. Originally encompassing everything south of Lake Okeechobee, today only a comparatively small section around Florida's southern tip is under the federal protection of **Everglades National Park**.

Everglades ecology

Appearing as flat as a tabletop, the limestone on which the Everglades stands (once part of the sea bed) actually tilts very slightly – a few inches over seventy miles – toward the southwest. For thousands of years, water flowed as a sixty-mile-wide sheet through the Everglades, from Lake Okeechobee to the coast. This sheet flow replenishes the **sawgrass**, which grows on a thin layer of soil – or "marl" – formed by decaying vegetation on the limestone base, and gives birth to the algae at the foot of a complex food chain that sustains much larger creatures, most importantly alligators.

Alligators earn their "keepers of the Everglades" nickname during the dry winter season. After the summer floodwaters have reached the sea, drained through the bedrock, or simply evaporated, the Everglades is barren except for the water accumulated in ponds or "gator holes" – created when an alligator senses water and clears the soil covering it with its tail. Besides nourishing the alligator, the pond provides a home for other wildlife until the summer rains return.

Sawgrass covers much of the Everglades, but where natural indentations in the limestone fill with marl, tree islands – or "**hammocks**" – appear, just high enough to stand above the flood waters and fertile enough to support a variety of trees and plants. Close to hammocks, often surrounding gator holes, you'll find wispy green-leafed willows. Smaller patches of vegetation, like small green humps, are called "**bayheads**." **Pinewoods** grow in the few places where the elevation exceeds seven feet and, in the deep depressions that hold water the longest, dwarf cypress trees flourish, their treetops forming a distinctive "cypress dome" when large numbers cover an extensive area.

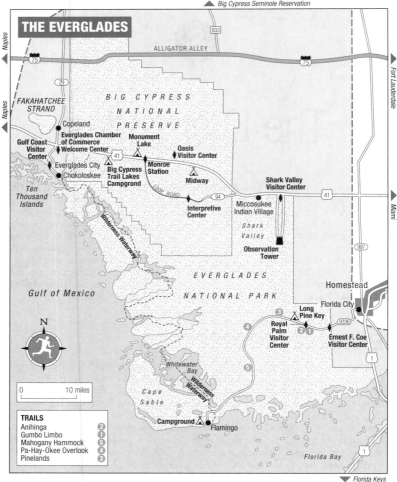

▲ Big Cypress Seminole Reservation

THE EVERGLADES

Threats and preservation

As Florida's population grew, the damage caused by uncontrolled hunting, road building and draining the Everglades for farmland gave rise to a significant conservation lobby. In 1947, a section of the Everglades was declared a national park, but unrestrained commercial use of nearby areas continued to upset the Everglades' natural cycle. The 1200 miles of canals built to divert the flow of water away from the Everglades toward the state's expanding cities, the poisoning caused by agricultural chemicals from the farmlands around Lake Okeechobee, and the broader changes wrought by global warming and invasion by non-native species, threaten to turn Florida's greatest natural asset into a wasteland.

In an attempt to increase the natural sheet flow in the Everglades, Congress authorized a thirty-year, $7.8 billion plan in 2000 to dismantle miles of levees and canals, and divert and store part of the 1.7 billion gallons of water lost each day (in the flow from Lake Okeechobee to the ocean) for later use. A potentially major step forward was made in 2008 when the government purchased sugarcane plantations to the south of Lake Okeechobee for $1.34bn, though it remains to be seen how much of this land will actually be set aside for restoration. Given the complexity of the project, it will be some time before it's clear whether the plan will produce any of the desired results.

Everglades practicalities

Everglades National Park has three main entrances. The popular **southern section** of the park can be reached by taking the **Florida's Turnpike Extension** to Homestead, where it drops you on US-1 South. Make a right at the first traffic light (onto West Palm Drive, or 344th Ave), and follow the signs for the park entrance. Centrally located **Shark Valley** can only be accessed from two-lane **US-41** (the **Tamiami Trail**), 25 miles from Florida's Turnpike. US-41 runs along the northern edge of the park between Miami and Naples, and also provides the only land access to the park entrance at **Everglades City**, the Big Cypress National Preserve, and the Miccosukee Indian Village.

Park entry is free at Everglades City, although from there you can travel only by boat or canoe. At the other entrances it's $10 per car and $5 for pedestrians and cyclists. Entry tickets are valid for seven days and can be used at any entrance. With the exception of the Wilderness Waterway canoe trail between Everglades City and Flamingo, you can't travel from one section of the park into another.

There is **no public transportation** along US-41, or to any of the park entrances, though day-trips are organized by almost every tour operator in Miami and Naples (see p.266).

The park is **open year-round**, but the most favorable time to visit is **winter**, when the receding floodwaters cause wildlife to congregate around gator holes, ranger-led activities are frequent, and the mosquitoes are bearable. In **summer**, afternoon storms flood the prairies, park activities are substantially reduced, and the mosquitoes are a severe annoyance. Visiting between seasons is also a good idea (April to early May, or late Oct to early Nov).

Accommodation

Apart from two drive-in camp sites (see p.172), **accommodation** within the park is limited to 47 backcountry **campgrounds**. In most cases these are raised wooden platforms with a roof and chemical toilet, accessible by boat or canoe. To stay, you need to pick up a **backcountry permit** ($10 plus $2 per person, free May–Nov), from the closest visitor center, no more than 24 hours beforehand. One backcountry site at Flamingo, Pearl Bay, is accessible to disabled visitors, with lower ground access to huts and other facilities.

In **Florida City**, ten miles east of the reserve, you'll find the *Everglades International Hostel*, 20 SW Second Ave (℡305/248-1122 or 1-800/372-3874, ⓦwww.evergladeshostel.com). In high season (Nov–March) dorm beds are $25 a night ($28 in advance), with private rooms $75. Camping is $18. Bike ($15 per day) and kayak ($30 per day) rental is also available, and the friendly staff will rent you racks ($6 per day) to transport equipment on your car or give you a lift to the park entrance for $10. Other convenient bases outside the park include **Everglades City** (see p.172), **Naples** (see p.266) and **Homestead** (see p.65). The park's lone **motel** at Flamingo sustained major damage during hurricanes Katrina and Wilma in 2005, and the ambitious eco-friendly replacement – dubbed "Alternative D" – is not expected to open until 2011 or later. Check the park website for updates.

Southern section

Flamingo Campground Flamingo ☎1-877/444-6777, ⓦwww.recreation.gov. Well-equipped though often buggy campground at the end of Rte-9336, with 234 drive-in sites (55 with a view of the water), cold-water showers, picnic tables and grills but no hook-ups. ($16 per tent site; free May–Nov). You can make reservations up to six months in advance.

Long Pine Key Campground off Rte-9336, 6 miles west of Ernest Coe Visitor Center ☎305/242-7873, ⓦwww.nps.gov/ever. Attractive campground with 108 sites for tents and RVs, restrooms and water, but no showers or hook-ups. No reservations – check the instructions on the bulletin board just inside the park entrance ($16 per tent site; free May–Nov).

Along US-41/Shark Valley

Gator Park 24050 SW 8th St (US-41) ☎305/559-2255, ⓦwww.gatorpark.com. Camping and RV hook-ups are available at this popular airboat and alligator park, 12 miles west of Florida's Turnpike and 13 miles east of Shark Valley. Sites from $30 per night.

Big Cypress National Preserve

Midway Campground US-41 ☎239/695-1201, ⓦwww.nps.gov/bicy. Best of the two designated campgrounds in the preserve, around two miles from Oasis Visitor Center and equipped with flush toilets, grills, drinking water, 26 RV sites with hook-ups ($19) and 10 tent sites ($16). No reservations.

Monument Lake Campground US-41, near Monroe Station ☎239/695-1201, ⓦwww.nps.gov/bicy. Set next to a small lake five miles west of Oasis Visitor Center, the other official preserve campsite also offers restrooms, drinking water and an outside cold-water shower. RV sites ($16) are without hook-ups here; camping is also $16. Fees charged Dec 15–April 15, otherwise free. Open Aug 28–April 15. No reservations.

Trail Lakes Campground 40904 US-41, Ochopee ☎239/695-2275, ⓦwww.skunkape.info. Privately owned campground around 17 miles west of the Oasis Visitor Center on US-41, sharing a site with the eccentric but oddly intriguing Skunk Ape Research Headquarters. It's $20 a night to pitch a tent, $25 for an RV.

Everglades City and around

Captain's Table 102 E Broadway ☎239/695-4211, ⓦwww.captainstablehotel.com. Wide choice of rooms, from basic but adequate doubles to luxury apartments. Has a great heated pool overlooking a lake and *Seafood Depot* on site (see p.180). ❸

Chokoloskee Island Park 1150 Hamilton Lane, Chokoloskee ☎239/695-2414, ⓦwww.chokoloskee.com. Family-oriented budget resort, with 22 sites for RVs ($43) or tents ($38) and 11 comfy two-bedroom cottages. Laundry and free wi-fi on site. Three miles south of Everglades City, off Rte-29. ❺

Ivey House Bed & Breakfast 107 Camellia St ☎239/695-3299, ⓦwww.iveyhouse.com. Offers accommodation with shared bathrooms in the lodge (closed April–Oct; ❹) or in a slightly nicer inn (❻) on the premises, where you get TV, phone, and private bathroom.

Parkway Motel & Marina 1180 Chokoloskee Drive, Chokoloskee ☎239/695-3261, ⓦwww.parkwaymotelandmarina.com. Immaculate and cozy motel rooms equipped with fridge, bathrooms and a/c. Knowledgeable owners can sort out boat rentals and guides. ❺

Rod & Gun Lodge 200 Riverside Drive ☎239/695-2101, ⓦwww.evergladesrodandgun.com. Used to be an exclusive club whose members included presidents, but now anyone can stay in this hunting-lodge-style hotel, with pool and antique cocktail lounge thrown in. Cottages are showing their age, but come with private bath and plenty of character. ❻

The Everglades: southern section

The **southern section** of the park – containing the Pine Island area and Flamingo – holds virtually everything that makes the Everglades tick. Spend a well-planned day or two here for an introduction to its complex ecology, starting at the park's largest information hub, the **Ernest Coe Visitor Center** (daily 9am–5pm; ☎305/242-7700). From here the road passes through the **park entrance**, and continues for 38 miles to the tiny coastal settlement of

Flamingo, a one-time pioneer fishing colony now comprising a marina and campground. The short **walking trails** (none longer than half a mile) along the route will keep you engaged for hours; devote at least one day to walking and another to the **canoe trails** close to Flamingo.

Pine Island walking trails

The first section of this part of the park is known as **Pine Island**, containing some of the most rewarding hiking trails in the Everglades. Your first stop should be the barebones **Royal Palm Visitor Center** (open 24hr), a mile from the main park entrance, which usually hosts ranger activities but has little in the way of information, though there is a small gift and book store (daily 8am–4.15pm).

Park visitors eager to spot an **alligator** tend to be satisfied by walking the **Anhinga Trail** here; the reptiles are easily seen during the winter, often splayed near the trail, looking like plastic props. They're notoriously lazy, but give them a wide berth, as they can be extremely swift if provoked. Turtles, marsh rabbits and the odd raccoon are also likely to turn up on the route, and keep an eye out for the bizarre **anhinga**, a black-bodied bird resembling an elongated cormorant, which, after diving for fish, spends ages drying itself on rocks and tree branches with its white-tipped wings fully spread. Get an early start on the trail to beat the crowds and then peruse the adjacent but very different **Gumbo Limbo Trail**, a hardwood jungle hammock packed with exotic subtropical growths: strangler figs, red-barked gumbo limbos, royal palms, wild coffee, and resurrection ferns. The latter appear dead during the dry season, but "resurrect" themselves in the summer rains to form a lush collar of green.

By comparison, the **Pinelands Trail**, three miles further on, offers an undramatic half-mile ramble through a forest of slash pine, though the solitude comes as a welcome relief after the busier trails. The hammering of woodpeckers is often the loudest sound you'll hear. More birdlife – including egrets,

▲ Wildlife along the Anhinga Trail

red-shouldered hawks, and circling vultures – is viewable six miles ahead from the **Pa-hay-okee Overlook Trail**, which emerges from a stretch of dwarf cypress to face a sweeping expanse of sawgrass. Although related to California's giant redwoods, the mahogany trees of the **Mahogany Hammock Trail**, seven miles from the Overlook Trail, are comparatively small despite being the largest of the type in the country. A greater draw is the colorful snails and golden orb spiders lurking among their branches.

Flamingo and around

A century ago, the only way to reach **FLAMINGO** was by boat, a fact that failed to deter a small group of settlers who came here to fish, hunt, smuggle, and get paralytic on moonshine whiskey. It didn't even have a name until the opening of a post office made one necessary: "Flamingo" was eventually chosen due to an abundance of roseate spoonbills – pink-plumed birds, killed for their feathers – wrongly identified by locals. The completion of the road to Homestead in 1922 was expected to bring boom times to Flamingo, but as it turned out, most people seized on this as a chance to leave. None of the old buildings remain, and the main trade of present-day Flamingo is servicing the needs of sport fishing fanatics. The **marina store** (Sun–Thurs 7am–7pm, Fri & Sat 6am–8pm) is likely to be the only place to buy supplies and snacks until the completion of the new hotel complex. The nearby **visitor center** (Dec–April 7.30am–5pm, May–Oct 9am–4.30pm; ☎239/695-2945) has a great viewing deck overlooking the bay, maps on local walks, and a small exhibition on local fauna and flora.

You'll find several walking trails within reach of Flamingo, but more promising are the numerous **canoe trails**. Rent a tandem canoe ($22 half day, $32 full day, $40 for 24hr) or kayak ($35 half day, $45 full day, $55 for 24hr) from the marina store, and get maps and advice from the visitor center. A good choice for novices (don't go it alone if you've no experience whatsoever) is the two-mile **Noble Hammock Trail**, passing through sawgrass and around dense mangroves. Segments of the trail are very narrow, though, and do require some agility. An alternative, the **Mud Lake Loop** (6.8 miles), links the Buttonwood Canal, Coot's Bay, Mud Lake, and the Bear Lake Canoe Trail, with plenty of opportunities for prime birdwatching.

If you lack faith in your own abilities, take a **guided boat trip** from the marina. The **Backcountry Boat Cruise** (daily 10am, 1pm, & 3.30pm, minimum 6 people; $18; reservations on ☎239/695-3101), makes a tranquil one-hour 45-minute foray around the mangrove-enshrouded Coot and White-water bays.

Wilderness Waterway

Anybody adequately skilled with the paddle, equipped with rough camping gear, and with a week to spare, should have a crack at the 99-mile **Wilderness Waterway**, a marked kayak trail between Flamingo and Everglades City, with numerous backcountry campgrounds en route. Take a compass, maps, and ample provisions, including at least a gallon of water per person per day. Carry supplies in hard containers, as raccoons can chew through soft ones. Be sure to leave a detailed plan of your journey and its expected duration with a park ranger. Finally, pay heed to the latest weather forecast and note the tidal patterns if you're canoeing in a coastal area. If you need help with planning the trip, kayak rentals or lifts to the waterway, contact the Flamingo marina (see above) or *Everglades International Hostel* (p.171).

Eating and drinking

It's a good idea to stop for a snack or drink before entering the southern section of the park – otherwise you'll have to wait until Flamingo, 38 miles on, where the **marina store** sells basic snacks and food. Your last chance for refreshments is enticing fruit stall *Robert Is Here* (see p.107), outside Homestead.

Shark Valley

In no other section of the national park does the Everglades' "River of Grass" tag seem as appropriate as it does at **Shark Valley** (daily 8.30am–6pm). From here the sawgrass plain stretches as far as the eye can see, dotted by hardwood hammocks and the smaller bayheads. Though the parking area closes at 6pm, the park itself is open 24 hours and is quite popular with hikers on full-moon nights; park your vehicle along the road near the entrance. You won't see any sharks here: the "valley" is actually part of the Shark River Slough, which ends up emptying into Florida Bay (where you will find sharks).

Seeing Shark Valley

Aside from a few simple walking trails close to the **visitor center** (daily 9.15am–5.15pm; ☏305/221-8776), you can see Shark Valley only from a fifteen-mile loop road. At the far point of the loop (seven miles), a 45-foot **observation tower** offers a panoramic overview of the plains. Too lengthy and lacking in shade to walk comfortably, and off limits to cars, the loop is ideally explored by **bike** (rental shop 8.30am–3pm; $6.50 per hr, return by 4pm). Alternatively, a highly informative two-hour **tram tour** (Dec–April 9am–4pm, hourly; May–Nov 9.30am, 11am, 1pm, & 3pm; $15.25, children $9.25; reservations recommended Dec–April; ☏305/221-8455, ⓦwww .sharkvalleytramtours.com) stops frequently to view wildlife.

If touring by bike, set out as early as possible (the wildlife is most active in the cool of the morning), ride slowly and stay alert: otters, turtles, and snakes are plentiful but not always easy to spot, and the abundant alligators often keep uncannily still. During September and October you'll come across female alligators tending their young; watch them from a safe distance. You can see more of the same creatures – and a good selection of birdlife – from the observation tower.

Miccosukee Indian Village

A mile west of Shark Valley, the **Miccosukee Indian Village** (daily 9am–5pm; $10, $5 for children; ☏305/223-8380, ⓦwww.miccosukee.com) symbolizes the tribe's uneasy compromise with modern America. In the souvenir shop good-quality traditional crafts and clothes stand side by side with blatant tat, and in the "village" men turn logs into canoes and women cook over open fires. Despite the authentic roots, it's such a contrived affair that anyone with an ounce of sensitivity can't help but feel uneasy. Since it's one of the few introductions to Native American life in the Everglades, it's hard to resist taking a look, though a plateful of home-made chili with the regulars at nearby *Gunny's* (see p.176), might be more enlightening. If you're visiting at the end of December, check out the **Indian Arts Festival** held at the village, when

Florida's Seminole and Miccosukee tribes

Against all the odds, Florida's **Seminole** and **Miccosukee** Indians have created a thriving community in the same swamps and sawgrass plains where their ancestors – less than two hundred survivors of the last Seminole war in 1858 – held out against the US army. They never surrendered to the US government, and there is still much pride in the epithet "unconquered people." Many more Seminoles live in the Mid-West, where they were deported in the nineteenth century.

Florida's original native inhabitants – tribes like the Calusa and the Tequesta – died out in the eighteenth century and by the 1760s bands of Creek Indians from Georgia and Alabama had moved into the state – Seminole was a transliteration of the Spanish word "cimarrones" meaning wild or free people, and came into use around this time. Pushed further into the Everglades in the nineteenth century, the Seminoles lived on hammocks in open-sided *chickee* huts built from cypress and cabbage palm, and traded, hunted, and fished across the wetlands by canoe. Development and drainage of the Everglades in the 1920s ended this way of life, and the tribe turned to tourism and farming (mainly cattle-ranching) to make a living. The division between the Miccosukee and Seminole occurred in the 1950s and is somewhat controversial. The Miccosukee are descendants of what were once known as Trail Seminoles, who lived along the Tamiami Trail; when the Seminole tribe re-organized in 1957, this group opted to remain independent. Despite recent attempts on both sides to emphasize differences, both tribes speak the same Mikasuki language.

In 1979 the Seminoles were the first Native American tribe to develop **gaming** as a form of income (see p.198), and today their million-dollar revenues pay for universal health care, financial support for education, full senior care and modern community centers. The six Seminole reservations at Hollywood (the headquarters), Big Cypress, Brighton, Fort Pierce, Immokalee and Tampa, (with a total population of around 3,300) exercise limited sovereignty and have plenty of spare cash; the tribe purchased the **Hard Rock Cafe** franchise in 2006.

Native American artisans from all over the country gather to display their work. Across the road, the tribe also runs **airboat tours** (☎305/552-8365), which take in a traditional Miccosukee hammock camp, where you can learn a little more about the local wildlife, and the history and culture of the tribe; thirty-minute tours start at $10 per person, but can be hit-and-miss (the enthusiasm of the guides tends to vary).

Eating and drinking

The tribe runs the official *Miccosukee Restaurant* (☎305/894-2349) across the highway, which serves decent tacos, pumpkin bread, Indian fry bread, frog legs and catfish, along with plenty of uninspiring burger and fries-type items, though service can sometimes be slow. A more interesting option is *Gunny's* (☎305/222-9130; closed Tues & Wed) little more than a shack along the reservation service road (turn left as you leave the Indian village), which is where hungry locals go to fill up on beans and chili. Opening times here can be erratic, however (while the *Miccosukee Restaurant* is usually open daily). You can also get reasonable meals at Gator Park and Coopertown (see box, p.178), featuring the obligatory alligator and catfish; the latter is best for gator tails and frogs legs.

Big Cypress National Preserve

The completion of US-41 in 1928 led to the destruction of thousands of towering bald cypress trees – whose durable wood is highly marketable – that lined the roadside sloughs. By the 1970s, attempts to drain these acres and turn them into residential plots posed a threat to nearby Everglades National Park and the government created the **Big Cypress National Preserve** in 1974 – a massive chunk of protected land mostly on the northern side of US-41. Today one third of the preserve is covered in cypress trees (mostly the dwarf pond variety), though the giant cypress has largely vanished.

Seeing the preserve

The only way to traverse the entire preserve is via a rugged 37-mile (one-way) hiking trail, part of the **Florida National Scenic Trail**. The **Oasis Visitor Center** (daily 9am–4.30pm; ☎239/695-1201) on US-41 divides the trail into a thirty-mile section north of US-41 and a seven-mile section south of the highway. Visitors are required to pick up a free backcountry permit, for either day or overnight access. More manageable hiking routes include the five-mile (round-trip) **Fire Prairie Trail** (on Turner River Rd, fourteen miles north of US-41); its slight elevation means it tends to be on the dry side, giving colorful prairie flowers a chance to bloom in the spring.

A half-mile east of the visitor center sits the **Big Cypress Gallery**, 52388 Tamiami Trail (daily 10am–5pm; ☎239/695-2428 or 1-888/999-9113, ⓦwww .clydebutcher.com), which exhibits the amazing pictures of Everglades photographer Clyde Butcher, capturing all the beauty and magic of the area. Framed pictures are on the expensive side ($450 and up), but they also come as smaller cards that make perfect souvenirs (boxes from $16.50).

▲ An airboat driver pilots his passengers through the Everglades

Airboat tours

Airboat tours are synonymous with the Everglades and all along US-41 operators will try and tempt you onto one of their trips. In the hands of a responsible operator they are not a problem; however, not all operators are so inclined and these tours can have a damaging impact on the environment. If you do want to take an airboat tour, be careful which operator you choose. The three tours listed here are on the south side of US-41 and run boats just inside the boundaries of the park.

Operating since 1945, **Coopertown** (daily 9am–5pm; $21, $10 for children; ☏305/226-6048, ⓦwww.coopertownairboats.com), eleven miles west of Florida's Turnpike, is the oldest airboat tour company in the area and offers an informative forty-minute tour through eight miles of sawgrass. Boat drivers are a font of Everglades knowledge. **Gator Park** (daily 9am–5pm; $21, $10.70 for children; ☏305/559-2255 or 1-800/559-2205, ⓦwww.gatorpark.com) offers a somewhat slicker tour, for 45 minutes, though it doesn't cover as much area inside the park. After the tour, you'll be subjected to the slightly disturbing "alligator wrestling" and wildlife show. **Everglades Safari** (daily 9am–5pm; $23, $10 for children; ☏305/226-6923, ⓦwww.evsafaripark.com) runs the shortest tour, at 30 minutes, and also offers the obligatory wildlife shows.

For a bone-shaking but wildlife-packed off-road excursion, turn left off US-41 at Monroe Station, four miles west of the Oasis Ranger Station, onto the 26-mile **Loop Road**, a gravel track that's potholed in parts and prone to sudden flooding as it winds its way through cypress stands and pinewoods. Once you reach Pinecrest, things get easier: the road becomes paved and, after another twenty minutes or so, rejoins US-41 at Forty Mile Bend, just west of the Miccosukee Indian Village. Alligators are as common as lizards on the road (sometimes blocking it), and you'll see plenty of white ibis and sometimes snakes; if you're very lucky, you might spot a black bear or panther.

Fakahatchee Strand Preserve State Park

After a trip to the Big Cypress National Preserve be sure to visit the nearby **Fakahatchee Strand Preserve State Park**, directly north of Everglades City on Route 29. This water-holding slough sustains dwarf cypress trees (gray and spindly during the winter, draped with green needles in summer), a stately batch of royal palms, and masses of orchids and spiky-leafed air plants. You should see plenty of wildlife from the Big Cypress Bend Boardwalk just off US-41, or along the eleven-mile Jane's Scenic Drive off Rte-29. If possible, see them on a **ranger-guided walk** (details on ☏239/695-4593).

Further north along Rte-29 (just beyond I-75), the **Florida Panther National Wildlife Reserve** protects the remaining 80 to 100 panthers that inhabit the Everglades, endangered after years of over-hunting. You can walk the 1.3-mile loop trail into the reserve, though realistically you're as likely to see a panther as you are to win the Florida lottery.

Eating and drinking

At ♨*Joanie's Blue Crab Café*, 39395 US-41 in Ochopee (Wed–Mon 10am–5pm; ☏239/695-2682), a colorful shack crammed with knickknacks, you can dine on a meal of frogs' legs, gator pieces, and Indian fry bread, or choose from the usual sandwiches and seafood dishes (lunch entrées $8–17). Opposite, make a stop at the **world's smallest post office**, squashed into a 7 by 8-foot hut that was originally an irrigation pipe shed built in 1953.

Everglades City and around

Created by advertising tycoon Barron Collier in the 1920s, sleepy **EVERGLADES CITY** serves as a good base from which to explore the **Ten Thousand Islands** section of the Everglades, but also warrants a visit in its own right. For local information, stop at the wooden, triangular building of the **Everglades Area Chamber of Commerce Welcome Center** (daily 9am–4pm; ☎239/695-3941, Ⓦwww.evergladeschamber.com), at the junction of Route-29 and US-41 (four miles north of the town center).

The Town

Smitten with southwest Florida, Collier began pouring money into the area in the early 1920s, and after the state named Collier County in his honor in 1923, he established Everglades City as the county seat. Despite the completion of the Tamiami Trail in 1928, the "city" never really took off, and after Hurricane Donna leveled the place in 1960, the county government and most businesses relocated to Naples. Everglades City has been a pleasant backwater ever since, existing largely to serve the tourist trade. Some of the properties left standing in the wake of Hurricane Donna have been restored, offering a glimpse into life before the destruction. One such building is the **Museum of the Everglades**, downtown at 105 W Broadway (Tues–Fri 9am–5pm, Sat 9am–4pm; free, suggested $2 donation; ☎239/695-0008), housed in what used to be the old laundry when it was built in 1928. It now displays a small but absorbing exhibition documenting the last two thousand years in the southwest Everglades, enhanced by a selection of artifacts and old photographs.

Ten Thousand Islands

The main attraction here lies offshore, the numerous mangrove islands scattered like jigsaw-puzzle pieces along the coastline – aptly named **Ten Thousand Islands** and forming part of the largest mangrove forest in North America. For an introduction, visit the dockside **Gulf Coast Visitor Center**, half-mile south of the town center, (daily: Nov–April 8am–4.30pm, May–Oct 9am–4.30pm; ☎239/695-3311), which has a small array of displays highlighting local flora and fauna (including a lead-like manatee rib), and DVDs played on demand.

The only way to really experience this part of the park is get onto the water. Ignore the ecologically dubious tours advertised along the roadside and take one of the park-sanctioned **boat trips**. Everglades National Park Boat Tours (daily 8.30am–5pm; ☎239/695-2591 or 1-866/628-7275), underneath the visitor center, has ninety-minute excursions starting at $26.50. Boats run every thirty minutes December to mid-April, and hourly for the rest of the year. Expect to see plenty of birds year-round (herons, egrets, and fish-feeding pelicans), though dolphins, turtles and manatees are less easy to spot. You can also **rent canoes** here for $25–44 per day.

Everglades Rentals and Eco Adventures (☎239/695-3299, Ⓦwww.everglades adventures.com), located at *Ivey House Bed and Breakfast* (see p.172), offers a range of activities from November through April, from an evening paddle ($99) to full-day kayak excursions ($119). Canoe rentals are $35 a day. *Ivey House* guests receive a 20 percent discount on all rates.

Chokoloskee Island

Beyond the visitor center the road continues for another four miles across the causeway to **Chokoloskee Island**, connected to the mainland in 1954. Archeologists believe the whole island started life as a vast shell midden created by the lost **Calusa** civilization. Nothing remains from that period, however, and the main reason to visit this sleepy boating community is for the old Indian trading post of **Smallwood's Store** at the end of Mamie St (Dec–April daily 10am–5pm, May–Nov Fri–Mon 11am–4pm; $3; ☎239/695-2989). Pioneer Ted Smallwood built this stilt house out of rock-hard Dade County pine in 1906, and it remains crammed with all sorts of bric-a-brac and curios, old medicinal bottles and machinery. The solid wood counter, rickety roof, and creaky veranda cooled by bay breezes are evocative of the days when Ted traded vegetables, tools and salt pork with the Seminoles. You'll also learn about the notorious vigilante killing of local strongman Edgar Watson near here in 1910, dramatized in Peter Matthiessen's novel *Killing Mr Watson*.

Eating and drinking

Seafood **restaurants** dominate the area, though despite providing 95 percent of the world's supply of **stone crab** since the 1940s, all the best claws tend to get sent elsewhere (see *Joe's Stone Crab* in Miami p.102). *The Seafood Depot*, 102 Collier Ave, Everglades City (☎239/695-0075), in the old 1928 train depot, offers stone crab and lobster, as well as a tasty selection of Mexican and Caribbean dishes, and will cook any fish you have caught (and cleaned). At the *Oyster House*, on Chokoloskee Causeway (☎239/695-2073), you can watch the sunset over the Ten Thousand Islands while you eat seafood baskets and sip cold beers.

Big Cypress Seminole Reservation

Located on the northern border of the Big Cypress National Preserve, but only accessible from Rte-833 off I-75, the **Big Cypress Seminole Reservation** features a couple of attractions that may hold your interest for an hour or two; as the largest **Seminole** reservation in Florida, it's also the best place to meet the locals and get some sense of how the modern tribe lives.

The main settlement begins fifteen miles north of I-75, where amongst an impressive array of schools, sports facilities, civic buildings and a new rodeo

Manatee tours

One of Florida's most endangered and endearing inhabitants is the hippo-like **manatee** (see box, p.396), with only an estimated 1000 to 1500 remaining in the state. Though you might see manatees anywhere along the coast, their dwindling numbers and the difficulty in spotting them means that in practice this is unlikely; if you really want to see a manatee, look for specialist operators such as **Captains Barry and Carol Berger** at the *Port of the Islands Resort* marina, just off US-41 eleven miles west of Rte-29 (☎239/642-8818, ⌨www.see-manatees.com; $38–48), who guarantee sightings (on 90min trips), or your money back. Advance bookings are essential. At the same marina, **Double R's Manatee Eco Tours** (☎239/642-9779, ⌨doublersmanateetours.com; $55) run similarly focused 2hr 30min tours around the Ten Thousand Islands.

arena, you'll find a few basic diners (see below) and the rather sparse **Seminole Country Gift Shop** (Mon–Sat 9am–6pm, Sun 1–6pm; ℡239/564-1114), which sells traditional clothing, jewelry and necklaces. On the northern side of town lies the principal attraction, the fascinating **Ah–Tah–Thi–Ki Museum** (daily 9am–5pm; $9; ℡863/902-1113), where a seventeen-minute audio-visual presentation, displays and a rare collection of clothing and artifacts highlight Seminole history and cultural traditions. The 1.5-mile boardwalk at the back cuts through a tranquil swamp, to a reproduction of a traditional camp. Boards along the way explain how local plants were used by the Seminole for medicinal purposes.

At **Billie Swamp Safari**, four miles north of the museum (daily 8.30am–5pm; ℡1-800/949-6101, ⓦwww.seminoletribe.com/safari), swamp buggy tours cruise through the Everglades (1hr narrated, $25; hourly 10am–5pm), where you're sure to spot alligators, egrets, and American buffalo. You can also take twenty-minute airboat rides (10am–4.30pm; every 30min; $15), and watch a 30–45 minute educational presentation on snakes and alligators (daily 2.15pm) or a swamp critter show (daily 1.15pm; both $8). Day packages, including all of these activities, start at $49. To round off the experience stay overnight in a native-style *chickee* (a traditional palm-thatched hut) and listen to ancient Seminole tales (two-person *chickee* is $35 per night, 8- or 12-person dorm $65).

Eating

The *Swamp Water Café* (℡863/983-6491) at Billie Swamp Safari offers plenty of Seminole specialties such as gator nuggets, frog legs and fry bread aimed squarely at tourists, but for a quick home-cooked meal, try the *Snake Road Café* (℡863/983-2595) inside the Big Cypress Trading Post at the U-Save gas station back in the main settlement. The "world's best burgers" ($4.75) here are certainly tasty, but the bowls of home-made chili are much better (from $4). You'll get a filling breakfast for under $5. Similar food is on offer at *Big Cypress Landing* (℡863/902-1783) convenience store down the street, which also does sandwiches at its canteen. Both places usually serve food between 7am and 7–8pm daily.

The Southeast

THE SOUTHEAST

CHAPTER 4

Highlights

✳ **Fort Lauderdale** The city's reputation as a haven for teens and retirees has all but disappeared, replaced by an emerging upmarket image that, along with some lovely buildings and a fine museum, makes it an inviting destination. See p.188

✳ **Boca Raton Resort and Club** Be sure to tour this resort, one of the most intriguing designs by quirky architect Addison Mizner. See p.201

✳ **Morikami Museum and Japanese Gardens** You'll feel like you've been transported to Japan after stepping into an intricate tea ceremony here. See p.205

✳ **Hobe Sound National Wildlife Refuge** This refuge on Jupiter Island, north of West Palm Beach, is an extraordinary sea turtle nesting ground during the summer. See p.218

✳ **Spring training** If you're here in early spring, take in an exhibition baseball game at Jupiter, Fort Lauderdale, or Port St Lucie. See p.218

✳ **Sebastian Inlet State Recreation Area** Sixteen miles north of Vero Beach, this inlet challenges surfers with its roaring ocean breakers. See p.225

▲ Boca Raton beach

The Southeast

S tretching from the fringes of northern Miami along nearly half of Florida's Atlantic shoreline, the **southeast** is the sun-soaked, subtropical Florida of popular imagination, with bodies bronzing on palm-dotted beaches as warm ocean waves lap idly against silky sands. With the exception of tranquil **Lake Okeechobee**, a prime fishing spot an hour inland and quite literally a world apart from the coastal settlements, the main attractions hug the ocean strip.

The **Gold Coast**, the first fifty-odd miles of the southeast coast up to Palm Beach, lies deep within the sway of Miami and comprises back-to-back conurbations with often little to tell them apart. However, the first and largest, **Fort Lauderdale**, is certainly distinctive. Its reputation for rowdy beach parties – stemming from years as a student Spring Break destination – is a thing of the past; the city has cultivated a cleaner-cut, sophisticated image, aided by an excellent art museum, an ambitious downtown improvement project, and a new wave of luxury oceanfront hotels. Further north, diminutive **Boca Raton** is renowned for its 1920s Mediterranean Revival buildings, as designed by the unconventional architect Addison Mizner. Ultimately, though, Mizner is best remembered for his work in **Palm Beach**, a city now inhabited almost exclusively by multi-millionaires, yet which remains accessible to visitors on all budgets.

North of Palm Beach, the population thins, and nature asserts itself forcefully throughout the **Treasure Coast**. Here, rarely crowded beaches flank long, pine-coated barrier islands such as Jupiter and Hutchinson, which boast miles of untainted, rugged shoreline peaceful enough for sea turtles to use as nesting grounds.

By car, the scenic route along the southeast coast is **Hwy-A1A**, which sticks wherever possible to the ocean side of the **Intracoastal Waterway**. Beloved of Florida's boat owners, this stretch was formed when the rivers dividing the mainland from the barrier islands were joined and deepened during World War II to reduce the threat of submarine attack. When necessary, Hwy-A1A turns inland and links with the much less picturesque **US-1**. The speediest road in the region, **I-95**, runs parallel to and about ten miles west of the coastline, splitting the residential sprawl from the state's flat and open interior, and is only worthwhile taking if you're in a hurry.

Frequent Greyhound connections link the bigger towns, and a few daily services run to the smaller communities. Local **buses**, plentiful from the edge of Miami to West Palm Beach, are nonexistent in the more rural Treasure Coast. Along the Gold Coast, there's the additional option of the dirt-cheap Tri-Rail service, and Amtrak has one daily **train** running as far north as West Palm Beach and inland to Okeechobee.

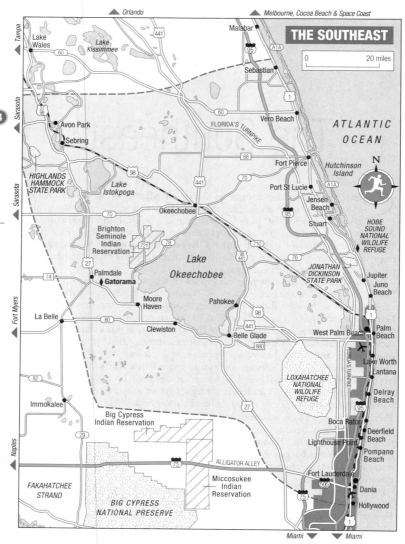

The Gold Coast

The widely admired beaches and towns occupying the fifty-mile commuter corridor north of Miami make the **GOLD COAST** one of the most heavily populated and tourist-besieged parts of the state. The sands sparkle, the nightlife rocks, and many of the communities have an assertively individualistic flavor – but you'll have to look hard for any peace and seclusion.

Hollywood

From Miami Beach, Hwy-A1A runs through undistinguished Hallandale Beach before reaching **HOLLYWOOD** – founded and named by a Californian in 1924 – a surprisingly diverse city with a wider beach and more cheerful persona than the better-known and much larger Fort Lauderdale, ten miles north. Pick up visitor information from the **Hollywood Office of Tourism**, 101 N Ocean Drive, Suite 204 (Mon–Fri 8am–5pm; ☎877/672-2468, ⓦwww .visithollywood.org), just north of the *Ramada Resort* near the beach.

Hollywood **beach** lies two miles east of downtown and is by far the town's premier attraction (the beach area is also a wi-fi hotspot). If the sand and surf don't tempt you, allocate an hour to the 2.5-mile-long, pedestrian-only **Broadwalk**, parallel to Hwy-A1A (called Ocean Drive here), a brick-lined promenade where restaurants and skateboarders enliven a casual amble. Metered parking ($1.25 per hr) is available on the side streets off N Ocean Drive – the best bars and restaurants face the beach north of the *Ramada Resort*.

Downtown Hollywood, linked to the beach by Hollywood Boulevard (Rte-820), offers plenty of bars and restaurants but little in the way of sights, though you could check out the temporary art exhibitions at the **Art and Culture Center of Hollywood**, at 1650 Harrison St just east of Young Circle (Mon–Sat 10am–5pm, Sun noon–4pm; $7; ☎954/921-3274, ⓦwww .artandculturecenter.org) – the center also hosts dance performances, theater, and concerts. The newly constructed ten-acre **ArtsPark** nearby (in the middle of Young Circle) is really just a pleasant green space, and not reason enough to leave the beach unless it hosts a concert or festival. Call the Downtown Hollywood Events Line (Mon–Fri 8am–5.30pm; ☎954/921-3016) to find out what's going on, or visit ⓦwww.downtown hollywood.com.

Accommodation

Reasonably priced **motels** line Hollywood's oceanside streets, but you'll save a few dollars by staying further inland, like along US-1, known here as Federal Highway.

Caroline 1515 N Ocean Drive ☎954/839-0744, ⓦwww.thehollywoodbeachhotel.com. A comprehensive renovation in 2008 makes this a good deal, with smart rooms steps away from the beach, all with microwaves and flatscreen TVs. ⑤
Hollywood Beach Marriott 2501 N Ocean Drive ☎954/924-2202 or 1-866/306-5453, ⓦwww .marriott.com. This oceanfront hotel is the best of the area's fashionable beach resorts, with luxurious rooms, spa, pool and beachside tiki bar. ⑧

Manta Ray Inn 1715 S Surf Rd ☎1-800/255-0595, ⓦwww.mantarayinn.com. The one-or two-bedroom suites here are great value, with the hotel right on the beach and all rooms equipped with kitchens and bright rattan furniture. Free parking. ⑥
Shell Motel 1201 S Federal Hwy (US-1) ☎954/923-8085, ⓦwww.shellmotelhollywood .com. Basic motel offering excellent rates on standard rooms and large efficiencies with kitchens. ②

Eating and drinking

What it lacks in terms of sights, downtown Hollywood more than makes up for with its restaurants and **nightlife**, especially around Harrison Street and Hollywood Boulevard, west of US-1 and Young Circle. You'll also find plenty of action along the Broadwalk at the beach.

Billy's Stone Crab Restaurant 400 N Ocean Drive ☎954/923-2300, ⓦwww.crabs.com. This local favorite serves up wicked crab, Key lime pie and fresh fish, with fabulous views of the yachts plying the Intracoastal.

Lola's on Harrison 2032 Harrison St ☎954/927-9851, ⓦwww.lolasonharrison.com. Offers appetizing pastas and burgers from $13, and excellent crab cake sandwiches ($14), but there's a much more sophisticated contemporary American dinner menu. Closed Mon.

Ocean Alley 900 N Broadwalk and Indiana St ☎954/921-6171, ⓦwww.oceanalley.net.

Specializing in seafood with an Italian flavor, but also perfect for a lazy afternoon beer drinking and people watching.

Sugar Reef 600 N Surf Rd (on the Broadwalk between New York and Fillimore sts) ☎954/922-1119, ⓦwww.sugarreefgrill.com. Solid choice for a drink right on the beach, accompanied by live jazz and Caribbean food. Closed Tues.

Sushi Blues Café and Blue Monk Lounge 2009 Harrison St ☎954/929-9560, ⓦsushiblues.com. You'll find live blues (Fri and Sat at 9.30pm), Japanese food and sidewalk seating at this small and somewhat pricey restaurant and bar. Closed Sun.

Dania

Ocean Drive continues north into **DANIA**, whose prime asset isn't the grouping of pseudo-English antique shops along US-1, but the sands and coastal vegetation of the **John U. Lloyd Beach State Park**, at 6503 N Ocean Drive (daily 8am–sunset; cars $3 for one person, $5 for two or more, pedestrians and cyclists $1; ☎954/923-2833). Sitting on a peninsula jutting out into the entrance to the shipping terminal of Port Everglades, the 251-acre park provides an enjoyable, 45-minute nature trail around its mangrove, seagrape, and guava trees, but as ever, the main attraction is the 2.5-mile **beach** – it has a wilder, unspoiled feel here, rare on the Gold Coast (though marred somewhat by the constant roar of jets from the nearby airport). In June and July the park runs a **sea turtle awareness program**, when every Wednesday and Friday evening rangers host campfire talks and a 20-minute slide show on turtles – if a nesting Loggerhead is spotted nearby, you'll be able to get a look at the real thing (from a distance). Reservations are essential, so call the park for details. The beachside *Loggerhead Café* (daily 9am–5pm; ☎954/923-6711) serves drinks and light meals, and **rents kayaks** ($15 per hr).

Downtown Dania is best known for its jai-alai court, or fronton, the second-oldest in the US (after Miami's). At **Dania Jai-Alai**, 301 E Dania Beach Blvd, Hwy-A1A (live games Tues–Sat 7pm, Tues & Sat noon, Sun 1pm; free; ☎954/920-1511, ⓦwww.betdania.com), spectators can bet on or just watch the ancient Basque sport in all its fast-paced glory from a comfortable indoor showplace.

If you're in need of sustenance, head to large, bustling *Islamorada Fish Company*, adjacent to the Bass Pro Shops Outdoor World at 220 Gulf Stream Way, just off I-95 on Rte-818 (☎954/927-7737), with some of the freshest (and biggest) sushi imaginable alongside the usual seafood dishes. Afterwards, gawk at live fish in Outdoor World's massive aquarium or at the world-record-setting catches next door at the **IGFA Fishing Hall of Fame & Museum** (Mon-Fri 10am–6pm, Sun noon–6pm; $8; ☎954/922-4212, ⓦwww.igfa.org), where you can also test your skills with virtual-reality fishing exhibits.

Fort Lauderdale

A thinly populated riverside trading camp at the start of the twentieth century, **FORT LAUDERDALE** came to be known as "the Venice of America" when its mangrove swamps were fashioned into slender canals during the 1920s.

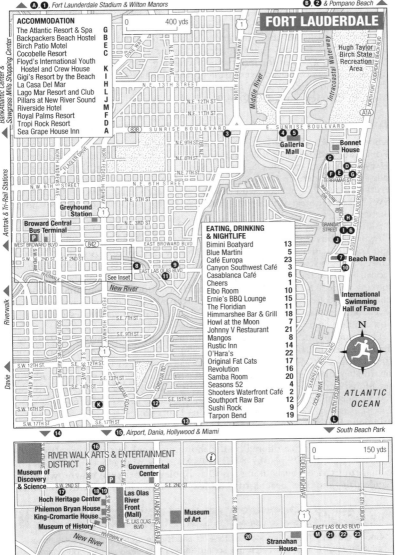

FORT LAUDERDALE

ACCOMMODATION

The Atlantic Resort & Spa	G
Backpackers Beach Hostel	B
Birch Patio Motel	E
Cocobelle Resort	C
Floyd's International Youth Hostel and Crew House	K
Gigi's Resort by the Beach	I
La Casa Del Mar	H
Lago Mar Resort and Club	L
Pillars at New River Sound	J
Riverside Hotel	M
Royal Palms Resort	F
Tropi Rock Resort	D
Sea Grape House Inn	A

0   400 yds

EATING, DRINKING & NIGHTLIFE

Bimini Boatyard	13
Blue Martini	5
Café Europa	23
Canyon Southwest Café	3
Casablanca Café	6
Cheers	1
Elbo Room	10
Ernie's BBQ Lounge	15
The Floridian	11
Himmarshee Bar & Grill	18
Howl at the Moon	7
Johnny V Restaurant	21
Mangos	8
Rustic Inn	14
O'Hara's	22
Original Fat Cats	17
Revolution	16
Samba Room	20
Seasons 52	4
Shooters Waterfront Café	2
Southport Raw Bar	12
Sushi Rock	9
Tarpon Bend	19

THE SOUTHEAST | Fort Lauderdale

ATLANTIC OCEAN

N

RIVER WALK ARTS & ENTERTAINMENT DISTRICT

Museum of Discovery & Science

Governmental Center

Hoch Heritage Center
Philemon Bryan House
King-Cromartie House
Museum of History

Las Olas River Front (Mall)

Museum of Art

Stranahan House

0   150 yds

Beginning in the 1930s, intercollegiate swimming contests drew the nation's youth here, a fact seized on by the 1960 teen-exploitation film *Where the Boys Are*, which instantly made Fort Lauderdale the country's premier Spring Break destination. Hundreds of thousands of students – around 350,000 in 1985 alone – congregated around the seven miles of sand for a six-week frenzy of underage drinking and lascivious excess. The students also brought six weeks of traffic chaos, and ultimately proved a deterrent to regular tourists, so in the 1990s the local authorities enacted strict laws to restrict boozing and wild behavior. Fortunately, it worked and the city began to forge a new identity.

Fort Lauderdale has since emerged as an affluent business and cultural center dominated by a mix of wealthy retirees and affluent yuppies keen to play up the city's status as a center for international yachting, and growing repute among upmarket travelers. Nevertheless, parts of downtown remain a bit rough around the edges, and you'll want to spend most of your time in the newly restored **historic district**, along **Las Olas Boulevard**, or on the **beach**.

Arrival, information, and getting around

Known as Federal Highway, US-1 plows through the center of **downtown Fort Lauderdale**, three miles inland from the coast. Just south of downtown, **Hwy-A1A** veers east off US-1 along SE 17th Street and runs through oceanside Fort Lauderdale as Beach Boulevard. You'll find metered **parking** everywhere ($1.25 per hr), while the Government Center Parking Garage on SW 2nd Street, near the historic district, is $2 for the first hour, $1 per hour thereafter.

All the long-distance public transport terminals are in or near downtown: the Greyhound **bus station** is at 515 NE Third St (☎954/764-6551), while the **train** and Tri-Rail station is two miles west at 200 SW 21st Terrace (Amtrak ☎1-800/USA-RAIL, ⓦwww.amtrak.com; Tri-Rail ☎1-800-TRI-RAIL, ⓦwww.tri-rail.com), linked to the center by regular bus #22 ($1.50). If you're flying in and are looking to rent a car, **Fort Lauderdale/Hollywood International Airport** conveniently offers shuttle buses to its new **Rental Car Center**, an indoor, four-level complex that's home to nearly all of the major rental companies. Otherwise you can take a taxi or bus #1 ($1.50) into the city.

The centrally located **Greater Fort Lauderdale Convention & Visitors Bureau** sits at 100 E Broward Blvd, Suite 200 (Mon–Fri 8.30am–5pm; ☎954/765-4466, ⓦwww.sunny.org), but can be hard to find; the entrance is on an alley between Broward and SE 1st Street (aim for the metered parking on SE 1st Ave). For **internet** access, try the *Calling Station*, 1422 SE 17th St ($0.17 per minute; wi-fi $5.25 per 30min, $9 per 1hr; ☎954/763-5721), or *Brew Urban Café*, 209 SW 2nd Ave (Mon–Thurs 7am–11pm, Fri & Sat 7am–midnight, Sun 8am–8pm; ☎954/523-7191), which has free wi-fi and rents out laptops for $5 an hour.

The handiest service offered by the thorough **local bus** network, Broward County Transit (☎954/357-8400, ⓦwww.broward.org/bct), is the #11, which runs twice hourly along Las Olas Boulevard between downtown Fort Lauderdale and the beach; **timetables** are available from Governmental

---

Professional sports venues

Sports enthusiasts will find the Greater Fort Lauderdale area a hub of professional athletic activity. You can catch the spring training and Grapefruit League games (Feb–March) of baseball's **Baltimore Orioles** at Fort Lauderdale Stadium, 1301 NW 55th St (Ticketmaster, ☎954/523-3309, ⓦwww.baltimore.orioles.mlb.com). Mid-July to August sees the preseason training of football's **Miami Dolphins** (☎305/620-2578, ⓦwww.miamidolphins.com) in nearby Davie at the Nova Southeastern University campus, 7500 SW 30th St. The BankAtlantic Center at One Panther Parkway, just west of Fort Lauderdale in Sunrise, is home to the **Florida Panthers** hockey team (☎954/835-7000, ⓦpanthers.nhl.com). It's also not far to Miami's major league sports venues (see p.34).

Center (115 S Andrews Ave at SW 2nd St), the Broward Central Bus Terminal at W Broward Avenue and NW 1st Street, or online. If you are using the buses, buy a **bus pass** ($3.50 per day), which allows unlimited travel on the buses throughout the county – otherwise it's $1.50 per journey, with no transfers.

A great – and cheap – way to get around is the **Sun Trolley** (☎954/761-3543, ⓦ www.suntrolley.com) which runs a downtown loop (Mon–Fri 7.30am–6pm; every 10min; $0.50) and between downtown and the beaches along Las Olas Boulevard (Thurs & Fri 6pm–12.45am, Sat 10am–1.30pm, Sun 10am–12.30am; every 10min; $0.50). You can hail the bus anywhere along the route.

Accommodation

Options for staying in downtown Fort Lauderdale are relatively limited, but the scores of **motels** clustered between the Intracoastal Waterway and the ocean can be exceptionally good value. The beachfront has the pick of the luxury **resorts**, with the opening of the *W Fort Lauderdale Hotel* and *Trump International Hotel* in 2009 cementing the city's jet-set appeal. Standard rates at these hotels range well above $300 in peak season, so book via discount websites or come offseason for the best bargains. If money is tight, note there are two **hostels** in town (see below).

The Atlantic Resort & Spa 601 N Fort Lauderdale Beach Blvd ☎954/567-8020, ⓦ www .theatlantichotelfortlauderdale.com. The first of a projected series of luxury residence properties facing the ocean, this Mediterranean-style hotel features elegant rooms and suites, a spa, an oceanfront pool and a superb restaurant, *Trina*. ❽

Backpackers Beach Hostel 2115 N Ocean Blvd ☎954/567-7275, ⓦ www.fortlauderdalehostel .com. Clean, friendly hostel offering free parking and internet use as well as a pleasant rooftop patio; dorm beds $20, private rooms ❷.

Birch Patio Motel 617 N Birch Rd ☎954/563-9540, ⓦ www.birchpatio.com. Superb value, a short walk from the beach. Standard doubles are comfy and clean, though the efficiencies have kitchens and a lot more space. Extras include a small swimming pool, free parking, coin operated washer and dryer, and internet. ❹

🏃 **Cocobelle Resort** 2831 Vistamar St ☎954/463-1723, ⓦ www.cocobelleresort .com. Two blocks from the beach, this hotel is a real bargain, with leafy tropical gardens, a tranquil pool and bright, beautifully decorated rooms with tiled floors, free wi-fi and microwave. ❻

Floyd's International Youth Hostel and Crew House 445 SE 16th St ☎954/462-0631, ⓦ www .floridahostel.com. Welcoming hostel with similar amenities to *Backpackers*, but also offers a $10 pick-up service from the airport. Dorm beds $25, private rooms ❷.

Lago Mar Resort and Club 1700 S Ocean Lane ☎954/523-6511 or 1-800/LAGO MAR, ⓦ www .lagomar.com. A luxury resort located a bit away from the action, with two pools, several restaurants and bars, a full-service spa, and its own private patch of sand. ❽

🏃 **Pillars at New River Sound** 111 N Birch Rd ☎954/467-9639, ⓦ www.pillarshotel .com. Quiet, intimate British-colonial-style hotel with plush rooms, antique furniture, lush gardens and a pool, sits just a block from the ocean on the Intracoastal. ❽

Riverside Hotel 620 E Las Olas Blvd ☎1800/325-3280, ⓦ www.riversidehotel.com. Built in 1936, this elegant and comfortable (if slightly overpriced) option is in the heart of downtown Las Olas. ❽

🏃 **Tropi Rock Resort** 2900 Belmar St ☎954/564-0523 or 1-800-987-9385, ⓦ www.tropirock.com. A block from the beach, this funky, family-owned hotel offers great value in artful environs that include hand-laid mosaics and local art. Rates for rooms and efficiencies include parking, wi-fi and internet access, and use of tennis courts and a small gym. ❺

Downtown Fort Lauderdale

Tall, anonymous, glass-fronted buildings make an uninspiring first impression, but **downtown Fort Lauderdale** boasts an outstanding modern art museum and the ambitious **Riverwalk Arts and Entertainment District**, bringing together new malls, art centers, and a number of restored older buildings. The area is anchored by the one-and-a-half-mile **Riverwalk** along the north bank of the New River, which starts near Stranahan House, skirts the Las Olas Riverfront entertainment complex and ends at the Broward Center for Performing Arts.

Stranahan House

For a reminder of early Fort Lauderdale life, start at the carefully restored **Stranahan House**, 335 SE Sixth Ave (by 45min tour only, daily 1pm, 2pm, & 3pm; $12; ☎954/524-4736, ⓦwww.stranahanhouse.org), just south of the *Cheesecake Factory* on Las Olas Boulevard. Erected in 1901, with high ceilings, narrow windows, and wide verandas, the city's oldest surviving structure is a fine example of Florida frontier style, and served as the home and trading post of the turn-of-the-twentieth-century settler Frank Stranahan, hailed as the father of Fort Lauderdale. Stranahan, who established his first trading post on the New River in 1893, was a prosperous dealer in otter pelts, egret plumes, and alligator hides, which he purchased from Seminole Indians who traded along river. Financially devastated by the late-1920s Florida property crash, Stranahan drowned himself in the same SE waterway.

The Museum of Art

In a postmodern structure shaped like a slice of pie, the **Museum of Art**, 1 E Las Olas Blvd (daily 11am–5pm, Thurs 11am–8pm, closed Tues June–Sept; $10; ☎954/525-5500, ⓦwww.moafl.org), provides ample space and light for the best art collection in the state, with an emphasis on modern painting and sculpture. From Stranahan House it's a short stroll along the **Riverwalk** (cut across Huizenga Plaza before you reach Andrews Ave).

The museum features occasional large-scale, high-profile exhibits (which cost extra to view); of the permanent collection, the strongest pieces are drawn from the museum's hoard of works from the avant-garde **CoBrA** movement, which began in 1948 with a group of artists from Copenhagen, Brussels, and Amsterdam (hence the acronym). CoBrA's art is typified by

▲ Stranahan House

bright, expressionistic canvases combining playful innocence with deep emotional power. Important names to look for include Asger Jorn, Carl-Henning Pedersen, and Karel Appel. Another attraction is the William Glackens wing, named for the early twentieth-century American Impressionist who painted most of his pieces exhibited here while in France, and which includes a period-outfitted drawing room.

Riverwalk Arts and Entertainment District

The most enticing part of downtown begins one block west of the art museum, an area collectively dubbed the Riverwalk Arts and Entertainment District (see p.195 for places to eat). Las Olas Riverfront dominates the first section, a mall and entertainment complex in faux Spanish Colonial style which has yet to really take off – it's nevertheless a good place to pick up a water taxi or boat cruise (see box, p.194).

For a glimpse into the city's past, keep walking west along the river to the **Old Fort Lauderdale Village** historic district (℡954/463-4431, Ⓦwww.oldfort lauderdale.org), at the center of which is the **Museum of History** on the Riverwalk at 231 SW Second Ave (Tues–Sat 10am–5pm, Sun noon–5pm; $10). The museum occupies the former **New River Inn**, completed in 1905 and the first hotel built in the area to serve Flagler's railway. Exhibits inside tackle the early history of the region – including displays on the Seminole Wars – and the modern history of the city from the 1890s to the 1960s.

Entry to the museum includes a tour of the next door **King-Cromartie House** (Tues–Sat 10am–4.45pm, Sun noon–4.45pm), built in 1907, where you'll find such futuristic-at-the-time fixtures as the first indoor bathroom in Fort Lauderdale. Beyond here, the 1905 **Philemon Bryan House** at 227 SW Second Ave was once the home of the Bryan family, who constructed many buildings in this area, and is now the home of the Historical Society's administrative offices. Closer to SW Second Street (also known as Himmarshee St), the **Hoch Heritage Center** (Mon & Sat noon–4pm, Tues–Fri 10am–4pm) at 219 SW Second Ave rounds off the stock of historic buildings here, though it serves primarily as a research center and there's little to see inside for the casual visitor.

Museum of Discovery & Science

Two blocks west of the historic district, the **Museum of Discovery & Science**, 401 SW Second St (Mon–Sat 10am–5pm, Sun noon–6pm; $10, kids (2–12) $8; ℡954/467-6637, Ⓦwww.mods.org), is among the best of Florida's many child-orientated science museums, where exhibits present the basics of science in numerous ingenious and entertaining ways. You can, for example, pretend to be an astronaut, rising in an air-powered chair to realign an orbiting satellite or making a simulated trip to the moon. The museum also contains a towering 3-D IMAX film theater that screens daily (check admissions booth for times); you can pay $15 (kids $12) to see the museum and one IMAX film or just $9 (kids $7) for the film alone.

Las Olas Boulevard and the beach

Downtown Fort Lauderdale is linked to the beach by **Las Olas Boulevard** – the city's upmarket shopping strip, with no shortage of fashion, art, and dining options – and by the canal-side Las Olas Isles, where residents park their cars on one side of their mega-buck properties and moor their luxury yachts on the other. Once across the arching Intracoastal Waterway Bridge, about two miles on, you're within sight of the ocean and the mood changes appreciably. Where

Water taxis and boat tours

Though the nickname "**Venice of America**" is a little misleading, you haven't really seen Fort Lauderdale unless you explore its miles of waterways lined with opulent mansions and million-dollar motorboats. Try **Water Taxi** (daily 10am–11:30pm; ☎954/467-6677, ⓦwww.watertaxi.com), which operates small covered boats that will pick up and deliver you almost anywhere along the water, from the restaurants near East Oakland Park Boulevard down to the 17th Street Causeway and west to the Las Olas Riverfront and Riverwalk area. These taxis are the best way to see the city, especially because the friendly captains often give unofficial tours, dishing the gossip behind the multimillion-dollar homes and yachts along the way. An all-day pass with unlimited usage costs only $13 (single tickets are $7). Water Taxi also runs a day-trip to Miami's South Beach for $35 (daily 9.30am; reservations required). **River Taxi** (☎954/880-7060, ⓦwww.rivertaxifortlauderdale.com) runs a similar service at similar prices.

If you'd prefer a more structured **water tour** of the city and its Millionaire's Row, try **Riverfront Cruises**, Las Olas Riverfront at 300 SW 1st Ave (☎954/463-3220, ⓦwww .anticipation.com; $20), which offers enlightening daily 1hr 30min tours departing 11am, 12.30pm, 2pm, and 3.30pm for the rest of the year. For a bit of kitschy fun try the **Jungle Queen Riverboat**, 801 Seabreeze Blvd at Hwy-A1A (☎954/462-5596, ⓦwww.junglequeen.com), an old-style steamboat that makes daily cruises at 9.30am and 1.30pm ($16.50).

Las Olas Boulevard ends, **beachside Fort Lauderdale** begins – T-shirt and swimwear shops suddenly spill out between clusters of restaurants and hotels, punctuating over 25 miles of "Blue Wave" beaches (those certified as clean, safe, and environmentally friendly).

Along the seafront, **Fort Lauderdale Beach Boulevard (also known as Atlantic Boulevard)**, which once bore the brunt of heavy Spring Break partying, has benefited from a multimillion-dollar facelift. Now only a few beach-front bars bear any trace of the carousing of the past, though the sands, flanked by graciously aging coconut palms and an attractive promenade, are by no means deserted or dull: joggers, rollerbladers, and cyclists create a stereotypical beach scene, and a small number of whooping students still turn up each spring.

South along Beach Boulevard

A short way south of the Las Olas Boulevard junction, the **International Swimming Hall of Fame**, 1 Hall of Fame Drive (daily 9am–5pm; $8; ☎954/462-6536, ⓦwww.ishof.org), salutes aquatic sports with a collection even dedicated nonswimmers will enjoy. The two floors are stuffed with medals, trophies, and press cuttings pertaining to the heroes and heroines of swimming, diving, and many other obscure watery activities. If the museum puts you in the mood for a swim, the giant outdoor pools of the **Fort Lauderdale Aquatic Complex** (Mon–Fri 8am–4pm & 6.30–7.30pm, Sat & Sun 8am–2pm; $4; ☎954/828-4580) are right next door.

North along Beach Boulevard

At the flashy commercial complex called **Beach Place** (☎954/760-9570) just north of the Las Olas Boulevard junction, you'll find three levels of shops, restaurants like *Hooters* and *Fat Tuesday*, and a few of the still-remaining rowdy bars. The good thing about Beach Place is you can hop up from the sand to grab a bite to eat, buy souvenir paraphernalia, or use the restroom. Otherwise, it's just an overhyped mall with a spectacular waterfront location.

Further north, amid the high-rise hotels and apartment blocks dominating the beachside area, Fort Lauderdale's pre-condo landscape can be viewed in the jungle-like 35-acre grounds of **Bonnet House Museum & Gardens**, 900 N Birch Rd (Tues–Sat 10am–4pm, Sun noon–4pm; last tour 2.30pm; $20, or $10 for grounds only; ☎954/563-5393, ⓦwww.bonnethouse.org), a few minutes' walk off Fort Lauderdale Beach Boulevard. The house and its tranquil surroundings – including a swan-filled pond and resident monkeys – were designed and built by Chicago muralist Frederic Clay Bartlett in 1920. The tours of the vaguely plantation-style abode highlight Bartlett's eccentric passion for art and architecture – and for collecting ornamental animals, dozens of which fill nearly all of the thirty rooms.

Another green pocket is nearby. Beside E Sunrise Boulevard, the tall Australian pines of the **Hugh Taylor Birch State Park** (daily 8am–sunset; cars $3 for one person, $4 for two or more, pedestrians and cyclists $1; ☎954/564-4521) form a shady backdrop for canoeing on the park's mile-long freshwater lagoon (**canoe** rentals $5 per hr, kayaks $12.50 per hr). You can **rent bikes** ($12.50 per hr, $35 per day) and take guided **Segway** tours (daily 11am, 1pm, & 3pm; $50–100) from the park concession, M. Cruz Rentals (☎954/235-5082, ⓦwww .mcruzrentals.com), at the beach entrance at Sunrise Boulevard.

Eating

Fort Lauderdale has many affordable, enjoyable **places to eat** featuring everything from Asian creations to home-made conch chowder. The best and most convenient restaurants tend to be grouped on Las Olas Boulevard, along the beachfront, and in the **Riverwalk Arts and Entertainment District**.

Riverwalk Arts and Entertainment District

Himmarshee Bar & Grill 210 SW 2nd St ☎954/524-1818, ⓦwww.himmarshee.com. Stylish contemporary design and cuisine, featuring gourmet sandwiches (from $9), and an eclectic menu of entrées, from addictive mac and cheese and pastas, to Thai chicken and sautéed snapper (lunch plates from $9).

Tarpon Bend 200 SW 2nd St ☎954/523-3233, ⓦwww.tarponbend.com. Popular lunch spot, serving decent burgers and other standard American grill-type food – best known for its daily happy hour cocktails (from 4pm), and handy location near the museum.

Las Olas Boulevard

Café Europa 726 E Las Olas Blvd ☎954/763-6600. Funky, moderately priced café, always packed, serving largely Italian food including a wide variety of salads, unusual pizza toppings, good selection of veggie options and mouthwatering desserts.

The Floridian 1410 E Las Olas Blvd ☎954/463-4041. Also known as "the Flo," this decades-old and inexpensive downtown 24hr diner is popular for its mammoth breakfasts.

Johnny V Restaurant 625 E Las Olas Blvd ☎954/761-7920, ⓦwww.johnnyvlasolas.com.

Trendy, upmarket creative American restaurant serving excellent wine and food from local celebrity chef Johnny Vinczencz, such as "Duck Duck Duck" (seared duck breast, leg of duck confit and duck liver; $30) and sage-grilled Florida dolphin ($29).

Sushi Rock 1515 E Las Olas Blvd ☎954/462-5541. Don't be put off by the neon lights and dark interior: This is a cool, rock'n'roll-inspired café with good sushi and other Japanese food on its funky menus.

The beach and Intercoastal Waterway

Canyon Southwest Café 1818 E Sunrise Blvd ☎954/765-1950, ⓦcanyonfl.com. Extremely hip restaurant, offering a sophisticated, modern take on southwestern, Mexican and Asian cuisines; expect dishes like jalapeño panko-crusted jumbo shrimp and *añejo tequila guajillo* chili (entrées from $24). Dinner only.

Casablanca Café 3049 Alhambra St ☎954/764-3500, ⓦwww.casablancacafeonline.com. Great atmosphere and excellent beachfront location, with an enticing menu of Mediterranean-influenced American food (with a focus on seafood), reasonable prices, and live music Wed–Sun nights.

Seasons 52 2428 E Sunrise Blvd at the Galleria Mall ☎954/537-1052, ⓦwww.seasons52.com.

A friendly grill and wine bar boasting an extensive wine list and a fresh, seasonally inspired menu; every item has less than 475 calories.

Shooters Waterfront Café 3033 NE 32nd Ave ⊤954/566-2855, ⓦ www.shooterscafe.com. This popular café is right on the Intracoastal and accessible by water taxi. It draws large crowds for generous – though fairly pricey – portions of seafood (from $16.99) burgers (from $11), and salads (from $7).

South Fort Lauderdale

Bimini Boatyard 1555 SE 17th St ⊤954/525-7400, ⓦ www.biminiboatyard.com. Well-prepared and presented salads and seafood, served in a great waterfront location. Less expensive than it looks, with burgers and sandwiches from $10, and dinner entrées $13–29.

Ernie's BBQ Lounge 1843 S Federal Hwy ⊤954/523-8636. The somewhat scruffy but likeable *Ernie's*, south and west of downtown, is a local legend for its glorious conch chowder ($9.50; add sherry to taste), though the ribs can be hit-and-miss.

Rustic Inn 4331 Ravenswood Rd ⊤954/584-1637, ⓦ www.rusticinn.com. At this ultra-casual crabhouse, on a waterway near the airport, crack open mountains of delicious steamed garlic blue crabs onto newspaper-covered tables (crab sampler $29.99).

Southport Raw Bar 1536 Cordova Rd ⊤954/525-CLAM or 877/646-9808, ⓦ www.southportrawbar .com. Boisterous local bar offering succulent crustaceans and well-prepared fish dishes at inexpensive prices (shellfish baskets from $5.95, fresh fish from $8.95). Has an open deck on the water.

Drinking and nightlife

In addition to the bars listed below, some of the restaurants above, particularly *Shooters* and *Tarpon Bend*, are also notable drinking spots. You should also check out **Jazz Brunch** at Riverwalk Park on the first Sunday of each month, when crowds gather for cocktails and snacks sold at food stalls, serenaded by live music (10am–2pm). In general, you'll find more locals partying along Himmarshee Street in the historic district, while tourists tend to stick to the beach.

Many bars double as live venues for rock, jazz and blues bands; to find out who's playing where, check the events calendar at ⓦ www.broward.org/arts, pick up the free *New Times* (ⓦ www.browardpalmbeach.com) from newsstands, or consult the "Showtime" segment of the Friday edition of the local *Sun-Sentinel* newspaper. For high culture, check out the **Broward Center for the Performing Arts**, 201 SW Fifth Ave (ticket information ⊤954/462-0222, ⓦ www.browardcenter.org).

Blue Martini 2432 E Sunrise Blvd at the Galleria Mall ⊤954/653-BLUE, ⓦ www.bluemartinilounge .com. Classy bar with an outdoor patio offering over two dozen types of martinis, a tapas menu, live music, and dancing. Open from 2pm daily.

Cheers 941 E Cypress Creek Rd ⊤954/771-6337, ⓦ www.cheersfoodandspirits.com. Live rock music and DJs bring the house down until 4am most nights of the week.

Elbo Room 241 S Fort Lauderdale Beach Blvd ⊤954/463-4615, ⓦ www.elboroom.com. This former Spring Break favorite, made famous by the film *Where the Boys Are* is now a friendly, no-frills beach bar with live bands and a good happy hour.

Howl at the Moon 17 S Fort Lauderdale Beach Blvd at Beach Place ⊤954/522-7553, ⓦ www .howlatthemoon.com. Boisterous, dueling-pianos bar, where everyone's encouraged to sing along. Cover charge $5 (Thurs), $10 (Fri & Sat).

Mangos 904 E Las Olas Blvd ⊤954/523-5001, ⓦ www.mangosonlasolas.com. The airy outdoor area is perfect for people watching along Las Olas, while

the roaring live rock, R&B, and jazz inside keeps things lively. You can also munch on decent food.

O'Hara's 722 E Las Olas Blvd ⊤954/524-1764, ⓦ www.oharasjazzcafe.com. This dark bar has live jazz and blues music every night around 9pm.

Original Fat Cats 217 SW 2nd St ⊤954/713-8500. Right in the heart of the Himmarshee party strip, this lively pub serves as a rocking venue for local bands, with shows usually starting 11.30pm. Open from 5pm daily.

Revolution 200 W Broward Blvd ⊤954/727-0950, ⓦ www.jointherevolution.net. Cavernous club with two stages, two full bars, an outdoor patio, and plenty of space for dancing; also features occasional live national concerts, for which tickets are available. Tickets for live shows vary (usually $12–30).

Samba Room 350 E Las Olas Blvd ⊤954/468-2000, ⓦ www.sambaroom.net. The festive atmosphere is fueled by potent, Cuban-inspired drinks, live Latin and reggae bands, and spicy Latin-fusion food, served all day and night.

Gay and lesbian Fort Lauderdale

Fort Lauderdale has been one of **gay** America's favorite holiday haunts for years and has been called San Francisco by the Sea. Like the rest of Fort Lauderdale, the scene has quieted down considerably over recent years, but there's still plenty going on. For more information, contact the Gay and Lesbian Community Center of South Florida at 1717 N Andrews Ave (Mon–Fri 10am–10pm, Sat & Sun noon–5pm; ☎954/463-9005, ⓦwww.glccsf.org); pick up free copies of *411 Magazine* (ⓦwww.the411mag.com) and *HOTspots! Magazine* (ⓦwww.hotspotsmagazine.com) around town or a Rainbow Vacation Planner from the Convention and Visitors Bureau; and visit the Fort Lauderdale section of Fun Maps (ⓦwww.funmaps.com).

Accommodation

Gigi's Resort by the Beach 3005 Alhambra St ☎954/463-4827 or 1-800/910-2357, ⓦwww .gigisresort.com. Comfortable and friendly Art Deco guesthouse, very close to the St Sebastian gay beach, with a choice of twelve stylish rooms and suites, all with wi-fi and fridge. Breakfast in the tranquil, leafy courtyard is included. ❹

La Casa Del Mar 3003 Granada St ☎954/467-2037, ⓦwww.lacasadelmar.com. The rooms of this attractive hotel are each themed to – and named after – a particular artist or musician (though the Dali room is disappointingly tame). Each is equipped with kitchenette and wi-fi. ❻

Royal Palms Resort 2901 Terramar St ☎954/564-6444 or 1-800/237-PALM, ⓦwww .royalpalms.com. This clothing-optional hotel offers more luxury, with a heated pool, spa and complimentary breakfast and happy hour. Rooms come with Frette linens, wi-fi, flatscreen TVs and iPod docking stations. ❼

Sea Grape House Inn 1109 NE 16th Pl ☎954/525-6586, ⓦwww.seagrape.com. Further inland, this small bed and breakfast is convenient for the popular gay bars of Wilton Drive in Wilton Manors, a neighborhood northwest of downtown Fort Lauderdale. ❹

Bars and clubs

Gay **bars** and **clubs** in Fort Lauderdale fall in and out of fashion; check the magazines listed above or ⓦwww.gayftlauderdale.com for the latest hot spots, many of which are located in nearby Wilton Manors.

Boom 2232–36 Wilton Drive ☎954/630-3556. Loud, high-energy club for dancing at the weekends, with karaoke Monday and Tuesday, open drag night Wednesday and cheap drinks Thursday. Opens at 8pm nightly.

Chardees 2209 Wilton Drive ☎954/563-1800. For eating as well as drinking try this lively piano bar and restaurant, which features a fabulous Sunday brunch.

Copa 2800 S Federal Hwy ☎954/463-1507, ⓦwww.copaboy.com. This long-running dance club draws all ages, with Friday and Saturday the big DJ nights, though you'll find plenty of action Wednesdays and Thursdays; also boasts a game room, live entertainment, shows, and indoor and outdoor bars. Closed Mon & Tues.

Cubby Hole 823 N Federal Highway ☎954/728-9001, ⓦwww.thecubbyhole.com. Another place to drink and eat daily from 11am; known for its excellent burgers and cruising scene. Pool tables and video games add to the fun.

Georgie's Alibi 2266 Wilton Drive ☎954/565-2526, ⓦwww.georgiesalibi.com. Casual sports and video bar, with a decent menu of hot sandwiches and burgers, and plenty of special events from football nights to comedy.

Steel 1951 NW 9th Ave ☎954/522-9985, ⓦwww .steelftl.com. The best club in recent years, with a multi-room venue, video lounge and outdoor patio – the biggest party night is Saturday.

Around Fort Lauderdale

North of Fort Lauderdale, Hwy-A1A passes through a succession of sleepy towns inhabited by a mixture of retirees, "snowbirds" from the northeast and the super rich, and though the beaches remain enticing, there's little in the way of sights. A diversion inland can prove slightly more rewarding, the otherwise dreary suburbs punctured by the eccentric town of Davie, and the Hollywood Seminole Reservation.

Davie

An exception to the prevailing factories, housing estates, and freeway interchanges surrounding Fort Lauderdale, **DAVIE** lies twenty miles from the coast on Griffin Road, circled by citrus groves, sugar cane, and dairy pastures. Davie's roughly 80,000 inhabitants are besotted with the Old West: jeans, plaid shirts, and Stetsons are the order of the day. Davie's cowboy origins hail from settlers who came here in the 1910s to herd cattle and work the fertile black soil, an agricultural history embodied by the restored **Old Davie School Historical Museum**, 6650 Griffin Rd (Tues–Sat 10am–2pm; $10; ☎954/797-1044, Ⓦ www.olddavieschool.org). The Davie Pro Rodeo is generally held the last Saturday of each month, at 8pm at the Davie Arena, on the Bergeron Rodeo Grounds, 4271 Davie Rd (☎954/680-3555, Ⓦ www.davieprorodeo.com; $15, children $8) – look for the rearing white horse sign. You can also check out the cheaper Jackpot Rodeos (with local riders) here every Wednesday night at 7pm ($4, children $2).

Hollywood Seminole Reservation

Fifteen minutes southwest from downtown Fort Lauderdale on State Rd 7/ US-441 is the **Hollywood Seminole Reservation** (Ⓦ www.seminoletribe .com), the headquarters of the **Seminole** tribe and their biggest source of income (see box, p.176 for more on Florida's Native American tribes). Here you'll find tourist attractions ranging from somewhat depressing to downright glitzy.

The **Seminole Okalee Indian Village**, 5716 Seminole Way (Wed–Sun 10am–5pm; $10; ☎954/797-5560), falls into the former category, with a touristy arts and gift shop and disturbing alligator wrestling shows, though the replica of a Seminole village at least provides a basic introduction to tribal traditions; cooking, dollmaking and woodworking are often demonstrated. The whole thing lies within the fashionable Seminole Paradise complex, where the biggest attraction is the **Seminole Hard Rock Hotel & Casino** (☎1-866-2-CASINO or 954/327-7625, Ⓦ www.seminolehardrock hollywood.com; ❽). It's the casino that draws most visitors; laws against gaming don't apply to Indian reservations, so you can play slot machines, high stakes bingo and poker, as well as buy your fill of tax-free cigarettes. Also inside, *Hard Rock Live* showcases popular performance and sporting events; call ☎954/523-3309 or visit the website for its upcoming schedule. You'll find a slew of trendy nightclubs in the Seminole Paradise complex, like the upmarket, African-decorated *Pangaea* (Thurs–Sat; $20 cover; ☎954/581-5454, Ⓦ www.pangaea-lounge.com) with bottle-service-only; its attached sister dance club *Gryphon*, with house music and international DJs (Fri & Sat only; same phone; Ⓦ www.gryphon-club.com); or the huge, multilevel *Spirits* (Wed–Sat; $20 cover; ☎954/327-9094, Ⓦ www.spiritshardrock.com), also featuring guest DJs and a variety of dance music.

North to Boca Raton

The seventeen miles between Fort Lauderdale and Boca Raton are marked by several sedate beachside communities; Hwy-A1A (much preferable to US-1) is rarely busy, but note hotels and condos largely block the sea views once you leave north Fort Lauderdale. The most worthy stop is **Lauderdale-By-The-Sea**, around four miles up the coast and one of the best places to don **scuba-diving** gear and explore the reefs, many of which are within one hundred yards of the beach. Try **Deep Blue Divers** (☎954/772-7966, ⓦwww.deepbluedivers.net) at 4348 Ocean Drive, or inquire at the little **Chamber of Commerce**, 4201 Ocean Drive (daily 9am–5pm; ☎954/776-1000, ⓦwww.ltbs.com), for more information.

Accommodation

Cheap **motels** abound along the stretch of Hwy-A1A coming into Lauderdale-By-The-Sea, but you'll also find many pleasant **B&Bs**, most along beachfront El Mar Drive, one block east of Hwy-A1A (or Ocean Drive, as it's also known here).

A Little Inn by the Sea 4546 El Mar Drive ☎954/772-2450 or 1-800/492-0311, ⓦwww.alittleinn.com. Friendly beachside B&B, with spacious rooms (some with sea views), complimentary bicycles, breakfast buffet, and an oceanside pool. ❻

Best Florida Resort 4628 N Ocean Drive ☎954/772-2500, ⓦwww.bestfloridamotel.com. Cozy motel with a tropical garden and pool; the spotless rooms and grounds are decked out with rattan furnishings and Polynesian-style art, and the owners are exceptionally friendly. ❹

Blue Seas Courtyard 4525 El Mar Drive ☎954/772-3336, ⓦwww.blueseascourtyard.com. This hacienda-style hotel is one of the most distinctive in town, with snappy rooms decked out in an ebullient Mexican style, replete with terra-cotta tiles and arts and crafts from south of the border. ❻

Courtyard Villa 4312 El Mar Drive ☎954/776-1164 or 1-800/291-3560, ⓦwww.courtyardvilla.com. Attractive faux-antique European hotel with a rooftop sundeck and patio, where rates include a full breakfast. ❼

Eating and drinking

Good **places to eat** include the *Aruba Beach Café*, 1 E Commercial Blvd (☎954/776-0001, ⓦwww.arubabeachcafe.com), serving Caribbean-inspired American food amid live music and three tropical bars, and decades-old *The Village Grill and Village Pump*, 4404 El Mar Drive (☎954/776-5092, ⓦwww.villagegrille.com) – a good place for seafood, steaks and cocktails on the beach.

Three miles north of Lauderdale-By-The-Sea, Hwy-A1A crosses the Hillsboro Inlet, which lends its name to the posh canal-side community of **Hillsboro Beach**. There's nothing to detain you here except the offshore *Cap's Place* (dinner only, booking recommended; ☎954/941-0418, ⓦwww.capsplace.com), which can only be reached by ferry (call for directions to the dock). The food – lots of fresh seafood, with entrées ranging from $23 to $31.50 – is the main attraction, but the fact the restaurant doubled as an illegal gambling den during Prohibition adds appeal.

Boca Raton and around

You can practically smell the money as you cross into Palm Beach County's southernmost town, **BOCA RATON**. Smartly dressed valets park your car at supermarkets, and golf-mad retirees and executives from numerous hi-tech industries hibernate year-round; Northeasterners fleeing the winter chill make

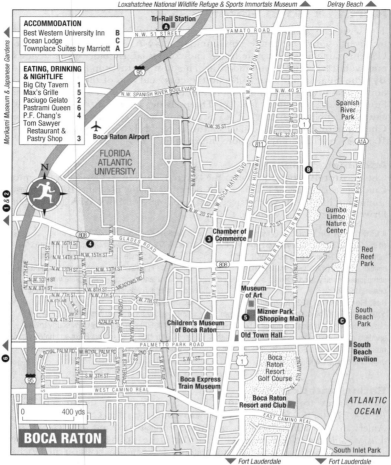

up 60 percent of the population. In 2007 America's mortgage crisis took the sheen off the opulence somewhat, and 2008 was the first year in which the population is thought to have declined.

More noticeably, Boca Raton has an abundance of Mediterranean Revival architecture, a style prevalent here since the 1920s and preserved by strict building codes. Other than the architecture, the town boasts some fine, under-recognized beaches and parks.

Arrival and information

Boca Raton covers a large area, and it's much easier to get around if you have your own car. Roads are rarely busy, but with the exception of Mizner Park (which is free, see p.202), parking can be expensive, especially at the beaches. Getting here by public transport is tough, as the nearest Greyhound **bus** terminal is in Delray Beach, 402 SE Sixth Ave (☎561/272-6447) and the Tri-Rail station is off I-95, at 680 Yamato Rd (☎1-800/TRI-RAIL), though their shuttle buses connect with the town center. Palm Tran bus #91 ($1.50 each way, $3.50 daily unlimited; ☎561/841-4BUS, ⊛www.palmtran.org) operates daily one to two times an hour between Mizner Park through downtown west via Glades Road to the Sandalfoot Square shopping center. The Boca Raton Historic Society runs **trolley tours** of the city as well, for $15 (Jan–April, second and fourth Thur 10am–noon; ☎561/395-6766).

The Chamber of Commerce, 1800 N Dixie Hwy (Mon 9.30am–5pm Tues–Fri 8.30am–5pm; ☎561/395-4433, ⊛www.bocaratonchamber.com), supplies the usual information on area hotels and attractions.

Accommodation

You can stay in luxury at places like the *Boca Raton Resort and Club* (see below); otherwise, one of the better-value **motels** near the beaches is the *Ocean Lodge*, 531 N Ocean Blvd (☎561/395-7772, ⊛www.oceanlodgeflorida.com; ❺), which also has kitchen units. West of the Intracoastal Waterway, North Federal Highway has its fair share of hotels, some made more affordable by the slightly inland location; of these, try the *Best Western University Inn*, 2700 N Federal Hwy (☎561/395-5225, ⊛www.bestwestern.com; ❺), which offers a free shuttle to the beach. If you're staying for an extended period, a good place for a deal might be *Towneplace Suites by Marriott*, 5110 NW Eighth Ave (☎561/994-7232, ⊛www.towneplacebocaraton.com; ❼).

Downtown Boca Raton

Boca Raton lacks a definitive central area marked by the landscaped palm trees and upmarket shops of most other South Florida cities. Instead, **downtown** is a bit more spread out, and generally focused around Palmetto Park Road, Federal Highway, and their junction, including the Mizner Park shopping and entertainment complex. Throughout, you'll see signs of Boca Raton's Mediterranean-flavored architecture, the influence of **Addison Mizner**, who furnished the fantasies of Palm Beach's fabulously wealthy (see box, p.210) during the 1920s. Unable to give reign to his megalomaniacal desires elsewhere, Mizner swept into Boca Raton on the tide of the Florida property boom after World War I, bought 1600 acres of land, and began selling plots of a future community, advertised as "beyond realness in its ideality." Envisaging gondola-filled canals, a luxury hotel, and a great cathedral dedicated to his mother, Mizner had big plans that were ultimately nipped in the bud by the economic crash of 1926; shortly thereafter, he crawled back to Palm Beach with his tail between his legs.

The few buildings Mizner did manage to complete left an indelible mark on Boca Raton. His million-dollar *Cloister Inn* grew into the present **Boca Raton Resort and Club**, 501 E Camino Real (☎561/447-3000 or 1-888-491-BOCA, ⊛www.bocaresort.com; ❽). A pink palace of marble columns, sculptured fountains, and carefully aged wood (the centuries-old effect was accomplished by the hobnailed boots of Mizner's workmen), its tall towers are visible for miles around. Like most exclusive clubs, unless you're staying here, you'll have to be satisfied with a drive-by, unless you join the **guided walking tour** (Nov–April, Tues 2–3.30pm; $12, plus $9 valet ticket; ☎561/395-6766) run by the Boca Raton Historical Society – casual visitors are strictly forbidden.

The Historical Society itself resides in Mizner's more accessible gold-domed **Old Town Hall**, 71 N Federal Hwy (Mon–Fri 10am–4pm; free; ☎561/395-6766, ⊛www.bocahistory.org), completed in 1927. For a glimpse into Boca's formative years, history buffs should check out the society's library, which features historic maps, photos, and documents; once you're inside, turn left along the corridor from the building's rear entrance.

Boca Raton's museums

Mizner Park, off of N Federal Highway between Palmetto Park Road and Glades Road, isn't a park at all but one of several stylish, open-air shopping and entertainment malls that improved downtown Boca Raton in the 1990s, where the well heeled pay tribute with their credit cards. Outfitted in a very Floridian scheme of pink and yellow pastels, and landscaped with the palm trees and fountains of Plaza Real, Mizner Park is packed with haute couture stores, specialty merchants, and a range of restaurants, from chain to upmarket.

At its north end, Mizner Park contains an open amphitheatre for concerts and the airy **Museum of Art** (Tues, Thurs & Fri 10am–5pm, Wed 10am–9pm, Sat & Sun noon–5pm; $8; ☎561/392-2500, ⊛www.bocamuseum.org), which has benefited from generous patrons and inspired curatorship to become one of Florida's finest small art museums. Besides temporary exhibitions by both international and Florida artists, the museum has a permanent collection featuring an outdoor sculpture garden, the Mayers Collection of Modern Masters – 53 works including drawings by Degas, Matisse, Picasso, and Seurat – and a formidable trove of West African art, among other displays.

To escape the Mizner influence altogether, head for the beaches (see below) or turn to the **Children's Museum of Boca Raton**, 498 Crawford Blvd (Tues–Sat noon–4pm; $3; ☎561/368-6875, ⊛www.cmboca.org). Housed in a 1913 driftwood "cracker" cottage – the simple abode of early Florida farmers (see Contexts, p.465) – the museum stocks entertaining remnants from the pioneer days alongside exhibitions aimed at kids.

Near the old Town Hall (see p.201), at the junction of Dixie Highway and SE Eighth Street, is the Historical Society-owned **Boca Express Train Museum** (first and third Fri only, Nov–April, 1–4pm; $4; ☎561/395-6766 ext 100), a historic site comprising the old 1930 railroad depot and two restored 1947 streamliner rail cars. Admission includes a guided tour of the museum and rail cars, courtesy of the society.

Sports fans, meanwhile, will revel in the **Sports Immortals Museum and Memorabilia Mart**, 6830 N Federal Hwy (Mon–Fri 10am–6pm, Sat 10am–5pm; $7; ☎561/997-2575), which houses an overwhelming assortment of sporting mementoes, from Muhammad Ali's championship belt to the baseball that killed the ballplayer Ray Chapman in 1920. The main focus, however, is the **memorabilia store**, one of the largest in the US, where you can buy balls, plaques, helmets, and autographs from every major sport.

Boca Raton's beaches

All four of Boca Raton's fine **beaches** are open to the public (daily 8am–sunset), but they are walled in by tall rows of palm trees, sea grape and Australian pine, so it's unlikely you'll stumble across them as you drive along Hwy-A1A, also known as Ocean Boulevard here. The three that are also city-owned parks come with hefty daily **parking fees** so they tend to be the preserve of select Floridians who can purchase permits, rather than long-distance travelers. To avoid the steep costs, your best bet is to park elsewhere and walk, or head north to Delray Beach, which is much cheaper (see p.204).

The southernmost patch, **South Inlet Park**, at 1298 S Ocean Blvd (cars $4 weekdays, $6 weekends and holidays), is the smallest and quietest of the quartet, often deserted in midweek save for a few people fishing along its short jetty. To reach it, look for the entrance on the right off Hwy-A1A, just before the Boca Raton Inlet. **South Beach Park** (cars $15 weekdays, $17 weekends), about a mile north, is a surfers' favorite, though the actual beach is a fairly tiny area of coarse sand; the park's entrance is about a quarter-mile north of the attractive **South Beach Pavilion**, where a small parking lot offers free one-hour parking (time limit is enforced). **Red Reef Park** (cars $16 weekdays, $18 weekends), a mile further, is far better for sunbathing, swimming, and snorkeling – activities that should be combined with a walk around the twenty-acre **Gumbo Limbo Nature Center** (Mon–Sat 9am–4pm, Sun noon–4pm; $3 donation suggested; ☏561/338-1473, ⓦwww .gumbolimbo.org), directly across Hwy-A1A at 1801 N Ocean Blvd. The center's wide boardwalks take you through a tropical hardwood hammock and a mangrove forest between the Intracoastal Waterway and the Atlantic Ocean; watch for ospreys, brown pelicans, and the occasional manatee lurking in the warm waters. Between the end of May and early July, you can join the center's scheduled walks ($8) to observe **sea turtles**. These can be extremely popular, however, and tickets must be purchased in person.

Boca Raton's most explorable beachside area is **Spanish River Park** (cars $16 weekdays, $18 weekends), a mile north of Red Reef Park on Hwy-A1A (entrance on the left). Here, sandwiched between the Intracoastal Waterway and the ocean, you'll find fifty acres of lush vegetation, most of which is only penetrable on secluded trails through shady thickets. Aim for the forty-foot observation tower for a view across the park and much of Boca Raton. The adjacent beach is a slender but serviceable strip, linked to the park by several tunnels beneath the highway. If you get here early enough, you may find free parking in the few curbside spaces at the end of Spanish River Boulevard, a short walk from the park's entrance.

Loxahatchee National Wildlife Refuge

Boca Raton makes a good base from which to visit the excellent **Arthur R. Marshall Loxahatchee National Wildlife Refuge**, about twenty miles northwest of here, just off US-441 at 10216 Lee Rd (daily sunrise–sunset; cars $5, pedestrians and cyclists $1; ☏561/732-3684, ⓦwww.fws.gov/loxahatchee).

The 220-odd square miles of sawgrass marshes – the northerly extension of the Everglades (see p.169) – are penetrable on two easy walking trails from the **visitor center** (Wed–Fri 9am–4pm, Sat & Sun 9am–4.30pm; ☏561/734-8303). One trail is a half-mile boardwalk that meanders above a cypress swamp, while the grassy Marsh Trail (0.8 miles) loops around one area of wetlands to an observation tower, with the option to walk further around additional marshes. You're likely to see quite a bit of the local wildlife – alligators, snakes, turtles, and a wide variety of local birds, including the endangered snail kite.

Another option is to explore the refuge by **airboat**, which you can arrange at **Loxahatchee Everglades Tours**, 15490 Loxahatchee Rd, off State Road 7/US-441, fifteen miles due west of downtown Boca Raton (daily tours leave hourly 10am–4pm; $44 per person for 55min tour, $32 for 45min; ☏561/482-6107 or 1-800/683-5873, ⓦwww.evergladesairboattours.com).

Eating and drinking

When it comes to **eating**, there are plenty of choices in Boca Raton, albeit spread out all over town.

Big City Tavern 5250 Town Center Circle, just west of I-95 ☎561/361-4551, ⓦwww .bigcitytavernboca.com. Serves tasty dishes from seafood to pastas to steaks mostly in the $17–27 range, but is also a great place for a cocktail.
Max's Grille 404 Plaza Real ☎561/368-0080, ⓦwww.maxsgrille.com. One of the best options at Mizner Park, featuring upmarket American dishes with Asian influences; try the Shanghai duck salad or hefty grilled tuna club sandwich for lunch. Most entrées $17–25.

🏃 **Paciugo Gelato** 8903 Glades Rd, West Boca (in Somerset Shoppes mall) ☎561/479-0343, ⓦpachiugo.com. Worth a detour for the freshest and tastiest gelato in south Florida; choose from a vast range of flavors including coconut cinnamon, roasted banana and pumpkin pie.

🏃 **Pastrami Queen** 7132 Beracasa Way, off W Palmetto Park Rd (Rte-798)

☎561/391-8989. This classic Jewish deli offers a slice of old Brooklyn in Boca, with giant pastrami and corned beef sandwiches, perfect matzah balls and thick split-pea soup you can eat with a fork.
P.F. Chang's 1400 Glades Rd, off N Federal Highway ☎561/393-3722, ⓦwww.pfchangs .com. Contemporary Chinese bistro chain, just one of several dining options found in the University Commons shopping complex. Start the meal with their fabulous lettuce wraps ($8) before moving on to crispy honey chicken or *lo mein* ($11–12).
Tom Sawyer Restaurant & Pastry Shop 1759 NW 2nd Ave ☎561/368-4634. Old-fashioned diner, with big portions and an especially vast range of omelets and pancake specials at the weekends. Try "breakfast in a pot", featuring crab as well as bacon combos, all for under $10. Open till 2pm.

North toward Palm Beach

Heading north from Boca Raton along Hwy-A1A it's 26 miles to Palm Beach, a generally stress-free route through shoulder-to-shoulder towns **with** pleasant beaches but little else to see; only **Delray Beach** warrants a lengthy stop, with the **Morikami Museum** a worthy detour inland. If you're reliant on public transportation, you can take the local Palm Tran bus #1 ($1.50; ☎561/841-4BUS), which runs every twenty to thirty minutes (hourly on Sun) through towns between Boca Raton and West Palm Beach.

Delray Beach

Five miles north of Boca Raton, **Delray Beach** justifies at least a half-day visit; its powdery-sanded **municipal beach**, at the foot of Atlantic Avenue, is rightly popular and is one of the few in Florida where you can sometimes see the Gulf Stream current – a cobalt-blue streak about five miles offshore. Metered **parking** is available along the seafront ($1 per hr). For a greater understanding of South Florida's fragile marine and freshwater environments, visit the **Sandoway House Nature Center**, 142 S Ocean Blvd (Tues–Sat 10am–4pm; $4; ☎561/274-7263, ⓦwww.sandowayhouse.com), located within a 1936 beachfront house, just south of Atlantic Avenue. Exhibits include a shell gallery and a coral reef ecosystem display, home to reef fish and nurse sharks (call for feeding times).

A mile inland along Atlantic Avenue, on the corner of Swinton Avenue, an imposing schoolhouse dating from 1913 is now the **Cornell Museum** (Tues–Sat 10.30am–4.30pm, Sun 1–4.30pm; closed Sun May–Oct; $6, children free; ☎561/243-7922), part of **Old School Square** (ⓦwww.oldschool.org), a group of buildings restored and converted into a cultural center. The spacious two-floor museum hosts rotating American art and craft exhibitions in its six gallery spaces; featured artists are usually south Florida-based, and the standard of work is usually high.

Nearby the **Delray Beach Historical Society** (☎561/243-2577) runs the **Cason Cottage Museum**, 5 NE First St (Oct–April Thurs–Sat 11am–3pm; $3), a house erected circa 1915 for Rev John R. Cason, member of an illustrious local family; the cottage warrants a look for its simple woodframe design based on pioneer-era Florida architecture. The society's **History Learning Center** at the restored 1908 Hunt House around the corner, at 111 N Swinton Ave, should be open by the end of 2009. The society also organizes edifying **historic trolley tours** on the second Saturday of the month (Sept–May; $15), taking in all the town's sights with an expert guide.

Nature lovers, meanwhile, will enjoy the **American Orchid Society Visitors Center and Botanical Garden**, 16700 AOS Lane (daily 10am–4.30pm; $10; ☎561/404-2000, ⊛www.aos.org), where they can linger in a steaming orchid jungle as well as formal gardens and a habitat entirely populated by native Florida plants. You'll find it by driving six miles inland along Atlantic Avenue, then heading south for just under two miles on Jog Road (it's next to the Morikami Museum).

Accommodation

Bermuda Inn 64 S Ocean Blvd ☎561/276-5288, ⊛www.thebermudainn.com. Reasonably priced beachside accommodation, with simple but comfy sea-view rooms equipped with microwaves, fridge and wi-fi; there's also a small pool. ➎

Colony Hotel & Cabana Club 525 E Atlantic Ave ☎561/276-4123, ⊛www.thecolonyhotel.com. This resort-style place, with its garnet-and-pale-yellow awning, has been a fixture since 1926; rooms come with many of the original mahogany furnishings. Its private beach is located two miles away, reachable by complimentary shuttle. ➐

Crane's BeachHouse 82 Gleason St ☎561/278-1700 or 1-866/372-7263, ⊛www.cranesbeachhouse.com. For something different, try this gracefully laid-back resort, featuring tropical-themed rooms, bamboo tiki huts, and miniature waterfalls. One block from the beach. ➎

Wight by the Sea 1901 S Ocean Blvd ☎561/278-3355, ⊛www.wbtsea.com. Friendly oceanside hotel, with helpful staff, spacious rooms with well-equipped kitchens, and a fabulous location close to all the action. Thoughtful extras include free daily newspapers, cabanas on the beach, wi-fi and laundry. Rates halve in the summer. ➑

Eating

Boston's on the Beach 40 S Ocean Blvd ☎561/278-3364, ⊛www.bostonsonthebeach.com. This New England-style restaurant offers incredibly fresh seafood and fish at reasonable prices (entrées from $7.95), plus a separate fine dining menu on the upper deck and a downstairs lounge with live music.

Caffe Luna Rosa 34 S Ocean Blvd ☎561/274-9404, ⊛www.caffelunarosa.com. Serves casual Italian-style food in an attractive exposed-brick space hung with unusual artwork, and features occasional live music – you can also sit outside. Lunchtime pastas $8–16, pizzas from $11.50 – add around $6 for dinner, which also

features a bigger choice of Italian seafood dishes from $18.

🏃 **Doc's** 10 N Swinton Ave at Atlantic Avenue ☎561/278-3627. Best for a quick bite downtown, this old-school diner has been in business since 1951; try the burgers ($3.75) and hefty sandwiches ($5.95) washed down with shakes ($2.99) and hand-whipped ice cream ($2.45). Cash only.

Sandwiches by the Sea 1214 E Atlantic Ave ☎561/272-2212. This tiny but excellent lunch spot has good salads, sandwiches (from $6–7), and amazing frozen yogurt shakes ($3.50). No seating – take your subs to the beach. Cash only.

The Morikami Museum and Japanese Gardens

The flat, featureless suburbs west of Delray Beach might be the last place you'd expect to find a formal Japanese garden, Shinto shrine, teahouse, and a museum recording the history of a Japanese agricultural colony, but next door to the Orchid Society, at the **Morikami Museum and Japanese Gardens**, 4000 Morikami Park Rd (Tues–Sun 10am–5pm; adults $10, children $6;

▲ Morikami Museum and Japanese Gardens

☎561/495-0233, ⓦwww.morikami.org), you'll find all four. These are reminders of a group of Japanese farmers who came here in the early twentieth century at the behest of the Florida East Coast Railway to grow tea and rice and to farm silkworms in a colony called Yamato, but wound up selling pineapples until a blight killed off the crop in 1908. Most of the settlers departed by the 1920s.

A permanent exhibit of artifacts and photographs commemorate the colony in the site's original building, the Yamato-kan, which also serves as a model of a traditional Japanese residence. Across the beautifully landscaped grounds, additional galleries in the principal museum stage themed exhibitions drawn from their 5000-piece archive of Japanese art objects and artifacts. A traditional **teahouse**, assembled here by a Florida-based Japanese craftsman, is used every third Saturday of the month (Oct–June) for tea ceremonies ($5). The **open-air café** (Tues–Sun 11am–3pm) serves pan-Asian fare and makes for a great lunch stop.

Lantana and Lake Worth

One of the first towns established on the Gold Coast, **LANTANA** retains a few original wood buildings on its main street, Ocean Avenue, but the real highlight here is the ⚤ *Old Key Lime House* (☎561/582-1889, ⓦwww.oldkeylimehouse .com) restaurant at 300 E Ocean Ave, just off US-1 on the way to the beach. One of the oldest structures in South Florida, the creaky pinewood house was built in 1889 by pioneer Morris Lyman, but the most enticing section today is the outdoor deck (protected by a Seminole palm-thatched *chickee* roof) looking out over Lake Worth, replete with resident pelicans. The seafood is excellent – standouts are the crab cakes ($25) and fish dip ($10) – but you have to try the Key lime pie ($7 per slice), a wedge of creamy lime heaven.

From Lantana Hwy-A1A charts a picturesque course along ten-odd miles of slender barrier islands, with ocean views on one side and the Intracoastal Waterway – plied by luxury yachts and lined with opulent homes – on the other. Three miles north of Lantana, **Lake Worth**'s distinct downtown district, east of I-95 along the parallel Lake and Lucerne avenues, can get lively on weekend nights with a handful of outdoor bars and cafes. You'll find a couple of good places to **eat**, like the cozily eclectic *Bizarre Avenue Café*, 921 Lake Ave (T 561/588-4488, W www.bizaareavecafe.com; closed Sun), where stylish dining, moderately priced tapas and an antique garage sale collide – everything, from comfy sofas to coffee tables, is for sale. For a burger and a beer, head to *Brogue's on the Avenue*, 621 Lake Ave (T 561/585-1885), an Irish pub with an attractive bar and nightly live music. Across from the **beach**, *John G's*, 10 S Ocean Blvd (T 561/585-9860, W www.johngs.com; breakfast and lunch only), is known nearly as much for its long weekend waiting lines as it is for its delicious french toast and omelet.

From Lake Worth, Palm Beach (via Hwy-A1A) and West Palm Beach (via US-1) are just a few miles north.

Palm Beach

A small island town of palatial homes, pampered gardens, and streets so clean you could eat your dinner off them, **PALM BEACH** has been synonymous for nearly a century with the kind of lifestyle only limitless loot can buy. A bastion of conspicuous wealth, with pomposity – banning clothes lines, for example – that knows no bounds, Palm Beach is, for all its faults, irrefutably unique.

The nation's upper crust began wintering here in the 1890s, after **Henry Flagler** brought his railway south and built two luxury hotels on this then-secluded, palm-filled island (only *The Breakers* is still open, see p.209). Throughout the 1920s, **Addison Mizner** began a vogue for Mediterranean-style architecture, blanketing the place in arcades, courtyards, and plazas – and the first million-dollar homes. Since then, corporate tycoons, sports heroes, jet-setting aristocrats, rock stars, and CIA directors have all flocked here, eager to become part of the Palm Beach elite and enjoy its aloofness from mainland life.

Summer is very quiet and easily the least costly time to stay here. The pace heats up between November and May, with the winter months a whirl of elegant balls, fund-raising dinners, and charity galas. Winter also brings the **polo season** – watching a chukka or two is one of the few times Palm Beach denizens show themselves in the less particular environs of West Palm Beach (on the mainland), where the games are held.

Even by walking – generally the best way to see the moneyed isle – you'll get the measure of Palm Beach in a day. Drive in along Hwy-A1A from the south, or use one of the three bridges over Lake Worth from West Palm Beach, the nearest bus and train stop.

Arrival and information

If you're arriving by **car** from US-1 or I-95, take Okeechobee Blvd east into Palm Beach; otherwise, Hwy-A1A is the most direct route. Metered **parking** is available on the seafront ($2 per hr), but you can usually park for free (2hr maximum) on most streets.

Public transportation to Palm Beach is limited, and all long-distance terminals are located in West Palm Beach (see p.213). To get to Palm Beach

ACCOMMODATION

Best Western Palm Beach Lakes Inn	C
Brazilian Court	E
Chesterfield	F
Colony	H
Hibiscus House	B
Hotel Biba	I
Marriott Fairfield Inn & Suites	J
Palm Beach Historic Inn	G
Queens Lodge	A
West Palm Beach Marriott	D

EATING, DRINKING & NIGHTLIFE

Amici	16
Brewzzi	11
Blue Martini	13
Cabana	7
Café Delamar	18
Café L'Europe	15
Charley's Crab	19
Feelgoods Rock Bar & Grill	4
Hamburger Heaven	14
Hotel Nightclub	12
Leila	8
O'Shea's Irish Pub	3
Pizza Al Fresco	17
Renato's	17
Respectable Street Café	5
Rocco's Tacos	6
Sloan's	9
Spoto's Oyster Bar	10
Testa's	2
Tom's Place for Ribs	1

PALM BEACH AND WEST PALM BEACH

from West Palm Beach, take any PalmTran bus ($1.50; ☎561/841-4BUS) to the hub at Quadrille Boulevard and Clematis Street, then transfer to the #41 (no Sun service).

The **Palm Beach Chamber of Commerce**, 400 Royal Palm Way, Suite 106 (Mon–Fri 8am–6pm; ☎561/655-3282, ⓦwww.palmbeachchamber.com) provides all the usual free **maps**, **brochures**, and **information**.

Accommodation

You'll need plenty of money **to stay** in Palm Beach. Comfort and elegance are the key words, and prices vary greatly depending on the time of year. To save money, visit between mid-April and mid-November, when you can often find deals. It's always cheaper to stay outside Palm Beach and visit by day, something easily done from West Palm Beach even without a car (see p.214 for more). For *The Breakers*, see below.

Brazilian Court 301 Australian Ave ☎561/655-7740 or 1-800/552-0335, ⓦwww.thebrazilian court.com. An elegant and intimate hotel, comprising Spanish-style villas surrounding a fountained courtyard. It's also the home of internationally acclaimed chef Daniel Boulud's French–American *Café Boulud* and the Frederic Fekkai Salon & Spa. ❽

Chesterfield 363 Cocoanut Row ☎561/659-5800 or 1-800/243-7871, ⓦwww.chesterfieldpb.com. Opulent boutique hotel, with antique-filled rooms and a popular nightclub, the *Leopard Lounge*. Serves a traditional English tea every afternoon in the wood-paneled library. ❽

Colony 155 Hammon Ave ☎561/655-5430 or 1-800/521-5525, ⓦwww.thecolonypalmbeach.com.

Steps away from chic Worth Avenue, the lovely and convenient *Colony* has hosted former presidents, sheiks, and Hollywood royalty. ❽

Marriott Fairfield Inn & Suites 2870 S Ocean Blvd ☎561/582-2581 or 1-800/347-5434. One of the cheaper options and catering to the business set, with clean, decent-sized rooms and complimentary newspaper, continental breakfast, and wi-fi. Located about 5 miles south of Worth Avenue. ❼

Palm Beach Historic Inn 365 S County Rd ☎561/832-4009 or 1-800/918-9773, ⓦwww.palmbeachhistoricinn.com. A friendly, centrally located B&B, offering complimentary in-room continental breakfasts and some of the best rates in town – if you visit off-season. ❽

The Town

The main residential section of Palm Beach is where you should spend most of your time, and **Worth Avenue**, cruised by classic cars and filled with designer stores and upmarket art galleries, is a good place to start your stroll, if only to window-shop.

Other than expense-account spending, the most appealing aspect of the street is its architecture: stucco walls, crafted Romanesque facades, and narrow passageways leading to small, charming courtyards called "vias" that might be adorned with miniature bridges, spiral staircases, quirky statues or fountains.

County Road

The government and business heart of Palm Beach lies along **County Road** north of Worth Avenue, where Mizner's Mediterranean Revival themes are displayed in Palm Beach's tidy local administration offices and bank buildings. By contrast, the 1926 **Episcopal Church of Bethesda-by-the-Sea**, a fifteen-minute walk further north at 141 S County Rd, is a handsome imitation-Gothic pile replacing the island's first church, which had been built in 1889. The hushed interior features a timber ceiling, wooden pews and a series of large stained-glass windows depicting saints and Biblical scenes, but the hidden gem here is the **Cluett Memorial Garden** (daily 8am–5pm; free), a peaceful spot behind the echoing cloisters in which to claim a stone pew and tuck into a picnic lunch. Free guided tours 12.15pm (second and fourth Sun Sept–Nov & Jan–May; 11.15am every fourth Sun June–Aug).

A little further north, County Road is straddled by the golf course of *The Breakers* (☎1-888/BREAKERS, ⓦwww.thebreakers.com; ❾), a castle-like hotel established by Flagler in 1896, and the greatest of Palm Beach's ultra-swanky resorts (the current building dates from 1926, modeled on the Villa Medici in Rome). Though security is tighter than in the past, you can still catch

Palm Beach's architect: Addison Mizner

A former miner and prizefighter, **Addison Mizner** was an unemployed architect when he arrived in Palm Beach in 1918 from California to recuperate from the recurrence of a childhood leg injury. Inspired by the medieval buildings he'd seen around the Mediterranean, Mizner, financed by the heir to the Singer sewing machine fortune, built the *Everglades Club* at 356 Worth Ave, which is now off-limits to the public. Described by Mizner as "a little bit of Seville and the Alhambra, a dash of Madeira and Algiers," the Everglades Club was the first public building in Florida erected in the Mediterranean Revival style, and fast became the island's most prestigious social club.

The success of the club, and the house he subsequently built for society bigwig Eva Stotesbury, won Mizner commissions all over Palm Beach as the wintering wealthy decided to swap their suites at one of Henry Flagler's hotels for a "million-dollar cottage" of their own.

Brilliant and unorthodox, Mizner's loggias and U-shaped interiors made the most of Florida's pleasant winter temperatures, while his twisting staircases to nowhere became legendary. Pursuing a medieval look, Mizner used untrained workmen to lay roof tiles crookedly, sprayed condensed milk onto walls to create an impression of centuries-old grime, and fired shotgun pellets into wood to imitate worm holes. By the mid-1920s, Mizner had created the Palm Beach Style – which Florida architecture buff Hap Hattan called "the Old World for the new rich" – and would go on to fashion much of Boca Raton (see p.201).

a glimpse of the ornate lobby on a trip to the hotel's high-end shops or restaurants. For a closer look, take the **guided tour** on Tuesdays at 2pm (free for guests, $15 for the public; for information, call ☎561/655-6611).

Society of the Four Arts and Flagler Museum

Four blocks west of County Road, Royal Palm Way leads to the stuccoed buildings and gardens of the **Society of the Four Arts**, at 2 Four Arts Plaza (galleries open Dec–April Mon–Sat 10am–5pm, Sun 2–5pm; $5; ☎561/655-7226, ⓦ www.fourarts.org). Aside from presenting art shows, concerts, films and lectures of an impressive standard between early December and mid-April, the organization also has a library worth browsing (open year-round; free).

Head north along Cocoanut Row for half a mile from here and you'll see the white Doric columns fronting Whitehall, also known as the **Henry Morrison Flagler Museum** (Tues–Sat 10am–5pm, Sun noon–5pm; tours at 11am, 12.30pm, and 2pm, Sun at 12.30pm, 1.30pm, and 2.30pm; $15; ☎561/655-2833, ⓦ www.flagler.org). The most overtly ostentatious home on the island, Whitehall was a $4-million wedding present from Flagler to his third wife, Mary Lily Kenan, whom he married (after controversially persuading the Florida legislature to amend its divorce laws) in 1901. Like many of Florida's first luxury homes, Whitehall's interior design was created by pillaging the great buildings of Europe. Among the 73 rooms are an Italian library, a French salon, a billiard room with a Swiss-style mantel, a hallway modeled on the Vatican's St Peter's Basilica, and a Louis XV ballroom. All are richly stuffed with ornamentation but, other than their mutual decadence, lack any aesthetic cohesion. Flagler was in his 70s when Whitehall was built, 37 years older than his bride and not enamored of the banquets and balls she continually hosted. He often sloped off to bed using a concealed stairway, perhaps to ponder plans to extend his railway to Key West – a display on the project, which was completed in 1912 (a year before his death), fills his former office. From the 110-foot hallway, informative

▲ Palm Beach condominiums

45-minute free guided tours depart three times a day, depending on availability, and will leave you giddy with the tales and sights of the earliest Palm Beach excesses. Don't miss the spectacular views of West Palm Beach from Flagler's enormous backyard.

Next door to the house, back on Cocoanut Row, you'll notice the square bell tower of the **Royal Poinciana Chapel** at no. 60, which dates from 1898. Flagler had built the original structure on the grounds of his *Royal Poinciana Hotel*, but the shingled church was moved to its current locale and reconstructed in 1973. It still has interdenominational services every Sunday morning, but is otherwise usually locked up. Look out for **Sea Gull Cottage** at the back of the church, Flagler's first home in Palm Beach and the town's oldest remaining house, built in 1886; it was originally located on the Intracoastal Waterway, and moved here in 1984. Now owned and used by the church, it's recently undergone a massive restoration that should be complete by the end of 2009.

The Lake Trail

The limited points of interest beyond Royal Poinciana Way are best viewed from the three-mile **Lake Trail**, a bicycle and pedestrian path skirting the edge of Lake Worth, almost to the northern limit of the island. A bicycle is the ideal mode of transportation here; rent one from **Palm Beach Bicycle Trail Shop**, 223 Sunrise Ave (Mon–Sat 9am–5.30pm, Sun 10am–5pm; ☎561/659-4583), a few blocks north of Royal Poinciana Way, for $39 for 24hr or $12 an hour. Most locals use the trail as a jogging strip, and certainly there's little other than exercise and fine views across the lake to make it worthwhile.

Peanut Island

Just off the north coast of Palm Island, in the middle of Lake Worth, **Peanut Island** makes for an off-beat day-trip, though it can get crowded at the weekends. Home to the JFK bunker, most of the island is now a county park;

Thrift stores

Amazingly high-class threads, some of them discarded after only a single use, turn up in Palm Beach's thrift stores, though you'll usually pay above normal thrift-store prices. Worth perusing are The Church Mouse, 378 S County Rd (Mon–Sat 10am–4pm; ☎561/659-2154; open Oct–May only); Goodwill Embassy Boutique, 210 Sunset Ave (Mon–Sat 9am–5pm, Sun 10am–5pm; ☎561/832-8199); and Deja Vu, at the back of the Via Testa Mall at 219 Royal Poinciana Way, but more easily accessed from Sunset Avenue (Mon–Sat 10am–5pm; ☎561/833-6624). Be warned: many shops in Palm Beach close for the summer or operate on reduced hours, so call before you go.

it's relatively unspoiled and thickly forested, surrounded by clear, calm water and can only be reached by boat, making it blissfully free of traffic.

The island was created in 1918 from landfill excavated from Lake Worth, and though it covers 86 acres, only the outer sections are open to the public – you can walk the entire perimeter along a 1.25-mile path. Other than taking in the fresh air and lake views, you can swim at **Boater Beach** or spot tropical fish and occasional manatees at the **snorkeling lagoon** which has a shallow-water reef. If the sun gets too much, check out the **Palm Beach Maritime Museum** (Fri–Sun 11am–5pm; by guided tour only, $10; ☎561/832-7428, ⓦwww .pbmm.org) on the south-side of the island, comprising a former US Coast Guard Station and **President Kennedy's command post and bomb shelter**, a barebones but atmospheric bunker constructed during the Cuban Missile Crisis in the early 1960s (the Kennedys had a home in Palm Beach at the time). Food is not sold on the island, so bring a picnic.

Practicalities

Palm Beach Water Taxi (☎561/683-8294, ⓦwww.sailfishmarina.com) can take you to the island ($10), and also does shuttles around the area and guided tours from Sailfish Marina, 98 Lake Drive, in Palm Beach Shores on Singer Island. You could also try **Peanut Island Ferry** (☎561/339-2504) from Riviera Beach Marina, at the end of E 13th Street in Riviera Beach, opposite the island and just north of West Palm Beach on US-1. Alternatively, rent a **paddle boat** ($15 per hr, $95 per day), **jet ski** ($90 per hr) or **powerboat** (from $85 per hr) from here (☎561/840-7470, ⓦwww.bluewaterboatrental .com). You can also take a ferry from the Palm Beach Maritime Museum's center in Currie Park (561/832-7428), West Palm Beach – ferries depart Fri–Sun to coincide with tours of the JFK bunker. If you want to stay the night, the island **campground** (with restrooms and indoor showers) can be reserved three months in advance by calling ☎561/845-4445 or 1-866/383-5730. Sites are $20 (plus $4.60 tax).

Eating

Though it may be difficult to land affordable accommodation in Palm Beach, it's still possible to **eat** relatively cheaply here. Dining options are more abundant in West Palm Beach, however (see p.215).

Amici 375 S County Rd ☎561/832-0201, ⓦamicipalmbeach.com. Comfortable, popular Italian restaurant, with a wood-fired oven; pizzas go for around $16–18 and pastas from $25 at dinner (lunch is around $10 cheaper).

Café Delamar Via De Mario, 326 Peruvian Ave ☎561/659-3174. A Worth Ave rarity: a casual café serving light breakfasts ($2–4), salads, and sandwiches (around $7.75). Open breakfast and lunch only; closed Sun.

Café L'Europe 331 S County Rd ☎561/655-4020, ⓦwww.cafeleurope.com. If money's no object (you'll spend at least $70 a head) and you're dressed to kill, make for this super-elegant French restaurant, where the menu includes an award-winning wine list, a variety of caviar ($38–230), and dishes like Maine lobster risotto and Muscovy duck confit. Closed Mon.

Charley's Crab 456 S Ocean Blvd ☎561/659-1500, ⓦwww.muer.com. Serves up a mean shrimp cocktail among other scrumptious seafood offerings (and a killer Sunday brunch) in a lovely location overlooking the dunes. Entrées start at $17.

Hamburger Heaven 314 S County Rd ☎561/655-5277. Since 1945, this inexpensive diner-style restaurant has been dispensing delicious ground-beef burgers, as well as breakfast, salads and sandwiches. Open breakfast and lunch only; closed Sun.

Pizza Al Fresco 14 Via Mizner ☎561/832-0032. This attractive, European-style restaurant with courtyard seating is a great alternative to pricier Worth Ave restaurants, serving tasty brick-oven pies ($14–19), calzones ($14.50), and baked pastas ($12.50–16.50). It's also one of the only places around here selling pizza by the slice (until 6pm).

Renato's 87 Via Mizner ☎561/655-9752, ⓦwww.renatospalmbeach.com. Romantic Italian restaurant in beautiful setting, hidden among the courtyards of Via Mizner. Entrées $14.50–23.50. Closed Sun in summer.

Testa's 221 Royal Poinciana Way ☎561/832-0992, ⓦwww.testasrestaurants.com. Long-running Italian–American restaurant serving exquisite seafood, pasta and steak, with alfresco seating. As with most places here, dinner is pricey (average entrée $28), but you can eat well at lunch for under $20.

West Palm Beach and around

Founded to house the workforce of Flagler's Palm Beach resorts, **WEST PALM BEACH** has long been in the shadow of its glamorous neighbor across the lake. Only during the last two decades has the town gained a life of its own, with smart new office buildings, a scenic lakeside footpath – and less seemly industrial growth sprouting up on its western edge. Above all, West Palm Beach holds the promise of accommodation and food at more reasonable prices than in Palm Beach, and it's the closest you'll get to the island using public transportation – PalmTran buses from Boca Raton and Greyhound services stop here, leaving a short walk to Palm Beach over one of the Lake Worth bridges.

Arrival and information

If arriving by car, try the **parking lot** at Dixie Highway and Datura Street (first hr free, $1 per hr thereafter; free Sun). Similarly priced parking garages circle the CityPlace shopping mall.

   Palm Beach International Airport, 1000 Turnage Blvd (☎561/471-742, ⓦwww.pbia.org) is just off I-95 (special exit between junctions 68 and 69), a few miles southwest of downtown West Palm Beach. You can take Palm Tran bus #2 ($1.50) or a taxi into the city – free shuttles connect with the Tri-Rail station (see below). All the major car rental companies have counters at the airport.

   The West Palm Beach Amtrak (☎1-800/USA-RAIL), Tri-Rail (☎1-800/TRI-RAIL), and Greyhound (☎561/833-8536) stations are all located at 201–205 S Tamarind Ave, and linked by regular shuttle buses to the downtown area. Most local PalmTran (☎561/841-4BUS) bus routes converge at Quadrille Boulevard and Clematis Street.

   The **Chamber of Commerce**, 401 N Flagler Drive, at Fourth S (Mon–Fri 8.30am–5pm; ☎561/833-3711, ⓦwww.palmbeaches.org), has stacks of free leaflets and can answer questions on the Palm Beach County area. Coming from I-95, stop at the Palm Beach County Convention and Visitors Bureau, 1555

The waters around Palm Beach County – including Boynton Beach, Delray Beach, Boca Raton, Palm Beach, and Jupiter – are near the **Gulf Stream**, allowing for warm temperatures (especially in summer), outstanding visibility (especially in winter), and ideal drift diving conditions. Large game fish, spiny lobsters, stingrays, moray eels, angelfish, parrotfish, sea turtles, and nurse sharks are among the wide variety of marine life you can spot in the reefs, wrecks, tunnels and crevices. Most outfitters offer reef dives (45–65ft), wreck dives (85–95ft), and night dives; prices range depending on what, if any, of your own equipment you might have. Generally, you can expect to pay about $65 for a two-tank day dive, plus $20–55 for air tanks and other equipment. Reputable outfitters include the following:

Narcosis 200 E 13th St and US-1, Riviera Beach (℡561/630-0606 or 1-866/627-2674, Ⓦ www.narcosisdivecharters.com).

The Scuba Club 4708 N Flagler Drive, West Palm Beach (no Mon dives; ℡561/844-2466 or 1-800/835-2466, Ⓦ www.thescubaclub.com).

Splashdown Divers 700 Casa Loma Blvd, Boyton Beach (℡561/736-0712 or 1-877/724-2342, Ⓦ www.splashdowndivers.com).

Palm Beach Lakes Blvd, Suite 800 (Mon–Fri 9am–5pm; ℡561/233-3000, Ⓦ www.palmbeachfl.com), which also provides free maps, brochures, and information on the whole region.

Accommodation

For **places to stay**, West Palm Beach offers a wider selection than Palm Beach and includes a number of lower-priced options.

Best Western Palm Beach Lakes Inn 1800 Palm Beach Lakes Blvd ℡561/683-8810 or 1-800/331-9569, Ⓦ www.bestwesternwestpalm.com. You can often find good bargains at this motel, which has standard comfy rooms, a small tropical pool and free continental breakfast; it's across from the Palm Beach Mall, about 15min from downtown. ❹

Hibiscus House 501 30th St ℡561/863-5633 or 1-800/203-4927, Ⓦ www.hibiscushouse.com. For a real treat that won't cost an arm and a leg, head north of downtown to this pretty 1922 B&B loaded with beautiful antiques – including a baby grand piano – and five color-themed rooms, most with private terraces and four-poster beds, in addition to a full breakfast served garden-side. ❺

Hotel Biba 320 Belvedere Rd ℡561/832-0094 or 1-800/789-9843, Ⓦ www.hotelbiba.com. Historic boutique hotel with a popular wine bar and sleek, modern rooms with a subtle Eastern feel. ❼

Queens Lodge 3712 Broadway ℡561/842-1108. You'll find the best deals in town at this simple budget option by the highway. ❹

West Palm Beach Marriott 1001 Okeechobee Blvd ℡561/833-1234 or 1-888/376-2292, Ⓦ www.marriott.com/pbimc. Centrally located, reliable business hotel, very close to the shops and restaurants of CityPlace. Rooms come with all the usual upmarket amenities, including wi-fi ($12.95 per day). ❽

Downtown West Palm Beach

In the late 1950s, the boom of shopping malls in Palm Beach practically shut down the street life in **downtown West Palm Beach**. Today, thanks to major renovation projects started in the late 1990s, the area is undergoing something of a renaissance, though the national real estate bust in 2008 stalled plans to build more condos – you'll see plenty of unused stores and office buildings, and the whole district is often deserted at the weekends.

The best place to hang out is **Clematis Street**, home to a diverse mix of restaurants, shops, galleries, and a busy schedule of cultural activities like daytime lunch concerts. Colorfully landscaped, the street stretches from the heart of downtown (where the 500 block contains some of its original 1920s buildings), to the Intracoastal Waterway, culminating with the attractive **fountain** in Centennial Square. Here you can enjoy the popular and free "Clematis by Night" (Ⓦ www.clematisbynight.net) every Thursday evening (6–9.30pm). The Clematis Street downtown district includes the spacious outdoor Meyer Amphitheatre on S Flagler Drive, where the concert series "Sunday at the Meyer" is held once a month (May–Oct), and nearby City Hall on W 2nd Street, where a farmer's market turns everything green on Saturday mornings (Oct–April 8am–1pm).

The faux-European plazas of **CityPlace**, at Okeechobee Boulevard and S Rosemary Avenue (Ⓣ 561/366-1000, Ⓦ www.cityplace.com), a huge and airy shopping, dining and entertainment complex, is conveniently connected to Clematis Street by a free daily trolley (Sun–Wed 11am–9pm, Thurs–Sat 11am–11pm; every 20–30min).

Other than shopping and eating, one reason to linger in downtown is the **Norton Museum of Art**, 1451 S Olive Ave (Mon–Sat 10am–5pm, Sun 1–5pm; closed Mon May–Oct; $8, children 13–21 $3; volunteer tours given Mon–Fri 12.30–1pm; Ⓣ 561/832-5196, Ⓦ www.norton.org), a mile south of the downtown area. Together with some distinctive European paintings and drawings by Braque, de Chirico, Degas, Picasso, and others, the museum boasts a solid grouping of twentieth-century American works: Duane Hanson's eerily lifelike sculpture *Young Worker* and Roger Brown's dark *Guilty Without Trial: Protected by the Bill of Rights* are among the most impressive.

You should also visit the entertaining **Richard and Pat Johnson Palm Beach County History Museum** (Tues–Sat 10am–5pm, Sun 1–5pm; free; Ⓣ 561/832-4164, Ⓦ www.historicalsocietypbc.org), at the restored 1916 courthouse, 300 North Dixie Hwy. Inside you'll find an absorbing interpretation of Palm Beach history, utilizing touch-screen maps on a fifty-inch screen (highlighting the most dramatic events), and special exhibits on city notables such as Addison Mizner.

Eating

The majority of good **places to eat** can be found downtown in the Clematis Street district or at CityPlace.

Brewzzi 700 S Rosemary Ave, at CityPlace, section P (2/F) Ⓣ 561/366-9753, Ⓦ www.brewzzi.com. The home-made microbrews add gusto to this classy but casual Italian–American restaurant-pub, with a wide selection of pizzas, salads, burgers, and pastas ($12–30).

Cabana 118 Clematis St Ⓣ 561/833-4773, Ⓦ www.cabanarestaurant.com. Try the mouthwatering *chuletas do cerdo* (pork chops) and *pollo asado* at this moderately priced and not strictly Cuban restaurant (they serve paellas and Brazilian *churrasco* as well). Entrées $16–25.

Leila 120 S Dixie Hwy Ⓣ 561/659-7373, Ⓦ www.leilawpb.com. Middle Eastern cuisine,

including a full mezze menu, with an alluring atmosphere that includes belly dancers and tableside hookahs. Entrées $17–38. Dinner daily, lunch Mon–Fri only.

Rocco's Tacos 224 Clematis St, Ⓣ 561/650-1001, Ⓦ www.roccostacos.com. Popular weekend brunch spot, with freshly made tacos ($2.95) and TexMex classics ($15–17) washed down with $26 jugs of margarita (and 175 varieties of tequila).

Sloan's 112 Clematis St Ⓣ 561/833-3335, Ⓦ www.sloansonline.com. Great downtown spot for ice cream and baked goods, with fanciful pink decor and cool bathrooms with seemingly transparent walls. Scoops from $4.59.

Spoto's Oyster Bar 125 Datura St ℡561/835-1828, ⓦ www.spotosoysterbar.com. Enjoy delicious oyster shooters (raw oysters in tomato juice and vodka) and pasta, fish, and shellfish dishes (from $17.50) in a fun, casual environment, including pet-friendly alfresco dining.

Tom's Place for Ribs 1225 Palm Beach Lakes Blvd ℡561/832-8774, ⓦ www .tomsplaceforribs.com. Locals' choice for juicy ribs and barbeque, accompanied by an irresistible line-up of black-eyed peas, collard greens, corn muffins, fried chicken, and sweet potato pie. Full rack dinners from $17.75. Closed Sun & Mon.

Drinking and nightlife

Some of the restaurants listed above, such as *Brewzzi*, make for pleasant cocktail spots, but there are plenty of clubs and bars in town; note, though, turnover is relatively high, so call ahead before you head out.

Blue Martini 550 S Rosemary Ave, no. 249 at CityPlace, Plaza Q ℡561/835-8601, ⓦ www .bluemartinilounge.com. Stylish bar which has more than 25 versions of the cocktail on the menu, along with tapas dishes and live jazz and rock.
Feelgoods Rock Bar & Grill 219 Clematis St ℡561/833-6500, ⓦ www.drfeelgoodsbar.com. You'll get thumping rock music and plenty of dancing here, enhanced by drink specials, live rock bands and theme nights (Tues is Ladies Night). Closed Sun & Mon.
Hotel Nightclub 700 S Rosemary Ave, at CityPlace, Plaza Q ℡561/491-7376 ⓦ www .hotelrocklobby.com. Fancy club with glitzy lounge

bars, a big sound system, live acts and blinged-up clientele; don't even think about wearing sneakers.
O'Shea's Irish Pub 531 Clematis St ℡561/833-3865, ⓦ www.osheaspub.com. This fun bar does a fine job of reproducing all the usual Irish pub classics: gut-busting breakfast plates, Guinness and Murphy's stout on draft, and live Irish folk music at the weekends.
Respectable Street Café 518 Clematis St ℡561/832-9999, ⓦ www.respectablestreet.com. Check out this long-standing loud, dark dance club with DJs, live local and national acts (cover usually $5–20), and frequent drink specials. Open Wed–Sat.

Lion Country Safari

West Palm Beach makes a good base for a day-trip to the **Lion Country Safari** (daily 9.30am–5.30pm; last vehicles admitted 4.30pm; $24, children 3–9 $18; parking fee $5; ℡561/793-1084, ⓦ www.lioncountrysafari.com), off Hwy-80/Southern Boulevard (20 miles inland from West Palm Beach and 15.5 miles west of I-95), where African and Asian wildlife is the star attraction. Lions, elephants, giraffes, chimpanzees, zebras, and ostriches are among the creatures roaming a 500-acre preserve in which human visitors are confined to their cars. There's also a walk-through park with a petting zoo. It's a bit awkward to reach and expensive to visit, but if you can't leave Florida without photographing a flamingo this place could well be for you.

The Treasure Coast

West Palm Beach marks the end of the southeast coast's heavily populated (and moneyed) sections. The next eighty miles – dubbed the **TREASURE COAST** for the booty of a Spanish galleon that sank here in 1715 – has seen a much slower rate of expansion than its neighbors to the south, leaving wide open spaces, ruggedly beautiful barrier islands, and magnificent swathes of quiet beach that attract Florida's nature lovers, as well as a small band of well-informed tan-seekers.

Singer Island and Juno Beach

North of West Palm Beach, Hwy-A1A swings back to the coast at **SINGER ISLAND**, which gets its name from the sewing-machine heir Paris Singer. The island is predominantly residential, and the most appealing section is the northern end where you'll find the **John D. MacArthur Beach State Park** (daily 8am–sunset; nature center open daily 9am–5pm; cars $4, pedestrians and cyclists $1; ☎561/624-6950, ⊛www.macarthurbeach.org). A 20-minute nature walk winds through a mixed maritime hammock; elsewhere, a 1600-foot boardwalk (with a daily tram service along it between 10am and 4pm) crosses a mangrove-fringed estuary – popular among manatees, wading birds (at low tide), and a wide variety of fish – to a picturesque beach bordered by sea grape trees. From the boardwalk's end, some worthwhile dirt trails lead off behind the barrier beach's dunes; the park also offers kayak rentals (starting at $10 per hour), ranger-led kayak tours ($20 per single, $35 per double), free evening concerts in its covered amphitheatre and summertime turtle walks.

The next few miles are mostly golf courses and planned retirement communities, but one good stop is **JUNO BEACH**, where Hwy-A1A follows a high coastal bluff from which it's relatively easy to find paths down over the protected dunes to the uncrowded sands below – leave your car at **Juno Beach Park**, where you'll find a beach with amenities (snack bar, lifeguards on duty, restrooms, and fishing pier), and a big parking lot (free).

Or you could set your sights on the **Loggerhead Marinelife Center** (entrance on Hwy-1, Mon–Sat 10am–5pm, Sun noon–3pm; free; ☎561/627-8280, ⊛www.marinelife.org), intended for kids but good for adults interested in brushing up on their knowledge of marine life and **sea turtles** in particular. There's a turtle hospital and informative displays on their life cycles here, and it's one of a few places along the Treasure Coast where you can go on expeditions to watch the turtles as they steal ashore to lay eggs under cover of darkness (June and July only). Reservations for this are essential and accepted from May onwards; the center can provide you with further details.

Jupiter and Jupiter Island

Splitting into several colorless districts around the wide mouth of the Tequesta River, **JUPITER**, about six miles north of Juno Beach, was a rumrunners' haven during the Prohibition era; these days it's better known as the hometown of Florida's favorite son, actor Burt Reynolds. Fans can visit the kitschy Burt Reynolds and Friends Museum, 100 N US-1 (Fri–Sun 10am–4pm; $5; ☎561/743-9955, ⊛www.burtreynoldsmuseum.org), which displays Burt's movie memorabilia among gifts and autographed pictures from his celebrity pals.

One remarkable attraction in the area, however, has nothing to do with Reynolds – the **Hibel Museum of Art**, 5353 Parkside Drive (Tues–Fri 11am–4pm; free; ☎561/622-5560, ⊛www.hibelmuseum.org). Forget Warhol and Rothko; the most commercially successful artist in the US is Edna Hibel, a nonagenarian resident of Singer Island and the only female artist ever to paint for nine decades straight. Hibel often works seven days a week, churning out coy, sentimental portraits, usually of serene Asian and Mexican women. Pay a visit, though, if only to admire the unflappable devotion of the guides, and to figure out why Hibel originals change hands for $100,000 at the gallery shop.

For a well-presented introduction to the ecology of the Loxahatchee River, visit the **River Center**, 805 N US-1 in Burt Reynolds Park (Tues–Sat 9am–4pm; free; ☎561/743-7123), which has interactive displays and live tanks full of fish and river animals. To gain more insight into the lives of the area's first settlers, you can walk through the **Dubois Pioneer Home**, a house dating to 1898, located in nearby Dubois Park (Tues & Wed 1–4pm; $2). Also worth a stop – and a climb – is the red-brick **Jupiter Inlet Lighthouse & Museum** on the north bank of Jupiter Inlet (Tues–Sun 10am–5pm, last tour 4pm; $7; ☎561/747-8380, Ⓦwww.jupiterlighthouse.org); it was completed in 1860 – making it the oldest building in Palm Beach County – and has an absorbing museum detailing the history of the region. You'll see the lighthouse from US-1, off Beach Road (Rte-707) – keep following the latter route for Jupiter Island (see below).

For a bite to eat in Jupiter, try ★ *Little Moir's Food Shack*, 103 S Hwy-1 (closed Sun; ☎561/741-3626, Ⓦwww.littlemoirsfoodshack.com). Festively decorated with bamboo, surfboards, and tropical paintings, it serves up some of the area's best seafood in creative, Caribbean- and Asian-inspired ways, with an extensive beer list. It's tucked into a Publix strip mall off the highway.

Jupiter Island

Two miles into **Jupiter Island** on Beach Road (which starts back in Jupiter town on US-1, at the lighthouse), pull up at the **Blowing Rocks Preserve** (daily 9am–4.30pm; $2; ☎561/747-3113). Here a limestone outcrop covers much of the beach and powerful incoming tides are known to drive through the rocks' hollows, emerging as gusts of spray further on. At low tide, it's sometimes possible to walk around the outcrop and peer into the rock's sea-drilled cavities. Visit the **Hawley Education Center** (same hours; free) across the road from the parking lot, which has displays on Jupiter Island habitats (and a DVD presentation), as well as a couple of trails into the thick mangroves on Indian River Lagoon.

Beach Road continues for another 6.5 miles through the exclusive residences of Jupiter Inlet Colony and Jupiter Island, before reaching shell-strewn **Hobe Sound Beach Park** (free parking) – frustratingly, you'll hardly glimpse the sea the whole way. The beach here is pleasant enough, but you're better off heading two miles north on N Beach Road to the 1000-plus acres of **Hobe Sound National Wildlife Refuge** (daily sunrise–sunset; $5; ☎772/546-6141). Having achieved spectacular success as a nesting ground for sea turtles during the

▲ Spring training

summer (turtle hikes available May–July Tues & Thurs evenings, reservations accepted beginning April 1; ☎772/546-2067), the refuge is also rich in birdsong, with scrub jays among its tuneful inhabitants. To learn more about the refuge's flora and fauna, retrace your steps to Hobe Beach and head inland on County Road 708, turning south when you hit US-1; a short drive from here lies the refuge's small **nature center** (Mon–Fri 9am–3pm; free; ☎772/546-2067, ⓦwww.hobesoundnaturecenter.com), which has a few exhibits (including tanks with baby alligators) and two short nature trails, one of which leads down to the pretty shores of the Indian River Lagoon.

The parking lot of Hobe Sound National Wildlife Refuge is the farthest point north your vehicle can travel on Jupiter Island, but there's still more to see. The more than 900 acres of **St Lucie Inlet Preserve State Park** (daily 8am–sunset; fee for boats $2, kayaks and canoes $1; ☎772/219-1880) include mangrove-lined creeks and over two miles of beach, accessible only by water or by walking the nearly five miles of beach from the Hobe refuge. The park's remoteness makes it a special place to visit, and also a very difficult one to get to. There is a kayak launch site directly across the **Intracoastal Waterway** in Stuart (at the eastern end of Cove Rd), and a kayak rental outfitter five miles from there (South River Outfitters, 7647 SW Lost River Rd; Thurs–Fri 10am–4pm, Sat & Sun 9am–5pm; ☎772/223-1500, ⓦwww.southriveroutfitters.com), but you have to find your own (outfitter-approved) way of getting the kayak to the water. Kayaks are $26 for half a day, and $46 for 24 hours.

Jonathan Dickinson State Park

Two miles south of the Hobe Sound nature center on US-1, the **Jonathan Dickinson State Park** (daily 8am–sunset; cars $4, pedestrians and cyclists $1; ☎772/546-2771), named for a Quaker who washed ashore here in 1696, preserves a natural landscape quite different from what you'll see at the coast. Climb up the observation tower atop **Hobe Mountain**, one mile from the entrance, an ancient 86-foot-high sand dune, for sweeping views of the ocean, the Intracoastal, and the entire park, including the sand pine scrub and *palmetto* (a stumpy, tropical palm fan) flatlands.

The more adventurous can drive four miles to the end of the park road, **rent a canoe** ($16 for 2hr, $5 for each additional hour) from the concession store (daily 9am–5pm; ☎561/746-1466), and explore the mangrove-lined **Loxahatchee River**, Florida's first river to be federally designated as "wild and scenic." Don't be put off by the preponderance of alligators; continue paddling to the **Trapper Nelson Interpretive Center**, (Thurs–Mon 9am–5pm; by river only), where rangers give guided tours of the former homestead of a "wild man" pioneer from the 1930s who, in his 38 years here, built log cabins, tropical gardens and a wildlife zoo. Allow three to four hours for a round-trip. A less strenuous way to reach it is to take a two-hour guided **boat tour** (9am, 11am, 1pm, and 3pm; $18.78, children $11.50); call the concession to make reservations. Also near the concession, the **Kimbell Center** (daily 9am–5pm; free; ☎561/745-5551) highlights the cultural and natural resources of the park with interactive displays.

The park also offers a network of **hiking trails**, including the leisurely, one-hour Kitching Creek trail and the nine-mile East Loop trail, which starts and ends at the entrance and passes through two primitive campgrounds (obtain maps at the entrance office). Keep your eyes open for snakes, birds, alligators, deer, bobcats, and some of the park's 140 species of birds.

Campgrounds with water and electricity are also available, but space must be booked in advance (campsites $22; ☎1-800/326-3521 or Ⓦwww.reserveamerica.com). Rustic cabins are $85–95, and can be reserved by calling the concession.

Stuart and Hutchinson Island

HUTCHINSON ISLAND, another long barrier island, lies immediately north of Jupiter Island. To reach it (with either US-1 or Hwy-A1A), you'll first pass through the surprisingly congested and fairly depressing strip malls of **STUART**, which nevertheless has a small but attractive downtown district on the south bank of the St Lucie River. Here you'll find an attractive riverside walk, specialty stores, restaurants and century-old wooden buildings proudly preserved on and around Flagler Avenue, including the 1901 general store that now houses the **Stuart Heritage Museum**, 161 SW Flagler Ave (Mon–Sat 10am–3pm; free; ☎772/220-4600). Staffed by enthusiastic volunteers, it's built of rock-hard Dade County Pine and filled with memorabilia and artifacts from the town's early years, with displays on diverse topics such as the local Seminole Indians, the pineapple industry and the great Flagler himself. You can pick up a free walking guide from the **Chamber of Commerce** at 1650 S Kanner Hwy, a half-mile west of US-1 (Mon 9am–5pm, Tues–Thurs 8.30am–5pm; Fri 8.30am–1pm; ☎772/287-1088, Ⓦwww.goodnature.org).

For a bite to **eat** in downtown Stuart, try the cozy *Riverwalk Café*, 201 SW St Lucie Ave (closed Sun; ☎772/221-1511), located at the start of the Riverwalk, or the tasty but more expensive *Flagler Grill*, 47 SW Flagler Ave (dinner only; ☎772/221-9517), for local seafood, steak, and an extensive wine list.

Avoid the island's often-pricey accommodation rates by staying at the tropical-themed *Four Fish Inn & Marina*, near the banks of the Indian River at 2100 NE Indian River Dr (☎772/334-2152, Ⓦwww.aamarina.com; ❹) in **Jensen Beach**, a small town just northeast of downtown Stuart. All units are colorful and fully equipped studio apartments.

Hutchinson Island

Largely hidden behind thick vegetation, several beautiful beaches line twenty-mile-long **Hutchinson Island**, located to the east of Stuart along Hwy-A1A, which is also known as Ocean Boulevard once it traverses the Indian River.

Once you're on the island, a right turn onto MacArthur Boulevard brings you past the *Marriott* and a mile of condos to **Gilbert's Bar House of Refuge**, 301 SE MacArthur Blvd (Mon–Sat 10am–4pm, Sun 1–4pm; $5, children $2; ☎772/225-1875, ⓦwww.houseofrefugefl.org), a convincingly restored refuge for shipwrecked sailors that was one was one of ten erected along Florida's east coast in 1876, and is the only one still standing.

Another mile south of the House of Refuge, **Bathtub Reef Park** (24hr; free parking) lives up to its name; at low tide, a series of exposed reefs just offshore creates a protected, bath-like swimming area ideal for snorkelers and just about anybody else looking to loll about in calm, warm waters.

A second dose of education and beach-going awaits just to the north. Back on Hwy-A1A and next to **Stuart Beach**, a wide and low-key stretch of sand where locals generally outnumber tourists, you'll find the **Elliott Museum**, 825 NE Ocean Blvd (Mon–Sat 10am–4pm, Sun 1–4pm; $7, children $2; ☎772/225-1961, ⓦelliottmuseumfl.org). Initially established to commemorate inventor Sterling Elliott, the museum has been totally redesigned, and is expected to re-open in 2010 when it will feature interactive exhibits, a simulated underwater shipwreck and an expanded vintage car collection.

Across the street, the **Florida Oceanographic Coastal Center**, 890 NE Ocean Blvd (Mon–Sat 10am–5pm, Sun noon–4pm; $8, children $4; ☎772/225-0505, ⓦwww.floridaoceanographic.org) offers hands-on opportunities for learning about Florida's marine life, including a stingray touch tank, a large game fish lagoon, and looping mile-long nature trail. If you want to know what you're looking at, take one of the guided nature walks (Mon–Sat 11am, Sun 2pm). You can also participate in the daily feeding of game fish and stingrays (check website for times).

Driving four miles north you'll reach **Jensen Beach**, which straddles the Indian River and has a small, pleasant beach on its ocean side. To reach the northern half of the island (known as North Hutchinson Island), you'll need to pass through Fort Pierce, another eighteen tranquil miles on Hwy-A1A, though there's little point in stopping along the way.

Fort Pierce

The bulk of workaday **FORT PIERCE** (looped through by Hwy-A1A) lies two miles inland, across the Intracoastal Waterway, where tourism plays second fiddle to processing and transporting the produce of Florida's citrus farms. If you're driving north along Hwy-A1A, you'll hit the scrappy beach side of town first, where the motley assembly of motels, bars, and restaurants have seen better days. The Fort Pierce area, with several offshore shipwrecks – some dating back to the time of the Spanish galleons – and an abundance of Florida lobsters, is known for good **scuba diving**, especially in the summer months when the waters are warmer and calmer. Try Dive Odyssea, 621 N Second St (☎772/460-1771, ⓦwww.diveodyssea.com), for local diving trips in the $110 range (including equipment and a wetsuit).

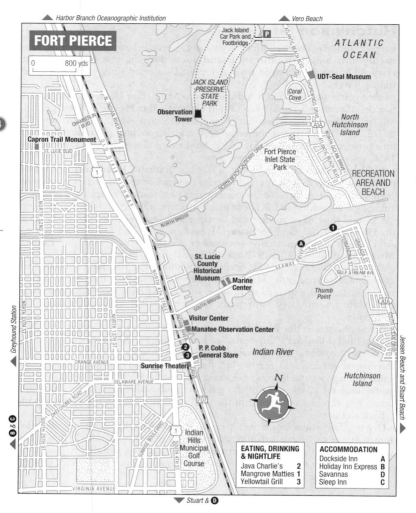

FORT PIERCE

Harbor Branch Oceanographic Institution

Vero Beach

0   800 yds

Jack Island
Car Park and
Footbridge

ATLANTIC
OCEAN

JACK ISLAND
PRESERVE
STATE
PARK

UDT-Seal Museum

Observation
Tower

Coral
Cove

North
Hutchinson
Island

Capron Trail Monument

ST. LUCIE BLVD

N. INDIAN RIVER DRIVE

CHAMBERLIN BLVD

DIXIE HIGHWAY

NORTH BEACH CAUSEWAY DRIVE

NORTH OCEAN DRIVE

Fort Pierce
Inlet State
Park

NORTH AMERICAN DRIVE

ATLANTIC BEACH BLVD

SHOREWINDS DRIVE

RECREATION
AREA AND
BEACH

NORTH 52ND ST

NORTH 4TH STREET

NORTH BRIDGE

St. Lucie
County
Historical
Museum

Marine
Center

SEAWAY DRIVE

FERNANDINA ST

ORANGE ST

GULF STREAM AVE

Thumb
Point

NORTH 13TH ST

SOUTH BRIDGE

Visitor Center
Manatee Observation Center

P. P. Cobb
General Store

Indian River

Hutchinson
Island

Greyhound Station

NORTH 35TH ST

Sunrise Theater

N

INDIAN RIVER DRIVE

SOUTH OCEAN DRIVE

Jensen Beach and Stuart Beach

ORANGE AVENUE

DELAWARE AVENUE

OKEECHOBEE ROAD

SOUTH 25TH ST

SUNRISE BOULEVARD

SOUTH 4TH ST

707

Indian
Hills
Municipal
Golf
Course

VIRGINIA AVENUE

Stuart & D

EATING, DRINKING & NIGHTLIFE		ACCOMMODATION	
Java Charlie's	2	Dockside Inn	A
Mangrove Matties	1	Holiday Inn Express	B
Yellowtail Grill	3	Savannas	D
		Sleep Inn	C

On route to downtown Fort Pierce, and beside the South Bridge to the mainland at 420 Seaway Drive, the **Marine Center** (Tues–Sat 10am–4pm; $3; free first Tues of month; ☎772/462- 3474) houses the **Smithsonian Marine Ecosystems Exhibit**, a thoughtful introduction to the marine life within Indian River Lagoon, through aquariums, touch tanks and displays. Nearby, the **St Lucie County Historical Museum** (Tues–Sat 10am–4pm; $4; ☎772/462-1795) features a full-sized Seminole Indian *chickee* (a palm-thatched hut), a solid account of the Seminole Wars, the 1838 fort from which Fort Pierce took its name, and a re-creation of P.P. Cobb's general store, the hub of the early twentieth-century town. Outside the museum at the **Gardner House**, a 1907 "cracker" cottage, note the tall ceilings and many windows that allowed the muggy Florida air to circulate in the days before air conditioning.

Downtown Fort Pierce and around

Much of Fort Pierce is starkly industrial, but there are a few worthwhile stops in the **downtown area**. From Hwy-A1A, take a first left onto Indian River Drive just beyond the South Bridge for Fort Pierce's **visitor information center**, **located** in the historic Seven Gables House at no. 482 (Tues–Fri 9am–5pm, Sat 10am–4pm, Sun 1–4pm; ☎772/468-9196). Next door, if you're visiting between mid-November and early April, you might catch sight of manatees in Moore's Creek from the viewing bridge of the **Manatee Observation & Education Center** (July–Sept Thurs–Sat 10am–5pm; Oct–June Tues–Sat 10am–5pm, Sun noon–4pm; $1; ☎772/466-1600 ext 3333, ⓦwww.manateecenter.com).

From here it's a short drive into the expertly restored **historic downtown district**; highlights include the refurbished **Sunrise Theatre**, 117 S Second St, which dates from 1923, was closed in 1983 and reopened following a $12-million-dollar renovation in late 2005. Identifiable by its retro neon sign, the theatre hosts a wide variety of national acts, performances, and concerts (☎772/461-4775, ⓦwww.sunrisetheatre.com). Stroll along nearby Avenue A towards the harbor to see some fine examples of original wooden houses, including the **P.P. Cobb General Store** at no. 100 (closed Sun; ☎772/465-7010; ⓦppcobbgeneralstore.com), now a deli serving sandwiches and a over 400 brands of bottled beer. You can park on most of the streets downtown for free (maximum 2hr).

The Harbor Branch Oceanographic Institution

Five miles north of St Lucie Boulevard, the **Harbor Branch Oceanographic Institution**, 5600 N US-1 (☎772/465-2400, ⓦwww.fau.edu/hboi), is a phenomenally well-equipped deep-sea research center belonging to Florida Atlantic University. You can learn more about the work conducted here at the **Ocean Discovery Center** (Mon–Fri 10am–5pm, Sat 10am–2pm; free; ☎772/465-2400 ext 293), which features interactive exhibits, tanks of tropical fish, and regular screenings of research-related videos.

Practicalities

There are inexpensive accommodation options in and around Fort Pierce (many of them just off I-95), as well as some good seafood restaurants and coffee shops. A range of options for both categories appears below.

For transport, the Greyhound **bus station** (☎772/461-3299) is six miles from downtown at 7150 Okeechobee Rd, near the junction of Hwy-70 and Florida's Turnpike. A taxi from here to the beach will cost around $20, and downtown $15 to $20; try Checker Cab (☎772/878-1234).

Accommodation

Dockside Inn 1160 Seaway Dr ☎772/468-3555 or 1-800/286-1745, ⓦwww.docksideinn.com. You can join fishing locals at this comfortable inn, which has five fishing piers, numerous boat slips, and waterfront BBQ grills for cooking up your catch, in addition to a pool and a variety of rooms and apartments. ❹
Holiday Inn Express 7151 Okeechobee Rd ☎772/464-5000, ⓦwww.hiturnpike.com. One of the smarter motels in the area, with spacious rooms and all the usual amenities, including laundry, a small pool, filling complimentary breakfast and free wi-fi. ❹
Savannas 1400 E Midway Rd ☎772/464-7855. For camping, head inland and seven miles south of downtown Fort Pierce along Rte-707 to this sizeable square of reclaimed marshland beside the Indian River where you can pitch a tent for $13. You can explore the surrounding unspoiled landscape on one of the site's nature trails or, rent a kayak ($4 per hr, $10 deposit).

Sleep Inn 2715 Cross Road Parkway ☎772/595-6080, ⓦwww.sleepinn.com. Worthy alternative to the *Holiday Inn*, this relatively new chain motel features neat, comfy rooms, a small pool, free wi-fi and breakfast, as well as a computer in the lobby for those without a laptop. ❹

Eating

Café La Ronde 221 Orange Ave ☎772/595-1928, ⓦwww.cafelaronde.com. This popular gourmet restaurant offers a creative blend of New Floridian and French styles of cooking, with exquisite classics such as escargot ($7.99) and French onion soup ($6.99), as well as excellent burgers ($6.49), sweet potato soup ($3.99) and seafood stuffed bread ($23.99). Closed Sun (lunch Mon–Fri, dinner Wed–Sat).

Java Charlie's 116 Avenue A ☎772/429-1550. Best choice for potent Kona coffee and soft drinks, as well as lighter food such as bagels and ice cream. (Closes 5pm, closed Sun.)

Mangrove Matties 1640 Seaway Drive ☎772/466-1044. Knocks out fabulous coconut shrimp and conch chowder, and boasts a fantastic waterside location – stick with seafood for the best dishes. Dinner entrées usually range $20–40, though the "early bird" menu (come at 5.30pm) is $8–10 cheaper.

Yellowtail Grill and Raw Bar 101 N 2nd St ☎772/466-5474. Handy for downtown, serving upmarket pizza, sandwiches and great shellfish, with main entrées averaging $15–25; expect to pay $100 for a full dinner for two. (Closed Sun).

North Hutchinson Island

Covering 340 acres at the southern tip of North Hutchinson Island, **Fort Pierce Inlet State Park** (daily 8am–sunset; cars $5, pedestrians and cyclists $1; ☎772/468-3985), entrance just off Hwy-A1A, overlooks the Fort Pierce Inlet and the community's beach. It's a scenic setting for a picnic, as well as a launch site for local surfers. Just over a mile north on Hwy-A1A, a concrete footbridge from the parking lot of the **Jack Island Preserve State Park** (daily 8am–sunset; free) leads to the Marsh Rabbit Run, a mile-long trail cutting through a thick mangrove swamp crawling with tiny crabs (and occasionally, marsh rabbits). It ends at an observation tower overlooking the Indian River. Keep alert to spot the great blue herons and ospreys nesting in the area.

Located between the two parks at 3300 N Hwy-A1A, the **Navy UDT-SEAL Museum** (Jan–April Tues–Sat 10am–4pm, Sun noon–4pm, Mon 10am–4pm; $6; ☎772/595-5845, ⓦwww.navysealmuseum.com), is dedicated to the US Navy's Frogman demolition teams. During World War II, the UDTs (Underwater Demolition Teams) trained on Hutchinson Island, which, like most of Florida's barrier islands, was off-limits to civilians at the time. The more elite SEALs (Sea Air Land) came into being later during the 1960s. The museum's outdoor exhibits include a Vietnam-era Huey helicopter, Apollo training crafts, and several beach obstacles used for training that have been recovered from the ocean.

Vero Beach and around

For the next fourteen miles north, lush vegetation and a wearisome preponderance of private communities block Hwy-A1A's ocean view until North Hutchinson Island imperceptibly becomes Orchid Island and you reach **VERO BEACH**, the area's sole community of substance and one with a pronounced upmarket image. It makes an enjoyable hideaway, however, with a

Kayaking the Indian River Lagoon

Boating opportunities abound in southern Florida, but the some of the best flat-water **kayaking** in the world can be found on the **Indian River Lagoon**, home to a wide array of wildlife including pelicans, ospreys, dolphins, manatees, stingrays and sea turtles. The lagoon is actually a salt-water estuary, stretching 156 miles from the Space Coast to Jupiter, with a width that varies between a half-mile and five miles.

A few outfitters in the area offer guided excursions to various parts of the lagoon – a great idea if you're new to the area. Call ahead to check schedules or make a reservation.

Adventure Kayaking Tours, 3435 Aviation Blvd, Vero Beach (T772/567-0522 or 1-800/554-1938, Wwww.paddleflorida.com). Daily three-hour tours from $45. Longer camping trips are offered from November through May.

Kayaks, Etc, 2626 US-1, Vero Beach (T772/794-9900 or 1-888/652-9257, Wwww.kayaksetc.com). Three-hour tours most days from $35. You can just a kayak for $35 for four hours ($45 for 24hr).

fine group of beaches around Ocean Drive, parallel to Hwy-A1A. There's little to tempt you from the sands but it's worth checking out the *A Driftwood Resort*, 3150 Ocean Drive (T772/231-0550, Wwww.thedriftwood.com; ⑤), a 1930s hotel now home to fully equipped studios and apartments, erected from a jumble of driftwood, bells, religious statuary, mosaics, flea-market finds, and pieces of demolished Palm Beach mansions.

Good **restaurants** in Vero Beach include *Waldo's*, the ocean- and poolside restaurant bar of the *Driftwood Resort* (T772/231-7091) serving items like beer-battered dolphin fingers, salads, and cheesesteak sandwiches (around $12 for lunch) and more substantial dinner selections. *Ti Amo Sempre*, 3001 Ocean Drive (T772/231-1550; closed Sun), cooks up some stylish Italian dishes, including a magnificent Bolognese sauce.

North of Vero Beach: Sebastian Inlet

Tiny beachside communities dot the rest of the island, but you'll find most activity – and campgrounds (around $23 per night) – near the **Sebastian Inlet State Park**, 9700 S Hwy-A1A (open 24hr; cars $3 for one person, $5 for two or more, pedestrians and cyclists $1; T321/984-4852), sixteen miles north of Vero Beach. Roaring ocean breakers lure surfers here, particularly over the Easter holiday when contests are held, and anglers cram the jetties for the finest saltwater fishing on Florida's east coast. You can also visit the **McLarty Treasure Museum** (Thurs–Mon 10am–4.30pm; $1; T772/589-2147), which tells the story of the 1715 Spanish Fleet that ran aground just offshore (and gave its name to this stretch of coast), through artifacts, displays and video presentations. More history is on show at the **Sebastian Fishing Museum** (daily 10am–4pm; free) which contains a replica of an original fish house, a home-made fishing boat, nets, fishing gear, and old photos of the Indian River Lagoon.

You can rent powerboats (from $139 per day) and kayaks ($38 a day) at the Inlet Marina, 9502 S Hwy-A1A; T321/724-5424, Wwww.sebastianinlet.com). For manatee and dolphin watching, contact River Queen Cruises (at *Captain Hiram's Restaurant & Marina*, 1606 Indian River Drive; T772/589-6161 or 1-888/755-6161, Wwww.riverqueencruises.net), which runs daily cruises on Indian River Lagoon for $20 to $28 (1.5–3hr).

South central Florida

Trapped in the triangle between the affluent beaches of Palm Beach and Tampa Bay, and the vacation haunts of Orlando, **SOUTH CENTRAL FLORIDA** seems a world away. The area is worth a pit stop primarily for a taster of rural Florida, which has seen little of the wealth or tourism from the coast, and where farming rules; orange groves, cattle herds and sugarcane plantations laced with small towns and depressing RV parks.

Traditional tourism, such as it is, is focused on the region's numerous **lakes**, though unless you enjoy **fishing** (which is, to be fair, top-notch), these tend to be fairly dull. More interestingly, several of the region's small towns were formerly big towns around the turn of the twentieth century and are keen to flaunt their pasts – and near them can be found several refreshingly under-hyped attractions, which were bringing tourists into the state back when Walt Disney was still in short trousers.

Lake Okeechobee and around

Completely encircled by a massive dike and invisible from nearby roads, it can be frustratingly difficult to get your first glimpse of **Lake Okeechobee**. Drive up to the top of the dike and you're in for a bit of a shock; this vast expanse of water can seem like a mini sea, with the far shore too distant to make out. After that first look, though, it's hard to get excited about Lake Okeechobee; utterly featureless, it's surrounded by pancake-flat farm land. The main draw is some of the best **freshwater fishing** in the US, with large-mouthed bass, speckled perch and blue gill the most prized targets. Bird-lovers will also enjoy the lake, as over 120 varieties have been spotted, including the endangered snail kite. Other inhabitants include bobcats, alligators, turtles, otters, snakes, and, occasionally, manatees, and you'll definitely see great flocks of white egrets.

For centuries, the lake was home exclusively to Native Americans (who named the lake Ok Ichobi or "Big Water" in their Seminole language). The area's first farming settlers began arriving in 1910, encouraged by the work carried out by wealthy Philadelphian Hamilton Disston, who, in the nineteenth century, started dredging canals and draining the surrounding land for agriculture. Next came the railroads, extending around three-quarters of the lake by the late 1920s and providing easy access to the rest of the state. Today the area is also served by three **highways**, which join to encircle the lake and allow access to the towns dotted around its shores.

The lake

Covering 730 square miles and ranging from ten to fourteen feet in depth, **Lake Okeechobee** is fed by the several rivers, creeks, and canals that make up the state-traversing Okeechobee Waterway. The lake has always played an important role not only in the lives of communities close to its shores, but also in the life cycle of the **Everglades**. After a devastating hurricane in 1928, a retaining wall, the 35-foot-high Herbert Hoover Dike, was built to ring the lake, and the lake has since served as both a flood-control safety valve during hurricane season and a freshwater storage reservoir. Traditionally, the lake has drained slowly south to nourish the Everglades after the summer rains, but ever-increasing demands on its fresh water for the agriculture industry and human consumption have put strains on the Everglades' delicate ecosytem (see p.170).

Although tourist brochures herald the lake as an unspoiled natural landscape, its condition has been a hot environmental issue in Florida for several years. Specifically, environmentalists and fishermen have long contested the pumping of billions of gallons of polluted farm runoff into the lake, via the massive pumps along its southern edge. Only time will tell if the long-promised clean-up will actually occur. **Boat tours** are the only way to get onto the water, but fishing fans will get the most out of the lake.

If you fancy a challenge, the 110-mile **Lake Okeechobee Scenic Trail** circles the entire lake (most of it along the dike), with several campgrounds along the way, though hiking the whole thing gets extremely monotonous – **cycling** at least some of it is more fun. For more information, call the Florida Trail Association (℡1-877/HIKE-FLA, Ⓦwww.floridatrail.org).

Okeechobee town

The lakeside community of **OKEECHOBEE**, with plenty of accommodation, food, and entertainment, is a prime base from which to explore the area, though its main highways roar with traffic and are lined with miles of grim strip malls.

The town was originally designed by the ubiquitous Henry Flagler (see Contexts, p.465), whose grandiose plan demanded wide streets and wood-framed buildings, some of which remain in the historic downtown area. The best examples are the **Historical Society Museum & Schoolhouse**, 1850 Hwy-98 N (by appointment only; free; ℡863/763-4344) and the 1926 **County Court House** at 304 NW 2nd St (private offices), a pretty example of Mediterranean Revival architecture, a style much favored by Flagler. Details on other places of interest, as well as local events, can be found at the **Chamber of Commerce** at the intersection of Rte 70 and US-441 at 55 S Parrott Ave (Mon–Fri 9am–noon, 1.30–4pm; ℡863/763-6464, Ⓦwww.okeechobee chamberofcommerce.com).

Most people come here for the superb **fishing**. Contact Garrard's Tackle Shop, 4259 US-441 S (℡863/763-3416, Ⓦwww.okeechobeebassguides.com) for all the gear and a guide to help ensure you catch something (full-day guide service $325). The Lake Okeechobee Guide Association (℡1-800/284-2446, Ⓦwww .fishokeechobee.com) provides a similar service and prices.

One of the offbeat highlights of the town is the **Okeechobee Livestock Market**, 1055 Hwy-98 N (℡863/763-3127, Ⓦwww.floridacattleauction.com), Florida's largest cattle market and a riveting spectacle of braying cows and modern-day cowboys. Auctions usually take place at noon on Mondays and 11am Tuesdays, July to February, but call to make sure. You can also check out the **Okeechobee County Cattlemen's Association Rodeo Arena**, Hwy-441 N (℡863/763-3959), where a lively rodeo is held on the second weekend in March and Labor Day weekend (first weekend in Sept).

Practicalities

Although the town is relatively easy to get to – Amtrak has a depot at 801 N Parrott Ave (℡1-800/872-7245) – there is no local public transportation system, and taxis generally stop running at 9pm. Of places to **stay**, the quiet and unassuming *Wanta Linga Motel*, 3225 US-441 SE (℡863/763-1020 or 1-800/754-0428; ❷), has reasonably priced rooms with microwaves and mini fridges. More centrally located are the *Flamingo Motel*, 4101 US-441 S (☎863/763-6100; ❸), with internet and wi-fi, and the familiar *Budget Inn*, 201 S Parrott Ave (☎863/763-3185; ❹); both have pools. The *Holiday Inn Express*, 3101 US-441 S (☎863/357-3529; ❻), offers a step up in comfort and includes a free breakfast bar. For **camping**, you'll find the largest KOA campground in North America just outside the town as you're heading toward the lake on US-441 S (☎863/763-0231 or 1-800/562-7748, ⓦwww.koa.com). In high season, tent sites are $50, RV sites $75, and a one-room cabin (sleeping up to four) around $82. A nine-hole golf course is on the premises, as well as miniature golf, tennis courts, pools, and a restaurant and lounge.

For **eating**, try the *Clock Family Restaurant*, 1111 S Parrott Ave (☎863/467-2224), best for American-style breakfasts ($7–8 entrées) and cheap lunch buffets ($7). You'll find plenty of cheap options on this stretch of Hwy-441. Alternatively, heading further south on Hwy-78, a few miles out of town, *Lightsey's*, 10435 Hwy-78 W (☎863/763-4276), serves a selection of fresh fish and home-style food at reasonable prices, along the banks of the Kissimmee River. You should also try locals' favorite *Speckled Perch*, 105 US Hwy-98, (☎863/763-998), a no-frills diner in a concrete building serving luscious, freshly cut steaks – the signage is virtually non-existent, so just park at the back and walk in.

Brighton Seminole Indian Reservation

Leaving Okeechobee via Hwy-441, follow Rte-78, which charts a 34-mile course along the west side of the lake, crossing over the Kissimmee River and continuing into the treeless expanse of Indian Prairie, part of the 35,000-acre **Brighton Seminole Indian Reservation**. To drive into the heart of the reservation, head up Rte-721 (21 miles from Okeechobee).

The Seminole Indians migrated here in the eighteenth century from Georgia and Alabama (see box, p.176); about 450 remain here, as successful cattle farmers. Although they live in houses rather than traditional Seminole thatched huts, the current residents maintain many aspects of their ancient culture (like consulting medicine men and speaking their native language), and while handicrafts may be offered from the roadside, you won't find any of the tacky souvenir shops common to reservations in more populous areas.

Heading north along Rte-721 you'll pass the entrance to the reserve two miles from the lake, and another mile on is the **Brighton Seminole Trading Post and Campground** (☎863/357-6644). This is really just a basic convenience store, though it does sell some simple arts and crafts, including wooden flutes. You can camp here for $40 (full hook-ups). Another three miles north the tribe runs the **Seminole Casino** (☎1-866/2-CASINO, ⓦwww .seminolecasinobrighton.com), which is open from 10am and features video gaming, poker, and "high stakes" bingo (call or check website for schedule). The casino acts as a sort of social club for the entire area (mostly non-Seminole) and you've a better chance of meeting Seminole locals in nearby *Alice's Restaurant*, 17410 Reservation Rd (Mon–Fri 6am–3pm, Sat 7am–3pm; ☎863/467-2226), a tiny diner on the main road nearby – try the Indian tacos.

Accommodation is limited to camping in these parts. If you'd rather stay near the lake, try *Twin Palms Resort* (☎863/946-0977), located twenty miles south of Okeechobee on Hwy-78. This RV park offers a few self-contained cottages for $75 and tent sites for $25 per night for two people.

Clewiston

From the reservation you can continue around the lake for around 27 miles to **CLEWISTON**, which is dominated by the US Sugar Corporation and the company's multimillion-dollar profits. On the way you'll pass miles of **sugar cane** – evidence of Florida being the top sugar producer in the country. First impressions aside – the town is a dreary looking place, lined with fast-food outlets and cheap motels – Clewiston is one of the more rewarding stops around the lake.

The **Chamber of Commerce**, 109 Central Ave, just off US-27 (☎1-877/693-4372 or 863/983-7979, ⓦwww.clewiston.org) occupies the same space as the **Clewiston Museum** (Mon–Fri 9am–4pm; $4; ☎863/983-2870, ⓦwww.clewistonmuseum.org), which provides an interesting rundown of the agricultural and cultural history of the area. The chamber runs the more engaging **Sugarland Tour** from here, a half-day bus tour (Mon–Fri mid-Oct to April only; 10am–2.30pm; $37.50, includes lunch at the *Clewiston Inn*) that takes in a sugar cane farm, a sugar refinery, a look at the lake, and an insect lab where mites beneficial to the sugar industry are bred. Reservations are essential.

To get out onto Lake Okeechobee itself (Clewiston is lauded for its large-mouth bass **fishing**), contact Big "O" Airboat Tours (☎863/983-2037, ⓦwww.bigofishing.com) at Roland & Mary Ann Martin's Marina, 920 E Del Monte Ave. You can also rent powerboats here from $79 per day.

Practicalities

Accommodation is relatively plentiful, though squarely aimed at fishing folk – if that's not your scene, you may as well stay away. The nicest place by far is the historic *Clewiston Inn*, 108 Royal Palm Ave (☎863/983-8151 or 1-800/749-4466, ⓦwww.clewistoninn.com; ⑥), notable for its Southern-style hospitality, simple yet comfortable rooms, and a 360-degree mural of local wildlife in its "Everglades" cocktail lounge. Another option is *Roland & Mary Ann Martin's Resort*, 920 E Del Monte Ave (☎863/983-3151 or 1-800/473-6766; ④), which has a variety of room options as well as RV hook-ups ($35), tent sites ($15), an outfitter shop, and the popular *Galley* restaurant (great burgers from $5.50), and *Tiki Bar* on the premises.

North of Lake Okeechobee

The section of US-27 that runs **north from Lake Okeechobee** is among Florida's least eventful roads: a four-lane snake through a landscape of gentle hills, lakes, citrus groves, and sleepy communities dominated by retirees. Busy

Pick-your-own Florida fruits

South central Florida is littered with tropical fruit farms, many offering seasonal pick-your-own rates. The **Erickson Farm**, 13646 Hwy-441, at Canal Point on the eastern shore of Lake Okeechobee (Mon–Fri 10am–6pm; ☎561/924-7714, ⓦwww.ericksonfarm.com) sells fresh mangoes, sweet white onions and avocados (seasonal), while at **Grapes of Kath Vineyards**, 9233 Muscadine Drive in Sebring (☎863/382-4706, ⓦwww.grapesofkath.com) you can pick your own grapes July to September and even make your own wine. The shop is open year-round but always call ahead. In Lake Placid, **Henscratch Farms** (closed June & July; ☎863/699-2060, ⓦwww.henscratchfarms.com) sells strawberries, blueberries, grapes and free-range eggs – you can pick your own fruit in season.

with farm trucks, the highway itself is far from peaceful, but provides an interesting course off the beaten track if you're making for either coast.

Sebring and Avon Park

From Okeechobee town it's 48 miles via US-27 or US-98 to **SEBRING**. Other than a few old wooden buildings, and a handful of stores and restaurants, the main feature of the town is pretty but unspectacular Lake Jackson, lined with motels on its south side (along US-27).

Sebring's tranquility is shattered each March when thousands of motor-racing fans arrive for the grueling **12 Hours of Sebring** race (℡1-800/626-RACE, Ⓦwww.sebringraceway.com), held at Sebring International Raceway about ten miles east of town; if you're passing through around this time, plan accordingly.

If you decide to **stay**, the historic *Kenilworth Lodge*, 1610 Lakeview Drive (℡863/385-0111 or 1-800/423-5939, Ⓦwww.kenlodge.com; ❹), is a mammoth Spanish-style hotel restored to some of its former grandeur, with lake views. For authentic American and local specialties, like home-made burgers and lemon pepper grouper, try the Art Deco *Sebring Diner*, 4040 US-27 S (℡863/385-3434).

The orange groves and cypress swamp trails inside **Highlands Hammock State Park**, four miles west of Sebring on Route 634 Hammock Rd (daily 8am–sunset; cars $3 for one person, $4 for two or more, pedestrians and cyclists $1), make a worthy diversion. Watch out for white-tailed deer and time your visit to coincide with the popular and informative ranger-guided **tram tour** (Tues–Fri 1pm, Sat & Sun 1pm & 2.30pm; $4; ℡863/386-6094). The park also offers campsites ($18) and a full-service restaurant.

Twelve miles north of Sebring on Rte-17 is **AVON PARK**. Rte-17 becomes Main Street in **downtown**, another sleepy area of older buildings and a few antique stores. The **Avon Park Museum**, 3 N Museum Ave, just off Main St (Tues–Fri 10am–3pm; free; ℡863/453-3525) contains a simple display of local history.

If you're **staying** the night, try the restored *Hotel Jacaranda*, 19 E Main St (℡863/453-2211, Ⓦwww.hoteljac.com; ❸). Built in 1926, it's now owned by South Florida Community College, while its restaurant specializes in Southern-style lunch **buffets** (Mon–Fri & Sun 11am–2pm; $8.49–10.49). Grab breakfast or lunch at the *Depot*, 21 W Main St (closes at 2pm and all day Sun; ℡863/453-5600).

Travel details

Trains (Amtrak and Tri-Rail)

Hollywood to: Boca Raton (45min Tri-Rail); Delray Beach (52min Amtrak; 51min Tri-Rail); Fort Lauderdale (16min Amtrak; 17min Tri-Rail); West Palm Beach (1hr 30min Amtrak; 1hr 17min Tri-Rail).

Buses (Greyhound)

Fort Lauderdale to: Daytona Beach (5 daily; 7hr–8hr 30min); Delray Beach (1 daily; 55min);

Fort Pierce (8 daily; 2hr–2hr 40min); Miami (11 daily; 45min–50min); Orlando (8 daily; 4hr 20min–5hr 10min); Vero Beach (2 daily; 3hr 10min–3hr 35min); West Palm Beach (8 daily; 50min–1hr 25min).

West Palm Beach to: Daytona Beach (5 daily; 5hr 25min–7hr 30min); Fort Pierce (8 daily; 1hr); Miami (6 daily; 1hr 50min–2hr 15min); Tampa (5 daily; 6hr 35min–8hr 10min); Vero Beach (2 daily; 1hr 55min–2hr 5min).

Sarasota and the Southwest

ALABAMA

GEORGIA

ATLANTIC OCEAN

Gulf of Mexico

N

0   100 miles

CHAPTER 5

Highlights

✳ **Cà d'Zan and the Ringling Museum** Experience the source of Sarasota's circus legacy: an imposing home, a circus museum, and a breathtaking art museum rolled into one. See p.237

✳ **Edison and Ford Winter Estates** Visit the historic off-season homes of two men who changed the world. See p.253

✳ **Lee County Manatee Park** This low-key park is the best place to see the endangered manatee from dry land, especially in winter. See p.256

✳ **Sanibel Island** The antithesis of the standard Florida beach town, offering a wildlife refuge and miles of gorgeous beaches. See p.258

✳ **Corkscrew Swamp Sanctuary** Best seen from its impressive boardwalk, which meanders several miles through wet prairie, pine flatlands, and a bald cypress forest. See p.264

✳ **Naples** This pampered and surprisingly friendly town is all about indulgent relaxation, with a fine stretch of beach, fashionable shops and jaw-dropping sunsets. See p.264

▲ Ringling Brothers and Barnum & Bailey circus poster, circa 1919

Sarasota and the Southwest

A string of barrier-island beaches runs the length of the Gulf in Florida's **SOUTHWEST**, and although the beaches tend to draw the biggest crowds, the mainland towns providing access to them have a lot in their favor as well. The first of any consequential size is **Sarasota**, the custodian of an arts legacy passed down at the turn of the twentieth century by John Ringling, the circus entrepreneur. Further south, Thomas Edison was one of a number of scientific pioneers who took a fancy to palm-studded **Fort Myers**, a small and attractive city that somehow feels like a metropolis next to its intimate island neighbors, **Sanibel** and **Captiva**, both of which offer a good mix of lovely beaches, quiet nature, and charming restaurants. **Naples** dominates further south, with a plethora of shopping, dining, and beach-going options for visitors on any budget. However, for those prepared to venture off the tourist trail, there is more to Florida's southwest coast than sun, sand, and sea. A healthy mixture of history, culture, and wildlife awaits discovery in this fine balance of mainland sights and beaches begging for exploration.

Sarasota and around

Rising on a gentle hillside beside the blue waters of Sarasota Bay, **SARASOTA** is both affluent and welcoming, cosmopolitan and laid-back. This is the city where golf was first introduced to Florida from Scotland and it remains a popular sport, with more than thirty courses within minutes of the downtown area. Sarasota is also one of the state's leading cultural centers, home to galleries, museums, artists, and respected performing arts companies. Opera and theatergoers in formal attire join hip students in coffee and wine bars, and the tone of the town is intelligently upbeat – far less stuffy than its wealth might suggest. Sarasota is also recognized for its strong circus ties; a few miles north up the Tamiami Trail (US-41), the **Ringling Museum Complex** – home of the late art-loving circus magnate – makes for an enlightening diversion. And the sugary barrier-island **beaches**, a couple of miles away across the bay, are a lounger's paradise.

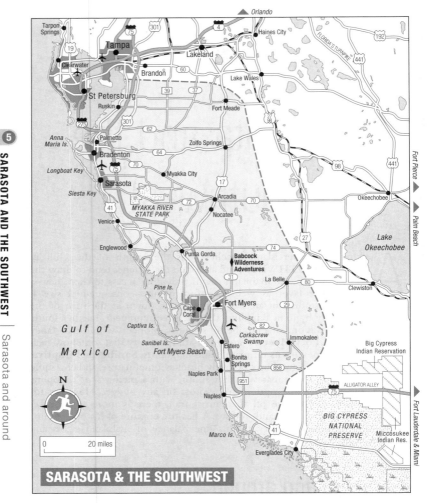

SARASOTA & THE SOUTHWEST

Arrival, transport, and information

Whether you're arriving from the north or south, **US-41** (usually referred to here as the Tamiami Trail) zips through Sarasota, passing the main causeway to the islands just west of downtown and skirting the Ringling estate to the north. Parallel to the Tamiami, the less enticing I-75 is the quickest way to travel longer distances into and out of town. Downtown Sarasota is an easy grid of streets mostly named for fruits, while Main Street boasts many of the area's restaurants and nightlife venues. You can **park** for up to two hours for free along most downtown streets.

Sarasota Bradenton International Airport (☎941/359-5200, ⓦwww .srq-airport.com) is a around four miles north of downtown, just off US-41; bus #2 runs into downtown Sarasota every hour (Mon–Sat), and taxis meet most flights. All the major car rental companies have branches at the airport.

Local **bus** routes run by Sarasota County Area Transit, or SCAT (Mon–Sat 4.30am–8.30pm; reduced service Sun; ☎941/861-1234), radiate out from the downtown Sarasota terminal on Lemon Avenue, between First and Second streets. **Useful routes** are #99 to the Ringling estate; #4 to Lido Key; #18 to Longboat Key; #11 to Siesta Key; and #17 to Venice Beach. Fares are 75¢ per journey; day passes are $3.

The **Amtrak bus** from Tampa pulls in a few blocks east, at the Hollywood 20 cinema, 1993 Main St (see p.244), while **Greyhound** passengers are dropped a few blocks north at 575 N Washington Blvd (☎941/955-5735). The Sarasota–Tampa Express provides a direct connection with Tampa's **airport**, running frequently throughout the day ($40 one way, $20 for children; ☎941/355-8400 or 1-800/326-2800, ⊛www.stexps.com) from the Publix Supermarket, at Tuttle Avenue and University Parkway; note this is four miles north of downtown, so you'll need to call a cab or walk to the nearest bus stop (#12), one long block east. For a **taxi**, try Diplomat Taxi (☎941/365-8294 or 1-877/859-8933) or Yellow Cab of Sarasota (☎941/955-3341).

If you're around for a week or more, a good way to explore the town and the islands is by **renting a bike** for $15 per day ($40 per week) from Sarasota Bicycle Center, 4084 Bee Ridge Rd (☎941/377-4505). For bike and kayak rentals on Siesta Key, see p.242. For **Segway tours** of the city, contact Florida Ever-Glides, 200 S Washington Blvd, Suite #11 (tours 9am and 2pm daily; $68; ☎941/363-9556, ⊛www.floridaever-glides.com), which runs two-and-a-half-hour tours taking in the city's historic district, downtown waterfront area, and artists' colony.

Information

For all the usual help and brochures, stop at the excellent **Visitor Information and History Visitor Center**, 701 N Tamiami Trail (Mon–Sat 10am–4pm; ☎941/957-1877 or 1-800/522-9799, ⊛www.sarasotafl.org). Look out for the free magazines *Sunny Day* (⊛www.sunnydayguide.com) and *See* (⊛www.see-sarasota.com), and the Friday edition of the *Sarasota Herald Tribune* (⊛www.heraldtribune.com), which has a pullout section, 'Ticket', with entertainment listings.

Accommodation

On the **mainland**, you're most likely to end up in the corridor of chain hotels and motels running the length of US-41 between the Ringling estate and south of downtown Sarasota. Prices are generally higher at the **beach resorts**, but there are a few budget options close to the sand.

Downtown

Holiday Inn Lakewood Ranch 6231 Lake Osprey Drive ☎941/782-4400 or 1-866/782-4401, ⊛www.hilr.com. Flashy contemporary design characterizes this standby, about 15min northeast of downtown near I-75, with LCD TVs, microwaves, a nice pool, fitness center, and nature trails. ⑥

Hotel Indigo 1223 Boulevard of the Arts ☎941/487-3800, ⊛www.hotelindigo.com. Fabulous boutique hotel, with bright, bold colors and tropical art splashed across the walls, wooden floors and spotlessly clean rooms, all with CD players and fridge. ⑥

Hotel Ranola 118 Indian Place #6 ☎941/951-011 or 866/951-0111, ⊛www.hotelranola.com. Small but hip hotel, with just nine rooms and excellent service; crisp, stylish rooms come with hung plasma TVs, hardwood floors, iPod docks, full kitchens and free wi-fi, and it's an easy walk to Main St. ⑤

Hyatt Sarasota 1000 Blvd of the Arts ☎941/953-1234, ⊛www.hyatt.com. Centrally located hotel near the Ringling Causeway, with funky, stylish rooms boasting iPod docks, LCD TVs and soothing views of Sarasota Bay (request a high floor). You also get a lagoon-style pool and fitness center – but internet is $9.99 a day. ⑦

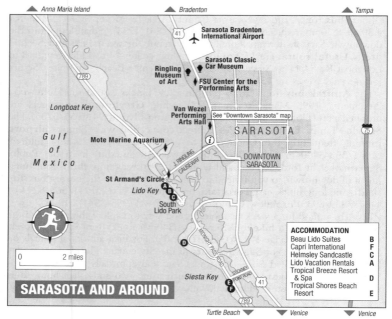

Springhill Suites 1020 University Parkway
☎ 941/358-3385 or 1-888/287-9400. You'll find
all the usual amenities, including wi-fi and mini
kitchens, in the tidy rooms at this *Marriott*
property by the airport, not far from the Ringling
Museum. ❼

The beaches

Beau Lido Suites 149 Tyler Drive, Lido Key
☎ 941/388-3227, ⓦ www.beaulido.com. Steps
from the beach and offering a variety of basic
rooms, houses, and an apartment; all have
kitchenettes with stove, refrigerator, and
microwave. ❹
Capri International 6782 Sara Sea Circle, Siesta
Key ☎ 941/349-2626, ⓦ www.capriinternational
.com. Plain, though pleasant, motel located near
Stickney Point Bridge, and right on the beach.
Rates drop by 50 percent off-season. ❼
Helmsley Sandcastle 1540 Ben Franklin Drive,
Lido Key ☎ 941/388-2181 or 1-800/225-2181,
ⓦ www.helmsleysandcastle.com. Decent-sized
rooms, accented in yellows and floral prints, plus

two pools, a restaurant, and an enticing
stretch of sand. ❼
Lido Vacation Rentals at the Lido Islander, 528
S Polk Drive, Lido Key ☎ 941/388-1004 or
1-800/890-7991, ⓦ www.lidovacationrentals.com.
Offers the best rates on Lido Key, a variety of room
types, and friendly service, in a central spot near
St Armands Circle. ❸
Tropical Breeze Resort & Spa 5150 Ocean Blvd,
Siesta Key ☎ 941/349-1125 or 1-800/300-2492,
ⓦ www.tropicalbreezeinn.com. Rooms are average
size, a bit colorless and worn, but there are three
pools, a day spa, and a fitness center, and it's
walking distance to the beach and Siesta Key
Village. ❺
Tropical Shores Beach Resort 6717 Sara
Sea Circle, Siesta Key ☎ 941/349-3330,
ⓦ www.tropicalshores.com. Great family resort
with a variety of rooms, all with kitchens and free
wi-fi. The hotel faces a lovely stretch of beach, and
there's plenty of games and activities to keep the
kids amused. ❻

Downtown Sarasota

Restored architectural oddities, excellent theater, and some of the best
bookstores in Florida make **downtown Sarasota** a worthy break from the
beaches. Start at the **History Visitor Center** on US-41 (see p.235), where a

small but detailed exhibition (free) charts the development of Sarasota from pre-colonial days to the post-World War II years.

Closer to the water lies the enormous purple form of **Van Wezel Performing Arts Hall**, 777 N Tamiami Trail (℡941/953-3368 or 1-800/826-9303, ⓦwww.vanwezel.org), designed by the Frank Lloyd Wright Foundation in 1968 to resemble a seashell. The program includes musicals, dance, comedy, and plays (see "Entertainment," p.243). For those who wish to explore behind the scenes (and see the collection of the local Fine Arts Society, displayed inside), backstage **tours** are conducted on the first Tuesday of the month (Oct–May 10am; $5; ℡941/953-3368).

Heading into the heart of downtown, don't miss the **Selby Public Library**, 1331 First St (Mon–Thurs 10am–8pm, Fri & Sat 9am–5pm, Sun 1–5pm; ℡941/861-1100), with an exterior that could have been lifted out of a grandiose Hollywood epic. Inside, it's a clean, functioning library, complete with a fish tank and loads of computers with free **internet** access (it also has free wi-fi). Opposite the library on the corner of First Street and Pineapple Avenue sits the **Sarasota Opera House**, 61 N Pineapple Ave (℡941/366-8450 or 1-888/OPERA-12, ⓦwww.sarasotaopera.org). Opened in 1926, this Mediterranean Revival building hosted the Ziegfeld Follies and a young Elvis Presley. The best time to catch a performance (or four) is during the Winter Opera Festival every February and March, when Opera Lovers' Weekends feature four operas in three days, starting at around $95; the box office is open Mon–Sat 10am–4pm.

South of Main Street, a few blocks past the pretty Methodist Church on Pineapple Avenue, lies **Burns Court**, a hidden lane of 1920s bungalows with Moorish details. Almost all the Spanish/Mediterranean buildings in town were built just before the Depression, when the style was most in vogue. At the end of this lane stands the startlingly pink **Burns Court Cinema**, a great alternative film house run by the Sarasota Film Society (see also listing on p.244). Walk a few blocks east to reach the **Towles Court Arts District**, a cluster of wooden bungalows and cottages taking up a two-block stretch of Morrill Street and Adams Lane (between Osprey Ave and US-301/Washington Boulevard; ℡941/866-0267, ⓦwww.towlescourt.com). You can browse the galleries here, which are usually open to the public (Tues–Sat noon–4pm, also 6–10pm on third Friday of each month). The district forms part of the **Laurel Park Historic Neighborhood**, packed with graceful wooden homes; you'll find a parking lot on nearby Adams Lane.

The Ringling Museum of Art and around

Two miles north of downtown Sarasota is the **Ringling Museum of Art**, containing the house and art collections of John Ringling, a multimillionaire who

Sarasota bookstores

Anyone bemoaning the lack of decent **bookstores** in Florida should take heart at the selection in Sarasota, though the long-standing Main Bookshop closed in 2008. Good bets are Book Bazaar, which stocks used and out-of-print titles, and rare book dealer A. Parker's – both located at 1488 Main St (Mon–Sat 10am–5pm; ℡941/366-2898 or 941/366-1373, ⓦwww.aparkers.com). There are also Sarasota News & Books at 1341 Main St (℡941/365-6332, ⓦwww.sarasotanewsandbooks.com), which boasts a cute café, and Circle Books at 478 John Ringling Blvd, near St Armand's Circle (℡941/388-2850, ⓦwww.circlebooks.net).

SARASOTA AND THE SOUTHWEST | Sarasota and around

DOWNTOWN SARASOTA

▲ **A** *Airport & Ringling Museum of Art*

10TH STREET

Van Wezel
Performing
Arts Hall

History Visitor Center ⓘ **C**
BLVD OF THE ARTS **D**

6TH STREET
Greyhound ★

5TH ST

4TH STREET

3RD STREET
Local
Bus
Station

Chamber of
Commerce

Selby Public Library

FST Gompertz Theater
FST Goldstein Cabaret
and Box Office **1**
1ST STREET
Golden Apple
Dinner Theater **2**
Sarasota
Opera House **4**
Sarasota
News and Books

Amtrak
Bus Stop ★
Hollywood 20 **3**

MAIN STREET

Book
Bazaar **E**

RINGLING BLVD

5
ADAMS LANE

EATING, DRINKING
& NIGHTLIFE
Bijou Café   1
Canvas Café   5
First Watch   2
Main Bar
  Sandwich Shop   3
Phillippi Creek
  Village Oyster Bar 7
Solorzano's Italian
  Restaurant   8
Two Señoritas   4
Yoder's   6

Bayfront

MORRILL STREET

Towles Court
Art District

LAUREL STREET

Burns
Court
Cinema

Park

*Sarasota
Bay*

Marie Selby
Botanical
Gardens

MOUND STREET

ACCOMMODATION
Holiday Inn
  Lakewood Ranch   **B**
Hotel Indigo   **C**
Hotel Ranola   **E**
Hyatt Sarasota   **D**
Springhill Suites **A**

BAHIA VISTA STREET

▼ **7**   *Siesta Key &* **8** ▼

not only poured money into the fledgling community beginning in 1911 (when he moved here), but also gave it a taste for fine arts it has never lost. Ringling, who made his money as part owner of the fantastically successful Ringling Brothers Circus (which began touring the US during the 1880s and acquired the Barnum & Bailey show in 1907), plowed the business's profits into railways, oil, and land. By the 1920s, he had acquired a fortune estimated at $200 million. Charmed by Sarasota and recognizing its investment potential, Ringling built the first causeway to the barrier islands and made the town his circus's winter base, saving a fortune in northern heating bills and generating tremendous publicity for the town in the process. His greatest gift to Sarasota, however, was a Venetian Gothic mansion – a combination of European elegance and American-millionaire extravagance – and an incredible collection of European Baroque paintings, displayed in a museum built for the purpose beside the house. Grief-stricken following the death of his wife Mable in 1929, Ringling, already financially overextended, was unprepared for the stock market crash of the same year, and lost much of his wealth. He died in 1936, reportedly with just $300 to his name.

The Ringling House: Cà d'Zan

Begin your exploration of the Ringling estate by walking through the gardens to the former Ringling residence, the 32-room **Cà d'Zan** ("House of John," in Venetian dialect). A lavish but not tasteless piece of work situated serenely beside Sarasota Bay, it was the dilapidated setting for the 1998 film adaptation of *Great Expectations*. Completed in 1926, at a cost of approximately $1.5 million, the house was planned around an airy, two-story living room marked

Ringling Museum practicalities

The Ringling Museum of Art, beside US-41 at 5401 Bay Shore Rd (daily 10am–5.30pm; $19, children $6; ☏941/359-5700, recorded info at ☏941/351-1660, ⓦwww.ringling.org), ranges over 66 acres. Its buildings are linked by clearly signposted and easily walked pathways; trams connect the main areas as well. To get there from downtown Sarasota via public transport, take bus #99.

on one side by a fireplace of carved Italian marble and on the other by a $50,000 Aeolian self-playing pipe organ. The other rooms are similarly decorated with expensive items, but unlike their mansion-building contemporaries elsewhere in Florida, the Ringlings knew the value of restraint. Their spending power never exceeded their sense of style, and the house remains a triumph of taste and proportion. You can tour the first floor, but to see the bedrooms on the second floor (husband and wife had separate suites), you must join a regular volunteer-led tour ($5); to see it all, take the 45-minute "Private Places" tour ($20), which explores the upper floors, guest rooms, game room and, weather permitting, visits the top of the sixty-foot Belvedere Tower.

The Art Museum

On trips to Europe to scout for new circus talent, Ringling became obsessed with **Baroque art** – then wildly unfashionable – and over seven years, led largely by his own sensibilities, he acquired an impressive collection of Old Masters now totaling around 750 and regarded as one of the finest of its kind in the US. To display the paintings, Ringling selected a patch of Cà d'Zan's grounds and erected a spacious **museum** around a mock fifteenth-century Italian palazzo, decorated by his stockpile of high-quality replica Greek and Roman statuary. As with Cà d'Zan, the very concept initially seems absurdly pretentious but, like the house, the idea works, and the architecture matches the art with great aplomb. Take the free **guided tour** departing regularly from the entrance, before wandering around at your leisure. Five enormous paintings by **Rubens**, commissioned in 1625 by a Hapsburg archduchess, and the painter's subsequent *Portrait of Archduke Ferdinand*, are the undisputed highlights of the collection, but they shouldn't detract from the excellent canvases in succeeding rooms: a wealth of talent from Europe's leading schools of the mid-sixteenth to mid-eighteenth centuries. Watch out, in particular, for the finely composed and detailed *The Rest on the Flight to Egypt* by Paolo Veronese, and the entertaining *Building of a Palace* from Piero de Cosimo.

Museum of the Circus and Tibbals Learning Center

The Ringling fortune had its origins in the big top, and the **Museum of the Circus** is worth a visit for a glimpse into the family business. The museum also includes the next door **Tibbals Learning Center**, featuring vintage circus posters and comprehensive displays on the history of the American circus. Its star attraction, however, is the largest **miniature circus** in the world – the astonishingly meticulous Howard Bros Circus, a 3800-square-foot, three-quarte-inch-to-one-foot replica of the Ringling Bros and Barnum & Bailey circus, built by Howard Tibbals, a master model builder and circus fan. It was a forty-year labor of love for Tibbals; he grew up fascinated by the traveling circus and its many detailed components, all of which he painstakingly re-created in his exhibit: 41,000 pieces, including eight tents, 55 railroad cars, 152 wagons, 7000 folding chairs, hundreds of animals, and thousands of performers and circus personnel.

The rest of the Circus Museum contains tiger cages and wagons once used to transport animals and equipment; a spotlight on Cecil B. DeMille's film, *The Greatest Show on Earth* (some of which was filmed in Sarasota); memorabilia of famous dwarfs and performers; and a tribute to Gunther Gebel-Williams, the legendary animal trainer who never missed a day of work in over 12,000 performances, before passing away in 2001. Nearby, a banyan tree shades the circular *Banyan Café* (☎941/359-3183), where you can grab lunch for $10–12.

The Visitors Pavilion and Asolo Theater

In the 1950s, the museum transported and reassembled an eighteenth-century, Italian-court playhouse from the castle of Asolo to the grounds of the estate. The fully restored **Asolo Theater** is the centerpiece of the **Visitors Pavilion**, which also includes the elegant *Treviso* restaurant and a gift shop. The buzz, though, mostly surrounds the historic Asolo, which is open for performances, lectures, films, and concerts (see Ringling website for program).

FSU Center for the Performing Arts

Just outside the main entrance to the museum you'll see the **Florida State University Center for the Performing Arts**, home to the Asolo Repertory Theatre company (ⓦwww.asolo.org) – not to be confused with the historic theater of the same name inside the Ringling complex – and a strong program of theatrical events throughout the year. In addition to the modern Cook Theatre, shows are held in the elegant, gilded interior of the Mertz Theatre, originally built in 1903 as an opera house and brought over from Dunfermline, Scotland. If you'd like a behind-the-scenes look, join one of the free backstage tours (Nov–May Wed–Sat 10am and 11am; for contact and performance details, see p.244).

Sarasota Classic Car Museum

Vintage car enthusiasts and devotees of old music boxes will love the **Sarasota Classic Car Museum**, across US-41 from the entrance to the Ringling Museum Complex (daily 9am–6pm; $8.50; ☎941/355-6228, ⓦwww.sarasota carmuseum.org). Nearly 200 aged vehicles – including John Lennon's Mercedes Roadster and Stephen King's "Christine" – are gathered together with hurdy-gurdies, cylinder discs, an enormous Belgian pipe organ, and nickelodeons. You'll also find an antique game room filled with arcade games from the 1930s and 40s. Even if you don't pay to enter the museum, check out the gift shop for some unusual souvenirs, antiques, and collectibles including posters, guitars, and gas station artifacts.

The Sarasota beaches

Increasingly the stomping ground of European package tourists spilling south from the St Petersburg beaches, the powdery white sands of the **Sarasota beaches** – fringing several barrier islands which continue the chain beginning off Bradenton – haven't exactly been spared the attentions of property developers. Regardless, they are worth a day of anybody's time, either to lie back and soak up the rays, or to seek out the few remaining isolated stretches. The sunsets alone make this area worth a visit, but one of the islands, **Siesta Key**, is also renowned for its powdery-fine, quartz-like sand. Siesta Key and **Lido Key** are both accessible by car or bus from the mainland, but there's no direct link between the two. If you're traveling by car, be forewarned: the beach roads are very busy in high season, and the tailbacks heading away from the beach near the day's end might ruin any relaxation you gained on the sands.

Sarasota's circuses

The circus spirit is alive and well in Sarasota, and it's well worth catching a performance if you're here during the season of one of the following Sarasota-based circus companies (call or check websites for schedule information). The **Royal Hanneford Circus** (☎941/922-4358, ⓦwww.hannefordcircus.com), which originated in England in 1608 and is now the second largest touring circus in the US, performs at the Robarts Arena, 3000 Ringling Blvd, every April or May. Kids will delight in the family-oriented one-ring **Walker Bros Circus** (☎941/922-8387, ⓦwww.walkerbrotherscircus.com), which likewise travels much of the year but returns for annual performances at the Sarasota Fairgrounds, also at 3000 Ringling Blvd, in late October. The professionals in **Circus Sarasota** amaze every February (☎941/355-9805, ⓦwww.circussarasota.org) at their Big Top adjacent to the Ed Smith stadium at the corner of 12th Street and Tuttle Avenue, five miles west of I-75 (Exit 210). And at perhaps the most unique show in town, you can catch the community's high school performers in the professional-caliber circus offered by **PAL Sailor Circus** (☎941/361-6350, ⓦwww.sailorcircus.org), which runs holiday (Dec) and spring (March/April) performances in their arena at 2075 Bahia Vista St, south of downtown.

Lido Key

The Ringling Causeway crosses yacht-filled Sarasota Bay from the foot of Main Street to **Lido Key** and flows into **St Armands Circle**, (take bus #4 or #18) a traffic circle packed with mostly upmarket shops and restaurants (you can park here for 3hr for free) two miles from downtown. At its center is the **Circus Ring of Fame**, a series of plaques commemorating famous circus performers that encircles a small park dotted with some of Ringling's replica classical statuary. Once you've browsed the park and shops, continue west on Ringling Boulevard to **Lido Key Beach**, which is relatively condo-free at its northern end (though the main parking lot is further south). Heading south for around two miles, Benjamin Franklin Drive passes more accessible beaches until you come to the first of two entrances to the attractive **South Lido Nature Park** (daily 8am–sunset; free); this one leads to a kayak trail through the mangroves (see p.242 for rentals) and a refreshing 45-minute hiking trail along the coast. The second entrance lies at the end of Benjamin Franklin Drive, where a belt of dazzlingly bright sand faces the ocean beyond a large grassy park, although with no lifeguards and exceptionally strong currents, swimming is not advised; you can swim or just loll on the smaller patch of sand facing the calmer waters of Sarasota Bay near the parking lot, shaded by Australian pines.

Away from the beaches, the only place of consequence on Lido Key is the **Mote Aquarium**, 1600 Ken Thompson Parkway (daily 10am–5pm; $17, children $12; ☎941/388-2451, ⓦwww.mote.org), a mile north of St Armands Circle. The aquarium is the public off-shoot of a marine laboratory that studies the ecological problems threatening Florida's sea life, like the red tide, a mysterious algae that blooms every few years, devastating sea life. You'll see plenty of live sea creatures, including sea horses, and also manatees, sea turtles, dolphins, and whales at the Marine Mammal Center, which houses its rehabilitation program. Other highlights are ghostly jellyfish, preserved giant squid, and the massive outdoor shark tank.

Siesta Key

Far more refreshing and laid-back than Lido Key, **Siesta Key** (reached via Siesta Drive off US-41, about five miles south of downtown Sarasota; take bus #11) attracts a younger crowd. Clusters of shops, businesses, restaurants, and bars form **Siesta Key Village**, along Ocean Boulevard, but beach-lovers should head straight to **Siesta Key Beach**, beside Beach Road, where the sand has an uncommon sugary texture due to its origins as quartz (not the more usual pulverized coral). It's a wide, white strand that can – and often does – accommodate thousands of sun-worshippers. To escape the crowds, continue south on Beach Road, (which becomes Midnight Pass Road when it meets Stickney Point Road from the mainland), for six miles to **Turtle Beach**, a small, secluded stretch of sand not as soft or floury as what you'll find further north, but much quieter. **Parking** is free throughout the island, though spaces go fast in peak season.

You'll find a small and friendly **Chamber of Commerce** at 5118 Ocean Blvd (Mon–Fri 9am–5pm, also Sat 9am–5pm Feb–Easter; ☏941/349-3800, ⓦwww.siestakeychamber.com). In addition to **bikes** ($5 per hr, $15 per day), Siesta Sports Rentals, 6551 Midnight Pass Rd (☏941/346-1797, ⓦwww.siestasportsrentals.com), also rents out kayaks ($13 per hr, $45 per day), motor scooters ($65 per day), and beach equipment.

Eating

Sarasota's **restaurant** and **cafe culture** is particularly vibrant, and while exquisite restaurants (with prices to match) are everywhere, you'll still find plenty of budget options. The **Downtown Farmers' Market** (Sat 7am–noon; ☏941/951-2656), at the corner of Main Street and Lemon Avenue, is also worth checking out for its freshly baked pastries and coffee.

Downtown

Bijou Café 1287 First St ☏941/366-8111, ⓦwww.bijoucafe.net. Popular fine-dining restaurant, with French-influenced seafood, fowl, and meat served in surprisingly basic surroundings. Entrées average $25.

Canvas Café 239 S Links Ave ☏941/366-2233, ⓦwww.canvascafesrq.com. Great choice for lunch or dinner, especially if browsing the galleries of Towles Court, with a menu of eclectic American cuisine utilizing local ingredients. Lunch entrées $12–13, which isn't bad considering the quality. Closed Sun.

First Watch 1395 Main St ☏941/954-1395. There isn't much character to the place, but the excellent American-style breakfast and brunch plus inexpensive lunch offerings, like turkey burgers and Reuben sandwiches ($6–9), assure there's always a line. Closes 2.30pm.

Main Bar Sandwich Shop 1944 Main St ☏941/955-8733. Admire the circus memorabilia on the walls and dig into the delicious, reasonably priced sandwiches that have been served here since 1958. Closes at 4pm; also closed Sun.

Phillippi Creek Village Oyster Bar 5353 S Tamiami Trail ☏941/925-4444, ⓦwww.creekseafood.com. Excellent seafood, a tropical waterfront setting, and reasonable prices make this casual spot a good bet; get there early as it tends to get very crowded.

Solorzano's Italian Restaurant 2117 Siesta Drive ☏941/906-9444. A little slice of Italy in the tropics, with some of the best pizza and Italian food in the state, friendly owners, and live piano adding to the old-school ambience.

Two Señoritas 1355 Main St ☏941/366-1618, ⓦwww.twosenoritas.com. Cute and cozy spot serving inexpensive TexMex standards like quesadillas ($9–10) and fajitas ($13.50–14.50), great margaritas and sangria.

Yoder's 3434 Bahia Vista St ☏941/955-7771, ⓦwww.yodersrestaurant.com. Sarasota has thriving Mennonite and Amish communities, and this local favorite has won awards for the homemade goodness of its old-fashioned Amish cuisine, especially its massive peanut butter cream pies ($3.95 a slice). Closed Sun.

St Armands Circle and Lido Key

Blue Dolphin Café 470 John Ringling Blvd ☏941/388-3566, ⓦwww.bluedolphincafe.com. Come to this convivial, informal blue diner just off St Armands Circle for hearty breakfasts ($6–9) guaranteed to fill you up. Closes at 3pm.

Café L'Europe 431 St Armands Circle ☏941/388-4415, ⓦwww.cafeleurope.net. Innovative and award-winning, if pricey (dinner entrées start at $26), cuisine with French, Italian, and Spanish influences, popular with tourists and locals alike. Serves lunch and dinner.

Cha-Cha Coconuts 417 St Armands Circle ☎ 941/388-3300. A young crowd spills out of this very busy, very loud bar (next to *Café L'Europe*), which showcases nightly live entertainment. The inexpensive menu claims to be "Caribbean cuisine," but it's mostly just fish sandwiches and burgers ($8–10).

Hemingway's Retreat 325 Ringling Blvd, 2/F (just off St Armands Circle) ☎ 941/388-3948, Ⓦ www.hemingwaysretreat.com. Tasty steak and seafood standards served in upmarket, but comfy, surroundings; try their infamous rumrunner cocktails at happy hour (daily 2–7pm). Entrées $16–34.

Old Salty Dog 1601 Ken Thompson Parkway (on City Island) ☎ 941/388-4311, Ⓦ www.theoldsalty dog.com. Near the bridge to Longboat Key (opposite Mote Aquarium), you'll find this ultra-casual beach shack serving delicious grouper sandwiches and more – its laid-back vibe and location are the main reasons for a visit, with grand views across the bay.

Siesta Key

The Broken Egg 140 Avenida Messina, Siesta Key Village ☎ 941/346-2750, Ⓦ www .thebrokenegg.com. Popular with locals for the all-American breakfasts and lunches. Try the gut-busting broken egg breakfast for $6.59 or the home-made banana nut bread French toast for about $5.

Javier's 6621 Midnight Pass Rd ☎ 941/349-1792, Ⓦ www.javiersrestaurant.com. Come here for a taste of Peru and an extensive menu of seafood, steaks, ribs, pasta, and decadent desserts. Entrées are $16–25. Dinner only; closed Sun and Mon.

Mattison's Siesta Grille 1256 Old Stickney Point Rd ☎ 941/349-2800, Ⓦ www.mattisons.com. Tuck into Mediterranean-inspired food in elegant but casual surroundings at this latest restaurant from renowned Gulf Coast chef Paul Mattison (there's also one in downtown Sarasota). Entrées start at $18; pizzas at $16.

Turtles 8875 Midnight Pass Rd, Turtle Beach ☎ 941/346-2207, Ⓦ www.turtlesrestaurant.com. Outstanding, nicely priced seafood dinners ($13–20) served at tables overlooking Little Sarasota Bay, at the southern tip of Siesta Key.

Drinking and nightlife

On the weekends, **nightlife** along Sarasota's Main Street attracts students looking to chill and a more rough-and-ready, good-old-boys crowd. Siesta Key Village on Siesta Key also offers a hot bar-hopping scene.

Beach Club 5151 Ocean Blvd, Siesta Key Village ☎ 941/349-6311, Ⓦ www.beachclubsiestakey.com. You'll find special events and rock 'n' roll here every night, including local and small national acts. No food, but you can bring some TexMex specials over from the nearby *Hub*, which also has live music.

Daiquiri Deck 5250 Ocean Blvd, Siesta Key Village ☎ 941/349-8697, Ⓦ www.daiquirideckgrill.com. Cool down with frozen daiquiris at this hugely popular after-beach venue. They also do great snacks and burgers (from $8.50).

Fred's Restaurant & Bar 1917 S Osprey Ave, Downtown ☎ 941/364-5811. This restaurant has a dark, popular bar and cushioned sidewalk seating, with a good buzz on weekends and a large assortment of wine, cocktails, and beers. Happy hour starts at 3pm daily.

The Gator Club 1490 Main St, Downtown ☎ 941/366-5969, Ⓦ www.thegatorclub.com.

The Gator continually wins the prize for loudest bar. Set in a huge warehouse, it features dance-style music performed live every night at 9.30pm, and a scotch bar and pool tables upstairs.

Old Salty Dog 5023 Ocean Blvd, Siesta Key Village ☎ 941/349-0158, Ⓦ www.theoldsaltydog.com. One of the more popular bars on Siesta Key; English-themed, fish and chips optional. Sister bar to the *Salty Dog* on City Island restaurant (see above).

Sarasota Brewing Company 6607 Gateway Ave ☎ 941/925-2337. Easy-going sports bar and micro brewery (with six homebrews offered).

Speakeasy 5254 Ocean Blvd, Siesta Key Village ☎ 941/346-1379, Ⓦ www.speakeasysiestakey .com. Cozy, laid-back spot showcases a variety of live bands Fri–Sun; otherwise enjoy the fireplace, pool table, and the island's largest selection of beers.

Entertainment

The Sarasota area lives up to its billing as "Florida's Cultural Coast". For full details of arts events, pop into the Visitor Information Center (see p.235) or check out the Sarasota County Arts Council website (Ⓦ www.sarasota–arts.org).

Drama devotees are well catered to as some of the state's top small theatrical groups are based in Sarasota.

Theaters and cinemas

The Burns Court Cinema 506 Burns Lane ☎ 941/955-3456 ⓦ www.filmsociety.org. The cinema that hosts Sarasota's Cine-World film festival in November, showing over fifty of the best international films of the year on its three screens. To purchase tickets ($7.75) and hear a schedule for regular shows, call the box office.

Florida Studio Theatre 1241 N Palm Ave ☎ 941/366-9000, ⓦ www.floridastudiotheatre.org. Hosts Sarasota's most contemporary theatrical events in three downtown venues: the Keating Theater, the Gompertz Theater and the Goldstein Cabaret (tickets from $20).

FSU Center for the Performing Arts 5555 N Tamiami Trail ☎ 941/351-8000 or 1-800/361-8388, ⓦ www.asolo.org. The center's major repertory, the Asolo Theatre Company, stages plays both classic (Shaw, Miller, Coward) and contemporary (tickets $40–60, balcony seats from $22).

Golden Apple Dinner Theatre 25 N Pineapple Ave ☎ 941/366-5454, ⓦ www.thegoldenapple .com. For a wide range of theater, including Broadway favorites, with cocktails and candlelit dining. Tickets $40–45.

Hollywood 20 1993 Main St ☎ 941/365-2000 or 941/954-5768 for recorded info, ⓦ www .regmovies.com. All mainstream films are shown at this distinctive (and popular) Art Deco theater. Inside, a neon-lilac glow bathes the popcorn-devouring crowds.

The Van Wezel Performing Arts Hall 777 N Tamiami Trail ☎ 941/953-3368 or 1-800/826-9303, ⓦ www.vanwezel.org. Affectionately called "the Purple Cow" or "the Purple Palace" – depending on who you ask – this hall has a varied program of musicals and dance performances.

Gay nightlife

Despite its cultural advancements, Sarasota doesn't have much to offer in the way of **gay nightlife**. The only gay bar in town is *Witness Café*, 5100 N Tamiami Trail (☎ 941/351-4949, ⓦ www.witnesscafe.com), open 2pm to 2am daily for food, drinks, dancing and live acts. For information on local events and news, visit ⓦ www.outinsarasota.com or pick up a copy of *Watermark* magazine (ⓦ www.watermarkonline.com).

North of Sarasota: Bradenton and around

A major producer of tomato and orange juice, **BRADENTON**, across from Palmetto on the south side of the broad Manatee River, is a hard-working town with a center comprising several unlovely miles of strip mall and office buildings along the river. While mainland Bradenton is far from exciting, **Anna Maria Island** (the northernmost point of a chain of barrier islands running from here to Fort Myers) and the **Bradenton beaches** eight miles west of downtown make up for Bradenton proper's lack of charm. Rather than travel inland, take Rte-789 for a more picturesque (if slightly longer) route to and from Sarasota.

The town and around

It's well worth spending some time away from the beach and paying a visit to the **South Florida Museum**, Bishop Planetarium, and Parker Manatee Aquarium, 201 Tenth St W (Tues–Sat 10am–5pm, Sun noon–5pm; Jan–April and July also Mon 10am–5pm; $15.95, $11.95 children, includes one plane-tarium show; ☎ 941/746-4131, ⓦ www.southfloridamuseum.org). The museum takes a wide-ranging look at the region's past through artifacts and exhibits

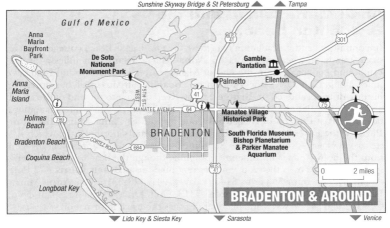

Gulf of Mexico

Anna
Maria
Bayfront
Park

De Soto
National
Monument Park

Gamble
Plantation �🏛

Palmetto   Ellenton

Anna
Maria
Island

75TH STREET WEST

41

N

Holmes
Beach

789

MANATEE AVENUE 64

Manatee Village
Historical Park

BRADENTON

South Florida Museum,
Bishop Planetarium
& Parker Manatee
Aquarium

Bradenton Beach

CORTEZ ROAD

684

Coquina Beach

75

0   2 miles

Longboat Key

BRADENTON & AROUND

5

related to its early settlers and natural history. The most popular attraction here, however, is the **aquarium**, home to Snooty the manatee. Born in 1948, Snooty is the oldest manatee born in captivity, and the community celebrates his birthday every July (thousands turned up for his sixtieth birthday party in 2008). The aquarium is intelligently laid out to provide varying views of Snooty and his poolmates, but ten minutes of watching them glide about is generally enough. The **Bishop Planetarium** is open throughout the day, although weekday mornings are reserved for school visits; the public is still welcome during these times, but the programs will vary with the kids' ages. Shows like "Secret of the Cardboard Rocket" and "Extreme Planets" present educational tours (and probing questions) of the universe, and are generally scheduled twice daily.

In central Bradenton, the **Manatee Chamber of Commerce**, 222 Tenth St W (Mon–Fri 9am–5pm; ☎941/748-3411, Ⓦwww.manateechamber.com), offers the usual tourist information.

De Soto National Memorial

Five miles west of central Bradenton, Manatee Avenue (the main route to the beaches) crosses 75th Street W, at the northern end of which sits the pretty **De Soto National Memorial** (daily 9am–5pm; free; ☎941/792-0458, Ⓦwww .nps.gov/deso), its waterfront lawn dotted by twisted gumbo limbo trees. This is believed to be near the spot Spanish conquistador **Hernando de Soto** came ashore in 1539. The four-year de Soto expedition, hacking through Florida's dense subtropical terrain and wading through its swamps, led to the European discovery of the Mississippi River – and numerous pitched battles with Native Americans. The park's **visitor center** contains artifacts and exhibits explaining the expedition's effect on American Indians, and an engrossing twenty-minute film depicting the expedition is shown on demand. The interpretive De Soto Expedition Trail (0.75 miles) invites visitors to experience a coastal landscape similar to that encountered by de Soto and his men centuries ago, and you can poke a replica of Camp Uzita, the first Spanish base, near the parking lot. From mid-December to mid-April, park rangers dressed as sixteenth-century Spaniards offer informative tidbits on the lifestyles of Florida's first adventurers (including weapons demonstrations and kid-friendly hands-on exhibits). For more about the de Soto expedition, see Contexts, p.458.

Anna Maria Island and the Bradenton beaches

In contrast to central Bradenton's grayness, the ramshackle beach cottages, seaside snack stands, and beachside bars on **Anna Maria Island** ten miles away are bright and convivial. From the end of Manatee Avenue, turn left and head two miles along Gulf Drive for **Bradenton Beach**, with its small but attractive historic district centered on **Bridge Street**. Keep driving to the end of the island and **Coquina Beach**, where the swimming is excellent. If you're after tranquility, take a right at the end of Manatee Avenue instead for **Anna Maria Bayfront Park**, at the eastern end of Pine Avenue at the island's northern tip, which has stellar views across the bay to the Sunshine Skyway; you can watch pelicans feed from the nearby pier, and sometimes dolphins, though the beach itself is nothing special. Further down the road, you can rent bikes from **Beach Bums**, 427 Pine Ave (daily 9am–5pm; $5 per hr, $14 per day; ☎941/778-3316). The **Anna Maria Island Chamber of Commerce**, 5313 Gulf Drive (Mon–Fri 9am–5pm; ☎941/778-1541, ⓦwww.amichamber.org) has the usual information.

Accommodation

Accommodation is plentiful on the beaches, but for those on a budget, suitable places tend to be a long way from the sands – rates always increase on weekends.

Harrington House 5626 Gulf Drive, Holmes Beach ☎941/778-5444, ⓦwww.harringtonhouse.com. This cozy B&B is a restored 1925 country-style inn that's right on the Gulf, with a variety of rooms and three other beachside properties to choose from. Book ahead. **❼**

Queen's Gate Resort 1101 Gulf Drive, Bradenton Beach ☎941/778-7153 or 1-800/310-7153, ⓦwww.queensgateresort.com. Just across the road from the beach, all the comfortable rooms here have porches with views of the sea, while larger cottages overlook the pool. **❻**

Siam Garden Resort 512 Spring Ave, Anna Maria Island ☎941/778-2000, ⓦwww.siamgardenresort.com. Tucked away in the village a short stroll from the beach, this laid-back resort boasts just sixteen suites decked out with antique bathrooms, tiki huts, tropical gardens and some unique architectural features such as the Thai "spirit house" by the pool. **❻**

Silver Surf Gulf Beach Resort 1301 Gulf Drive N, Bradenton Beach ☎941/778-6626 or 1-800/441-7873, ⓦwww.silverresorts.com. Best of the motel-style resorts near the beach, with a heated pool, a virtually private strip of sand, and big rooms that can accommodate three or four people. **❺**

Eating

You'll find a number of pleasant **restaurants** near the beaches. Look out for the local **stone crabs**, which feature on most menus from October to May.

Gulf Drive Café 900 Gulf Drive, Bradenton Beach ☎941/778-1919. Popular local breakfast spot, especially noted for its divine Belgian waffles; for lunch go for the crab-cake sandwiches and luscious desserts. Be prepared to wait for a table. Most dishes range $5–15.

Joe's Eats and Sweets 219 Gulf Dr S, Bradenton Beach ☎941/778-0007, ⓦwww.joeseatsandsweets.com. For sweet treats head to this raised wooden beach house selling fabulous home-made ice cream such as Key lime cheesecake, pumpkin and almond turtle fudge.

Mr Bones BBQ 3007 Gulf Drive S, Holmes Beach ☎941/778-6614, ⓦwww.misterbonesbbq.com. For a break from seafood, try this sumptuous barbecue joint, which cooks up some mean baby back ribs ($14.99), apricot-brandied ham ($15.99) and filling rice plates (from $7.99).

Sandbar 100 Spring Ave, Anna Maria Beach, just off Gulf Drive ☎941/778-0444, ⓦwww.sandbar-restaurant.com. Top choice for fresh, moderately priced seafood lunches or dinners, with innovative dishes like wasabi-encrusted salmon ($14.99) and legendary grouper sandwiches (market prices) on its beachfront patio.

Starfish Company 12306 46th Ave W, Cortez ☎941/794-1243, Ⓦwww.starfishcompany .com. Heading back to the mainland on Rte-684 (Cortez Rd), it's worth stopping at the fishing shacks of Cortez, where you'll find this friendly place serving huge fresh shellfish platters for under $15. **Waterfront Restaurant** 111 Bay Blvd S, near the end of Pine Ave, Anna Maria Beach

☎941/778-1515, Ⓦwww.thewaterfront restaurant.net. Come here for more upmarket seafood dishes, enhanced by soothing views of the pier and Gulf. Highlights include the Spring Street bouillabaisse ($24) and choice of local fish including grouper, but they also do plenty of grilled meats. Dinner entrées $15–35.

The Gamble Plantation

If you have time, head across the Manatee River from downtown Bradenton and along Tenth Street (US-301) to riverside **ELLENTON**, where the 1840s **Gamble Plantation Historic State Park**, 3708 Patten Ave (visitor center open Thurs–Mon 8am–4.30pm; free; ☎941/723-4536, Ⓦwww .floridastateparks.org/gambleplantation), contains one of the oldest homes on Florida's West Coast and the only slave-era plantation this far south. Composed of thick, tabby walls (a mixture of crushed shell and molasses) and girded on three sides by sturdy columns, the house belonged to Confederate major Robert Gamble, a failed Tallahassee cotton planter who ran a sugar plantation here before financial uncertainty caused by the impending Civil War forced him to leave. In 1925, the mansion was designated the **Judah P. Benjamin Confederate Memorial** in remembrance of Confederate Secretary of State Benjamin, who reportedly took refuge here in 1865 after the fall of the Confederacy. With Union troops in hot pursuit, he is believed to have hid here until friends found him a boat in which he sailed from Sarasota Bay to England, where he began practicing law. A showcase of wealthy (and white) Old South living, the house – stuffed to the rafters with period fittings – is open Thursday to Monday, and admission is by a **guided tour** (six times daily, beginning at 9.30am; $5 adults, $3 children).

Inland from Sarasota: Myakka River State Park

If all you've seen thus far are beaches and theme parks, broaden your horizons by traveling fourteen miles east of Sarasota on Rte-72. Here you'll find the marshes, pinewoods, and prairies of **Myakka River State Park**, 13207 Rte-72 (daily 8am–sunset; $2 for one person, $5 for two to eight people; ☎941/361-6511, Ⓦwww.myakkariver.org), a great tract of rural Florida barely touched by humans. On arrival, drop into the interpretive **visitor center** for insight into this fragile (and threatened) ecosystem, and then explore the park on its numerous walking paths, enjoy the seven-mile scenic drive, or rent a canoe or kayak ($20 first hr, $5 per hr thereafter; ☎941/923-1120) and glide the calm expanse of the **Upper Myakka Lake**. Myakka Wildlife & Nature Tours (☎941/365-0100) offer narrated one-hour tram and airboat tours through the wildlife habitats, explaining the ecology of the area and pointing out animals; both tours cost $12 (children $6) with three to four boat tours and two tram tours daily (no tram tours June–Dec). If you're equipped for hiking, following the forty miles of trails through the park's wilderness preserve is a better way to get close to the cotton-tailed rabbits, deer, turkey, bobcats, and alligators living in the park; before commencing, register at the entrance office, get maps, and check weather conditions – be prepared for wet conditions during the summer months. Other than the six primitive **campgrounds** on the hiking trails ($4 per night), park accommodation (details and reservations: ☎941/361-6511, for cabins, ☎800/326-3521; both at ⊛www.reserveamerica.com) comprises two well-equipped campgrounds ($22 per night) and five log cabins ($60 a night) that can sleep up to six people; these are very popular, so it's a good idea to book well in advance.

South from Sarasota: Venice and around

In 1960, the Ringling Circus moved its winter base twenty miles south from Sarasota to **Venice**, a laid-back small town best visited for its gorgeous **beaches**, which draw everyone from watersports enthusiasts to pensioner sunbathers.

The **downtown area** is centered on palm-lined Venice Avenue (which runs one mile from the Tamiami Trail, US-41, to the beach), with plenty of small shops and cafés along the way; though traces of Italianate architecture remain, you'll need a vivid imagination to see any connection to its European namesake. Head to the **Chamber of Commerce**, 597 Tamiami Trail S (Mon–Fri 8.30am–5pm; ☎941/488-2236, ⊛www.venicechamber.com) for local information. **Parking** at the beachfront is limited to a couple of small lots, but you can also leave your car along Venice Avenue (both free of charge). Alternatively, **local bus #13** (☎941/316-1234; 75¢) runs up and down Venice Avenue to the beach. You can always entertain yourself by searching for the sharks' teeth commonly washed ashore here – Venice does, after all, bill itself as the "Shark's Tooth Capital of the World." The fishing pier, two miles south of downtown off of Harbor Drive, is a beautiful spot from which to watch the sun dip below the horizon, and offers a good perspective on the town's extensive beaches and (gratefully) not-so-developed seafront.

Practicalities

Spending a night in this quiet community is an attractive proposition, though as always prices can be steep between February and April. Of the motels, try the various rooms at *Venice Beach Villas* (☎941/488-1580, ⊛www .venicebeachvillas.com; ❻), which has two locations near the beach: 501 W Venice Ave and 505 Menendez St. *The Inn at the Beach Resort*, 725 W Venice Ave (☎941/484-8471 or 1-800/255-8471, ⊛www.innatthebeach.com; ❻) aims for a resort-like feel, with more personalized service, free continental breakfast and newspapers, and a heated palm-fringed pool. The *Venice Campground*, near I-75 at 4085 E Venice Ave (☎941/488-0850, ⊛www .campvenice.com), offers both primitive and equipped tent sites ($50–52 peak season), as well as simple cabins ($75; reserve well in advance) in an old-growth oak hammock by the Myakka River.

Among the **places to eat**, don't miss *The Soda Fountain*, 349 W Venice Ave (☎941/488-7600), a charmingly old-fashioned diner, for delicious milkshakes, ice creams, and sandwiches; *The Frosted Mug*, 1856 S Tamiami Trail (☎941/497-1611), which has been here since 1957 and serves the area's best root beer and burgers; and *TJ Carney's Pub and Grill*, 231 W Venice Ave (☎941/480-9244), for evening entertainment as well as moderately priced pub food and seafood throughout the day. At the base of the pier, *Sharky's*, 1600 S Harbor Drive (☎941/488-1456, ⊛www.sharkysonthepier.com), is *the* spot to enjoy the sunset while munching on seafood, pastas and steak.

Continuing south: Punta Gorda

PUNTA GORDA, about thirty miles south of Venice, might easily be dismissed as another West Coast retirement community, but it does warrant exploring. While you won't find impressive beaches, you will encounter large, Southern-style houses on the riverfront and an unhurried pace of life that contrasts sharply with the frantic US-41 running through the town.

After crossing the Peace River on US-41, take the first right for the **Charlotte County Chamber of Commerce**, 311 West Retta Esplanade (Mon–Thurs 8am–5pm, Fri 8am–4.30pm; ☎941-639-2222, ⊛www.charlottecountychamber .org), housed in the gracious 1903 A.C. Freeman House (volunteers give free tours of the house Mon–Fri, 11am–3pm). Get maps here for the monuments and grand mansions scattered around the well-preserved **downtown district**, which spans several blocks south of the river, as well as for the fourteen historic **murals** painted along the walls of its main streets. Further along the banks of the river on West Retta Esplanade lies **Fishermen's Village**, a quaint collection of unusual shops and restaurants with a working marina housed in the old city docks – an appropriate extension to a town that got its name from Cuban fishermen in the early nineteenth century. A collection of boat-tour operators line the pier, offering trips around the harbor and further afield to Cayo Costa Island and Cabbage Key (see p.263); **King Fisher Fleet** (☎941/639-0969, ⊛www.kingfisherfleet.com) runs full- and half-day cruises and shorter nature and sunset boat trips, starting at $13.95 for ninety minutes, as well as deep-sea and back-bay fishing excursions.

Practicalities

If you are charmed enough by Punta Gorda to want to stay the night, skip the motels on US-41 and try one of the waterfront **accommodation** options in the town itself. You can rent two-bedroom villas at the *Fishermen's Village*, 1200 W Retta Esplanade (☎941/639-8721 or 1-800/639-0020, ⊛www.fishville .com; ❼), where amenities include a beach area, tennis courts, free use of bikes, and a heated pool. If you don't require a whole villa, you'll find similar amenities at the *Best Western Waterfront*, 300 W Retta Esplanade (☎941/639-1165, ⊛www .bwpuntagorda.com; ❺). The *Banana Bay Motel*, 23285 Bayshore Rd (☎941/743-4441, ⊛www.bananabaymotel.com; ❹), has a secluded waterfront setting, across the bridge from Fishermen's Village Marina in Charlotte Harbor.

One of the more adventurous **eating** options includes the *Nav-a-Gator Grill* (☎800/308-7506; ⊛www.nav-a-gator.com) at 9700 SW Riverview Circle in Lake Suzy, further up the Peace River; you can drive here, but it's far more fun to take a ferry from Laishley Park Marina, slip E-8, at the end of Nesbit Street just off US-41 (departures usually 9.30am, back at 2.30pm; $26.95). Contact Punta Gorda River Boat Tours for details (☎941/627-3474). The grill serves up gator tails, shrimp, burgers, conch, duck, and even peanut butter sandwiches, with live rock bands most weekends. Less effort is required for *Harpoon Harry's* (☎941/637-1177, ⊛www.harpoonharrys.com) at the end of the pier in Fishermen's Village Marina; enjoy raw oysters, clams, and hearty sports pub food to the accompaniment of live music on weekends.

Telegraph Cypress Swamp

For a glimpse of untamed Florida – without having to traipse through the wild for days – try **Babcock Wilderness Adventures**, 8000 State Rd 31 (☎1-800/500-5583, ⊛www.babcockwilderness.com). Forty miles northeast of Fort Myers (take Exit 143 on I-75) and about 25 miles east of Punta Gorda (Exit 164 on I-75, or east on Rte-74), this ecotourism outfit offers ninety-minute swamp-buggy tours through the privately owned Crescent B Ranch and **Telegraph Cypress Swamp** (Nov–May 9am–3pm, June–Oct mornings only, reservations essential; $17.95, children $10.95). From open fields with wild pigs and bison to swamp areas where alligators carpet the pathway, the tours will take you through wild, ever-changing terrain. Highlights include the **bald cypress swamp**, a primeval scene of stunning trees and blood-red bromeliads reflected in still, tea-colored water, and the gold Florida panthers, although they're not pure-bred (only around fifty of those are left). In the movie set-turned-museum, where Warner Brothers shot the 1995 film *Just Cause* with Sean Connery, you can take a break from the wilderness and learn more about the ranch's history, and that of the surrounding area. For food, bring a picnic lunch or snack on fried gator bites, hot dogs, and burgers at the ranch's seasonal restaurant, *Gator Shack*.

Fort Myers

Though lacking the sophistication of Sarasota (fifty miles north) and the exclusivity of Naples (twenty miles south), **FORT MYERS** is one of the southwest coast's up-and-coming communities. The town took its name from Abraham Myers, who helped re-establish a fort here in 1850 during the Seminole Indian Wars. Fortunately, most of the town's late-twentieth-century growth occurred in North Fort Myers, across the wide Calusahatchee River, and so the traditional center has been left relatively unspoiled. The workplace of inventor **Thomas Edison**, who passed more than forty winters in Fort Myers, provides the strongest cultural interest, while balmy sands await at **Fort Myers Beach** and on the islands of **Sanibel** and **Captiva**, fifteen miles south and west, respectively.

Arrival and information

Fort Myers, like many south Florida towns, sprawls farther than you initially imagine. Around nine miles southeast of downtown, **Southwest Florida International Airport** (☎239/590-4800, ⓦwww.flylcpa.com) is accessible from I-75 via Daniels Parkway. LeeTran bus #50 (Mon–Sat 7am–9pm; $1.25) links the airport with Daniels Parkway and US-41, but you'll need to change at least once to get to the beach or downtown. **Taxi** rates from the airport are charged according to a zone system: the historic downtown area is $30, Fort Myers Beach $50, and Sanibel and Captiva islands $56–75. The major car rental companies are all represented at the airport.

If **driving**, US-41 is known here as Cleveland Avenue; Hwy-80 runs through downtown Fort Myers and curves into McGregor Boulevard (also called 867) to the west, where you'll find the Edison home (see p.253). If you're arriving from US-41, the exit for McGregor Boulevard is clearly marked, and although the **local buses** don't travel the length of McGregor, the #20 ($1.25; ☎239/533-8726, ⓦwww.rideleetran.com; limited Sun service) will get you closest to the Edison home. To get from downtown Fort Myers to the beaches, take the #140 south to Bell Tower and change to the #50 to Summerlin Square, where you can catch the **Beach Trolley** (50¢) to Fort Myers Beach; this continuously runs the full length of Fort Myers Beach to Lovers Key and Bonita Springs along Estero Boulevard, daily from approximately 6am to 7pm. The **Greyhound station** is in downtown Fort Myers at 2250 Peck Street (☎239/334-1011).

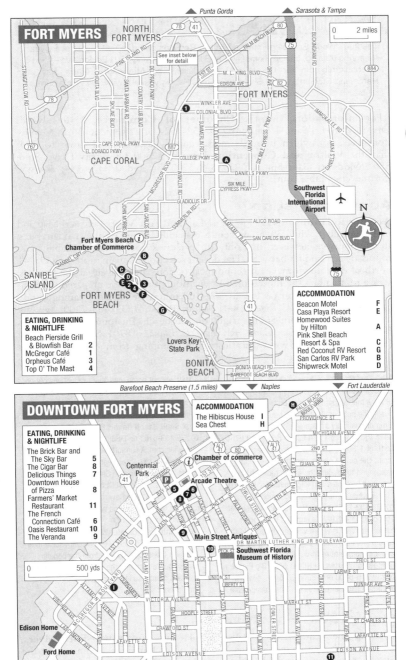

FORT MYERS

▲ *Punta Gorda*   ▲ *Sarasota & Tampa*

NORTH FORT MYERS

See inset below for detail

FORT MYERS

CAPE CORAL

SANIBEL ISLAND

FORT MYERS BEACH

Fort Myers Beach Chamber of Commerce

Southwest Florida International Airport

N

Lovers Key State Park

BONITA BEACH

0   2 miles

EATING, DRINKING & NIGHTLIFE

Beach Pierside Grill & Blowfish Bar	2
McGregor Café	1
Orpheus Café	3
Top O' The Mast	4

ACCOMMODATION

Beacon Motel	F
Casa Playa Resort	E
Homewood Suites by Hilton	A
Pink Shell Beach Resort & Spa	C
Red Coconut RV Resort	G
San Carlos RV Park	B
Shipwreck Motel	D

Barefoot Beach Preserve (1.5 miles) ▼   ▼ *Naples*   ▼ *Fort Lauderdale*

DOWNTOWN FORT MYERS

ACCOMMODATION

The Hibiscus House	I
Sea Chest	H

EATING, DRINKING & NIGHTLIFE

The Brick Bar and The Sky Bar	5
The Cigar Bar	8
Delicious Things	7
Downtown House of Pizza	8
Farmers' Market Restaurant	11
The French Connection Café	6
Oasis Restaurant	10
The Veranda	9

Centennial Park

Chamber of commerce

Arcade Theatre

Main Street Antiques

Southwest Florida Museum of History

Edison Home

Ford Home

0   500 yds

Baseball in Fort Myers

The 2007 World Series champions **Boston Red Sox** come to Fort Myers every year for spring training, basing themselves at City of Palms Park, 2201 Edison Ave – check Ⓦredsox.mlb.com for tickets and schedules. The **Minnesota Twins** play at Hammond Stadium, 14100 Six Mile Cypress Parkway (see Ⓦwww.twins.mlb.com).

For **information**, visit the **Chamber of Commerce**, 2310 Edwards Drive (Mon–Fri 9am–4.30pm; ☏239/332-3624 or 1-800/366-3622, Ⓦwww.fortmyers.org), which is much more centrally located (and easier to find) than the **Visitor and Convention Bureau**, 12800 University Drive, Suite 550 (Mon–Fri 8am–5pm; ☏239/338-3500 or 1-800/237-6444; Ⓦwww.fortmeyers-sanibel.com).

Accommodation

Accommodation costs are low in and around Fort Myers between May and mid-December, when 30–60 percent is generally lopped off the standard rates. In high season, however, not only do prices skyrocket, but available spare rooms are few and far between. The decent selection of chain motels on US-41 north of downtown make an economical option; alternatively, at the beaches, seek a room along the motel-lined Estero Boulevard and be prepared to spend at least $150 in season (as low as $60–100 otherwise). Of the campgrounds, only *Red Coconut RV Resort*, 3001 Estero Blvd (☏239/463-7200, Ⓦwww.redcoconut.com; from $60), is right on the beach. En route to Fort Myers Beach, you'll pass *San Carlos RV Park & Islands*, 18701 San Carlos Blvd (☏239/466-3133, Ⓦwww.sancarlosrv.com; camping from $46), which has plenty of bayfront sites.

Hotels and motels

Beacon Motel 1240 Estero Blvd ☏239/463-5264, Ⓦwww.thebeaconmotel.com. Cozy 1940s beachside hotel on the bustling boulevard; prices jump dramatically in high season. ❻

Casa Playa Resort 510 Estero Blvd ☏239/765-0510 or 1-800/569-4876, Ⓦwww.casaplayaresort.com. The potted plants painted on the facade are a welcoming touch, and the ample rooms have screened balconies and kitchenette facilities. ❼

The Hibiscus House 2135 McGregor Blvd ☏239/332-2651, Ⓦwww.thehibiscushouse.net. This pretty 1912 B&B is outfitted in Victorian furnishings and is within walking distance of the Edison and Ford Winter Estates, as well as dining and entertainment options. ❻

Homewood Suites by Hilton 5255 Big Pine Way ☏239/275-6000 or 1-800/225-5466, Ⓦwww.homewoodsuitesftmyers.com. For considerable luxury without pomp, and sharp reductions out of season, try the *Homewood Suites*, which offers a complimentary hot breakfast, heated pool, fitness center, and business amenities. ❼

Pink Shell Beach Resort & Spa 275 Estero Blvd ☏239/463-6181 or 1-888/222-7465, Ⓦwww.pinkshell.com. A comfortable beachfront resort with a full-service spa, three heated pools, two tennis courts, a fishing pier, and Gulf-view rooms. ❼

Sea Chest 2571 E First St ☏239/332-1545 or 1-800/438-6461. This riverfront motel has basic rooms, a heated pool, and waterfront access – you can fish from the pier. ❹

Shipwreck Motel 237 Old San Carlos Blvd ☏239/463-4691, Ⓦwww.shipwreckmotel.com. On the lagoon, a block from the popular Times Square area and the Gulf, this motel offers standard rooms, suites, two pools, and shuffleboard. ❻

Downtown Fort Myers

Crossing the Calusahatchee River, US-41 hits **downtown Fort Myers**, which nestles by the river's edge. Modern office buildings dominate, but the historic riverfront area, dubbed the **Fort Myers River District**, has far more appeal. Ambitious and largely successful renovations have transformed this area, particularly along Main and First Streets between Broadway and Jackson St, though like much of the state, the property bust of 2008 means business is likely to remain sluggish and some units will remain empty for a few years yet. Highlights include colorful **Arcade Theatre**, 2267 First St (℗239/332-4488 or 1-877/787-8053, ⓦwww.floridarep.org), home to the top-notch Florida Repertory Theater, and stores such as Main Street Antiques and Collectibles, 2229 Main St (Mon–Sat 11am–5pm; ℗239/689-6246). Note also the Sidney & Berne Davis Art Center (℗239/337-1933, ⓦwww.fl-arts.org), housed in the wonderfully restored 1933 Federal Building on First Street, which hosts concerts and art shows. **Parking** is usually easy downtown, with plenty of curbside spaces (2–10hr free) and a parking lot near the river.

For a thorough insight into the town's past, stop by the **Southwest Florida Museum of History**, 2300 Peck St (Tues–Sat 10am–5pm; $9.50, $5 children; ℗239/332-5955), where exhibits include a full-sized "cracker" house and the rusty 84-foot-long *Esperanza*, one of the longest private Pullman rail cars built in the United States. Not aiming to compete, it leaves details of the most recent star of Fort Myers' history – Thomas Edison – to the museum estates a mile southwest of downtown on McGregor Boulevard (the same route to Fort Myers Beach and the Sanibel Island causeway).

The Edison and Ford Winter Estates

In 1885, six years after inventing the light bulb, workaholic **Thomas Edison** collapsed from exhaustion and was instructed by his doctor to find a warm working environment or face an early death. While on holiday in Florida that year, the 37-year-old Edison noted a patch of bamboo sprouting from the banks of the Calusahatchee River and bought and cleared fourteen acres of it. Henry Ford, a close friend of Edison's, bought the house next door in 1916, by which time he was established as the country's top automobile manufacturer. The combined **Edison and Ford Winter Estates**, 2350 McGregor Blvd (daily 9am–5.30pm, last tour at 4pm; guided tours every 30min; $20 for homes and gardens tour, children $11; ℗239/334-3614 or 239/334-7419, ⓦwww.efwefla .org), provide some small insight into these men of innovation. If you're here in February, try to catch the annual Festival of Lights celebration (ⓦwww .edisonfestival.org), a three-week event culminating in a grand parade held each year in commemoration of Edison's birthday.

Edison was a keen horticulturist and often used the chemicals produced by plants and trees in his experiments. The **gardens** of the house (in-depth botanical tours Thurs and Sat at 9am; $24) are sensational. Edison nurtured more than 100 varieties of plants from Africa, South America, and Asia, including an abundance of tropical foliage – from the extraordinary African sausage tree to a profusion of wild orchids, intoxicatingly scented by frangipani.

Getting to Key West

If you're heading to **Key West** from Fort Myers, opt for the high-speed catamaran, a trip that takes about three-and-a-half hours each way. Key West Express (℗888/539-2628 or 239/463-5733, ⓦwww.seakeywestexpress.com) has boats leaving from Salty Sam's Marina, 2500 Main St, in Fort Myers Beach, as well as from its bridge location on San Carlos Island, 706 Fisherman's Wharf, just before the bridge to the beach. Trips cost approximately $85 one-way or $129 round-trip, with flexible return dates. Call for schedules.

▲ Thomas Edison's laboratory

By contrast, Edison's **house**, where he spent each winter with his wife Mina until his death in 1931, is an anticlimax: a palm-cloaked wooden structure with an ordinary collection of period furnishings glimpsed only through windows from the porch. A reason for the abode's plainness may be that Edison spent most of his waking hours inside the **laboratory**, attempting to turn the latex-rich sap of *solidago Edisoni* (a giant strain of goldenrod weed he developed) into natural rubber. A mass of test tubes, files, and tripods are scattered over the benches, unchanged since Edison's last experiment, which he performed just before his death.

Not until the tour reaches the **museum** does the full impact of Edison's achievements become apparent. A design for an improved ticker-tape machine provided him with enough funds to conduct the experiments that led to the creation of the phonograph in 1877, and financed research into passing electricity through a vacuum, which resulted in the creation of a practical, safe, and economical incandescent lightbulb two years later. Scores of cylinder and disc phonographs with gaily painted horn-speakers, bulky vintage lightbulbs, and innumerable spin-off gadgets make up an engrossing collection. Here, too, you'll see some of the ungainly cinema projectors derived from Edison's Kinetoscope, which brought him nearly a million dollars a year in patent royalties from 1907.

Unlike the Edison home, you can go inside the **Ford Winter Home**, though the interior, restored to the style of Ford's time, lacks almost all of the original fittings and bears an unassuming appearance. Ford, despite becoming the world's first billionaire, lived with his wife in quite modest surroundings.

Before leaving the old homes, pause to admire the sprawling **banyan tree** outside the ticket office – it's worth a visit in its own right. Grown from a four-foot-tall seedling given to Edison by tire-king Harvey Firestone in 1925, it's now the largest banyan tree in the United States, second in the world only to its mother tree in India.

Fort Myers Beach

En route to **Fort Myers Beach**, a separate town fifteen miles south of downtown Fort Myers, you'll pass the helpful **Chamber of Commerce** (Mon, Thurs & Fri 9–5pm, Sat 10–5pm; 17200 San Carlos Blvd; ☎239/454-7500, ⓦwww.fortmyersbeach.org) before crossing a small bridge into the tiny fishing and sailing community of **San Carlos Island**, where you'll find the Key West boat (see box, p.253) and half-day fishing trips aboard the *Sea Trek* (702 Fisherman's Wharf; 9.30am–4pm; $50; ☎239/765-7665, ⓦwww.seatrekfishing.com). The longer causeway from San Carlos Island brings you to central Fort Myers Beach on seven-mile **Estero Island**, a cheerfully commercialized town a bit less refined than the southwest's other popular beach strips – think T-shirt, swimsuit, and ice-cream shops, and plenty of blaring beach bars. Most of the action happens where the bridge ends, near the short fishing pier, the **Lynne Hall Park**, and the pedestrian-only area called Times Square, identified by the great clock in its middle and the street performers that often pull in crowds (**parking** is $1 per hr). If that's your scene, this place is for you; otherwise, you might want to head for quieter stretches of beach further south. You'll find over thirty beach access points (clearly marked from the road) and lots of accommodation (see p.252) on Estero Boulevard, which runs the length of the **island**.

Lovers Key State Park

Fort Myers Beach becomes quieter and increasingly residential as you press south. Estero Boulevard eventually swings over a slender causeway to **Lovers Key State Park** (daily 8am to sunset; cars $3 for one person, $5 for two or more, pedestrians and cyclists $1; ☎239/463-4588), actually a series of interconnecting mangrove islands forming a chain to **Bonita Beach**. The main park entrance is around a mile from the causeway, and you can reach the beaches – among the quietest and prettiest in the region – via a short footpath over a couple of mangrove-fringed islands and several mullet-filled, man-made canals. If you don't fancy the walk, or are lugging beach chairs ($6 a day), a free tram (daily 9am–4.30pm) runs regularly between the beach and the main concession shop, near the parking lot. If you crave some outdoor action, hike the worthwhile **Black Island Trail** (2.5 miles, but shortcuts are built in), or go exploring by canoe or kayak ($42 full day, $32 half day), or bicycle ($25 full day, $18 half day), all of which can be rented at the concession shop (daily 9am–5pm; ☎239/765-7788).

Eating

You'll find clusters of **restaurants** downtown, as well as near Times Square on the northern section of Estero Boulevard in Fort Myers Beach.

Fort Myers

Delicious Things 2262 First St ☎239/332-7797, ⓦwww.deliciousthings.us. Cozy restaurant serving fresh Italian food including tasty pastas (from $15), meat, and fish (from $27) for lunch and dinner. Also has free wi-fi.

Downtown House of Pizza 1520 Hendry St ☎239/337-3467, ⓦwww.downtownhouse ofpizza.com. Best pizza pie (from $13.75) and slices (from $2) in town, with $1 draft beers to wash them down. Also does sandwiches from $3.75.

Farmers' Market Restaurant 2736 Edison Ave ☎239/334-1687, ⓦwww.farmersmarket restaurant.com. Despite its somewhat grim appearance and 1950s signs, try this reasonably priced spot for hearty country favorites like smoked ham hocks or fried ribs and breakfasts of eggs, biscuits, and grits.

The French Connection Café 2282 First St ☎239/332-4443, ⓦwww.frenchconnectioncafe .com. Convivial café for inexpensive French onion soup ($3), crepes ($6), and excellent hot Reuben sandwiches ($7).

McGregor Café 4305 McGregor Blvd ☎239/936-1771. Enjoy a delicious breakfast or an Italian-inspired dinner on the outdoor patio dominated by a great live oak tree. Closed Mon; no dinner on Sun.

Oasis Restaurant 2260 Dr Martin Luther King Blvd ☎239/334-1566. Stop in at this friendly, family-owned, always busy spot for cheap all-day breakfasts and large burgers. Open breakfast and lunch only.

The Veranda 2122 Second St ☎239/332-2065, ⓦwww.verandarestaurant.com. The casual elegance of the Old South lives on in this restaurant, which occupies two 1902 houses and a lush courtyard of mango trees. Tuck into regional specialties like Southern grit cakes and pan-seared

grouper. While dinner can be pricey ($24–36), lunch is very reasonable ($10–16). Reservations recommended.

Fort Myers Beach

Beach Pierside Grill & Blowfish Bar 1000 Estero Blvd ☎39/765-7800 ⓦwww.piersidegrill .com. Festive oceanfront bar and restaurant on Times Square, heavy on seafood, pasta, "beachy drinks," and live music. Entrées $12–21.

Orpheus Café 1165 Estero Blvd ☎239/463-1549. Across the street from the beach, this Greek restaurant serves a popular all-day breakfast of the usual favorites – omelets, pancakes, French toast – at about $7 per dish, as well as Mediterranean foods and specialty pizzas.

Nightlife

Fort Myers' **nightlife** scene is small but constantly changing and you'll usually find some lively bars on a stroll through downtown or along Estero Boulevard in Fort Myers Beach; alternatively, check ⓦwww.downtownftmyers.com for more options. There's also a gay and lesbian scene in the city, which we've indicated in the lisitngs below.

The Bottom Line 3090 Evans Ave ☎239/337-7292, ⓦwww.clubtbl.com. This long-running gay nightspot is a cavernous bar and club tucked away in a desolate stretch of downtown; nightly events range from drag shows to DJs to karaoke.

The Brick Bar and The Sky Bar 2224 Bay St ☎239/332-7425. Two different venues housed in the same attractive converted warehouse; the former is a sleek, second-floor spot with live music and light food, while the latter is an inviting outdoor rooftop bar with frequent DJs and a slightly younger crowd.

The Cigar Bar 1502 Hendry St ☎239/337-4662, ⓦwww.cigarbarlive.com. Laid-back yet stylish bar, filled with leather chesterfields and the mounted

heads of bison, oryx, and bears (often sporting cigars themselves). Choose from a huge range of bourbons, single malts, and smokes.

The Office 3704 Cleveland Ave ☎239/936-3212, ⓦwww.officepub.com. This congenial gay pub in the Pizza Hut Plaza has a lively happy hour and various themes like "underwear night."

Top O' The Mast 1028 Estero Blvd ☎239/463-9424. All-day and late-night hot-spot on the beach with live music or DJs; they also serve inexpensive light meals with beach service.

Tubby's 4350 Fowler St ☎239/274-5001, ⓦwww.tubbysbar.com. The friendly gay pub has a dancefloor and karaoke on Thursday nights.

Around Fort Myers: Lee County Manatee Park

As might be guessed, manatees are the center of attention at the **Lee County Manatee Park**, northeast of downtown Fort Myers at 10901 Hwy-80 (Oct–March 8am–5pm; April–Sept 8am–8pm; visitor center closed in summer; $1 per hr parking fee or $5 per day; ☎239/694-3537), Exit 141 off I-75. Here, along the banks of the Orange River, large information boards explain how manatees are identified by their scar patterns, which are caused by collisions with boat propellers. Those most often sighted – usually the most scarred – are given names. Due to its proximity to the interstate and the Florida Power & Light plant, the park isn't too aesthetically pleasing. Still, the manatees enjoy the warm water generated by the plant, especially in the winter. You're likely to see a number of them, especially if you come early in the morning, in the first inlet, where they tend to congregate because it's calm and shallow.

Sanibel and Captiva islands

Despite being mobbed by tourists in high season, Sanibel and Captiva islands, 25 miles southwest of Fort Myers, have managed to retain some of their old Florida charm; a laid-back island aura, natural beauty, and fabulous beaches. Despite vociferous opposition from locals, **Sanibel Island**, the most southerly of an island grouping around the mouth of the Calusahatchee River, was linked by road to the mainland in 1963. Thankfully, strict land-use laws have since prevented the island from sinking beneath holiday homes and hotels; there are no high resorts to mar the view, and environmental groups continue to buy up land, thereby blocking future development. North of Sanibel, a road continues to the much smaller, less populated **Captiva Island**, which, with fewer restaurants and people, has even more of a tranquil island vibe.

Arrival and information

The lack of public transport both to and on the islands makes day-trips virtually impossible without a car – though once you're here, all you really need is a bicycle. To reach Sanibel and Captiva from mainland Fort Myers, take College Parkway west off of US-41, turning almost immediately south onto Summerlin Road which winds its way to Sanibel Causeway, a series of three bridges linking to the island. There's a $6 vehicle **toll** to get onto Sanibel.

Stop in at the very thorough **Chamber of Commerce and Visitor Center**, 1159 Causeway Rd (Mon–Fri 9am–5pm, Sat–Sun 9am–5pm; ☏239/472-1080, ⓦwww.sanibel-captiva.org), packed with essential information and free publications. The lack of public transport on the island means that without a car, you'll have to rent a **bike** – a great way to get around regardless because of the island's flat terrain and well-maintained bike paths. Bear in mind bikes are generally not allowed on the beaches. Finnimore's Cycle Shop, 2353 Periwinkle Way (daily 9am–4pm; ☏239/472-5577, ⓦwww.finnimores.com), and Billy's Rentals, 1470 Periwinkle Way (☏239/472-5248, ⓦwww.billysrentals.com), both offer good selections; a single-speed bike rental costs $15 a day, mountain bikes $25 (Finnimore's is $1 cheaper). Billy's also rents scooters for $70 a day. Opposite at no. 1509 is Segway of Sanibel, offering 90-minute guided tours of the island atop Segways (daily 9am, 11am, 3pm; $60; ☏239/472-3620, ⓦwww.segwaysanibel.com).

Accommodation

Accommodation on the islands is always more expensive than on the mainland, and per-day rates can be $100 higher than usual during high season.

Sanibel

Anchor Inn & Cottages 1245 Periwinkle Way ☏239/395-9688 or 1-866/469-9543, ⓦwww.sanibelanchorinn.com. One of the island's more reasonable offerings, this comfortable inn has a heated pool, outdoor grills, and is just a ten-minute walk from the beach. ⑥

Gulf Breeze Cottages 1081 Shell Basket Lane ☏239/472-1626 or 1-800/388-2842, ⓦwww.gbreeze.com. Choose between a Victorian house or one of the more expensive cottages; all are clean, well furnished, and right on the Gulf. ⑦

Kona Kai Motel & Cottages 1539 Periwinkle Way ☏239/472-1001 or 1-800/820-2385, ⓦwww.konakaimotel.com. Sits less than a mile from the beach, with a large freshwater pool and garden. The motel also rents bikes to go to the beach. Check website for special discounts – rates start at $90 in low season. ⑥

Periwinkle Trailer Park 1119 Periwinkle Way ☏239/472-1433, ⓦwww.sanibelcamping.com. The only campground on either of the two islands, this centrally located site features a popular onsite aviary and costs £35–45 to pitch a tent.

Seahorse Cottages 1223 Buttonwood Lane
☎239/472-4262, ⊛www.seahorsecottages.com.
Comfortable, thoughtfully decorated cottages on
the island's eastern end offer an intimate, adults-
only environment with antique oak furniture, a
garden pool, and complimentary bikes. ❼
Waterside Inn on the Beach 3033 W Gulf Drive
☎239/472-1345 or 1-800/741-6166, ⊛www
.watersideinn.net. A colorful, friendly place right on
the beach, with spacious accommodation in rooms,
efficiencies, and cottages. ❻

Near the island's restaurants and shops, and a
short walk to the beach, this charming bed and
breakfast offers everything from rooms to houses,
plus complimentary bikes. Low season rates from
$99 (weeknights only). ❼
'Tween Waters Inn 15951 Captiva Rd
☎239/472-5161 or 1-800/223-5865, ⊛www
.tween-waters.com. Nestled between the Gulf and
Pine Island Sound, this historic resort has rooms
and cottages, and also tennis courts, a marina,
pool, and day spa. Inquire about walk-in specials,
when rates are discounted. ❻

Captiva

Captiva Island Inn 11509 Andy Rosse Lane
☎239/395-0882, ⊛www.captivaislandinn.com.

Sanibel Island

Although **SANIBEL ISLAND** boasts plenty of enticing attractions away from
the sands, most people come here for the beaches. While these are certainly
appealing, public access is limited and they're not as spectacular as the glossy
brochures might have you believe. Signs prohibit parking everywhere you look
(parking and speeding regulations are strictly enforced), and in winter the
parking lots tend to get clogged (parking is $2 per hr in lots on both islands,
7am–7pm daily). The further west and north you travel, the more likely you are
to find space.

When you come over on the toll bridge, you'll first see the 98-foot **Sanibel
Lighthouse** (erected in 1884), an unattractive iron-framed relic most arrivals
feel obliged to inspect (from the outside only; park at the beach) before
spending time on the presentable beach at its foot, a popular shell-collecting
spot. After the beach, follow Periwinkle Way and turn right onto Dunlop Road,
passing the island's tiny city hall on your way to no. 950, the **Sanibel Historical
Village and Museum** (May to mid-Aug Wed–Sat 10am–1pm; Nov–April
10am–4pm; $5; ☎239/472-4648, ⊛www.sanibelmuseum.org). The museum is
a 1913 "cracker" style home with furnishings and photos of early Sanibel
arrivals – those who weren't seafarers tried agriculture until the soils were
ruined by saltwater blown up by hurricanes – and the village consists of a cluster
of restored island buildings, including an old schoolhouse and post office.

Continue along Periwinkle Way to Tarpon Bay Road, which cuts north–south
across the island; going south, you'll pass the 100-acre **Bailey Tract** (daily
sunrise–sunset; free) a freshwater marsh that is part of the Wildlife Refuge (see
p.260). Here, four clearly marked, color-coded hiking and biking trails take you
past ponds, canals, and a red mangrove island – a habitat of bobcats, alligators,
snakes, and multiple freshwater bird species.

Further south, resorts and tourists line the beaches along West Gulf Drive, but
if you head east along Casa Ybel Road, and then all the way down Algiers Lane,
you'll find the more promising **Gulfside City Park**, 47 acres of palm forest and
wetlands, as well as a slender sandy strip of beach and a nicely secluded picnic
area. If you follow the narrow bike path veering off Algiers Road (no parking;
cycle or walk from the beach), you'll find two little gems, hidden from the street
by thick vegetation: a tiny **cemetery**, where a few wooden markers commemorate those who perished over a century ago, and the 22-acre **Gulfside Park
Preserve**, which encircles a pond and has an interpretative walking trail
through palm groves and sea grape trees.

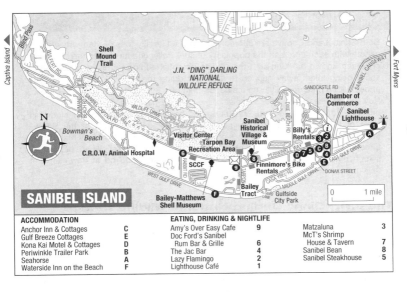

ACCOMMODATION		EATING, DRINKING & NIGHTLIFE			
Anchor Inn & Cottages	C	Amy's Over Easy Cafe	9	Matzaluna	3
Gulf Breeze Cottages	E	Doc Ford's Sanibel		McT's Shrimp	
Kona Kai Motel & Cottages	D	Rum Bar & Grille	6	House & Tavern	7
Periwinkle Trailer Park	B	The Jac Bar	4	Sanibel Bean	8
Seahorse	A	Lazy Flamingo	2	Sanibel Steakhouse	5
Waterside Inn on the Beach	F	Lighthouse Café	1		

Bailey-Matthews Shell Museum, SCCF and CROW

Taking the local love of shells to its logical conclusion, the nonprofit **Bailey-Matthews Shell Museum**, at 3075 Sanibel-Captiva Rd (daily 10am–5pm; $7; ☎ 239/395-2233, ⓦ www.shellmuseum.org), is devoted entirely to mollusks from all over the world. A cornucopia of colors, shapes, and sizes is spread before you in such a way as to inform as well as entertain, revealing the formation of shells, their diversity and uses, and the life cycle of the critters inside. The museum's several rooms merit an hour or two of quiet contemplation, but you can also just visit the onsite shell store (free).

A bit further west on Sanibel-Captiva Road, at no. 3333, the **Sanibel-Captiva Conservation Foundation**, or SCCF (Mon–Fri: Oct–May 8.30am–4pm; June–Sept 8.30am–3pm; Dec–April also Sat 10am–3pm; $3, kids under 17 free; ☎ 239/472-2329, ⓦ www.sccf.org) runs a nature center with four miles of trails (with an observation tower), exhibits, a touch tank, butterfly house and bookstore. You'll learn about the many nearby habitats and the work of the SCCF, which manages over 1300 acres of land on both islands (and owns an additional 500 acres on nearby Pine Island). Check the website for special tours and programs.

Still on Sanibel-Captiva Road, at no. 3884, near the entrance to the Wildlife Refuge, you'll find the absorbing **CROW Visitor Center** (Tues–Sun 10am–4pm; donation $5; ☎ 239/472-3644, ⓦ www.crowclinic .org). **CROW** (Clinic for the Rehabilitation of Wildlife), is a "hospital" for injured, orphaned, and sick native and migratory wildlife from all over southwest Florida. Several thousand patients are treated here each year (over 80 percent suffer injuries due to interaction with humans), and the center's interactive displays show how these animals are assessed, treated and ultimately released. There's a short introductory video, interactive games such as "Be the Vet", and a live video feed from the hospital, though the clinic itself is off-limits to the public.

Shelling on Sanibel and Captiva islands

Both Sanibel and Captiva are littered with **shells**. Literally tons of them are washed ashore with each tide, and the popularity of shell collecting has led to the bent-over condition known as "Sanibel Stoop." The potential ecological upset of too many shells being taken away has led to laws forbidding the removal of any live shells (those with a creature still living inside) on pain of a $500 fine or a prison sentence. Novices and seasoned conchologists alike will find plenty to occupy them on the beaches; to identify your find, consult one of the illustrated shell charts included in most of the giveaway tourist magazines – or check the exhibits at the Bailey-Matthews Shell Museum (see p.259) or at the **Sanibel Shell Fair** in early March. Top three shelling tips: hit the sands after storms, when numerous shells are deposited; search during low tide, when more shells are exposed; and go at dawn for first pickings.

The J.N. "Ding" Darling National Wildlife Refuge

In contrast to the fluffy white beaches along the Gulf side of Sanibel Island, the opposite edge comprises shallow bays, creeks, and a vibrant wildlife habitat under the protection of the **J.N. "Ding" Darling National Wildlife Refuge** (wildlife drive daily, except Fri, 7.30am–sunset; cars $5, cyclists and pedestrians $1; ☎239/472-1100). The main entrance and **information and education center** (daily: May–Dec 9am–4pm; Jan–April 9am–5pm) are just off Sanibel-Captiva Road, two miles west of Tarpon Bay Road (and about a mile on from the SCCF). The refuge is home to many species, including bobcats, marsh rabbits, and gopher tortoises; most commonly spotted are alligators, raccoons, and a wide variety of birds including brown pelicans, ospreys, double-breasted cormorants, herons and egrets, red-shouldered hawks, and red-bellied woodpeckers. Keep an eye out for bald eagles, physically distinguishable from ospreys by their pure-white heads, necks and tails, and graceful roseate spoonbills. The four-mile, one-way **Wildlife Drive** requires slow speeds and plenty of stops if you're to see the well-camouflaged residents by car; for this reason, bikes are really the way to go (see p.257 for rentals). Additionally, the **Indigo Trail**, a less-traveled, two-mile path for hikers and bikers only, begins just beyond the information center; look out for alligators and the park's elusive American crocodile in the brackish water canal on the trail's south side. You'll also find a second, much shorter (quarter-mile) trail close to the north end of Wildlife Drive – the **Shell Mound Trail**, a twisty boardwalk through a hardwood hammock of mangrove, buttonwood and a few lime trees (which remain from efforts to cultivate the island), all of which have grown atop an ancient Calusa Indian shell mound.

To see the reserve from the water, head to the **Tarpon Bay Recreation Area** at the northern end of Tarpon Bay Road, where Tarpon Bay Explorers (daily 8am–6pm; ☎239/472-8900, ⓦwww.tarponbayexplorers.com) runs a variety of boat and kayak tours, in addition to an interpretative tram tour of Wildlife Drive ($13, children $8). Popular options include the kayak tour ($30) through the mangrove tunnels of the Commodore Creek Water Trail, and sea life cruise ($20). You can also **rent kayaks** here (first hr $20; $10 per hr thereafter).

Bowman's Beach

Sanibel's loveliest, and most popular, swathe of crushed-shell sand is wide **Bowman's Beach** on the island's western end, reachable via Bowman's Beach Road off Sanibel-Captiva Road just before Blind Pass. Attracting shell-hunters

▲ Blind Pass, between Sanibel & Captiva islands

and suntan-seekers, it offers showers and a shady picnic spot, along with spectacular sunsets, though you won't find much shade on the beach itself.

Captiva Island

Immediately north of Bowman's Beach, Sanibel-Captiva Road becomes Captiva Drive as it crosses Blind Pass by bridge and reaches **CAPTIVA ISLAND**, markedly less developed than Sanibel and inhabited year-round by only a few hundred people. It makes for a pleasant day-trip, especially if you stay to enjoy the sunset: unlike Sanibel, Captiva faces due west on its Gulf side. It lacks the bike paths of Sanibel, and narrow streets make riding risky, so you're best off driving here.

The beach can be accessed at two principal parking lots; just beyond the bridge from Sanibel, and at the other end of Captiva Drive, where the public road terminates at the *South Seas Island Resort*. Besides the few attractive restaurants and beaches, the sole site of note is the tiny, inter-denominational **Chapel-by-the-Sea**, at 11580 Chapin Lane (down Wiles Drive). Often used for weddings, the chapel, built in 1904, is open most days mid–November to mid-April from 9am to 5pm. Don't miss the nearby **cemetery**, an unusual and historic spot where many of the island's original settlers are buried. Half a mile further north, Captiva's tip is covered by the picturesque golf course, eighteen pools and tennis courts, multiple restaurants, and Polynesian-style villas of the ultra-posh *South Seas Island Resort* (☎239/472-5111, ⓦ www.southseas.com), where it's hard to find a bed for less than $200, even in low season. You can also catch a **boat trip** here to the neighboring islands (see box, p.262).

Eating and drinking

The islands' isolation offers a relaxing **eating** and **drinking** experience, with shrimp and grouper, among other seafood options, the islands' specialties. You'll find restaurants all over Sanibel, while Captiva has fewer haunts, and most are clustered near the island's northern end. As for nightlife, don't expect to find a wild scene – young locals head to Fort Myers and Fort Myers Beach for that.

Boat and kayak trips from Captiva Island

Organized **boat trips** by Captiva Cruises (daily 8am–5pm; ☏239/472-5300, ⓦwww
.captivacruises.com) leave from either the docks of the *South Seas Island Resort*, or
from **McCarthy's Marina** on the bay side of Andy Rosse Lane. The trips on offer
include dolphin spotting, sunset serenade, and shelling trips (to North Captiva or
Cayo Costa), but the best of them is the lunch cruise, departing at 10am and
returning at 3pm, allowing two hours ashore on either Cabbage Key (see opposite)
or the private Useppa Island, home to the gourmet *Collier* Inn and a more casual,
seasonally open bar-restaurant; cost is $35. The price does not include food while
ashore – there's no obligation to eat once you land, but taking your own food on the
boat isn't allowed. Another option, offered seasonally only, is the six-hour trip to the
seaside village of Boca Grande on Gasparilla Island for $45. Whenever you sail,
you're likely to see **dolphins**.

Captiva Kayaks (daily 9am–5pm; ☏239/395-2925, ⓦwww.captivakayaks.com)
rents **kayaks** and organizes tours from McCarthy's Marina.

Restaurants:

Sanibel

Amy's Over Easy Cafe 630-1 Tarpon Bay Rd
☏239/472-2625, ⓦwww.overeasycafesanibel
.com. Feast on breakfast – served all day – in this
brightly colored, amiable diner. Try the Egg Reuben
sandwich on a bagel ($7.95) or the Gulf shrimp,
tomato, and cheese omelet ($9.50).

🏃 **Lazy Flamingo** 1036 Periwinkle Way
☏239/472-693, ⓦwww.lazyflamingo.com.
Popular, moderately priced raw bar and seafood
grill with a nautical theme and two Sanibel
locations (this one is more central).

Lighthouse Café 362 Periwinkle Way
☏239/472-0303, ⓦwww.lighthousecafe.com. Tuck
into breakfast or lunch in a diner-like setting, with
tasty dishes like the red-sauce frittata ($8.95) and
turkey Benedict ($8.95). Dinner runs the gamut from
burgers and steak to seafood and pasta ($7–15).

Matzaluna 1200 Periwinkle Way ☏239/472-1998.
A reasonably priced Italian restaurant, where you
can fill up on pasta, pizza, or classics like veal
marsala ($18.95) and chicken cacciatore ($15.95).

Sanibel Bean 2240-B Periwinkle Way ☏239/395-
1919, ⓦwww.sanibelbean.com. Cozy café for coffee
and light food – bagels, salads, and sandwiches.

Sanibel Steakhouse 1473 Periwinkle Way
☏239/472-5700, ⓦwww.thesanibelsteakhouse
.com. One of the few restaurants catering to meat-
eaters; it isn't cheap (steaks start at $32), but you
can top your slab with home-made steak sauces.

Captiva

Bubble Room 15001 Captiva Drive ☏239/472-
5558, ⓦwww.bubbleroomrestaurant.com. "Bubble
scouts," complete with uniforms, take your order at
this campy restaurant. Portions are huge, with such

creative dishes as the appetizer "carolina moons"
(home-made potato chips, topped with melted
cheese and bacon). Dinner entrées $20 and up.

Keylime Bistro 11509 Andy Rosse Lane, Captiva
☏239/395-4000. Daily live entertainment and a
cheerful atmosphere accompany the fresh seafood-
and pasta-heavy menu. Good selection of specialty
cocktails and a Sunday jazz brunch. Entrées $19–26.

🏃 **Mucky Duck** 11546 Andy Rosse Lane,
Captiva ☏239/472-3434, ⓦwww
.muckyduck.com. This prime sunset-watching spot
serves an affordable lunch ($5–13) but gets pricier
at dinner ($20–30). The menu is heavy on seafood,
with specials including fish cakes and fried grouper
fingers, but also has steak, chicken, and roasted
duck. Save room for the Key lime pie ($5). The
English-themed bar serves fourteen beers on draft
($3.49) and pints of margarita ($5.29). Closed Sun.

Bars

🏃 **Doc Ford's Sanibel Rum Bar & Grille** 975
Rabbit Rd, Sanibel ☏239/472-8311,
ⓦwww.docfordssanibel.com. This friendly sports
bar sits near the Wildlife Refuge. The rum bar
boasts more than 40 varieties, and the excellent,
tropical-inspired lunch and dinner dishes include
"spicy shake & shuck shrimp" and "Campeche"
(grilled) fish tacos. Open until 1am.

The Jac Bar 1223 Periwinkle Way, Sanibel
☏239/472-1771. The livelier side of the *Jacaranda*
restaurant, this bar attracts a slightly older crowd
with live music (jazz, reggae, Top 40, or classic
rock) every night and an appealing open-air feel,
thanks to the adjacent patio.

McT's Shrimp House & Tavern 1523 Periwinkle
Way, Sanibel ☏239/472-3161. Locals flock here to
lift a few lagers; the excellent restaurant specializes in shrimp prepared fifteen different ways.

Beyond Captiva Island: Cabbage Key

Of a number of small islands just north of Captiva, **Cabbage Key** is the one to visit. Even if you arrive on the lunch cruise from Captiva (see box opposite), skip the unexciting food in favor of prowling the footpaths and small marina: there's a special beauty to the isolated setting and the panoramic views across Pine Island Sound. Take a peek into the **restaurant and bar** of the *Cabbage Key Inn* to see an estimated $30,000 worth of dollar bills, each one signed by the person who pinned it up. The lunchtime menu is reasonable, but if you're planning to stay for dinner expect to pay at least $120 (for two). In case you get the urge **to stay** longer, the inn offers six simple rooms for $119 a night in season and seven rustic one- to three-bedroom cottages starting at $150; reserve at least a month in advance (☎239/283-2278, ⓦwww.cabbagekey.com).

South of Fort Myers

While Sanibel and Captiva islands warrant a few days of exploration, there's less to keep you occupied on the mainland on the seventy-mile journey **south of Fort Myers** towards Naples. The towns you'll pass through aren't as appealing as the nearby beaches or the interesting vistas of Florida's interior. Set aside a few hours, however, to examine one of the stranger footnotes to Florida's history: the oddball religious community of the Koreshans.

The Koreshan State Historic Site

One of the most bizarre episodes in Florida history opened in 1894, when followers of a new faith, Koreshanity, came from Chicago to establish their "New Jerusalem" 22 miles from Fort Myers. The Koreshans are long gone, but you can learn more about their Utopian beliefs by exploring their quixotic former settlement, preserved today as the tranquil **Koreshan State Historic Site**, just south of Estero beside US-41 (daily 8am–sunset; cars $3 for one person, $4 for two or more, pedestrians and cyclists $1; ☎239/992-0311, ⓦwww.floridastateparks.org/koreshan).

The flamboyant leader of the Koreshans, **Cyrus Teed**, believed that the entire universe existed within a giant, hollow sphere (he later changed his name to "Koresh," which is Hebrew for Cyrus and means "the anointed of God"). Among the other tenets of Koreshanity were celibacy outside marriage, shared ownership of goods, and gender equality. The aesthetes who came to this desolate outpost, accessible only by boat along the alligator-infested Estero River, quickly learned new skills in farming and house building, and marked out thirty-foot-wide boulevards, which they believed would one day be the arteries of a city inhabited by ten million enlightened souls. In fact, at its peak in 1907, the community numbered just two hundred. After Teed's death in 1908, the Koreshans fizzled out, with the last real member – who arrived in 1940, fleeing Nazi Germany – dying in 1982.

Along the crushed shell paths of the site, several of the Koreshan buildings have been restored, including Teed's 1896 home (also known as the Founder's House), where exhibits and a video help put the site into context, and the Planetary Court (1904), meeting place of the seven women – each named for one of the seven known planets – who governed the community. You can take ranger-led tours on weekend mornings (10am; 1hr–1hr 30min; $2), and there are sixty campsites in the pinelands along the river for $22 a night.

Corkscrew Swamp Sanctuary

Head fifteen miles **inland** on Rte-846 (branching from US-41 a few miles south of Bonita Springs) and you'll get a real contrast to coastal Florida at the National Audubon Society's **Corkscrew Swamp Sanctuary**, 375 Sanctuary Rd, Naples (Oct to mid-April daily 7am–5.30pm; mid-April to Sept 7am–7.30pm; $10; ☎239/348-9151, ⓦwww.corkscrew.audubon.org). Here you'll find a well-maintained 2.25-mile **boardwalk trail** through the largest stand of virgin bald cypress trees in North America. The trees loom amid a dark and moody swamp landscape of pine flatwood, wet prairie, and sawgrass ponds. Much of the surrounding area – presently safeguarded by the Big Cypress National Preserve (see "The Everglades," p.169) – used to look like this; however, uncontrolled logging felled the 500-year-old trees, partly for war efforts, and severely reduced Florida's population of wood stork, which nest a hundred feet up in the treetops. The remaining wood stork colony is still the largest in the country, but now faces the threat of falling water levels and never-ending development. Look out also for river otters, white-tailed deer, anhinga birds, herons, alligators, red-shouldered hawks, and black bears (in summer).

You'll find one of the park's unique features near the restrooms. Here, a remarkably simple "living machine" aids water management in the park by recycling waste from the restrooms to produce purified water. Within a visually pleasing, plant-filled greenhouse, the cycle relies on sunlight, bacteria, algae, and snails to break down the waste, a process later continued by vegetation, small insects, and animals.

Naples

Like the rest of South Florida, it's easy to forget **NAPLES** was a frontier town little more than a hundred years ago. The first trading posts appeared in the 1870s, followed by the first hotel in 1889, and when millionaire Barron Collier (see p.179) bought most of the town in the 1920s Naples had become a winter resort for the rich and famous. The area remained a sleepy outpost until the 1950s, when condominium development began in earnest. Thirty-six miles south of Fort Myers, Naples is still cushioned in wealth. On lazy summer days, the most action in town is from the sprinklers spraying obsessively manicured lawns. While the city has its fair share of wealthy retirees, it's surprisingly accessible, more diverse, and less snobby than you might expect; the beaches are magnificent, and away from the Gulf coastline, the town itself has plenty to amuse you.

Arrival and information

Greyhound **buses** (☎239/774-5660) stop in Naples at 2669 Davis Blvd, but the city is very spread out and best explored by car. Downtown, the beaches and most sights are easily accessible from US-41 (Tamiami Trail), though the fastest route from Miami and the east coast is I-75, which bypasses Naples around four miles east of US-41. The nearest Amtrak **bus** connection and **airport** are at Fort Myers (see p.250).

For **information**, head to the plush **Visitor Information Center**, 2390 Tamiami Trail North (Mon–Sat 9am–5pm; ☎239/262-6141, ⓦwww .napleschamber.org), one of the best stocked in the state; they also offer

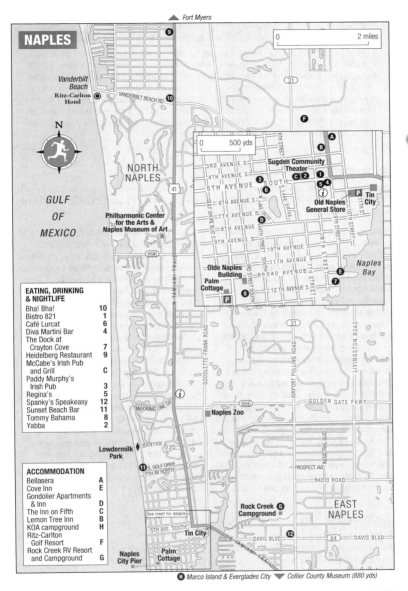

NAPLES

Fort Myers

0 ——— 2 miles

Vanderbilt
Beach
Ritz-Carlton
Hotel

VANDERBILT BEACH RD

N

GULF

OF

MEXICO

NORTH
NAPLES

0 ——— 500 yds

3RD AVENUE S
4TH AVENUE S
5TH AVENUE SOUTH
6TH AVENUE S
7TH AVENUE S
8TH AVENUE S
9TH AVENUE S

Sugden Community
Theater

Old Naples
General Store

Tin
City

Philharmonic Center
for the Arts &
Naples Museum of Art

GULF SHORE BLVD

LAKE DRIVE

Olde Naples
Building
Palm
Cottage

10TH AVENUE
11TH AVENUE
BROAD AVENUE S
12 TH AVENUE S

Naples
Bay

TAMIAMI TRAIL

GOODLETTE-FRANK ROAD

AIRPORT PULLING ROAD

LIVINGSTON ROAD

GOLDEN GATE PKWY

MOORING LINE DR

Naples Zoo

**EATING, DRINKING
& NIGHTLIFE**

Bha! Bha!	10
Bistro 821	1
Café Lurcat	6
Diva Martini Bar	4
The Dock at Crayton Cove	7
Heidelberg Restaurant	9
McCabe's Irish Pub and Grill	C
Paddy Murphy's Irish Pub	3
Regina's	5
Spanky's Speakeasy	12
Sunset Beach Bar	11
Tommy Bahama	8
Yabba	2

ACCOMMODATION

Bellasera	A
Cove Inn	E
Gondolier Apartments & Inn	D
The Inn on Fifth	C
Lemon Tree Inn	B
KOA campground	H
Ritz-Carlton Golf Resort	F
Rock Creek RV Resort and Campground	G

Lowdermilk
Park

BANYAN BLVD

S. GOLF DRIVE
7TH AVE NORTH

PROSPECT AVE

RADIO ROAD

INDUSTRIAL BLVD

EAST
NAPLES

See inset for details

5TH AVE. SOUTH

Rock Creek
Campground

Tin City

DAVIS BLVD

E TAMIAMI TRAIL

Naples
City Pier

Palm
Cottage

Marco Island & Everglades City ▼ Collier County Museum (880 yds)

complimentary use of high-speed computers. The trolley bus (see p.268)
stops here, and you'll find information on various boat, manatee and
Everglades tours (see box, p.266). In downtown, the smaller **Downtown
Information Center** at 800 5th Ave S (Mon–Sat 9am–5pm, Sat 10am–2pm
in summer; ☏239/435-3741) is also very helpful – the entrance is on 8th
Street, just south of 5th Avenue.

Getting to the Everglades from Naples

There's no public transport to the Everglades (see p.169), so if you don't have a car, a good option is to take a day-trip from Naples or Marco Island (see p.269). **Everglades Excursions** (☏239/262-1914 or 1-800/592-0848, ⓦ www.everglades -excursions.com), runs full- and half-day tours that include guided safari transportation, a jungle cruise and an airboat ride through Everglades National Park, and a tour of Everglades City. Half-day tours cost $79; full-day $119, including lunch. You can usually find discount coupons of up to $5 in the tourist booklets at the Visitor Center (see p.264). See also the trolley tour box, p.268.

Accommodation

As always, accommodation is more expensive the closer you get to the beach, but you'll find plenty of cheaper motels on US-41, and excellent bargains everywhere in the summer.

Bellasera 221 Ninth St S ☏239/649-7333 or 1-888/612-1115, ⓦ www.sunstream.com. Centrally located, romantic resort hotel with Italianate architecture, a fitness center, an attractive pool and courtyard, and a popular Mediterranean restaurant and lounge. ❻

Cove Inn on Naples Bay 900 Broad Ave S ☏239/262-7161 or 1-800/255-4365, ⓦ www .coveinnnaples.com. This comfortable inn is a condo-hotel, so each room is decorated a bit differently according to the owner's individual taste – although all feature private balconies and are convenient for walking everywhere in Old Naples. ❼

Gondolier Apartments & Inn 407 8th Ave S ☏239/262-4858, ⓦ www.gondolierinn.com. Dated but well-maintained studio and one-bedroom efficiencies lack phones but offer good value otherwise, and are central to both downtown areas. ❻

The Inn on Fifth 699 Fifth Ave S ☏239/403-8777 or 1-888/403-8778, ⓦ www.innonfifth.com. This Mediterranean-style boutique hotel on Naples' main drag fits right in with the subdued wealth and chic stores. Well-appointed rooms all have terraces. ❽

Lemon Tree Inn 250 Ninth St S ☏239/262-1414 or 1-888/800-LEMO, ⓦ www.lemontreeinn.com. This homey inn offers a complimentary continental breakfast and lemonade in the lobby, plus a pool and garden. ❺

Naples KOA 1700 Barefoot Williams Rd ☏239/774-5455 or 1-800/562-7734, ⓦ www .napleskoa.com. You can pitch a tent at this place, the nearest campground to the city, for $57 a night in peak season or rent a rustic cabin for $82.

Ritz-Carlton Golf Resort 2600 Tiburon Drive ☏239/593-2000, ⓦ www.ritzcarlton.com. Similar to Naples' other *Ritz-Carlton* (which is on the beach), but cheaper and a bit more low-key, with lusher grounds and a cordial staff. All the amenities you could possibly think of (for a price). Check for off-season specials. ❼

Rock Creek RV Resort & Campground 3100 North Rd ☏239/643-3100, ⓦ www.rockcreekrv .com. Lush campground three miles from the beach, just east of downtown Naples. Extras include hot showers and a heated pool, but it's primarily geared towards RVs ($50 per day in peak season).

Downtown

Downtown Naples is split by opulent Fifth Avenue S running east–west, with its high-end clothes shops, boutique hotels, and restaurants. You can park anywhere along the street (free), but get here early to secure a space. Look out for the **Sugden Community Theater** (box office ☏239/263-7990), tucked away between the glitzy shops at no. 701, home of the well-regarded **Naples Players** (ⓦ www.naplesplayers.com); check the website for upcoming shows, which can be anything from musicals and comedies to more serious plays.

Just a few blocks away, at the end of Sixth Avenue S, are the unique shops and restaurants of the colorful **Tin City** complex (Mon–Sat 10am–9pm, Sun noon–5pm), a former 1920s clam shelling and oyster processing plant. While here, pop in for complimentary tropical fruit wine tastings at The Naples Winery (☏239/732-9463, ⓦ www.thenapleswinery.com – try the Mango

Mamma). Fishing tours (half day $75) and sightseeing and sunset cruises of the bay ($30 for 1.5hr) depart from the river here (℡239/263-4949, Ⓦwww .tincityboats.com). Dolphin sightings are fairly common. Leave your car in the Tin City Park-n-Walk Lot on Sixth Avenue (free).

The second main downtown area to explore lies seven blocks south along Third Street S (between Broad and 14th aves), where you'll find yet more shopping, cafés, and Gallery Row (a concentration of art galleries along Broad Ave). Look out for the **Olde Naples Building**, 1148 Third St (on the corner of Broad Ave), which, since its construction in 1922, has been everything to Naples – its first town hall, a courthouse, drugstore, movie theater, community church, tap dance school, and most recently a café (at the time of writing it remained empty).

A block away at 137 12th Ave S, the 1895 **Palm Cottage** is the oldest house in town and one of the few houses left in Florida built of tabby mortar (made by burning seashells). Once the home of Walter N. Haldeman, who built the first hotel in Naples, it's now owned by the historical society. To see the beautifully preserved interior, take a guided tour (May–Oct Wed & Sat 1–4pm; Nov–April Tues–Sat 1–4pm; $8 donation; ℡239/261-8164, Ⓦwww.naples historicalsociety.org). You can also pick up walking tours of the neighborhood here (May–Oct first Wed of the month 10am; Nov–April Wed 10am; $15).

You can park on the street outside Palm Cottage, or in the parking lot opposite, which serves historic **Naples City Pier**, one block away (both options 25¢ for 15min). Started in 1888 as a passenger dock, the pier has been rebuilt many times, and the latest incarnation dates from 1960. Unusually, you can fish here without a license, but it's also a popular place to watch the sunset and access the beach.

Beaches

Stretching north from Naples City Pier are eleven miles of gorgeous public **beaches**, though as ever, the condo-lined shore means access can be tricky. The most gregarious of the local sands, especially on weekends, is **Lowdermilk**

▲ Tin City shopping district

5

Park, off Gulf Shore Boulevard N, about one mile from US-41 and two miles north of the pier; extras include two beach volleyball courts and a handful of resident ducks in the pond opposite. Most of the **parking** lot is reserved for residents so make sure you park in the visitor section and pay at the machine (25¢ for 15min).

To ogle the fruits of Naples' wealth, head north up US-41 to **Vanderbilt Beach** and the *Ritz-Carlton Hotel* (☎239/598-3300, ⓦwww.ritzcarlton.com) at the end of Vanderbilt Beach Road. While you'd need around $5000 for a night in the presidential suite, sweeping through the grand entrance for a coffee at the bar is an inexpensive way to appreciate the hotel's towering splendor. The building looks like a 1930s vision of classical decadence, but it actually appeared in the late 1980s. You'll have to park valet at the hotel ($5 a day), while the parking garage for the beach (just beyond the Ritz entrance), is $6 a day.

Philharmonic Center for the Arts and Naples Museum of Art

Enjoy Naples' growing cultural arts scene at the **Philharmonic Center for the Arts**, 5833 Pelican Bay Blvd (☎239/597-1900 or 1-800/597-1900, ⓦwww .thephil.org), with an orchestra hall, a black box theater, and several art galleries; programs run the gamut from Broadway to Beethoven, and events include film screenings and music lectures. Here you'll also find the **Naples Museum of Art** (Tues–Sat 10am–4pm, Sun noon–4pm; closed July–Oct; $8, $12 Feb–April; ☎239/597-1900), a three-story museum with rotating national and international exhibits and a permanent collection including American Modernists (Alfred Stieglitz, Stuart Davis) and 20th-century Mexican masters (Diego Rivera, Rufino Tamayo). Don't miss the Persian ceiling and spectacular chandeliers by glass artist Dale Chihuly. You can eat under one of them in the *Garden Café*, which has indoor and outdoor seating and serves salads, quiche, and sandwiches.

Collier County Museum

The sprawling Naples suburbs east of US-41 hold little interest, but the **Collier County Museum**, 3301 E Tamiami Trail (Mon–Fri 9am–5pm, Sat 9am–4pm; free; ☎239/252-8476), is definitely worth seeking out. The small but well-presented exhibition room covers local events from prehistory to World War II, with particular attention paid to Seminole history, and the arrival of advertising magnate and founding father Barron Gift Collier in 1911. Outside, the tranquil gardens contain an eclectic assortment of exhibits, including a Sherman tank, steam engine and reproduction of a Seminole village. The museum is tucked away behind the county government center just off US-41 at Airport Pulling Road, east of downtown Naples.

Eating and drinking

There's a welcome lack of the usual fast-food chains in Naples. Even the food in casual restaurants is done well here, though not surprisingly, it's often more expensive than elsewhere in the state. To dine at the nicer spots without blowing your budget, keep your eyes open for early bird and prix-fixe specials.

Restaurants

Bha! Bha! 847 Vanderbilt Beach Rd, Pavilion Shopping Mall, ☏239/594-5557, ⓦwww .bhabhapersianbistro.com. Classical and new Persian cuisine, with most dishes around $20–25 and occasional live music and belly dancing. Try the delicious lamb *bademjune*, in a tomato and lemon sauce, with grilled vegetables, sautéed eggplant, and sour grapes.

Bistro 821 821 Fifth Ave S ☏239/261-5821, ⓦwww.bistro821.com. Local favorite offering Italian-, French- and Asian-inspired entrées, from seafood risotto ($15.95–28.95) to bouillabaisse ($31.95) to coconut, ginger and lemongrass-encrusted snapper ($29.95). Dinner only (happy hour 5–7pm).

Café Lurcat 494 Fifth Ave S ☏239/213-3357, ⓦwww.cafelurcat.com. Romantic, two-story Spanish Revival building, with fine American cuisine (try the well-priced early bird menu) and a lighter downstairs bar menu of small plates like the popular Lurcat burger ($7.50), yellowtail snapper sashimi ($9.75), and warm cinnamon-sugar doughnuts ($6).

The Dock at Crayton Cove 845 Twelfth Ave S ☏239/263-9940, ⓦwww.dockcraytoncove.com. Next to the Naples City Dock, this casual, open-air restaurant overlooks the bay and features fresh fish ($22–30) – it's a prime spot for grouper and fries ($20.95) and a tropical rum cocktail.

Heidelberg Restaurant 10711 Tamiami Trail N ☏239/592-7900. An Old-World German-style restaurant, where you can expect to find *sauerbraten* and plenty of meat on the menu.

McCabe's Irish Pub and Grill 699 Fifth Ave S ☏239/403-7170, ⓦwww.mccabesirishpub.com. Seafood grills ($15–22.95) alongside breakfasts, traditional Irish food and ale, pub standards and pizza ($11–14), and live Irish entertainment attract a young crowd. Free wi-fi.

Regina's 824 Fifth Ave S ☏239/434-8181. Old-fashioned ice cream parlor, selling sundaes, home-made ice cream and frozen custard from $3.69 a scoop.

Spanky's Speakeasy 1550 Airport Pulling Rd ☏239/643-1559, ⓦwww.spankysnaples.com. Worth seeking out for its unique old-America atmosphere, complete with a 1924 Model T truck and antiques in every nook and cranny. Try the fried fish sandwich ($10) or the Louisiana barbecue shrimp ($16).

Tommy Bahama 1220 Third St S ☏239/262-5500. You'll always find a crowd at this tropical café which has a large outdoor patio and sits between the Tommy Bahama clothing stores. Enjoy sandwiches, salads, and grilled seafood, washed down with a glass of wine or two.

Bars

Diva Martini Bar at *Mangrove Café*, 878 Fifth Ave S ☏239/262-7076. Once the seafood dishes are cleared away, this space turns into a dance club with DJ Top 40 and hip-hop music. Fri and Sat, 10.30pm–2am; between Christmas and Easter, also open Wed and Thurs nights.

Paddy Murphy's Irish Pub 457 Fifth Ave S ☏239/649-5140, ⓦwww.paddymurphys.com. Staff from the local bars and restaurants descend on this pub for a drink when it's quitting time. Listen to live music (usually Irish earlier in the night) seven nights a week; they serve food until 1am and close at 2am (midnight on Sun).

Sunset Beach Bar at *Naples Beach Hotel & Golf Club*, 851 Gulf Shore Blvd N ☏239/261-2222 ext 2938. Casual pool- and Gulf-side bar also open to non-guests of the hotel, and the best spot to sip tequila while watching the sunset. Serves lunch and light dinner fare, with daily live music. Park in the *Broadwell's* lot across the street, and follow signs to *HBs on the Gulf*.

Yabba 711 Fifth Ave S ☏239/262-5787. The tables are moved aside at this yummy Caribbean grill after 10.30pm on Fri and Sat nights to make way for a DJ, dancefloor, and the young crowd that works it.

Marco Island

Home to several ritzy beach resorts and a largely residential community of palm-lined boulevards, **MARCO ISLAND** (about twenty miles south of Naples; take US-41 to Rte-951) makes a pleasant detour if you need a break from the crowds elsewhere. To avoid driving in circles, stop at the **Chamber of**

Commerce, 1102 N Collier Blvd (Mon–Fri 9am–5pm, ☎239/34-7549, ⓦwww.marcoislandchamber.org) and pick up a map.

Long before white settlers arrived here in the 1870s, Marco Island was an important Calusa settlement, and in 1896 archeologists unearthed one of the most sensational caches of wooden artifacts ever found in North America – the most famous being a six-inch wooden panther-like figure, dubbed the **Key Marco Cat** (dating from 500–800 AD), and now housed in the Smithsonian Museum (Washington, DC) The local historical society is currently raising money for a flashy new museum near the library, which it hopes will convince the Smithsonian to return the cat; until then, you can check out a replica along with Calusa shell tools, masks, necklaces and exhibits at the tiny **Key Marco Museum** (Mon–Fri 9am–4pm; free; ☎239/394-6917, ⓦwww.themihs.org), awkwardly located in the lobby of a local realtors at 140 Waterway Drive (at the corner of Bald Eagle Drive), and its twin, the **Museum at Old Marco** (daily 7am–7pm; free), a small second-floor room next to the *Old Marco Inn* at the shops on Royal Palm Drive (take Bald Eagle Drive to the northern end and turn left).

The whole western edge of Marco Island is lined with brilliant white crushed-shell beaches, though access can be an issue. The best spot is **Tigertail Beach Park** (daily 8am–sunset; $6 to park; ☎239/591-8596) on Hernando Drive (accessed from Kendall Drive off Collier Boulevard).

Eating and drinking

Sand Bar 826 E Elkcam Circle ☎239/642-3625. No-frills local bar that doubles as a relatively cheap place to eat; try the eggs and bacon ($4.25) for breakfast, or massive steakburgers ($6.95) and fish platters ($9.95) for lunch or dinner.

Snook Inn 1215 Bald Eagle Drive ☎239/394-3313, ⓦwww.snookinn.com. Another good bet for lunch or dinner, this local seafood-and-steak institution in the north of the island boasts an enticing waterside location on the Marco River (look out for pelicans and dolphins). Try the grouper sandwiches ($13) or excellent broiled seafood combo ($13).

Stan's Idle Hour 221 Goodland Drive ☎239/394-3041, ⓦwww.stansidlehour.net. Located in Goodland, a fishing village at the eastern end of the

island (south off San Marco Rd), this ramshackle fish shack – one of many in the area – serves fresh seafood in baskets or sandwiches and features live music most nights, as well as a dance known as "buzzard lope", invented by the restaurant's wacky owner. Seafood entrées range $14.95 to $19.95. Closed in Sept.

Susie's Diner 1013 N Collier Blvd (Marco Town Center Mall) ☎239/642-6633. The old-style diner is one of the best options for breakfast or lunch, offering a vast menu of staples, including excellent waffles and French toast (from $6.95), while the grouper Reuben is one of the best sandwiches on the coast ($9.95). Usually closes at 2pm.

Travel details

Fort Myers to: Fort Lauderdale (3 daily; 3hr); Miami (3 daily; 4hr); Naples (3 daily; 1hr); Orlando (5 daily; 6hr–8hr 40min); Sarasota (4 daily; 1hr 45min–2hr 15min); Tampa (4 daily; 3hr 35min–4hr 5min).

Sarasota to: Fort Lauderdale (3 daily; 5hr 15min–5hr 25min); Ft Myers (4 daily; 1hr 45min–2hr 15min); Miami (3 daily; 6hr 10min–6hr 25min); Orlando (4 daily; 3hr 45min–4hr 40min); Tampa (4 daily; 1hr 40min–1hr 50min).

Orlando and Disney World

CHAPTER 6 **Highlights**

✱ **Downtown Orlando nightlife**
Hop from grungy bars to wine
bars to lively clubs in one of
Florida's after-dark hot spots.
See p.284

✱ **Blizzard Beach**
Demonstrating it can work its
magic in all domains, Disney
has created this excellent
water park to provide a break
from trudging around the
theme parks. See p.297

✱ **Islands of Adventure** The
rides don't get more thrilling
than here. See p.303

✱ **Gatorland** Watch the
alligators being fed
– or wrestled – at this less
heralded theme park between
Orlando and Kissimmee.
See p.309

✱ **Celebration** An easy day-
trip from Orlando, this essay
in urban planning – if not
incredibly compelling in itself
– has provoked a storm of
controversy. See p.311

✱ **Cassadaga** This spiritualists'
village deep in the forest is
just about as far from the
classic Orlando vacation
experience as you can get.
See p.316

✱ **Blue Spring State Park** The
St John's River, which runs
through the park, is a prime
place to spot manatees.
See p.318

▲ The Kraken rollercoaster at SeaWorld Orlando

6

Orlando and Disney World

I t's highly ironic that **Orlando**, an insubstantial, quiet farming town in the heart of peninsular Florida a little over thirty years ago, now has more people passing through its environs than any other place in the state. Reminders of the old Florida are still easy to find in and immediately north of Orlando. Most people, however, get no closer to Orlando's heart than a string of cheap hotels along US-192, just south of Walt Disney World, or **International Drive**, five miles southwest of downtown Orlando: a long boulevard of chain hotels, more upmarket establishments used by convention-goers, shopping malls, and schmaltzy restaurants.

The cause of the area's transformation is, of course, **Walt Disney World**, a group of state-of-the-art theme parks southwest of central Orlando that lure millions of people a year to a 43-square-mile plot of previously featureless scrubland. It's possible to pass through the Orlando area and not visit Walt Disney World, but there's no way to escape its impact – even the road system was reshaped to accommodate the place, and, whichever way you look, billboards tout multiple ways to spend your money there. Amid a plethora of fly-by-night, would-be tourist targets, only **Universal Orlando** and **SeaWorld Orlando** offer serious competition to the most finely realized concept in escapist entertainment anywhere on earth.

Orlando's tentacles have wrapped themselves firmly around much of what lies **south of Orlando**, especially the seemingly perfect, Disney-like town of **Celebration**. Venture a few miles **north of Orlando**, however, and the "real world" starts to reassert itself, albeit very gently, in the form of a quaint Victorian-era town called **Mount Dora** and the hidden village of **Cassadaga**, populated almost entirely by spiritualists.

Arrival and information

The region's primary **airport**, **Orlando International** (☎407/825-2001, ⓦwww.orlandoairports.net), is nine miles southeast of downtown Orlando. Shuttle buses will carry you from the airport to any hotel or motel in the Orlando area. The flat rate from the airport to downtown Orlando is $16; to

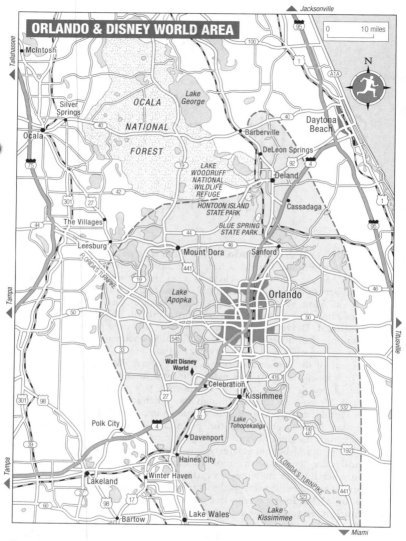

International Drive it's $17; and to Lake Buena Vista or US-192, the fare is $19. Mears Transportation (☎407/423-5566, ⓦwww.mearstransportation .com) is one of the largest and most reliable shuttle bus operators. For those staying at Walt Disney World, **Disney's Magical Express Transportation** (reservations: ☎1-866/599-0951) provides a free transfer from the airport to your hotel and vice versa. Upon arrival at the airport, make your way to the Disney Welcome Center on Level 1 of the airport's Main Terminal (on the "B Side" concourse). Lynx Buses, which serve Orlando and surrounding areas, link the airport with downtown Orlando (#11 or #51, both about a 45-minute journey) and International Drive (#42, around 60 minutes).

Orlando area orientation: the major roads

The major cross-Florida **roads** form a web-like mass of intersections in or around Orlando and Walt Disney World: **I-4** passes southwest–northeast through Disney and continues in elevated form through downtown Orlando; **US-192** (the **Irlo Bronson Memorial Highway**) crosses I-4 just south of Disney and charts an east–west course through the towns of Kissimmee and St-Cloud; **Hwy-528** (the **Beeline Expressway**) stems from International Drive and heads for the east coast; and **Florida's Turnpike** (for which there is a toll) cuts northwest–southeast, avoiding Disney World and downtown Orlando altogether.

All buses depart from Level 1 (on the "A Side" concourse) every thirty minutes between 5am and 11.30pm for #11, 5.30am and 10.30pm for #51, and 6am to 10.30pm for #42. A taxi to downtown Orlando, International Drive, or the hotels on US-192 will cost from $30 to $60; Walt Disney World is $50 to $60.

A second airport, **Orlando Sanford International** (☏ 407/585-4000, ⓦ www.orlandosanfordairport.com), is a smaller facility twenty miles north of downtown Orlando that receives charter flights from the UK, as well as Allegiant Air (see p.22) flights from a selection of more obscure US cities, such as Bangor ME and South Bend IN. A taxi from Sanford to downtown Orlando costs about $55. A cheaper alternative is to take a taxi to the Seminole Center, a shopping center on the corner of US-17/92 and Lake Mary, and then catch Lynx #39 into downtown Orlando (every 30min from 5am–10.30pm; 70min).

Arriving by **bus**, you'll wind up near downtown Orlando at the Greyhound terminal, 555 N John Young Parkway (☏ 407/292-3424); take Lynx #25 (every 30min from 5.30–1.20am; 10min) into downtown. The Amtrak **train** station is one and a half miles south of downtown at 1400 Sligh Blvd (☏ 407/843-7611); take Lynx #40 (every hour from 5.30–1.20am; 10min) to downtown. If you're staying along US-192 in Kissimmee, consider going to the Kissimmee Greyhound terminal, 103 E Dankin Ave (☏ 407/847-3911) or the Kissimmee Amtrak station, 111 E Dankin Ave (☏ 407/933-1170), both of which provide easier access to the US-192 hotels than their Orlando counterparts.

Masses of brochures and magazines are available almost everywhere you look; leaf through them for the discount coupons. The best source of **information**, however, is the **Official Visitor Center**, 8723 International Drive (daily 8.30am–6.30pm; ☏ 407/363-5872 or 1-800/972-3304, ⓦ www .orlandoinfo.com), where you can pick up the free *Orlando Official Fun Guide*. Another useful acquisition is the Orlando Magicard (download it for free from the Official Visitor Center website), which gives savings at a range of attractions, accommodation, restaurants, and shops. The **Winter Park Welcome Center**, 151 W Lyman Ave (Mon–Fri 9am–5pm; ☏ 407/644-8281, ⓦ www.winterpark.org), has good local information and brochures not found at the Official Visitor Center. If you're using the hotels along US-192, drop by the equally well stocked **Kissimmee–St Cloud Convention & Visitors Bureau**, 1925 E US-192 in Kissimmee (Mon–Fri 8am–5pm; ☏ 407/944-2400 or 1-800/333-KISS, ⓦ www.floridakiss.com). The best entertainment guide to the area is the Friday "Calendar" section of the *Orlando Sentinel* newspaper.

Getting around

Local **Lynx buses** (☏ 407/841-5969, Ⓦ www.golynx.com) converge at the downtown Lynx Central Station, 455 N Garland Ave. Most routes operate from 6.30am to 8pm on weekdays, 7.30am to 6pm on Saturdays, and 8am to 6pm on Sundays (although some routes don't operate at all on Sundays). You'll need **exact change** ($1.75 one way; $4 day pass) if you pay on board; a weekly pass for $14 is available at the central station. The single fare includes a free transfer to another Lynx service, valid for travel within 90 minutes of the initial ticket purchase. Given the expanse of the network and the considerable journey times, you'll often be hard-pressed to catch your second bus before the ticket expires. The Lynx system comprises roughly 4000 stops in three counties, and the Official Visitor Center (see p.275) has a useful handout entitled *Using the Lynx Bus System*, which explains how to get to many points of interest by bus starting from International Drive. The **most useful bus routes** (from downtown Orlando) are #1 or #9 to Loch Haven Park and Winter Park; #11 or #51 to the airport; #8 or #38 (which has limited stops and takes just 20min) to International Drive – where you can connect with #42 to **Orlando International Airport** (an hour-long journey) – and #50 to Disney's The Magic Kingdom (limited stops; 40min journey time). The **I-Ride Trolley** (☏ 407/354-5656 or 1-866/243-7483, Ⓦ www.iridetrolley.com) serves all points along International Drive (including SeaWorld Orlando), operating roughly every twenty minutes daily from 8am to 10.30pm, and costing $1 one way (seniors 25¢); exact change is required, and children 12 and under ride free. One-day passes for unlimited travel are also available for $3.

Orlando **taxis** are expensive; rates begin at $3.25 for the first mile, plus $1.75 for each additional mile. For nondrivers, however, they're the most convenient way to get around at night – try Town & Country (☏ 407/828-3035), Star Taxi (☏ 407/857-9999), or Diamond Cab (☏ 407/523-3333).

Cheaper than taxis, but more expensive and quicker than local buses, are the **shuttle buses**, minivans, or coaches run by private companies connecting the main accommodation areas, such as International Drive and US-192, with Walt Disney World, SeaWorld Orlando, Universal Orlando, and other attractions. You should book at least a day in advance, and confirm a time for your return. Mears Transportation (see p.274) charges $14–16 for a round-trip ride from International Drive or US-192 to all the major attractions.

All the main **car rental** firms have offices at or close to Orlando International Airport. Demand is strong throughout the year despite the high rates (around $45 per day or $250 per week for a mid-sized car), so always try to book in advance (for phone numbers, see "Getting around" in Basics).

Orlando

Given the preponderance of Walt Disney World and its rival theme parks, it's easy to overlook the fact Orlando is an important city in its own right. The compact **downtown**, with a small but growing crop of high-rise buildings and smart residential neighborhoods, features several good museums and galleries, and the best nightlife in Central Florida – all providing a welcome change of pace from the theme parks. This said, most visitors haven't come to Orlando to sample more than an afternoon or two of its unheralded cultural refinement, and will inevitably gravitate southwest of the downtown area before too long

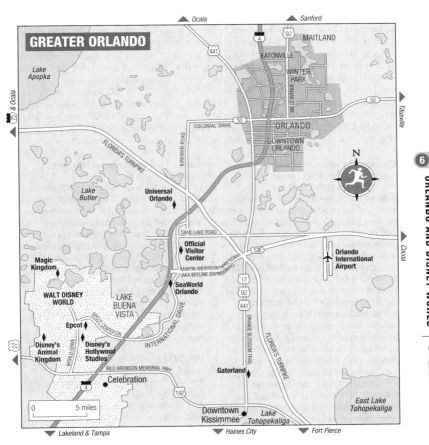

to join the fun and frolics at the parks. Here, along the strip of hotels, restaurants, shopping malls, and multitude of other tourist traps that is **International Drive**, the Orlando you had always expected rears its mouse-eared head, to the delight of kids and kids-at-heart.

Accommodation

In a sprawling city like Orlando, your choice of **accommodation** will be guided as much by location as by price. If you don't have your own transport, consider staying along or near International Drive, an area dominated by chain hotels, or in downtown Orlando, where you'll find a few privately owned hotels and bed and breakfasts – both areas have plenty of good local bus connections. You'll also find numerous hotels within Walt Disney World itself (see p.289), dotted around Disney property in an area called Lake Buena Vista (see p.289), and at Universal Orlando (see p.301). Budget hotels line US-192 (see p.311), just south of Disney, where you'll also find campgrounds and a hostel.

   Prices at the Disney and Universal resorts are generally the highest you'll pay, with some of the fancier places demanding in excess of $300 per night. The hotels in Lake Buena Vista, International Drive, and downtown Orlando tend to be mid-range, usually not costing more than $150. For the cheapest rates head to US-192, where you can get a room for around $50 per night.

If you have a car and are traveling in a group or with a family, an excellent – and economical – option is to **rent a villa**. Most agencies offer three- to seven-bedroom houses with their own pools, garages, kitchens, and washing machines, normally located in communities within a 30-minute drive of Orlando and Walt Disney World. Rates for a three-bedroom house typically start at around $110 per night. Orlando Vacation Rentals, 8815 Conroy Winder-mere Rd, Suite 311, Orlando, FL 32835 (☎407/297-8663 or 1-877/311-7368, ⓦwww.orlandovacationrentals.com), offers a particularly good selection.

Downtown Orlando

The Courtyard at Lake Lucerne 211 N Lucerne Circle E ☎407/648-5188, ⓦwww.orlandohistoricinn.com. A lush flower garden and four separate buildings, one of which is the oldest house in Orlando, comprise this peaceful oasis of grace and hospitality nestled right in the busy downtown area. The eclectic accommodations range from elegantly furnished Victorian- and Edwardian-era rooms to airy Art Deco suites. ❺
Eö Inn 227 N Eola Drive ☎407/481-8485 or 1-888/481-8488, ⓦwww.eoinn.com. Facing Lake Eola, this chic boutique hotel has stylish rooms with modern furnishings; some of the more expensive rooms have lake views. An onsite spa offers a full range of massages and facials, while the hot-tub on the rooftop terrace is another good place to unwind. Gay-friendly. ❺
Parliament House Resort 410 N Orange Blossom Trail, just east of downtown ☎407/425-7571, ⓦwww.parliamenthouse.com. A party atmosphere reigns at this well-known gay resort with its six clubs and bars, restaurant, pool, lakeside beach, and drag shows. The 130 simple, yet comfortable, renovated rooms are good value. ❸
Travelodge Orlando Downtown Centroplex 409 N Magnolia Ave ☎407/423-1671, ⓦwww.travelodgemagnolia.com. Inexpensive motel-style accommodation within walking distance of the Orange Ave bars and clubs, so reserve well in advance if staying Friday or Saturday nights. There's a tiny pool. ❷
Veranda Bed & Breakfast Inn 115 N Summerlin Ave ☎407/849-0321 or 1-800/420-6822, ⓦwww.theverandabandb.com. In the trendy Thornton Park neighborhood, one block from Lake Eola, this pretty, but slightly precious, ten-room bed and breakfast is housed in five period buildings nestled around a courtyard garden and swimming pool. ❺
Westin Grand Bohemian 325 S Orange Ave ☎407/313-9000 or 1-866/663-0024, ⓦwww.grandbohemianhotel.com. Downtown's most luxurious hotel is centrally located and has classy rooms decorated in soothing, earthy tones. Guests also have access to a heated outdoor pool and a fitness center. ❽

International Drive and around

Days Inn Maingate Universal Orlando 5827 Caravan Court ☎407/351-3800 or 1-800/327-2111, ⓦwww.orlandoflus.com. The rooms here are nothing fancy, but do sleep up to four. Kids under 12 also eat free if accompanied by a paying adult. The main advantage is that it's within walking distance of Universal Orlando. ❸
DoubleTree Castle Hotel 8629 International Drive ☎407/345-1511 or 1-800/952-2785, ⓦwww.doubletreecastle.com. Elaborate theme hotel, complete with Renaissance music and medieval

Hiking, biking, and picnicking

Just north of Universal Orlando, next to Florida's Turnpike, lies **Bill Frederick Park and Pool at Turkey Lake**, 3401 S Hiawassee Rd (daily: Nov–March 8am–5pm; April–Oct 8am–7pm; cars $4, pedestrians and cyclists free; ☎407/299-5581), a quiet place to have lunch by a lake, a swim in the pool, or let the kids run around a terrific playground. Five miles west of downtown Orlando off Hwy-50 (take Hwy-50 towards Clermont and look for the County Line Station on your right) is the start of the **West Orange Trail** (☎407/654-1108), nineteen miles of scenic, paved walkways that end in the town of Apopka. You can rent bikes at West Orange Trail Bikes and Blades, located along the trail at 17914 Hwy-438, Winter Garden (☎407/877-0600 or 1-888/281-3341, ⓦwww.orlandobikerental.com).

decor, such as suits of armor, with surprisingly understated rooms and free transportation to the theme parks. ❸

Imperial Swan Orlando 7050 S Kirkman Rd ☎407/351-2000 or 1-800/327-3808, ⓦwww .imperialswanorlando.com. Cheap, decently sized rooms, two pools, free shuttle buses to the theme parks, and an I-Ride Trolley stop nearby make this a good base for nondrivers on a tight budget. ❷

Renaissance Orlando Resort at SeaWorld 6677 Sea Harbor Drive ☎401/351-5555 or 1-800/327-6677. An upmarket hotel with spacious and comfortable rooms, a bright and airy atrium, an onsite spa, and a good location directly opposite SeaWorld Orlando. ❼

🏃 **Staybridge Suites International Drive** 8480 International Drive ☎407/352-2400

or 1-800/866-4549, ⓦwww.sborlando.com. This friendly and popular hotel has numerous shops and restaurants accessible by foot. The spacious one- and two-bedroom suites have well equipped kitchens and free internet access. A buffet breakfast and a thrice-weekly evening cocktail reception is also included. ❻

🏃 **Ritz-Carlton Orlando** 4040 Central Florida Parkway ☎407/206-2400 or 1-800/682-3665, ⓦwww.grandelakes.com. One of Orlando's most luxurious hotels, this elegant building with an intimate feel and superb rooms shares the 500-acre Grande Lakes Orlando – the hotel's landscaped grounds – with another excellent hotel (the *J.W. Marriott*) and a golf course. The immaculate facilities include several restaurants, a fitness center, and a full-service spa. ❽

Downtown Orlando

Orlando's sprawling and often unattractive layout is redeemed by its vibrant **downtown**, an area still largely ignored by visitors. Ongoing urban rejuvenation has led to an appealing mix of luxury condos, trendy restaurants, and excellent nightspots (see p.284), which, coupled with the fact that everything of consequence can be visited on foot within an hour, makes downtown an increasingly enticing area to explore.

Begin by dawdling along **Orange Avenue**, trawled by lunch-seeking office workers by day and revelers sampling its numerous bars and clubs at night. Sightseeing here is limited to one building of architectural interest: the late-1920s **First National Bank** building (now Valencia Community College) on the corner of Church Street. One block east of Orange Avenue on Heritage Square, you'll find the informative **Orange County Regional**

▲ Lake Eola, downtown Orlando

DOWNTOWN ORLANDO

EATING & DRINKING

Bravissimo Wine Bar & Café	4
Dexters of Thornton Park	7
Eola Wine Company	12
The Globe	8
HUE – A Restaurant	11
Independent Bar	6
Little Saigon	3
Numero Uno	13
Panera Bread	5
Pulse	14
Roxy	2
Shari Sushi	10
The Social	9
Tabu	9
White Wolf Café	1

ACCOMMODATION

The Courtyard at Lake Lucerne	F
Eö Inn	C
Parliament House Resort	B
Travelodge Orlando Downtown Centroplex	A
Veranda Bed & Breakfast Inn	D
Westin Grand Bohemian	E

History Center, housed in the restored 1927 Orange County Courthouse (Mon–Sat 10am–5pm, Sun noon–5pm; $9; T407/836-8500 or 1-800/965-2030, Wwww.thehistorycenter.org). Interactive exhibits trace the history of the area from 10,000 BC to the present day, but the most effective displays are the old photos and re-created hotel lobbies and grocers' stores which give a revealing glimpse of Orlando's pre-Disney days as the epitome of an American frontier town.

Some of the wooden homes built by Orlando's first white settlers in the mid-1800s stand next to fancy high-rise condos around scenic **Lake Eola**, a ten-minute walk east of Orange Avenue. Stroll the one-mile path skirting the lake, or get on the water by renting a paddleboat shaped like a swan for a pricey $12 per half-hour. The several streets on the eastern side of the lake comprise **Thornton Park**, a trendy, upmarket neighborhood full of hip restaurants and bustling coffee shops – a pleasant spot to relax in what feels like a village within the city.

Loch Haven Park

A large lawn wedged between two small lakes, **Loch Haven Park**, three miles north of downtown Orlando, contains several buildings of varying degrees of interest. The **Orlando Museum of Art**, 2416 N Mills Ave (Tues–Fri 10am–4pm, Sat & Sun noon–4pm; $8; ☏407/896-4231, ⓦwww.omart.org), is likely to take up at least an hour; permanent collections of recent and ancient American art and African artifacts back up the usually excellent temporary exhibitions of modern paintings, sculptures, and the like, culled from some of the finest collections in the world.

Children will enjoy roaming around the nearby **Orlando Science Center**, 777 E Princeton St (Mon–Fri & Sun 10am–6pm, Sat 10am–9pm; $17, children 3–11 $12; ☏407/514-2000 or 1-888/672-4386, ⓦwww.osc.org), a multi-level complex where plentiful interactive exhibits explain the fundamentals of many branches of science to formative minds. The main draw for adults is the CineDome, a huge cinema and planetarium, where documentary-style films (included in the ticket price) about various natural phenomena are shown daily.

Harry P. Leu Gardens

A green-thumbed Orlando businessman purchased the fifty-acre **Harry P. Leu Gardens**, a mile east of Loch Haven Park at 1920 N Forest Ave (daily 9am–5pm; $7, including a tour of Leu House; ☏407/246-2620, ⓦwww.leugardens.org), in 1936 to show off plants collected from around the world. After seeing and sniffing the orchids, roses, azaleas, and the largest camellia collection outside of California, take a trip around **Leu House** (guided tours only; Aug–June daily 10am–3.30pm), a late-nineteenth-century farmhouse bought and lived in by Leu and his wife, now maintained in the simple but elegant style of their time and laced with family mementos.

International Drive

Devoid of any of the traditional charm one might find in downtown Orlando and adjacent communities (see p.309), **International Drive (or "I-Drive")**, five miles southwest of downtown, is still worth a short visit for the myriad attractions – some good, others not so good – located here. The strip boasts **Wet 'n' Wild** and the brand new **Aquatica**, two water parks to rival those on offer at Disney World, as well as other attractions such as **WonderWorks,** a quirky museum imaginatively housed in an upside-down house (for more on all these attractions, see p.308). I-Drive is also good for **shopping**, with several malls competing for your business. The best of these is the massive Prime Outlets International, at the northern end of I-Drive at no. 4951 (☏407/352-9600), which has 175 shops offering discounted prices on popular name brands.

Eating

Given the amount of competition among restaurants hoping to attract hungry tourists, **eating** in Orlando is never difficult and – if you escape the clutches of the theme parks – need not be expensive. In **downtown Orlando**, the need to satisfy a regular clientele of lunch-breaking office workers keeps prices low during the day, while at night the increasingly wide selection of smart restaurants is testament to downtown's new, hipper image. With a car, you might also investigate the local favorites scattered in the outlying areas away from downtown, especially the northern suburb of **Winter Park** (see p.312).

Tourist-dominated **International Drive** offers the complete range of restaurants, all easily accessible by foot, while nearby, around the intersection of Sand Lake Road and Dr Philips Boulevard, a cluster of trendy restaurants known as **Restaurant Row** is very popular with locals.

Budget travelers will relish the opportunity to eat massive amounts at one of several buffet restaurants – all for less than they might spend on a tip elsewhere. Buffet eating reaches its ultimate expression along **US-192**, where virtually every buffet restaurant chain has at least one outlet, leaving the discerning glutton spoiled for choice.

Note that **discount coupons** in tourist magazines bring sizeable reductions at many restaurants.

Downtown Orlando

Bravissimo Wine Bar & Cafe 337 N Shine Ave ☎407/898-7333. Authentic Italian cuisine and outdoor garden seating in a quiet, residential location about ten blocks from central downtown. Main dishes for around $15.

Dexters of Thornton Park 808 E Washington St ☎407/648-2777, ⊛www.dexwine.com. A young, urban clientele come here for fresh, tasty foods priced right – imaginative sandwiches and salads for lunch (around $10) and more gourmet dinner entrées such as chicken with chorizo stuffing (around $20) – plus an extensive beer and wine list.

The Globe 25 Wall St Plaza ☎407/849-9904. A perfect spot for inexpensive Nouveau American snacks and light meals, like noodle bowls and chicken masala, not usually costing more than around $10. Tables on the pedestrian-only street make for good people watching.

HUE – A Restaurant 629 E Central Blvd ☎407/849-1800, ⊛www.huerestaurant.com. Another of Thornton Park's hip restaurants, as popular for a cocktail at the bar or on the outside terrace as for its stylish, expensive ($20–35), but sometimes mediocre nouveau cuisine, such as wood-grilled meat and fish dishes with chive mashed potatoes.

Little Saigon 1106 E Colonial Drive ☎407/423-8539, ⊛www.littlesaigonrestaurant.com. One of the biggest and best of the many economical Vietnamese restaurants on Colonial Drive around the intersection with Mills Ave. Most dishes cost around $6.

Numero Uno 2499 S Orange Ave ☎866/495-7187, ⊛www.numero-uno-restaurant.com. An authentic Cuban restaurant, reputed to be the best *comida Cubana* in town, where lunch specials cost under $10 and dinners include paella Valencian. Closed Sat & Sun.

🏃 **Panera Bread** 227 N Eola Drive ☎407/481-1060, ⊛www.panerabread.com. This branch of an inviting local "bakery-café" chain serving up a wide array of baked goods, soups, salads, and sandwiches to go with the drinks enjoys a great location opposite Lake Eola. Plan on spending around $8 for lunch. Also a wi-fi hotspot.

Shari Sushi 621 E Central Blvd ☎407/420-9420, ⊛www.sharisushilounge.com. Fresh and expensive sushi and sashimi – using both classic and Western-inspired ingredients – served in a sleek lounge to beautiful people. Sushi platters $15–50.

White Wolf Café 1829 N Orange Ave ☎407/895-9911, ⊛www.whitewolfcafe.com. Down-to-earth café/antique store with creative salads and sandwiches for under $10, plus home-made lasagna, quiche, and meatloaf.

International Drive and Restaurant Row

Bahama Breeze 8849 International Drive ☎407/248-2499, ⊛www.bahamabreeze.com. This bar-restaurant serves decent Caribbean food ($15–20) in an upbeat atmosphere. It's particularly busy Fri and Sat evenings. Dinner only; open late (until 1am most nights).

Orlando has many well-publicized **"Show Restaurants,"** where you'll be served a multi-course meal and (usually) limitless beer, wine, and soft drinks while you watch live entertainment ranging from intriguing whodunits to medieval knights jousting on horseback. The all-inclusive cost is usually around $50 for adults or $30 for children, although discounts are often available if you book online.

Arabian Nights Dinner Show 6225 W Irlo Bronson Hwy, Kissimmee ☎407/239-9223 or 1-800/553-6116, ⑩www.arabian-nights.com. Seventy beautiful live horses are the highlight of this comic version of the classic story. The steak, chicken, or pasta dinners are better than the ham acting.

Makahiki Luau Dinner Show Seafire Inn SeaWorld Orlando ☎1-800/327-2424, ⑩www.seaworld.com. The rhythmic music, traditional dance, and superb costumes of this South Seas-style show overshadow the so-so Hawaiian and Pacific Rim food. Alcoholic drinks are not included in the ticket price.

Medieval Times Dinner & Tournament 4510 W Irlo Bronson Hwy, Kissimmee ☎407/396-1518 or 1-888/935-6878, ⑩www.medievaltimes.com. Knights joust on horseback as wenches serve roast chicken and spare ribs inside this replica of an eleventh-century castle. Two rounds of drinks per person.

Pirate's Dinner Adventure 6400 Carrier Drive ☎407/248-0590 or 1-800/866-2469, ⑩www.piratesdinneradventure.com. Shivering timbers, peg-leg buccaneers, scalawags, cannons, sword fights, and a host of stunts will divert your attention from the ordinary roast chicken, pork tenderloin, or seafood dinners. Arrive early to take advantage of the free appetizers before the show.

Sleuth's Mystery Dinner Show 8267 International Drive ☎407/363-1985 or 1-800/393-1985, ⑩www.sleuths.com. If you know red herring isn't a seafood dish, you're well on the way to solving the whodunit (which changes throughout the week) acted out by reasonably skilled actors in the dining room as you eat a copious roast hen dinner. Expect some audience interaction.

Bergamo's Festival Bay Mall, 5250 International Drive ☎407/352-3805, ⑩www.bergamos.com. Authentic Italian dishes (around $20) like meatballs, risotto, and several pasta choices served by singing waiters who perform Broadway hits, opera, and Neopolitan folk songs while you eat. Good selection of Italian wines. Dinner only.

Café Tu Tu Tango 8625 International Drive ☎407/248-2222, ⑩www.cafetututango.com. Original, imaginative dishes ($7–11) such as mango duck quesadillas and alligator bites served in small portions so you'll need two or three to fill you up. All the artwork on the walls is for sale.

Christini's Ristorante Italiano 7600 Dr Phillips Blvd ☎407/345-8770, ⑩www.christinis.com. One of Orlando's best Italian restaurants, boasting elegant decor, excellent service, and well prepared dishes including clams and linguini in a red or white clam sauce and several meat and seafood options. Pasta dishes cost around $20, meat and seafood $30 and up. Dinner only.

The Crab House 8291 International Drive ☎407/352-6140, ⑩www.crabhouseseafood .com. Lively seafood restaurant specializing in many kinds of crab. The all-you-can-eat seafood and salad bar for $29.99 is very popular, so expect to wait for a table. Another location at 8496 Palm Parkway, in the Vista Center ☎407/239-1888.

Cricketers Arms Festival Bay Mall, 5250 International Drive ☎407/354-0686, ⑩www.cricketersarmspub.com. Fish and chips, pies, and pasties, all for under $15, complement a range of imported ales and lagers at this cozy nook with nightly live music and sometimes televised soccer matches. A wi-fi hotspot.

Ming Court 9188 International Drive ☎407/351-9988, ⑩www.ming-court.com. Chinese cuisine of an exceptionally high standard, including meticulously prepared dim sum or sumptuous sushi; given the flash decor, it's less costly than you might expect (around $15) .

Passage to India 5532 International Drive ☎407/351-3456, ⑩www.passagetoindia restaurant-orlando.com. Northern Indian dishes ($15–20), including *biryani* and plenty of vegetarian choices, emphasizing the "rich but not fatty" and "spicy but not hot" nature of the food.

Punjab 7451 International Drive ⓣ407/352-7887, ⓦwww.punjabindianrestaurant.com. Dig into a wide range of curries (around $15) – spiced to your personal taste – including a tasty vegetarian selection.

Roy's 7760 W Sand Lake Rd ⓣ407/352-4844, ⓦwww.roysrestaurant.com. One of a chain founded in Hawaii and offering innovative island-fusion cuisine. Try the fixed-price, three-course menu ($35), with prosciutto-wrapped tiger shrimp and Hawaii koi beef ribs, for a good sampling of what's on offer.

Seasons 52 7700 W Sand Lake Rd ⓣ407/354-5212, ⓦwww.seasons52.com. All items on the menu are under 475 calories, a feat achieved by using plenty of chicken, fish, and vegetables rather than skimping on quantity. The desserts, meanwhile, come in "four-bite" portions. Most main dishes cost around $15. There are tables outside overlooking a lake, while the busy piano bar is a popular venue for cocktails, particularly on Wed, Fri, and Sat evenings. Dinner only.

Nightlife and entertainment

Orlando can now make a justifiable claim to have Florida's second best **nightlife** after Miami – and many consider Orlando's less pretentious after-dark scene preferable to the pompous attitudes that often prevail in South Beach. An eclectic and ever-growing collection of bars, lounges, and clubs pack the city's **downtown**, with many of the liveliest spots found along Orange Avenue. For all its restaurants and attractions, **International Drive** has only a smattering of nightlife options; restaurants such as *Bahama Breeze*, the *Cricketers Arms*, and *Seasons 52* tend to function more as bars as the night progresses. Elsewhere, Universal Orlando has created its own after-dark entertainment venue in the form of **CityWalk** (see p.305), but this can seem somewhat artificial and predigested in comparison with downtown.

Downtown Orlando

Eola Wine Company 500 E Central Blvd ⓣ407/481-9100, ⓦwww.eolawinecompany.com. Escape the noise and crowds at this refined, laid-back wine bar across from Lake Eola, where you can order by the glass or in "flights" (two-ounce servings of three or four different wines for $13–16).

Independent Bar 70 N Orange Ave ⓣ407/839-0457, ⓦwww.independentbar.net. This longstanding downtown bar caters to the alternative crowd, including plenty of Goths who mope around the adjoining nightclub listening to melancholic tunes from the 80s.

Pulse 1912 S Orange Ave ⓣ407/649-3888, ⓦwww.pulseorlando.com. A justifiably popular gay nightclub a mile or so south of downtown with great lighting and sound, plus cabaret performers, drag acts, and erotic dancers.

Roxy 740 Benett Rd ⓣ407/898-4004, ⓦwww.roxyorlando.com. Hip-hop predominates at this two-level dance club a couple of miles east of downtown, where a large video screen overlooking the dance floor and gogo dancers contribute to a frenzied atmosphere. Closed Mon.

The Social 54 N Orange Ave ⓣ407/246-1419, ⓦwww.thesocial.org. Grunge, alternative rock, and everything else non-mainstream is played at this important venue showcasing the talents of bands with local and national followings. Check the website for a full list of coming attractions.

Tabu 46 N Orange Ave ⓣ407/648-8363, ⓦwww.tabunightclub.com. Housed in an old theater, this large-scale dance club has a down-to-earth atmosphere – hardly "taboo" – typified by student-friendly "all-u-can-drink" promotions and rather bland commercial dance music.

Walt Disney World

As significant as air conditioning in making the state what it is today, **WALT DISNEY WORLD** turned a wedge of Florida grazing land into one of the world's most lucrative vacation venues within a decade of its opening in 1971. Bringing growth and money to Central Florida for the first time since the citrus boom a century earlier, the immense and astutely planned empire (and

Walt Disney World really *is* an empire) also pushed the state's profile through the roof: from being a down-at-heel and slightly seedy mixture of cheap motels, retirement homes, and clapped-out alligator zoos, Florida suddenly became a showcase of modern international tourism and in doing so, some would claim, sold its soul for a fast buck.

Whatever your attitude toward theme parks, there's no denying Disney World is the pacesetter: it goes way beyond Walt Disney's original "theme park" – Disneyland, which opened in Los Angeles in 1955 – delivering escapism at its most technologically advanced and psychologically brilliant in a multitude of ingenious guises across an area twice the size of Manhattan. In a crime-free environment where wholesome all-American values hold sway and the concept of good clean fun finds its ultimate expression, Disney World often makes the real world – and all its problems – seem like a distant memory.

Here, litter is picked up within seconds of being dropped (by any of the "cast members," as all employees are called, who happen to spy it), subtle mind-games ease the tedium of standing in line, the special effects are the best money can buy, and Disney minions grin merrily as snotty-nosed kids puke down their legs. It's not cheap, forward planning is essential, and there are times when you'll feel like a cog in a vast machine – but Walt Disney World unfailingly, and with ruthless efficiency, delivers what it promises.

A brief history of Disney

When brilliant illustrator and animator Walt Disney devised the world's first theme park, California's **Disneyland** – which brought to life his cartoon characters Mickey Mouse, Donald Duck, Goofy, and the rest – he had no control over the hotels and restaurants that quickly engulfed it, preventing growth and missing out on profits he felt were rightfully his. Determined this wouldn't happen again, the Disney Corporation secretly began to buy up 27,500 acres of Central Florida farmland, and by the late 1960s had acquired – for a comparatively paltry $6 million – a site a hundred times bigger than Disneyland. With the promise of a jobs bonanza for Florida, the state legislature gave the corporation – thinly disguised as the Reedy Creek Improvement District – the rights of any major municipality: empowering it to lay roads, enact building codes, and enforce the law with its own security force.

Walt Disney World's first park, the Magic Kingdom (see p.291), opened in 1971; based, predictably, on Disneyland, it was an equally predictable success. The far more ambitious **Epcot** (see p.292), unveiled in 1982, represented the first major break from cartoon-based escapism. Millions visited, but the rose-tinted look at the future received a mixed response. Partly because of this reaction, and some cockeyed management decisions, the Disney empire (Disney himself died in 1966) faced bankruptcy by the mid-1980s.

Since then, clever marketing has brought the corporation back from the abyss, and despite being subject to a (failed) hostile takeover bid by Comcast in 2004, it now steers a tight and competitive business ship, always looking to increase Walt Disney World's daily attendance figures of over 100,000 visitors and stay ahead of its rivals, notably Universal Orlando. **Disney's Hollywood Studios** (see p.295), for example, puts a sizeable dent in Universal Studios Florida's trade (see p.302), while **Downtown Disney** (see p.298) has considerably more shops and restaurants than Universal's CityWalk (see p.305). It may trade in fantasy but, where money matters, the Disney Corporation's nose is firmly in the real world.

6

ORLANDO AND DISNEY WORLD | Walt Disney World

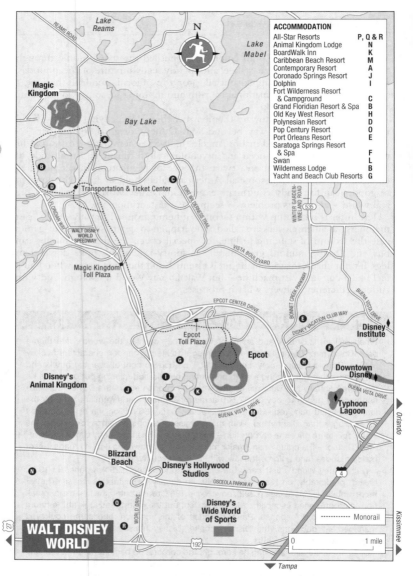

ACCOMMODATION

All-Star Resorts	P, Q & R
Animal Kingdom Lodge	N
BoardWalk Inn	K
Caribbean Beach Resort	M
Contemporary Resort	A
Coronado Springs Resort	J
Dolphin	I
Fort Wilderness Resort & Campground	C
Grand Floridian Resort & Spa	B
Old Key West Resort	H
Polynesian Resort	D
Pop Century Resort	O
Port Orleans Resort	E
Saratoga Springs Resort & Spa	F
Swan	L
Wilderness Lodge	B
Yacht and Beach Club Resorts	G

Costs may come as a shock, especially to families (children under 3 are admitted free of charge, though note little is designed specifically for their entertainment), but the basic admission fee allows unlimited access to all the shows and rides in a particular park. There are **four main parks** and you'll need *at least* a day per park. Remember Disney World comprises over 46 square miles in all and is not easy to take in, even if spread over a week. On crowded days (and there are many) it's even more daunting. Restaurants and snack bars –

each as clinically themed as the parks – are plentiful but pricey. No alcohol is served in the Magic Kingdom.

Getting around

With its multiple attractions and similarly named resort hotels (see p.288), Disney property seems at first glance complicated to get around. In fact, it's quite easy, with Disney's fleet of free **buses** serving all points of interest. As a general rule, buses to all destinations depart at roughly twenty-minute intervals from all of the resorts. Intra-park travel, meanwhile, will sometimes involve changing buses at the Transportation and Ticket Center (near the Magic Kingdom) or another park. For example, to get to Disney's Wide World of Sports, you'll have to catch a bus from Disney's Hollywood Studios. Note that buses to Downtown Disney depart from the resorts only. Transport between the Transportation and Ticket Center, the Magic Kingdom, and Epcot is via the **monorail**. Although in theory it's possible to **walk** from one park to another, distances are deceptively long and there are few pedestrian walkways.

The charge for using the Disney World parking lots is $12, which covers you for the whole day. These lots are enormous, so make a note of exactly where you're parked.

Accommodation

If you want to escape the all-pervasive influence and high prices of Disney World for the night, refer to the accommodation listings under "Orlando," p.277, or opt to stay at one of the hotels around Disney property in the area known as **Lake Buena Vista** (see p.289), from where it's only a few minutes' drive to any of the parks (most of these hotels offer complimentary shuttles to and from the parks). If you can't bring yourself to leave – and staying within easy access of the parks is, after all, the most convenient way of experiencing Disney World – you'll be relieved to find a large number of **hotels** on Disney property, most of which are, in fact, fully equipped resorts. Predictably, each follows a particular theme to the nth degree, and prices are much higher – sometimes more than $300 per night – than you'll pay elsewhere. *All-Star Resorts* and *Pop Century Resort*, however, are specifically intended for the less affluent visitor, costing from $82 a night.

Each resort occupies its own landscaped plot, usually encompassing several swimming pools and a beach beside an artificial lake, and has several restaurants and bars. The Disney resorts are located in several areas, and transport, be it by boat, bus, or monorail, between them and the main theme parks is free (see "Getting around," above). Resort guests also have free use of Disney **parking** lots and free **airport transfers** (see "Arrival and information," p.273). Theme park admission tickets are available at each resort, saving valuable time otherwise spent lining up at park ticket booths. The standard of service should be excellent; if it isn't, make a stiff complaint and you'll probably be treated like royalty throughout the remainder of your stay. Another advantage of staying at a Disney resort comes in the shape of the **Extra Magic Hours**, when each day one of the four parks either opens one hour earlier or closes up to three hours later exclusively for resort guests, giving them the opportunity for some quality time with Mickey and relatively unimpeded access to the wildest rides.

At quiet times, rooms may be available at short notice, but with Disney resorts pitching themselves to convention-goers as much as vacationers, you may turn up only to find everywhere fully booked. To be assured of a room, reserve as far ahead as possible – nine months is not unreasonable. You can make **reservations** by phone or internet (☎ 407/939-6244, ⓦ www.disneyworld.com).

Disney's Animal Kingdom Resort Area

🏃 **All-Star Resorts** ☎ 407/939-6000 (*Music*), ☎ 407/939-5000 (*Sports*), ☎ 407/939-7000 (*Movies*). The most affordable of Disney's resorts, divided into the *All-Star Music Resort*, which is decorated with giant, brightly colored cowboy boots and guitar-shaped swimming pools; the *All-Star Sports Resort*, complete with huge Coca-Cola cups, American football helmets, and so on; and the *All-Star Movies Resort*, which is littered with humongous reminders of Disney movies. Each complex has its own pools and nearly 2000 functional and garishly decorated rooms; *All-Star Music Resort* also has family suites (sleeping six) with kitchenettes. ❹ suites ❼

🏃 **Animal Kingdom Lodge** ☎ 407/938-3000. One of Disney's most spectacular luxury accommodations, where from some of the rooms – all of which are done in warm colors and decorated with African handicrafts – you can wake up to see wildlife grazing outside your window. ❼

Coronado Springs Resort ☎ 407/939-1000. Moderately priced resort paying homage to the cultures of Mexico and the American Southwest, with its nearly 2000 colorfully Latino inspired rooms built around a faux-Mayan pyramid. ❻

Downtown Disney Resort Area

Old Key West Resort ☎ 407/827-7700. Caribbean-style wooden homes and shaded verandas create a tropical ambience based on a late-nineteenth-century Key West resort. Accommodation is in studios or villas with kitchens and washer dryers. ❽

Port Orleans Resort ☎ 407/934-5000 (*French Quarter*), ☎ 407/934-6000 (*Riverside*). This resort combines two Southern themes: the row houses and cobbled streets of New Orleans at the *French Quarter*, and the grandiose manors overlooking the Mississippi River at the *Riverside*. Rooms at both have a somewhat spartan feel. ❻

Saratoga Springs Resort & Spa ☎ 407/827-1100. Spacious studios or well-equipped villas (complete with whirlpool tubs) are offered at this resort modeled on America's first vacation resort, Saratoga Springs, in the late-1800s. ❽

Epcot-Disney's Hollywood Studios Resort Area

BoardWalk Inn ☎ 407/939-5100. Styled after a 1930s mid-Atlantic seaside resort, complete with a waterfront promenade full of shops and restaurants, this place proves no theme is too humble for the Disney treatment. The rooms have a spacious, if not overly warm, feel, and all come with balconies. ❽

Caribbean Beach Resort ☎ 407/934-3400. Reasonably priced hotel where the comfortable but unremarkable rooms are located in one of six "island villages," each with its own pool and beach surrounded by nicely landscaped grounds. ❻

Dolphin ☎ 407/934-4000. Topped by a giant dolphin sculpture and decorated in dizzying pastel shades and reproduction artwork from the likes of Matisse and Warhol, this hotel has pricey rooms with a fresh, contemporary design. ❽

Pop Century Resort ☎ 407/938-4000. Devoted to mammoth pop icons from each decade of the second half of the twentieth century, this is Disney's largest hotel with nearly 3000 budget-priced rooms along the same lines as the *All-Star Resorts* (see opposite). ❹

Swan ☎ 407/934-3000. Sister hotel to the *Dolphin* (see above), from which it's separated by an artificial lake and beach, and likewise whimsically decorated, though with sharper, more vibrant colors, and equipped with every conceivable luxury. ❽

Yacht and Beach Club Resorts ☎ 407/934-7000 (*Yacht Club*), ☎ 407/934-8000 (*Beach Club*). Late-nineteenth-century New England is the cue for these twin hotels, complete with clapboard facades, a miniature lighthouse, and bright, airy rooms inspired by nautical themes. Amusements include a mini water park reminiscent of a Nantucket beach. ❽

Magic Kingdom Resort Area

Contemporary Resort ☎ 407/824-1000. The Disney monorail runs right through the center of this hotel, which takes its exterior design from the futuristic fantasies of the Magic Kingdom's Tomorrowland, but is disappointingly characterless inside. All the modern, minimalist rooms have balconies, some affording good views of the Magic Kingdom. ❽

Fort Wilderness Resort & Campground ☎ 407/824-2900. A 700-acre site where you can pitch your tent or hook up your RV (from $43), or rent an a/c six-berth cabin (from $265) – a good deal for larger groups. Entertainment includes nightly open-air screenings of classic Disney movies. ❽

Grand Floridian Resort & Spa ☎ 407/824-3000. Gabled roofs, verandas, and crystal chandeliers are among the frivolous variations on early Florida resort architecture at Disney's most upmarket hotel, complete with a full-service spa. ❽

Polynesian Resort ☎407/824-2000. Accessible via the monorail, this effective, if somewhat tacky, imitation of a Polynesian beach hotel is most enjoyable if you spend your time on the lakeside beach under the shade of coconut palms. The brightly colored rooms continue the tropical theme. ❽

🏃 **Wilderness Lodge** ☎407/824-3200. This magnificent, oversized replica of a frontier log cabin is furnished with massive totem poles, a wood-burning fire in the lobby, and Southern-style rocking chairs, while the welcoming rooms have a close-to-nature motif. ❼

Lake Buena Vista

Nickelodeon Family Suites by Holiday Inn 14500 Continental Gateway ☎407/387-5437 or 1-877/642-5111, ⓦwww.nickhotel.com. The leader in kid-friendly resorts, with one-, two-, and three-bedroom suites sleeping up to six, two giant swimming pools with water slides, free kids' meals (for under 5s), and even a spa for the little ones. ❻

Orlando World Center Marriott Resort 8701 World Center Drive ☎407/239-4200, ⓦwww .marriottworldcenter.com. Looking like a small city, the 2000 rooms here are comfortable enough, but it's the recreational activities on offer – a giant lagoon-shaped swimming pool, full-service spa, and well-manicured golf course – that are the main draws. ❽

Perri House Acres Estate B&B Inn 10417 Vista Oaks Court ☎407/876-4830 or 1-800/780-4830, ⓦwww.perrihouse.com. This eight-room bed and breakfast hidden on four wooded acres – also a bird sanctuary – just a stone's throw from the opulent resorts of Disney is the perfect antidote to all the theme-park frenzy. The clean, bright rooms have their own private outside entrances and access to a shared kitchen. There's also a swimming pool and hot tub. ❺

🏃 **Sheraton Vistana Resort** 8800 Vistana Center Drive ☎407/239-3100, ⓦwww .starwoodhotels.com. With the atmosphere of a small village, this sprawling resort is dotted with plenty of swimming pools and restaurants, and has activities for the kids. The attractive one- and two-bedroom villas come with large kitchens and washer dryers. Within walking distance of the entrance to Downtown Disney (see p.298). ❻

Staybridge Suites at Lake Buena Vista 8751 Suiteside Drive ☎407/238-0777, ⓦwww .sborlando.com. With similar facilities to its sister property on I-Drive (see p.279), this relaxing hotel is about a mile from the entrance to Downtown Disney. ❻

The main parks: an overview

Walt Disney World's four main theme parks are quite separate entities. The **Magic Kingdom** is the Disney park everyone imagines, the signature Cinderella Castle towering over it all, where Mickey Mouse mingles with the crowds and the emphasis is on fantasy and fun – very much the park for kids. Recognizable for its giant, golfball-like geosphere, **Epcot** is Disney's attempted celebration of science and technology, coupled with a very Disneyfied trip around various countries and cultures; not as compelling for young kids, it's a sprawling area involving a lot of walking. **Disney's Hollywood Studios** suits almost everyone; its special effects are enjoyable even if you've never seen the movies they're derived from, and the fact this is also a working production studio lends a welcome – and rare – touch of reality to your Disney experience. The more relaxed **Disney's Animal Kingdom** is part new-age zoo, part theme park, remarkable in bringing an African and Asian feel to the swamp-lands of southwest Orlando.

Doing any kind of justice to all four parks will take at least five days – one should be set aside for rest – and you shouldn't tackle more than one on any single day. If you only have a day to spare, pick the park that appeals most and stick to it, as day tickets are only valid for one location anyway. For visiting several parks over a few days, the Magic Your Way ticket is the economical solution.

When to visit

While Epcot in particular absorbs crowds easily, it's best to avoid the **busiest periods**: summertime, over Thanksgiving (fourth Thurs in Nov), Christmas,

Disney's FASTPASS

In an effort to keep outrageous waiting times from wiping the smiles off visitors' faces, Disney set up a system to give people the chance to avoid the long lines – provided they are prepared to return to the attraction later in the day. At certain sites you can obtain a FASTPASS by simply inserting your ticket into a special FASTPASS ticket station at the entrance. The machine then prints out a slip indicating the time you should return. In effect, you book a time to enter the FASTPASS line, which bypasses the regular line and gets you in with little or no wait. You can save lots of time booking ahead all day long, but remember you can only hold one FASTPASS for one attraction at any one time. We have stated whether FASTPASSes are available in the account for each attraction.

and Easter. The quieter months of the year for the theme parks are January, May, September, and the first three weeks in December. The busiest days vary from park to park, though Mondays and Tuesdays are traditionally seen as busier than normal while Fridays and Sundays tend to be quieter.

Provided you **arrive early** at the park (just before opening time is best), you'll get through the most popular rides before the mid-afternoon crush, when lines can become monstrously long. Each park has regularly updated notice boards showing the latest **waiting times** for each show and ride – at peak times often about an hour and a half for the most popular rides and up to forty minutes for others.

Beating the crowds

Other than trying to avoid the busiest times of the year, the best way to beat the crowds is to use the FASTPASS system. It also pays to avoid standing in line at attractions where FASTPASSes are available if you don't want your waiting position constantly usurped by FASTPASS holders waltzing to the front of the line. Savvy Disney visitors use different time-saving tactics depending on the park they are in. At the **Magic Kingdom** most people turn right (counter-clockwise) when reaching the Cinderella Castle at the end of Main Steet, USA; therefore, consider starting your tour in a clockwise direction, starting at Adventureland and working your way toward Tomorrowland. At **Epcot**, new arrivals tend to make straight for the geosphere, beside the entrance, to wait in line for Spaceship Earth. Therefore, a sensible, time-saving plan is to head for Mission: SPACE, Test Track (where there's a single-rider line), or Soarin', the three most popular rides, and obtain a FASTPASS for one and then join the line for one of the others (which should be short enough if you arrive early). At **Disney's Hollywood Studios**, the Lights, Motors, Action! Extreme Stunt Show can take as many as 5000 people out of circulation for around thirty minutes, making this a good time to go on the park's two thrill rides, The Twilight Zone Tower of Terror and Rock 'n' Roller Coaster. By far the most popular attraction at **Disney's Animal Kingdom** is Expedition Everest, so visit this one at off-peak times or use a FASTPASS for it. And finally, it might be worth avoiding a park on days when it opens early for guests of the Disney resorts – when it's sure to be more crowded than usual.

Opening times and tickets

Opening times vary greatly depending on what park you are visiting and at what time of year. The parks are generally **open** daily from 9am to around 9pm or 10pm during holidays and in the summer, and from 9am to 6pm or later the rest of the year. Disney's Animal Kingdom closes at 5pm. During peak seasons the *Orlando Sentinel* lists each park's hours on the front page.

A one-day, one-park ticket costs $75 (children 3–9 $63; under-3s get in free), is available from any park entrance, and allows entry to one park only. The **Magic Your Way** ticket saves money if you spread your visit over a number of days; for example, a seven-day Magic Your Way ticket would cost $228 (children 3–9 $193). You can buy a Magic Your Way ticket for a maximum of ten days and you can only visit one park per day. If you want to move from park to park in the same day, you must add the **Park Hopper** option for an additional flat fee of $50. The **Water Park Fun & More** option allows you to add from two to ten extra admissions (the exact number depends on the length of your basic Magic Your Way ticket) to Blizzard Beach, Typhoon Lagoon, DisneyQuest, and Disney's Wide World of Sports for a flat fee of $50. There's also a $469 **annual pass** (children 3–9 $414), strictly for fanatics.

Magic Kingdom

Anyone who's been to Disneyland in California will recognize much of the Magic Kingdom, not least the dramatic Cinderella Castle sitting smack in the middle of the park, surrounded by several themed sections, each with its own identity. Building facades, rides, gift shops, even the particular characters giving hugs contribute to the distinct feel of each section, while the park as a whole emphasizes fantasy and family fun over thrills and spills. The areas are called **Main Street USA**, **Adventureland**, **Tomorrowland**, **Fantasyland**, **Frontierland**, **Liberty Square**, and **Mickey's Toontown Fair**. Some of the rides are identical to their Californian forebears, while others are greatly expanded and improved – and a few are much worse. Like its older sibling, the place is best experienced with enthusiasm: jump in with both feet and go on every ride possible.

A warning: don't promise the kids (or yourself) too much beforehand. Even with clever use of the FASTPASS system (see box opposite), lines are sometimes so long it may be better to pass up some attractions. Although waiting times are usually posted, lines can be deceiving – Disney masterfully disguises their true length and keeps you cool with shade, fans, and air-conditioning wherever possible.

The park

From the main gates, you'll step into **Main Street USA**, a bustling assortment of souvenir shops selling the ubiquitous mouse-ear hats and other Disney paraphernalia in old-fashioned, town-square stores. Don't spend too much time here, as you can buy most of the same items throughout the park and all over Disney property.

At the end of Main Street USA you'll see **Cinderella's Castle**, a stunning 189-foot pseudo-Rhineland palace that looks like it should be the most elaborate ride in the park. In fact, it's merely a shell that conceals all the electronics and machinery that drive the whole extravaganza. You simply walk through a tunnel in its center, and use it as a reference point if you lose your bearings.

If you arrive early, beat the lines by heading immediately for the popular thrills-and-spills rides, which tend to draw the biggest crowds. The most nerve-jangling of these is **Space Mountain** (minimum height 44"/112cm; FASTPASS accepted), in essence an ordinary rollercoaster, yet one whose total darkness makes every jump and jolt unexpected (taller riders may find the small cars a little cramped). **Splash Mountain** (minimum height 40"/102cm; FASTPASS accepted) employs water to great effect, enhancing the cute Br'er

Rabbit storyline, although the only really exciting moment is a 52-foot drop down a waterfall that's sure to get you wet. **Big Thunder Mountain Railroad** (minimum height 40"/102cm; FASTPASS accepted) puts you on board a runaway train, which trundles through Gold Rush California in about three minutes at a modest pace that won't upset too many younger riders. Otherwise, kids can try **The Barnstormer at Goofy's Wiseacre Farm** (minimum height 35"/89cm), a milder attraction perfect for thrillseekers-in-training.

You don't have to be a rollercoaster junkie to enjoy the Magic Kingdom. Many of the best rides in the park rely on "Audio-Animatronics" characters – impressive vocal robots of Disney invention – for their appeal. Some of the best are seen in **Stitch's Great Escape** (minimum height 38"/95cm; FASTPASS accepted), in which the mischievous monster wreaks havoc on the audience, who feel, hear, and smell strange things in the dark. A slew of realistic robots appear in **Pirates of the Caribbean**, the classic boat ride through a pirate-infested Caribbean island full of drunken debauchery. A large cast of Audio-Animatronics characters is also used to good effect in the **Haunted Mansion**, a mildly spooky ghost ride through a well devised set, memorable for the ghouls depicted by the clever use of holograms. The leisurely **Jungle Cruise** (FASTPASS accepted) is narrated by a pun-loving guide, who takes you down the Amazon, Nile, Congo, and Mekong, each river inhabited by the appropriate Audio-Animatronics animals, from crocodiles to elephants, which look slightly less realistic in the cold light of day.

One of the park's recent additions, **Monsters, Inc. Laugh Floor**, is an interactive comedy show in which the Monsters send up members of the audience who are singled out by a roaming camera – amusing enough for extroverts; terrifying for introverts.

The kid-orientated Fantasyland is the one place where the Magic Kingdom shows its age, with a generally rather dated collection of attractions. Among the merry-go-rounds and flying elephants found here, there's the excellent **Mickey's PhilharMagic** (FASTPASS accepted), an enchanting 3-D journey with Daffy Duck and other well-known characters, set to classic Disney soundtracks. **It's a Small World** is a slow, pleasant boat ride past multi-ethnic dolls who sing the theme song over and over and over again. **Peter Pan's Flight** (FASTPASS accepted), **Snow White's Scary Adventures**, and **The Many Adventures of Winnie the Pooh** (FASTPASS accepted) are creaky, low-tech amusements, still very popular with fairytale-loving youngsters, but which wouldn't be out of place in a fairground.

Adjoining Fantasyland, Mickey's Toontown Fair is the top spot in the park to **meet Disney characters**; all the usual suspects hang around throughout the day for autographs and handshakes in the **Toontown Hall of Fame Tent**. Alternatively, stay for the character-saturated **parade** (daily 3pm). The best vantage-point is from a bench in Frontierland, at the parade's departure point, which will also allow you to save time and get back to touring the park more quickly. Do make an effort to see **Wishes**, held just before the park closes. Of all the imaginative efforts to create an aura of fantasy, this simple but stunning twelve-minute fireworks display is the most magical of them all. It's best viewed facing the Cinderella Castle at the end of Main Street, USA.

Epcot

Even before Orlando's Magic Kingdom opened, Walt Disney was developing plans for the Experimental Prototype Community of Tomorrow, or **Epcot**. It was conceived in the 1960s as a real community that would experiment and work with the new ideas and materials of a technologically advancing US. The

▲ EPCOT geosphere

idea failed to take shape as Disney had envisaged. Epcot didn't open until 1982, when global recession and ecological concerns had put a damper on the belief in the infallibility of science, and the park became a general celebration of human achievement. Epcot is twice as big as the Magic Kingdom and, ironically, given its futuristic themes, very sapping on mankind's oldest mode of transport – the feet.

The park

Epcot's 180-foot-high **geosphere** (unlike a semicircular geodesic *dome*, the geo*sphere*, invented by futurist Buckminster Fuller, is completely round) sits in the heart of the **Future World** section of the park, which keeps close to Epcot's original concept of exploring the history and researching the future of agriculture, transport, energy, and communication. Inside the geosphere is the recently revamped **Spaceship Earth**, a slow-moving buggy ride through the past, the present, and into the future, with narration by actress Judi Dench and interactive features such as touch screens in the buggies which allow you to choose your own vision of the future. The highlight of the ride is a final poignant ascent into the star-filled core of the geosphere.

Future World is divided into several pavilions (including Spaceship Earth), each corporate-sponsored, and having its own rides, films, interactive computer exhibits, and games.

Currently, the park's most popular ride is the superb **Soarin'** (minimum height 40"/102cm; FASTPASS accepted) in The Land Pavilion, which employs the latest flight-simulator technology to take you on a magical hang-glider ride over breathtaking Californian landscapes, the seats banking and turning and wind blowing through your hair as you soar. Epcot's two thrill rides also attract big crowds. Disney worked with NASA advisors, astronauts, and scientists to build **Mission: SPACE** (minimum height 44"/112cm; FASTPASS accepted), which re-creates as realistically as possible the sensations of being launched in a rocket to Mars, including real G-force on take-off. Opt for the "Orange Team" if you want to experience the ride in all its intensity or the "Green Team" for a gentler voyage. The park's only rollercoaster-style ride is **Test Track** (minimum height 40"/102cm; FASTPASS accepted), where you put a high-performance car through various tests, with only the final thirty seconds or so, when the speed tests are carried out, being really exciting. Like Spaceship Earth, the Mission: SPACE and Test Track rides form their own pavilions.

The **Universe of Energy Pavilion**, a celebration of the harnessing of the earth's energy, is dominated by **Ellen's Energy Adventure** starring actress Ellen DeGeneres. Although ultimately educational and with some impressive cinematography on enormous screens, the undoubted highlight is a buggy ride through the primeval forests where dinosaurs roamed and today's fossil fuels originated.

In the **Imagination! Pavilion**, a 3-D cinematic thrill called **Honey, I Shrunk the Audience** (FASTPASS accepted) keeps an audience "shrunk" by an inventor's Shrinking Gun amused with some low-tech "feelies" – which add sensations of touch and smell to the 3-D visuals and surround-sound effects (like the movies of the future as imagined in Aldous Huxley's *Brave New World*).

The Seas with Nemo & Friends Pavilion contains the park's newest attraction, the only vaguely realistic **The Seas with Nemo & Friends**, which takes you on a terrestrial buggy ride through an aquatic world full of characters from the *Finding Nemo* movie. For real marine life, check out the Pavilion's giant **aquarium**, the world's largest artificial saltwater environment, occupied by a multitude of fish, sharks, turtles, and other sea creatures – the fish are best viewed at the regular feeding times throughout the day.

Along with Soarin', **The Land Pavilion** offers the rich and informative **Living with the Land** (FASTPASS accepted), a boat tour of the world's various biomes and alternative means of food production – including Disney's own successful attempts to produce Mickey Mouse-shaped vegetables (pumpkins and cucumbers among them, if you're wondering). **The Circle of Life** is another worthwhile stop; this animated fable based on the film *The Lion King*, carries a powerful message about keeping the earth a viable habitat for all of its creatures, not just humans. Consider having a bite to **eat** in the food court, where the options are more varied than the burgers-and-fries found elsewhere in Future World.

Innoventions is the least interesting of Future World's pavilions and merits only a cursory glance. It's divided into two sections: Innoventions **East** is for the young and old; Innoventions **West** is mainly for the kids. Both are full of the latest in gizmos and gadgetry, much of which you can fiddle and play with. For example, try designing and building a plastic robot at East's **Fantastic Plastic Works**, or give your kids a crash course in fire safety at West's **Where's the Fire?** Note the exhibits at Innoventions change regularly.

World Showcase

Arranged around a forty-acre lagoon, the **World Showcase** section of Epcot attempts to mirror the history, architecture, and culture of the eleven nations that responded to Disney's worldwide appeal when the original idea of creating a futuristic ideal community using the latest technology was being developed in the 1970s. Each section features an instantly recognizable landmark – Mexico has a Mayan pyramid, France an Eiffel Tower – or a stereotypical scene, such as a British pub or a Moroccan bazaar. The elaborate reconstructions show careful attention to detail, and each country also offers its own cuisine in often excellent restaurants where the decor can be as impressive as the food – notably at the *San Angel Inn* (see p.300) – and the staff are almost all natives of the specific country. The most crowded Pavilion is usually **The American Adventure** inside a replica of Philadelphia's Liberty Hall, where Audio-Animatronics versions of Mark Twain and Benjamin Franklin give a somewhat sanitized account of two centuries of US history in under half an hour. If you're pressed for time, bypass this in favor of the two excellent film presentations in the Chinese and French pavilions featuring a mouth-watering resume of these countries' treasures. At night, the lagoon transforms into the spectacular sound-and-light show, **IllumiNations: Reflections of Earth**, which starts half an hour before closing. During the rest of the day, a boat crosses the lagoon at regular intervals, linking the entrance to Future World, Morocco, and Germany. Note that World Showcase opens daily at 11am.

Disney's Hollywood Studios

When the Disney Corporation began making films and TV shows for adults – most notably *Who Framed Roger Rabbit?* – it also began plotting the creation of a theme park geared as much to adults as kids. After signing an agreement in the 1980s with Metro-Goldwyn-Mayer (MGM) to exploit its many movie classics, Disney had an ample source of instantly recognizable images to mold into rides. The park opened in 1989 as Disney-MGM Studios, but since then, the addition of attractions encompassing music, television, and theater led to the decision to rename the park **Disney's Hollywood Studios** to reflect the broader focus on "entertainment." Most of the attractions here take the form of rides or shows, and there are fewer exhibit-style attractions compared with the other Disney parks. This, combined with its relatively small size, makes Disney's Hollywood Studios the easiest park to see in a day.

The park

The first of several highly bowdlerized imitations of Hollywood's famous streets and buildings – which cause much amusement to anyone familiar with the seedy state of the originals – **Hollywood Boulevard** leads into the park, its length animated by re-enactments of famous movie scenes, strolling film-star lookalikes, and the odd Muppet.

Avoid a long wait by arriving early and going straight to either of the park's top-notch thrill rides. The better one is **The Twilight Zone Tower of Terror** (minimum height 40"/102cm; FASTPASS accepted), which gives you the dubious pleasure of experiencing several sudden drops – including moments of weightlessness – on one of four, randomly selected sequences, so no matter how many times you ride this one, you'll never quite know what's coming next. Conveniently located next door, **Rock 'n' Roller Coaster** (minimum height 48"/122cm; FASTPASS accepted) starts with a breakneck-speed launch and maintains an exhilarating pace through several loop-the-loops – all done in complete darkness and accompanied by Aerosmith's high-energy music.

The park doubles as a working production studio and in the 35-minute **Backlot Tour** a narrated tram-ride tour takes you behind the scenes, whisking you past the windows of animation studios and production offices (where you might see costumes and props being created) toward the undoubted highlight: the exploding "**Catastrophe Canyon**," an ingenious set that demonstrates special effects – notably pyrotechnics – at disturbingly close range.

Enjoy good laughs courtesy of Kermit, Miss Piggy, and the gang at **Muppet Vision 3-D**, a three-dimensional film whose special effects and "feelies" put you right inside the *Muppet Show*. Within a replica of Mann's Chinese Theater in Hollywood is **The Great Movie Ride**, a nostalgic jaunt through sets from classic movies such as *The Wizard of Oz* and *Public Enemy*, where real-life actors interact entertainingly with the Audio-Animatronics movie stars. Sharp turns and collisions with asteroids make **Star Tours** (minimum height 40"/102cm; FASTPASS accepted), a flight-simulator trip to the Moon of Endor piloted by *Star Wars* characters R2D2 and C-3PO, one of the more physical rides in the park, although it's somewhat outdated when compared with the newer flight-simulator rides in Orlando. **The Magic of Disney Animation** explains how a Disney character is thought up in the first place, and kids can try their hand at drawing cute mice and ducks.

The park has some very worthwhile live shows. Don't miss **The Indiana Jones Epic Stunt Spectacular!**, which re-creates and explains many of the action-packed set pieces from the Steven Spielberg films. In a similar vein, the very noisy **Lights, Motors, Action! Stunt Show** features equally eye-catching stunts, this time involving cars, motorbikes, and jet skis speeding through a Mediterranean village. Adding a welcome dimension to the park are two theater productions: **Beauty and the Beast – Live on Stage** and **Voyage of The Little Mermaid**. Both are live performances of shortened versions of the Disney movies. The wonderful costumes and Broadway-style sets rather than the ham acting make them worth seeing. Then check out **Fantasmic!**, the dramatic laser, light, and fireworks show that takes place just before the park closes (arrive early if you want a seat).

Disney's Animal Kingdom

DISNEY'S ANIMAL KINGDOM was opened in 1998 as an animal-conservation park with Disney's trademark over-the-top twist. The result is a 500-acre theme park, Disney World's largest by far, divided into six major "lands" – **Africa, Asia, Discovery Island, Camp Minnie-Mickey, DinoLand USA**, and **Rafiki's Planet Watch** – with Africa and Asia being the most visually impressive, each re-creating the natural landscapes and exotic flavors of these two continents with admirable attention to detail.

The park

Upon entering the park, visitors pass through **The Oasis**, with its flamingoes and other exotic birds, reptiles, and mammals, before crossing a bridge to **Discovery Island**. Here you'll find **The Tree of Life**, a 145-foot-high concrete imitation tree with depictions of animals cleverly and intriguingly woven into the trunk and branches. In the tree's root system, the amusing 3-D presentation **It's Tough to be a Bug!** shows you what an insect's life is really like, and includes some moments that can be a little intimidating for the very young.

The park's newest and most exciting ride is **Expedition Everest – Legend of the Forbidden Mountain** (minimum height 44"/112cm; FASTPASS accepted) in **Asia**, in which a train careers (both forwards and backwards) around a well-detailed replica of a Himalayan mountain, building up to a memorable encounter with a yeti. Fearsome creatures also generate the excitement in **DINOSAUR** (minimum height 40"/102cm; FASTPASS accepted) in **DinoLand USA**, where your "Time Rover," on a mission to save a friendly Iguanadon from extinction, makes lots of short drops and sudden stops in the dark as beasts spring menacingly from the prehistoric forest, roaring all the while.

In **Africa**, you'll find one of the most involving and best realized attractions: **Kilimanjaro Safaris**. Climb into a good facsimile of a jeep transport and be swept into what feels very much like a real safari through the African savannah (local oak trees have been trimmed to look like African acacias). Throughout the tour, the driver keeps up a running commentary, pointing out the animals while at the same time helping other park rangers track down make-believe poachers. In addition to Expedition Everest, Asia offers **Kali River Rapids** (minimum height 38"/97cm; FASTPASS accepted), a raft ride where, like most water-based rides at Disney, the excitement lies in the (very real) prospect of getting drenched.

The remainder of the park requires no more than casual strolling, yet all of its corners warrant exploration. **Rafiki's Planet Watch**, accessible by a ten-minute ride on the **Wildlife Express Train**, features **Conservation Station**, the most educational part of the park. Here you can view interactive exhibits promoting nature conservation and experience **Song of the Rainforest**, a simple yet extremely effective attraction where sounds from screeching birds to buzzing chainsaws come alive as you sit with earphones in a small, dark booth. Rafiki's is also home to **Affection Section**, where kids can pet docile sheep and goats. To see more of the park's impressive collection of animals from around the globe, head back to Africa and saunter along the **Pangani Forest Exploration Trail**, home to a troop of lowland gorillas, hippos (view them underwater at the hippo pool), and innumerable exotic creatures; or experience Asia's **Maharajah Jungle Trek**, which gives you an astoundingly up-close look at the healthiest-looking tigers in captivity frolicking amid ruins, as well as a host of other creatures from that continent.

Disney's Animal Kingdom has four live shows, three for all ages, and one targeted at younger visitors. Head to DinoLand USA for *Finding Nemo – The Musical*, where singing actors armed with piscean puppets on sticks tell the *Finding Nemo* story. At **Camp Minnie–Mickey** you'll find the *Festival of the Lion King*, a Broadway-style production of upbeat music with some nifty acrobatics, loosely based on its namesake film. Also in Camp Minnie-Mickey, *Pocahontas and Her Forest Friends* is an understated show very much for kids, featuring the legendary Native American lass and a few cute live animals. Asia's charming 'Flights of Wonder' animal show showcases falcons, vultures, owls, and other wonderful birds interacting deftly with the audience.

The water parks

If you're planning to visit the four main Disney parks, consider splitting your itinerary with a day at either **Blizzard Beach** or **Typhoon Lagoon**. Both water parks follow the fantastical themes typical of Disney, and the thrilling slides, along with artificial white sand beaches and hundreds of deckchairs, should appeal to kids and worn-out parents alike.

Blizzard Beach

Near Disney's Hollywood Studios and *All-Star Resorts* (see "Accommodation," p.288). Daily 10am–5pm in winter, 9am–6pm or later in summer; ☎ 407/560-3400; $40, children 3–9 $34.

Blizzard Beach is based on the fantasy that a hapless entrepreneur has opened a ski resort in Florida and the entire thing has started to melt. A combination of sand and fake snow surround Melt Away Bay, which lies at the foot of a snow-covered "mountain," complete with a ski lift and water slides. The quickest way down is via **Summit Plummet**, designed to look like a ski jump but in fact an incredibly steep water slide 120 feet high. This ride offers possibly the most exhilarating ten seconds in Orlando – and there are panoramic views over Disney property as you wait in line. The chairlift transporting you to the starting point of this and most of the park's other rides is really considered an attraction in itself (complete with waiting lines); walking up the stairs is a far quicker option. Alternatively, you can lounge around in deckchairs on the sand

and soak up some rays, then cool off in one of the pools rippled by wave machines. Arrive early in summer to beat the inevitable crowds and secure a deckchair. If you want a locker, there's an additional charge of $10; towel rental is $1. Unlike the major parks, you can bring **food** (but no alcohol or glass containers) to both of the Disney water parks.

Typhoon Lagoon
Just south of Downtown Disney (see below). Daily 10am–5pm in winter, 9am–6pm or later in summer; ☏ 407/560-4141; $40, children 3–9 $34.

Typhoon Lagoon, busiest in the summer and on weekends (often reaching full capacity), consists of an imaginatively constructed "tropical island" around a two-and-a-half-acre lagoon called the **Surf Pool**, where a powerful wave machine generates slow-building six-foot waves. The rides are generally less daunting than what's on offer at Blizzard Beach, but exciting enough to justify the price of entrance. **Humunga Kowabunga**, three speed-slides fifty feet up the "mountain" beside the lagoon, is the most exhilarating ride, followed by several smaller slides and a saltwater **Shark Reef** where you can snorkel among benign sharks and pretty tropical fish.

Typhoon Lagoon is the better choice for picnicking, with the Surf Pool's large sandy beach the obvious place to eat.

The rest of Walt Disney World

Several other **Disney-devised amusements** exist to keep people on Disney property as long as possible and to offer therapeutic recreation and relaxation to those suffering theme-park burn-out.

Downtown Disney
Buena Vista Drive (take Exit 26B off I-4). Most shops and restaurants open daily 9.30am–11pm; ☏ 407/939-2648, ⓦ www.downtowndisney.com.

Bordered by a lake on one side and the I-4 on the other, **Downtown Disney** is in essence a sprawling shopping mall. Divided into three areas – **West Side**, **Pleasure Island**, and **Marketplace** – you'll find a good range of shops and restaurants (see "Eating," p.300), a Cirque du Soleil show, and a complex dedicated to video games.

As well as some interesting dining alternatives, **West Side**, occupying the western part of Downtown Disney, has the five-story, high-tech arcade **DisneyQuest** (Mon–Thurs & Sun 11.30am–11pm, Fri & Sat 11.30am–midnight; $40, children 3–9 $34; ☏ 407/828-4600), a bastion of virtual-reality games, including a raft ride where you paddle through digital rapids, getting splashed with real water. West Side is also the permanent home of the **Cirque du Soleil's** La Nouba (shows Tues–Sat 6pm & 9pm; $53–117, children 3–9 $43–94; ☏ 407/939-1298, ⓦ www.cirquedusoleil.com), a fascinating and surreal 90-minute show full of the spellbinding acrobatics for which the company is famed.

Pleasure Island, a six-acre island in the middle of Downtown Disney, was formerly crowded with nightclubs. However, in 2008, Disney decided to withdraw from the Orlando nightlife scene, closing all of the clubs. Plans for the future include a new batch of restaurants and shops for Pleasure Island, which will be opening gradually during 2009 and 2010.

On the eastern side of Pleasure Island sits **Marketplace**, a shopping emporium crammed with the world's largest Disney merchandise store, a Disney art gallery, and a Lego store where kids can play while adults marvel at the massive creations of robots, dinosaurs, and the like outside.

Disney Institute

Buena Vista Drive, north of Downtown Disney; ☎321/939-4600, ⓦwww.disneyinstitute.com.

The **Disney Institute**, modeled on a university campus done in Florida-style architecture, offers various business-related courses. The interest for visitors, however, are the **tours** giving a behind-the-scenes look at many aspects of Walt Disney World. The best – and most expensive at $199 (including lunch) – is the "Backstage Magic" tour, which takes you along the tunnel system beneath the Magic Kingdom and offers a look at some of the backstage goings-on at Epcot and Disney's Hollywood Studios, including the technology required to put on a show such as The American Adventure (see p.294) and a peek at the elaborate costumes inside the Disney wardrobe. The tour lasts about seven hours and you must be over 16, not to mention rather dedicated to gaining a greater inside perspective on the parks; it's probably of less interest to first-time visitors trying to bag as many rides as possible. If you're on this tour, there is no admission charge to the three parks.

Disney's Wide World of Sports

Two miles east of Disney's Animal Kingdom on Osceola Parkway. Hours depend on daily events; $11.75, children 3–9 $9; ☎407/939-GAME, ⓦwww.disneyworldsports.com.

Professional and amateur sporting events (check the website for schedules) are frequently held at **Disney's Wide World of Sports**, a 200-acre complex of stadiums, arenas, and sports fields bustling on any given day with soccer moms, high-school wrestling teams, or pro baseball players. A small section called **The Sports Experience** allows you to ascertain your baseball pitching speed, kick a field goal, and test various other sporting skills, but this feels more like a fun diversion for competing athletes than an attraction for visitors. The complex is only really worth a special trip if you time it to coincide with a particular sporting event. The most publicized of these are the games played by the **Atlanta Braves** during March spring training, which take place in the 9500-seat baseball stadium (tickets $14.50–23.50).

Richard Petty Driving Experience

Walt Disney World Speedway (at the south end of the Magic Kingdom parking lot). Ride-Along daily 9am–4pm, other experiences Mon, Wed & Fri–Sun at 8am & 1pm; ☎1-800/237-3889, ⓦwww.1800bepetty.com.

The **Richard Petty Driving Experience** offers NASCAR fanatics (for more on NASCAR, see "Daytona International Speedway," p.337) four ways to get a realistic feel for stock-car racing: they can take a three-lap stock-car ride around

Disney Line cruises

Disney is also solidly in the cruise business. On the **Disney Wonder** and **Disney Magic**, you can book three- four-, and seven-day voyages, or trips combining days at sea with days at a Disney resort. The elegant ships – the luxurious decor includes inlaid Italian woodwork – depart from Port Canaveral, an hour from the theme parks (parking $36, $48, and $84 for the three-, four-, and seven-day cruises respectively), and sail to Nassau and then Disney's own Bahamian island, **Castaway Cay**. Live shows change nightly and separate entertainment areas are provided for children, adults, and families. Prices vary considerably depending on when you go and the cabin (or Disney resort) that you choose. Three-day cruises range from $429 to $2999 per person (excluding airfare); four-day cruises are $499 to $3999; and the different types of seven-day cruises are $849 to $5399. For more information, call ☎1-800/951-3532 or visit ⓦwww.disneycruiseline.com.

a one-mile tri-oval track driven by an expert in the $199 "Ride-Along;" for $399–499 (depending on the time of year), an intensive three-hour "Rookie Experience" course lets participants drive eight laps themselves; and the "King's Experience" ($799–849) or the "Experience of a Lifetime" ($1249–1299) are longer variations whereby participants get to drive eighteen and thirty laps respectively. In all cases, a valid driver's license must be presented.

Eating

Besides the generally mundane and overpriced food available at the theme parks, there are plenty of **places to eat** on Disney property. You'll find some upmarket dining opportunities at the resorts, while Downtown Disney is a safe bet for dinner, where you can choose from restaurants that are generally more varied and interesting than those at the theme parks. Epcot's World Showcase, with its multi-ethnic cuisines, offers the tastiest food among the theme parks.

Artist Point at *Wilderness Lodge* ☎407/939-3463. Tuck into hearty cuisine from the Pacific Northwest – including buffalo and the recommended house specialty, cedar plank-roasted salmon – washed down with wines from Oregon and Washington, all served under high wood-beamed ceilings. Most main dishes around $30 and up.

Bongo's Cuban Café Downtown Disney West Side, 1498 E Buena Vista Drive ☎407/828-0999. Created by Gloria and Emilio Estefan, the reasonable Cuban cuisine here ($15–20) is outshone by the wildly fabulous decor and lively salsa shows Fri & Sat.

California Grill on the 15th floor of *Contemporary Resort* ☎407/939-3463. One of Disney's best all-round restaurants, with a pricey menu dominated by fresh sushi ($20–25) and some excellent fish dishes (around $35), all served in an unpretentious dining room. A great selection of Californian wines – and impressive views over the Magic Kingdom.

Chefs de France/Bistro de Paris the French Pavilion at Epcot's World Showcase ☎407/939-3463. Fresh produce is flown in daily to create the most authentic, and beautifully presented, French cuisine around, including foie gras, goat cheese salad, and snails. *Chefs de France* is less formal and slightly cheaper (around $30) than *Bistro de Paris* ($30 and up) upstairs.

Hollywood Brown Derby Disney's Hollywood Studios ☎407/939-3463. A faithful re-creation of the mythic Hollywood landmark, with the famous recipes to match (including Cobb salad, invented by the Derby's original chefs). The relaxing, softly lit dining room gets you away from the park's general hustle and bustle. Most dishes $20–30.

House of Blues Downtown Disney West Side, 1490 E Buena Vista Drive ☎407/934-2583. Decent Creole- and Cajun-inspired food ($15–25) with live music Thurs–Sat. Try the popular all-you-can-eat Gospel brunch ($33.50) every Sun.

Jiko – The Cooking Place at *Animal Kingdom Lodge* ☎407/939-3463. Enjoy typical American food such as steaks and ribs with a welcome cosmopolitan flavor of curried sauces and exotic grains and spices, all washed down with no fewer than 65 different choices of exclusively South African wine. Most dishes cost around $30.

Raglan Road Irish Pub Downtown Disney Pleasure Island ☎407/938-0300. This Irish-owned and operated pub has stereotypical dishes such as fish and chips, pies, and stews (mainly $15-20), but it's the beer (served throughout the day) that's the main draw.

San Angel Inn the Mexican Pavilion at Epcot's World Showcase ☎407/939-3463. Savor dishes ($20-28 for dinner) that are more adventurous – using ingredients such as cactus and cocoa – than the standard TexMex food at this atmospheric re-creation of a Mexican village on a balmy night.

Victoria & Albert at *Grand Floridian Resort & Spa* ☎407/939-3463. Elk, caviar, fine wines, and harp music in the background set a refined tone at one of Central Florida's top rated restaurants. Reserve far in advance to sit at the Chef's Table in the kitchen, where you'll be attended to by the chef himself. The seven-course menu costs $125 (or $185 with wine).

Wolfgang Puck Downtown Disney West Side, 1482 E Buena Vista Drive ☎407/938-9653. Four restaurants in one multi-level location: *The Dining Room* upstairs for upmarket dining (dinner only); *The Café* for casual; *The Express* for self-service; and *B's Lounge & Sushi Bar* for sushi. Meals are moderately priced except at *The Dining Room*, which features the celebrity chef's signature dishes ($25-35). Pizzas, rotisserie chickens, and good sandwiches are available at *The Express*, which has another location in Downtown Disney Market-place ☎407/828-0107.

In the hopes of prying tourists from Disney's clutches, competitors have teamed up to offer special multi-park passes. The **Orlando FlexTicket** provides unlimited admission for fourteen days to the two Universal Orlando theme parks, SeaWorld Orlando, and two water parks, Aquatica and Wet 'n' Wild, for $234.95 (adults), $194.95 (children 3–9). For $279.95 (adults) or $233.95 (children 3–9), you can add Busch Gardens in Tampa (two hours away), with a free shuttle from Orlando to Busch Gardens included. For details on Busch Gardens, see p.371.

Universal Orlando

For some years, it seemed US TV and film production would be shifting away from expensive California to Florida, which, with its lower taxes and cheaper labor, was more amenable, and the opening of Universal Studios Florida in 1990 appeared to confirm that trend. So far, for various reasons, Florida has not proved to be a fully realistic alternative, but that hasn't stopped the Universal enclave here, known as **UNIVERSAL ORLANDO**, from expanding enormously and becoming even more successful.

The sequel to the long-established and immensely popular tour of its studios in Los Angeles, **Universal Studios Florida**, like its rival Disney's Hollywood Studios, is a working studio, filling over 400 acres with high-tech movie-themed attractions. In addition to Universal Studios Florida there's **Islands of Adventure**, boasting a high concentration of some of the best thrill rides in Orlando. And with all the nightclubs at Downtown Disney now closed, **CityWalk** has become the main competition to downtown Orlando for nightlife dollars (see "Nightlife and entertainment," p.284).

Overall, the mood at Universal Orlando is more hip and the rides more intense than at Disney, but the atmosphere is less magical, service can be variable, and the parks can feel less welcoming – as though almost everything is aimed primarily at hyper-energetic adolescent boys who want things louder, faster, and with more attitude. For most visitors, two days will be sufficient.

Accommodation

A sign of Universal Orlando's popularity has been the relatively recent opening of three resort hotels on Universal property, all of them luxurious, expensive, and incredibly convenient for visiting Universal Studios Florida, Islands of Adventure, and CityWalk (regular complimentary water taxis operate between the three resorts and a dock at CityWalk). To make reservations at any of the Universal resorts, call ☎1-888/273-1311 or visit ⓦ www.uescape.com.

Hard Rock Hotel Stuffed with rock memorabilia, and with familiar tunes blaring out at poolside, this is the least tranquil of the park's resorts – and the most popular with the younger generation. The simple yet stylish rooms are equipped with high-quality CD players and flatscreen TVs. ❽

Loews Portofino Bay Hotel A lavish re-creation of the Italian seaside village of Portofino, complete with vintage Alfa Romeos and Fiats parked in the piazza. The luxurious rooms are decorated with marble and Italian furnishings, and there's a full-service spa. ❽

Loews Royal Pacific Resort The comfortable rooms here are decked out in bamboo to enhance the "tropical" theme, while the kids will enjoy the lagoon-style pool. ❽

Universal Studios Florida

The park is arranged around a large lagoon and nominally divided into several areas: New York, Hollywood, San Francisco, and Amity (the New England town where *Jaws* took place) are impeccably replicated in street sets; Production Central, World Expo, and Woody Woodpecker's KidZone are less distinctive. There's no real need to follow a particular order in your explorations.

Replacing one of the park's best rides, **Back to the Future The Ride**, **The Simpsons Ride** (minimum height 40"/102cm) combines the same cutting-edge flight-simulator technology that was employed to such great effect in the old attraction with the irreverent humor of the Simpsons cartoon family. The other flight-simulator ride is the popular but comparatively inferior **Jimmy Neutron's Nicktoon Blast** (minimum height 40"/102cm), most memorable for its impressive animated graphics. The park's only rollercoaster is **Revenge of the Mummy** (minimum height 48"/122cm), a relatively slow-paced ride through scenes from the eponymous movie, perked up by some nifty effects, such as exploding fireballs. Be sure not to miss **Shrek 4-D**, a delightful 3-D presentation brought even more to life by an overdose of superb "feelies" (including a few too many water sprays). Another worthwhile stop is at **Disaster**, which gives you an intensely claustrophobic two minutes of terror as you experience what it's like to be caught on a subway train during an 8.0 Richter-scale earthquake. Along the same lines, **TWISTER … Ride It Out** is a gripping and frighteningly realistic re-creation of a tornado tearing through a small Oklahoma town, complete with simulated lightning, flying objects, and rain (cover all camera equipment). **JAWS** owes its success to anticipation of horror and classy special effects, but the ride is over all too quickly. Special effects – like the "plasma blasts" that let the audience feel the heat and shock of its explosions – are also the main draw at **Terminator 2: 3-D**, which also has 3-D imagery and some live action. **MEN IN BLACK Alien Attack** (minimum height 42"/107cm) puts you smack inside a video game as you rack up points zapping monsters – a chaotic and unsatisfying experience, although the monsters are well designed. For something a little more sedate, check out **Lucy: A Tribute**, made up of memorabilia associated with the zany, irrepressible redhead comedienne Lucille Ball.

Visiting Universal Orlando

Universal Orlando (☏407/363-8000, ⊛www.uescape.com) is located half a mile north of exits 74B or 75A off I-4. Both parks open daily at 9am and close at any time between 6pm and 10pm depending on the season. A one-day, one-park ticket costs $73 for adults, $61 for children 3–9; a two-day, two-park ticket is $104.99 for adults, $94.99 for children 3–9. **Parking** at Universal Orlando costs $12 per day.

Universal has also devised **Universal Express** – a system similar to Disney's FASTPASS (see box, p.290) and which includes virtually every attraction – to help get visitors around long waits in line. To avoid the limitation of being able to hold only one Universal Express pass for one attraction at any one time you can pay $25.99–50.99 depending on the time of year for **Universal Express Plus**, which allows you to enter the Express line whenever and wherever you want. Another good way to **beat the crowds** at Universal is to join the much quicker single rider lines – where you fill up the odd seat not taken by groups wishing to experience the attraction together – that you'll find at some rides. All guests at the Universal resorts can join the Express lines simply by presenting their room key-card.

▲ The Simpsons at the opening of their eponymously named ride

Other attractions will appeal especially to the kids. **E.T. Adventure** is a rather dull ride on pretend bicycles to ET's home planet, redeemed somewhat by ET speaking your name (recorded earlier by a computer) as you leave. Playgrounds and fairground rides dominate Woody Woodpecker's KidZone, where the best attraction is **A Day in the Park with Barney**, a show involving lots of singing and clapping along with Barney the dinosaur and friends.

You'll also find a number of live stage shows on offer throughout the park: the best is the **Universal Horror Make-Up Show**, where horror-movie special effects are revealed amid amusingly tasteless jokes; **Fear Factor Live!** has contestants confront their worst fears in a series of challenges that mimic, albeit in watered-down form, those of the hit TV show (to register as a contestant for this show, present yourself at the venue 90 minutes in advance); **Animal Actors on Location!** explains some of the tricks used to turn animals into film actors; and **Beetlejuice's Graveyard Revue** features high-tempo renditions of catchy tunes and risqué humor.

Islands of Adventure

Universal Orlando's other theme park, **ISLANDS OF ADVENTURE**, is a five-minute walk from Universal Studios Florida. The park is divided into five sections, each with its own unique character: **Marvel Super Hero Island** and **The Lost Continent** have the most exciting rides, molded on the comic-book heroes of your youth and ancient myths and legends respectively; **Jurassic Park** goes to town on the well-worn dinosaur motif in a scientific as well as scary way; **Toon Lagoon** uses cartoon characters to get you completely soaked; and the garishly eye-catching **Seuss Landing** is where the kids hang out. The park is bursting with excellent thrill rides and outshines anything Disney World has to offer in that department – even though no one has yet equaled Disney for the seamless perfection of its imagined environments made real. There's also a live show (though Disney still holds the edge in this area) and a number of decent hands-on play areas spread throughout.

The very best of the rides is **The Amazing Adventures of Spider-Man** (minimum height 40"/102cm), which employs every trick imaginable – 3-D, sensory stimuli, motion simulation, and more – to spirit you into Spider-Man's battles with villains across a high-rise city. **Dueling Dragons** (minimum height 54"/137cm) is the next most exciting ride: twin rollercoasters ("Fire" and "Ice", separate waiting lines for each) engineered to provide harrowing head-on near-misses with one another – which makes sitting in the front row especially thrilling; the seats also leave your feet dangling precariously in mid-air, adding to the sense of danger. Another exciting ride is the **Incredible Hulk Coaster** (minimum height 54"/137cm), with its catapult start (apparently packing the same thrust as an F-16 fighter jet) and plenty of loop-the-loops and plunges, which would be more scary if they were higher up.

Heading the second tier of thrill rides is **Jurassic Park River Adventure** (minimum height 42"/107cm), a generally tame boat-trip through a primeval zoo, spiced up by special effects, pyrotechnics and an unexpected 85-foot drop. **Doctor Doom's Fearfall** (minimum height 52"/132cm) looks frightening enough with its imposing twin towers (affording good views over the park), but the very short ride – a controlled drop during which you experience a few seconds of weightlessness – is an anti-climax. **Storm Force Accelatron** is a ride for all ages, placing visitors in tub-like cars that spin and whirl in a domed space enveloped by a noisy light show. **Poseidon's Fury** offers some impressive effects using water and fire as you play your part in an Indiana Jones-style tour of the ancient ruins of Poseidon's temple, even if the storyline is only mildly engaging.

In somewhat less adrenaline-pumping mode, you could try **Dudley Do-Right's Ripsaw Falls** (minimum height 44"/112cm), a flume ride where the final 60-foot drop will drench all four passengers in the hollowed-out-log boats (avoid on cooler days); **Popeye & Bluto's Bilge-Rat Barges** (minimum height 42"/107cm), a raft-ride that's only slightly drier; and **The Flying Unicorn** (minimum height 36"/91cm), a mini-rollercoaster that takes you on a fanciful flight through an enchanted forest.

Seuss Landing has even tamer, but enchanting, offerings for the little ones, including **Caro-Seuss-el**, a merry-go-round adorned with Seussian characters; the interactive playround **One Fish, Two Fish, Red Fish, Blue Fish;** a Flying Dumbo-style ride called **If I Ran the Zoo**; and **The Cat in the Hat**, which retells the famous story as you sit in spinning sofas. For an aerial perspective of Seuss Landing's incredibly colorful scenery, take a trip on **The High in the Sky Seuss Trolley Rain Ride!**

There's one live performance offered throughout the day: **The Eighth Voyage of Sinbad**, an action-packed extravaganza of swashbuckling adventure and great pyrotechnics, where the set, stunts, and effects are as good as the jokes are bad.

Eating

CityWalk, Universal Orlando's nightlife venue, has a good selection of restaurants – at least better than those on offer inside neighboring Universal Studios Florida and Islands of Adventure.

Emeril's CityWalk, 6000 Universal Blvd ☏407/224-2424, ⓦwww.emerils.com. CityWalk's most upmarket and expensive dining option, overseen by TV chef Emeril Lagasse, serves gourmet food such as filet mignon and hickory smoked-lemongrass duck in a somewhat austere dining room.

Hard Rock Café CityWalk, 6050 Universal Blvd ☏407/351-7625. Orlando boasts the world's largest *Hard Rock Café*, known as much for its T-shirts and music memorabilia as for its All-American menu – hamburgers generally cost $10–15.

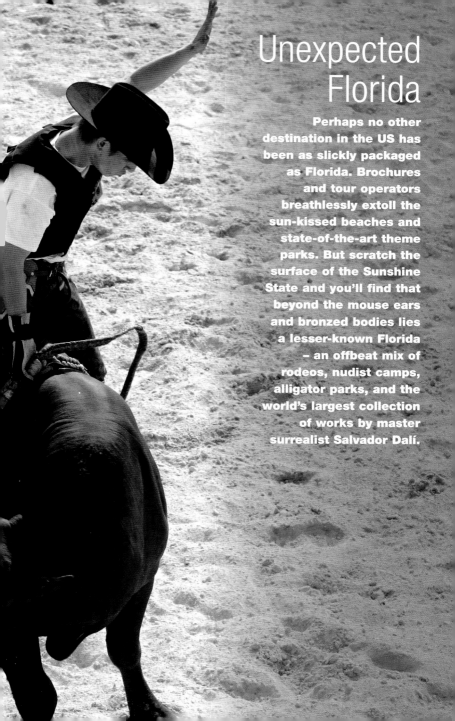

Unexpected
Florida

Perhaps no other
destination in the US has
been as slickly packaged
as Florida. Brochures
and tour operators
breathlessly extoll the
sun-kissed beaches and
state-of-the-art theme
parks. But scratch the
surface of the Sunshine
State and you'll find that
beyond the mouse ears
and bronzed bodies lies
a lesser-known Florida
– an offbeat mix of
rodeos, nudist camps,
alligator parks, and the
world's largest collection
of works by master
surrealist Salvador Dalí.

Unshowy side shows

In a state where almost nothing has escaped the showy theme park treatment, some of the most memorable attractions are the understated ones that don't try too hard to impress. Nothing demonstrates this better than the voyeuristic appeal of the **Reptile World Serpentarium**, where the fangs of vipers, rattlesnakes, and cobras are pried open to extract venom for sale to research laboratories.

The theme parks of yesteryear, decidedly low-tech and one-dimensional, still survive against the odds, thanks to their quirky charm. Orlando's **Gatorland** has been around since 1949 – quite an achievement in a city where attractions come and go with alarming regularity. The alligators and crocodiles here usually lie motionless all day, but at a twice-daily show leap from the water to tear into whole chickens held on sticks.

Reptile World Serpentarium ▲

Celebration ▼

Planned living

Many of Florida's cities and towns may have grown organically, spreading out as and when the population dictated. But there are some rather eerily perfect places, designed and planned down to the last streetlamp and cornice. Prefab towns like **Seaside** and **Celebration** are the best examples, with their dollhouse architecture and scrubbed streets. The latter is an exercise in Disney expansion and must be seen to be believed.

Cassadaga has an altogether more ethereal origin. It was founded in 1875, after a man was told in a séance he would found a spiritualist community there. It still thrives, full of psychics, mediums, and palm readers dispensing advice and healing with as much enthusiasm as Mickey Mouse expends entertaining.

Seniors have long been flocking to Florida to spend their twilight years, and **retirement communities** have cropped up everywhere. But what's often amazing is their size and infrastructure: **The Villages**, near Ocala, is so sprawling and crammed full of facilities – including its own hospital – that it's marked on maps and appears in TV weather forecasts as a town.

Divisions

In a state of divides – coastal versus interior, north versus south – the greatest extremes may well be found in liberal versus conservative attitudes, though these do somewhat follow geographical lines. America's southernmost town, Key West, is among the most liberal anywhere in the US, a fact celebrated during the decadent week-long **Fantasy Fest**. This Mardi Gras–style extravaganza, which has a strong Gay Pride element, ranks as one of North America's not-to-be-missed events for anyone leading an alternative lifestyle.

Meanwhile, visitors to the northern part of the state will notice similarities with the **Deep South**; up in the Panhandle and around Jacksonville you could easily believe you were in Alabama or Georgia. The **plantation houses** clustered around Tallahassee are reminiscent of Florida's slavery past and provide some historical

▲ Plantation-style house

▼ Fantasy Fest, Key West

▼ Salvador Dalí Museum, St Petersburg

Dalí Museum

That the largest collection of works by Spanish artist **Salvador Dalí** is found in sleepy St Petersburg is perhaps as surreal as some of the paintings themselves. The phenomenal **museum** displays more than a thousand of his works, including examples from his Impressionist, Cubist, and Surrealist periods; look for the famed melting watches in *The Disintegration of the Persistence of Memory*.

Racehorses, Hallandale Beach ▲

Paradise Lakes ▼

insight into why the northern part of the state has a distinctly southern feel: people are friendly and hospitable, yet wary of outsiders, while conservative attitudes dominate and religion plays an important part in daily life.

Horse country

Florida's beaches and swampland are well known. However, around Ocala in Marion County, the land is green and softly undulating – the perfect place for raising **thoroughbred racehorses**. Over seventy-five percent of the country's thoroughbred breeding and training facilities are located here, and the last Triple Crown winner, *Affirmed* (1978), was born on one of the many **horse farms** in the area. There is also a brisk trade in fifty breeds of horse, prompting the US Department of Agriculture to allow Marion County to promote itself as the "Horse Capital of the World."

Horse farming flourishes, but the days of cattle farming being a significant industry are long past. Nevertheless, **cowboy culture** remains alive and well in the region around Kissimmee, as well as in Davie, just west of Fort Lauderdale; both hold well-known rodeo events.

As nature intended

In the middle of nondescript Pasco County, fifty miles south of The Villages, you'll find no less than six **nudist resorts**, including **Paradise Lakes**, the largest in the US, with over 72 acres of palm-shaded pools, spas, a lake, and every activity under the sun, including "co-ed naked water volleyball." The clothing-optional resort attracts more than 100,000 visitors per year, making this small patch of Florida the epicenter of North American naturism.

Jimmy Buffett's Margaritaville CityWalk, 6000 Universal Blvd ☎407/224-2155, ⓦwww .margaritavilleorlando.com. Caribbean-style food like jerk salmon and coconut shrimp served in an appropriately tropical setting, complete with a volcano exploding with margarita mix. Busy and moderately priced, with dishes costing under $20.
Latin Quarter CityWalk, 6000 Universal Blvd ☎407/224-3663. Traditional dishes of Latin America – defined broadly to include fajitas and barbecue ribs – are given a "Nuevo Latino"

contemporary touch, including a sumptuous paella containing several different types of seafood and chorizo. Most main dishes cost $15–20. Dinner only.
NBA City 6860 Universal Blvd ☎407/363-5919. The moderately priced dishes such as blue-cheese pasta and maple-glazed pork chops are more imaginative than at most themed restaurants. There's also an interactive area where you can test your basketball-shooting skills and see how high you can jump.

Nightlife: CityWalk

With the closure of the nightclubs at Downtown Disney (see p.298), **CITYWALK** ($11.99 for all-night access to every club, $15 if you want to take in a movie, plus free parking after 6pm ☎407/363-8000, ⓦwww.citywalkorlando.com), a friendly mix of restaurants, live music, dance clubs, bars, and a multi-screen cinema, has become the main after-dark alternative to downtown Orlando (see p.284). However, compared with downtown's extensive and diverse options, CityWalk's clubs can seem a little sterile and monotonous.

If you want to dance, try **the groove**, with its huge dancefloor, flashing lights, and good sound system. Elsewhere, live music provides much of the entertainment. **Bob Marley – A Tribute to Freedom** celebrates the "King of Reggae" with endless covers of Marley songs; the live island-style music and potent margaritas at **Jimmy Buffett's Margaritaville** capture the famous laidback Florida mood perfectly; **Red Coconut Club** is an attractive martini lounge with live music to suit most tastes; and **Pat O'Brien's** offers an Old New Orleans vibe of dueling pianos and wrought-iron balconies. CityWalk's latest addition, **CityWalk's Rising Star**, is a karaoke bar where the twist is that you can sing accompanied by a live band. Finally, **Hard Rock Live**, a 3000-capacity auditorium, hosts live performers – occasionally famous ones – almost every evening. Visit ⓦwww .hardrocklive.com or call ☎407/351–LIVE for show schedules and ticket prices.

SeaWorld Orlando

It may have as many souvenir shops as fish, but **SEAWORLD ORLANDO** is the cream of Florida's sizeable crop of marine parks and as such shouldn't be missed. Like Busch Gardens in Tampa (see p.371), SeaWorld Orlando is owned by Anheuser-Busch (which explains the incongruous homage to the brewery's Clydesdale horses, the company symbol, at SeaWorld's **Clydesdale Hamlet**). To see it all and get the best value for your money, you'll need to allocate a whole day and be certain to pick up the free map and show schedule at the entrance. To **beat the crowds**, try going on the park's thrill rides during one of the immensely popular live animal shows, when the number of people milling about the park can be significantly reduced.

The signature event, held at the Shamu Stadium, is **Believe** – thirty minutes of tricks performed by playful killer whales (the first fourteen rows will get drenched during the performance). In a similar vein, **Blue Horizons**, at the Whale and Dolphin Theatre, has dolphins doing the tricks, with trapeze artists, high-divers, and even parrots adding a welcome change of pace. Perhaps the best show for kids takes place at the **Sea Lion and Otter Stadium**, where

SeaWorld Orlando (☎407/351-3600 or 1-800/327-2424, ⊛www.seaworld.com) is located on Sea Harbor Drive, at the intersection of I-4 and the Central Florida Parkway, or I-4 and the Beeline Expressway; Exit 71 if you're coming from the west on I-4, Exit 72 if you're coming from the east on I-4. The park opens daily at 9am and closes at any time between 6pm and 10pm depending on the season. Tickets cost $69.95, children 3–9 $59.95.

the mammals put on a grand pantomime-style entertainment entitled *Clyde and Seamore Take Pirate Island*. Be sure not to miss the mime artist on hand fifteen minutes or so before the show making fun of spectators as they file into the stadium – very amusing and, in the context of Orlando theme parks, daring entertainment. At the **Seaport Theatre**, you'll be charmed by **Pets Ahoy!**, in which animals, many of them rescued from local shelters, do their best to win you over by performing a multitude of very cute routines. The last of the park's live shows, **Odyssea**, at the Nautilus Theater, has humans rather than animals performing acrobatics, accompanied by music and special effects that transport you into an underwater fantasy world.

SeaWorld's first thrill ride – billed a "water coaster" – **Journey to Atlantis** (minimum height 42"/107cm) travels on both water and rails. However, it's not as exciting as it sounds, with the only exciting moment being a sheer drop that will soak everyone in the front row. Inside the adjacent gift shop are two aquariums: a 25,000-gallon, underfoot aquarium filled with stingrays, and another one overhead (6000 gallons) with hammerhead sharks. **Kraken** (minimum height 52"/132cm) is a much better bet for thrills and spills; this incredibly high rollercoaster reaches speeds of up to 65mph, performing numerous loop-the-loops as your feet dangle unnervingly in mid-air. A brand new rollercoaster, **Manta**, is due to open in the summer of 2009. The **Wild Arctic** complex (complete with artificial snow and ice) brings you close to beluga whales, walruses, and polar bears, which are accessible by foot or via a bumpy but enjoyable flight-simulator ride (minimum height 42"/107cm) which takes you on a perilous helicopter trip through an Arctic blizzard.

With less razzmatazz, plenty of smaller tanks and displays around the park offer a wealth of information about the underwater world. Among the highlights, **Penguin Encounter** re-creates Antarctica – right down to being more dimly lit in summer – with scores of the waddling birds scampering over a make-believe iceberg and swimming underwater; **Shark Encounter** includes a walk through a 60-foot-long, acrylic-sided and -roofed tunnel, offering as realistic an impression on dry land of what swimming with sharks must feel like; and at **Manatee Rescue**, the world's largest manatee rehabilitation facility, you'll get a close-quarters look at these endangered creatures and learn about the threats faced by their species (for more on Florida's manatees, see box, p.396). Elsewhere, buy plates of fish ($4) to feed to the slimy – but safe – stingrays at **Stingray Lagoon**, the sociable dolphins at **Dolphin Cove**, or the dexterous sea lions and seals at **Pacific Point Preserve**.

When you're ready for a change of scene from the animals, head to the **Anheuser-Busch Hospitality Center** for two free glasses of beer, or attend the Brewmaster's Club (sign up in advance), where you'll sample malts, stouts, and lagers, and learn how to pair them with food. The area set aside for kids is **Shamu's Happy Harbor**, offering inner tubes, slides, and climbing nets, as well as more challenging equipment such as remote-control boats and cars.

▲ A killer whale in mid-dive

The Waterfront, a five-acre themed area reminiscent of a Mediterranean village, is where you'll find the bulk of the park's **restaurants**, including *Spice Mill*, offering sandwiches with some spicy fillings like Cajun, Jambalaya, and Caribbean jerk chicken.

Discovery Cove

DISCOVERY COVE is slightly different from anything else you'll find in Orlando: a theme park without a theme; a water park without the slides; an aquarium without the glass tanks. It's billed as a multi-environment tropical paradise where the star attraction is swimming – or, more accurately, standing waist-deep in water – with actual dolphins in the chilly salt waters of the **Dolphin Lagoon**. On entry to the park you'll be given a time for your (optional) dolphin encounter, which lasts for about half an hour and involves stroking, playing, and riding on the dorsal fin of the docile creatures. Other attractions in the park include an **Aviary** packed with tame exotic birds that you have to swim under a waterfall to get to; a **Coral Reef** where you can snorkel with colorful fish; the **Ray Lagoon**, offering the chance to wade with hundreds of harmless Southern and Cownose rays; and a swimmable **Tropical River** that winds around the Coral Reef and Ray Lagoon, and past a sandy **beach**. Access to Discovery Cove is limited to about a thousand visitors a day, so you must reserve in advance (one to three months if you want to take the dolphin swim; at least three weeks if not). The high cost of admission does include use of equipment (wet suits, snorkeling gear, towels, lockers, animal-friendly sunscreen) and a meal with soft drinks, although once you've done your business with the dolphins and been on a few snorkeling expeditions, there's not much else to do than lounge around on the beach.

Other attractions in Orlando

Orlando's small-time entrepreneurs are nothing if not inventive. No end of
tacky, short-lived, would-be attractions spring up each year and a large number
of them swiftly sink without a trace. The list below represents the best – or just
the longest-surviving – of the thousand-and-one little places to visit in Orlando.
You'll also find several other highly worthwhile attractions just to the south of
Orlando in and around the town of Kissimmee (see opposite).

Aquatica

5800 Water Play Way, on International Drive across from Seaworld Orlando. Daily 9am–6pm, closes at 8pm in
summer; $41.95, children 3–9 $35.95; ☎407/351-3600 or 1-888/800-5447, ⊛www.aquaticabyseaworld.com.

Combining live animal attractions with wave pools, slides, and beaches, this new
water park by SeaWorld Orlando represents an original take on a well-worn
idea. In the **Dolphin Plunge** slide, for example, the clear-sided tube passes
through a pool full of black and white Commerson's dolphins, providing brief
glimpses of the creatures as you go down.

The Holy Land Experience

4655 Vineland Rd, at Conroy Rd, next to the I-4 (Exit 78). Mon–Sat 10am–6pm (sometimes closes at
9pm during holidays); $35, children 6–12 $20; ☎407/872-2272 or 1-800/447-7235, ⊛www
.theholylandexperience.com.

Orlando's newest theme park opened in 2001 with the primary aim to educate
rather than wow the crowd – don't expect Noah's Ark flume rides and David
vs Goliath rollercoasters. The Christian message is instead preached through the
park's architecture – an evocative rebuilding of ancient Jerusalem – various
religious exhibits, and films and shows recounting pivotal events during Jesus'
lifetime, most notably the musical retelling of the crucifixion.

Pirate's Cove Adventure Golf

Two locations: 8501 International Drive (☎407/352-7378) and Crossroads Shopping Center, corner of I-4
and Hwy-535, Lake Buena Vista (☎407/827-1242); ⊛www.piratescove.net. Daily 9am–11.30pm;
$9.95–13.95, children 3–12 $8.95–12.50, depending on which course you choose.

This is miniature golf at its inventive best. Choose from several challenging,
fanciful courses, and putt your way through caves, over footbridges, and under
waterfalls, with pirates scrutinizing your every stroke.

SkyVenture

6805 Visitors Circle, off International Drive, across from Wet 'n' Wild. Mon–Thurs & Sun 11.30am–9pm, Fri
& Sat 11.30am–10pm; $44.95; ☎407/903-1150 or 1-800/759-3861, ⊛www.skyventureorlando.com.

Fly on a column of air without a parachute in this realistic freefall skydiving
simulator. The whole process takes about an hour, although the actual diving, in
an indoor wind tunnel, only lasts for a couple of minutes or so.

Wet 'n' Wild

6200 International Drive. Daily 10am–5pm, longer hours in summer; $41.95, children 3–9 $35.95. After 2pm, $10 off regular prices; ☎407/351-1800 or 1-800/992-9453, @www.wetnwildorlando.com.

Orlando's original water park has stood the test of time very well indeed and continues to offer stiff competition to Disney's water parks and SeaWorld's Aquatica. Unfettered by Disney's predilection for fantastical themes, Wet 'n' Wild has put all of its energy into providing the most fun and exciting attractions possible. There are very scary, no-nonsense speed slides such as the 250-foot "Der Stuka"; more elaborate but slightly less intimidating flume and tube rides like the twisting "Mach 5" and "The Storm", which feels rather like being flushed down the toilet; and multi-person raft rides like "The Flyer", with plenty of sharp turns.

Wonderworks

9067 International Drive at Pointe Orlando. Daily 9am–midnight; $19.95, children 4–12 $13.95; ☎407/351-8800, @www.wonderworksonline.com.

This collection features more than a hundred high-tech interactive gizmos inside an upside-down creaking house. Many of the exhibits rely on simulators to re-create various exciting situations such as landing the Space Shuttle and riding a virtual rollercoaster, while quirkier exhibits let you feel what it's like, for example, to lie on a bed of 3500 nails.

South of Orlando

The area **south of Orlando**, stretching fifteen miles or so south and east from Walt Disney World, contains more of the same kind of attractions found in Orlando itself, many of them, such as the venerable Gatorland, based on animals. The main towns in these parts are **Kissimmee**, just as sprawling as Orlando to the north, and the smaller, quainter **Celebration**, a more amenable place for a leisurely stroll – although you'll really need your own car to explore this area effectively.

Gatorland

Gatorland, 14501 S Orange Blossom Trail (daily 9am–5pm; $22.99, children 3–12 $14.99; ☎407/855-5496 or 1-800/393-5297, @www.gatorland.com) has been giving visitors an up-close look at the state's most feared and least understood animals since the 1950s. Along with the alligators, the park's inhabitants now include crocodiles (whose noses are more pointed than alligators'), llamas, snakes, and flamingoes, but the undisputed highlight remains the twice-daily "Gator Jumparoo Show", where hunks of chicken are suspended from a wire and the largest alligators, using their powerful tail muscles, propel themselves out of the water to ferociously snatch their dinner. When you arrive, pick up a schedule for the other main shows: along with Gator Jumparoo, there's "Gator Wrestlin'", where a small gator is pinned down and it's mouth pried open by a staff member; and "Up Close Encounters", where assorted creepy-crawlies are shared with the most terrified-looking members of the audience. You can easily see the whole park and the shows in half a day.

Kissimmee

Continuing south from Gatorland along Orange Blossom Trail brings you to the downtown portion of **KISSIMMEE**, a town spread across much of the rough acreage south of Orlando. Although easy to walk around, Kissimmee's downtown holds little of interest except for the **Monument of States**, a funky forty-foot obelisk on the corner of Monument Avenue and Johnston Street comprising garishly painted concrete blocks adorned with pieces of stone and fossil representing all of the American states and twenty foreign countries, erected in 1943 to honor the former president of the local All-States Tourist Club. Afterwards, take a stroll to Lakeshore Boulevard and admire pretty **Lake Tohopekaliga**, headwaters to the Everglades and home to many of Florida's native birds and also alligators and bald eagles. If you want to get a closer look at the wildlife, take a thirty-minute airboat ride with **Boggy Creek Airboat Rides** (daily 9am–5pm; $24.95, children 3–10 $18.95; ☎407/344-9550, Ⓦ www.bcairboats.com), which leave from Southport Park, about 18 miles south from the intersection of Poinciana Boulevard and US-192.

Kissimmee's other attractions are spread out along US-192 or just to the south of US-192. **Old Town**, 5770 W Irlo Bronson Memorial Hwy (shops daily 10am–11pm, rides daily noon–11pm or later at weekends; free to enter, buy individual tickets for each ride or an all-day pass for $15 (limited rides) or $25 (all rides); ☎407/396-4888, Ⓦ www.old-town.com), is a throwback to a traditional fairground complete with Ferris wheel and bumper cars – not overly exciting unless you visit on a Saturday night, when, at 8.30pm, hundreds of classic cars are paraded up and down the streets. With a peaceful, rural setting a couple of miles south of Old Town, **Green Meadows Petting Farm**, 1368 S Poinciana Blvd (daily 9.30am–4pm; $21; ☎407/846-0770, Ⓦ www.greenmeadowsfarm.com), is a refreshing change of pace from the bustle of the major parks. The two-hour guided tour takes in all the usual farm animals, and hands-on experience is encouraged, from simple petting to the full-blown milking of a cow. Kids also enjoy pony and tractor rides. Horse rides for adults are offered a little further down the road at **Horse World Riding Stables**, 3705 S Poinciana Blvd (daily 9am–5pm; $43.95–74.95 depending on the ride chosen; ☎407/847-4343, Ⓦ www.horseworldstables.com).

Traveling east along US-192 brings you to the town of St-Cloud, where, at 5705 E Irlo Bronson Memorial Hwy, you'll find the wonderfully offbeat **Reptile World Serpentarium** (Oct–Aug Tues–Sun 9am–5.30pm; $5.75, children 6–17 $4.75, children 3–5 $3.75) presided over by George VanHorn, who has been extracting snake venom for sale to anti-venom research laboratories for years. He handles several moody vipers, rattlesnakes, and cobras; the stub at the end of one of his fingers is testament to the occupational hazards. You can view the fascinating extraction process twice daily at noon and 3pm; the rest of the place – basically a small collection of snakes in glass tanks – can be perused quickly.

Practicalities: Eating and accommodation

Along with a couple of high-profile dinner shows that are reviewed in the box on p.283, US-192 is lined with predictable **chain restaurants**, many of them offering cheap and cheerful all-you-can-eat meals. Downtown Kissimmee has a few restaurants catering to lunching office workers, such as *Susan's Courtside Café*, 18 S Orlando Ave (☎407/518-1150; lunch only, closed Sat & Sun), where you can get good sandwiches and home-made pizza for around $7 and up. By far the most appealing selection of restaurants, however, is to be found in Celebration (see opposite).

Many people choose to stay in the budget **hotels** and **motels** that line **US-192** (also known as Irlo Bronson Memorial Highway). Not only do these establishments tend to be cheaper than their Orlando equivalents (you can usually get a room for around $50 per night), but they are also close to Disney World (often with free shuttles to the parks), and are most likely to have rooms available at busy times. We've provided a range of options, including two **campgrounds**, below.

Cypress Cove Nudist Resort & Spa 4425 Pleasant Hill Rd ☎407/933-5870 or 1-888/683-3140, ⓦwww.cypresscoveresort.com. For something a little different, ditch the clothes and head to this full service resort catering to those who prefer to vacation in the nude. Choose from spacious apartments or smaller hotel rooms; camping (from $51) and RV hook-ups (from $60) are also available. ❸

Howard Johnson Maingate Resort West 8660 W Irlo Bronson Memorial Hwy ☎407/396-4500 or 1-800/638-7829, ⓦwww.orlandohojomaingate .com. An elaborate *HoJo* with renovated rooms, three pools, two restaurants, tennis courts, a fitness center, and even a sports field. ❷

Inn Nova Motel 9330 W Irlo Bronson Memorial Hwy ☎407/424-8420 or 1-800/440-4473. Bright, cheerful rooms and free local calls are good reasons to try this motel, just 5min west of Disney. ❷

Kissimmee/Orlando KOA 2644 Happy Camper Place ☎407/396-2400 or 1-800/562-7791, ⓦwww.koa.com/where/fl. A bit pricey (from $48) but suited to tents and RVs, and offers a large heated pool as well as a playground and game-room for kids.

Palm Lakefront Resort & Hostel 4840 W Irlo Bronson Memorial Hwy ☎407/396-1759, ⓦwww .orlandohostels.com. The obvious choice for backpackers, this hostel has six-bed, single-sex dorms ($19), private rooms, a pool, and a pleasant lakefront location. ❶

Richardson's Fish Camp 1550 Scotty's Rd ☎407/846-6540. For those looking for a peaceful setting, pitch your tent at this laid-back campground a few miles south of Kissimmee, beside West Lake Tohopekaliga. Tent sites are £24.50

🏃 Sevilla Inn 4640 W Irlo Bronson Memorial Hwy ☎407/396-4135, ⓦwww.sevillainn .com. This unpretentious, privately owned inn provides a refreshing change from the chain hotels, offering simple, cheap, but perfectly satisfactory rooms and a humble pool. ❷

Celebration

If you just can't get enough of the squeaky-clean Disney concept, you might consider buying a home in **CELEBRATION** (ⓦwww.celebrationfl.com), a 4900-acre town nestled between Kissimmee and Disney's theme parks (off US-192) created by Disney and officially opened in 1996. The Disney people did massive sociological research before settling on the design they believed would capture the American ideal of community: old-fashioned exteriors, homes close to the road so neighbors are more likely to interact, and a congenial old-fashioned downtown area beside a tranquil lake. World-famous architects were brought in to design major buildings: Phillip Johnson, Ritchie & Fiore designed the Town Hall; Michael Graves the post office; Cesar Pelli the 1950s-style moviehouse; and Robert A.M. Stern the health center. The first 350 home sites sold out before a single model was even complete. Enthusiasts applaud Celebration's friendly small-town feel, where town events are well attended and children can walk carefree to school, all without being a gated community, as spokespersons are quick to point out. Detractors use words such as "contrived" and "sterile" to describe the atmosphere, and criticize stringent rules, like the insistence all window treatments facing the outside must be white. The town, though, is growing rapidly and is worth a short visit – not least for its several good restaurants (see below) and virtually traffic-free streets that are ideal for a leisurely stroll. Stop by to determine for yourself whether this homogeneous blandness is an evolutionary stage of the American Dream, a touch of elitist Big Brother, or some sort of smug cult.

Practicalities

Celebration's only **hotel**, *Celebration Hotel*, 700 Bloom St (☎407/566-6000 or 1-888/499-3800, ⓦwww.celebrationhotel.com; ❸), is a predictably upmarket and classy place, with elegant rooms overlooking the town's picturesque lake.

The town has the area's best selection of **restaurants**, most of them facing the lake along Front Street. *Café d'Antonio*, 691 Front St (☎407/566-2233), is a good, but expensive, Italian restaurant, serving predominantly meat and pasta dishes in an upmarket atmosphere bordering on being a little stuffy. *Colombia*,

649 Front St (☎407/566-1505; live Spanish folk music Fri evenings), is famous for high-standard, moderately priced Spanish food, notably paella, eaten appropriately enough in a dining room that looks like something straight out of a luxurious Iberian villa. *Celebration Town Tavern*, 721 Front St (☎407/566-2526), specializes in New England seafood – although the barbecued baby back ribs ($22) is possibly the tastiest item on the menu. Light meals are available at the bar until 2am, making this a favorite among Celebration's night owls.

The northern suburbs

Head a few miles north from downtown Orlando for a taste of Florida living without the mouse-ear hats. The northern suburbs are an area of smart residential neighborhoods such as **Winter Park**, **Eatonville**, and **Maitland**, adorned by parks, lakes, and a smattering of decent museums and art galleries which, for all their varying degrees of quality, offer a refreshing change of pace for those with theme-park fatigue.

Winter Park

A couple of miles northeast of Loch Haven Park (see p.281), **WINTER PARK** has been socially a cut above Orlando since it was launched in 1887 as "a beautiful winter retreat for well-to-do people." For all its obvious money – a mix of new yuppie dollars and old wealth – Winter Park is a very likeable place, with a pervasive sense of community and a touch of California-style, New Age affluence.

On Fairbanks Avenue, which brings traffic from Loch Haven Park into Winter Park, stand the Mediterranean Revival buildings of **Rollins College**, the oldest recognized college in the state, boasting a tiny but respected liberal arts faculty. Other than its neat landscaping, the campus has just one point of interest: the **Cornell Fine Arts Museum** (Tues–Fri 10am–4pm, Sat & Sun noon–5pm; $5; ☎407/646-2526, ⓦwww.rollins.edu/cfam), where a few Italian Renaissance paintings brighten the otherwise staid bundle of modest nineteenth-century European and American art. The temporary exhibitions are often more contemporary and vibrant.

You'll find a more personal art collection a mile east of the college on Osceola Avenue, at the **Albin Polasek Museum and Sculpture Gardens**, no. 633 (Sept–June Tues–Sat 10am–4pm, Sun 1–4pm; gardens only July & Aug Mon–Fri 10am–4pm; $5; ☎407/647-6294, ⓦwww.polasek.org), the former home of Czech-born sculptor Albin Polasek, who arrived penniless in the US in 1901 and spent most of his time over the next fifty years winning big-money commissions, many of the profits from which have been plowed back into this museum. The most striking sculptures – technically accomplished, Realist works with classical, mythical, and liturgical themes – are on display amid the colorful flowers and plants of the three-acre gardens.

Park Avenue: the Morse Museum and boat tours

The showpiece of Winter Park's upmarket status is **Park Avenue**, the town's main north–south thoroughfare, which meets Fairbanks Avenue near Rollins College. This eminently strollable street is lined with chic boutiques, spick-and-span restaurants, and diverse art galleries, of which Scott Laurent Collection, 348 N Park Ave (Mon–Sat 10.30am–5.30pm, Sun noon–5pm; ☎407/629-0278, ⓦwww.scottlaurentcollection.com), is worth a special look for its impressive selection of objets d'art, particularly the colorful glasswork.

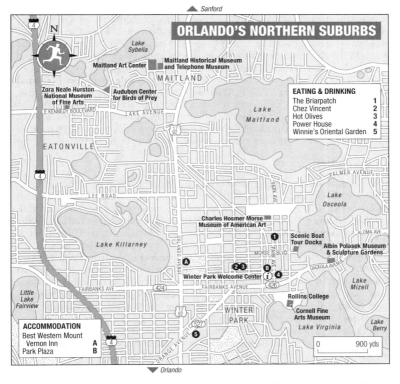

ORLANDO'S NORTHERN SUBURBS

Lake Sybelia

Maitland Art Center

Maitland Historical Museum and Telephone Museum

MAITLAND

Zora Neale Hurston National Museum of Fine Arts

Audubon Center for Birds of Prey

E KENNEDY BOULEVARD

LAKE AVENUE

Lake Maitland

EATONVILLE

EATING & DRINKING
The Briarpatch	1
Chez Vincent	2
Hot Olives	3
Power House	4
Winnie's Oriental Garden	5

PALMER AVENUE

LEE ROAD

Lake Osceola

Charles Hosmer Morse Museum of American Art

ALOMA AVE.

Lake Killarney

ORLANDO AVENUE

MORSE BLVD.

PARK AVE.

Scenic Boat Tour Docks

Albin Polasek Museum & Sculpture Gardens

OSCEOLA AVENUE

Winter Park Welcome Center

FAIRBANKS AVE.

FAIRBANKS AVENUE

Lake Mizell

Little Lake Fairview

Rollins College

WINTER PARK

Cornell Fine Arts Museum

Lake Virginia

Lake Berry

ACCOMMODATION
Best Western Mount Vernon Inn	A
Park Plaza	B

ORANGE AVENUE

0   900 yds

Should window–shopping not appeal, drop in to the **Charles Hosmer Morse Museum of American Art**, 445 N Park Ave (Tues–Sat 9.30am–4pm, Sun 1–4pm; Nov–April also Fri 9.30am–8pm; $3; ☎407/645-5311, ⓦwww.morse museum.org), which houses the collections of its namesake, one of Winter Park's founding fathers. The major exhibits are drawn from the output of Louis Comfort Tiffany, a legend for his innovative Art Nouveau lamps and windows that furnished high-society homes around the turn of the twentieth century. Great creativity and craftsmanship went into Tiffany's work: he molded glass while it was still soft, imbuing it with colored images of water lilies, leaves, and even strutting peacocks. Tiffany's work is so stunning the rest of the museum's possessions, including paintings by Hermann Herzog and John Singer Sargent, pale in comparison.

To discover why those who can afford to live anywhere choose Winter Park, take the **Scenic Boat Tour** from the dock at 312 E Morse Blvd, three blocks east of Park Ave (departures on the hour daily 10am–4pm; $10; ☎407/644-4056, ⓦwww.scenicboattours.com). The one-hour, narrated voyage of attractive Lake Osceola and adjoining lakes focuses on the rich flora and fauna – including plenty of alligators – although a good part of the fun is in staring enviously at the expensive lakeside homes.

Eatonville

Just to the east of Winter Park lies the small town of **EATONVILLE**, the first incorporated African-American municipality in the United States. The town was founded by three black men in 1875 so that, according to an 1889 notice published in the local newspaper, black Americans could "solve the great race problem by securing a home … in a Negro city governed by Negroes," and land was sold for $5–10 an acre to encourage relocation. Renowned author Zora Neale Hurston, an Eatonville native, used the town as the setting for novels such as *Their Eyes Were Watching God*. Stop by the **Zora Neale Hurston National Museum of Fine Arts**, 227 E Kennedy Blvd (Mon–Fri 9am–4pm; donation suggested; ☎407/647-3307), which features rotating exhibits relating to African American life. Here you can pick up the pamphlet *A Walking Tour of Eatonville, Florida*, which gives exhaustive historical explanations of every possible point of interest, all of which you can explore on foot in less than an hour.

Maitland

The luscious sunsets over Lake Sybelia in **MAITLAND**, directly north of Winter Park, inspired a young artist named Jules André Smith to buy six acres on its banks during the 1930s. With the financial assistance of Mary Bok (wealthy widow of Edward Bok; see p.392), Smith established what is now the **Maitland Art Center**, 231 W Packwood Ave (Mon–Fri 9am–4.30pm, Sat & Sun noon–4.30pm; free; ☎407/539-2181, ⓦwww.maitlandartcenter.org), a collection of stuccoed studios, offices, and apartments decorated with Aztec- and Mayan-style murals and grouped around garden courtyards. Smith invited other American artists to spend working winters here, but his abrasive personality scared many potential guests away. The colony continued in various forms until Smith's death in 1959, never becoming the aesthetes' commune he'd hoped for. There are temporary exhibitions and a permanent collection of Smith's etchings, paintings, and sculpture, but it's the unique design of the place that warrants a visit. While here, spare a thought for Smith's ghost, which, according to a number of local painters and sculptors who claim to have felt its presence, dispenses artistic guidance.

A few steps from the Maitland Art Center sit the **Maitland Historical Museum** and the **Telephone Museum**, 221 W Packwood Ave (Wed–Sun noon–4pm; $3; ☎407/644-1364, ⓦwww.maitlandhistory.com). The front rooms of the combined museums host rotating exhibits with some bearing on Maitland life – not overly exciting unless you have a particular interest in the area. The back room, on the other hand, is filled with wonderful vintage telephones, commemorating the day in 1910 when a Maitland grocer installed telephones in the homes of his customers, enabling them to order groceries from the comfort of their armchairs. The only other reason to linger in Maitland is the **Audubon Center for Birds of Prey**, 1101 Audubon Way (Tues–Sun 10am–4pm; $5, children 3–12 $4; ☎407/644-0190), run by the Florida Audubon Society, the state's oldest and largest conservation organization. The house is primarily an educational center and gift shop, but the adjacent rehabilitation facility is one of the largest in the southeast US, treating injured and orphaned birds, such as ospreys, owls, hawks, eagles, falcons, and the odd vulture, with the aim of returning them to the wild.

Accommodation and eating

Few tourists choose to base themselves this far away from the theme parks, but if you do want to soak up Winter Park's refined atmosphere, the best place **to stay** is the *Park Plaza*, 307 S Park Ave (☎407/647-1072 or 1-800/228-7220, ⓦwww.parkplazahotel.com; ❻), a 1920s "vintage" boutique hotel reminiscent of New Orleans' French Quarter, where some of the rooms have balconies overlooking

Park Avenue. Alternatively, the *Best Western Mount Vernon Inn*, a twenty-minute walk west of Park Avenue at 110 S Orlando Ave (☎407/647-1166 or 1-800/992-3379; ❺), offers tastefully decorated rooms, a pool, and a cocktail lounge.

Winter Park has a good and burgeoning selection of **restaurants**, many of which are along Park Avenue and cater to most tastes and budgets. We've listed a range of options below.

The Briarpatch 252 N Park Ave ☎407/628-8651. Known for its huge slices of cake, which are best sampled with a coffee on the outside tables; otherwise, the sandwich-dominated menu is overpriced (around $10 for a sandwich) and unexciting.
Power House 109–111 E Lyman Ave ☎407/645-3616. Just off Park Ave, this economical spot ($5–7 for most of the food items) serves up tasty Middle Eastern-style sandwiches and soups, as well as vitamin-packed smoothies.
Hot Olives 463 W New England Ave, just west of Park Ave ☎407/629-1030, ⊕www.hotolives restaurant.com. The menu here features simple, healthy dishes prepared with a gourmet touch, like

tapenade-encrusted halibut and filet mignon stuffed with gorgonzola. Main dishes $20–30. Closed Sun.
Chez Vincent 533 W New England Ave ☎407/599-2929, ⊕www.chezvincent.com. This intimate French restaurant where local ingredients such as grouper and snapper are prepared with capers, shallots, and white wine is well worth a try. Main dishes $20–30.
Winnie's Oriental Garden 1346 Orange Ave ☎407/629-2111. Where the southern end of Winter Park merges with downtown Orlando features the best Chinese restaurant in these parts. Savory specialties like spicy orange-flavored beef and roast pork asparagus mostly costing $10–15. Closed Mon.

North of Orlando

Back-to-back residential areas dissolve into fields of fruit and vegetables **north of Orlando**'s city limits. Around here, in slow-motion towns harking back to Florida's frontier days, farming still has the upper hand over tourism. Although it's easy to skim through on I-4, consider a more leisurely drive along the older local roads giving access to the major settlements.

Sanford and around

Once called "Celery City" on account of its major agricultural crop, **SANFORD**, fifteen miles north of Maitland on US-92 (also known as US-17 along this section), hasn't had a lot going for it since the boom years of the early twentieth century. Visit the **Sanford Museum**, 520 E First St (Tues–Fri 11am–4pm, Sat 1–4pm; free; ☎407/688-5198) for more about the town's history – and Henry Shelton Sanford, the turn-of-the-nineteenth-century lawyer and diplomat who created it – or pick up a self-guided tour map and venture around several buildings of divergent classical architecture in the adjacent old downtown district, most of which are now doing business as drugstores and insurance offices. As you leave Sanford to return to Orlando on US-17/92, you'll pass the vast warehouse that is **Flea World** (Fri–Sun 9am–6pm; free), a massive flea market selling items nobody in their right mind would ever buy; meticulous browsing is required to find the odd gem.

If Sanford's historic buildings, antique shops, and quiet charm appeal, **stay** at *Higgins House*, a Victorian B&B just a few blocks from downtown, at 420 S Oak Ave (☎407/324-9238, ⊕www.higginshouse.com; ❺), featuring four rooms with antiques and wicker furniture, huge, healthy breakfasts, and its very own pub. For lunch or dinner, try *Two Blondes and a Shrimp*, 112 E First St (closed Sun; ☎407/688-4745), with a fine, mid-priced international menu, including a few interesting vegetarian options like black bean patties and tomato pie.

Mount Dora

To see an authentic Victorian-era Florida village on a pristine lake, take Rte-46 west of Sanford for 21 miles and feast your eyes on the picket fences, wrought-iron balconies, and fancy wood-trimmed buildings making up **MOUNT DORA**. The Chamber of Commerce, 341 Alexander St (Mon–Fri 9am–5pm, Sat 10am–3pm; ☎352/383-2165, ⊕www.mountdora.com), has a free brochure containing a walking tour around the old houses of the town's compact center, which can be strolled easily in a couple of hours. Alternatively, board the Mount Dora Trolley, which offers narrated historic tours of the parks, monuments, and significant buildings, as well as a lovely view of Lake Dora. The tour lasts about an hour and leaves from next to the *Lakeside Inn* (Mon–Sat 11am, noon, 1pm, & 2pm; fewer tours if less demand; $13, children $11; ☎352/385-1023). Antique-lovers should check out **Renningers Antique Center**, just east of Mount Dora at 20651 US-441 (Sat & Sun 9am–5pm; ☎352/383-8393, ⊕www.renningers .com), a large weekend market where you'll find most of the area's antique dealers conveniently grouped under one roof.

A **stay** at Mount Dora's genteel *Lakeside Inn*, 100 N Alexander St (☎352/383-4101 or 1-800/556-5016, ⊕www.lakeside-inn.com; ❻), might just transport you to Old Florida, with a long front porch where you can watch sunsets over the lake. Bed and breakfasts fit in perfectly with Mount Dora's quaintness, and they're not in short supply. A good, central option is *Simpson's Bed & Breakfast*, 441 N Donnelly St (☎352/383-2087, ⊕www.simpsonsbnb.com; ❻), with six suites, all with kitchenettes and some eccentrically decorated with palm trees and watering cans on the walls.

At the popular, mid-priced *The Goblin Market*, hidden down a quiet side street at 311b N Donnelly St (☎352/735-0059, ⊕www.goblinmarketrestaurant .com), enjoy gourmet **food** like veal with spinach risotto and beef with pepper brandy cream sauce; reservations recommended. Another good bet, this time easier to find opposite the park, is the *5th Avenue Café*, 116 E Fifth Ave (☎352/383-0090, ⊕www.5thavenuecafe.com), which uses mainly organic ingredients in its meat, poultry, seafood, pasta, and vegetarian dishes, most of which cost $15–20 for dinner. It would be sacrilegious to come to Mount Dora and not take tea and scones at one of the many English-inspired teahouses dotted around town. *The Windsor Rose Tea Room*, 144 Fourth Ave (☎352/735-2551, ⊕www.windsorrose-tearoom.com), serves tea and scones for around $20, plus other English delicacies such as Cornish pasties and Scotch eggs.

Cassadaga

A village in the deep forest populated by spiritualists may conjure up images of beaded curtains and thumping tabletops in forbidding houses, but the few hundred residents of **CASSADAGA**, just east of I-4, fifteen miles north of Sanford, are disarmingly conventional citizens in normal homes, offering to reach out and touch the spirit world for a very down-to-earth fee. Cassadaga has been around since 1875, when a young New Yorker bought 35 acres of land here after being told during a séance he would one day be instrumental in founding a spiritualist community.

These days, several **spiritual centers** offer a range of services, from palm and tarot readings to full-blown sessions with a medium. Prices vary little from center to center: $60 for 30 minutes, $75 for 45 minutes, and $100 for one hour are the going rates. The Cassadaga Spiritualist Camp (☎386/228-2880, ⊕www .cassadaga.org), in the Andrew Jackson Davis Building, on the corner of Route 4139 (Cassadaga Rd) and Stevens Street, offers regular seminars and lectures covering topics from UFO cover-ups to out-of-body traveling, and also has a well-stocked psychic bookshop. Rival enclaves include The Universal Centre of Cassadaga, across the street at 460 Cassadaga Rd (☎386/228-3190, ⓦwww .universalcentre.net), which gives readings over the telephone; and the (predictably) haunted *Cassadaga Hotel*, back on the other side of the street at 355 Cassadaga Rd (☎386/228-2323, ⓦwww.cassadagahotel.net; ❸), which uses hypnosis to help you lose weight.

Just outside Cassadaga, on the way to nearby Lake Helen, the friendly *The Ann Stevens House*, 201 E Kicklighter Rd (☎386/228-0310 or 1-800/220-0310, ⓦwww.annstevenshouse.com; ❻), makes for a wonderful, woodsy place **to stay**; four of the ten individually decorated rooms are in a Victorian-era house.

DeLand and around

Intended as the "Athens of Florida" when founded in 1876, **DELAND**, four miles north of Cassadaga, west off I-4, is really just an old-fashioned central Florida town featuring a domed courthouse, an old theater, and a welcoming atmosphere. It boasts the state's oldest private educational center, **Stetson University**, on Woodland Boulevard (☎386/822-7100, ⓦwww.stetson.edu), whose red-brick facades have stood since the 1880s. The school is named after hat manufacturer John B. Stetson, a generous donor to the university and one of its founding trustees. Pick up a free tour map from easy-to-spot DeLand Hall for a walk around the vintage buildings.

Practicalities

For general information, visit the **Chamber of Commerce**, 336 N Woodland Blvd (Mon–Fri 9.30am–3pm; ☎386/734-4331, ⓦwww.delandchamber.org), which has brochures on local points of interest. If you're spending the night in DeLand, **stay** at the pleasant *DeLand Artisan Inn*, 215 S Woodland Blvd (☎386/736-3484, ⓦwww.delandartisaninn.com; ❹), where each room has a different theme, such as Literary, Mediterranean, or Tropical. The hotel's lively restaurant (closed Sun) serves tasty pasta, meat, and fish dishes. At the *Holiday House*, 704 N US-17/92, across from Stetson University (closed Mon; ☎386/734-6319, ⓦwww.holidayhouserestaurant.com), you can enjoy great buffet meals for around $10, with salads and a carvery in a lush garden setting.

DeLeon Springs, Lake Woodruff National Wildlife Refuge, and Barberville

DeLeon **Springs State Park** (daily 8am–sunset; cars $5, pedestrians and cyclists $1; ☎386/985-4212), ten miles north of DeLand on US-17, is one of the better-known sites in the area where thousands of gallons of pure water bubble continuously up from artesian springs. These labyrinths of underground water permeating north central Florida are popular with both visitors and tourists. At **DeLeon Springs**, you can swim, canoe, and picnic in and beside the spring, and even make your own pancakes at the *Old Spanish Sugar Mill Grill & Griddle House* (Mon–Fri 9am–5pm, Sat & Sun 8am–5pm; ☎386/985-5644), set in a historic sugar mill on the park grounds, at the corner of Ponce de León Boulevard and Burt Parks Road, west of US-17.

Following US-17 a few miles west to Grand Avenue, you'll come upon the stunning **Lake Woodruff National Wildlife Refuge** (open sunrise to sunset; free; ☎386/985-4673), 22,000 acres of untouched wetlands and home to over 200 species of birds, including the endangered Southern bald eagle, many types of fish, and other creatures. For dinner or Sunday brunch in the town of DeLeon Springs, try *Karling's Inn*, 4640 N US-17 (closed Mon;

⊕386/985-5535), a restaurant specializing in German cuisine such as chicken schnitzel and apple strudel (main dishes around $10).

Seven miles further north on US-17, the tiny crossroads community of **Barberville** celebrates rural Florida with its **Pioneer Settlement for the Creative Arts**, 1776 Lightfoot Lane (Mon–Sat 9am–4pm; $6; ⊕386/749-2959, ⓦwww.pioneersettlement.org), a small collection of turn-of-the-nineteenth-century buildings, including a train station, a log cabin, a turpentine still, a bridgehouse, and a general store. Here, an assembly of pottery wheels, looms, and other tools are put to use during the informative guided tour, which generally lasts just under two hours.

Blue Spring and Hontoon Island

The year-round 72°F (22°C) waters at **Blue Spring State Park** (daily 8am–sunset; cars $5, pedestrians and cyclists $1; ⊕386/775-3663), seven miles south of DeLand (off US-17/92, on W French Ave) in Orange City, attract **manatees** between mid-November and mid-March. Affectionately known as "sea cows," these best-loved of Florida's endangered animals swim here from the cooler waters of the St John's River, so the colder it is there the more manatees you'll see here. Aside from staking out the manatees from several observation platforms (early morning on a cold winter's day is the best time for sightings), you also get the chance to see **Thursby House**, a large frame dwelling built by pioneer settlers in 1872. **Accommodation** in the park includes a $20-a-night campground and air-conditioned cabins for $85 that sleep up to four people (for reservations, call ⊕1-800/326-3521).

Not far from Blue Spring is **Hontoon Island State Park** (⊕386/736-5309), a striking dollop of wooded land set within very flat and swampy terrain. Without a private boat, Hontoon Island is reachable only by the free **ferry** that runs daily from 8am to about one hour before sunset from a landing stage off Rte-44 (the continuation of DeLand's New York Avenue). Remarkably, the island once held a boatyard and cattle ranch, but today it's inhabited only by the hardy souls who decide to stay over in one of its six rustic **cabins** ($25 for four people, $30 for six people; for reservations, call ⊕1-800/326-3521), or at one of its very basic **campgrounds** ($12).

Travel details

Trains (Amtrak)

Orlando to: DeLand (2 daily; 1hr); Jacksonville (2 daily; 3hr 15min); Kissimmee (2 daily; 25min); Miami (2 daily; 5hr 45min–7hr 35min); Tampa (2 daily; 2hr); Winter Park (2 daily; 20min).

Buses

Orlando to: Daytona Beach (5 daily; 1hr 5min); Fort Lauderdale (10 daily; 4hr 15min–10hr); Fort Pierce (10 daily; 2hr–3hr 15min); Gainesville (5 daily; 2hr 40min); Jacksonville (7 daily; 2hr 30min–3hr 10min); Kissimmee (3 daily; 40min); Lakeland (3 daily; 1hr 30min); Miami (10 daily; 4hr 40min–11hr); Ocala (7 daily; 1hr 20min); Panama City (3 daily; 8hr 25min–9hr 25min); Pensacola (3 daily; 11hr 10min–12hr 40min); St Augustine (3 daily; 2hr 15min); Tallahassee (5 daily; 4hr 35min–7hr 55min); Tampa (6 daily; 1hr 40min–2hr 20min); West Palm Beach (9 daily; 3hr 20min–4hr 35min); Winter Haven (3 daily; 1hr).

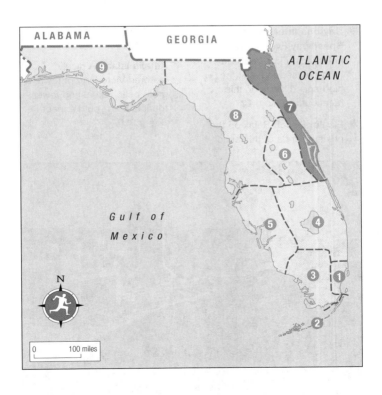

The Northeast

CHAPTER 7

Highlights

* **Kennedy Space Center**
The history (and future) of America's space program is thoughtfully and entertainingly explained. See p.323

* **Merritt Island National Wildlife Refuge** Spot an incredible array of wildlife, from bald eagles to bobcats. See p.326

* **Daytona International Speedway** Even if you're not a racing fan, you'll be hard-pressed to resist the high-speed thrills on this racecourse. See p.337

* **Flagler Beach** Relax on the pristine sands of this beach, just fourteen miles from crowded Daytona. See p.339

* **St Augustine** America's oldest city, with European charm, narrow streets, and an eventful history. See p.340

* **Jacksonville museums** The stand-out Cummer Museum and Gardens and the Jacksonville Museum of Modern Art feature intriguing collections. See p.353

* **Amelia Island** A nicely restored Victorian-era town, a great beach area, and fewer tourists than you'd expect. See p.356

▲ Jacksonville

The Northeast

S ubstantially free of commercial exploitation, the 190 miles of coastline dominating Florida's **NORTHEAST** are tailor-made for leisurely exploration. You'll often feel like doing nothing more strenuous than settling down beside the ocean, but throughout the region signs of the forces that have shaped Florida – from ancient Native American settlements to the launch site of the space shuttle – are easy to find and worth exploring. When planning your trip, remember that, owing to the less tropical climate, the northeast coast's tourist **seasons** are the reverse of those of the southeast coast: the crowded time here is the summer, when accommodation is more expensive and harder to come by than during the winter months.

Besides sharing a shoreline, the towns of the northeast coast have surprisingly little in common. Those making up the **Space Coast**, the southernmost area, primarily serve the hordes passing through to visit the impressively efficient **Kennedy Space Center** (KSC), birthplace of the nation's space exploits. The Space Center largely lives up to its unrelentingly positive public image and is definitely worth a look, as is the wildlife refuge that surrounds it. Seventy miles north of the Space Coast lies **Daytona Beach**, a small town with a big-name stretch of sand, where the legendary excesses of Spring Break gained international notoriety in the 1980s until local authorities began to discourage all sorts of teenage carousing – though the equally high-spirited bikers that roar into town haven't made the place any quieter.

Along the northerly section of the coast, the plentiful evidence of Florida's early European landings is on display in **St Augustine**, where sixteenth-century Spaniards established the oldest permanent settlement in the US. The surrounding coastline extends to the **Jacksonville Beaches**, twenty miles north, where lying in the sun and tuning in to the sprightly local nightlife will fill a few decadent days. Just inland, the city of **Jacksonville merits** more than a cursory glance, as you strike out toward the state's northeastern extremity. Here, flirting with the coast of Georgia, slender **Amelia Island** is fringed by gorgeous silver sands and features a quirky, posh Victorian-era main town.

The **road network** is very much a continuation of the southeast coast's system: **Hwy-A1A** hugs the coastline, with occasional breaks, while **US-1** charts a less appealing course on the mainland and is a lot slower than **I-95**, which divides the coastal area from the eastern edge of central Florida. Traveling by Greyhound **bus** is quite practical between Jacksonville and Daytona Beach, but if you want to explore the Space Coast, the best way to get around is by car, as with the rest of Florida.

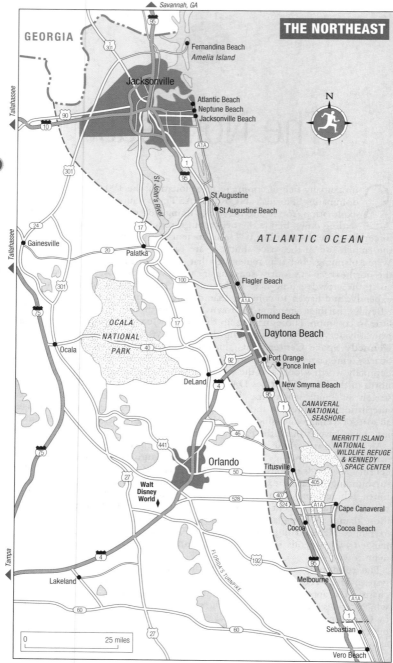

Savannah, GA

GEORGIA

Fernandina Beach
Amelia Island

Jacksonville

Atlantic Beach
Neptune Beach
Jacksonville Beach

N

St Augustine
St Augustine Beach

ATLANTIC OCEAN

Tallahassee

Gainesville

Palatka

Flagler Beach

St John's River

OCALA

NATIONAL

PARK

Ormond Beach

Daytona Beach

Ocala

Port Orange
Ponce Inlet

DeLand

New Smyrna Beach

CANAVERAL
NATIONAL
SEASHORE

MERRITT ISLAND
NATIONAL
WILDLIFE REFUGE
& KENNEDY
SPACE CENTER

Orlando

Titusville

Walt
Disney
World

Cape Canaveral

Cocoa

Cocoa Beach

Tampa

FLORIDA'S TURNPIKE

Melbourne

Lakeland

Sebastian

Vero Beach

West Palm Beach & Miami

0   25 miles

The Space Coast

The barrier islands that occupy much of the Treasure Coast (see "The Southeast," p.215) continue north into what's known as the **SPACE COAST**, the base of the country's space industry and site of the KSC, which occupies a flat, marshy island bulging into the Atlantic just fifty miles east of Orlando. Many of the visitors who flock here are surprised to find that the land from which the space shuttle leaves earth is also a sizeable wildlife refuge framed by several miles of rough coastline. Except for the beach-oriented communities on the ocean, the towns of the Space Coast are of little interest other than for low-cost overnight stops on the way to St Augustine or points north, or for meal breaks. You can get general information about the area on the 24-hour Space Coast hotline (℡ 1-800/93-OCEAN) or by checking out Ⓦ www.space-coast.com.

The Kennedy Space Center

Justifiably the biggest attraction in the area, the **KSC** is the nucleus of the US space program: it's here that space vehicles are developed, tested, and blasted into orbit. The first launches actually took place across the water at the US Air Force base on Cape Canaveral (renamed Cape Kennedy in 1963 and changed back to the original in 1973), from which rockets still lift off. After the space program was expanded in 1964 and the Saturn V rockets proved too large to launch from there, the focus of activity was moved to Merritt Island, positioned between Cape Canaveral and the mainland, and directly north of Cocoa Beach.

The Space Center is well worth a visit for its solid documentation of US achievements, revealing how closely success in space is tied to the nation's sense of well-being.

The Kennedy Space Center: practical info and tips

At the time of writing, the shuttle program was set to mothball in 2010 so space buffs will soon have to settle for watching unmanned rocket launches. If that's not a deterrent, then head for the only **public entry roads** to the KSC: Hwy-405 from Titusville and Rte-3 off Hwy-A1A between Cocoa Beach and Cocoa. On either approach, follow signs for the KSC Visitor Complex (daily 9am–6pm), which contains a museum, a life-size Space Shuttle Explorer replica, the Universe Theater, exhibit halls, the Astronaut Memorial, the Rocket Garden, and an IMAX film theater.

Arrive early to be able to devote the better part of a day here; unfortunately, many others do the same, so plan accordingly. The complex fills up during the summer and school vacations. Regular admission ($38, children 3–11 $28) covers Kennedy Space Center Visitor Complex, including the bus tour, IMAX movies, attractions and programs plus access to the US Astronaut Hall of Fame in Titusville (see p.350). **Add-on** tours take in other attractions: "Cape Canaveral: Then and Now" visits the now retired launch sites of the Mercury, Gemini, and Apollo programs; while "NASA Up Close" takes you to Kennedy Space Center's industrial area to see NASA KSC's headquarters, the closest possible view of the Space Shuttle launch pads, Shuttle Landing Facility and the massive Vehicle Assembly Building, (both tours: $21, children 3–11 $15; reservations recommended). You can buy most tickets online at Ⓦ www.kennedyspacecenter.com.

Visit the website or call ℡ 321/449-4444 for the dates and times of **real-life launches** from the Space Center. There is a special restricted viewing area six miles away, although the magnitude of the blast is awesome enough from anywhere within a forty-mile radius of the launch pad. Night-time send-offs are especially spectacular.

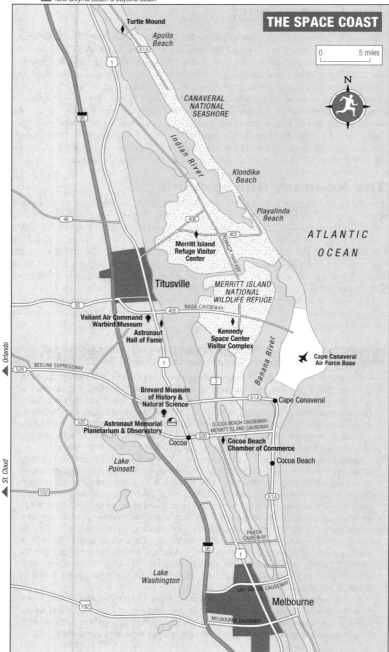

New Smyrna Beach & Daytona Beach

Turtle Mound

Apollo Beach

A1A

1

THE SPACE COAST

0   5 miles

N

CANAVERAL NATIONAL SEASHORE

95

Indian River

Klondike Beach

Playalinda Beach

ATLANTIC OCEAN

46

406

402

Merritt Island Refuge Visitor Center

Titusville

MERRITT ISLAND NATIONAL WILDLIFE REFUGE

50

405

NASA CAUSEWAY

Valiant Air Command Warbird Museum

Astronaut Hall of Fame

Kennedy Space Center Visitor Complex

Cape Canaveral Air Force Base

Orlando

528

BEELINE EXPRESSWAY

1

3

Banana River

Brevard Museum of History & Natural Science

A1A

Cape Canaveral

520

Astronaut Memorial Planetarium & Observatory

Cocoa

520

COCOA BEACH CAUSEWAY/ MERRITT ISLAND CAUSEWAY

St. Cloud

Cocoa Beach Chamber of Commerce

Cocoa Beach

Lake Poinsett

532

A1A

PINEDA CAUSEWAY

95

1

Lake Washington

EAU GALLIE CAUSEWAY

Melbourne

192

MELBOURNE CAUSEWAY

Fort Pierce & Miami   Fort Pierce

The Kennedy Space Center Visitor Complex

Everything at the **KSC Visitor Complex** is within easy walking distance of the parking lot, as is the departure point for the bus tour (see below). The complex will keep anyone with the faintest interest in space exploration entertained for at least an hour or two. Everything you might expect to see is here: actual mission capsules, space suits, lunar modules, a granite memorial to those who gave their lives in the quest to explore space, a full-sized, walk-through mock-up of the space shuttle, and a light-hearted interactive mission to Mars.

In the center of the complex, the IMAX **theater** shows two films, which change sporadically, although you can count on both focusing on a space theme and containing at least some footage shot by actual astronauts in space. Other offerings include the **Astronaut Encounter**, a daily chance to meet and question a real-life astronaut, and **Exploration in the New Millennium**, a futuristic exhibit tracing the history of human civilization's urge to go where no one has gone before, an educational journey that includes the chance to touch an actual piece of the planet Mars – or at least a meteorite that scientists claim originally came from Mars. The newest attraction is the **Shuttle Launch Experience**, a simulation ride, where passengers get to experience what it's like to be an astronaut, vertically "launching" into space and orbiting Earth aboard the space shuttle.

As far as **eating** goes, there are four canteens and various snack bars scattered around the Visitor Complex that provide standard pizza-and-hot-dog fare at just short of stratospheric prices.

The Kennedy Space Center Tour

The **bus tour** (daily; tours leave from 10am to 2.15pm; included with admission) around the rest of the Merritt Island complex provides a dramatic insight into the colossal grandeur of the space program. After zooming through the main gate and passing countless alligators on the side of the road, you'll see the **Vehicle Assembly Building** (VAB), where space shuttles, like the Apollo and Skylab spacecraft before them, are put together and fitted with payloads, or equipment carried by spacecraft, looming ahead. At 52 stories and equivalent in volume to three-and-a-half Empire State Buildings, it's the largest single-story scientific building in the world. Unfortunately, access is prohibited, but if a door is open you can peek inside. The VAB is the first stop for the "crawlerway" – the huge tracks along which space shuttles are wheeled to the launch pad.

The bus continues swiftly on to a vantage-point from where you can gaze at the **launch pad**, which, unless a space shuttle is not in place ready for take-off, is no more interesting than any other large pile of scaffolding.

Besides a nose-to-nozzle inspection of a Saturn V rocket, which took the first Apollo mission into space and produced enough power on blast-off to light up New York City for over an hour, the most impressive part of the rest of the bus tour is a simulated Apollo countdown and take-off, watched from behind the blinking screens of an actual control room that has been retired.

The **Air Force Space and Missile Museum**, situated a mile inside the gate of Cape Canaveral (on launch pad 26A), is included on the "Cape Canaveral: Then and Now" tour (covered in box, p.323). A testament to NASA's skill at making money out of its old hardware, the museum consists of a large expanse of land rather akin to the Rocket Garden at the KSC Visitor Complex (see above), and two buildings containing exhibits and information on rocket development, some of which prove fascinating: one such nugget is the fact that all the extraordinary developments of the space program stem from V2 rockets, originally fired by the Nazis against Britain in the closing years of World War II. These were subsequently launched into orbit by America in 1950.

Americans in space

The growth of the Space Coast started with the "**Space Race**," which followed President John F. Kennedy's declaration in May 1961 to "achieve the goal, before the decade is out, of landing a man on the moon and returning him safely to Earth." This statement came in the chill of the Cold War, when the USSR – which had just put the first man into space following its launch of the first artificial satellite in 1957 – appeared scientifically ahead of the US, a fact that dented American pride and provided great propaganda for the Soviets.

Money and manpower were pumped into the National Aeronautics and Space Administration (**NASA**), and the communities around Cape Canaveral expanded with a heady influx of scientists and would-be astronauts. The much-hyped Mercury program helped restore prestige, and the later Apollo moonshots captured the imagination of the world. The moon landing by *Apollo 11* in July 1969 not only turned the dreams of science fiction writers into reality, but also meant that for the first time – and in the most spectacular way possible – the US had overtaken the USSR.

During the 1970s, as the incredible expense of the space program became apparent and seemed out of all proportion to its benefits, pressure grew for NASA to become more cost-effective. The country entered a period of economic recession and NASA's funding was drastically slashed; unemployment – unthinkable in the buoyant 1960s – threatened many on the Space Coast.

After the internationally funded Skylab space station program, NASA's solution to the problem of wasteful one-use rockets was the reusable **space shuttle**, first launched in April 1981, and able to deploy commercial payloads and carry out repairs to orbiting satellites. The shuttle's success silenced many critics, but the *Challenger* disaster of January 1986 – when the entire crew perished during take-off – not only imbued the country with a deep sense of loss but highlighted the complacency and corner-cutting that had crept into the space program after many accident-free years. (A memorial inside the KSC Visitor Complex bears the names of astronauts who have lost their lives since the inception of the US space program, among them the crews of the *Challenger* shuttle and the ill-fated *Apollo 1* mission of 1967.)

Despite numerous satisfactory missions since, technical problems were to cause serious delays to the space shuttle program over the next two decades, as well as another catastrophic accident: the *Columbia* shuttle disaster of 2003, in which the vehicle burned up during re-entry, killing all on board. The subsequent investigation concluded that NASA had failed to learn from its earlier technical mistakes (and could have given even more consideration to safety controls). Since the accident, work has continued apace on the **international manned space station** in the earth's orbit, scheduled for completion before 2010, with Russian Soyuz rockets being used in place of shuttles to ferry the parts into space. These same rockets have already transported three (very rich) "**space tourists**" in what looks to be the new phenomenon in space travel.

For yet another angle on space travel, visit the **Astronaut Hall of Fame** (see Titusville, p.350; entrance included with regular admission), just down the road from the Kennedy Space Center.

Merritt Island National Wildlife Refuge

NASA shares its land with the **Merritt Island National Wildlife Refuge** (daily sunrise–sunset; free), entered via Rte-402 from Titusville. Here you'll find alligators, armadillos, raccoons, bobcats, and one of Florida's greatest concentrations of birdlife living alongside some of the world's most advanced technology.

▲ Nine-banded armadillo, Merritt Island National Wildlife Refuge

Even if you're only coming for a day at the Space Center, it would be a shame to pass up such a spectacular place – though it has to be said that Merritt Island, on first glance, looks anything but spectacular, comprising acres of estuaries and brackish marshes interspersed with occasional hammocks of oak and palm, and pine flatwoods where a few bald eagles construct nests ten feet in circumference. Winter (Oct–March) is the **best time to visit**, when the island's skies are alive with thousands of migratory birds from the frozen north, and when mosquitoes are absent. At any other period, and especially in summer, the island's Mosquito Lagoon is worthy of its name; bring ample insect repellent.

Seeing the refuge

Seven miles east of Titusville on Rte-406, the seven-mile **Black Point Wildlife Drive** gives a solid introduction to the basics of the island's ecosystem. At the entrance you can pick up a highly informative free leaflet that describes specific stops along the route. From one you'll spot a few bald-eagle nests, while another by the mudflats affords a good vantage point for watching a wide variety of wading and shore birds angling for their dinner.

Be sure to do some walking within the refuge, too. Off the wildlife drive, the five-mile **Cruickshank Trail** weaves around the edge of the Indian River. If the whole length is too strenuous for you, make use of an observation tower just a few minutes' walk from the parking lot. For a more varied landscape, drive a few miles further east along Rte-402 – branching from Rte-406 just south of the wildlife drive – passing the **visitor center** (Mon–Fri 8am–4.30pm, Sat & Sun 9am–5pm; closed Sun April–Oct; ☎321/861-0667), and tackle the three-quarter-mile **Oak Hammock Trail** or the two-mile **Palm Hammock Trail**, both accessible from the parking lot.

The Canaveral National Seashore

A slender, 25-mile-long beach dividing Merritt Island's Mosquito Lagoon from the Atlantic Ocean, the **Canaveral National Seashore** (Nov–March 6am–6pm; April–Oct 6am–8pm; $3 per day; ☎321/267-1110) begins at **Playalinda Beach** on Rte-402, seven miles east of the refuge's visitor center. The National Seashore's entire length is top-notch beachcombing and surfing territory and also suitable for swimming. Except when rough seas and high tides submerge it completely, you should take a wind-bitten ramble along the palmetto-lined path to wild **Klondike Beach**, north of Playalinda Beach, its sands often coated with intriguing shells and marked from May through September by the tracks left by sea turtles crawling ashore at night to lay eggs. The Space Coast is the second largest **turtle nesting** area in the world and, not surprisingly, turtle-watching is a popular local pastime. **Turtle-watches** with a park ranger are offered in June and July (reserve one month in advance; ☎321/867-4077 or 386/428-3384 ext 10).

At the northern tip of the National Seashore, on **Apollo Beach** (accessible only by road from New Smyrna Beach, eight miles north of Apollo; see "Heading north: New Smyrna Beach," p.331), is **Turtle Mound**. Known as a "midden," the mound is a 35-foot heap of oyster shells and other refuse left by the Timucua Indians over several generations of living here. The site became prominent enough over time to be marked on maps by Florida's first Spanish explorers, being visible several miles out to sea. Take a few minutes to walk along the boardwalks, through the dense, fragrant vegetation to the top of the mound – aside from its historical significance, the greenery provides some welcome shade in an otherwise desert-like environment.

Cocoa Beach

A few miles south of the Kennedy Space Center, **Cocoa Beach** comprises just a ten-mile strip of shore and a few residential streets off Atlantic Avenue (Hwy-A1A). As well as being unquestionably the best base from which to see the Space Coast, it's also a favored haunt of surfers, who are drawn here by some of the choicest waves in Florida. Major (and minor) surfing contests are held here during spring and summer, and throughout the year the place has a perky, youthful feel. There's also a big beach volleyball contingent, setting and spiking on four permanent courts, as well as free music around the pier and beachside parks often on weekends. To get an idea of the community's prime concerns you need only take a walk around the original **Ron Jon Surf Shop**, 4151 N Atlantic Ave (☎321/799-8888 or 1-888/RJ-SURFS; ⓦwww.ronjons.com), a surfing superstore, with its colorful, high-energy vibes, and its rental shop just a stone's throw away. It's open 24 hours a day and packed with surfboards (rental per day is $30 for a fiberglass board), bicycles ($15 per day), kayaks ($30 per day), wetsuits ($30 for three days), and extrovert beach attire. Located in the rental shop across the street, the **Cocoa Beach Surf Museum** (daily 8am–8pm; $2) features an eclectic collection of old photos, magazines, memorabilia, and surfboards dating from the 1960s and 1970s. If you can't find what you want at Ron Jon's, try the Cocoa Beach Surf Company next door at 4001 N Atlantic Ave (☎321/799-9930), another good spot to shop for surfing gear.

Arrival, information, and getting around

The nearest stations are in Titusville and Melbourne. The Cocoa Beach Shuttle (☎321/784-3831 or 1-888/784-4144) runs to and from Orlando International Airport for $36 one way; call to be collected from any hotel on Hwy-A1A.

Tourist information is available seven days a week at 8501 Astronaut Blvd (Hwy-A1A) Suite Four (8.30am–6pm; ☎321/454-2022) or from the Cocoa Beach **Chamber of Commerce**, located on Merritt Island at 400 Fortenberry Rd (Mon–Fri 9am–5pm; ☎321/459-2200 or 1-877/321-8474).

A local **bus** service (Space Coast Area Transit; ☎321/633-1878, ⓦwww .ridescat.com) runs daily (Mon–Sat 6.30am–8.30pm, Sun 8am–5pm) to and from Cape Canaveral through Cocoa Beach (#9: Beach Trolley), and #6 runs from downtown Cocoa to Cocoa Beach; a ride costs $1.25 each way. To get around the beach area, rent a **bike** from the Ron Jon Surf Shop (see opposite).

Accommodation

Accommodation bargains are rare in Cocoa Beach. Prices are generally highest in February, March, July, and August – and during space shuttle launches. The most tent-friendly **campground** is *Jetty Park*, 400 E Jetty Rd (T 321/783-7111; $25–47), five miles north at Cape Canaveral

Days Inn 5500 N Atlantic Ave T 321/784-2550 or 1-800/245-5225, W www.daysinncocoabeach.com. Next door to the Cocoa Beach pier, half the rooms here feature balconies and all have microwaves and mini-fridges. **4**

Fawlty Towers 100 E Cocoa Beach Causeway T 321/784-3870 or 1-800/887-3870, W www .fawltytowersreseort.com. Nothing like the television show, this friendly, roomy, pink-towered motel on the beachfront has a pool and free videos to borrow. **4**

Luna Sea 3185 N Atlantic Ave T 321/783-0500 or 1-800/586-2732, W www.lunaseacocoabeach.com. This bed and breakfast/motel features clean and neat rooms and a heated pool. **4**

Sea Esta Villas 686 S Atlantic Ave T 321/783-1739 or 1-800/872-9444, W www.seaestavillas .homestead.com. Apartments in this little oasis are cheaper if rented by the week. The two-bedroom units come with full kitchens, spacious baths, and access to the pool, gardens, and beach across the street. **6**

Eating and drinking

For great oysters and excellent riverfront views, head for *Sunset Café*, 500 W Cocoa Beach Causeway (T 321/783-8485, W www.sunsetwaterfrontcafe andbar.com) – but go early as it's frequently mobbed. Another great seafood option is right next door at *Florida's Seafood* (T 321/784-0892, W www .floridaseafood.com) – try the shrimp volcano: shrimp topped with more shrimp, scallops and a spicy Cajun sauce. Another great dinner option is *Atlantic Ocean Grille*, on the pier (closed Mon; T 321/783-7549), which has a quality (and somewhat expensive) menu especially strong on seafood and also a Sunday champagne brunch.

Nightlife is most enjoyable if you start early at one of the beachside **happy hours**: try *Marlins' Good Time Grill*, also part of the pier complex (T 321/783-7549). As the evening draws on, the *Pig and Whistle*, 240 N Orlando Ave (T 321/799-0724), offers TV soccer and English bitter, while the party-hearty *Coconuts on the Beach*, 2 Minuteman Causeway (T 321/784-1422, W www .coconutsonthebeach.com), has bikini contests to accompany the drinking and **live music** on the beach (with no cover).

Inland: Cocoa and Titusville

The chief attractions of the Space Coast's sleepy **inland towns**, strung along US-1, are cheaper accommodation and food than at the beaches, plus areas of historical interest that provide a welcome change from the usual tourist drag.

Cocoa

In **Cocoa**, thirty miles north of Melbourne and eight miles inland from Cocoa Beach, the brick-paved sidewalks and turn-of-the-nineteenth-century buildings of **Cocoa Village** (W www.cocoavillage.com) fill several small blocks south of King Street (Hwy-520) and make for a relaxing stroll. Among the rather quaint antique shops and boutiques, seek out the Porcher House, 434 Delannoy Ave (Tues–Fri 9am–5pm; free; T 321/639-3500), a grand Neoclassical abode built in 1916 (and currently occupied by a rental agency).

For a greater insight into the town's origins, head a few miles west to the **Brevard Museum of History and Natural Science**, 2201 Michigan Ave (Tues–Sat 10am–4pm; $6; ☎321/632-1830, ⓦwww.brevardmuseum.org), whose displays recount Cocoa's birth as a trading post when the first settlers arrived in the 1840s by steamboat and mule. There's also a respectable exhibit of Florida wildlife and some informative leaflets that are particularly useful if you're planning to visit the Merritt Island National Wildlife Refuge (see p.326) further north.

The **BCC Planetarium and Observatory**, 1519 Clearlake Rd (Wed 1.30–4.30pm, Fri & Sat 6.30–10.30pm; $16 for all three shows, or $7 per show; ☎321/634-3732, ⓦwww.brevardcc.edu/planet), which offers a planetarium show, a large-screen movie, and a laser show, is a half-hearted attempt to attract tourist dollars from the overflow of the nearby Kennedy Space Center and will interest only the most devoted of space enthusiasts.

If you're **staying** in Cocoa, you'll find some cheap chain motels lining Cocoa Boulevard, two miles from Cocoa Village. One of the better options in town is the *Holiday Inn Express* at 301 Tucker Lane (☎321/635-9975 or 1-888/465-4329; ❹), which has a pool and a full hot breakfast. For **eating**, try *Lone Cabbage Fish Camp*, 8199 W Hwy-520 (☎321/632-4199), good for catfish, frog legs, and alligator tail (and 30min airboat rides as well; 10am–5:30pm; $22). Alternatively, the stylish *Café Margaux*, 220 Brevard Ave (closed Sun; ☎321/639-8343, ⓦwww.margaux.com), features French and European cuisine, including veal, duck, and some good soups.

Titusville

If you don't visit the Kennedy Space Center, you'll at least get a great view of the towering Vehicle Assembly Building from **Titusville**, twenty miles north of Cocoa. If you have time, visit the **Valiant Air Command Warbird Museum**, 6600 Tico Rd (daily 9am–5pm; $12; ☎321/268-1941, ⓦwww.vacwarbirds .org), a celebration of slightly more pedestrian flying machines than those at the Kennedy Space Center. Originally formed to commemorate the US Air Force's involvement in preventing Japan's invasion of mainland China in 1941, the museum today exhibits lovingly restored planes, with examples from all wars since that date, as well as a variety of artifacts and memorabilia from both world wars. The old warbirds take to the skies in March, when the VAC holds an air show at which those remaining war veterans take the wheel again.

Titusville provides easy access to the Kennedy Space Center (via Hwy-405) and the Merritt Island National Wildlife Refuge (via Hwy-402). On the way to either place, be sure to visit the **Astronaut Hall of Fame** (daily 9am–6.30pm; $17, children 3–11 $13 separately or included in the $38 Kennedy Space Center ticket; ☎321/449-4444), one of Florida's most entertaining interactive museums, where simulation rides allow visitors to experience stomach-churning G-forces or a ride across the bumpy surface of Mars.

You'll find plenty of inexpensive **hotels and motels** along Washington Avenue (US-1): try the *Clarion Inn KSC*, no. 4951 S (☎321/269-2121, ⓦwww .clarionspacecenter.com; ❺). Otherwise, try the slightly overdone but nonetheless quirky *Casa Coquina*, 4010 Coquina Ave (☎321/268-4653, ⓦwww .casacoquina.com; ❹) a B&B originally built in the 1920s, and now offering seven suites, each named for a gemstone, and a complimentary happy hour each night from 5pm to 7pm.

For **food**, search out the seafood at locally famous *Dixie Crossroads*, 1475 Garden St (☎321/268-5000, ⓦwww.dixiecrossroads.com).

When it's time to move on, there's a Greyhound **bus** station at 1220 S Washington Ave (☎321/267-8760).

Heading North: New Smyrna Beach

After the virgin vistas of the Canaveral National Seashore, the likeable, low-key beach community of **New Smyrna Beach**, thirty miles north of Titusville on US-1, is a gentle reintroduction to tourism along the coast, with a few beachside hotels fronting a stretch of water that's protected from dangerous currents by offshore rock ledges, making it perfect for **swimming** and **surfing**, especially at Smyrna Dunes State Park, located on the south side of Ponce Inlet, to the north. To reach the beach (or the northern section of the Canaveral National Seashore, see p.327), you have to pass through the inland section of the town, before swinging east on Hwy-A1A.

New Smyrna Beach started life as a Mediterranean colony founded by wealthy Scottish physician **Andrew Turnbull**, who bought land here in the mid-1700s and set about recruiting Greeks, Italians, and Minorcans to work for seven years on his plantation in return for fifty acres of land per person. The colony didn't last: bad treatment, language barriers, culture clashes, disease, and financial disasters hastened its demise, and many of the settlers moved north to St Augustine (see p.340). The immigrants worked hard, however (by most accounts, they had little choice), laying irrigation canals, building a sugar mill, and commencing work on what was to be a palatial abode for Turnbull. Close to US-1, the **ruins** of the mill, at the junction of Canal Street and Mission Road, and his unfinished house, at Riverside Drive and Julia Street, are substantial enough to merit a look. The nearby **visitor center**, 2238 State Rd 44, just off I-95 (Mon–Sat 9am–5pm, Sun 10am–2pm; ☎386/428-1600 or 1-800/541-9621, ⓦwww.nsbfla.com), has a handy historical brochure, as well as the usual local information. For surfing tips, visit Quiet Flight (☎386/427-1917) and Inlet Charley's (☎386/423-2317), surf shops right next door to each other at nos. 508 and 510 Flagler Blvd.

Practicalities

If you want to stay over, there are a few good choices right by the beach, as well as luxurious and welcoming *Night Swan Intracoastal B&B*, within walking distance of downtown at 512 S Riverside Drive (☎386/423-4940 or 1-800/465-4261, ⓦwww.nightswan.com; ❻), with its own dock. Across the arching causeway bridge and out to the beach itself, the aquamarine stucco *Sea Vista Resort*, 1701 S Atlantic Ave, Hwy A1A (☎386/428-2210 or 1-800/874-3917, ⓦwww.seavistaresort.com; ❹), offers satisfactory motel rooms, efficiencies, or one-bedroom apartments, as well as a pool and a beachside tiki bar serving cocktails and snacks – the grouper sandwich is a favorite. Less than a block from the beach and in the heart of the Flagler Avenue action is *The Seahorse Inn*, 423 Flagler Ave (386/428-8081, ⓦwww.seahorseinnflorida.com; ❹), a 20-unit motel with clean, 1950s-style retro rooms with terrazzo floors and driftwood decor.

For the area's finest upmarket **dining**, head to *Norwood's*, on the beach side of the causeway at 400 Second Ave (☎386/428-4621, ⓦwww.norwoods.com); stop by on a Friday (5–7pm), when they have one of their popular wine tastings to complement the mouthwatering seafood. If you'd rather sample some Florida seafood, stop in to *JB's Fish Camp*, on the corner of Hwy-A1A and Pompano (☎386-427-5747). Try the justly famous crab cakes and grouper sandwich on the weathered deck overlooking the Halifax River, or take your dinner inside where bumper stickers behind the bar read "finish your beer, there are sober people in China." If you're counting calories, *Heavenly Sandwiches & Smoothies*, 115 Flagler Ave (☎386/427-7475) runs toward healthy drinks and wraps (not counting their home-made ice cream).

Daytona Beach

The consummate Florida beach town, with plentiful T-shirt shops, amusement arcades, and motels, **DAYTONA BEACH** owes its existence to twenty miles of light brown sand where the only pressure is to relax and enjoy yourself.

For decades, Daytona Beach was invaded by half a million college kids going through the Spring Break ritual of underage drinking and libido liberation. In the mid-1990s, the town ended its love affair with the nation's students and tried to emulate Fort Lauderdale (see "The Southeast," p.188) by cultivating a more refined image – an attempt that has been only partially successful, to say the least, since now it seems to cater mainly to bikers and race-car fanatics.

The resort is the center of three major annual events: the world-famous **Daytona 500** stock-car meeting, held at the Daytona International Speedway; **Bike Week**, when thousands of leather-clad motorcyclists converge for lively street festivals and races at the Speedway; and the relatively new **Biketoberfest**, which is a more family-oriented and slightly scaled-down copy of Bike Week (for more info on all of these events, see box, p.337).

Even before the students and bikers, the beach was a favorite with pioneering auto enthusiasts such as Louis Chevrolet, Ransom Olds, and Henry Ford, who came here during the early 1900s to race their prototype vehicles beside the ocean. The land speed record was regularly smashed, five times by millionaire British speedster Malcolm Campbell who, in 1935, roared along at 276mph. As a legacy of these times, Daytona Beach is one of the few Florida towns where the dubious thrill of **driving on the beach** is permitted; 11 of the area's 23 miles of beach are open to motor vehicles. Pay $5 (Feb–Nov only) at any of these beach entrances, stick to the marked track, observe the 10mph speed limit, park at right angles to the ocean – and beware of high tide.

Arrival, information, and getting around

As Ridgewood Avenue, **US-1** steams through **mainland Daytona Beach**, passing the Greyhound station, at no. 138 S (☎386/255-7076). By car, you should keep to **Hwy-A1A** (known as Atlantic Avenue), which enters the beachside area – filling a narrow sliver of land between the ocean and the Halifax River (part of the Intracoastal Waterway) a mile from the mainland.

The **Convention and Visitors Bureau**, in the Chamber of Commerce building at 126 E Orange Ave (Mon–Fri 9am–5pm; ☎1-800/854-1234, Ⓦwww.daytonabeach.com), is on the way to the beach and has a wealth of free information.

Local buses (Votran: $1.25 a ride; ☎386/761-7700, Ⓦwww.votran.org) connect the beaches with the mainland and the Greater Daytona Beach area,

---

Buses between Daytona Beach and Orlando International Airport

If you're enjoying yourself at the beach but have to fly home from Orlando, you can take advantage of the **Daytona–Orlando Transit Service** (DOTS; ☎386/257-5411 or 1-800/231-1965, Ⓦwww.dots-daytonabeach.com), whose shuttle buses run every ninety minutes (4am–7pm) from the corner of Nova Road and Eleventh Street to Orlando International Airport. On request, the buses also make stops in DeLand and Deltona. The one-way fare is $35 ($65 round-trip). Call ahead for details and reservations.

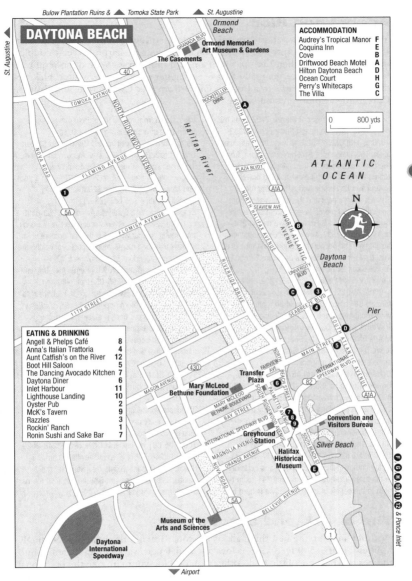

DAYTONA BEACH

Bulow Plantation Ruins & ▲ Tomoka State Park   ▲ St. Augustine

◄ St. Augustine

Ormond Beach

Ormond Memorial Art Museum & Gardens

The Casements

GRANADA BLVD

ROCKEFELLER DRIVE

SOUTH ATLANTIC AVENUE

Halifax River

ACCOMMODATION

Audrey's Tropical Manor	F
Coquina Inn	E
Cove	B
Driftwood Beach Motel	A
Hilton Daytona Beach	D
Ocean Court	H
Perry's Whitecaps	G
The Villa	C

TOMOKA AVENUE

NORTH RIDGEWOOD AVENUE

FLEMING AVENUE

NOVA ROAD

40

1

5A

FLOMISH AVENUE

11TH STREET

RIVERSIDE DRIVE

PLAZA BLVD

A1A

NORTH HALIFAX AVENUE

NORTH SEAVIEW AVE

NORTH ATLANTIC AVENUE

ATLANTIC OCEAN

0   800 yds

N

Daytona Beach

A

B

C   2   3

4

D

5

Pier

EATING & DRINKING

Angell & Phelps Café	8
Anna's Italian Trattoria	4
Aunt Catfish's on the River	12
Boot Hill Saloon	5
The Dancing Avocado Kitchen	7
Daytona Diner	6
Inlet Harbour	11
Lighthouse Landing	10
Oyster Pub	2
McK's Tavern	9
Razzles	3
Rockin' Ranch	1
Ronin Sushi and Sake Bar	7

MASON AVENUE

430

FAIRVIEW AVE

Transfer Plaza

Mary McLeod Bethune Foundation

MARY MCLEOD BETHUNE BOULEVARD

BAY STREET

SOUTH RIDGEWOOD AVENUE

INTERNATIONAL SPEEDWAY BOULEVARD

MAGNOLIA AVENUE

ORANGE AVENUE

NOVA ROAD

92

5A

BELLEVUE AVENUE

Museum of the Arts and Sciences

Daytona International Speedway

▼ Airport

MAIN STREET

SEABREEZE BLVD

UNIVERSITY BLVD

NORTH STREET

BEACH STREET

PALMETTO AVENUE

82

6

7   8

9

Greyhound Station

Halifax Historical Museum

E

INTERNATIONAL SPEEDWAY BLVD

A1A

SOUTH ATLANTIC AVENUE

Convention and Visitors Bureau

SOUTH BEACH ST

Silver Beach

F G H I J & Ponce Inlet

and also provide limited night and Sunday services. The bus terminal, called **Transfer Plaza**, sits at the junction of Ridgewood Avenue and Mary McLeod Bethune Boulevard in mainland Daytona Beach. At the beach, **trolleys** ($1.25 a ride) run until midnight along the central part of Atlantic Avenue from mid-January to early September. Several **taxi** companies operate in Daytona Beach and the surrounding communities: try AAA Metro Taxi (☎386/253-2522) or Yellow Cab (☎386/255-5555).

Accommodation

You'll get the lowest rates – **motel** rooms dip as low as $40–50 – from after Labor Day (early Sept) to the end of January. Prices rise sharply (at least double) during big events, when five- or seven-night minimum stays are often required. In summer, prices are generally $20 or so higher than during winter. Pick up the free *Daytona Beach Area Visitor's Guide* from the Convention and Visitors Bureau for helpful hints on where to stay.

Audrey's Tropical Manor 2237 S Atlantic Ave, Daytona Beach Shores ☏386/252-4920 or 1-800/253-4920, ⓦwww.tropicalmanor .com. This oceanfront pink motel is a gem, from the personal service to the lovingly maintained rooms to the charming hand-painted flowers, foliage and fish inside and outside the rooms. There's a large pool and the rooms range from standard motel rooms to oceanfront suites. ❺

Coquina Inn 544 S Palmetto Ave ☏386/254-4969 or 1-800/805-7533, ⓦwww.coquinainndaytona beach.com. Homespun bed and breakfast sits a bit inland, close to the nightlife on Beach Street. Free use of bikes for guests. ❺

Cove 1306 N Atlantic Ave ☏386/252-3678 or 1-800/828-3251, ⓦwww.motelcove.com. Family-friendly 38-room motel has some rooms that come with kitchenettes and private balconies. ❸

Daytona Beach Campground 4601 S Clyde Morris Blvd ☏386/761-2663, ⓦwww.rvdaytona .com. Tent sites from $20, with pool access and a small store on the grounds.

Driftwood Beach Motel 657 S Atlantic Ave, Ormond Beach ☏386/677-1331 or 1-800/490-8935, ⓦwww.driftwoodmotel.com. Motel on the beach a couple of miles north of the action. Well-appointed rooms of varying sizes; the larger ones (with kitchens) are ideal for families. ❷

Hilton Daytona Beach 100 N Atlantic Ave ☏386/254-8200 or 1-866/536-8477, ⓦwww .hilton.com. Definitely the biggest and certainly one of the more luxurious options, this 744-room resort right in the center of the Atlantic Ave is hard to

miss. Oceanfront rooms have great views over a three-mile stretch of car-free beach. ❻

Nova Family Campground 1190 Herbert St, Port Orange ☏386/767-0095, ⓦwww.novacamp.com. Ten miles south of mainland Daytona Beach (accessible by buses #7, #12, or #17B), with a pool and laundromat. Tent sites $20 (more during special events – see box, p.337).

Ocean Court 2315 S Atlantic Ave ☏386/253-8185 or 1-800/532-7440, ⓦwww.oceancourt.com. Beach-front motel popular with the British on account of its kitchen-equipped rooms, heated pool overlooking the beach, and gregarious English owners. ❸

Perry's White Caps 2209 S Atlantic Ave, Daytona Beach Shores ☏386/255-0581 or 1-800/447-0002, ⓦwww.perryswhitecaps.com. Right next to the larger – and more impersonal – *Perry's Resort*, and sharing a front desk are seven charming standalone cottages, featuring living rooms, full kitchens and access to all the next-door resort's amenities like two outdoor pools and a 700-foot stretch of beach. ❹

Tomoka State Park seven miles north of mainland Daytona, in Ormond Beach ☏386/676-4050, 1-800/326-3521 for reservations, ⓦwww .floridastateparks.org/tomoka. Tent sites in this attractive, leafy park cost $20. Bus #1B stops a mile down the road or $4 per car.

The Villa 801 N Peninsula Drive ☏386/248-2020 or 1-888/248-7060, ⓦwww.thevillabb.com. Situated in a Spanish-style mansion near the Halifax River, this pleasant B&B has opulent rooms, a pool, and gardens. ❻

The beach and around

Without a doubt, the best thing about Daytona Beach *is* the **beach**: a seemingly limitless affair – 500 feet wide at low tide and, lengthways, fading dreamily into the heat haze. There's little to do other than develop your tan, take the occasional ocean dip, or observe one of the many pro volleyball tournaments that set up camp during the summer. Most activity centers on the **pier**, at the end of Main Street, where you can take the Sky Ride ($7), a run-down cable-car-like convey-ance that ferries you slowly from one end of the pier to the other over the heads of patient anglers or play a variety of carnival games along the pier.

Nearby, Main Street – the main drag for motorcyclists – and Seabreeze Boulevard have better bars and cafés (see "Eating," p.338, and "Drinking and nightlife," p.339), but for more diverse pursuits – such as rambling around sand

▲ Daytona Beach

dunes, climbing an old lighthouse, or discovering Daytona Beach's history – head twelve miles south to Ponce Inlet, three miles north to Ormond Beach, or cross the Halifax River to the mainland.

South to Ponce Inlet

As you travel south along Atlantic Avenue, small motels and fast-food chains give way to the towering beachside condos of affluent Daytona Beach Shores. On your right as you reach the southern extremity of these condos, at 3140 S Atlantic Ave, you'll spot a large patch of grass between the ocean and the Halifax River; this is the **Daytona Beach Drive-In Christian Church** (Sunday services at 8.30am & 10am; ☎386/767-8761), where worshipers praise the Lord from the comfort of their cars. Approaching **Ponce Inlet**, four miles ahead, the outlook changes again, this time to single-story beach homes and large sand dunes.

Here, at the end of Peninsula Drive – parallel to Atlantic Avenue – the 175-foot-high Ponce Inlet Lighthouse (Sept–May 10am–6pm; June–Aug 10am–9pm; $5; ☎386/761-1821) illuminated the treacherous coast from the late 1800s until 1970, giving seaborne access to New Smyrna Beach (see p.331). Stupendous views make climbing the structure (the tallest of its kind in Florida) worthwhile, and the outbuildings hold engaging artifacts from its early days, as well as mildly interesting displays on US lighthouses in general. Two rickety rafts carrying Cuban immigrants washed up here in 1989 and 1994 and are on display next to the administration building. It's hard to imagine they were ever capable of floating – a harsh reminder of the passengers' desperation to reach American shores. Several **nature trails** scratch a path through the surrounding scrub-covered dunes to a (usually) deserted **beach**; pick up a map from the **ranger station** at the end of Riverside Drive. Once you've checked out the lighthouse, pop next door to the **Marine Science Center**, 100 Lighthouse Drive (Tues–Sat 10am–4pm, Sun noon–4pm; $5; ☎386/304-5545, ⓦwww .marinesciencecenter.com), where you can see sick and injured sea turtles and birds being nursed back to health.

In 1890, as part of his plan to bring his East Coast railway south from St Augustine, oil baron Henry Flagler bought the local hotel, built a beachside golf course, and helped give **Ormond Beach**, three miles north of Main Street, the refined tone that it retains to this day. Millionaires like John D. Rockefeller wintered here, and the car-happy fraternity of Ford, Olds, and Chevrolet used Flagler's garage to fine-tune their cars before powering them along the beach. Note, however, that beach driving is now prohibited in Ormond Beach, from north of Granada Boulevard.

Facing the Halifax River on Granada Boulevard, Flagler's **Ormond Hotel** stood until 1993, when it was demolished to much public mourning. However, the **Casements**, a three-story villa on the other side of Granada Boulevard that Rockefeller bought in 1918, is in fine shape (most of the original furniture, though, was sold, and what remains resides in the Rockefeller period room). Guided tours of the house (25 Riverside Drive; Mon–Fri 10am–2.30pm, Sat 10–11.30am; free; ☎386/676-3216) – which, oddly enough, now also holds displays of Hungarian folklore and Boy Scouts of America bric-a-brac – run every thirty minutes and tell you more than you'll ever need to know about Rockefeller and his time here, which was mostly spent playing golf and pressing dimes into the hands of passers-by.

At 78 E Granada Blvd, the **Ormond Memorial Art Museum and Gardens** (Mon–Fri 10am–4pm, Sat & Sun noon–4pm; suggested donation $2; ☎386/676-3347, ⊛www.ormondartmuseum.org) puts on decent temporary art shows – if they don't appeal, the gallery's jungle-like **gardens**, with shady pathways winding past fishponds to a gazebo, just might.

For **information** on Ormond Beach, drop by the Chamber of Commerce, 165 W Granada Blvd (Mon–Fri 9am–5pm, ☎386/677-3454, ⊛www.ormond chamber.com), which is located west of the museum, across Halifax River.

The mainland

When you're tired of the sands or nursing your sunburn, cross the river to **mainland Daytona Beach**, where several waterside parks and walkways contribute to a relaxing change of scene, and four museums will keep you out of the sun for a few hours.

Near the best of the parks, on Beach Street, a few turn-of-the-nineteenth-century dwellings have been tidied up and turned into office space. At no. 252 South is the **Halifax Historical Museum** (Tues–Sat 10am–4pm; $5, free on Thurs; ☎386/255-6976, ⊛www.halifaxhistorical.org), which captures, with an absorbing stock of objects, models, and photos, the frenzied growth of Daytona Beach and Halifax County. Amid the fine stash of prehistoric archeological artifacts and historic memorabilia, don't overlook the immense wall paintings of long-gone local landscapes.

One former Daytona Beach resident mentioned in the museum is better remembered by the **Mary McLeod Bethune Foundation**, a mile or so north at 640 Mary McLeod Bethune Blvd. Born in 1875 to freed slave parents, Mary McLeod Bethune was a lifelong campaigner for racial and sexual equality, founding the National Council of Negro Women and serving as a presidential advisor to Calvin Coolidge and Franklin Roosevelt on racial issues, especially the education of African American women. In 1904, against the odds, she founded the state's first black girls' school here – with savings of $1.50 and five pupils. The white-framed **house** (Mon–Fri 9am–4pm; free; ☎386/481-2122), where Bethune lived from 1914 until her death in 1955, contains scores of awards and citations alongside furnishings and personal effects, and sits within the campus of Bethune-Cookman College, which has grown up around the original school.

A mile south of International Speedway Boulevard sits the diverse **Museum of the Arts and Sciences**, 352 S Nova Rd (Tues–Fri 9am–4pm, Sat & Sun noon–5pm; $13 including the planetarium; ☏386/255-0285, ⓦwww.moas .org), which is well worth a visit. Those keen on paleontology and prehistory can scrutinize bones and fossils dug up from the numerous archeological sites in the area. These include the ferocious-looking reassembled remains of a million-year-old giant ground sloth, measuring thirteen feet long. The other sections of the constantly expanding museum are equally riveting, such as the crowd-pleasing collection of Americana amassed by the Root family (the Root Family Glass Works was responsible for designing the Coca-Cola bottle), which includes a huge contingent of Teddy Bears, the first Coca-Cola can sent to space, and two magnificently luxurious railroad cars used by the Roots to travel the length and breadth of the country. A major African collection displays domestic and ceremonial objects from thirty of the continent's cultures, including the world's largest collection of Ashanti gold and pieces donated – strangely enough – by some bygone television stars. Cuban paintings spanning two centuries (donated by Cuba's former dictator, Fulgencio Batista, who spent many years of exile in a comfortable Daytona Beach house) provide a glimpse of the island nation's important artistic movements.

Daytona International Speedway

About three miles west along International Speedway Boulevard, at no. 1801 West, accessible by bus #9, #10, and #60, stands an ungainly configuration of concrete and steel that has done much to promote Daytona Beach's name around the world: the **Daytona International Speedway** (☏386/254-2700, ⓦwww.daytonainternationalspeedway.com), home of the Daytona 500 stock-car rally and a few other less famous but similar events. When high speeds made racing on Daytona's sands unsafe, the solution was this 150,000-capacity temple to high-performance thrills and spills, which opened in 1959.

Though it doesn't quite capture the excitement of a race, the guided **trolley tour** (daily 9.30am–5pm, except on race days; every 30min) gives visitors a chance to see the sheer size of the place and the remarkable 33 degree gradient of the curves, which help make this the fastest racetrack in the world – reaching speeds of 200mph is not uncommon.

Daytona speed weeks and more

The Daytona Speedway hosts several major race meetings each year, starting in late January with the **Rolex 24**, a 24-hour race for GT prototype sports cars. A week or so later begin the qualifying races leading up to the biggest event of the year, the **Daytona 500** stock-car race in mid-February. Tickets (see below) for this are as common as Florida snow, but many of the same drivers compete in the **Coca Cola 400**, for which tickets are much easier (and cheaper) to get, held on the first Saturday in July. The track is also used for motorcycle races. **Bike Week**, in early March, sees a variety of high-powered clashes, highlighted by **American Motorcycle Association** championship racing; and the **Fall Cycle Scene**, held the third week in October to coincide with **Biketoberfest**, features the **Championship Cup Series races**.

Tickets for the bigger events sell out well in advance, and it's advisable to book accommodation at least six months ahead (expect to pay $30–50 for car-racing and $99 and up for the Daytona 500, while some motorcycle races cost only $10). For **information** and ticket details call ☏877/306-RACE or check the website.

Inside, the interactive exhibits that comprise the **Daytona 500 Experience** (daily 9am–5pm; $24, children 6–12 $19 including trolley tour, ☎386/947-6800, ⓦwww.daytona500experience.com) bring you closer still to the action: see how fast you can jack a race car off the ground during a sixteen-second pit stop; feel the engines revving in your chest as you watch two wide-screen films, the mildly-interesting *Daytona 500*, and the much more engaging *NASCAR 3-D*, which features a good resume of what National Association of Stock Car Auto Racing (NASCAR) is all about, aided by fantastic 3-D effects. Other exhibits showcase the history of NASCAR and the evolution of the race car.

If all of this isn't enough, you can actually get behind the wheel of a stock car yourself – for a price – at the **Richard Petty Driving Experience** in Orlando; for details, see "Walt Disney World," p.299.

North to Tomoka State Park and the Bulow Ruins

At the meeting point of the Halifax and Tomoka rivers, just off US-1 six miles north of International Speedway Boulevard (bus #1B, then a mile's walk), the attractive **Tomoka State Park** (daily 8am–sunset; cars $4, cyclists and pedestrians $1; ☎386/676-4050, ⓦwww.floridastateparks.org/tomoka) comprises several hundred acres of marshes and tidal creeks, bordered by magnolias and moss-draped oaks. It's ripe for exploration by canoe ($10 per hour or $50 per day) or on foot along its many paths.

Take full advantage of the park by camping overnight (see "Accommodation," p.334), which leaves time to visit the **Bulow Plantation Ruins**, five miles north of the park off Rte-201 (Thurs–Mon 9am–5pm; cars $4, cyclists and pedestrians $1; ☎386/517-2084) – scant and heavily vegetated remains of an eighteenth-century plantation destroyed by Seminole Indians. Picnicking is encouraged and canoe rentals are available.

Eating

While most visitors satisfy themselves with the casual and fast-food **restaurants** along Atlantic Avenue, you'll find more interesting options around town, particularly on the mainland along Beach Street.

Angell & Phelps Café 156 S Beach St ☎386/257-2677, ⓦwww.angellandphelpscafe .com. Creative American-style gourmet food served in an informal setting, with live local talent (often jazz) Wed–Fri. Closed Sun.

Anna's Italian Trattoria 304 Seabreeze Blvd ☎386/239-9624. If you had an Italian grandma, this is how she'd cook. Home-made pastas like cannelloni and house favorite seafood risotto insure that you won't leave hungry.

Aunt Catfish's on the River 4009 Halifax Drive, Port Orange ☎386/767-4768, ⓦwww.auntcatfish ontheriver.com. Mighty portions of ribs and seafood prepared in traditional Southern style. Lunch from $7, dinner from $13.

Dancing Avocado Kitchen 110 S Beach St ☎386/947-2022. Health-conscious café serving salads, vegetarian sandwiches, and Mexican snacks, including a filling breakfast burrito.

Daytona Diner 290 1/2 N Beach St ☎386/258-8488. A Harley-Davidson presence dominates this

1950s-style diner (there's a dealership next door), where huge breakfasts cost around $6.

Inlet Harbor 133 Inlet Harbor Rd, Ponce Inlet ☎386/767-5590, ⓦwww.inletharbor .com. Enjoy shrimp cooked in a number of different ways (try one of the tasty pasta dishes) at this restaurant right on the marina. Live music nightly.

Lighthouse Landing 4940 S Peninsula Drive, beside the Ponce Inlet Lighthouse ☎386/761-9271, ⓦwww.lighthouselandingrestaurant.com. Offering fresh seafood for $15–20 in a quirky and festive setting.

McK's Tavern 218 S Beach St ☎386/238-3321, ⓦwww.mckstavern.com. A relaxed spot for a filling meal, with juicy burgers, Guinness stew, and an extensive beer selection. Closed Sun.

Ronin Sushi and Sake Bar 111 West International Speedway Blvd ☎386/252-6320, ⓦwww.roninsushiandbar.com. The newest sushi joint in town has become a local favorite, offering the freshest rolls and a chic atmosphere.

Drinking and nightlife

Daytona Beach **nightlife** is more varied than its biker reputation would suggest. Main Street has the biker bars while Seabreeze Boulevard offers Spring Break-style entertainment.

Boot Hill Saloon 310 Main St ☎386/258-9506, ⓦwww.boothillsaloon.com. They say it's "better here than across the street," referring to the neighboring cemetery, but this slightly rowdy biker bar is at least several notches above that.
Oyster Pub 555 Seabreeze Blvd ☎386/255-6348, ⓦwww.oysterpub.com. Lively sports bar with dirt-cheap oysters and a loud jukebox.
Razzles 611 Seabreeze Blvd ☎386/257-6236, ⓦwww.razzlesnightclub.com. Large disco with

headache-inducing light shows and throbbing music for dancers, plus four pool tables and twenty TVs for everyone else. Drink specials every night.
Rockin' Ranch 801 S Nova Rd ☎386/673-0904, ⓦwww.rockinranchdaytona.com. If country and western is your thing, come here Wed, Fri, or Sat for live C&W or anytime 6pm–2am Mon–Sat for free line-dancing lessons.

North of Daytona Beach

Assuming you don't want to cut twenty miles inland along I-4 or Hwy-92 to DeLand and the Orlando area (see "Orlando and Disney World," p.273), keep on Hwy-A1A **northward** along the coast toward St Augustine. The first community you'll encounter is **Flagler Beach**, fourteen miles from Daytona Beach, comprising a few houses and shops, a pier, and a very tempting beach. Nearby, at the **Gamble Rogers Memorial State Recreation Area**, 3100 S Hwy-A1A (daily 8am–sunset; cars $4, cyclists and pedestrians $1; ☎386/517-2086; camping $23 ☎1-800-326-3521 for reservations), spot a good cross-section of coastal birdlife and during the summer months sea turtles lay their eggs on the beach. If the relative peace and solitude of Flagler Beach persuades you to stay, try the antique-filled *Topaz Motel/Hotel*, 1224 S Ocean Shore Blvd (☎386/439-3301 or 1-800/555-4735; ❸), which offers standard rooms with or without kitchens as well as a few that carry on the antique theme (❺).

Further north, soon after passing the blazing blooms of **Washington Oaks State Gardens**, 6400 N Oceanshore Blvd (daily 8am–sunset; cars $3–4, pedestrians and cyclists $1; ☎386/446-6780), you can't miss the streamlined, yet crumbling, architecture of **Marineland**, 9600 N Oceanshore Blvd (daily 8.30am–4.30pm; $6, children 3–11 $3; ☎904/471-1111 or 1-888/279-9194, ⓦwww.marineland.net), Florida's original sea-creature theme park. Established as marine studios for underwater research and photography, and the state's biggest tourist draw when it opened in 1938, Marineland is now a shadow of its former glory. The shows have gone, and a few dolphins are all that remain. The low entrance fee allows you to observe the dolphins playing, but the real idea is to fork out $189 (reservations required) to swim with them – for twenty minutes in shallow water, plus another ten minutes with a mask in deep water.

Hwy-A1A crosses a narrow inlet three miles beyond Marineland onto **Anastasia Island**, close to the Spanish-built eighteenth-century **Fort Matanzas** on Rattle-snake Island. Never conquered, partly due to the sixteen-foot-thick walls and the surrounding moat, the fort is accessible only by **ferry** (daily 9.30am–4.30pm every hour on the half-hour; free; call ☎904/471-0116 to confirm schedule), but it's of minor appeal in comparison with history-packed St Augustine.

A better stop is the **St Augustine Alligator Farm** (daily 9am–5pm, or 6pm in summer; $21.95, children 3–11 $10.95; ☎904/824-3337, ⓦwww.alligator farm.us), a few miles further north along Hwy-A1A, where visitors can take a walk through a wildlife-infested swamp. It's the only place in the world where you can meet all 23 members of the crocodilian family, including an Australian saltwater crocodile measuring over fifteen feet. It's also home to thousands of wading birds, who come to roost in the rookery in the late afternoons. From April through July these birds are in full breeding plumage – a great time for budding photographers to snap away. Time your visit to coincide with the alligator, reptile, or bird shows (one or two shows daily, call for exact times) or the alligator feeding demonstration – heart-stopping stuff, especially when you're listening to the crunch of capybara (a large South American rodent) bone between reptilian teeth.

St Augustine

Few places in Florida are as immediately engaging as **ST AUGUSTINE**, the oldest permanent settlement in the US and one with much from its early days still intact. Looking like a small Mediterranean town, St Augustine's eminently strollable narrow streets are lined by carefully renovated buildings whose architecture carries evidence of Florida's broad European heritage and the power struggles that led up to its statehood. There's plenty here to fill a day or two, and for variation you can visit two alluring lengths of beach located just across the small bay on which the town stands.

Ponce de León, the Spaniard who gave Florida its name, touched ground here on *Pascua Florida* (Easter Sunday) in 1513, but it wasn't until Pedro Menéndez de Aviles put ashore that settlement began with the intention of subduing the Huguenots based to the north at Fort Caroline (see "The Jacksonville beaches," p.348). Sir Francis Drake's ships razed St Augustine in 1586, but Spanish control was only relinquished when Florida was ceded to Britain in 1763, by which time the town was established as an important social and administrative center – soon to become the capital of East Florida. Spain regained possession twenty years later, and kept it until 1821, when Florida joined the US. A railway and a posh hotel stimulated a tourist boom at the turn of the twentieth century, but otherwise expansion bypassed St Augustine – which inadvertently made possible the restoration program that started in the 1930s

Arrival, information, and tours

From Anastasia Island, **Hwy-A1A** crosses over Mantanzas Bay into the heart of St Augustine; **US-1** passes a mile west along Ponce de León Boulevard. The Greyhound **bus** will drop you at an inconvenient location a couple of miles from the center at 1711 Dobbs Rd (☏904/829-6401). The only way to get into town from here is to take a taxi (see p.342) or walk.

The main **Visitor Center**, 10 Castillo Drive (daily 8.30am–5.30pm; ☏904/825-1000 or 1-800/653-2489, ⓦwww.visitoldcity.com), offers the usual tourist brochures and discount coupons (it costs $7.50 to park there for the day or $1.25 per hour, but is convenient if you're strolling the streets). It also has a film on the town's history, recommendations for a variety of historical guided tours, including those of Tour Saint Augustine (☏904/825-0087 or 1-800/797-3778, ⓦwww.staugustinetours.com), who offer well-organized and informative walking tours, tailored itineraries, and information on the numerous local festivals (including torch-lit processions and a Menorcan Fiesta). Consider indulging in "A Ghostly Experience," a more historical than scary guided walking tour that reveals local legends, tall tales, and haunted and spook-filled

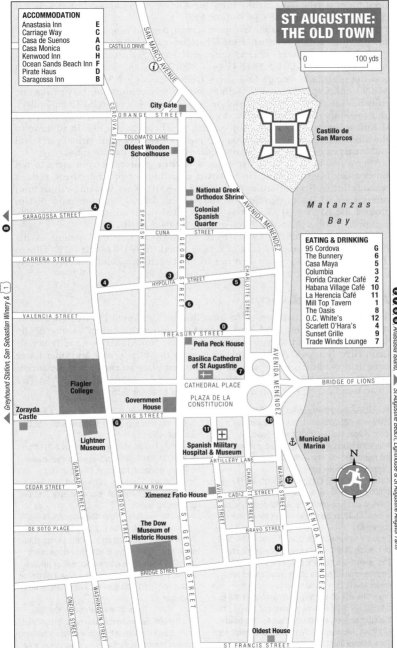

Mission of Nombre de Dios, The Fountain of Youth & Vilano Beach

ST AUGUSTINE: THE OLD TOWN

ACCOMMODATION

Anastasia Inn	E
Carriage Way	C
Casa de Suenos	A
Casa Monica	G
Kenwood Inn	H
Ocean Sands Beach Inn	F
Pirate Haus	D
Saragossa Inn	B

0   100 yds

SAN MARCO AVENUE

CASTILLO DRIVE

City Gate

ORANGE STREET

CORDOVA STREET

TOLOMATO LANE

Oldest Wooden Schoolhouse

Castillo de San Marcos

SPANISH STREET

National Greek Orthodox Shrine

Colonial Spanish Quarter

AVENIDA MENENDEZ

Matanzas Bay

SARAGOSSA STREET

CUNA STREET

ST GEORGE STREET

CARRERA STREET

CHARLOTTE STREET

EATING & DRINKING

95 Cordova	G
The Bunnery	6
Casa Maya	5
Columbia	3
Florida Cracker Café	2
Habana Village Café	10
La Herencia Café	11
Mill Top Tavern	1
The Oasis	8
O.C. White's	12
Scarlett O'Hara's	4
Sunset Grille	9
Trade Winds Lounge	7

HYPOLITA STREET

VALENCIA STREET

TREASURY STREET

Peña Peck House

Basilica Cathedral of St Augustine

CATHEDRAL PLACE

PLAZA DE LA CONSTITUCION

BRIDGE OF LIONS

Flagler College

Government House

KING STREET

Zorayda Castle

Lightner Museum

Spanish Military Hospital & Museum

Municipal Marina

ARTILLERY LANE

N

GRANADA STREET

CEDAR STREET

CORDOVA STREET

PALM ROW

Ximenez Fatio House

AVILES STREET

CADIZ STREET

CHARLOTTE STREET

MARINE STREET

AVENIDA MENENDEZ

DE SOTO PLACE

The Dow Museum of Historic Houses

ST GEORGE STREET

BRAVO STREET

BRIDGE STREET

ONEIDA STREET

WASHINGTON STREET

Oldest House

ST FRANCIS STREET

Greyhound Station, San Sebastian Winery & (1)

Anastasia Island, St Augustine Beach, Lighthouse & St Augustine Alligator Farm sites; tours start at 8pm across from the Oldest Schoolhouse (for tickets call ☎904/461-1009 or 1-888/461-1009; $12).

St Augustine has no public transport system, but this poses no problem in the town, which is best seen **on foot**. There are two **sightseeing trains**, distinguishable only by their colors: the red Ripley's Sightseeing Train (170 San Marco Ave; $21; ☎904/829-6545 or 1-800/226-6545; ⓦwww.redtrains.com) and the green-and-orange Old Town Trolley Tours (167 San Marco Ave; $21, $18.90 online only; ☎904/829-3800, ⓦwww.trolleytours.com). They operate daily 8.30am to 5pm (Ripley's Sightseeing Train) or 4.30pm (Old Town Trolley), and make approximately twenty stops during an hour-long narrated circuit of the main landmarks; you can hop on and off whenever you like. In addition to the aforementioned addresses, you can purchase **tickets** from virtually any bed and breakfast or motel, and tickets entitle you to three days of travel.

After a few hours of hard exploration, **harbor cruises**, leaving eight to ten times a day from the Municipal Marina near the foot of King Street, make a relaxing break; Scenic Cruise (☎1-800/542-8316, ⓦwww.scenic-cruise.com) offers four to six (depending on the season) daily 75-minute guided trips around the bay for $15.75. There is also a two-hour sunset sail on the fully equipped 72-foot schooner *Freedom* ($35; ☎904/810-1010).

After delving into the town's trove of historical treasures, getting to the beaches means a two-mile hike or calling a **taxi** (☎904/824-8161). Old Town Trolley tour tickets include free use of the Beach Bus, which departs hourly from the south side of the Plaza de la Constitucion.

Accommodation

St Augustine attracts plenty of visitors, and its Old Town has many excellent restored inns offering **bed and breakfast**. Note that prices usually go up $15–50 on weekends. Several chain **hotels** line San Marco Ave and Ponce de León Blvd (Hwy-A1A) for a mile or two north of the center, and offer lower rates than the hotels in the Old Town. The best place to **camp** is the Anastasia State Recreation Area (☎904/461-2033), four miles south, off Hwy-A1A (see "The Beaches," p.347), where you can pitch a tent for $25.

Anastasia Inn 218 Anastasia Blvd ☎904/825-2879 or 1-888/226-6181, ⓦwww.anastasiainn.com. Across the bay from the Old Town, on Anastasia Island, well within striking distance of all the sights and the beach, the *Anastasia Inn* has clean, simple motel rooms.
Carriage Way 70 Cuna St ☎904/829-2467 or 1-800/908-9832, ⓦwww.carriageway.com. Canopy and four-poster beds, clawfoot tubs, and antiques add to the period feel of this 1880s house. ❻
Casa de Suenos 20 Cordova St ☎904/824-0887 or 1-800/824-0804, ⓦwww.casadesuenos.com. This sumptuous bed and breakfast with five Spanish-themed rooms offers all amenities (even cream sherry in your room). ❼
Casa Monica 95 Cordova St ☎904/827-1888 or 1-800/648-1888, ⓦwww.casamonica.com. By far the most elegant, and costly, choice in the heart of Old Town. The magnificently restored, Spanish-style *Casa Monica* has 138 uniquely furnished rooms

and an air of royalty – in fact, the tower suite has hosted the king and queen of Spain. Book well in advance. ❽
Kenwood Inn 38 Marine St ☎904/824-2116 or 1-800/824-8151, ⓦwww.thekenwoodinn.com. Enjoying a peaceful location, this charming, immaculate inn features its own pool, and there's a complimentary cocktail hour every day. Free use of bikes for guests. ❺
Ocean Sands Beach Inn 3465 Coastal Hwy (Hwy-A1A) ☎904/824-1112 or 1-800-609-0888, ⓦwww.oceansandsinn.com. All the rooms at this small beachfront hotel, a little over three miles from Old Town, have either balconies or private patios, some with ocean or Intracoastal Waterway views. The hotel also puts on a nice spread for breakfast. ❺
Pirate Haus 32 Treasury St ☎904/808-1999, ⓦwww.piratehaus.com. A renovated pirate-themed hotel/hostel with a giant kitchen and a common room stuffed with local guidebooks. All

of the five private rooms have a/c, and you can make your own pancake breakfast. Rooms ❸. Dorms $20.

 Saragossa Inn 34 Saragossa St ☎ 904/808-7384 or 1-877/808-7384,

ⓦ wwwsaragossainn.com. This lovely little pink cottage began life in 1924 as a prefab bungalow and now holds four comfortable guest rooms and two suites, just a bit west of the beaten path. ❻

Old Town

St Augustine's historic area – or **Old Town** – along St George Street and south of the central plaza contains well-tended evidence of the town's various periods. Worth a look, too, are the lavish "Spanish Renaissance" structures along King Street, just west of the plaza, surviving from the turn-of-the-nineteenth-century resort era. Although St Augustine is small, there's a lot to see: an early start, around 9am, will give you a lead on the crowds, and you should ideally allow three days to explore the town fully.

The fortress

Given the fine state of the **Castillo de San Marcos** (daily 8.45am–4.45pm; $6), on the northern edge of the Old Town beside the bay, it's difficult to believe that the fortress was built in the late 1600s. The secret of its longevity is the design: a diamond-shaped rampart at each corner maximized firepower, and fourteen-foot-thick coquina (a type of soft limestone found on Anastasia Island) walls reduced vulnerability to attack – as British troops found when they waged a fruitless fifty-day siege in 1702. The fort is now a National Monument run by the National Park Service; time schedules for the free and very informative twenty-minute talks on the fort and local history are posted at the entrance.

Inside, there's not a lot to admire beyond a small museum and echoing rooms – some of them with military and social exhibits – but venturing along the 35-foot-high ramparts gives an unobstructed view over the low-lying city, which the castle protected so successfully, and its waterborne approaches. Look for the eerie graffiti on the walls, scrawled by soldiers in the 1600s.

Along St George Street

Leaving the Castillo, you'll pass through the little eighteenth-century **City Gate** marking the entrance to **St George Street**, once the main thoroughfare and now a tourist-trampled pedestrianized strip – but home to plenty of genuine history. At no. 14, the **Oldest Wooden Schoolhouse** (daily 9am–5pm; $3.50; ☎904/824-0192) still has its original eighteenth-century red-cedar and cypress walls and tabby floor (a mix of crushed oyster shells and lime). The building was put into use as a school some years later, thereby inadvertently becoming the oldest wooden schoolhouse in the US. Pupils and teacher are now unconvincingly portrayed by speaking wax models.

Further along, at no. 41, an unassuming doorway leads into the petite **National Greek Orthodox Shrine** (daily 9am–5pm; free), where tapes of Byzantine choirs echo through the halls, and icons and candles stand alongside hard-hitting accounts of the experiences of Greek immigrants to the US – some of whom settled in St Augustine from New Smyrna Beach (see p.331) in 1777.

More directly relevant to the town, and taking up a fair-sized plot along St George Street between Tolomato Lane and Cuna Street, the **Colonial Spanish Quarter** (daily 9am–5.30pm last ticket sold at 4:45pm; $7; ☎904/823-4569) includes nine reconstructed homes and workshops. Volunteers disguised as Spanish settlers go about their daily tasks at anvils, and foot-driven wood lathes. The museum should be visited either early in the day or during an off-peak period; lines of camera-wielding tourists and rowdy school groups substantially lessen the effect. The main entrance is through the Triay House, at 29 St George St.

For a more intimate look at local life during a slightly later period, head for the **Peña Peck House**, at no. 143 (Mon–Fri & Sun 12.30pm–4.15pm, Sat 10.30am-4.15pm; donation requested; ℡904/829-5064). Thought to have originally been the Spanish treasury, by the time the British took over in 1763 this was the home of a physician and his gregarious spouse, who turned the place into a high-society rendezvous. The Pecks' furnishings and paintings, plus the enthusiastic spiel of the guide, make for an enjoyable tour.

The Dow Museum of Historic Houses, 246 St George St (entrance at 147 Cordova St; Mon–Sat 10am–4.30pm, Sun 11am–4.30pm; $9; ℡904/823-9722), presents a group of nine period buildings that have been beautifully restored from every period and cultural stripe, not just Spanish. Particularly fascinating is the **Prince Murat House** (1790), briefly home to Napoleon's nephew (for whom it was named), whose main room and upstairs bedroom is graced by ravishing French Empire furniture.

The plaza

In the sixteenth century, the Spanish king decreed all colonial towns had to be built around a central plaza, and St Augustine was no exception: St George Street runs into **Plaza de la Constitucion**, a marketplace dating from 1598 that nowadays attracts shade seekers and the occasional wino. On the north side of the plaza, the **Basilica Cathedral of St Augustine** (daily 7am–5pm; donation requested) adds a touch of grandeur, though it's largely a 1960s remodeling of the late eighteenth-century original, with murals by Hugo Ohlms depicting life in St Augustine. Inside, pick up free **self-guided tour** leaflets explaining the church's main features. The ground floor of **Government House** (daily 9am–3.45pm; $4; ℡904/825-5079), on the west side of the plaza, contains small displays of objects from the city's various renovation projects and archeological digs.

South of the plaza

Tourist numbers lessen as you cross south of the plaza into a web of quiet, narrow streets with as much antiquity as St George Street.

Close by, at 3 Aviles St, the small 1791 **Spanish Military Hospital & Museum** (Mon–Sat 10am–4pm, Sun noon–4pm; $5.30; ℡904/827-0807) is worth a short visit. The museum re-creates the spartan care wounded soldiers received and includes displays of rusty surgical instruments and also the "mourning room," where the priest administered last rites to doomed patients. A little further along at 20 Aviles St, the **Ximenez Fatio House** Tues–Sat 11am–4pm; $5; ℡904/829-3575, ⊛www.ximenezfatiohouse.org) was built in 1789 for a Spanish merchant and proved popular with travelers during the late eighteenth century, drawn by the airy balconies added to the original structure. Although the upper floor is a bit rickety, a walk around is safe and quick in the company of a guide who points out illuminating details such as a kitchen in a detached building. More substantial history is unfurled a ten-minute walk away at the **Oldest House**, 14 St Francis St (daily 9am–5pm, last admission 4.30pm; $8; ℡904/824-2872, ⊛www.staugustinehistoricalsociety.org), occupied from the early 1700s (and, indeed, the oldest house in town) by the family of an artillery hand at the castle. The second floor was grafted on during the British period, a fact evinced by the bone china crockery belonging to a former occupant, one Mary Peavitt. Her disastrous marriage to a hopeless gambler provided the basis for a popular historical novel, *Maria*, by Eugenia Price (the gift shop has copies). A smaller room shows the pine-stripped "sidecar" style made popular by the arrival of Flagler's railway, copying as it does the decor of a train carriage.

West of the plaza: along King Street

A walk west from the plaza along **King Street** bridges the gap between early St Augustine and its turn-of-the-twentieth-century tourist boom. You'll soon notice, at the junction with Cordova Street, the flowing spires, arches, and red-tiled roof of **Flagler College**. Now a liberal arts campus, a hundred years ago it was the *Ponce de León Hotel*, an exclusive winter retreat of the nation's rich and mighty. The hotel was an early attempt by entrepreneur Henry Flagler to exploit Florida's climate and coast, but as he developed properties further south and extended his railway, the *Ponce de León* fell from favor – not helped by several freezing winters. There are **guided tours** explaining the building's storied past (daily 10am and 2pm; $6, ⊕904-819-6400, Ⓦwww.flagler.edu), but you can also walk around on your own through the **campus** and to the first floor of the **main building** to admire the Tiffany stained glass and the painstakingly restored painted ceiling in the dining room.

Flagler commissioned the same architects who were working on the *Ponce de León* to build the *Alcazar Hotel* right across the street in 1887. Fronted by a courtyard of palm trees and fountains, the Spanish Renaissance building now holds the **Lightner Museum** (daily 9am–5pm, last admission 4pm; $10; ⊕904/824-2874, Ⓦwww.lightnermuseum.org), where you can easily pass an hour poring over the Victorian cut glass, Tiffany lamps, antique music boxes, and more. There's even a Russian malachite and ormolu urn from the Winter Palace of imperial St Petersburg. Much of the booty was acquired by publishing ace Otto C. Lightner from once-wealthy estates hard hit by the Depression.

A rather incongruous sight in St Augustine is eccentric Bostonian architect Franklin W. Smith's re-creation of the famed Alhambra. The architect was so impressed by the Moorish architecture he'd seen in Spain that he built a copy of one wing of the thirteenth-century palace here, in the late nineteenth

▲ Flagler College

century, at a tenth of the original size. The **Villa Zorayda Museum** at 83 King St (Mon–Sat 10am–5pm, 4.30pm last admission, $10 audio tour, ☎904/829-9887, ⓦ www.villazorayda.com) has undergone extensive renovations in the last few years and is home now to a fascinating collection of Smith's personal belongings.

A bit further along King Street, at no. 157, the **San Sebastian Winery** (Mon–Sat 10am–6pm, Sun 11am–6pm; ☎904/826-1594 or 1-888/352-9463, ⓦ www.sansebastianwinery.com) is worth a look, especially for oenophiles. St Augustine wineries were around 150 years before their counterparts in California, and regular free **guided tours** explain the various stages in the wine-making process. You can taste several of the local wines after the tour; some are made with Florida's native muscadine grape, and have a very distinctive bouquet – not dissimilar to jet fuel – and a sickly sweet taste.

North of Old Town: San Marco Avenue and around

Leading away from the tightly grouped streets of the Old Town, the traffic-bearing **San Marco Avenue**, beginning on the other side of the City Gate from St George Street, passes the sites of the first Spanish landings and settlements as well as some remains of the Timucua Indians who greeted them.

Five blocks north along San Marco Avenue, a dull, modern church now stands in the grounds of the **Mission of Nombre de Dios** (Mon–Fri 8am–5pm, Sat–Sun 10am–5pm; donation requested). This sixteenth-century mission was one of many in the southeast US established by Spanish settlers to convert Native Americans to Christianity, simultaneously exploiting their labor and seeking their support in possible confrontations with rival colonial powers.

A pathway leads to a 208-foot-tall stainless steel cross, glinting in the sun beside the river on the spot where Menéndez landed in 1565. Soon after, Father Francisco Lopez de Mendoza Grajales celebrated the first Mass in North America, recording that "a large number of Indians watched the proceedings and imitated all they saw," which was a bit unfortunate since the arrival of the Spanish signalled the beginning of the end for the Indians. A side path takes a mildly interesting course around the rest of the squirrel-patrolled lawns, passing a few relics of the mission, on the way to a small, ivy-covered re-creation of the original chapel.

In addition to the prospect of finding gold and silver, it's said that Ponce de León was drawn to Florida by the belief that the fabled life-preserving "fountain of youth" was located here. Rather tenuously, this fact is celebrated at a mineral spring touted as **The Fountain of Youth**, 11 Magnolia Ave (daily 9am–5pm; $7.50; ☎904/829-3168 or 1-800/356-8222) in a park at the end of Williams Street (off San Marco Ave), very near the point where he landed in 1513, and three blocks north of the old mission site. When leaving the mission, instead of walking along San Marco Avenue and turning right at Williams Street, walk along Magnolia Avenue, which is lined with a canopy of beautiful oak trees dripping with Spanish moss. As you enter the springhouse, you'll be handed a cup of the fresh spring water (with a smelly bouquet of sulfur), but it's the expansive acres of the park that have far more significance as an archeological site. Beside the remains of the Spanish settlement, many Timucua Indian relics have been unearthed here, and you'll also come across some of the wiry plants that were the base of the "Black Drink," a thick, highly potent concoction used by the Timucuans to help them achieve mystical states.

The Beaches

If you've reached St Augustine via Hwy-A1A, you'll need no introduction to the fine **beaches** that lie just a couple of miles from the Old Town. Few other people need one either, especially on weekends when the bronzers, beach-combers, and watersports fanatics descend in droves. A fine view of St Augustine and up and down the beaches is afforded by the **Lighthouse and Museum**, 81 Lighthouse Ave (daily 9am–6pm, last admission 5:45pm; $9; ☏904/829-0745, Ⓦwww.staugustinelighthouse.com), which tells the story of the keepers and the lights they tended.

Across the bay on Anastasia Island, **St Augustine Beach** is family terrain, but here you'll also find the **Anastasia State Recreation Area** (daily 8am–sunset; cars $3–5, cyclists and pedestrians $1; ☏904/461-2033), offering a thousand protected acres of dunes, marshes, scrub, and a wind-beaten group of live oaks, linked by nature walks – though most people come here to catch a fish dinner from the lagoon. In the other direction (take May St, off San Marco Ave), **Vilano Beach** pulls a younger crowd and marks the beginning of a dazzling strand of vegetation hemming the road on both sides that continues for twenty undeveloped miles all the way to Jacksonville Beach (see p.348).

Eating

The tourist throng on and around St George Street makes **eating** in the Old Town an often-pricey affair, particularly for dinner. You'll find a few cheaper café-style spots in the Old Town, while the usual chain restaurants start to appear as you head north along San Marco Avenue.

95 Cordova 95 Cordova St, at the *Casa Monica Hotel* ☏904/810-6810. You'll need to make reservations to partake of the masterful nouvelle continental cuisine at this elegant bistro. Expect to pay $25 and up for entrées or $15 for a sumptuous Sunday brunch.
The Bunnery 121 St George St ☏904/829-6166. All the tempting goodies in this old Spanish bakery are made in-house except the strudel. There's also good coffee and economical breakfasts, plus tempting sandwiches and paninis.
🏃 **Casa Maya** 17 Hypolita St ☏904/823-1739. Didn't expect to find "organic Mayan cuisine" in Florida? Everything on the eclectic menu at this little four-table restaurant is good, from the Apocalypto breakfast sandwich with chorizo, egg, avocado, beans, tomato and bacon ($8.50) to the marinated Aztec pork dinner entrée ($15).
Columbia 98 St George St ☏904/824-3341, Ⓦwww.columbiarestaurant.com. Enjoy traditional

Spanish and Cuban food, from tapas to sumptuous paellas, amid splashing fountains, wood beams, candlelight, and painted tiles. Dinner entrées around $25.
Florida Cracker Café 81 St George St ☏904/829-0397, Ⓦwww.floridacrackercafe.com. Especially good for lunch, with eclectic and reasonably priced combo salads (blackened shrimp and spinach), conch fritters, and home-made desserts.
La Herencia Café 4 Aviles St ☏904/829-9487, Ⓦwww.laherenciacafe.com. You'll get some of the best Cuban food in town at this cute little breakfast and lunch spot, as well as great omelets like the Tropical, featuring sweet plantains. Closed Thurs.
The Oasis 4000 Ocean Trace Rd (Hwy-AIA) ☏904/471-3424, Ⓦwww.worldfamousoasis.com. Satiate yourself with excellent burgers, featuring a multitude of toppings, at this fun shack at St Augustine Beach.

Nightlife

You'll find plenty of **live music** in St Augustine, even in the afternoon and especially on weekends, though most of it takes place in restaurants rather than full-fledged bars.

Habana Village Café 1 King St ☏904/827-1700. Dance to live Latin jazz Wed–Sun at this upbeat hideaway, followed by potent home-made

sangria, and yummy Cuban appetizers such as fried yucca. Also open for lunch.

Mill Top Tavern 19 1/2 St George St ☎ 904/829-2329, ⓦ www.milltop.com. Lots of local folk hang out at the top of the millwheel, where there's a terrific, funky atmosphere, live music in the afternoons and evenings, and an open-air view of the Castillo and harbor.

O.C. White's 118 Avenida Menéndez ☎ 904/824-0808, ⓦ www.ocwhites.com. A lively crowd pervades this bayfront bar-restaurant, which has nightly live entertainment, an attractive outside patio, and grouper and crab cakes to absorb the beer.

Scarlett O'Hara's 70 Hypolita St ☎ 904/824-6535, ⓦ www.scarlettoharas.net. Tuck into full meals (barbecue is the specialty) and enjoy a variety of live music, including karaoke, at this cedar and cypress building that was once an old Florida crackers house.

Sunset Grille 421 Beach Blvd, St Augustine Beach ☎ 904/471-5555, ⓦ www.sunsetgrilleA1A.com. Parrotheads (ardent Jimmy Buffett fans) will feel right at home at this Key West-style bar and restaurant across from the beach. The menu offers a variety of sandwiches as well as seafood entrées and there's live music on Sundays.

Trade Winds Lounge 124 Charlotte St ☎ 904/826-1590, ⓦ www.tradewindslounge.com. Convivial bar where you can tap your feet to country and western and rock 'n' roll bands. Hopeful wannabes test their skills on Thursdays' open-mic nights.

The Jacksonville beaches

However good the beaches around St Augustine may be, they're just the start of an unblemished coastal strip running northwards for twenty miles alongside Hwy-A1A, with nothing but the ocean on one side, and the swamps and marshes of the Talamato River (the local section of the Intracoastal Waterway) on the other. The scene begins to change when you near the sculptured golf courses and million-dollar homes of **Ponte Vedra Beach** – one of the most exclusive communities in northeast Florida. The crowd-free sands are prime beachcombing terrain – retreating tides often leave sharks' teeth among the more common ocean debris.

Four miles on, the much less snooty **Jacksonville Beach** (visitor center at 380 Pablo Ave ☎ 904/242-0024 or 1-866/JAX-BCHS, ⓦ www .visitjacksonville.com) is an affable beachside community; most residents commute to work in the city of Jacksonville, twelve miles inland. Much cleaner than Daytona, the beach is inexplicably – and refreshingly – neglected by tourists outside of the summer months, when it's as busy as any other beach in northern Florida. The **pier** (entrance $1) is the center of activity. Munch on a fried-fish sandwich from the snack bar while checking out novice surfers grappling with modest-sized breakers. If you start itching for some action of your own, you could do worse than visit **Adventure Landing**, 1944 Beach Blvd (Mon–Thurs & Sun 10am–10pm, Fri & Sat 10am–midnight; ☎ 904/246-4386, ⓦ www.adventurelanding.com). Getting in is free, but you pay for the attractions that most strike your fancy: highlights include a go-kart race track ($7), a game of laser-tag with pirates in the dark ($7), baseball batting cages ($2), and a water park with three slides ($27); the "Night Splash" evening reduced-rate ticket lets you in for $17 between 3pm and 8pm.

Once you cross Seagate Avenue, less than two miles north of the pier, Jacksonville Beach merges with the more commercialized **Neptune Beach**, which in turn blurs (at Atlantic Boulevard) with the identical-looking **Atlantic Beach**. These last two places are more family-oriented than Jacksonville Beach, but all are great to visit for eating and socializing. A good way to get from beach to beach is to **rent a bike** from Champion Cycling, 1303 N 3rd St (☎ 904/241-0900; $7 per hr, $20 per day). Just north of Atlantic Beach, downbeat **Mayport** is dominated by its naval station, berth to some of the biggest aircraft carriers in the US Navy. It's best seen through a car window on the way to the Mayport ferry, which crosses the St Johns River, and the barrier islands beyond (see "Toward Amelia Island," p.355).

In contrast to the naval station is the **Kathryn Abbey Hanna Park**, 500 Wonderwood Drive (April–Oct 8am–8pm; Nov–March 8am–6pm; $1 per person until 10am, then $3 per car; ☎904/249-4700), just south of Mayport. Besides its mile and a half of unblemished beachfront, the park boasts 450 acres of woodland surrounding a large lake, around which wind ten miles of enjoyable biking and hiking trails. There's also a campground here (see "Accommodation," below).

Fort Caroline National Memorial

A few miles inland on Fort Caroline Road (several miles off Atlantic Blvd), the **Fort Caroline National Memorial** (daily 9am–5pm; free; ☎904/641-7155, ⓦ www.nps.gov/foca) offers a historical interlude: a small museum details the significance of the restored Huguenot fort here, which provoked the first Spanish settlement in Florida (see "St Augustine," p.340). Another reason to visit is the great view from the fort across the mile-wide St Johns River and its ocean-going freighters.

Accommodation

Along the coast prices will be lower in winter and on weekdays; rates generally start at around $80 and you should book ahead in summer.

Best Western Oceanfront 305 N 1st St, Jacksonville Beach ☎904/249-4949 or 1-800/897-8131, ⓦ www.jaxbestwestern.com. A reliable standby where the comfortable rooms come with fridge and microwave, although the tiny pool next to the road is uninviting. ⑥

Casa Marina Hotel and Restaurant 1st St north, Jacksonville Beach ☎904/270-0025, ⓦ www.casamarinahotel.com. This Mediterranean-style hotel first opened in 1925, and still boasts elegant touches like hardwood floors and period furniture in the rooms, as well as a great rooftop cocktail lounge. ⑥

Kathryn Abbey Hanna Park 500 Wonderwood Drive ☎904/249-4700. Great campground for woodsy isolation. Tent sites are $20 per night, while sleeping cabins with electricity (but no furniture) are $34 per night (two-night minimum).

One Ocean 1 Ocean Blvd, Atlantic Beach ☎904/247-0305, ⓦ www.oneoceanresort.com. There's an art gallery in the lobby of this new luxury hotel, and each floor has a volunteer eager to escort you to your room. Though the museum/gallery theme is a little over-the-top, you can't argue with the elegant rooms and serene setting. ⑧

Pelican Path Bed & Breakfast 11 N 19th Ave, Jacksonville Beach ☎904/249-1177 or 1-888/749-1177, ⓦ www.pelicanpath.com. Rooms with bay windows look onto the sands at this cozy inn, and bicycles are available for guests' use. Adults only; no smoking. ⑦

Sea Horse Oceanfront Inn 120 Atlantic Blvd, Neptune Beach ☎904/246-2175 or 1-800/881-2330, ⓦ www.seahorseoceanfrontinn.com. This beachside two-story pink stucco hotel has fairly ordinary, but clean, rooms and a pool. ⑤

Eating, drinking, and nightlife

You'll find good **eating** and **nightlife** options at the beaches, especially near the pier at Jacksonville Beach, which tends to be a bit louder and younger than the others. Check out restaurants like *Ragtime* (Thurs–Sun) and *Sun Dog Diner* (nightly) for live music as well.

Restaurants

Al's Pizza 303 Atlantic Blvd, Atlantic Beach ☎904/249-0002, ⓦ www.alspizza.com. Widely considered to have the best pizza in Jacksonville;

also serving other tasty Italian favorites such as calzone and lasagna.

Beach Hut Café 1281 S 3rd St, Jacksonville Beach ☎904/249-3516.

Popular breakfast spot – as the frequent lines out the door (particularly on Sun) will attest – with generous portions of biscuits and gravy, pancakes, French toast, and the like at reasonable prices. Serves breakfast and lunch, closes at 3.30pm

Ragtime Tavern Seafood Grill 207 Atlantic Blvd, Atlantic Beach ☎ 904/241-7877, ⓦ www .ragtimetavern.com. Boasting an extensive seafood menu with most dishes in the $15–20 range, this restaurant is a favorite among locals and visitors alike. Enjoy your meal alfresco in the garden at the back.

Sliders Oyster Bar 218 1st St, Neptune Beach ☎ 904/246-0881. The fresh seafood is superb; a platter of a dozen local oysters will only cost you $6.95.

Sun Dog Diner 207 Atlantic Blvd, Neptune Beach ☎ 904/241-8221, ⓦ www.sundogjax.com. Better than your usual diner food, with creative specials like pan-seared red snapper with black bean and sweet corn salsa.

Bars and clubs

Fly's Tie Irish Pub 177 E Sailfish Drive, Atlantic Beach ☎ 904/246-4293. An authentic Irish pub, the *Tie* usually features traditional Irish music on weekends and other musical acts during the week.

Freebird Live 200 N 1st St, Jacksonville Beach ☎ 904/246-2473, ⓦ www.freebirdlive.com. Named for Lynyrd Skynyrd's best-known song, this concert venue has a slightly rough atmosphere that's softened by the spirited music, from funk to rock to jazz to bluegrass. Cover varies from $10 to $30.

Ocean Club 401 N 1st St, Jacksonville Beach ☎ 904/242-8884, ⓦ www.oceanclubjax.com. This club has the loudest music on the beaches, with either a live band or DJs spinning every night. Chill out on the beachfront terrace to the occasional live reggae band.

Pete's Bar 117 1st St, Neptune Beach ☎ 904/249-9158. Novelist John Grisham based a bar in his novel *The Brethren* on this pool-hall-cum-local-dive, where a game of pool costs only 25¢ and the drinks are also cheap.

The Ritz 185 N 3rd Ave, Jacksonville Beach ☎ 904/246-2255. Standard bar with a couple of pool tables and a reputation as one of the beaches' best meeting places for singles. Unlike most other spots, you can also smoke here.

Jacksonville

Most outsiders know **JACKSONVILLE** only as an industrial city, with a dusty seaport that remains a major transit point for cargo on the deep St Johns River, and a deeply conservative population. It's known in the south of Florida as the most "Northern" city but residents, on the other hand, would call it the most "Southern." The city's insurance, technology, and service industries have generated enough buzz to attract commerce, construction projects, good restaurants and plenty of new blood into the area. Efforts to increase the city's appeal have created parks and riverside boardwalks, though the sheer size of the city – at 841 square miles, the largest in the US – dilutes its character and makes it difficult to walk around and get a real feel for the place. For all that, Jacksonville is not an unwelcoming place and is gearing up for tourism, though the Super Bowl football championship held here in 2005 didn't bring the deluge of visitors that the local brass had hoped for. Thanks to increased funding for its museums, however, the city's cultural attractions are now among the best in the state.

Arrival, information, and city transportation

The Greyhound **bus** station is downtown at 10 N Pearl St (☎ 904/356-9976). The **train** station, meanwhile, lies an awkward six miles northwest of town at 3570 Clifford Lane. A **taxi** (Gator City Taxi ☎ 904/355-TAXI) to the center will cost around $15. Alternatively, you can hop on local bus #K2.

In downtown Jacksonville, the **Convention and Visitors Bureau**, 550 Water St, Suite 1000 (Mon–Fri 8am–5pm; ☎ 904/798-9111 or 1-800/733-2668, ⓦ www.visitjacksonville.com), is an easy walk from the bus station and has plenty

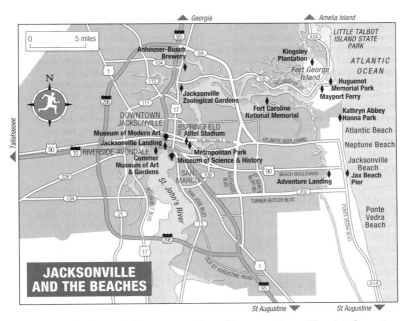

of tourist leaflets and discount vouchers (there are also affiliated information booths at the airport and in the Jacksonville Landing Mall; see p.353).

The local bus service, JTA ($1.00 a ride, or $1.50 to the beaches, exact change only; ☏ 904/630-3100, ⓦ www.jtafla.com), is comprehensive but confusing, so be sure to pick up a system map on JTA buses or at the CVB. In addition, free trolleys run on three routes through the north bank and to the beach during the summer, while the Skyway monorail (Mon–Fri 6am–11pm, Sat 10am–11pm; 50¢) links the north bank with the San Marco neighborhood south of the river.

Though maddening in spots, the city does offer ample opportunities for cycling. You can rent a bike from Open Road, 3544 St Johns Ave (☏ 904/388-9066), for $25 per day, $100 for a week. Outside of downtown, be sure to check out the Jacksonville–Baldwin Rail Trail, where a bike path wends its way through fifteen miles of parkland along the track bed of a defunct railroad. The trail starts about ten miles outside of downtown's north bank and stretches west to Baldwin; call (☏ 904/630-4100) for further information.

Accommodation

Accommodation is concentrated in several neighborhoods: the business-oriented hotels are in downtown's bustling Riverwalk, while you'll find the bed and breakfasts in the suburban Riverside-Avondale area – a good base for exploring the nearby residences and the Cummer Museum (see p.353). Most of the cheaper chain hotels lie near the airport, nine miles north of downtown Jacksonville.

Hampton Inn Central 1331 Prudential Drive ☏ 904/396-7770, ⓦ www.hampton-inn.com. Free parking makes this downtown hotel a good choice for drivers. Rooms are standard but comfortable, and there's a complimentary hot breakfast. ❻

The House on Cherry Street 1844 Cherry St, Riverside-Avondale ☏ 904/384-1999, ⓦ www .houseoncherry.com This cozy Colonial-style bed and breakfast is the only one on the riverfront, and some rooms have river views. Afternoon tea is also included. ❺

Hyatt Regency Jacksonville Riverfront 225 E Coastline Drive ☏ 904/558-1234, ⓦ www .jacksonvillehyatt.com. Great riverfront location just a few steps from Jacksonville Landing. Rooms have all the amenities and there's a rooftop pool, hot tub, sauna, and fitness center. ❼

The Inn at Oak Street 2114 Oak St, Riverside-Avondale ☏ 904/379-5525, ⓦ www.innatoakstreet .com. Dark polished wood and comfy sleigh beds are among the draws at this well-kept 1902 house. Also serves an excellent breakfast. ❻

Omni Jacksonville 245 Water St ☏ 904/355-6664, ⓦ www.omnijacksonville.com. The city's most luxurious business hotel, smack in the center of downtown with large, elegantly furnished rooms and a host of services and facilities. ❽

Wyndham Jacksonville Riverwalk Hotel 1515 Prudential Drive ☏ 904/396-5100, ⓦ www .wyndhamjacksonville.com. Over half of the stylish rooms here afford scenic views over the St John's River. Facilities include a swimming pool and fitness center, and there is free parking. ❼

Downtown Jacksonville

Leaning on local businesses to divert some of their profits into area improvement schemes, an enlightened city administration has helped make **downtown Jacksonville** much less the forbidding forest of corporate high-rises than it initially resembles. As a result, it has become an increasingly relaxing place to wander, particularly along the banks of the St Johns River, which snakes through the city center, dividing downtown Jacksonville in two.

The north bank

Within four blocks of Bay Street on the **north bank** of the river, you'll find the few structures that survived a major fire in 1901 – which claimed much of early Jacksonville – as well as some of the more distinctive buildings from subsequent decades. One of these is the **Florida Theater**, 128 E Forsyth St, which opened in 1927 and became a center of controversy thirty years later when Elvis Presley's pelvic thrusts shocked the city's burghers. Though rather nondescript from the outside, its interior has been restored with a dazzling gold proscenium arch, and the theater is now used for a variety of performances (box office ☏ 904/355-2787, ⓦ www.floridatheatre.com). Two blocks north, the **Morocco Temple**, 219 N Newman St, currently occupied by an insurance company, was built by Henry John Klutho, a classically minded architect who arrived to rebuild Jacksonville after the 1901 fire but later converted to Frank Lloyd Wright-inspired Modernism and erected this sphinx-decorated curiosity in 1912.

After the fire, many of the city's rich relocated to **Springfield**, a compact neighborhood of about one square mile beginning at Main and 1st streets, a ten-minute walk north of the Morocco Temple. After years of steady decline, the area has recently re-emerged as a trendy arts district attracting, once again, well-off homebuyers, and the quiet streets are full of gorgeous homes in varying states of repair.

In this city of commerce and industry, you might not expect much from the **Museum of Contemporary Art** (Tues, Wed, Fri, & Sat 10am–4pm,

---

Downtown Ambassadors

As part of recent attempts to rejuvenate Jacksonville's downtown area, in 2001 the city established a team of volunteers known as **Downtown Ambassadors**. Identifiable by their orange shirts and safari-style hats, these men and women are on hand to provide directions, clear litter, and help out in emergencies; some have a good knowledge of local history, which they are happy to share. To contact a Downtown Ambassador, call ☏ 904/634-0303 or 904/465-7980.

Thurs 10am–8pm, Sun noon–4pm; $8, free Wed 5–9pm; ☎904/366-6911, Ⓦwww.mocajacksonville.org), in the heart of downtown on Hemming Plaza at 333 N Laura St. However, the scope and depth of its offerings in photography, painting, and sculpture pleasantly surprise, including the large Ed Paschke and James Rosenquist canvases on permanent display. Beyond maintaining its collection and hosting traveling exhibits, the museum's small theater screens acclaimed foreign and independent films on Thursday evenings in spring and fall (tickets $8).

The lively **Jacksonville Landing** shopping mall, between Water Street and the river, is where you can catch a River Taxi ($3 one way) to the south bank. You can also take the Skyway or walk across Main Street bridge, next to Jacksonville Landing.

The south bank

The River Taxi to the **south bank** will drop you next to a mile-long pathway called the **Riverwalk**, a downtown boardwalk from where you can view the city's colorful bridges and its skyline. Opposite the River Taxi dock, you'll find the oversized **Friendship Fountain**, best seen at night when colored lights illuminate its gushing jets. Just behind the fountain, the **Museum of Science and History**, 1025 Museum Circle (Mon–Fri 10am–5pm, Sat 10am–6pm, Sun 1–6pm; $9, children 3–12 $6; ☎904/396-6674, Ⓦwww.themosh.org) has educational hands-on exhibits primarily aimed at kids, plus a planetarium offering hi-tech trips around the cosmos.

Beyond the museum, walking south for roughly twenty minutes will bring you to the **San Marco** neighborhood. Worth a stroll of an hour or two, it's filled with sleepy shops and restaurants, particularly along San Marco Boulevard, that give something of a small-town feel to sprawling Jacksonville. Pop into the heavenly smelling **Peterbrooke Chocolatier**, a local chocolate-maker at 1470 San Marco Blvd (Mon–Fri 10am–5pm; ☎904/398-2489, Ⓦwww.peterbrooke.com), where you can watch grinning workers making chocolate behind glass screens.

Beyond downtown

You'll find a few interesting diversions scattered around Jacksonville's downtown area, including a good art collection at the Cummer Museum, the laid-back, pedestrian-friendly neighborhood of Riverside-Avondale, and the green fields of Metropolitan Park, all of which can be reached by foot or a short bus ride from downtown. For the Jacksonville Zoological Gardens and the Anheuser-Busch Brewery, however, you'll need to drive.

The Cummer Museum and around

Just south of the Fuller Warren Bridge (I-95) lies the **Cummer Museum of Art and Gardens**, 829 Riverside Ave (Tues 10am–9pm, Wed–Fri 10am–4pm, Sun noon–5pm; $10, free Tues after 4pm; ☎904/356-6857, Ⓦwww.cummer .org), on the former estate of the wealthy Cummer family. The spacious rooms and sculpture-lined corridors contain works by prominent European masters from the twelfth to nineteenth centuries, but American art – especially from the nineteenth century – is the strongest feature: Edmund Greacen's smoky cityscape *Brooklyn Bridge East River* and Martin Heade's *St Johns River* are particularly moving. The museum's signature piece is Thomas Moran's *Ponce de León in Florida*, a striking painting of the explorer's meeting with local Native Americans (though this event never occurred). Also worth lingering over is an extensive collection of eighteenth-century Meissen porcelain. Afterwards, take a stroll through the flower-packed formal English and Italianate **gardens**, which roll down to the river's edge, providing a view of Jacksonville's sleek office towers.

If you have time to spare, take a short walking tour of the surrounding **Riverside-Avondale district**, home to an eclectic assortment of residential architecture. Georgian Revival, Tudor, Mediterranean, and Prairie School are all represented, amid a number of Gothic Revival churches.

Metropolitan Park and Alltel Stadium

The riverside greenery of **Metropolitan Park** is an enjoyable venue for free events most weekends plus some big free rock concerts during spring and fall. In midweek it's often deserted and makes a fine spot for a quiet riverside picnic. The "Northside Connector" NS-20 **bus** stops close by, and the water taxi stops here ($4) on event days. Next door, the 73,000-seat **Alltel Stadium** is home to the NFL's Jacksonville Jaguars (game tickets $50–250; ☎904/633-2000 or 1-877/4-JAGS-TIX, ⊛www.jaguars.com) and also the scene of the late October Florida-Georgia college football clash (an excuse for 48 hours of citywide drinking and partying); tickets for the actual match are notoriously hard to get.

Jacksonville Zoo and Gardens

The **Jacksonville Zoo and Gardens**, on Hecksher Drive, just off I-95 north of downtown Jacksonville (March–Aug Mon–Fri 9am–5pm, Sat & Sun 9am–6pm; Sept–Feb daily 9am–5pm; $13, children 3–12 $8; ☎904/757-4463, ⊛www.jaxzoo.org), is hoping to develop into one of the better zoos around and affords its inmates plenty of space to prowl, pose, and strut. A justifiable source of pride are the white rhinos, seldom bred in captivity, and the "Range of the Jaguar," where the majestic beasts roam around a landscape of lush vegetation, waterfalls and pools.

Anheuser-Busch Brewery

After trekking about the largest city in the US, you'll inevitably have worked up a thirst, and the **Anheuser-Busch Brewery**, 111 Busch Drive (Mon–Sat 10am–4pm; free; ☎904/696-8373, ⊛www.budweisertours.com), purveyor of Budweiser, would like to quench it for you. After taking the free tour, which follows the Germanic and Czech roots of America's most popular beer, including informative exhibits like a mural on the evolution of beer-can openers, visitors can indulge in the main attraction: free beer.

Eating

You'll find decent restaurants throughout the city, with the most appealing spots in the San Marco and Riverside-Avondale neighborhoods.

Biscotti's 3556 St John's Ave, Riverside-Avondale ☎904/387-2060, ⊛www.biscottis.net. Part-coffeehouse, part-restaurant, with Mediterranean and pasta specials, large portions, and a superb Sunday brunch.

Bistro Aix 1440 San Marco Blvd, San Marco ☎904/398-1949, ⊛www.bistrox.com. Enjoy well-prepared entrées (pasta, pizzas, grilled fish, steaks) on the inviting terrace or in the chic dining room. At lunch, $10–15 will buy you anything on the menu; dinner's slightly more costly.

Burrito Gallery 21 E Adams St, downtown – north bank ☎904/598-2922, ⊛www.burritogallery.com. Dark, grungy restaurant with no-nonsense burritos, tacos, and wraps for $5–7. The interior is given a welcome splash of color by the local artwork on the walls (all of which is for sale) and there's also an outside patio. Closed Sun.

Cool Moose Coffee Company 2708 Park St, Riverside-Avondale ☎904/381-4242. Sandwiches, wraps, and gourmet coffees served in rustic New England-style surroundings.

European Street Café 1704 San Marco Blvd, San Marco ☎904/398-9500, ⓦwww.europeanstcafe .com. Huge sandwich selection, plus several economical German sausage dishes, all of which play second fiddle to the unrivalled beer list, which includes brews from Greece, Honduras, and China.

Henrietta's 1850 Main St, Springfield ☎904/353-6002. Decent Southern-style dinners featuring pork, plantains, and catfish, and a liquor bar with daily happy hours to help wash it all down. Closed Sun.

Matthew's 2107 Hendricks Ave, San Marco ☎904/396-9922, ⓦwwwmatthewsrestaurant.com. One of the finest restaurants in the city, featuring venison, duck, and foie gras on changing prix-fixe menus ($70 or $115 with wine pairings). Reservations recommended. Closed Sun.

Mossfire Grill 1537 Margaret St, Riverside-Avondale ☎904/355-4434, ⓦwww.mossfire.com. Come to this casual, reasonably priced spot for fresh Southwestern fare such as yellowfin tacos and chicken tortilla soup, and vegetarian dishes.

River City Brewing Company 835 Museum Circle, downtown, south bank ☎904/398-2299, ⓦwww.rivercitybrew.com. Top-notch home-brews, seafood, and steaks (dinner entrées $17–33), served in an airy space with river views.

Wine Cellar 1314 Prudential Drive, downtown, south bank ☎904/398-8989, ⓦwww .winecellarjax.com. The ambience is rustic French at this local favorite; dine on classic cuisine (steaks, lobster, tuna, salmon) in the attractive garden. Over 200 wines available. Menus $20 and up. Closed Sun.

Nightlife

Downtown Jacksonville nightlife tends to be slightly older and more laid back than at the beaches (see p.349).

The Grotto 2012 San Marco Blvd, San Marco ☎904/398-0726, ⓦwww.grottowine.com. Cozy wine bar with comfy chairs in the back; diverse wines are served by the glass or bottle.

London Bridge Pub 100 E Adams St, downtown's north bank ☎904/359-0001. English-owned pub providing homesick Anglo Saxons with warm beer, fish and chips, and World Cup games.

 Pearl 1101 N Main St, Springfield ☎904/791-4499. Spacious bar with eccentric decor, including three pillars in the shape of tree trunks, a British-style phone box, and ornately decorated toilets.

Twisted Martini 2 Independent Drive, Jacksonville Landing ☎904/353-8023, ⓦwww.thetwisted martini.com. Jacksonville's professionals flock to this meat market to sip martini cocktails, listen to live music, and dance the night away.

Toward Amelia Island

Around thirty miles from Jacksonville lie the barrier islands that mark Florida's northeast corner, of which **Amelia Island** is particularly appealing. To reach the islands, Hwy-105 will take you from Jacksonville along the north side of the St Johns River, but a much more enjoyable route is Hwy-A1A from the Jacksonville beaches, which crosses the river on the tiny **Mayport ferry** (6.10am–10pm; every half hour; cars $5, cyclists and pedestrians $1). During this short voyage, you can spot pelicans swooping overhead to pluck morsels off the nearby shrimp boats.

The Kingsley Plantation

Near the ferry's landing point, Hwy-A1A combines with Hwy-105. Continuing north, you'll soon cross onto Fort George Island and, before long, encounter the entrance to the seemingly endless, tree-lined driveway of the **Kingsley Plantation** (daily 9am–5pm; free; ☎904/251-3537), the centerpiece of which is the elegant riverside house bought in 1814 by

Scotsman Zephaniah Kingsley – though it's currently closed due to structural instability. The house and its 1100 acres were acquired with proceeds from slavery, of which Kingsley was an advocate and dealer, amassing a fortune through the import and export of Africans. A pragmatic man, he wrote a treatise on the virtues of a patriarchal slave system more in keeping with the Spanish approach than the extremely brutal methods of the United States; he simply believed that well-fed, happier, and freer (though not free) slaves made better workers. Nonetheless, the restored plantation grounds and some original tabby slave quarters reveal much about the plight of the forced arrivals. Kingsley's remarkable wife, a Senegalese woman, ran the plantation and lived in extravagant style – perhaps compensating for her years as his servant. After returning to Hwy-A1A, keep an eye out for the **Huguenot Memorial Park** (April–Oct daily 8am–8pm; Nov–March daily 8am–6pm; $1 per person before 10am, $3 per vehicle after 10am) on the east side of the road, another nesting area for Florida's shorebirds, and one of the few parks up north where you can drive on the beach. There's a **campground** here (☎904/251-3335) where you can pitch a tent for $11.30–17 per night, depending on whether you choose the interior or the waterfront sites.

The Talbot Islands

One mile further on from the park, Hwy-A1A runs through **Little Talbot Island State Park** (daily 8am–sunset; cars $3–4, cyclists and pedestrians $1; ☎904/251-2320), which takes up 1900 acres of a thickly forested 3000-acre barrier island inhabited by 194 species of birdlife. The park has 13 picnic areas and a superb four-mile **hiking trail**, which winds through a pristine landscape of oak and magnolia trees, wind-beaten sand dunes, and a chunk of the park's five-mile-long beach. You can rent **bikes** for $2 an hour ($10 a day). If you're smitten by the natural charms and want to save the bother of finding accommodation on Amelia Island (see below), use the **campground** (☎1-800/326-3521; $19) on the western side of the park beside Myrtle Creek.

Alternatively, carry on across the creek, onto tiny Long Island and over onto **Big Talbot Island**, which has three points of interest. First, **Bluffs Scenic Shoreline** (signposted off the road), where the bluffs have eroded, depositing entire trees on the beach, some of them still standing upright with all their roots intact. Second, the **Blackrock Trail**, a one-and-a-half-mile hike through woods onto the Atlantic coast, to rocks once made from peat.

Amelia Island

Most first-time visitors to Florida would be hard-pressed to locate **AMELIA ISLAND**, at the state's northeastern extremity, which perhaps explains why this finger of land, thirteen miles long and never more than two across, is so peaceful and only modestly commercialized despite the unbroken silver swathe of Atlantic beach gracing its eastern edge. Matching the sands for appeal, **Fernandina Beach**, the island's sole town, was a haunt of pirates before transforming itself into an outpost of Victorian-era high society – a fact proven by its immaculately restored old center.

Some parts of the island are being swallowed by upmarket resorts – much of the southern half is taken up by the *Amelia Island Plantation* (☎904/261-6161 or 1-888/261-6161, ⓦwww.aipfl.com; ❼–❽), a golf and tennis resort with

▲ Amelia Island

private walking and biking trails, expensive restaurants, and pricey rooms – but it's still worth coming here. In Fernandina, at least, they concern themselves more with the size of the shrimp catch than with pandering to tourists.

Fernandina Beach

Hwy-A1A runs more or less right into the effortlessly walkable town of **Fernandina Beach**, whose Victorian heyday is apparent in the restored painted wooden mansions with manicured lawns that line the short main drag, Centre Street. The English spelling of the street name reflects bygone political tug-of-wars (the Spanish named the town but the British named the streets), but an old-fashioned charm and Southern gentility are still very much in evidence. Beside the marina, at the western end of Centre Street you'll spot the useful **visitor center** (Mon–Fri 9am–5pm, Sat 11am–4pm, Sun 11–4pm; ☎904/261-3248), where you can pick up the booklet *Walking Tour of Centre St*, produced by the local tourist board (☎1-800/2AMELIA, ⓦwww.ameliaisland.com), highlighting the forty historical buildings in the neighborhood.

The Museum of History and around Centre Street

The obvious place to gain insights into the town is the **Museum of History**, 233 S Third St (Mon–Sat 10am–4pm, Sun 1–4pm; $7; ☎904/261-7378, ⓦwww.ameliamuseum.org) – once the county jail – with a scattering of memorabilia backed up by photographs and maps. The 45-minute **guided tours** (Mon–Sat at 11am & 2pm, Sun at 2pm) of the museum are excellent, informatively covering 4000 years of the island's varied history with humor. Away from the museum, learn more about the town's past on the recommended **historical walks** (Fri & Sat at 3.30pm from the visitor center; $10) and ghost tours (Fri at 6pm; $10), which feature many of the old buildings on and around Centre Street. The longer 90-minute North and South Fernandina walking tours ($10 for North, $15 for South) are conducted by appointment during the summer. Horse-drawn carriage tours ($15, children under 13 $7.50; ☎904/277-1555) cover the fifty-block historic downtown area, complete with commentary on all of the major landmarks.

Amelia Island history: the eight flags

Amelia Island is the only place in the US to have been under the rule of **eight flags**. Following settlement by Huguenots in 1562, the Spanish arrived and founded a mission here. This was destroyed in 1702 by the British, who returned forty years later to govern the island (naming it in honor of King George II's daughter). The ensuing Spanish administration was interrupted by the US-backed "Patriots of Amelia Island," who ruled for a day during 1812; the Green Cross of the Florida Republic flew briefly in 1817; and, oddest of all, the Mexican rebel flag appeared over Amelia Island the same year. US rule has been disturbed only by Confederate occupancy during 1861.

These shifts reflect the ebb and flow of allegiances between the great sea-trading powers over many years, as well as the island's geographically desirable location: Amelia Island offered a harbor to ocean-going vessels outside US control but within spitting distance of the American border.

Even if you miss the tours, **walking around** on your own is far from dull. Centre Street and the immediate area are alive with Victorian-era turrets, twirls, and towers, plus many notable later buildings. Among them, **St Peter's Episcopal Church**, on the corner with Eighth Street, was completed in 1884 by New York architect Robert S. Schuyler, whose name is linked to many local structures and who never used the same style twice. The Gothic church is a long way from the painted folly of the Italianate **Fairbanks House**, also by Schuyler, which sits at the corner of Seventh and Cedar streets. This building, designed like a Florentine palace with a square tower rising above the center, was commissioned by a newspaper editor as a surprise for his wife, who hated it and refused to step over the threshold – at least according to local legend. Today it has been transformed into a sumptuous bed and breakfast (see "Accommodation," opposite).

The beach

Well suited to swimming and busy with beach sports, the most active of the island's **beaches** is at the eastern end of Fernandina's Atlantic Avenue, a mile from the town center. If you don't mind a long hike with sand between your toes, you can walk along the beach to Fort Clinch State Park, three miles north (see below). In the fall, you may spot **whales** in the waters off Amelia Island. The right whale, an endangered species, moves into inland waterways to calve.

North to Fort Clinch State Park

After Florida came under US control in 1819, a fort was built on Amelia's northern tip, three miles from Fernandina, to protect seaborne access to Georgia. The fort now forms part of **Fort Clinch State Park** (daily 8am–sunset; cars $5, pedestrians and cyclists $1) and provides a home for a gang of Civil War enthusiasts who pretend they're Union soldiers of 1864, the only time the fort saw action. Entrance to the fort itself costs $2, and the most interesting way to see it is with the soldier-guided **candle-lit tour** (every Fri and Sat June–Aug and the first Sat of every other month; $3; reservations essential: ☏904/277-7274). With the faux Civil War garrison moaning about their work and meager rations, the tour may sound like a ham job, but in fact it is a convincing, informative – and quite spooky – hour-long affair.

You'll see the rest of the park on the three-mile drive en route to the fort, passing an animal reserve (from which overgrown alligators often emerge, so if you do fancy a spot of hiking, stick to the marked 30- and 45-minute **nature trails**) and a turn-off for the stunning 2.5-mile long **beach**, where legions of crab catchers cast their baskets off a long fishing jetty. From both jetty and fort there's an immaculate view of Cumberland Island (only accessible by ferry from St Mary's, on the Georgia mainland), a Georgian nature reserve famed for its wild horses – if you're lucky, a few will be galloping over the island's sands. You might also catch a glimpse of a nuclear-powered submarine gliding toward Cumberland Sound and the massive Kings Bay naval base. You can **camp** in the park for $22.

Accommodation

The best way to savor Fernandina's unique historic atmosphere is by staying in one of the town's antique-filled **bed and breakfasts**, but you'll also find more basic motels on the way to or on Fletcher Avenue (Hwy-A1A).

The Addison on Amelia 614 Ash St ⊤904/277-1604 or 1-800/943-1604, ⊛www.addisononamelia.com. Each of the 14 rooms of this elegantly restored 1876 antebellum bed and breakfast is a study in understated luxury. From the high-quality linens to the rain shower-heads, to the breakfast cooked to order, you'll feel pampered within an inch of your life. ➐

Best Western Inn at Amelia Island 2707 Sadler Rd ⊤904/277-2300, ⊛www.bestwestern.com. A better budget inn than most, a bit away from the center of town, but with a pool and tennis courts. ➍

Elizabeth Pointe Lodge 98 S Fletcher Ave ⊤904/277-4851, ⊛www.elizabethpointelodge .com. The location alone, right on a gorgeous stretch of sugary beach, would sell this friendly bed and breakfast, but the rooms are also lovely, the veranda is wide, and the fresh-baked cookies are available all day. ➑

Fairbanks House 227 S Seventh St ⊤904/277-0500 or 1-800/261-4838, ⊛www.fairbankshouse .com. At this historic 12-room bed-and-breakfast (see opposite), ask for the top-floor Tower Suite ($395, sleeps four), with private turret. ➐

Florida House Inn 20 S Third St ⊤904/261-3300 or 1-800/258-3301, ⊛www.floridahouseinn.com. You can sleep where Ulysses S. Grant and the Carnegies stayed at the state's oldest hotel. Some rooms have working fireplaces and there's also a cozy restaurant and pub. Children and pets are welcome. ➏

Hampton Inn & Suites 19 S Second St ⊤904/491-4911 or 1-800/426-7866, ⊛www .hamptoninn.com. A chain hotel directly on the harbor and harmoniously designed so as not to clash with the surrounding historic architecture; some of the rooms have a cozy B&B feel. ➏

Eating and drinking

For its size, the island has an exceptionally good number of **places to eat**, the bulk of them on and around Fernandina's Centre Street. If you're just looking to tip one back, try the *Palace Saloon*, 117 Centre St (⊤904/491-3332), which claims to have the oldest bar in Florida, forty feet of hand-carved mahogany, built in 1878; this was the last tavern in the country to close after Prohibition began, taking two years to deplete its supply of spirits. The *Palace* also has live music on weekends.

Beech Street Grill 801 Beech St ⊤904/277-3662, ⊛www.beechstreetgrill.com. The inventive menu at this pricey-but-worth-it spot features items such as grouper with macadamia crust and curry citrus cream ($28), while the wine list is extensive.

Brett's Waterway Café 1 S Front St, end of Centre St at the Fernandina Harbor Marina ⊤904/261-2660, ⊛www.brettswaterwaycafe .com. Generous portions of Florida seafood

accompanied by great views of the Intracoastal Waterway.

Café Karibo 27 N Third St ⊤904/277-5269, ⊛www.cafekaribo.com. Moderately priced salads, sandwiches, and flavorsome main dishes like Cajun gumbo and Thai burritos with peanut sauce. Live jazz Sat night.

Crab Trap 31 N Second St ⊤904/261-4749, ⊛www.crabtrapamelia.com. Once past the unappealing poured concrete facade, you'll find tempting dishes such as alligator tail appetizer ($9) and the Crabber's Delight (fish, oysters, shrimp, deviled crab, and scallops; $23). Dinner only; closed Mon.

The Marina 101 Centre St ☎904/261-5310. One of the island's oldest restaurants, with a convivial atmosphere. Choose from a seafood menu featuring everything that swims.

T-Rays 202 S Eighth St ☎904/261-6310. You can't get more local than this. T. Ray himself mans the grill of this former gas station, unsigned from the outside. Order the best burger on the island or the famed Friday shrimp fry. Be sure to get there before closing time – T. Ray has been known to turn away those arriving a minute after closing (Mon–Fri 7am–2.30pm and Sat 8am–1pm).

Travel details

Trains

Jacksonville to: Miami (3 daily; 9–11hr); Orlando (2 daily; 3hr); Tampa (2 daily; 5hr).

Buses

Daytona Beach to: Jacksonville (5 daily; 1hr 40min–2hr); Orlando (6 daily; 1hr); St Augustine (3 daily; 1hr).

Jacksonville to: Miami (5 daily; 9–11hr); Orlando (7 daily; 2hr 40min–3hr 30min); St Petersburg (2 daily; 6hr 30min–8hr); Tallahassee (3 daily; 3hr); Tampa (6 daily; 5hr–7hr 20min).

St Augustine to: Jacksonville (3 daily; 1hr).

Titusville to: Daytona Beach (2 daily; 4hr); Jacksonville (2 daily; 5hr 30min–6hr); Melbourne (2 daily; 50min); Orlando (2 daily; 50min).

8

Tampa Bay and the Northwest

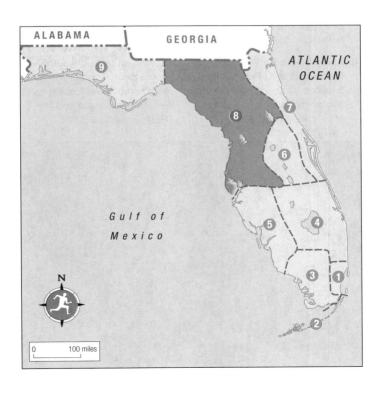

CHAPTER 8

Highlights

✳ **Ybor City** This neighborhood features Tampa Bay's most exciting nightlife and dining; sample the Cuban music and flamenco dancing at the *Columbia*. See p.370

✳ **The Salvador Dalí Museum** View Dalí masterpieces like *The Discovery of America by Christopher Columbus* at St Petersburg's unlikeliest art collection. See p.381

✳ **Fort de Soto Park** Escape the crowds at St Petersburg's beaches by spending a day or two on the five islands of this state park. See p.387

✳ **Swimming with manatees** Don't miss the chance to snorkel with these fascinating, endangered creatures. See p.396

✳ **Cedar Key** Oyster harvesting and an intoxicatingly slow pace of life still hold sway over tourism at this remote and picturesque spot along the northwest coast. See p.399

✳ **Gainesville** This university town is an oasis of youthful exuberance – combined with some fine old buildings – between Orlando and the Panhandle. See p.406

▲ Tarpon sponges

8

Tampa Bay and the Northwest

T he diverse and dynamic **TAMPA BAY** area, midway along Florida's three-hundred-mile west coast, is well placed to entice tourists away from nearby Orlando. Buzzing, youthful towns, a selection of good museums and galleries, a theme park of its own and, crucially, miles of beaches with sunset views rivaled only by those of the Florida Keys, have made Tampa Bay a firm, if somewhat unheralded, fixture on the Florida tourist circuit. Those wanting to get off the beaten track should head north along the coast of the largely beachless **NORTHWEST** or along I-75 toward the Panhandle and Georgia, where placid fishing hamlets, forests, horse ranches, and insular villages speak of a Florida largely ignored by the brochures – but one well worth exploring.

The largest city on Florida's west coast, 83 miles west of Orlando, **Tampa** itself probably won't detain you for long, but Ybor City, for example, is Tampa's – hippest and most culturally eclectic quarters. Directly across the bay, **St Petersburg** once took pride in being the archetypal Florida retirement community, but has managed in recent years to recast itself in a younger mold and is riding high on its acquisition of a major collection of works by the Surrealist Salvador Dalí and an infusion of hipsters along its once quiet streets and in formerly neglected bungalows. For most visitors, though, the Tampa Bay area begins and ends with the **St Petersburg beaches** – miles of sea, sun, and sand fringed by condos as far as the eye can see. The beaches are pure vacation territory but are also a good base for exploring the Greek-dominated community of **Tarpon Springs** just to the north.

The coast **north of Tampa** (known as the **Big Bend** for the way it curves toward the Panhandle) is consumed by flat marshes, large chunks of which are wildlife refuges with little public access. No settlement here boasts a population of more than a few thousand, and the area receives little attention from visitors bolting through on their way to the beach territories further south. It is, however, one of Florida's hidden treasures. Scattered throughout is evidence of much busier and prosperous times, like the prehistoric sun-worshipping site at **Crystal River**. **Cedar Key**, which was a thriving port in the mid-nineteenth century, is now the perfect retreat. Locals here have preserved a laid-back way of life, and the community is a time-warped enclave of excellent restaurants and rewarding sights. The wildlife park at **Homosassa Springs**,

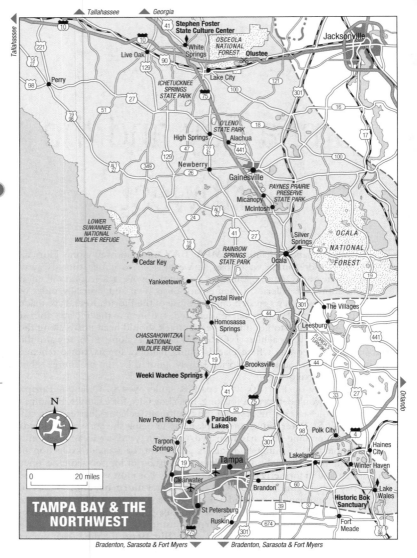

N

TAMPA BAY & THE
NORTHWEST

▼ Bradenton, Sarasota & Fort Myers   ▼ Bradenton, Sarasota & Fort Myers

fifteen miles south of Crystal River, offers the chance to view some of Florida's
endangered animals, like the manatee. The alternative route north from Tampa,
passing through **north central Florida** along I-75, is another area of
unexpected discoveries – the huge forest and numerous horse ranches around
Ocala and the historic villages and natural springs near the lively university
town of **Gainesville**.

The Tampa Bay area

The geographic and economic nerve center of the region, the **Tampa Bay area**, consisting of Tampa and St Petersburg, has a population greater than Miami's. The wide waters of the bay provide a scenic backdrop for Tampa itself, and the barrier-island beaches along the coast let the locals swap metropolitan bustle for luscious sunsets and miles of glistening beaches.

Tampa

TAMPA is a small city with an infectious, upbeat mood. Cradled by Old Tampa and Hillsborough bays, with the Hillsborough River running through downtown, it's surrounded by water – and the Gulf of Mexico lies less than an hour's drive west. You'll only need a day or two to explore the city thoroughly, but you'll depart with a lasting impression of a city on the rise. Tampa has been one of the major beneficiaries of the flood of people and money into Florida, and the city's main vibe is that of a business hub. Yet despite cultural and artistic offerings envied by many larger communities and an international airport in its back yard, Tampa rarely gets more than a passing glance. Tourists speed through to Busch Gardens, a theme park on the city's outskirts, and the Gulf Coast beaches half an hour's drive west – missing out on one of Florida's most youthful and energetic urban communities.

Tampa began as a small settlement beside Fort Brooke, (a US Army base built to keep an eye on local Seminole Indians during the 1820s), and remained tiny, isolated and insignificant until the 1880s, when the railway arrived and the Hillsborough River was dredged to allow seagoing vessels to dock. It became a booming port and simultaneously acquired a major tobacco industry as thousands of Cubans moved north in 1886 from Key West to the new cigar factories of neighboring Ybor City. Despite the city's optimistic, business-friendly atmosphere, the social problems blighting any moderately sized US city are evident here as well, especially directly north of downtown, where the prosperity of the office towers soon gives way to boarded-up buildings.

Downtown Tampa is quiet and compact. An art museum, a sensational film house built in the Spanish Revival style, and the *Tampa Bay Hotel* – one of the few remainders of earlier times – form the basis for a few hours' ramble. What downtown may lack in atmosphere and history is made up for in the Latin American character of **Ybor City**, one mile northeast. Ybor now boasts a plethora of historical markers commemorating the heady days of the struggle for Cuban independence.

Venture a mile south of downtown into **Hyde Park**, and you'll find the homes of Tampa's wealthiest early settlers. **Busch Gardens** and the **Museum of Science and Industry** are also worth a stop – or you could just amble into the wilds of the open country that appear remarkably quickly just north of the city.

Arrival, information, and city transportation

The city's international **airport** (☎813/870–8700, ⓦ www.tampaairport.com) is five miles northwest of downtown Tampa. Local bus #30 is the cheapest connection ($1.75) to downtown Tampa, while the **taxi** fare to downtown

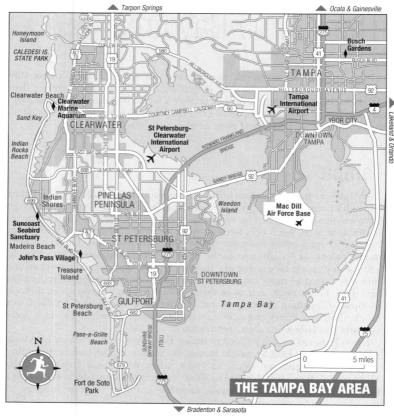

▲ Tarpon Springs   ▲ Ocala & Gainesville

Honeymoon
Island

CALEDESI IS.
STATE PARK

Busch
Gardens

CURLEW ROAD
19   580

HILLSBOROUGH AVE.

TAMPA

Clearwater Beach
Clearwater
Marine
Aquarium   GULF TO BAY
CLEARWATER

HILLSBOROUGH AVENUE   92

Sand Key

COURTNEY CAMPBELL CAUSEWAY   60
Tampa
International
Airport

Indian
Rocks
Beach

St Petersburg-
Clearwater
International
Airport

EAST BAY DR.
688
ULMERTON ROAD

HOWARD FRANKLAND
BRIDGE

YBOR CITY

DOWNTOWN
TAMPA

4

Lakeland & Orlando

699

Indian
Shores

PINELLAS
PENINSULA

PARK BLVD.
92   Weedon
Island

GANDY BRIDGE   92

Mac Dill
Air Force Base

Suncoast
Seabird
Sanctuary
Madeira Beach

John's Pass Village

19   ST PETERSBURG

92

Treasure
Island   5TH AVE.
19

275

DOWNTOWN
ST PETERSBURG

693

GULFPORT

41

St Petersburg
Beach   682

Tampa Bay

N

Pass-a-Grille
Beach

679

SUNSHINE
SKYWAY BRIDGE
(TOLL)

275

75

0   5 miles

Fort de Soto
Park

THE TAMPA BAY AREA

▼ Bradenton & Sarasota

Tampa is a $25 flat rate; to a Busch Boulevard motel or St Petersburg $35–45; to the St Petersburg beaches $65-70. The main firms are United (☎813/253-2424) and Yellow (☎813/253-0121). A cheaper option if you're jetting straight to the sand is the Super Shuttle (see p.377).

If you arrive **by car** from St Petersburg, the main route into Tampa is I-275, which crosses Old Tampa Bay and ends up in the west of downtown. From east or central Florida, you'll come in on the I-4, which intersects with I-75. Be advised that from I-75, it's essential to exit at Hwy-60 (signposted Kennedy Blvd) for downtown Tampa. There are seven less convenient exits and if you miss this one and end up in north Tampa, the city's fiendish one-way system could keep you in your car for hours.

Long-distance public transport terminates in downtown Tampa: Greyhound **buses** at 610 Polk St (☎813/229-2174) and **trains** at 601 N Nebraska Ave (☎1-800/872-7245).

Information

In downtown Tampa, collect vouchers, leaflets, and general information at the **Visitors Information Center**, 615 Channelside Drive, Suite 108A (Mon–Sat 9.30am–5.30pm, Sun 11am–5pm; ☎813/223-2752 or 1-800/44-TAMPA, ⓦwww.visittampabay.com).

For Ybor City, visit the **Ybor City Visitor Information Center**, 1600 E Eighth Ave, Suite B104 (Mon–Sat 10am–6pm, Sun noon–6pm; ☎813/241-8838, ⓦwww.ybor.org) for the usual helpful brochures and maps. You can also catch the informative seven-minute movie, offered throughout the day, on the history of the Ybor district.

City transportation

Although downtown Tampa and Ybor City are easily covered on foot, to travel between them – or to reach Busch Gardens or the Museum of Science and Industry – without a car, you'll need to use **local buses** (HARTline ☎813/254-4278, ⓦwww.hartline.org; one-way $1.75; day pass $3.75), whose routes fan out from Marion Street at the northern edge of downtown Tampa. **Useful bus numbers** are the #8 to Ybor City; #5 to Busch Gardens; #6 to the Museum of Science and Industry; and #30 to the airport. Commuter (express) buses run **between Tampa and the coast**: #100X to St Petersburg and #200X to Clearwater. Alternatives are the numerous daily Greyhound buses.

Another way to travel between downtown Tampa and Ybor City is on the **TECO Line Streetcar System** (☎813/254-4278, ⓦwww.tecolinestreetcar .org), a vintage replica streetcar running daily several times an hour, and until 2am on Fridays and Saturdays. The route takes you via Harbour Island and the Florida Aquarium (see p.368) and costs $2.50 one way. You can buy a $4 souvenir day pass on the streetcar that works on all public transportation, or you can stick with the $3.75 one sold on the buses, which does the same job.

Accommodation

Except for the area around Busch Gardens, Tampa is not generously supplied with low-cost **accommodation**. Within Tampa, the cheaper **motels** are all on East Busch Boulevard close to Busch Gardens. Ybor city offers a few accommodation options and an agreeable alternative to downtown Tampa, since you'll probably be spending much of your time in this area anyway. The only local **campground** where tents are welcome is the Hillsborough River State Park (see p.373).

In Tampa

Best Western All Suites 3001 University Center Drive, behind Busch Gardens ☎813/971-8930 or 1-800/780-7234, ⓦwww.bestwestern.com. A reasonable base for seeing the city by car, and so close to Busch Gardens the parrots escape into the hotel's trees. Features a happy hour every afternoon and free breakfast. ❺

Gram's Place 3109 N Ola Ave ☎813/221-0596, ⓦwww.grams-inn-tampa.com. This funky motel-cum-hostel offers both private rooms – all themed in different musical styles – and rather tatty youth-hostel-style accommodation. $23 for a dorm bed; private rooms ❸.

Marriott Waterside 700 S Florida Ave ☎813/221-4900, ⓦwww.marriott.com. One of downtown Tampa's largest and most luxurious hotels, this waterfront hotel towers above the nearby Convention Center and Channelside entertainment complex. Top-notch facilities – spa, health club, and a beautiful pool – and stellar views of the bay. ❽

Sheraton Tampa Riverwalk 200 N Ashley Drive ☎813/223-2222, ⓦwww.tampariverwalkhotel .com. Very convenient downtown location, nicely situated on the banks of the Hillsborough River. ❼

Wingate by Wyndham 3751 E Fowler Ave ☎813/979-2828. With a free shuttle bus to Busch Gardens (5min away), great free breakfast, clean rooms and a solicitous staff, you can't go wrong here. ❻

In Ybor City

Don Vicente de Ybor Historic Inn 1915 Avenida Republica de Cuba ☎1-866/206-4545, ⓦwww.donvicenteinn.com. A luxurious B&B option in Ybor City, featuring sixteen beautifully restored suites with four-poster beds and Persian rugs, as well as swing dancing on Tuesday nights. ❻

Hampton Inn 1301 E Seventh Ave ☎813/247-6700, ⓦwww.hamptoninn.com. Ybor City's newest accommodation offers comfortable rooms and suites and includes a free breakfast, a free shuttle

within a five-mile radius, and a parking garage ($7.50 per day). ❼
Hilton Garden Inn 1700 E 9th Ave ☎813/769-9267, Ⓦwww.tampabayhistoricdistrict.gardeninn.com.

Comfortable digs, even if the decor is a little sterile to be in the heart of Tampa's most historically rich neighborhood. ❼

Downtown Tampa

Downtown Tampa's prosperity is most evident in its thoughtfully designed office towers, and aside from the riverside warehouses in various states of dilapidation around the northern end of pedestrian-friendly **Franklin Street** (once a pulsating main drag and still a good place to get your bearings), any hint of the city's past is left largely to plaques detailing everything from the passage of sixteenth-century explorer Hernando De Soto to the site of Florida's first radio station.

The single substantial relic is the **Tampa Theatre**, 711 Franklin St (☎813/274-8981, Ⓦwww.tampatheatre.org), one of the few surviving "atmospheric theaters" erected by designer John Eberson during the 1920s. When silent movies enthralled the masses, Eberson's moviehouses heightened the escapist mood: ceilings became star-filled skies, balconies were chiseled to resemble Moorish arches, gargoyles leered from stuccoed walls and replica Greek and Roman statuary filled every nook and cranny. Today, the place boasts a full program of movies (an added bonus – for some – is the Wurlitzer organ that rises from the orchestra pit fifteen minutes before each screening to serenade the crowd) and concerts. Paying $9 for a ticket (see p.375) is one way to gain access to the splendidly restored interior, another is the "Balcony to Backstage" guided tour ($5), which is highly entertaining but is held only twice a month (call theater for dates and times).

The Tampa Museum of Art

At the time of writing, the highly regarded **Tampa Museum of Art**, temporary location at 2306 N Howard Ave (Tues–Sat 10am–4pm, donation requested; ☎813/274-8130, Ⓦwww.tampamuseum.org) was in transition. The museum is set to open a new facility at the Curtis Hixon Waterfront Park in the fall of 2009, with 66,000 square feet of gallery space, making it 150 percent larger than the former location. The new museum will still specialize in classical antiquities and twentieth-century American art, as well as playing host to traveling exhibits.

The Florida Aquarium

The **Florida Aquarium**, 701 Channelside Drive (daily 9.30am–5pm; $19.95, parking $6; ☎813/273-4000, Ⓦwww.flaquarium.org), houses lavish displays of Florida's fresh- and saltwater habitats, ranging from springs and swamps to beaches and coral reefs. The permanent residents include an impressive variety of exotic fish and native creatures such as otters, turtles, baby alligators, and countless species of birds. Certified scuba divers can dive in the shark tank (reservations ☎813/273-4000).

Northeast from downtown Tampa

The northeast section of the city has an **unsafe reputation**; heading that way to Ybor City (see p.370) on foot takes you thorough a desolate area with little reason to linger. The only site worth noting is the **Oaklawn Cemetery**, at the junction of Morgan and Harrison streets, just north of downtown, which was set aside to bury the town's dead ("whites and slaves alike") in 1850. Along with the bones of one Florida governor and two Supreme Court judges, the picturesque graveyard contains the remains of soldiers from the Second Seminole War,

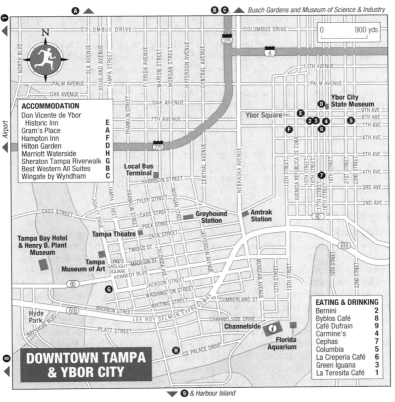

ACCOMMODATION

Don Vicente de Ybor Historic Inn	E
Gram's Place	A
Hampton Inn	F
Hilton Garden	D
Marriott Waterside	H
Sheraton Tampa Riverwalk	G
Best Western All Suites	B
Wingate by Wyndham	C

EATING & DRINKING

Bernini	2
Byblos Café	8
Café Dufrain	9
Carmine's	4
Cephas	7
Columbia	5
La Creperia Café	6
Green Iguana	3
La Teresita Café	1

DOWNTOWN TAMPA & YBOR CITY

the Mexican War, the Civil War, the Spanish American War, and both World Wars. Hidden away at the far end of the cemetery, in the shadow of the faceless Morgan Street Penitentiary, is the tomb of the **Ybor family** – whose name lives on in Tampa's most exotic quarter, Ybor City.

Across the river: the Tampa Bay Hotel

From the east bank of the Hillsborough River, you can't miss the silver minarets, cupolas, and domes of the main building of the University of Tampa – formerly the **Tampa Bay Hotel**. A fusion of Moorish, Turkish, and Spanish building styles, and financed to the tune of $2 million by steamship and railway magnate **Henry B. Plant**, the structure is as bizarre a sight today as it was on its opening in 1891, when its 500 rooms looked out on a community of just 700 people.

Plant had been buying up bankrupt railways since the Civil War and steadily inching his way into Florida to meet his steamships unloading at Tampa Harbor. Like Henry Flagler, whose tracks were forging a trail along Florida's east coast and whose upmarket resorts in St Augustine (see p.340) were the talk of US socialites, Plant was wealthy enough to realize his fantasy of creating the world's most luxurious hotel, which unfortunately for him stayed open for less than ten years. Neglect (the hotel was only used during the winter months and left to fester during the scorching summer), and Plant's death in 1899, hastened its transformation into a pile of musty, crumbling plaster. The city authorities bought the place in 1905 and halted the rot, before leasing the building to the fledgling University of Tampa 23 years later.

In a wing of the main building, the **Henry B. Plant Museum**, 401 W Kennedy Blvd (Tues–Sat 10am–4pm, Sun noon–4pm; $5; ☎813/254-1891, Ⓦwww.plantmuseum.com), has several rooms, including an original suite containing what's left of the hotel's furnishings. This is a gorgeous clutter of Venetian mirrors, elaborate candelabras, oriental rugs, Wedgwood crockery, and intricate teak cabinets – all the fruits of a half-million-dollar shopping expedition undertaken by Plant and his wife across Europe and Asia.

The hotel was Florida's first building to be installed with electricity, and low-wattage Edison carbon filters are used today to ensure the original, authentic gloom, which is perfect for taking in the richness of the Cuban mahogany doors. Note the reassembled *Rathskellar*, a gentleman's social room, previously in the hotel basement (now a student snack bar), complete with a German wine cooler and billiard tables.

Hyde Park

Hyde Park, a mile southwest of downtown Tampa just off Bayshore Boulevard, is a mostly residential area of lovingly restored homes. Attracted by the glamour of the *Tampa Bay Hotel*, well-heeled arrivals in the 1890s duplicated the architectural mold that defined the wealthier sections of that era's American towns: a mishmash of Mediterranean, Gothic, Tudor, and Colonial revival jobs, interspersed with Queen Anne cottages and Prairie-style bungalows – rocking chairs on porches being the sole unifying feature. Such complete "blasts from the past" are rare in Tampa and, provided you're driving (they don't justify a slog around on foot), the old homes are easy to appreciate on a twenty-minute drive on and around Swann and Magnolia avenues and Hyde Park and South boulevards. **Hyde Park Village**, beside Snow Avenue, is home to a few classy restaurants (see "Eating," p.374). If you want to browse or lunch here, go to one of the three free parking garages right in the village, one at each corner of S Dakota Avenue and Swann Avenue, and one at the corner of Bristol Avenue and S Rome Avenue.

Ybor City

In 1886, as soon as Henry Plant's ships (see p.465) ensured a regular supply of Havana tobacco into Tampa, cigar magnate Don Vicente Martínez Ybor cleared a patch of scrubland three miles northeast of present-day downtown Tampa and laid the foundations of **Ybor City**. Around 20,000 immigrants – mostly Cubans drawn from the strife-ridden Key West cigar industry – settled here, creating an enclave of Latin American life and producing the top-class hand-rolled cigars that made Tampa the "Cigar Capital of the World" for forty years. Yet mass-production, the popularity of cigarettes and the Depression proved a fatal combination for skilled cigar makers; Ybor City lost its *joie de vivre* and, while the rest of Tampa expanded, its twenty tight-knit blocks of cobbled streets and red-brick buildings were engulfed by drab and dangerous low-rent neighborhoods.

Today, Ybor City buzzes with tourists and at night the atmosphere can become raucous, especially at weekends. It is trendy, culturally diverse and a terrific place to wander at will. Yet commercialism is taking hold fast. Shops still sell hand-rolled cigars, but, owing to rising rents, the little hole-in-the-wall cafés that once doled out freshly baked Cuban bread and fresh-brewed coffee have all but disappeared, replaced by a *Starbucks* on every corner. There are still some sensational, authentic places to savor Cuban cooking, but they are being forced further and further off the main drag.

The Ybor City Museum

Ybor City's Cuban roots are immediately apparent, and explanatory background texts adorn many buildings. Soak up the atmosphere during the day, but don't expect the place to really get going until the evening. The **Ybor City Museum** (which is officially designated a state park), 1818 Ninth Ave (daily 9am–5pm; $3; ☎813/247-6323, ⓦwww.floridastateparks.org/yborcity), offers just enough to help you grasp the main points of Ybor City's creation and its multi-ethnic make-up. Enormous wall photographs show cigar rollers at work: thousands sat in long rows at bench-tables making 25¢ per cigar and cheering or heckling the *lector* (or reader), who recited the news from Spanish-language newspapers.

Ybor Square

The old Martínez Ybor Cigar factory building, where cigar rolling actually took place, at 1901 Thirteenth St on the corner of Eighth Avenue, is now called **Ybor Square**. This cavernous – three stories supported by sturdy oak pillars – structure's current incarnation is as an office block essentially closed to the public. Standing on the cigar factory's iron steps in 1893, the famed Cuban poet and independence fighter José Martí spoke to thousands of Ybor City's Cubans, calling for pledges of money, machetes, and manpower for the country's struggle for independence against Spain. It's estimated expatriate Cuban cigar workers contributed ten percent of their earnings, most of which was spent on the illicit purchase and shipment of arms to rebels in Cuba. A stone marker at the foot of the steps records the event and, across the street, the eponymous **José Martí Park** commemorates the man with a statue.

Ybor's social clubs

From the earliest days, each of Ybor City's ethnic communities ran its own **social clubs**, published newspapers, and even organized a medical insurance scheme leading to the building of two hospitals. Several of the clubs still function as neighborhood nerve centers. Stepping inside one (opening hours vary wildly) reveals patriotic paraphernalia and lots of old photographs. For a look at Ybor City life most visitors miss, visit the *The Cuban Club*, 2010 Ave Republica de Cuba N; *Centro Asturiano*, 1913 N Nebraska Ave; or *L'Unione Italiana*, 1731 E Seventh Ave. One Ybor City institution out-of-towners invariably do find is the *Columbia* restaurant, 2117 E Seventh Ave. Now filling a whole block, the *Columbia* opened in 1905 as a humble coffee stop for tobacco workers; inside, newspaper cuttings plaster the walls and recount the restaurant's lustrous past. For more in dining in Ybor City, see Listings on p.374.

Around Tampa

The collar of suburbia around downtown Tampa offers few reasons to stop, though the city's least expensive motels cluster around the **Busch Gardens** theme park, which ranks among the state's top tourist attractions. The **Lowry Park Zoo**, the **Museum of Science and Industry**, and (provided you're driving, for it's unreachable by public transport) the 3000 pristine acres of the **Hillsborough River State Park** will also compete for your attention.

Busch Gardens

Incredible as it may seem, most people are drawn to Tampa by a theme-park re-creation of colonial Africa in the grounds of a brewery, at 3000 E Busch Blvd (two miles east of I-275 or two miles west of I-75, Exit 54, signposted Fowler Ave). In glossing over a period of imperialist exploitation in the name of entertainment, **Busch Gardens** (hours vary according to season, check website for

Despite the exotic names given to each section of the park, on the whole, the landscaping and design of Busch Gardens lacks the imagination and attention to detail of the Orlando theme parks, and the overall impression is less enchanting. Predictably, **waiting times** can be long and, in the absence of an express line system akin to those at Disney and Universal, unavoidable. Ask a member of staff for actual waiting times, which are often considerably shorter than the gloomy predictions of the clocks at the entrance (at times up to 90min). Bear in mind you'll have to store your bags in a **locker** (50¢) while riding the rollercoasters.

details; $67.95, children $57.95; parking $10 a day; ☏1-888/800-5447, ⓦwww .buschgardens.com), which opened in 1959 as a brewery and was developed into a theme park six years later, brazenly reshapes world history just as much as its arch-rival, Walt Disney World.

Traversable on foot or by pseudo-steam train, the 335-acre park divides into several areas. You'll first enter **Morocco**, where Moroccan crafts are sold at un-Moroccan prices and snake-charmers and belly dancers weave through the crowds. Then comes the **Myombe Reserve**, where a collection of chimps and gorillas are kept in a tropical environment complete with waterfall. Follow the signs to **Nairobi** and you'll find small gatherings of elephants, giant tortoises, alligators, crocodiles, and monkeys in varying states of liveliness. Directly ahead in **Timbuktu**, animals are less in evidence than amusement rides: a small roller-coaster and a children's fairground ride called "Sandstorm," neither of which comes near to matching the park's larger coasters. If the Ubanga-Banga bumper cars in the **Congo** don't hold lasting appeal, gird your loins for the swirling and very wet raft trip around the "Congo River Rapids" – which may induce you to cross Stanleyville Falls on a rollercoaster, the best feature of neighboring **Stanleyville**. Whatever you do, don't miss the park's excellent **thrill rides**: "SheiKra," (minimum height 54"/137cm) at 200 ft is the tallest in Florida and features a 90-degree drop and speeds of up to 70 miles per hour; Congo's devastating "Kumba," (minimum height 54"/137 cm) which, along with "Gwazi" (minimum height 48"/122cm), near the entrance, and "Montu" (minimum height 54"/137cm), tucked away in the park's eastern corner, are among the largest and fastest rollercoasters in the southeastern US, with all the high-speed drops, twists and turns to satisfy the most serious of adrenaline junkies.

The biggest single section of the gardens, the eighty-acre **Serengeti Plain** – where giraffes, buffaloes, zebras, antelopes, black rhinos, and elephants roam – is the closest the place gets to showing anything genuinely African, even if the exhibits are really no better than those at a good zoo; look down on the scene from the Skyride cable car or get a closer view from the train. After all this, retire to the *Hospitality House* of the Anheuser-Busch Brewery, purveyors of Budweiser and owners of the park, where the beer is free but limited to two drinks (in a paper cup) per person.

The Lowry Park Zoo

The lovely **Lowry Park Zoo** is five and a half miles north of downtown Tampa, two miles southwest of Busch Gardens and just west of I-275, at 1101 W Sligh Ave (daily 9.30am–5pm; $18.95; ☏813/935-8552, ⓦwww .lowryparkzoo.com). Tampa's first zoo, established in the late 1930s, is today home to about 2000 animals, many of them are rare and endangered, kept on some 56 acres of natural habitats. There are seven major exhibits: the Florida

Manatee and Aquatic Center, Primate World, Wallaroo Station, Florida Boardwalk, Asian Gardens, Free Flight Aviaries and Safari Africa. All are supported by regular educational events – including courses given at the "Zoo School" – and shows held in outdoor amphitheaters, which makes this a good place to learn about Florida's wildlife, especially if most of your trip centers on the beaches and theme parks.

The Museum of Science and Industry

Two miles northeast of Busch Gardens, at 4801 E Fowler Ave, the **Museum of Science and Industry** (Mon–Fri 9am–5pm, Sat–Sun 9am–6pm; $20.95; ☎813/987-6100, ⓦwww.mosi.org) will entertain adults as much as kids. Intended to reveal the mysteries of the scientific world, the hands-on displays and machines will easily fill half a day. To get the most from your visit, study the program schedule carefully on arrival: the main – and most interesting – features run at fixed times throughout the day. The Gulf Coast Hurricane is a convincing demonstration allowing begoggled participants to feel the force of the strongest winds known. High Wire Bicycle gives you the somewhat daunting opportunity to pedal a bike 98 feet along a one-inch steel cable suspended thirty feet above the ground. After this excitement, relax in the Saunders Planetarium and gaze at the stars or catch a movie in Florida's first IMAX film theater in a dome. The entrance fee includes admission to both the planetarium and a single IMAX screening.

Hillsborough River State Park

Twelve miles north of Tampa on US-301, shaded by live oaks, magnolias, and sable palms, the **Hillsborough River State Park** (daily 8am–sunset; cars $4, pedestrians and cyclists $1; ☎813/987-6771, ⓦwww.floridastateparks.org /hillsboroughriver) holds one of the state's rare instances of rapids – outside of a theme park. Here, the Hillsborough River tumbles over limestone outcrops before pursuing a more typical meandering course. Rambling the sizeable park's walking trails and canoeing the gentler sections of the river could fill a day nicely (and the park makes an enjoyable place for **camping**; $20; ☎1-800/326-3521), but on weekends you should devote part of the afternoon to the **Fort Foster Historic Site**, a reconstructed 1836 Seminole War fort that can only be seen on one of the **guided tours** (Sat 2pm, Sun 11am; $2). Stemming from US attempts to drive Florida's Seminole Indians out to reservations in the Midwest and make the state fit for the white man, the Seminole Wars raged throughout the nineteenth century and didn't officially end until 1858 (see Contexts, p.463). Occasionally, period-attired enthusiasts occupy the fort and recount historical details – like the fact more soldiers died from tropical diseases than in battle. Not surprisingly, the Seminoles give a somewhat different account of the conflict. For an extra $2 you can also swim in the pool (hours vary seasonally).

Canoeing on the Hillsborough River

To spend two hours or a whole day gliding past the alligators, turtles, wading birds, and other creatures that call the Hillsborough River home, contact **Canoe Escape**, 9335 E Fowler Ave (☎813/986-2067, ⓦwww.canoeescape.com), who have devised a series of novice-friendly routes along the tea-colored river. Prices range from $23.50 to $47 depending on length of trip and the type of kayak, and you should make a reservation at least 24 hours in advance.

Eating

Eating in Tampa means good quality and lots of choice – except in **downtown**, where street stands dispensing snacks to lunching office workers are the culinary norm. Some of the best and most interesting meals are served in **Ybor City**, whose Latin heritage and hip reputation have made it a food haven. Most restaurants here cluster on Seventh Avenue, with a few good options nestled in the surrounding area. **Hyde Park** also offers a diverse range of eating places, mostly on S Howard Avenue (also known as SoHo). Remember the majority of Tampa's downtown restaurants are only open for lunch.

Downtown

Byblos Café 2832 S MacDill Ave ☏ 813/805-7977, ⓦ www.bybloscafe.com. Middle Eastern music plays in the background and you can lounge on lushly embroidered cushions at this Lebanese restaurant just west of downtown. Traditional food includes falafel as well as many other excellent *mezah* (appetizers) from $6–10 and main dishes from $14–21.

Café Dufrain 707 Harbour Post Drive, Harbour Island, ☏ 813/275-9701, ⓦ www.cafedufrain.com. This great, moderately priced place overlooking the water on Harbour Island serves a variety of contemporary cuisine with mouth-watering meat and seafood dishes – try the Latin grilled salmon ($19.75) or the Argentinean skirt steak ($25).

La Teresita Cafeteria 3248 W Columbus Drive, north of downtown near the Raymond James Stadium ☏ 813/879-4909. Cuban sandwiches go for under $4, and dishes such as *patas de cerdo* (pigs' feet) and *rabo encendido* (oxtail) are served with superb Cuban coffee.

Hyde Park

Bella's Italian Café 1413 S Howard Ave ☏ 813/254-3355, ⓦ www.bellasitaliancafe.com. Reliable pasta dishes ($13–17) preceded by tasty starters such as lobster bisque ($9) and polished off with a slice of rich molten chocolate cake at this long-standing SoHo restaurant.

Bern's Steak House 1208 S Howard Ave ☏ 813/251-2421, ⓦ www.bernssteakhouse .com. The most memorable charcoal-broiled steaks you'll ever have, starting from around $35. The restaurant also boasts the largest working wine cellar in the world.

Restaurant BT 1633 W Snow Ave ☏ 813/258-1916, ⓦ www.restaurantbt.com. Fresh Asian-inspired food with some tasty vegetarian options like stuffed tofu, plus a lamb stew hearty enough to satisfy any carnivore. Mains start at around $19.

Ybor City

Bernini 1702 E Seventh Ave ☏ 813/248-0099, ⓦ www.berniniofybor.com. An Italian joint serving up wood-fired pizza and pasta in the lovely old Bank of Ybor City (note the giant-insect door handles).

Carmine's 1802 E Seventh Ave ☏ 813/248-3834. This long-time Tampa restaurant offers a variety of hearty pastas as well as the requisite Cuban sandwich for around $10.

Cephas 1701 E Fourth Ave ☏ 813/247-9022. The colorful Jamaican owner will try to push his healthy aloe shakes on you – first-timers often get one for free, even if they don't ask for one. Enjoy it with the curry goat or jerk chicken among other great Jamaican offerings from $7.

Columbia 2117 E Seventh Ave ☏ 813/248-4961, ⓦ www.columbiarestaurant.com. Serving refined yet moderately priced Spanish and Cuban food, this Tampa institution – the city's oldest restaurant – has become a fixture on the tourist circuit. Diners are entertained six nights a week by flamenco dancers, for an extra $6. There's another outpost in St Petersburg, if you've not gotten your fill. Its 15 rooms hold nearly 2000 people, yet reservations are recommended. Mains start around $25.

La Creperia Café 1729 E Seventh Ave ☏ 813/248-9700. Besides offering almost sixty delicious sweet and savory crepes, this little gem makes every kind of specialty coffee and has free wi-fi. Crepes from around $6.

Nightlife

Tampa's **nightlife scene** may have the reputation of being strong on drinking and live rock music, but there are alternatives for those seeking more from a night out. Although **Ybor City** has long been the focus of Tampa's nightlife possibilities, two other entertainment complexes – **Channelside**, in the downtown area next to the Florida Aquarium (☏ 813/223-4250), and the **International Plaza and Bay Street**, near the airport at the junction of West

Shore and Boy Scout boulevards (☎813/342-3790, ⓦwww.shopinternational plaza.com) – have proved popular with locals, and the clientele is generally slightly older than the crowds of teenagers flocking to Ybor City. For a list of all things nightlife-related, pick up a copy of the free *Creative Loafing Weekly* (every Thurs), or try their website ⓦwww.creativeloafing.com, or the Friday edition of the *Tampa Tribune*, (ⓦwww.tampatrib.com).

Drinking, live music, and nightclubs

Ybor City is brimming with clubs and music bars and many of the area's restaurants also offer entertainment, such as the famous Columbia restaurant (see opposite). One of the busiest places for a **drink** is the *Green Iguana*, 1708 E Seventh Ave (☎813/248-9555, ⓦwww.greeniguana.com), which also has rock bands playing daily and DJs to keep the young crowd very much in the party mood. Another friendly drinking spot in Ybor is the *James Joyce Irish Pub*, 1704½ E Seventh Ave (☎813/247-1896).

Outside of Ybor, one of the best-looking crowds congregates at the *Blue Martini* at the International Plaza and Bay Street (☎813/873-2583). Tampa's most dependable **live music** club is the blues- and reggae-dominated *Skipper's Smokehouse*, 910 Skipper Rd (☎813/971-0666, ⓦwww .skipperssmokehouse.com).

Performing arts and film

Tampa's cultural profile is improved by regular high-quality shows at the **Tampa Bay Performing Arts Center**, 1010 N W.C. MacInnes Place (box office Mon–Sat noon–8pm, Sun noon–6pm; ☎813/229-7827, ⓦwww.tbpac .org), a state-of-the-art performance venue featuring top US and international names. The **Gorilla Theatre**, 4419 N Hubert Ave (tickets $20 to $25; ☎813/879-2914, ⓦwww.gorilla-theatre.com), is a more intimate, but just as professional, theater with a program including contemporary comedies and dramas, as well as the classics. For a full list of **films** playing around the city, check the Friday edition of the *Tampa Tribune*. Foreign-language, classic, or cult films only crop up at the **Tampa Theatre**, 711 Franklin St, for $9 (see p.368); pick up a schedule from the building itself or call ☎813/274-8981. The multi-screen cinema at Channelside shows mainstream movies and IMAX films. For details on other upcoming arts and cultural events, phone the Arts Council of Hillsborough County at ☎813/276-8250.

Comedy clubs

Tampa has two notable **comedy clubs**. *Side Splitters*, 12938 N Dale Mabry Hwy (☎813/960-1197, ⓦwww.sidesplitterscomedy.com), is one of the best in the area and features a line-up of national and regional comedians. The other, also with well-known performers, is the *Improv Comedy Theatre* 1600 E Eighth Ave (☎813/864-4000, ⓦwww.improvtampa.com), right in the heart of Ybor City. Cover charges range from $17 to $35 at both venues.

Gay and lesbian Tampa

With the constant addition of more bars, clubs, and resource centers, **gay and lesbian** life in Tampa is improving all the time, and it's a very gay-friendly city. For information on Tampa's gay life, visit ⓦwww.gaytampa.com. Every October, Tampa hosts the International Gay and Lesbian Film Festival; check ⓦwww.pridefilmfest.com for up-to-date information.

The clean, dimly lit *Baxter's*, 1519 S Dale Mabry Hwy (☎813/258-8830, ⓦwww.baxterslounge.com), is currently enjoying its third reincarnation and

The clothing-optional option

Somewhat unsurprisingly given its plentiful sunshine and agreeable year-round temperatures, the Tampa Bay area has gained a reputation as the site of clothing-optional resorts. **Paradise Lakes**, 17 miles north of Tampa in the town of Land O' Lakes (☎813/949-9327 or 1-866/794-6683, ⓦwww.paradiselakes.com), is the largest nudist resort in North America, and definitely worth a visit – even for just a day – for those interested in shedding their clothes. Once inside the confines of the 81-acre resort, where accommodation ranges from cabanas to condos ($100–130 per night), you're free to be naked anywhere and at any time. Nudity is virtually uniform around the two pools; less common in the evenings at the restaurant and disco. Special events such as a weekly lingerie contest, a nude fashion show, and a massive Halloween party are organized by the dynamic staff, when, in most cases, the clothes go on. Holiday weekends at **Paradise Lakes** are extremely busy, so book well in advance; a day pass entitling you to use all of the resort's facilities costs $30 for a single female, $60 for couples and families.

features pool tables and dancers on Wed–Sat nights. Alternatively, *The Rainbow Room*, 421 S MacDill Ave (☎813/871-2265), is geared primarily toward lesbians.

Listings

Airport car rental Avis ☎813/396-3500; Budget ☎1-800/527-0700; Dollar ☎1-800/800-4000.
Hospital Tampa General on Davis Island ☎813/844-7000. Emergency room ☎813/844-7100, ⓦwww.tgh.org.

Police Emergencies ☎911, non-emergency ☎813/231-6130.
Post Office 401 S Florida Ave (downtown). In Ybor City, at 1900 E Twelfth Ave.

St Petersburg and around

Sitting on the eastern edge of the Pinellas Peninsula, **ST PETERSBURG**'s (named by a homesick Russian) clock runs at a little slower speed. It should come as no surprise that a city that holds the world record for the number of consecutive days of sunshine – 768 in total, set in 1967–69 – and enjoys on average 361 days of sunshine a year wasted no time in attracting the recuperating and the retired to its climate. By the early 1980s, few people under 50 lived in the town and although it remains a retirement haven, St Petersburg has worked hard to lure young blood and there's a definite hipster vibe along Central Avenue. In addition to the rejuvenated pier, which now offers something for every age, its diverse selection of museums and plethora of art galleries have contributed to its emergence as one of Florida's richest cultural cities. The mixture of old and new architecture and the landscaped parks around the seafront make this lovely city well worth a few days of your time and a nice break from the beaches nine miles west on the Gulf Coast (see "The St Petersburg beaches," p.383).

Arrival, information, and city transportation

St Petersburg-Clearwater International Airport (☎727/453-7800, ⓦwww.fly2pie.com) is served by several major carriers as well as charters. A shuttle van will cost $18 and a private taxi will cost around $40 to downtown St Petersburg. If you are arriving at Tampa airport (see p.365) and need to get

▲ St Petersburg pier

to St Petersburg or the beaches, Super Shuttle (☎727/572-1111 or 1-800/282-6817, ⓦwww.supershuttle.com) can get you there for $23–26 per person, or $46–52 for a round-trip ticket; reservations are recommended.

The main route **by car** into St Petersburg is I-275 – don't get off before the "Downtown St Petersburg" exit or you'll face a barrage of traffic lights. The Greyhound **bus** station is centrally located at 180 Ninth St N (☎727/898-1496 or 1-800/231-2222). A day-trip to Tampa is difficult without a car; there are no trains between Tampa and St Petersburg. The only **bus** service to Tampa is the #100X commuter service running between the out-of-town Gateway Mall, on Ninth Street and 77th Avenue, and downtown Tampa and is both inconvenient to reach and infrequent during the day. Most bus services arrive at and depart from the Williams Park terminal, at the junction of First Avenue N and Third Street N, where an information booth (Mon–Sat 7am–5.45pm, Sun 8–4pm) gives route details. Most bus journeys cost $1.75 (except the #100X, which is $3). The best option if you're planning to take several buses in one day is to purchase a **Go Card pass**, which allows unlimited travel for a day. It costs $4 and can be purchased on board. You can reach the St Petersburg beaches on PSTA local buses (☎727/540-1900, ⓦwww.psta.net), though these are not always direct. There is also a **Sun Coast Beach Trolley** to most of the beaches, which is probably your best option (for more on transportation, see the "Buses between St Petersburg and the beaches" box, p.385). The **Looper** is a light-blue trolley bus running every 15 minutes (Mon–Thurs & Sun 10am–5pm, Fri & Sat 10am–midnight), connecting all the museums and attractions. It costs 25¢ a ride and there are blue Looper stops all around the downtown area. The driver gives a guided tour to boot.

Gather the usual tourist **information** and discount coupons from the **Chamber of Commerce**, 100 Second Ave N (Mon–Fri 8am–7pm, Sat 9am–7pm; ☎727/821-4715, ⓦwww.stpete.com), and look out for the "Weekend" section of the *St Petersburg Times*, which comes with the Thursday edition of the paper, for entertainment and nightlife listings, also available on their website (ⓦwww.tampabay.com).

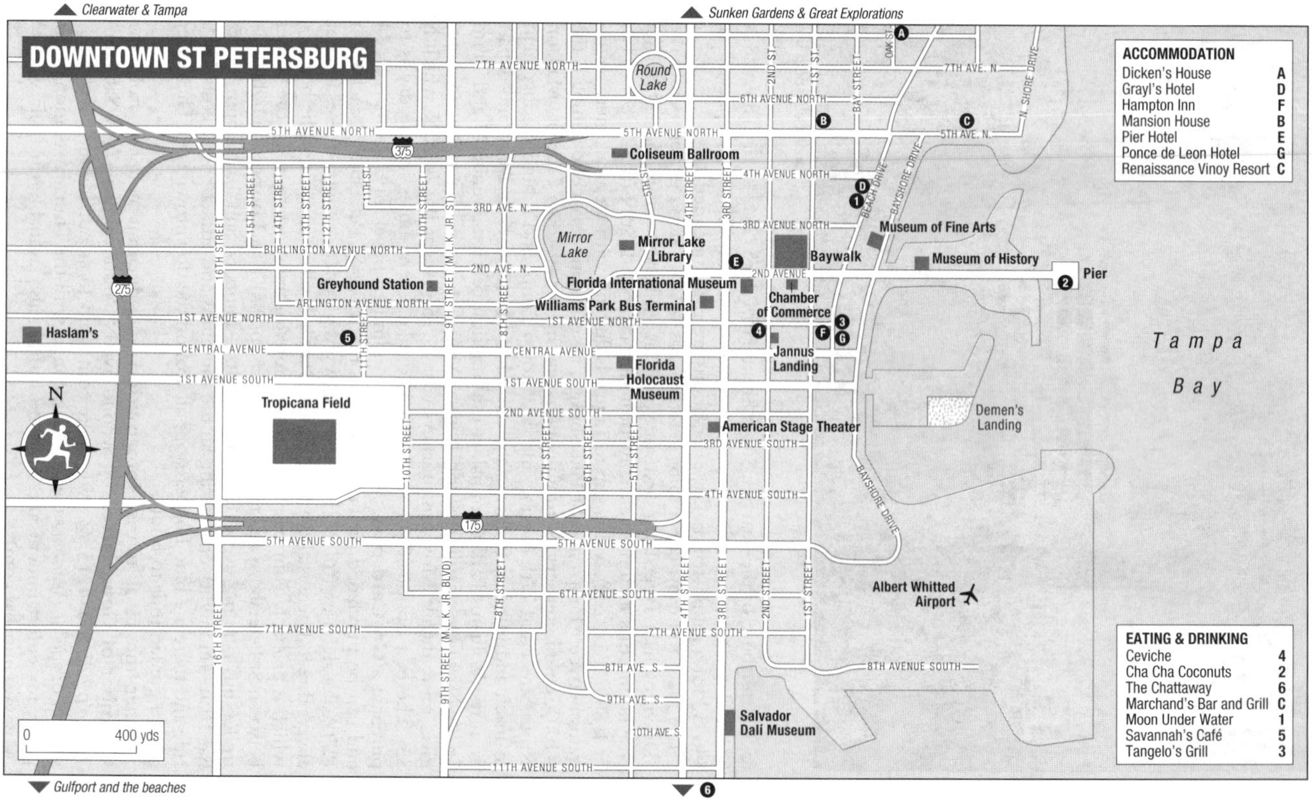

DOWNTOWN ST PETERSBURG

◀ Clearwater & Tampa

◀ Sunken Gardens & Great Explorations

ACCOMMODATION

Dicken's House	A
Gray's Hotel	D
Hampton Inn	F
Mansion House	B
Pier Hotel	E
Ponce de Leon Hotel	G
Renaissance Vinoy Resort	C

EATING & DRINKING

Ceviche	4
Cha Cha Coconuts	2
The Chattaway	6
Marchand's Bar and Grill	C
Moon Under Water	1
Savannah's Café	5
Tangelo's Grill	3

Tampa Bay

Pier

Museum of History

Museum of Fine Arts

Demen's Landing

Albert Whitted Airport

Baywalk

Chamber of Commerce

Jannus Landing

American Stage Theater

Salvador Dali Museum

Coliseum Ballroom

Mirror Lake Library

Florida International Museum

Williams Park Bus Terminal

Florida Holocaust Museum

Round Lake

Mirror Lake

Greyhound Station

Tropicana Field

Haslam's

N

0   400 yds

▶ Gulfport and the beaches

Accommodation

Sleeping in St Petersburg can be less costly than at the beaches. **Motels** are plentiful and can be easy on the pocket – between $60 and $120 year-round depending on location. Most, if not all, B&Bs offer free wireless internet.

Dickens House 335 Eighth Ave NE ☎727/822-8622 or 1-800/381-2022, ⓦ www.dickenshouse.com. Beautifully restored Craftsman bungalow B&B within walking distance of downtown. Plus, the affable owner serves up delicious gourmet breakfasts. ❼

Grayl's Hotel 340 Beach Drive NE ☎727/896-1080 or 1-888/508-4448, ⓦ www.graylshotel.com. Check out the excellent views of St Petersburg and the coast from the rooftop deck at this thirty-room boutique hotel in a distinctive white Spanish mission-style building. ❻

Hampton Inn 80 Beach Drive NE ☎727/892-9900, ⓦ www.stpetehamptonsuites.com. Perfectly nice, if a little pricey, rooms in a great downtown location. Free hot breakfast. ❽

Mansion House 105 Fifth Ave ☎727/821-9391 or 1-800/274-7520, ⓦ www.mansionbandb.com. Antique furnishings abound in this charming house just north of the pier. You can also take a dip in the backyard pool. ❼

Pier Hotel 253 Second Ave N ☎727/822-7500, ⓦ www.thepierhotel.com. Bright and tastefully decorated rooms at an upmarket hotel that offers free evening beer and wine to the strains of live piano music. ❻

Ponce de León Hotel 95 Central Ave ☎727/550-9300, ⓦ www.poncedeleonhotel.com. Rooms are rather ordinary, but the price is great for the location. Discounts available if you book online. ❺

Renaissance Vinoy Resort 501 Fifth Ave NE ☎727/894-1000 or 1-888/303-4430, ⓦ www .renaissancehotels.com/tpasr. If you want to stay over in style, try this pink hotel opened in 1925 as a haven for the rich and famous. Now beautifully restored, it offers two swimming pools, twelve tennis courts, a golf course, an excellent gym and health spa, grandiose ballrooms, and gourmet restaurants. ❽

The Town

However you reach downtown St Petersburg, the first thing you'll see is **Tropicana Field** on the western edge of town at 1 Stadium Drive. This huge building, shaped like a half-collapsed soufflé, opened in the spring of 1998 as home to the local major league baseball team, the **Tampa Bay Rays** (☎727/825-3137, ⓦ www.tampabay.rays.mlb.com), who've enjoyed new popularity as they went all the way to the World Series in 2008. To reserve tickets for a game (the season lasts from April to Oct) call or check the website.

Once in downtown, be sure to walk along **Fourth Avenue**, passing the grandstands of the **Shuffleboard Club**, at no. 536 N, the original home of this popular game. Directly across Fourth Avenue N is the Mediterranean Revival facade of the **Coliseum Ballroom**, built in 1924 and still throbbing to big-band sounds (see "Nightlife," p.382). If art galleries are more your style, try a Second Saturday Gallery Walk (☎727/895-1166), on the second Saturday of every month. Created by the St Petersburg Downtown Arts Association (ⓦ www.stpetearts.com), it incorporates around 16 downtown art galleries, showcasing local artisans as well as Caribbean handcrafts. Pick up a free leaflet at any of the downtown galleries.

If you want a swim, try the excellent **North Shore Pool**, 901 N Shore Drive NE (Mon–Fri 9am–4pm, Sat 10am–4pm, Sun 1–4pm; $3; ☎727/893-7727). In addition to the large pool, there is a sun terrace near the waterfront where you can soak up St Petersburg's abundant sunshine. Though a considerable trek west along Central Avenue, **Haslam's**, 2025 Central Ave (Mon–Sat 10am–6.30pm; ☎727/822-8616, ⓦ www.haslams.com), Florida's largest bookstore, will keep browsers occupied for hours. Opened in the Depression to provide avid readers with used magazines and books at bargain prices, the store stocks over 300,000 new and used books on all topics.

The pier and around

The focal point of downtown St Petersburg is its quarter-mile-long **pier** (open Mon–Thurs 10am–8pm, Fri & Sat 10am–9pm, Sun 11am–7pm, Ⓦwww .stpetepier.com), which juts from the end of Second Avenue N. There's a shuttle tram running between the parking lots and the end of the pier. You'll find stacks of tourist information at the Concierge Center desk (Mon–Thurs 10.30am–8pm, Fri 10.30am–9pm, Sat 10am–9pm, Sun 11am–6pm; Ⓣ727/821-6164), which is near the entrance. The five-story, inverted-pyramid-like building is packed with restaurants, shops, fast-food counters, and an aquarium with eight small tanks of sea life from oceans around the world. Outside at the bait house, you can buy fish to feed the pelicans that congregate at the end of the pier.

At 211 Third St you can see the oldest **theater** in the Tampa Bay area, The American Stage (Ⓣ727/823-7529, Ⓦwww.americanstage.org, tickets $31 to $39), a nonprofit organization with a mission to "entertain, educate, and enlighten." Each spring the theater stages a Shakespeare in the Park Festival at Demen's Landing, a waterfront park facing the pier.

Opposite the entrance to the pier is the **Museum of History**, 335 Second Ave NE (Mon noon–7pm, Tues–Sat 10am–5pm, Sun noon–5pm; $12; Ⓣ727/894-1052, Ⓦwww.spmoh.org). Modest displays recount St Petersburg's early twentieth-century heyday as a winter resort (which lasted until the wider and sandier Gulf Coast beaches became accessible), and the inaugural flight of the world's first commercial airline, KLM, which took off from St Petersburg in 1914. There's documentation, too, on **Weedon Island** (preserve open daily 7am–sunset, visitor's center Wed–Sun 10am–4pm; Ⓣ727/453-6800), five miles north of the town and once the base of a small film industry. Now a state-protected wildlife refuge, the island has two miles of boardwalk, hiking trails, and a two-mile paddling trail, with kayak and canoe rentals available. One block north of the pier, a group of Mediterranean Revival buildings houses the **Museum of Fine Arts** at 255 Beach Drive NE (Tues–Sat 10am–5pm, Sun 1–5pm; $12 including free guided tours; Ⓣ727/896-2667, Ⓦwww.fine-arts .org). Opened in 1965, the museum has more than 4500 works in its collection, and its 26 galleries hold objects from antiquity to the present day; the new airy and modern Hazel Hough wing more than doubles the museum's space. Inside, the works of seventeenth-century art are competent but not imposing; more inspiring is the section on modern European art, featuring Morisot's *Reading*, Monet's *Houses of Parliament* and Daumier's amusing *Connoisseur of Prints*. The American contemporary room displays include Georgia O'Keeffe's vibrant *Poppy* and George Luks' *The Musician*.

A short walk south of the Museum of Fine Arts lies the very worthwhile **Florida International Museum**, 244 2nd Ave N (during exhibition periods only, Tues–Sat 10am–5pm, Sun noon–5pm, last entry 4pm; $10; Ⓣ727/341-7900, Ⓦwww.floridamuseum.org). Exhibits change frequently so check the website or call ahead.

Florida Holocaust Museum

Dedicated to encouraging public awareness, education, and understanding of the Holocaust, the emotionally wrenching **Florida Holocaust Museum**, at 55 Fifth St S, on the western edge of the central part of downtown (Mon–Sun 10am–5pm, last entry 4pm; $12; Ⓣ727/820-0100, Ⓦwww.flholocaustmuseum .org), chronicles the genocide of Europe's Jewish population with sensitivity and intelligence, and puts the history of anti-Semitism, from the first anti-Jewish legislation in Europe in 1215 AD, into context. The museum has both permanent and temporary exhibits, including an expansive second-floor gallery focusing on Holocaust art, and eleven eternal flames – symbolizing the eleven million victims of the Nazis – form part of the building's facade.

The brainchild of local businessman and World War II veteran Walter Loebenberg, who escaped Germany in 1939, the museum includes among its exhibits a massive, original boxcar – #1130695-5 – that carried thousands of victims to their deaths and is one of four in the US. A child's ring, found wedged in the boxcar floor, is displayed alongside it. There are also some stunning sculptures on Jewish and secular themes, though for the best of these, you'll need to be here during the last week of January for the superb annual **art festival** at Temple Beth El, 400 Pasadena Ave S (℡727/347-6136, ⓦwww.templebeth-el.com).

The Salvador Dalí Museum

Few places make a less likely depository for the biggest collection of works by perhaps the world's best-known Surrealist artist than St Petersburg. However, the **Salvador Dalí Museum**, 1000 Third St S (Mon–Wed & Sat 9.30am–5.30pm, Thurs 9.30am–8pm, Fri 9.30–6pm, Sun noon–5.30pm; $15, $5 Thurs after 5pm; ℡727/823-3767, ⓦwww.salvadordalimuseum.org), a mile and a half south of the pier, stores more than 1000 Dalí works from the collection of a Cleveland industrialist and his wife, who struck up a friendship with the artist in the 1940s, bought stacks of his works, and ran out of space to show them – until this specially built gallery opened in 1982.

The hour-long **free tours** running continuously throughout the day trace a fact-filled path around the chronologically arranged paintings (some shown on rotation), from early experiments with Impressionism and Cubism to the ectoplasmic watches of the seminal Surrealist canvas *The Disintegration of the Persistence of Memory*. Works from Dalí's "Classic" period in the 1940s play upon the fundamentals of religion, science, and history, and include *Gala Contemplating the Mediterranean Sea*, with its double image of a woman's back and Abraham Lincoln's face. Some canvases – like the overwhelming *The Discovery of America by Christopher Columbus* and *The Hallucinogenic Toreador*, with its multiple double-images – are so big they have been hung in a specially deepened section of the gallery.

The Sunken Gardens

If you've had your fill of museums, head for the **Sunken Gardens**, 1825 Fourth St N (Mon–Sat 10am–4.30pm, Sun noon–4.30pm; $8; ℡727/551-3100, ⓦwww.stpete.org/sunken), a mile north of the pier. In 1935, a water-filled sinkhole was drained and planted with thousands of tropical plants and trees, forming what is now four acres of shady and sweet-scented gardens. Fifteen feet below street level, lush tropical gardens are combined with flowing ponds and waterfalls. For a crash-course in exotic botany, scrutinize the texts along the pathway, surrounded by bougainvillea, hibiscus, and staghorn ferns.

Eating

As the atmosphere in St Petersburg grows increasingly hipper, so does the array of choice of places to **eat**. The pier offers dining with a view, while the restaurants and bars on Central Avenue is where locals come to eat and play.

Cha Cha Coconuts 800 Second Ave N, 5th floor ℡727/822-6655, ⓦwww.cha-chadashcoconuts .com. Inexpensive Caribbean dishes, such as Blue Mountain voodoo ribs and Caribbean steak,

accompanied by tall, frosty island drinks and live entertainment on the pier. Entrées around $15.

 Ceviche 10 Beach Drive ℡727/209-2299, ⓦwww.ceviche.com. The tapas are tops at this fun spot next to the Ponce de León hotel. You can't go wrong with any of the six ceviches or many hot plates and you shouldn't deny yourself the pleasure of the *patatas bravas*, lightly fried potato wedges tossed in home-made *aioli*. Small plates starting around $8.

The Chattaway 358 22nd St S ℡ 727/823-1594. A one-time grocery store, gas station, and trolley stop, *The Chattaway* is now a great, inexpensive American diner, famous for its juicy Chattaburger, with all the trimmings. Burgers around $6.

Marchand's Bar & Grill at the *Renaissance Vinoy Resort* ℡ 727/824-8072. The best restaurant in St Petersburg's best hotel boasts well-presented and moderately expensive Mediterranean grill food in a lovely large dining room, which frequently reverberates with piano music and occasional live jazz.

Moon Under Water 332 Beach Drive NE ℡ 727/896-6160. Overlooking the waterfront, this inexpensive British Colonial tavern is well known for its cocktails, curries, and baked salmon. Try the killer Key lime pie for dessert.

🏃 **Savannah's Café** 1113 Central Ave ℡ 727/388-4371, ⓦ www.savannahsstpete.com. Traditional Southern food shines with a modern approach. Try the buttermilk fried chicken stuffed with goat cheese and herbs ($16), but be sure to save room for the bread pudding.

Tangelo's Grille 226 First Ave N ℡ 727/894-1695, ⓦ www.tangelosgrille.com. Excellent Cuban café offering hearty, economical meals, such as fantastic black beans and rice ($3.50), sweet potato fries ($4), and Cuban sandwiches ($5.50–7.50), plus great music.

Ted Peters' Famous Smoked Fish 1350 Pasadena Ave ℡ 727/381-7931. Indulge in hot smoked-fish dinners with all the trimmings. Order a menu item such as smoked mullet or catch your own fish and have it cooked in the restaurant's red oak smoker to go.

Nightlife and drinking

It's been said that if you fire a cannon down Central Avenue after 9pm on any night, you won't hit a soul, but enough bars and cafés have now opened to make this more risky.

The Garden 217 Central Ave ℡ 727/896-3800. A Mediterranean bistro with an outdoor martini lounge beneath an ancient banyan tree. Open every night until 2am.

A Taste For Wine Bar and Balcony 241 Central Ave ℡ 727/895-1623, ⓦ www.tasteforwine.net. Just up the stairs from *The Garden* you'll find this hidden gem – a chic wine bar with a comfortable art-filled lounge and live music on weekends.

Jannus Landing 16 Second St N ℡ 727/896-1244, ⓦ www.jannuslandingconcerts.com. This, the oldest (and one of the largest) outdoor concert venues in Florida offers a steady procession of bands playing rock, reggae, folk, and the like.

Coliseum Ballroom 535 Fourth Ave N ℡ 727/892-5202, ⓦ www.stpete.org/coliseum. Turn up with your own booze (there's no bar) at this big-band venue that boasts one of the largest dance floors in the US; weekend cover is around $15 depending on the event, less during the week, and $7 (including instruction 11.30am–12.30pm) for the Wednesday tea dances (1–3.30pm).

Gulfport

Absent from most tourist brochures and unseen by the thousands of visitors who hustle between downtown and the St Petersburg beaches, **GULFPORT** is a charming enclave of peaceful restaurants, eclectic art galleries, and unusual shops. There's little glamour to this former fishing community, making this one of the best places to stay in the area if you want to get off the tourist trail.

From downtown St Petersburg, travel a few miles south on I-275 to Exit 6, then turn right at the bottom of the exit onto Gulfport Boulevard (22nd Ave S), which, after about two miles, serves as the central axis for the town. If you are traveling by bus, catch #23 from the Williams Park terminal to Shore Boulevard. Turn off Gulfport Boulevard onto Beach Boulevard and you'll discover a stretch of antique shops and restaurants shaded by oak trees dripping with Spanish moss. At the end of the road is the **Gulfport Casino Ballroom**, 5500 Shore Blvd S (℡ 727/893-1070), where **ballroom dancing** with a live orchestra has the locals strutting their stuff on Sundays, while fans of swing have it their way on Wednesdays and salsa dancers sizzle on Thursdays.

Practicalities

The *Sea Breeze Manor*, 5701 Shore Blvd (☎727/343-4445 or 1-888/343-4445, ⓦwww.seabreezemanor.com; ❻), is a gloriously restored, seaside house with sumptuous beds, antique furnishings and home-baked breakfasts that makes a great alternative to staying in St Petersburg proper. Another comfortable place is the *Peninsula Inn & Spa*, 2937 Beach Blvd (☎727/346-9800 or 1-888/900-0466, ⓦwww.innspa.net; ❻), with its British Colonial-style decor, Indonesian hand-crafted furniture, full-service spa, and two restaurants. Renowned as one of the best Cuban restaurants in the Tampa Bay area, *Habana Café*, 5402 Gulfport Blvd (☎727/321-8855), serves shrimp of all sorts, all for around $14 for a main course. Try *Backfin Blue Café*, 2913 Beach Blvd S (☎727/343-2583), for fresh, creative dishes like crab-stuffed Portobello mushrooms for around $15; or *La Côte Basque*, 3104 Beach Blvd (☎727/321-6888), for moderately priced flounder, veal, liver, and lamb dishes ranging from $15 to $20. For **nightlife**, *O'Maddy's*, 5403 Shore Blvd (☎727/323-8643), has a good view of the sea and a happy hour between 4pm and 8pm. Otherwise, there's always the *Casino* (see opposite).

South from Tampa Bay

Taking I-275 south from St Petersburg (a preferable route to the lackluster I-75 or US-41 from Tampa), you'll soar over Tampa Bay on the **Sunshine Skyway Bridge** ($1 toll) high enough to allow ocean-going ships to pass beneath and for the outlines of land and sea to become blurred in the heat haze. A phosphate tanker rammed the original bridge during a storm in May 1980, causing the central span of the southbound section to collapse. With visibility reduced to a few feet, drivers on the bridge failed to spot the gap, and 35 people, including the occupants of a Greyhound bus, plunged 250 feet to their deaths. The southern and northern sections of the remains have been turned into the longest fishing piers in the world (access costs $3 per vehicle), while the central section, submerged in the waters at the mouth of Tampa Bay, creates an artificial reef. Tales of phantom hitchhikers who thumb rides across the new bridge – which cost $215 million to build – only to vanish into thin air before reaching the other side are rife.

Beyond the Sunshine Skyway Bridge you enter Florida's southwest coast, which is covered in Chapter 5, Sarasota and the Southwest.

The St Petersburg beaches

Framing the Gulf side of the Pinellas Peninsula – a bulky thumb of land poking out between Tampa Bay and the Gulf of Mexico – are 35 miles of barrier islands forming the **St Petersburg beaches**, a convenient name for one of Florida's busiest coastal strips. Although each beach area has a name of its own, collectively they are often referred to as "the Holiday Isles," or the "Pinellas County Suncoast," and in reality merge together in one long, built-up strip of overdevelopment. The beaches themselves are beautiful, the sea warm, and the sunsets fabulous, but in no way is this Florida at its best. That said, staying here can be very cost-effective (especially during the summer) and if you're prepared to travel beyond the major built-up areas, you will find some that deserve exploration.

A warning: alcohol is prohibited on all municipal beaches in Florida, and glass containers are also illegal. Police in this area are particularly vigilant in chucking the drunk and disorderly in jail.

The Pinellas Trail

If you're looking for an intriguing alternative to the usual beach-hopping paths of tourists up and down the coast, take the **Pinellas Trail** (ⓦwww.pinellascounty.org /trailgd), a 34-mile hiking/cycling track that runs between St Petersburg and Tarpon Springs (see p.393). You can pick up a free, informative, and portable guide to the trail at any of the Chambers of Commerce or visitor centers between these two destinations. The guide describes the route and picks out points of interest, providing easy-to-manage maps and mileage charts. Numerous exit and entry points encourage a leisurely approach, so allow yourself time to meander off the well-marked confines of the trail and, if you don't feel inclined to tackle its entirety, you can take a bus or drive to selected areas for day excursions. Despite some uglier sections through urban centers (tricky on a bike), the trail offers enjoyable scenery along its rural portions and a chance for contemplation away from tanning and watersports. Keep in mind that Florida law requires everyone under 16 to wear a helmet when they ride a bike – no matter where they ride.

Information

Several beach areas have **Chambers of Commerce** readily dispensing handy information: St Pete Beach, 6990 Gulf Blvd (Mon–Fri 9am–5pm; ☏727/360-6957, ⓦwww.tampabaybeaches.com); Treasure Island, 144 107th Ave (Mon–Fri 9am–5pm; ☏727/360-4121, ⓦwww.treasureislandchamber.org). In Clearwater Beach, visit the booth at Pier 60, 1 Causeway Blvd (daily 10am–6pm or 7pm depending on the season; ☏727/442-3604), or the Clearwater Welcome Center, 3350 Gulf-to-Bay Blvd (Mon–Sat 9am–5pm, Sun 10am–5pm; ☏727/726-1547).

Accommodation

The accommodation options along St Petersburg's beaches are limited to **hotels** – including resorts with facilities and activities galore for families – and less expensive **motels** lining mile after mile of Gulf Boulevard and the neighboring streets, though these smaller establishments are increasingly giving way to large condo developments. The ones that remain typically cost $75–100 in winter, $10–15 less during the summer, though if you're staying long enough, many offer discounted weekly rates. Some motels also have **self-catering** amenities for $5–10 above the basic room rate. A room on the beach side of Gulf Boulevard will cost more than an identical one across the street.

There are no **campgrounds** along the main beach strip, though the nearest and nicest spot, at Fort de Soto Park ($34–40; ☏727/582-2267, ⓦwww.pinellascounty .org/park), is adjacent to sand and sea. An inland alternative is *St Petersburg KOA*, 5400 95th St N (☏727/392-2233 or 1-800/562-7714). Situated five miles east of Madeira Beach and tucked away on a mangrove bayou, this campground rents cabins from $64 a night or primitive tent sites for $36. Bike rental is also available. *Clearwater/Tarpon Springs KOA*, 37061 US-19 N (☏727/937-8412 or 1-800/562-8743), six miles north of Clearwater, is handier for Clearwater Beach, charges $25 to pitch a tent, and has cabins available for $43.

The southern beaches

Don Cesar 3400 Gulf Blvd, St Petersburg Beach ☏727/360-1881 or 1-866/728-2206, ⓦwww.doncesar.com. The venerable hotel (see p.386) features 277 renovated rooms and "etiquette classes" in an attempt to regain its past glory. ❽

Island's End Resort 1 Pass-a-Grille Way, Pass-a-Grille ☏727/360-5023, ⓦwww.islandsend.com. Five one-bedroom cottages and a three-bedroom cottage with its own private pool, all occupying a tranquil spot at the southernmost tip of Pass-a-Grille. **7**

Lamara Motel & Apartments 520 73rd Ave, St Petersburg Beach ☎727/360-7521 or 1-800/211-5108, ⓦwww.lamara.com. The landscaped, flower-filled gardens give this motel a quiet and secluded feel despite the location in the heart of St Pete Beach. **3**

Plaza Beach Resort 4506 Gulf Blvd, St Petersburg Beach ☎727/367-2791, ⓦwww.plazabeach.com. Smack-dab on the sand, this friendly, comfortable motel is a great value for the money. There's also a large pool, free mini-golf and beach cabanas. **4**

Sun Burst Inn 19204 Gulf Blvd, Indian Shores ☎727/596-2500 or 1-877/384-8067, ⓦwww.sunburstinn.com. This eleven-room hotel has sunny, white-tiled rooms and a prime beachfront location. **4**

The northern beaches

Barefoot Bay 401 E Shore Drive, Clearwater Beach ☎727/447-3316, ⓦwww.barefootbayresort.com. This British family-owned

hotel, perched on Clearwater Bay, offers a variety of well-appointed, brightly painted rooms. **4**

Belleview Biltmore 25 Belleview Blvd, Clearwater ☎727/373-3000, ⓦwww.belleviewbiltmore.com. At the southern edge of Clearwater, on a bluff overlooking the water, this beautiful 1897 wooden structure was originally owned by the railroad magnate Henry B. Plant, who entertained shippers and celebrities here. All 244 rooms have been immaculately restored. **6**

Sea Captain Resort 40 Devon Drive, Clearwater Beach ☎727/446-7550 or 1-800/444-7488, ⓦwww.seacaptainresort.com. This local hotel offers comfortable, tropically decorated rooms and suites for reasonable rates. Boat slips are also available. **5**

Sheraton Sand Key 1160 Gulf Blvd, Sand Key ☎727/595-1611 ⓦwww.sheratonsandkey.com. One of the best and most popular hotels (especially for conferences) on the St Petersburg beaches. There's an attractive poolside area with pleasant gardens, a great restaurant, and the best-equipped gym hereabouts (where you can also treat yourself to a superb massage). **8**

The southern beaches

In twenty or so miles of heavily touristed coast, just one section has the feel of a genuine community with a history attached to it. The slender finger of **Pass-a-Grille**, at the very southern tip of the barrier island chain, was discovered in the early 1500s by Spanish explorers and became one of the first beach communities on the west coast. Settled by fishermen in 1911, it is now recognized in the National Historic Registry. Named by French fishermen "*la passe aux grilleurs*" – because they grilled their catch at this pass – modern Pass-a-Grille comprises two miles of tidy houses, well-kept lawns, small shops, and a cluster of bars and restaurants. On weekends, locals visit the beach to enjoy one of the area's liveliest stretches of sand and the unobstructed views of the tiny islands dotting the entrance to Tampa Bay. **The Gulf Beaches Historical Museum**,

---

Buses between St Petersburg and the beaches

The best way to access the beaches by bus is the **Suncoast Trolley** service. PSTA service #35 operates daily from the Williams Park terminal in St Petersburg to **St Pete Beach** (daily every half hour 5.50am–7.50pm, Fri & Sat until 11.50pm). Change here for the Suncoast Beach Trolley that travels along Gulf Boulevard and connects all the beaches from **Clearwater Beach** to **Pass-a-Grille** (daily every half-hour 5.45am–9.25pm, Fri & Sat until midnight). Alternatively, there's a direct connection from Williams Park to **Indian Rocks Beach** with #59 and to **Clearwater** with #18 and #52. PSTA bus fares are $1.75 one way.

If you are making a number of journeys in one day, a daily **Go Card** can be purchased on board for $4 and assures unlimited trips on any PSTA vehicle for one day, while $20 buys a seven-day unlimited pass – a real bargain if you're planning to explore the beaches over a number of days. Bicycles can be taken on buses. For further transport details, see box "Buses around Clearwater Beach," p.387.

115 Tenth Ave (hours vary so call ahead; free; ☎727/552-1610), is situated here in what was the first church built on the barrier islands. The museum traces the history of the islands through photographs, news clippings, and artifacts. The **Suncoast Beach Trolley** serves Pass-a-Grille (see box "Buses between St Petersburg and the beaches," p.385).

The Don Cesar Hotel and around

A mile and a half north of Pass-a-Grille, at St Petersburg Beach, you won't need a signpost to locate the **Don Cesar Hotel**, 3400 Gulf Blvd (☎727/360-1881 or 1-866/728-2206, ⓦwww.doncesar.com). Contrasting sharply with the turquoise sea, this grandiose pink castle with white-trimmed arched windows and vaguely Moorish turrets fills seven beachside acres and was conceived by 1920s property speculator, Thomas J. Rowe. The *Don Cesar* opened in 1928, but its glamour was short lived. The Depression forced Rowe to use part of the hotel as a warehouse and later to allow the New York Yankees baseball team to make it their spring training base. After decades as a military hospital and then as federal offices, the building received a $1-million facelift during the 1970s and became a hotel again (see p.384 for details). The current interior bears little resemblance to its original appearance, but you should check out the lounge, where you can soak up the understated elegance from the depths of a sofa or, just outside, from the poolside. The hotel offers live music every night, both indoors and outdoors and, of course, great sunsets.

Just beyond the *Don Cesar*, Pinellas County Bayway cuts inland and makes a good route to Fort de Soto Park (see opposite). Keeping to Gulf Boulevard, however, brings you into the main section of **St Petersburg Beach** (or St Pete Beach), row after row of hotels, motels, and restaurants grouped along the road and continuing for several miles. Further north, **Treasure Island** offers abundant watersports for those bored with lying in the sun. An arching drawbridge crosses over to **Madeira Beach** where you'll find **Hubbard's Marina** (☎727/393-1947 or 1-800/755-0677, ⓦwww.hubbardsmarina.com),

▲ Don Cesar Hotel

which offers deep-sea fishing, and the adjacent *Friendly Fisherman Seafood Restaurant* (Mon–Thurs & Sun 7am–9pm, Fri–Sat 7am–10pm; ☎727/391-6025) will cook the fish caught from their boats for you.

The Suncoast Seabird Sanctuary

Four miles north of Madeira Beach, at Indian Shores, the **Suncoast Seabird Sanctuary**, 18328 Gulf Blvd (daily 9am–sunset; donations suggested; ☎727/391-6211, ⊛www.seabirdsanctuary.com), offers a break from the sand. The sanctuary is the largest wild-bird hospital in North America, treating between 400 and 600 convalescing birds at any one time, in state-of-the-art facilities. These birds, commonly injured by fishing lines or environmental pollution, are released back into their natural habitat once well.

Fort de Soto Park

If you have a car, you can soak up some of the history surrounding the St Petersburg beaches by heading across the Pinellas County Bayway immediately north of the *Don Cesar*, then turning south along Rte-679 to spend a day on the five islands comprising **Fort de Soto Park** (sunrise–sunset; free; ☎727/582-2267, ⊛www.pinellascounty.org/park). The Spaniard credited with discovering Florida, Juan Ponce de León, is thought to have anchored here in 1513 and again in 1521 when the islands' indigenous inhabitants inflicted on him what proved to be a fatal wound. The islands later became a strategically important Union base during the Civil War, and in 1898 a fort was constructed to forestall attacks on Tampa during the Spanish-American War. The remains of the fort – which was never completed – can be explored on one of several **walking trails**, which wind through an untamed, thickly vegetated landscape, with plenty of palm-shaded picnic tables along the way. Pick up a leaflet for the self-guided walking tour of the fort, or join a guided walking tour offered on Saturdays at 10am. Free nature tours through the park are also available at weekends departing from various locations.

Three miles of swimmer-friendly **beaches** line the park, which possesses an intoxicating air of isolation during the week – a far cry from the busy beach strips. You can rent bikes from Wheel Fun Rentals (☎941/776-9962, ⊛www.wheelfunrentals.com; $7–18 per hr). The best way to savor the area is by **camping**; see "Accommodation," p.384.

The northern beaches

Much of the **northern section** of **Sand Key**, the longest barrier island in the St Petersburg chain, is lined by stylish condos and time-share apartments – this is one of the wealthier stretches of the coast. It ends with the pretty 65-acre **Sand Key Park**, where tall palm trees frame a scintillating strip of sand. This

---

Buses around Clearwater Beach

Clearwater Beach is good news for travelers without cars. **Around the beach strip**, the Jolly Trolley (☎727/445-1200) runs daily (10am–10pm) between Sand Key (from the **Sheraton Sand Key Resort**) and Clearwater Beach (along Gulfview Blvd, Mandalay Ave, and Acacia St); fares are $2. Alternatively, catch the Suncoast Beach Trolley, which operates between Clearwater Beach and Clearwater's Park Street terminal (info: ☎727/540-1900). **Useful routes** from the terminal are #18 and #52 to St Petersburg; #66 to Tarpon Springs; and #200X (weekdays and rush hours only) to Tampa.

classic beach vista is a good spot to watch dolphins, though the view is marred by the nearby high-rises.

The park occupies one bank of Clearwater Pass, across which a belt of sparkling white sands characterize **Clearwater Beach**, another community devoted to the holiday industry. Much of Clearwater Beach south of Pier 60 is completely taken over by condos and many, if not all, of the old mom-and-pop motels have been razed to make room. You'll see occasional vestiges of the small-town community in the local hotels near the beach north of the pier, and in shops on Mandalay Avenue. Clearwater has its own **information point** separate from that of Clearwater Beach at 1130 Cleveland St (Mon–Fri 8.30am–5pm; ☎727/461-0011, ⊛www.clearwaterflorida.org).

The Clearwater Marine Aquarium

The non-profit **Clearwater Marine Aquarium**, 249 Windward Passage (Mon–Thurs 9am–5pm, Fri-Sat 9am–7pm, Sun 10am–5pm; $11; ☎727/441-1790, ⊛www.cmaquarium.org), rescues and rehabilitates injured marine mammals and sea turtles. Visitors can learn ways to help protect these animals and examine exhibits on Florida's coastal ecology and tanks of stingrays and sharks. Beyond its sands and two long piers, there's not much else to do in Clearwater Beach: if the brine beckons, board a mock pirate vessel for a two-hour *Captain Memo's* "pirate cruise" (daily 10am & 2pm, no 10am cruise on Sun; $35; evening Champagne cruises at varying times through the year; $35; ☎727/446-2587, ⊛www.captainmemo.com) from the marina just south of the causeway; or, more adventurously, make a day-trip to the Caladesi or Honeymoon islands, a few miles north.

Honeymoon and Caladesi islands

These islands were created in 1921, when a hurricane tore the aptly named Hurricane Pass out of what was a single, five-mile island. Both are now protected state parks ($5 per car for Honeymoon and $1 pedestrians and cyclists, $4 per person for Caladesi) that offer a chance to see the jungle-like terrain that covered

▲ Clearwater Beach

the whole west coast before the bulldozers arrived. Of the two, only **Honeymoon Island** can be reached by road; take Rte-586 off US-19 just north of Dunedin. The island earned its name when Paramount newsreels and *Life* magazine gave away all-expenses-paid honeymoons on the island as a grand prize in a 1940s contest. Today the condos sprouting from Honeymoon Island dent its natural impact, but a wild pocket at the end of the road is well worth exploring by way of the walking trail running around the edge of the entire island.

For a glimpse of what these islands must have looked like before the onset of mass tourism, make for **Caladesi Island**, just to the south. From a signposted landing stage beside Rte-586 on Honeymoon Island, the **Caledesi Connections** ferry ($10 round-trip; ☎727/734-1501) crosses between the islands daily (on the hour, every hour) on weekdays and (if busy) every half-hour at weekends, between 10am and 5pm. Once ashore at Caladesi's mangrove-fringed marina, boardwalks lead to a beach of unsurpassed tranquility that's perfect for swimming, sunbathing, and shell collecting. While here, try and summon the strength to tackle the three-mile **nature trail**, which cuts inland through saw palmetto and slash pines. Bring food and drink to the island, as the poorly stocked snack bar at the marina is the sole source of sustenance.

Eating

The restaurants of the St Petersburg beaches are a jumble of diners, fast-food joints, casual and fine-dining establishments and, as you'd expect at any beach resort, buffets.

The southern beaches

Don Cesar 3400 Gulf Blvd, St Petersburg Beach ☎727/360-1881, ⊛www.doncesar.com. You'll find the pinnacle of buffet-style dining here, where from 10.30am to 2.30pm on Sundays you can tuck into as many made-to-order crepes and as much smoked salmon as you can eat for $39.95 per person.

Fetishes 6690 Gulf Blvd, St Petersburg Beach ☎727/363-3700, ⊛www.fetishesrestaurant.com. An intimate restaurant with expensive American cuisine and only eight tables, so reservations are essential. Try the roast pork tenderloin ($20) or the roast duckling ($32). There's also a good wine selection.

Guppy's on the Beach 1701 Gulf Blvd, Indian Rocks Beach ☎727/593-2032. Tasty meals, including sashimi tuna, potato-crusted salmon, and filet mignon, are served across from the beach in a setting ideal for sunset watching. Dinner entrées around $20.

Hurricane 807 Gulf Way, Pass-a-Grille ☎727/360-9558. Dine from a well-priced seafood menu on the terrace overlooking the Gulf of Mexico; the ubiquitous grouper is prepared a variety of ways. Entrées are $8–$20.

The Wharf 2001 Pass-a-Grille Way, Pass-a-Grille ☎727/367-9469, ⊛www.wharfrestaurant.org. Forming part of the marina and a popular place with locals. An enormous bowl of mouthwatering seafood chowder will only set you back around $4.

The northern beaches

Frenchy's Café 41 Baymont St, Clearwater Beach ☎727/446-3607, ⊛www.frenchysonline.com. This 1981 original has a funky, casual vibe and features favorites such as seafood gumbo, smoked fish spread, and some of the best grouper sandwiches on the beach. Sandwiches are $6.25–$10.

Frenchy's Rockaway Grill 7 Rockaway St, Clearwater Beach ☎727/446-4844, ⊛www .frenchysonline.com. A beachside grill with great atmosphere and decent grilled grouper, *mahi mahi* and chicken, along with a daily schedule of beach games and live music. Entrées $10–$19.

Island Way Grill 20 Island Way ☎727/461-6617, ⊛www.islandwaygrill.com. Owned by pro football players, this sleek spot, decked out in lots of glass and polished wood, offers a tasty seafood menu, including a wok-fried yellowtail snapper and steamed salmon wrapped in bamboo. There's also outdoor seating overlooking Mandalay Bay. Dinner entrées $20–$30.

🏃 **Rusty's Bistro** at *Sheraton Sand Key*, Sand Key ☎727/595-1611, ⊛www.sheraton sandkey.com. Seafood dishes like eastern spice-seared tuna are as good as the choice steaks and a prime rib buffet. All dishes are around $25, making this place excellent value, and worth a visit even if you aren't staying at the hotel.

Shephard's 619 S Gulfview Blvd, Clearwater Beach ☎727/441-6875, ⊛www.shephards.com.

Cheaper and more mundane buffet breakfasts (from $6.95), lunches (from $8.95), and dinners (menu and prices subject to change) are available at this waterfront resort.

Tio Pepe 2930 Gulf-to-Bay Blvd, Clearwater T727/799-3082, W www.tiopeperestaurant.com.

One of the area's longstanding restaurants, serving award-winning Spanish, Mediterranean, and Latin American cuisine, plus an extensive wine list, in a rich, Spanish-tiled interior. Closed Mon. Entrées around $20.

Nightlife and entertainment

Most of the **nightlife** is aimed at tourists, though there are exceptions. Many hotel and restaurant bars have lengthy **happy hours** and lounges designed for watching the sunset while sipping a cocktail – look for ads in the free tourist magazines.

Backyard Tiki Bar 601-619 S Gulfview Blvd, at *Shephard's Beach Resort*, Clearwater Beach T727/441-6875, W www.shephards.com. Features live reggae and rock music, bikini contests, and loads of people looking for a good time. Also has a grill if you're looking for a quick sandwich snack.
Sloppy Joe's on the Beach 10650 Gulf Blvd, at *Bilmar Beach Resort*, Treasure Island T727/367-1600, W www.sloppyjoesonthebeach.com. An ideal place to enjoy a sundowner and live music day and night in an informal setting.

Sunsets at Pier 60 Pier 60, Clearwater Beach T727/434-6060, W www.sunsetsatpier60.com. This free daily street festival celebrates the area's famed sunsets with street entertainers and live music of all kinds on offer around Pier 60 in the heart of Clearwater Beach.
The Wave also at *Shephard's*. This two-level nightclub is one of the more popular of the beaches' partying spots. It's massive sound system and light show attract a youngish crowd.

Inland from Tampa Bay: Lakeland and around

LAKELAND, thirty miles east of Tampa, plays the suburban big brother to its more rural neighbors and provides sleeping quarters for Orlando and Tampa commuters, who emerge on weekends to stroll the edges of the town's numerous lakes.

Aided by its busy railway terminal, Lakeland's fortunes rose in the 1920s, and a number of its more important buildings have been maintained as the **Munn Park Historic District** on and close to Main Street. Pay attention to the 1927 **Polk Theater**, 127 S Florida Ave (T863/682-7553), and the restored balustrades, lampposts, and gazebo-style bandstand on the promenade around Lake Mirror, at the east end of Main Street. A few minutes' walk from the town center, the spacious **Polk Museum of Art**, 800 E Palmetto St (Tues–Sat 10am–5pm, Sun 1–5pm; $5; T863/688-7743) hosts the latest innovative pieces by up-and-coming Florida-based artists.

A stronger draw, and something of a surprise in such a tucked-away community, is the largest single grouping of buildings by **Frank Lloyd Wright**, who redefined American architecture in the Twenties and Thirties. Maybe it was the rare chance to design an entire communal area that appealed to Wright – the fee he got for converting an eighty-acre orange grove into **Florida Southern College**, a mile southwest of Lakeland's center, certainly didn't; the financially strapped college paid on credit and got its students to provide the labor.

Much of the integrity of Wright's initial concept has been lost: buildings have been crudely adapted and used for purposes other than those for which they were intended, and newer structures have distorted the college's overall harmony. Even so, the campus is an inventive statement and easily negotiated using the free

maps provided in boxes along its covered walkways. Interestingly, Wright's contempt for air conditioning caused him to erect thick masonry structures to shield the students from the Florida sun, and his desire to merge his work with the natural environment allowed the creeping vegetation of the orange grove (which has now given way to lawns) to wrap around the buildings and provide further insulation. To sign up for the regular guided **tours** (Mon, Wed & Fri at 11am & 1pm; $10) of the Wright buildings, call ☎863/680-4444; otherwise, you can walk amongst them at your leisure (Mon–Fri 10am–4pm, limited hours and access on the weekend).

Practicalities

Get a descriptive **walking tour map** of the Munn Park Historic District from the **Chamber of Commerce**, 35 Lake Morton Drive (Mon–Fri 8.30am–5pm; ☎863/688-8551). For **eating**, the *Reececliff*, 940 S Florida Ave (☎863/686-6661), a spartan diner in business since 1934, has ridiculously cheap breakfasts and lunches, open for dinner as well; *Harry's Seafood Bar & Grille*, 101 N Kentucky Ave (☎863/686-2228), serves up Cajun and Creole-inspired food amid lots of dark wood and ferns. If you're in the mood for a posh meal, try the chic *Terrace Grille* (☎863/603-5420) in the historic *Terrace Hotel*, 329 E Main St (☎863/688-0800, ⓦwww.terracehotel.com; ❼), where you can tuck into superb dishes, such as rack of lamb with a chipotle-black-berry glaze. The hotel itself has been beautifully restored to its 1924 self, and some of the generously sized rooms overlook Lake Morton.

The *Lake Morton Bed & Breakfast*, 817 South Blvd (☎863/688-6788; ⓦwww.lakemortonbandb.com; ❹), is an oak-decorated period house near the campus and the main lake. All rooms have full kitchens. The well-maintained 1905 *Shaw House*, 605 E Orange St (☎863/687-7120; ❹), overlooks Hollis Gardens and Mirror Lake and offers guests wine and cheese on the wide second-story veranda.

Fantasy of Flight

Ten miles northeast of Lakeland, near Polk City, **Fantasy of Flight**, 1400 Broadway Blvd SE (daily 10am–5pm; ☎863/984-3500, ⓦwww.fantasyofflight.com; $29, children $15), draws both tourists and aviation enthusiasts. Part themed attraction and part private aircraft collection, Fantasy of Flight allows visitors to climb aboard a World War II B-17 Flying Fortress and pretend to drop bombs amid the sounds of anti-aircraft fire. Perhaps most interesting is the owner's collection of over forty vintage planes, including the Lockheed Vega, which was the first plane ever flown around the globe.

Lake Wales and around

Southeast of Lakeland (25 miles south of I-4 on US-27), **Lake Wales** (ⓦwww.cityoflakewales.com) is a lackadaisical town with more of note on its fringes than in its center, though the pink stucco **Lake Wales Depot Museum**, 325 S Scenic Highway (Mon–Fri 9am–5pm, Sat 10am–4pm; free; ☎863/678-4209), contains an entertaining collection of train parts, remnants of the turpentine industry on which the town was founded in the late 1800s, and a Warhol-like collection of crate labels from the citrus companies that prospered during the early 1900s.

At the museum, confirm directions to **Spook Hill**, an optical illusion that's been turned into a transparently bogus "legend" (which you can read about on a plaque), worth seeing as a unique example of local Florida kitsch (conveniently, it's on the way to Historic Bok Sanctuary; see p.392). By car, cross Central Avenue from the museum and turn right onto N Avenue, and then take a left at the T-intersection, following the one-way system. Just before meeting Hwy-17A, a sign indicates the spot to brake and put your vehicle into neutral. As you do so, the car appears to slide uphill. Looking back reveals the difference in road gradients that creates the effect.

Historic Bok Sanctuary

"A more striking example of the power of beauty could hardly be found, better proof that beauty exists could not be asked for," rejoiced landscape gardener William Lyman Phillips in 1956 on visiting **Historic Bok Sanctuary**, a rolling garden of greenery two miles north of Lake Wales on Hwy-17A (daily 8am–6pm, last admission 5pm; $10, children 5–12 $3; ☏863/676-1408, ⓦwww.boksanctuary.org). As sentimental as it may sound, Phillips' comment was, and is, accurate. Whether it's the effusive entanglements of ferns, oaks, and palms; the bright patches of magnolias, azaleas, and gardenias; or just the sheer novelty of a hill (this being the highest point in peninsular Florida), Bok Tower Gardens is one of the state's loveliest places.

Not content with winning the Pulitzer Prize for his autobiography in 1920, Dutch-born office-boy turned author and publisher **Edward Bok** resolved to transform the pine-covered Iron Mountain (as this red-soiled hump is named) into a "sanctuary for humans and birds," in gratitude to his adopted country for making his glittering career possible.

Marvelous though they are, these 250 acres would be just a glorified botanical garden were it not for the **Singing Tower** and the **mansion**. The tower, two hundred feet of marble and coquina, rises steeply above the foliage, poetically mirrored in a swan- and duck-filled lily pond. Originally intended to conceal the garden's water tanks, the tower features finely sculpted impressions of Florida wildlife on its exterior and fills its interior with a 60-bell carillon: richly toned chimes resound through the garden at regular intervals and during two recitals per day. The visitor's center provides plenty of details about the garden and tower. The twenty-room Mediterranean-style estate, named Pinewood, opened in 1995; its rooms are decorated with 1930s furnishings. Guided tours last for one hour and cost $6.

A portion of the grounds has been left in its raw state, allowing wildlife to roam and be surreptitiously viewed through the glass front of a wooden hut. Hardier visitors can hack their way for twenty minutes along the **Pine Ridge Trail**, through the pine trees, saw-edged grasses, and wild flowers that once covered the entire hill.

Chalet Suzanne

In 1931, gourmet cook and world traveler Bertha Hinshaw, recently widowed and made penniless by the Depression, moved to an isolated site two miles north of Lake Wales, beside US-17, to open a restaurant called **Chalet Suzanne**. Armed with her own recipes and tremendous powers of culinary invention – adding chicken livers to grilled grapefruit, for instance – Bertha created what's now among the most highly rated meal stops in the country, and one that's still run by her family.

Aside from the food (brunch runs $30, while a five-course dinner starts at $59; call for reservations ☏800/433-6011), the quirky architecture grabs the eye: part Arabic, part Renaissance, whimsical, Hobbit-like buildings painted in confectionery pinks, greens, and yellows, topped by twisting towers and exotic turrets. Even if you're not dining or staying in one of the boudoir-like guest rooms (ⓦwww.chaletsuzanne.com; ❼), you're free to wander through the public rooms, whose furnishings are as loopy as the architecture, with decorative pieces picked up from Bertha's seven around-the-world trips.

Tarpon Springs

Greek sponge-divers driven out of Key West by xenophobic locals during the early 1900s resettled in **TARPON SPRINGS**, ten miles north of Clearwater off US-19 (use Alt-19 – called Pinellas Ave here – to arrive in the center). These early migrants began what has become a sizeable Greek community in a town previously the preserve of wealthy wintering northerners. Demand for sponges was unprecedented during World War II (among other attributes, sponges are excellent for mopping up blood), but the industry was later devastated by a marine blight and the development of synthetic sponges. The Greek presence in Tarpon Springs remains strong, however, and is most evident every January 6 when around 30,000 participate in the country's largest Greek Orthodox Epiphany celebration. Each year, an even greater number of visitors traipse around the souvenir shops lining

the old sponge docks, largely neglecting the rest of the small town, which has much to offer.

The Town

Greek names appear on virtually every shop front throughout Tarpon Springs, and on Tarpon Springs Avenue, you'll find several that have been converted into curio-filled antique shops. While downtown, check out the restored **Historical Society Depot Museum**, 160 E Tarpon Ave (Tues–Sat 10am–3.30pm; free; ☎727/943-4624). Built in 1909, the depot was used until 1985 for freight before falling into disrepair. It now displays old photos of residents and artifacts of daily life. Note the two ticket windows near the entrance; the larger, nicer of the two was for white passengers, the smaller for black travelers.

Drop in to the **Tarpon Springs Cultural Center**, 101 S Pinellas Ave (Mon–Fri 9am–4pm, Sat noon–4pm; free except for special events; ☎727/942-5605), which regularly stages imaginative exhibitions about Tarpon Springs' past and present, as well as art exhibitions. The Neoclassical building housing the Cultural Center has served as the city hall since 1915.

Continuing north on Pinellas Avenue, following the "docks" signs, on the right you'll see the strongest symbol in this Greek community: the resplendent Byzantine Revival **St Nicholas Orthodox Cathedral**, 36 N Pinellas Ave, at Orange Street (Mon–Fri 9am–5pm; free; ☎727/937-3540). Partly funded by a half-percent levy on local sponge sales, the cathedral was finished in 1943. The full significance of the cathedral's ornate interior will inevitably be lost on those not of the faith, though the icons and slow-burning incense create an intensely spiritual atmosphere.

Pick up **information** and a map guide to all sites and points of interest in downtown from the **Chamber of Commerce**, 11 E Orange St, opposite the cathedral (Mon–Fri 9am–5pm; ☎727/937-6109, ⓦwww.tarponsprings.com). On weekends, when the chamber is closed, head for the **visitor center** at the City Marina (daily 10.30am–4.30pm; ☎727/937-8028).

The Unitarian-Universalist Church and George Innes Junior Collection

Walking west along Tarpon Avenue takes you downhill to **Spring Bayou**, a crescent-shaped lake ringed by the opulent homes of Tarpon Springs' pre-sponge-era residents, who were primarily a mix of tycoons and artists.

The **Unitarian-Universalist Church**, 230 Grand Blvd, at Read St (Nov–April Tues–Sat 1–4pm; donations suggested; ☎727/937-4682), is known for its collection of whimsical paintings by the early twentieth-century landscapist George Innes Junior. To mark what would have been the 100th birthday of his late father, Innes painted a delicate rendition of Spring Bayou (a crescent-shaped lake at the western end of Tarpon Ave), now a centerpiece of the church's collection. Innes spent much of his career mired in depression and mediocrity, but this particular work seemed to ignite a creative spark and prompted the series of hauntingly beautiful paintings (two of which once hung in the Louvre) dominating the church's walls today.

Just a few minutes' walk from the church, the simple wooden **Shrine of St Michael Taxiarchis**, at 113 Hope St (always open), was erected by a local woman in gratitude for the unexplained recovery of her "terminally ill" son in 1939. Numerous instances of the blind regaining their sight and the crippled throwing away their walking sticks after visiting the shrine have been reported, all detailed in a free pamphlet.

The sponge docks

Along Dodecanese Boulevard, on the banks of the Anclote River, the **sponge docks** are a disappointing conglomeration of one-time supply stores turned into restaurants and gift shops touting cassettes of Greek "belly-dancing music" and, of course, sponges. A boat departs regularly throughout the day on a half-hour **sponge-diving trip** from the St Nicholas Boat Line, 693 Dodecanese Blvd ($8; ☎727/942-6425). The trip includes a cruise through the sponge docks, a talk on the history of sponge diving, and a demonstration of harvesting performed in a traditional brass-helmeted diving suit. Only a few sponge boats still operate commercially today.

You'll pay less, and learn more about the local community and sponge diving, at the **Sponge Factory** (Mon–Fri Sun 10am–7pm, Sat 10am–10pm; ☎727/938-5366), a shop that includes the free Museum of Sponge Diving and a half-hour film detailing where sponges grow and how they are harvested. It also traces the history of Tarpon Springs' Greek settlers and shows the primitive techniques still used in the industry.

Once you've had your fill of sponges and tourist shops, the small **Konger Tarpon Spring Aquarium**, 850 Dodecanese Blvd (Mon–Sat 10am–5pm, Sun noon–5pm; $5.75; ☎727/938-5378, ⓦwww.tarponspringsaquarium .com), has a simulated coral reef, complete with native plants and tropical fish, and a tidal pool containing starfish and hermit crabs. For a really lazy and very pleasurable half day, you can take a **boat tour** to nearby **Anclote Key**, four miles of sandy beach with a lighthouse at its southern end. Sun Line Cruises,

776 Dodecanese Blvd, offers a variety of cruises, from environmentally themed journeys to Anclote Key sightseeing trips. ($16 to $19; ☎727/944-4478, ⓦwww.sunlinecruises.com).

Accommodation and eating

Tarpon Springs makes a sensible overnight stop if you're continuing north. For a lovely bed and breakfast, try either the *Spring Bayou Inn*, at 32 W Tarpon Ave (☎727/938-9333, ⓦwww.springbayouinn.com; ❺), or *Bavarian Lodge Bed and Breakfast*, 427 E Tarpon Ave (☎727/939-0850, ⓦwww.bavarianlodgeflorida .citymax.com; ❺).

Among the **eating** options, check out *Zánte Cafe*, 13 N Safford Ave (☎727/934-5558), an eclectic downtown café that resembles a grandmother's overstuffed attic. The Cajun–Greek cuisine includes such delicious dishes as the chicken gyro for under $10. For authentic Greek food, sample the offerings at *Costas*, 521 Athens St (☎727/938-6890), or *Plaka*, 769 Dodecanese Blvd (☎727/934-4752), which specializes in seafood, salads, and *souvlaki*. Main dishes start at around $8.

The Big Bend

Popularly known as the **BIG BEND** for the way it curves toward the Panhandle, Florida's **northwest coast** is one of its best-kept secrets. Far from the tourist beaches and theme parks, this sparsely populated coastline offers thousands of mangrove islands and marshlands, wide spring-fed rivers and quiet roads leading to small communities. Here you will find some of the best wildlife Florida has to offer and – in one instance – an outstanding Native American ceremonial site.

Homosassa Springs and around

The main highway out of Tampa Bay, US-19, is a roadside clutter of filling stations and used-car lots and something of a parking lot. A quicker route out of the area is to take I-275, which becomes I-75 after it leaves Tampa, then head west on US-98 at junction 61. By the time you reach US-19, after approximately twenty miles, it has become a more soothing, if often monotonous, landscape of hardwood and pine forests along with expanses of swamp. Those taking this quicker way to the Big Bend who are planning a visit to Weeki Wachee Springs should join Hwy-50 at Brooksville, while those on US-19 will remain on it until the junction with Hwy-50, about thirty miles north of Clearwater. **Weeki Wachee Springs State Park** (hours vary seasonally; $13.95, children 6–10 $10.95; ☎352/596-2062, ⓦwww.weekiwachee .com) opened in 1947 and has attracted numerous celebrities – including Elvis – to its thoroughly kitsch underwater shows performed by "mermaids" in one of the Big Bend's many natural springs. The park also offers a Wilderness River Cruise and bird shows and is now part of its own city. There are plenty of places to stay, although it can be visited as a day-trip from Clearwater. During the summer months the combination ticket for $25 allows access to the adjacent **Buccaneer Bay Water Park** (late March through mid June Sat–Sun 10am–5pm; June 8–August 30 Mon–Sun 10am–5pm; August 31–Sept 27 Sat–Sun 10am–4pm; ☎ 352/596-2062), where you can swim and play on the water slides to your heart's content.

Twenty miles north is **HOMOSASSA SPRINGS**, the first community of any size on US-19, and one of the best places anywhere in the world to catch tarpon (May and June are the prime fishing months). The **Homosassa Springs Wildlife State Park** (daily 9am–5.30pm, last ticket sold at 4pm; $9; ☎ 352/628-5343, ⓦ www.floridastateparks.org/homosassasprings) is a showcase of Florida's native wildlife, offering a chance to see animals, birds, and plants in their natural setting. Walking trails lead to a gushing spring and an underwater observatory where you can see numerous fish and manatees up close, while daily educational programs offer the opportunity of learning more about the wildlife on show. The park also serves as a rehabilitation center and refuge for endangered West Indian manatees orphaned or injured in the wild.

Practicalities

Homosassa Springs is a good option if you're seeking a place to stay off the beaten track. Avoid the usual chain motels on US-19 and spend a night at *MacRae's*, 5300 S Cherokee Way (☎ 352/628-2602, ⓦ www.macraesof homosassa.com; ❸), the place of choice for fishermen for kicking back in a rocking chair and barbecuing the day's catch, or the *Homosassa Riverside Resort*, 5297 S Cherokee Way (☎ 352/628-2474 or 1-800/442-2040, ⓦ www .riversideresorts.com; ❹). Boat rental is available at both establishments. Campers should head for the centrally located *Nature Resort Campground and Marina*, 10359 W Halls River Rd (☎ 352/628-9544 or 1-800/301-7880, ⓦ www .naturesresortfla.com), which charges $25 per night to pitch a tent. The

Manatees

Manatees are one of Florida's most beloved creatures, but sadly also one of its most endangered. More closely related to elephants and aardvarks than to other sea life, it's hard to believe these large animals – they can grow up to thirteen feet long and weigh up to 3500 pounds – are the source of the mermaid myth. Manatees are harmless and love to graze on seagrasses in shallow water, surfacing every three to four minutes to breathe. They have been on the endangered species list since 1973, and there are only a few thousand left in Florida waters. With no natural predators, a third of manatee deaths have human-related causes, such as accidents with boats, pollution, and flood control gates that automatically close. Although scientists believe manatees can live to 60 or longer, their slow development to sexual maturity and low birth rate do little to compensate for their disproportionately high death rate. Manatees may be endangered, but Florida law prohibits breeding them; resources, they say, are better spent on the care and rehabilitation of wild manatees that have suffered the blows of ship's propellers or river poisoning. You should never approach, feed, or touch manatees in the wild and if you see an injured or dead one, a calf with no adult around, or see anyone harassing one, call the Florida Fish and Wildlife Conservation Commission on ☎ 1-888/404-3922. To learn more about manatees and their conservation, read **Manatees: An Educator's Guide** produced by the Save the Manatee Club, 500 N Maitland Ave, Maitland, FL 32751 (☎ 1-800/432-5646, ⓦ www .savethemanatee.org). Most of the dive shops in Crystal River offer snorkeling trips geared to swimming with the manatees (starting from $30).

Chassahowitzka River Campground, 8600 W Miss Maggie Drive (☎352/382-2200), charges $15 per night for a primitive site and is within walking distance of the Chassahowitzka River, convenient for canoeing. The obvious place to eat is the *Riverside Crab House* at the marina next to the *Homosassa Riverside Resort* (☎352/628-2474), where the best spot to consume your blue crabs (from $15.95), grouper sandwiches ($8.95), and fried shrimp ($9.95) is at a table overlooking the river and small island inhabited by monkeys.

Crystal River and around

Seven miles further north along US-19, **CRYSTAL RIVER** is among the region's larger communities, with a population topping a whopping four thousand. **Manatees** take a shine to the sedate beauty of the clear river from which the town takes its name; they can be seen all year round, but in greater numbers during the winter, at the **Crystal River National Wildlife Refuge** (Mon–Fri 7.30am–4pm; mid-Nov to March also open weekends 8am–4pm; ☎352/563-2088), part of the larger **Chassahowitzka National Wildlife Refuge**, accessible by turning west on US-19 at Paradise Point Road in Crystal River. At the office you can gather information on swimming, snorkeling, scuba diving, and boat trips in the area. The American Pro Diving Center, 821 SE US-19 (☎352/563-0041 or 1-800/291-3483, ⓦwww.americanprodiving.com), offers all kinds of guided dives and snorkel trips from $30 to $70.

Crystal River's present dwellers are by no means the first to have lived by the waterway – it provided a source of food for Native Americans from at least 200 BC. To gain some insight into Indian culture, take State Park Road off US-19 just north of the town to the **Crystal River State Archaeological Site**, 3400 N Museum Point (daily 8am–sunset; cars $2, pedestrians and cyclists $1; ☎352/795-3817), where temple, burial, and shell midden mounds are still visible. Inside the **visitor center** (Thurs–Mon 9am–5pm) there is an enlightening

▲ Manatees at Crystal River

assessment of finds from the 450 graves discovered here, indicating trade links with tribes far to the north. More fascinating, however, are the connections with the south. The site contains two *stelae*, or ceremonial stones, much more commonly found in Mexico, and the engravings – thought to be faces of sun deities – suggest large-scale solar ceremonies were conducted here. The sense of the past and the serenity of the setting make the site a highly evocative educational experience. Right down the road from the archeological site is the **Crystal River Preserve State Park**, 3266 N Sailboat Ave (visitor's center Mon–Fri 9am–5pm, park open 8am–sunset; free; ☎352/563-0450). The park offers fishing, a canoe and kayak launch, and seven nature trails. Pick up a trail map in the visitor's center. If you're here on a Monday, Wednesday, or Friday catch the ninety-minute Heritage-Eco River Tour (10.30am and 1.30pm; $10; ☎352/563-0450). A guide discusses the ways pre-Columbian Indians may have used the abundant marine resources and gives an ecological interpretation of plants and wildlife. Passengers must register an hour before each tour.

Practicalities

If you're traveling by Greyhound (the station is at 640 SE 8th Terrace; ☎352/795-4445), Crystal River makes for a convenient overnight rest. The best **accommodation** is at the *Plantation Inn*, within walking distance of the bus station at 9301 W Fort Island Trail or Rte-44 (☎352/795-4211 or 1-800/632-6262, ⓦwww.plantationinn.com; ❻), surrounded by attractive bayfront lawns, with an onsite dive shop and a golf course nearby. The *Best Western*, at 614 NW US-19 (☎352/795-3171 or 800/435-4409, ⓦwww.crystalriverresort.com; ❺), also has a dive shop.

For **food**, try ☀ *Cravings on the Water*, 614 NW US-19, next to the *Best Western* (☎352/795-2027, ⓦwww.cravingsonthewater.com), a great place for authentic Cuban sandwiches and bread, as well as delicious home-made flan and Key lime pie. Alternatives include the seafood-based *Charlie's Fish House*, 224 NW US-19 (☎352/795-3949), with river views and an adjoining fish market.

Yankeetown and around

Ten miles north of Crystal River, US-19 spans the **Florida Barge Canal**. Conceived in the 1820s to provide a cargo link between the Gulf and Atlantic coasts, work on the canal only started in the 1930s and – thanks largely to the efforts of conservationists – was abandoned in the 1970s with just six miles completed. The bridge offers a view of the Crystal River nuclear power station, the area's major employer and the reason why local telephone books carry instructions on how to survive a nuclear catastrophe.

Further on, taking any left turn off US-19 will invariably lead to some tiny, eerily quiet community where fishing on the local river is the only sign of life. One such place is **YANKEETOWN**, five miles west of Inglis on Rte-40, reputedly named for some Yankee soldiers who moved here following the Civil War. Yankeetown's claim to fame is that in 1961 Elvis filmed *Follow That Dream* in several locations around the area: the bridge over Bird Creek was the main set, and Rte-40 is also known as Follow That Dream Parkway.

The area around Yankeetown contains many parks and preserves, most with something to recommend them. Two of the largest are **Withlacoochee State Forest** (main visitor's center at 15003 Broad St, Brooksville; $1 per person per day; Mon–Fri 8am–4.30pm; ☎352/754-6896) and **Chassahowitzka National**

Wildlife Refuge (west of US-19, see p.397). Withlacoochee has hiking and canoeing opportunities as well as camping ($10–13 per night). Call the visitor's center for details or stop in to the **Chamber of Commerce**, 167 Hwy-40 W (Mon–Fri 8am–5pm; ☎352/447-3383). A great way to see the area is on a canoe or kayak trip; try Rainbow River Canoe and Kayak, 12121 Riverview, Dunnellon (☎352/489-7854, ⓦwww.rainbowrivercanoeandkayak.com; from $30). You'll be shuttled to an entry point in either the Rainbow or Withlacoochee rivers and then allowed to paddle back to your vehicle. For cheap motel **accommodation** try the *Withlacoochee Motel*, 66 US-19 S (☎352/447-2211; ❷), or you can **camp** on the banks of the Withlacoochee River at *B's Marina*, 6621 Riverside Drive (☎352/447-5888, ⓦwww .bmarinacampground.net; $25). For slightly more upmarket accommodation, opt for the lovely *Pine Lodge Bed and Breakfast*, 649 Hwy-40 W (☎352/447-7463, ⓦwww.pinelodgefla.com; ❺), which has a great mid-week deal of only $68 Mon–Thurs. *Our Pub*, 253 Hwy-40 W (☎352/447-2406) in Inglis is a local favorite and a great place to grab a beer and some inexpensive pub grub.

Cedar Key

Whatever you do on your way north, don't deny yourself a day or two at the splendidly isolated and charmingly scenic community of **CEDAR KEY**. To find it, turn west off US-19 onto Rte-24 at the hamlet of Otter Creek and drive for 24 miles until the road ends. In the 1860s, the railroad from Fernandina Beach (see "The Northeast," p.357) ended its journey here, turning the community – which occupies one of several small islands – into a thriving port. When ships got bigger and moved on to deeper harbors, Cedar Key began cutting down its cypress, pine, and cedar trees to fuel a pencil-producing industry. Inevitably, the trees were soon gone, and by 1900 Cedar Key was all but a ghost town. The few who stayed eked out a living from fishing and harvesting oysters, as many of the thousand-strong population still do. Cedar Key has, however, undergone a revival, with many decaying, timber-framed homes becoming restaurants and shops. The town's remoteness, however (there's no public transport from other communities in the area), makes it unlikely it will ever be deluged with visitors – the only busy periods are during the Seafood Festival during the third full weekend in October and the fine-arts show during April – and the place remains a fascinating example of the old Florida. The **Chamber of Commerce**, 618 Second St (Mon, Tues, Wed, & Fri 9am–1pm, Sun 10am–2pm; ☎352/543-5600, ⓦwww.cedarkey.org), has a cozy visitor's center with all the usual information. When it's closed, try the Cedar Key State Museum (see p.400) or Cedar Key Bookstore on Second Street for information.

Accommodation

The accommodation options tend to reflect the town's picture-postcard setting, running the gamut from small, family-owned establishments to water-front hotels. All are perfectly serviceable, and most have fine waterfront views. Prices are higher in the center of town, while more reasonable rates can be found if you're prepared to stay on the islands closer to the mainland. You can pitch a **tent** at *Sunset Isle RV Park*, one mile from the center on Rte-24 (☎352/543-5375; $16).

Cedar Key Bed & Breakfast 810 Third St ☎ 352/543-9000 or 1-877/543-5051, Ⓦ www.cedarkeybandb.com. Relax on the back porch of this romantic wooden house, with a garden dominated by a 400-year-old live oak tree. Choose from eight comfortable, cozy rooms or a more private "Honeymoon Cottage." ❻

Dockside Motel 491 Dock St ☎ 352/543-5432 or 1-800/541-5432, Ⓦ www.dockside-cedarkey.com. You won't find anything cheaper or as centrally located as this motel, which sits on the dock a few steps away from the fishing-friendly pier. Ten well-furnished suites, one with a full kitchen, are also available. ❷

Island Hotel 373 Second St, at B St ☎ 352/543-5111 or 1-800/432-4640, Ⓦ www.islandhotel-cedarkey.com. This spot is full of character, with sloping wooden floors, overhanging verandas, and sepia murals. Ask about the ghosts that supposedly haunt three of the rooms. ❺

The Island Place First St, at C St ☎ 352/543-5307 or 1-800/780-6522, Ⓦ www.islandplace-ck .com. One- and two-bedroom suites with fully equipped kitchens and balconies overlooking the pool and the waters of the Gulf. ❺

Pirates' Cove Rte-24 ☎ 352/543-5141, Ⓦ www.piratescovecottages.com. The location about half a mile from the town center results in cheaper rates and views of the bayou, with its diverse birdlife. Accommodation is in six refurbished cottages. ❹

The island and around

With its rustic, ramshackle galleries, old wooden houses on Second Street, and the glittering reflections off the waters of Cedar Key's unspoiled bay, the island is perfect for exploring. The **Cedar Key State Museum**, 12231 SW 166 Court (Thurs–Mon 9am–5pm; $1; ☎ 352/543-5350), exhibits household items from the past and boasts an enormous collection of exotic shells from around the region. The **Historical Society Museum**, on the corner of D and Second streets (Mon–Fri & Sun 1–4pm, Sat 11am–5pm; $1; ☎ 352/543-5549), reveals this, in fact, is not the original site of Cedar Key. The uninhabited island cloaked in foliage across the water bore the town's name until the end of the nineteenth century, when a hurricane tore every building to pieces. The devastated ruins of a bed and breakfast still sulk near the dock and now serve as the adopted home of a troupe of pelicans, whose presence has helped make this Cedar Key's most popular postcard scene. The museum also supplies various leaflets, and sells maps of Cedar Key and a **historic walking tour** guide for $4.50.

If you're staying for several days, take a boat trip out to the twelve islands within a five-mile radius of Cedar Key – set aside in 1929 by President Hoover as the **Cedar Keys National Wildlife Refuge**. *Island Hopper*, at the City Marina on Dock Street (☎ 352/543-5904, Ⓦ www.cedarkeyisland hopper.com), operates daily cruises to **Seahorse Key** for $21 and also rents out boats. Seahorse Key boasts a pretty lighthouse built in 1851. At 52 feet, it stands on the highest point of land on the Gulf Coast. Landing is prohibited on the key between March and June when the island becomes a sanctuary for nesting birds; during this time the *Island Hopper* lands at another key, Atsena Otie. A more intimate option is Captain Doug's Tidewater Tours, at the City Marina (☎ 352/543-9523, Ⓦ www.tidewater tours.com). Captain Doug, a walking encyclopedia of the area's nature and history, leads the Backwater Tour ($35) where you're likely to spot a spectacular variety of birds, including nesting bald eagles and dolphins. Also worthwhile are the **kayak tours** run by Wild Florida Adventures (☎ 352/528-3984, Ⓦ www.wild-florida.com; all tours $50), which explore much of the Big Bend as well as the lower Suwannee River. Their half-day tours cover the **Lower Suwannee National Wildlife Refuge**, which fronts 26 miles of the Gulf of Mexico and is an ideal place to see the nesting grounds of the white ibis, egrets, blue herons, ospreys, and brown pelicans.

Eating

While there aren't a lot of places to eat in Cedar Key, it's nevertheless the best place in the Big Bend for dining out, offering the largest selection of restaurants and cafés between Tampa Bay and the Panhandle. Oysters, smoked mullet, and fried trout are among the local specialties.

Anne's Other Place 360 Dock St ☏ 352/543-5494. Locals flock to this casual waterfront spot for fresh seafood and the signature Heart of Palm salad. Entrées are around $7.

Blue Desert Café 12518 Rte-24 ☏ 352/543-9111. The food – all of it cooked from scratch, so be patient – includes fine pizzas, *bruschetta*, and a salsa dip to die for. A friendly ambience and thirty different types of beer add to the appeal. Closed Sun & Mon. Entrées range from $10–15.

Coconuts of Cedar Key 330 Dock St ☏ 352/543-6390, ⓦ www.coconutsofcedarkey.com. More of a sports bar than a restaurant, it's nonetheless a great spot to wile away an afternoon. Good pub food like shrimp and oyster baskets ($9, with coleslaw or fries included) will fill you up.

Cook's Café 434 Second St ☏ 352/543-5548. A good bet for breakfast as well as for the fresh grouper and shrimp served at reasonable prices during the day. Lunch mains are around $10.

The Island Room 192 Second St ☏ 352/543-6520, ⓦ www.islandroom.com. Cedar Key's most elegant restaurant, boasting a justly famous crab bisque and great home-made pastas ($15) and desserts.

North Central Florida

The alternative and quicker option to taking US-19 from the Tampa Bay area to the Panhandle would be to follow I-75 up through the center of the state, then, instead of continuing north into Georgia, turn west onto I-10 to Tallahassee. As unrelentingly ordinary as I-75 is, just a few miles to the east of the interstate are the villages and small towns that typified Florida before the arrival of mass tourism. The region has just two appreciably sized towns, one of which, **Ocala**, is the access point to a sprawling national forest. The other, **Gainesville**, holds a major university and a terrain that varies from rough scrub to resplendent grassy acres lubricated by dozens of natural springs. This part of Florida is definitely worth a day or two of your time, as much for its charming atmosphere compared with points further south as for things to see or do.

Ocala and around

Known throughout the US for the champion runners bred and trained at the thoroughbred horse farms occupying its green and softly undulating surrounds, **OCALA** itself is a town without much to shout about – though it makes an agreeable base for seeing some of the surrounding pristine natural springs. The **visitor center**, 110 E Silver Springs Blvd (Mon–Fri 8am–5pm; ☏ 352/629-8051), issues city maps, can direct you to the town's mildly interesting historic districts, and tell you which of the **horse farms** are open for free, self-guided tours.

The Don Garlits and Appleton museums

Ten miles south of Ocala, at Exit 341 off I-75, the **Don Garlits Museum of Drag Racing** (daily 9am–5pm; $15; ☎352/245-8661 or 1-877/271-3278, ⓦ www.garlits.com) parades dozens of low-slung drag-racing vehicles, including the "Swamp Rat" machines that propelled local legend Don Garlits to 270mph over the drag tracks during the mid-1950s. Yellowing press cuttings and grainy films chart the rise of the sport, and a subsidiary display of Chevys, Buicks and Fords – and classic hits pumped out by a Wurlitzer jukebox – evoke an *American Graffiti* atmosphere.

An outstanding assemblage of art and artifacts is found about seven miles east of I-75, inside the **Appleton Museum of Art**, 4333 NE Silver Springs Blvd (Tues-Sat 10am–5pm, Sun 12am-5pm, closed Mon; $6; ☎352/291-4455, ⓦ www.appletonmuseum.org). Spanning the globe and five thousand years, the exhibits go together with remarkable cohesion, and there's barely a dull moment over two well-filled floors. A Rodin *Thinker* cast from the original mold and paintings by Jules Breton, amid an exquisite stock of nineteenth-century French canvases are admirable enough, but the handicrafts are really special: look for the Nigerian Bo costume and mask, the brightly colored Peruvian Nazca ceramics, the Guinean Baga headdress, and the massed ranks of "Toggles" – Japanese *netsuke* figures carved from ivory.

Silver Springs

Silver Springs (hours vary; $35, children 3–10 $25; ☎352/236-2121, ⓦ www.silversprings.com) has been winning admirers since the late 1800s when Florida's first tourists came by steamboat to stare into the spring's deep, clear waters. It lies approximately one mile east of Ocala at the junction of the 5656 SR-40 and Silver Springs Boulevard.

During the 1930s and 1940s, six of the original *Tarzan* films, starring Johnny Weissmuller, were shot here. Today, the park is a rather tacky affair, with a menagerie of imported animals, such as monkeys, giraffes, and llamas marring an otherwise attractive spot. The admission fee is high, especially considering the proliferation of springs all across central and northern Florida, some of them just a few miles east in the Ocala National Forest (see p.404) or north of Gainesville (see p.406). From a conservationist point of view, Wakulla Springs near Tallahassee (see p.417) is a far better bet. However, if you do decide to visit Silver Springs, you'll get the most from the **Glass-Bottomed Boat Tour** (given a certain historical resonance by the fact the glass-bottomed boat was invented here in 1878), the **Fort King River Cruise**, and the **Wilderness Trail Ride**, all of which run regularly. If you feel like cooling off, or have kids in tow, buy a combo ticket, which allows entry to the adjacent **Wild Waters** (late March to mid-Sept, daily 10am–5pm; 10am–7pm during summer; $36, children 3–10 $27; ☎352/236-2121, ⓦ www.wildwaterspark.com), a typical water park with slides, wave pools, amusement arcades, and so on.

If you decide you want to spend a couple of days visiting Silver Springs and Wild Waters, the best choice for **lodging** is the *Days Inn*, right across from the entrance at no. 5751 (☎352/236-2575, ⓦ www.dieastsilversprings.com; ❸), an attractive establishment with two pools (one for the kids).

Rainbow Springs State Park

A more natural setting for a walk and a swim is **Rainbow Springs State Park**, about twenty miles west of Ocala and three miles north of Dunnellon, off US-41 (daily 8am–sunset; walk-in only, $1 per person; general information

352/465-8555, camping information ☎352/465-8550, and ☎1-800/326-3521 for reservations; $19 per night). From 1890 until the 1960s, this park rivaled Silver Springs as a commercial venture, but has thankfully been allowed to return to its natural state. A popular haunt for locals, it's busy on weekends, with families picnicking on the grass and splashing around in the springs. You can also explore woodland **trails** in peace and quiet, keeping an eye out for bobcats, raccoons, wild pigs, otters, and a great variety of birdlife, then have a swim in the cool, crystal-clear waters. Phone ahead to take advantage of the **ranger-led walks** (winter only) and **snorkeling** tours (summer). Day-trippers to the park can take advantage of canoe and kayak rentals for $10 per hour and **ranger-led canoe trips** from March to November. If you're camping, note that inner-tube rentals are also available for a leisurely drift down the Rainbow River.

Accommodation: Ocala and around

If you're staying over, there are plenty of **motels** lining I-75 on the way into town. Try the *Howard Johnson Inn*, 3591 NW Bonnie Heath Blvd. (☎352/629-7021; ❹), with comfortable rooms, free breakfast and a nice pool. The *Ocala Inn*, 1626 SW Pine Ave (☎352/622-4121; ❷), is another reasonably priced and central option. For real luxury, try the ⚜ *Seven Sisters Inn Bed & Breakfast*, in Ocala's historic district at 820 SE Fort King St (☎352/867-1170 or 1-800/250-3496, ⓦwww.sevensistersinn.com; ❻), where you can stay in Argentinian, Egyptian, or Indian-themed rooms. The inn also has a gift shop and hosts monthly murder mystery dinners.

Eating and drinking: Ocala and around

You'll seldom need to spend more than $10 for a filling **meal** in town, thanks to the wide selection of restaurants along East Silver Springs Boulevard. For lunch or dinner, *Piccadilly Cafeteria* at no. 1602 (☎352/622-7447), serves basic American food cafeteria-style, including four vegetables and bread for under $5, and meals with meat for a dollar or so more. At the other end of the scale, *Felix's*, 917 E Silver Springs (☎352/629-0339), is one of the area's most elegant choices and features a large, eclectic menu for lunch and dinner including five home-made soups. Alternatively, try *Harry's Seafood Bar & Grille*, 24 SE First Ave (☎352/840-0900), with outdoor seating directly on the central square. It specializes in New Orleans cooking and has great seafood and a fun-loving atmosphere.

Horseback riding

A visit to the Ocala area isn't really complete without seeing one of its numerous **horse ranches**, but you'll need a car to reach them. If you actually want to go horseback riding, rather than simply view the ranches from the road, try **Young's Paso Fino Ranch**, about four miles along SR-326, off I-75, at no. 8075 W (☎352/867-5305, ⓦwww.youngspasofino.com; book ahead). One of the country's top ranches for breeding and training Paso Fino horses (the name means "fine gait" in Spanish), Young's offers instruction before taking you out on a trail ($35 for 1hr 30min, including instruction). The horses' easy disposition and exceptionally smooth gait make them an ideal choice for beginners as well as more advanced riders.

An ideal place to rest your saddle-sore butt after a hard day's horseback riding is the **Heritage Country Inn**, set in ranch country at 14343 W Hwy-40, off I-75 (☎352/489-0023 or 1-888/240-2233, ⓦwww.heritagecountryinn.com; ❺). There are six unique bedrooms, ranging from The Plantation Room to The Thoroughbred Room.

Ocala National Forest

Translucent lakes, bubbling springs and a splendid 65-mile hiking trail bring weekend adventurers to the 400,000-acre **OCALA NATIONAL FOREST** (free), five miles east of Silver Springs on Rte-40. If you only have time for a quick look, take a spin along Rte-19 (meeting Rte-40, 22 miles into the forest) running north–south in the shade of overhanging hardwoods near the forest's eastern edge.

Juniper, Alexander, and Salt Springs

For swimming, canoeing (rent on the spot; $31.50 per one-way outing; ☎352/625-2808), gentle hiking, and lots of other people – especially on weekends and holidays – the forest has three warm-water springs that fit the bill, and each of them has a campground. The easiest to reach from Silver Springs is **Juniper Springs** (☎352/625-3147; $4 per person, $17 per primitive tentsite), fifteen miles ahead on Rte-40, particularly suited to hassle-free canoeing with a seven-mile marked course. **Alexander Springs** (☎352/669-3522; $4 per person, $17 per tentsite), on Rte-445 off SR-19 about ten miles southeast of Juniper Springs, has good canoeing, too, and its see-through waters are perfect for snorkeling.

To the north of the forest, reachable on Rte-314 or Rte-19, the most developed site – it even has a gas station and laundromat – is **Salt Springs** (☎352/685-2048; $4 per person, $17 per primitive tentsite, $23 for electric hook-up). Despite the name, the springs here flow with 52 million gallons of fresh water a day, and the steady 72°F temperature stimulates a semi-tropical landscape of vividly colored plants and palm trees.

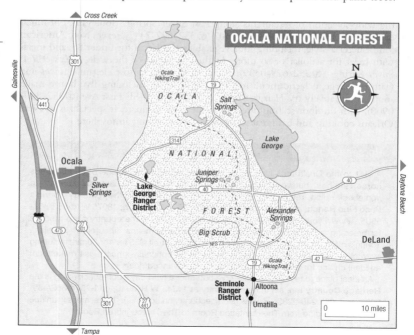

▲ Ocala National Forest

At the time of writing the springs were closed for refurbishment, so call ahead for details.

The Ocala Hiking Trail

The 67-mile **Ocala Hiking Trail** runs through the forest, traversing many remote, swampy areas, and passing the three springs mentioned opposite. Very **basic campgrounds** (free) appear at regular intervals (closed during the mid-Nov to early Jan hunting season). At the district rangers' offices (see box below), pick up the excellent leaflet describing the trail, which is part of the Florida State Scenic Trail.

However keen you might be, you're unlikely to have the time or stamina to tackle the entire trail, though one exceptional area that merits the slog required to get to it is **Big Scrub**, an imposingly severe, semi-arid landscape with sand dunes – and sometimes wild deer – moving across it. The biggest problem at Big Scrub is lack of shade from the scorching sun, and the fact the nearest facilities of any kind are miles away – don't come unprepared. Big Scrub is in the southern part of the forest, seven miles along Forest Road 573, off Rte-19, twelve miles north of Altoona.

Ocala National Forest information

The Ocala **Chamber of Commerce**, 110 E Silver Springs Blvd (Mon–Fri 10am–5pm; ☏352/629-8051), has a county map and general information, and visitor centers are located at three park entrances (daily 9am–4.30pm; ☏352/236-0288, 685-3070, or 669-7495), offering details on every campground. The latest camping updates are available by phoning the camping areas at Juniper, Alexander, and Salt Springs (see opposite). For specialist hiking tips, call one of the district ranger offices; the northern and southern halves of the forest are administered respectively by the Lake George Ranger District, 17147 E Hwy-40, Silver Springs (☏352/625-2520), and the Seminole Ranger District, 40929 Rte-19, Umatilla (☏352/669-3153).

North of Ocala

From the monotonous I-75, you'd never guess the thirty or so miles of hilly, lakeside terrain just to the east contain some of the most distinctive and insular villages in the state. Beyond the bounds of public transport, they can be reached only by driving; head **north from Ocala** on US-301.

Cross Creek and the Marjorie Kinnan Rawlings Home

Native Floridians often wax lyrical about Marjorie Kinnan Rawlings, author of the international classic *The Yearling*, the Pulitzer Prize-winning tale of the coming of age of a Florida farmer's son, and *Cross Creek*, which describes the daily activities of country folk in **CROSS CREEK**, about twenty miles from Ocala on Rte-325 (off US-301). Leaving her husband in New York, Rawlings spent her most productive years writing and tending a citrus grove here during the 1930s – her experience being faithfully re-created in the 1983 film *Cross Creek*.

The restored **Marjorie Kinnan Rawlings Home** (Thurs–Sun 10–11am & 1–4pm; guided tours on the hour; $3, children $2; grounds are open daily, $2, 9am–5pm; ☎352/466-3672) offers an eye-opening insight into the toughness of the "cracker" lifestyle.

Micanopy and Paynes Prairie

Four miles north of Cross Creek, Rte-346 branches off to meet US-441 just outside **MICANOPY**. A voguish vacation destination during the late 1800s, the town, named after a Seminole chief, has made an effort to win back visitors by restoring many of its century-old brick buildings and turning some into antique and craft shops. The atmosphere is most evocative of the slowed-down pace of the Old South, with its enormous live oak trees and the Spanish moss trailing down to the ground, and you may even be drawn to **stay**. The top choice would certainly be the glorious Greek-revival *Herlong Mansion*, 402 NE Cholokka Blvd (☎352/466-3322, ⓦwww.herlong.com; ⓺), whose facade of Corinthian columns will make you feel you've just stepped onto the set of *Gone with the Wind*.

Nearby, **Paynes Prairie Preserve State Park** (daily 8am–sunset ☎352/466-3397; cars $4, cyclists and pedestrians $1; camping ☎1-800/326-3521; $15 with electricity), filling 21,000 acres between Micanopy and Gainesville, is well-stocked with wildlife: cranes, hawks, otters, turtles, and various wading birds all make homes here, as do many alligators. During weekends from November to April, **ranger-led hikes** ($2 suggested donation; reservations ☎352/466-4100) uncover the fascinating natural and social history of the area: habitations have been traced back to 10,000 BC. Without a guide, you can bone up on the background at the **visitor center** (daily 9am–4pm), about a mile from Micanopy off US-441, and peer into the moody wilderness from the nearby **observation tower**.

Gainesville and around

Without the University of Florida, **GAINESVILLE**, 35 miles north of Ocala, would be just another slow-paced rural community nodding off in the Florida heartland. As it is, the daintily sized place, once called Hogtown, is

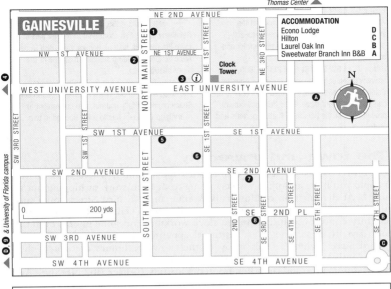

given a boost by its 40,000 students, who bring a lively, liberal spirit and account for the only decent **nightlife** in central Florida outside Orlando. This, combined with a few low-key targets in and around the town and some attractive and reasonable accommodation, makes Gainesville a deserving base for a day or two.

Arrival, information, and transportation

Gainesville's Greyhound **bus** station is centrally located at 101 NE 23rd Ave (☎352/376-5252), with services going either north to Tallahassee or south to Orlando and Miami. The old buildings are easily tracked down with the *Historic Gainesville* brochure issued by the **Visitors and Convention Bureau**, 30 E University Ave (Mon–Fri 8.30am–5pm; ☎352/374-5260 or 1-866/778-5002, ⊛www.visitgainesville.com). From the town center, it's an easy fifteen-minute walk along University Avenue to the university; though if you're feeling very lazy, take a **bus** (any number from #1 to #10) from beside the Clock Tower.

Accommodation

Although Gainesville has rows of low-cost **motels** a couple of miles outside the center along SW Thirteenth Street and scads of chain spots at the I-75 exits, these fill quickly when the University of Florida Gators are playing at home. Gainesville also has some of the most pleasant **B&Bs** in the state. The closest tent-friendly **campground** is ten miles south at the Paynes Prairie Preserve State Park (☎352/466-3397; $15 with electricity) – see opposite.

Econo Lodge 2649 SW Thirteenth St ☎352/373-7816. Nearer to downtown than many of the inexpensive motels, here you'll find reasonably priced, basic rooms, all with mini refrigerator and microwave. ❷

Hilton 1714 SW 34th St ☎352/371-3600, ⓦwww.hilton.com. The most luxurious hotel in Gainesville is strategically located right next to the campus (but about three miles from downtown), presumably for the benefit of visiting parents and professors. ❻

Laurel Oak Inn 221 SE Seventh St ☎352/373-4535, ⓦwww.laureloakinn.com. Relatively small, five-room B&B in a quiet part of town littered with historic homes; this 1885 Queen Anne Victorian building stands out as one of the more beautiful. ❻

Sweetwater Branch Inn B&B 625 E University Ave ☎352/373-6760, ⓦwww.sweetwaterinn.com. Spacious, beautifully laid out, and convenient to everything the town has to offer, housed in two gracefully restored period homes. ❻

The town and university

Impressive sights are few in Gainesville's quiet center, where most of the people you'll see are office workers going to or from work or nipping out to lunch. At the junction of University Avenue and NE First Street you'll spot the **Clock Tower**, an undramatic relic culled from Gainesville's nineteenth-century courthouse. Inside are the clock workings and some photos from the old days. If these whet your historical appetite, explore northwards along Third Street, which reveals many of the showcase homes of turn-of-the-nineteenth-century Gainesville – Queen Anne, Colonial and various Revival styles dominate – and the palm-fronted **Thomas Center**, 302 NE Sixth Ave (Mon–Fri 9am–5pm, Sat & Sun 1–4pm; free; ☎352/334-5064), once a posh hotel and restaurant, which now hosts small-scale art and historical exhibitions.

The University of Florida

Most of Gainesville's through traffic passes half a mile west of the town center along Thirteenth Street (part of US-441), from which the **University of Florida** campus stretches three miles west from its main entrance by the junction with University Avenue. Visit the **information booth**, facing SW Second Street, for a free map, without which it's easy to get lost in the extensive grounds.

After the university opened in 1906, the early alumni gave Florida's economy a leg-up by pioneering the state's fantastically successful citrus farms. These days, the curriculum is no longer devoted solely to agriculture and the university's modern buildings dominate the campus, though the first you'll see are the red-brick "Collegiate Gothic" structures favored by US turn-of-the-nineteenth-century academic institutions. In the center of the campus, the 1953 **Century Tower** serves as a navigational aid and a time-keeping device – its electric bells issue a nerve-shattering carillon every hour.

University sports venues

Beyond the tower, the 83,000-seat **Florida Field/Ben Hill Griffin Stadium**, nicknamed "The Swamp" – home of the Gators football team and a monument to the popularity of college sports in Florida – can hardly be missed, and neither can the adjacent **O'Connel Center** (☎352/392-5500), an indoor sports venue, entering which is akin to walking into a giant balloon. Aside from staging evening volleyball and basketball games, and entertaining design buffs, the building offers only a cool, refreshing breather from the Florida heat.

Take in the temporary shows in the **University Gallery**, inside the Fine Arts Building (Tues 10am–8pm, Wed–Fri 10am–5pm, Sat noon–4pm; free; T 352/273-3000), which capture the best student art. Head back outdoors and walk about two miles west along Museum Road to the tidy **University Garden**, where a concealed footpath leads to **Lake Alice** (overlooked by a wooden observation platform gradually losing its battle against the surrounding vegetation), where the constant scampering of lizards and the plentiful alligators mean keeping your guard up as you gaze over the sizeable lake.

At the corner of SW 34th Street and Hull Road is the **University of Florida Cultural Complex**, where the **Florida Museum of Natural History** (Mon–Sat 10am–5pm, Sun 1–5pm; $6 suggested donation; T 352/846-2000, W www.flmnh.ufl.edu) focuses on Florida's prehistory and wildlife. The **Harn Museum of Art** (Tues–Fri 11am–5pm, Sat 10am–5pm, Sun 1–5pm; free; T 352/392-9826, W www.harn.ufl.edu) has an intriguing permanent collection with an emphasis on ethnic works and hosts about twelve temporary exhibitions per year. The nearby **Center for the Performing Arts**, 315 Hull Rd (T 352/392-1900 for ticket information, W www.performingarts.ufl.edu), brings in traveling Broadway plays, symphonies, popular music, family entertainment, and educational programs.

Eating

You can find plenty of good restaurants in Gainesville. As a general rule, head to the town center for a more refined dining experience; the places around the campus offer filling meals at rock-bottom prices.

Burrito Brothers Taco Co 1402 W University Ave T 352/378-5948. This univeristy institution has been lining students' stomachs with tasty and very cheap burritos ($5) for over 25 years.

Emiliano's Café 7 SE First Ave T 352/375-7381, W www.emilianoscafe.com. Come here for pan-Latin cuisine, from a full tapas menu to Jamaican jerk pork loin. You can enjoy your meal at outdoor tables, and they also serve a hearty Sunday brunch and the best mojitos in town. Entrées around $15.

Leonardo's 706 706 W University Ave T 352/378-2001, W www.leonardos706.com. California pizzas and lots of seafood offerings. Don't miss the made-to-order Sunday brunch ($16) with such goodies as French toast made from home-made *challah* bread, and filet

mignon with eggs and hollandaise sauce. Entrées from $17.

Mark's US Prime 201 SE Second Ave T 352/336-0077, W www.marksprimesteakhouse.com. Upmarket steak restaurant with some great fish dishes as well like the pistachio tuna. Most main dishes cost over $25. Closed Sun.

The Top 30 N Main St T 352/337-1188. Young, arty, and hip – a good choice if all you want is a pleasant spot to refuel on salads or sandwiches for about $5. They also serve Sunday brunch.

The Wine and Cheese Gallery 113 N Main St T 352/372-8446. An amazing selection of international wines and cheeses, plus fresh breads, hors d'oeuvres, and crudités in a warm, inviting setting. Most dishes $5–15.

Drinking, entertainment, and nightlife

The town's students ensure a bright **nightlife**, with live rock music being especially easy to find. Check the "Scene" section of Thursday's *Gainesville Sun*, or the free *Insite* newspaper, found in most bars and restaurants, for details. From April to October in the Downtown Plaza, opposite the Clock Tower, you can catch special events such as jazz concerts and open-air film screenings on Friday evenings.

Hippodrome State Theatre 25 SE Second Place
☎352/375-4477, ⊛www.thehipp.org. This
grandiose building dominating the town center
hosts contemporary plays, films and exhibits by
local artists.
Lillian's Music Store 112 SE First St
☎352/372-1010. A Gainesville institution,
featuring live bands that play grunge, indie,
Southern, and acoustic rock. More of a local spot
than a student hangout.

Maude's 101 SE Second Pl ☎352/336-9646.
A smaller, more intimate place to enjoy a coffee
and a slice of cake than the *Starbucks* across the
street.
The University Club 18 E University Ave
☎352/378-6814. Downtown's no. 1 gay venue,
with three levels (a bar, club, and disco). Always
crowded and lively, with a deck out back.

Kanapaha Botanical Gardens

Flower fanciers shouldn't miss the 62-acre **Kanapaha Botanical Gardens**
(Mon–Wed & Fri 9am–5pm, Sat & Sun 9am–sunset; $6, children 6–13 $3,
☎352/372-4981, ⊛www.kanapaha.org), five miles southwest of central
Gainesville on Rte-24 (also known as Archer Rd), reachable on bus #75. The
summer months are a riot of color and fragrances, although the design of the
gardens means there's always something in bloom. Besides vines and bamboos,
and special sections planted to attract butterflies and hummingbirds, the
highlight is the herb garden, whose aromatic bed is raised to nose-level to
encourage sniffing.

Dudley Farm

Between Gainesville and Newberry, seven miles west of I-75 off Rte-26, a
worthwhile excursion is a trip to the **Dudley Farm Historic State Park**,
18730 W Newberry Rd (tours of the farm Wed–Sun 9am–4pm; cars $4,
pedestrians and cyclists $1; ☎352/472-1142), a working farm where park staff
– dressed in clothes the Dudley family would have worn when the farm was
at its peak in the late 1800s – perform daily chores and allow visitors to feed
the chickens and try their hand at harvesting and other rural activities. There's
also a rotating exhibit at the visitor center chronicling the history of the
Dudley family.

The Devil's Millhopper

Of the thousands of sinkholes in Florida, few are bigger or more spectacular
than the **Devil's Millhopper**, set in a state geological site (Wed–Sun
9am–5pm; cars $2, pedestrians and cyclists $1; ☎352/955-2008), seven miles
northwest of Gainesville at 4732 NW 53rd Ave. Formed by the gradual
erosion of limestone deposits and the collapse of the resultant cavern's
ceiling, the lower reaches of this 120-foot-deep bowl-shaped dent have a
temperature significantly cooler than the surface, allowing species of alpine
plant and animal life to thrive. A winding boardwalk delivers you into
the thickly vegetated depths, where dozens of tiny waterfalls trickle all
around you.

North of Gainesville

Traveling **north of Gainesville** puts you in easy striking distance of the
Panhandle to the west, and Jacksonville, the major city of the northeast coast,
but it's best not to be in a hurry. Choose to stop a night or two here and you'll

find yourself in the heart of some of the most pristine natural springs in the state – as well as some charming, out-of-the-way towns of the Florida of yesteryear.

High Springs and the Parks

Sticking to US-441 puts you in **HIGH SPRINGS**, a good base for exploring the area's plentiful freshwater springs. If you decide to stay, top choice for a few nights is the ⚐ *Grady House*, 420 NW First Ave (☎386/454-2206, ⒲www.gradyhouse.com; ➎), where the owners have poured their hearts into creating a gorgeous gazebo garden to go with the comfortable rooms (some have antique iron beds). For less expensive accommodation, there's *The High Springs Country Inn*, along US-441, 520 NW Santa Fe Blvd (☎386/454-1565, ⒲www.highspringscountryinn.com; ➋), with scrubbed oak and cherry wood furniture that give the motel-style rooms a homely feel.

The High Springs area is replete with crystal-clear springs, streams and rivers – waters that lend themselves to leisurely kayaking, canoeing or inner-tube rafting. You can rent **canoes** in most of the parks for $15–25 a day. Weekdays, when beavers, otters, and turtles sometimes share the river, are the best time to come to the area; weekend crowds scare much of the wildlife away. Try **Poe Springs** (9am–sunset; $6, children 6–13 $3; ☎386/454-1992), **Blue Springs** (9am–7pm 9am-5.30pm in winter; $10, children 5–12 $3; camping $15 per person, children 5–12 $6; ☎386/454-1369; ⒲www.bluespringspark.com), and **Ginnie Springs**, just to the west along County Road 340 (hours vary; $12, children 7–14 $3; camping $18 per person, children 7–14 $6, cottage $175 per night for up to four adults; ☎386/454-7188, ⒲www.ginniespringsoutdoors.com). The latter also has a full-service **scuba** shop onsite and offers scuba diving as well as snorkeling; costs start at $30. There's also **O'Leno State Park** (8am–sunset; cars $4, pedestrians and cyclists $1; ☎386/454-1853) and **Ichetucknee Springs State Park** (daily 8am–sunset; cars $5, pedestrians and cyclists $1, another $5 per person for river use; ☎386/497-4690) to the north and northwest, off US-441, which offers the possibility of cave diving to explore the labyrinthine domain of the underground rivers.

The Stephen Foster Folk Culture Center

Twelve miles north of Lake City, off US-41, the **Stephen Foster Folk Culture Center** (daily 8am–sunset; cars $4, pedestrians and cyclists $1; ☎386/397-2733, camping ☎1-800/326-3521; $16 per night or cabins $90 per night; ⒲www.floridastateparks.org/stephenfoster) offers a tribute to the man who composed Florida's state song *The Old Folks At Home*, immortalizing the waterway ("Way down upon the S'wanee river …") flowing by here on its 250-mile meander from Georgia's Okefenokee Swamp to the Gulf of Mexico. Foster never actually saw the river but simply used "S'wanee" as a convenient Deep South-sounding allusion. Besides exploring Florida's musical roots, the center has a sentimental display about Foster, who penned a hatful of classic American songs including *Camptown Races*, *My Old Kentucky Home*, and *Oh! Susanna* – instantly familiar melodies, which ring out through the oak-filled park from a bell tower.

Travel details

Trains (Amtrak)

Ocala to: Miami (bus to Lakeland; 1 daily; 8hr)
St Petersburg to: Orlando (bus to Tampa; 1 daily; 3hr).
Tampa to: Jacksonville (2 daily; 5hr); Miami (1 daily; 5hr 20min); Orlando (1 daily; 2hr).

Buses

Crystal River to: Tallahassee (2 daily; 3hr 35min); Tampa (2 daily; 2hr 40min).
Gainesville to: Miami (6 daily; 9–10hr); Ocala (6 daily; 1hr 25min); Orlando (6 daily; 3hr); Tallahassee (3 daily; 2hr 35min); Tampa (5 daily; 5hr 45min).

Lakeland to: Orlando (3 daily; 1hr 45min); Tampa (3 daily; 45min); West Palm Beach (3 daily; 6hr 20min–8hr 45min).
Ocala to: Gainesville (5 daily; 1hr 10min); Miami (7 daily; 8–9hr); Orlando (7 daily; 1hr 25min); Tallahassee (3 daily; 3hr 50min); Tampa (6 daily; 5–7hr).
St Petersburg to: Tampa (4 daily; 30min–1hr).
Tampa to: Crystal River (2 daily; 2hr 40min); Fort Myers (4 daily; 4hr); Gainesville (4 daily; 6–10hr); Jacksonville (6 daily; 5–7hr 30min); Miami (7 daily; 7–9hr); Ocala (6 daily; 4–8hr); Orlando (6 daily; 1hr 40min); Sarasota (4 daily; 2hr); St Petersburg (4 daily; 30min–1hr); Tallahassee (5 daily; 6–9hr).

The Panhandle

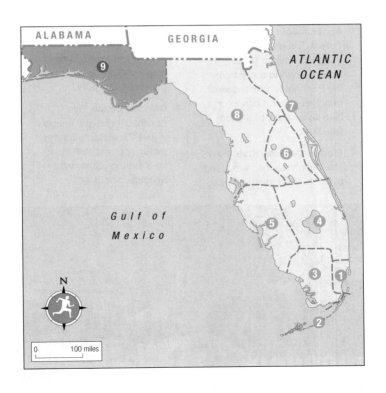

* **The Old City Cemetery** A good starting point for learning about African American history in Tallahassee. See p.422

* **Wakulla Springs** Take to the waters of the biggest and deepest natural springs in the world on a glass-bottomed boat tour. See p.428

* **Apalachicola National Forest** The great outdoors reasserts itself in these woods, a world away from the Panhandle's busy tourist beaches – rent a canoe or hike some trails to explore. See p.429

* **Florida Caverns State Park** The deep caverns here, used by Seminole Indians to hide from Andrew Jackson's army, hold magnificent calcite formations. See p.431

* **Scenic Route 30-A** Get off the beaten track on this eighteen-mile stretch of highway that runs through some of the prettiest beach communities the Panhandle has to offer. See p.441

* **Seaside** The dollhouse architecture and manicured streets and lawns of this resort should be seen to be believed. See p.442

* **Grayton Beach** This ramshackle artists' enclave is just the antidote for the picture-perfect sterility of neighboring community Seaside. See p.443

▲ Seaside

9

The Panhandle

Butting up against the southernmost borders of both Alabama and Georgia, the long, narrow **Panhandle** has more in common with the Deep South than it does with the rest of the state. Miami and Tampa residents tell countless jokes lampooning the folksy lifestyles of the people here – undeniably more rural and down-to-earth than their counterparts around the rest of the state – but the Panhandle has more to offer than many give it credit for. You certainly won't get a true picture of Florida without seeing at least some of it.

A century ago, the Panhandle actually *was* Florida. When Miami was still a swamp, **Pensacola**, at the Panhandle's western edge, was a busy port. Fertile soils lured wealthy plantation owners south and helped establish **Tallahassee** as a high-society gathering place and administrative center – a role it retains as the state capital. The great Panhandle forests fueled a timber boom that brought new towns and an unrivaled prosperity, but the decline of cotton, the felling of too many trees, and the building of the East Coast Railroad eventually left the Panhandle high and dry.

Today, the region divides neatly in two. Much of the **inland Panhandle** consists of small farming towns that see few visitors, despite their friendly rhythm, fine examples of Old South architecture, and proximity to springs, sinkholes, and the **Apalachicola National Forest** – perhaps the best place in Florida to disappear into the wilderness. The **coastal Panhandle**, on the other hand, is inundated with tourists who flock in from the southern states and wreak havoc during the riotous student Spring Breaks. Much of the coastline is marked by rows of hotels and condos, but there are also protected areas that are home to some of the finest stretches of unspoiled sand anywhere in the state. The blinding white sands are almost pure quartz, washed down over millions of years from the Appalachian Mountains, and they squeak when you walk on them. Not to be outshone, the Gulf of Mexico's waters here are two-tone: emerald green close to the shore and deep blue further out.

Provided you're driving, **getting around** is easy. Across the inland Panhandle, **I-10** carries the through traffic, and **US-90** links the little places and many of the natural sights between Tallahassee and Pensacola. It's simple, too, to turn south off I-10 or US-90 and get to the coast in under an hour. The main route along the coast is **US-98**, with a number of smaller, scenic roads leading off it. Several daily Greyhound **buses** connect the bigger centers, but rural and coastal services are fewer, and most parts see no bus services at all.

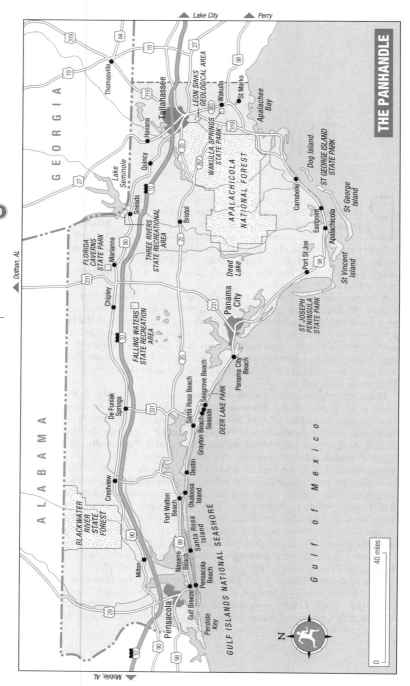

THE PANHANDLE

The inland Panhandle

Vast tracts of oak and pine trees, dozens of winding rivers, and a handful of moderately sized agricultural bases make much of the **inland Panhandle** powerfully evocative of Florida in the days before mass tourism took hold – and this distinct character is the main reason for making the effort to visit this part of the state. Despite the presence of the sociable state capital, **Tallahassee**, it's the insular rural communities strung along US-90 – between Tallahassee and the busy coastal city of **Pensacola** – that set the tone of the region. These small towns, including **Marianna**, **Chipley**, and **De Funiak Springs**, all grew rich from the timber industry at the turn of the twentieth century and now pull their earnings by working some of the richest soil in Florida. Thanks to some architectural gems, they warrant a look as you pass through to the area's compelling natural features, which include the state's only explorable caverns and two massive forests.

Tallahassee and around

State capital it may be, but **TALLAHASSEE** is a provincial city of oak trees and soft hills that won't take more than a day or two to explore. Around its small grid of central streets – where you'll find plenty of reminders of Florida's formative years – briefcase-clutching bureaucrats mingle with some of Florida State University's 35,000 students, who brighten the mood considerably and keep the city awake late into the night.

Though built on the site of an important prehistoric meeting place and taking its name from Apalachee Indian (*talwa* meaning "town," and *ahassee* meaning "old"), Tallahassee's **history** really begins with Florida's incorporation into the US and the search for an administrative base between the former regional capitals, Pensacola and St Augustine. Once this site was chosen, the local Native Americans – the Tamali tribe – were unceremoniously dispatched to make room for a trio of log cabins in which the first Florida government sat in 1823.

The scene of every major wrangle in Florida politics, Tallahassee's own fortunes have been hindered by the lightning-paced development of south Florida. Oddly distanced from most of the people it governs, the city has a slow tempo and a strong sense of the past.

Arrival and information

I-10 cuts across Tallahassee's northern perimeter; turning off along Monroe Street takes you into downtown Tallahassee. **US-90** (known as Tennessee St) and **US-27** (Apalachee Parkway) are more central – arriving in or close to downtown. Coming by **bus** presents few problems. The Greyhound terminal is at 112 W Tennessee St (☎850/222-4249), within walking distance of downtown and opposite the local bus station. Tallahassee's **airport** is twelve miles southwest of Tallahassee (☎850/891-7800); frustratingly, no public transport services link it to the city. A **taxi** from the airport to the center will cost around $20 (try City Taxi ☎850/562-4222, or Yellow Cab ☎850/580-8080). Some motels offer a free pick-up service.

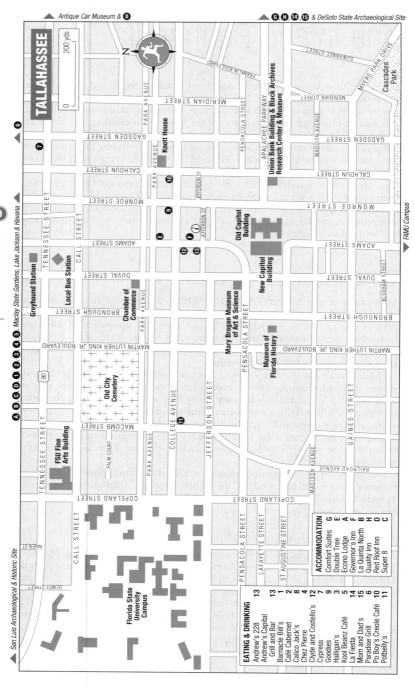

▲ San Luis Archaeological & Historic Site

▲ Antique Car Museum & **8**

▲ **6**, **H**, **14**, **15** & DeSoto State Archaeological Site

Maclay State Gardens, Lake Jackson & Havana ▲

A B C D 1 2 3 4 5

6 ▲ **7** ▲

TALLAHASSEE

0   200 yds

Antique Car Museum & **8**

SUWANNEE STREET

FRANKLIN BOULEVARD

MYERS PARK DRIVE

Cascades Park

PARK AVENUE

MERIDIAN STREET

PENSACOLA STREET

Union Bank Building & Black Archives
Research Center & Museum

APALACHEE PARKWAY

MADISON AVENUE

MERIDIAN STREET

GADSDEN STREET

GADSDEN STREET

Knott House

PARK AVENUE

CALHOUN STREET

CALHOUN STREET

10

JEFFERSON ST

MONROE STREET

MONROE STREET

9

E

ADAMS STREET

F **i**

Old Capitol Building

ADAMS STREET

CALL STREET

DUVAL STREET

12

13

New Capitol Building

DUVAL STREET

BLOXHAM STREET

Greyhound Station

TENNESSEE STREET

Local Bus Station

Chamber of Commerce

BRONOUGH STREET

Mary Brogan Museum of Art & Science

BRONOUGH STREET

PARK AVENUE

MARTIN LUTHER KING JR. BOULEVARD

Museum of Florida History

PENSACOLA STREET

MARTIN LUTHER KING JR. BOULEVARD

FSU Fine Arts Building

TENNESSEE STREET

(90)

Old City Cemetery

MACOMB STREET

COLLEGE AVENUE

11

JEFFERSON STREET

GAINES STREET

RAILROAD AVENUE

FAMU Campus ▶

FAMU Campus ▲

CALL STREET

RAVEN ST

DEWEY STREET

COPELAND STREET

PALM COURT

PARK AVENUE

COPELAND STREET

Florida State University Campus

PENSACOLA STREET

LAFAYETTE STREET

ST AUGUSTINE STREET

MADISON AVENUE

N

EATING & DRINKING

Andrew's 228	13
Andrew's Capital Grill and Bar	13
Barnacle Bill's	1
Café Cabernet	8
Calico Jack's	4
Chez Pierre	2
Clyde and Costello's	12
Cypress	7
Goodies	9
Halligan's	3
Kool Beanz Café	14
La Fiesta	15
Mom and Dad's	5
Paradise Grill	6
Po Boy's Creole Café	10
Potbelly's	11

ACCOMMODATION

Comfort Suites	G
Double Tree	E
Econo Lodge	A
Governor's Inn	F
La Quinta North	B
Quality Inn	H
Red Roof Inn	D
Super 8	C

Information

The **Tallahassee Area Convention and Visitor Information Center**, 106 E Jefferson St (Mon–Fri 8am–5pm, Sat 9am–1pm; ☎850/606-2305 or 1-800/628-2866, ⊛www.visittallahassee.com) stocks large numbers of leaflets and guides for the city. While there, be sure to pick up the engaging *Walking Guide to Historic Downtown Tallahassee* booklet, a free, comprehensive guide to the buildings and history of the area.

Getting around

Downtown Tallahassee can easily be explored **on foot**. Catch local buses at 111 W Tennessee St, across from the Greyhound station (StarMetro ☎850/891-5200, ⊛www.talgov.com) to reach outlying destinations. Rides cost $1.25 per journey. Collect a route map and timetable from the bus station (officially known as CK Steele Plaza) at the corner of Tennessee and Duval streets. Despite the area's hills, there is plenty of good **cycling** terrain. You can rent a bike from The Great Bicycle Shop, 1909 Thomasville Rd (☎850/224-7461).

Accommodation

Finding **accommodation** in Tallahassee is only a problem during two periods: the sixty-day sitting of the state legislature beginning with the first Tuesday in March – if you're arriving then, try to turn up on a Friday or Saturday when the power-brokers have gone home – and on fall weekends when the Seminoles (Florida State University's immensely popular football team) are playing at home. If you can't avoid these periods, book well ahead and be prepared to spend much more for a room. The cheapest **hotels** and **motels** are on N Monroe Street about three miles north of downtown, near the Interstate.

Comfort Suites 1026 Apalachee Parkway ☎850/224-3200, ⊛www.comfortsuites.com. The beds are heavenly at this comfortable, spotless motel, within walking distance of the capital. There's also a delicious, free continental breakfast. ➏

Double Tree 101 S Adams St ☎850/224-5000. Large, business-oriented hotel in the middle of downtown. Non-drivers will appreciate the complimentary airport shuttle and drivers can park for $6 a day in the hotel parking garage. ➐

Econo Lodge 2681 N Monroe St ☎850/385-6155 or 1-800/553-2666. This basic chain motel offers complimentary continental breakfasts. Some rooms have a microwave and a refrigerator, and there's a shopping mall within walking distance for stocking up on groceries and other supplies. ➌

Governors Inn 209 S Adams St ☎850/681-6855 or 1-800/342-7717. A good alternative to the chain hotels, this luxurious downtown inn is well worth splurging for. The rooms are decorated with antique furniture, reflecting the period of the governor each is named for. Free cocktails and newspapers are also included. ➑

La Quinta North 2905 N Monroe St ☎850/385-7172. This motel has much bigger and better

rooms than the exterior suggests. If you'd prefer to stay in south Tallahassee, there's *La Quinta South* at 2850 Apalachee Parkway (US-27) ☎850/878-5099. ➍

Quality Inn 2020 Apalachee Parkway (US-27) ☎850/877-4437. Bright, modern rooms, free evening cocktails Monday through Thursday, and complimentary use of the facilities at the nearby YMCA are reasons for choosing this slightly upmarket chain hotel. ➎

Red Roof Inn 2930 Hospitality St ☎850/385-7884 or 1-800/RED-ROOF. Right off I-10, this comfortable, clean chain motel is as close to the downtown action as any of the Monroe St hotels with considerably lower rates. ➋

Super 8 2801 N Monroe St ☎850/386-8286 or 1-800/800-8000. A reasonable option for the budget traveler, this chain motel offers simple rooms with basic amenities. ➌

Tallahassee East KOA 346 KOA Rd, just off the I-10, Monticello ☎850/997-3890, ⊛www.koa .com. Although it's 20 miles east of Tallahassee, this campground offers complimentary home-made cakes and cookies on arrival and a free continental breakfast upon departure. Primitive sites are $25, ones with electricity $36, or you can rent a cabin for $45.

Downtown Tallahassee

The soul of Tallahassee is the mile-square downtown area, where the main targets – the two Capitol buildings, the Museum of Florida History, and the two universities – are within walking distance of Adams Street, the peaceful main drag. A unique and charming feature of downtown Tallahassee is the **canopy roads**, thoroughfares lined with oak trees, whose branches, heavy with Spanish moss, arch across the road. Next to the allure of these splendid tree corridors – the best examples being Miccosukee, Centerville, Old St Augustine, Meridian, and Old Bainbridge roads – the **New Capitol Building**, at the junction of Apalachee Parkway and Monroe Street (Mon–Fri 8am–5pm; free), is an eyesore. Vertical vents make the seat of Florida's legal system resemble a gigantic air conditioning unit. The only way to escape the sight of the structure, unveiled to much outrage in 1977, is to go inside, where the 22nd-floor observation level provides an unobstructed view over Tallahassee and its environs; on a clear day you can see the Gulf of Mexico. If you're visiting from mid-February to April, stop off at the fifth floor for a glance at the state house of representatives or the senate in action.

Standing in the shadow of the New Capitol Building is the **Old Capitol Building** (Mon–Fri 9am–4.30pm, Sat 10am–4.30pm, Sun noon–4.30pm; free; main entrance facing Apalachee Parkway), an 1845 Greek Revival building. Designed on a more human scale than its modern counterpart, with playful red and white awnings over its windows, it's hard to imagine the Old Capitol's walls once echoed with the decisions that shaped modern Florida. Proof is provided, however, by a political history **museum**, where the various exhibits throughout the building lift the lid on the state's juiciest scandals and controversies, including a display of a ballot used for the contested 2000 Presidential election – with all of its chads successfully punched out.

Black Archives Research Center and Museum at the Union Bank

Along Apalachee Parkway from the Old Capitol's entrance is the nineteenth-century **Union Bank Building** (Mon–Fri 9am–4pm; free; ☎850/487-3803). The bank's past has been unsteady: going bust in the 1850s after giving farmers too much credit, reopening to administer the financial needs of emancipated

▲ Canopy road, Tallahassee

slaves after the Civil War, and later serving variously as a shoe factory, a bakery, and a cosmetics shop.

Today, the building serves as an extension of the Florida Agricultural and Mechanical University's **Black Archives Research Center and Museum** (Mon–Fri 9am–5pm; free; ☎850/599-3020). Both the Research Center and the Union Bank chronicle the history and persecution of Florida's black community. The first black Floridians arrived with Spanish explorers in the sixteenth century, and many more came as runaways in the early nineteenth century, taking refuge among the Creek and Seminole Indians. Exhibits rotate between the two locations, but among the permanent exhibits at the bank is a wall honoring the achievements of some famous black Floridians including Zora Neale Hurston and Mary McLeod Bethune. The museum also has some chilling Ku Klux Klan memorabilia, including an original Klan sword and a fairly recent application for membership, which proves the organization is far from being ancient history.

The Mary Brogan Museum of Art and Science

Situated one block to the northwest behind the Capitol buildings is the **Mary Brogan Museum of Art and Science**, 350 S Duval St (Mon–Sat 10am–5pm, Sun 1–5pm; $6; ☎850/513-0700, ⓦwww.thebrogan.org), a unique institution offering a hands-on science center combined with rotating exhibitions of national art. The museum also receives touring science shows and has a very active educational program providing lots of opportunities to learn more about the displays.

The Museum of Florida History

For a well-rounded history – easily the fullest account of Florida's past anywhere in the state – visit the **Museum of Florida History**, 500 S Bronough St (Mon–Fri 9am–4.30pm, Sat 10am–4.30pm, Sun noon–4.30pm; free; ☎850/245-6400, ⓦwww.museumoffloridahistory.com). Detailed accounts of Paleo-Indian settlements and the significance of their burial and temple mounds – some of which have been found on the edge of Tallahassee – provide valuable insights into Florida's prehistory. The colonialist crusades of the Spanish, both in Florida and across South and Central America, are also explained through displays of archeological finds. However, other than portraits of hard-faced Seminole chiefs, whose Native American tribes were driven south into Florida backcountry, there's disappointingly little on the nineteenth-century Seminole Wars – one of the sadder and bloodier skeletons in Florida's closet. There's plenty, though, on the railroads that made Florida a winter resort for wealthy northerners around the turn of the twentieth century, and on the subsequent arrival of the "tin can tourists," whose nickname refers to the rickety Ford camper vans (forerunners of the modern RV) they drove to what had by then been named the "Sunshine State."

Florida State University

West from Adams Street, fraternity and sorority houses along College Avenue line the approach to **Florida State University (FSU)**. The institution has long enjoyed a strong reputation for its humanities courses, taught from the late 1800s in the Collegiate Gothic classrooms you'll see as you enter the wrought-iron gates, but has recently switched its emphasis to science and business, and the newer buildings on the far side of the campus have far less character. Shady oaks and palm trees make the grounds a pleasant place for a stroll, but there's little cause to linger. The student art of the **University Museum of Fine Arts** (Mon–Fri 9am–4pm; free; ☎850/644-6836), in the Fine Arts Building, might consume a few minutes, but you'd be better occupied rummaging around inside Bill's Bookstore, just across Call Street at 111 S Copeland St (☎850/224-3178), where the large stock includes many student cast-offs at reduced prices.

The more interesting of Tallahassee's universities is the Florida Agricultural and Mechanical University (ⓦwww.famu.edu), about a mile south of the Capitol Buildings on Wahnish Way and Gamble Street. Founded in 1887 as the State Normal College for Colored Students, the university remains a major black educational center. Housed in the historic Carnegie Library on campus is the **Black Archives Research Center and Museum** (see p.420).

The Knott House

Another important landmark in Florida's black history, and one of the city's best-restored Victorian homes, is the **Knott House Museum**, 301 E Park Ave (Wed–Fri 1–3pm, Sat 10am–3pm; free; ☎850/922-2459), with guided tours on the hour. Probably built by George Proctor, a free black man, in 1843 the building later became home to Florida's first black physician. Florida's slaves were officially emancipated in May 1865 by a proclamation read from the steps of this house. It takes its name, however, from the Knotts, a white couple who bought it in 1928. William Knott, the state treasurer during a period of economic calamity (Florida had been devastated by two hurricanes just as the country entered the Depression), became one of Florida's most respected and influential politicians until his retirement in 1941. His wife, Luella, meanwhile, devoted her energies to the temperance movement (partly through her efforts, alcohol was banned in Tallahassee for a fifty-year period) and to writing moralistic poems, many of which you'll see attached to the antiques and furnishings filling this intriguing relic, and which give it the nickname of "the house that rhymes." The absence of intrusive ropes cordoning off the exhibits allows for an unusually intimate visit.

Old City Cemetery

A somewhat different perspective on Tallahassee's past is provided by walking around the **Old City Cemetery**, between Macomb Street and Martin Luther

---

Panhandle plantations

The largest concentration of plantations in the US lies between Tallahassee and the Georgia town of Thomasville, 28 miles to the northeast. In this relatively small section of the Panhandle, some seventy plantations – most of them cotton-growing – occupy an area totaling 300,000 acres, a reminder that Tallahassee's pre-Civil War days were notable less for their political events than for the wealthy people the town managed to attract. Plantation owners included descendants of the first three US presidents and a nephew of Napoleon Bonaparte, and their houses were the epitome of fine Southern living. Several of the more notable addresses have been preserved for public viewing, of which **Goodwood**, about two miles east of downtown Tallahassee at 1600 Miccosukee Rd (tours Mon–Fri 10am–4pm, Sat 10am–2pm; $6; ☎850/877-4202, ⓦwww.goodwoodmuseum.org), is one of the more elaborate examples, situated in attractive grounds with plenty of trees. All of the antiques on display are actually in use at one point or another during the 130-year period when the house was occupied, and they range from stately mirrors to a bath painted with flowers, reflecting the diverse tastes of the various owners. Five miles south of Thomasville (and still in Georgia), **Pebble Hill** provides another good opportunity to see how the well off of the time spent their money (see p.426), while **Bellevue**, a more modest 1840s plantation house, was once home to George Washington's great-grandniece.

King Jr Boulevard (daily sunrise–sunset; free), which was established outside the city's original boundaries in 1829 and restored in 1991. Its layout, consisting of four quadrants, is a striking testament to segregation, even in death. Graves of Union soldiers lie in the southwest quarter, while those of Confederates are kept at a distance in the southeast portion; slaves and free blacks were consigned to the western half of the ground, while whites occupied the eastern part. Among the names marked on gravestones, you'll find many of Tallahassee's former leading figures.

Eating

Tallahassee's **eating** options reflect the abiding presence of time-pressed bureaucrats and cash-strapped students. The downtown area is full of places to grab a sandwich or salad at lunchtime, while restaurants serving reasonably priced, stomach-lining food are most plentiful around the town's two college campuses. There is often live music at these establishments, which tend to become more bar than restaurant as the evening progresses, and while upmarket dining can be found, such places remain the exception rather than the rule.

Andrew's 228 228 S Adams St ☏850/222-3444, ⓦwww.andrewsdowntown.com. Fancier and more expensive than its near-namesake (the *Capital Grill & Bar*, see below), this elegant restaurant includes items such as tempura fried oysters and succulent roast lamb. Entrées begin at $19.

Andrew's Capital Grill & Bar 228 S Adams St ☏850/222-3444, ⓦwww.andrewsdowntown.com. A great lunch option with plenty of seating indoors and out. Choose from burgers and various chicken and pasta dishes, as well as a weekend brunch buffet. Sandwiches around $10.

Barnacle Bill's 1830 N Monroe St ☏850/385-8734. Reasonably priced seafood restaurant with a raucous atmosphere and occasional live music on the deck. Fish dinners starting around $15.

Café Cabernet 1019 N Monroe St ☏850/224-1175, ⓦwww.cafecabernet.com. A good choice for light California-style cuisine, this café also has one of the biggest wine selections in town. Try the Coho salmon and other entrées for around $18. You can hear live jazz here in Wed–Sat.

Chez Pierre 1215 Thomasville Rd ☏850/222-0936, ⓦwww.chezpierre.com. In a beautifully restored 1920s home, this French restaurant has a good lunch menu with options like a salmon niçoise sandwich. Dinner entrées are equally as creative with items like saffron scented lobster ravioli and range from $16 to $29.

Cypress 320 E Tennessee St ☏850/513-1100, ⓦwww.cypressrestaurant.com. This small and chic option offers a Southern take on upmarket dining, with Gulf coast oysters and biscuits replacing the more conventional side items. Entrées around $20. Closed Sun and Mon.

Goodies 116 E College Ave ☏850/681-3888. One of the few places serving all-day breakfasts in downtown. The lunchtime sandwiches (under $10) are tasty, if a little small and expensive.

Kool Beanz Café 921 Thomasville Rd ☏850/224-2466, ⓦwww.koolbeanz-cafe.com. Original and pricey starters, such as fried oysters and cheese grits and andouille gumbo, are followed by entrées ($15–19) like pecan-crusted *mahi mahi* and crawfish tacos. Be warned – the spice levels are set on hot. Closed Sun.

La Fiesta 2329 Apalachee Parkway ☏850/656-3392. Fill up on the very best Mexican food in the city. The portions are huge and the service solicitous. The number of cars outside at lunchtime gives away how good the food is. Entrées around $12.

Mom and Dad's 4175 Apalachee Parkway ☏850/877-4518. Delicious and affordable home-made Italian food served in a family atmosphere just outside town. Entrées around $10 to $12. Closed Sun–Mon.

Paradise Grill 1406 N Meridian Rd ☏850/224-2742, ⓦwww.paradisegrillandbar.com. This restaurant is a fun place to go for good seafood and gumbo. Also has live music on Wed, Fri, and Sat. Entrées around $18.

Po' Boys Creole Café 224 E College Ave ☏850/224-5400. A range of Creole dishes such as jambalaya and red beans and rice, plus a decent selection of seafood, generally for under $10. This restaurant is also a popular live music venue (see p.424).

9

Nightlife

Bolstered by its students, Tallahassee has a strong **nightlife** scene, with a leaning toward social drinking and live rock music. There's also a fair amount of **theater**, headed by the student productions at the University Theatre on the FSU campus (box office Tues–Sat 11am–4pm; ☎850/644-6500, ⓦ www.tickets.fsu.edu), and the Tallahassee Little Theatre, 1861 Thomasville Rd (box office Mon–Fri 10am–4pm; ☎850/224-8474 or 850/224-4597). Find out **what's on** from the "Limelights" section of the Friday *Tallahassee Democrat* newspaper; the *FSView* and *Florida Flambeau*, the FSU student papers, publish listings and recommendations.

American Legion Hall 229 Lake Ella Drive ☎850/222-3382. For a taste of the past, try this venue, which hosts a big-band dance night every Tues and old-fashioned Country and Western classes and dancing on Wed.

Bradfordville Blues Club 7152 Moses Lane ☎850/ 906-0766, ⓦ www.bradfordvilleblues.com. Drive down a rutted dirt road to this hole-in-the-wall club about ten miles north of downtown. You can enjoy live blues every weekend and the band's second set will likely be played outside around a bonfire.

Brothers 926 W Tharpe St ☎850/386-2399, ⓦ brothersnightclub.com. Touted as a "pan-sexual playground," this design-conscious venue draws a friendly crowd and is almost exclusively gay on Wed, Thurs, and Fri; there's an amateur drag show on Thurs.

Bullwinkle's 620 W Tennessee St ☎850/224-0651. Rock and blues dominate in this log-cabin-like setting, which also features DJs mixing the favorite dance music of the moment.

Calico Jack's 2745 Capitol Circle NE ☎850/385-6653. Come here for beer, oysters, and stomping Southern rock 'n' roll.

Clyde's & Costello's 210 S Adams St ☎850/224-2173. Pulls a smart and very cliquey crowd, which grows a bit rowdy during the early-evening happy hours.

Halligan's 1698 Village Square Blvd ☎850/668-7665. This joint, north of downtown, is popular for its pool tables and chilled mugs of beer.

Leon County Civic Center at the corner of Pensacola St and Martin Luther King Jr Blvd ☎850/487-1691, ⓦ www.tlccc.org. Major touring acts and Broadway shows play here – as does the FSU basketball team.

The Moon 1105 E Lafayette St ☎850/222-6666, ⓦ www.moonevents.com. Come for the indie bands or Friday night's "Stetsons Ladies Night" – a country music extravaganza with line dancing and much thigh slapping – and free drinks for the girls.

Po' Boys Creole Café 224 E College Ave ☎850/224-5400. Creole and acoustic music sets nicely complement the drink specials in this downtown bar.

Potbelly's 459 W College Ave ☎850/224-2233. On the frat house-filled approach to the FSU campus, this rather grubby bar – with a stage for live music – is a major student watering hole.

Listings

Art galleries Tallahassee has a credible arts scene centered around Railroad Square, close to the junction of Springhill Rd and Gaines St near the FSU campus. You'll find some innovative galleries here, and several local artists have open studios. Other contemporary art showcases include The 621 Gallery, 621 Industrial Drive (☎850/224-6163); and LeMoyne Art Foundation, 125 N Gadsden St (☎850/222-8800), which has an art museum and sculpture garden (Tues–Sat 10am–5pm, Sun 1–5pm; $1).

Car rental Most major companies have branches at the airport (see p.417)

Hospital Non-emergencies: Memorial Health Care Center, 1300 Miccosukee Rd ☎850/431-1155.

Sports Tickets for FSU baseball (March–May) and football (Sept–Nov) matches are on sale at the stadiums two hours before the games begin: ☎888/FSU-NOLE. For info on FAMU sports teams, all known as the Rattlers, call ☎850/224-6093.

Around Tallahassee

Scattered around the fringes of Tallahassee are half a dozen diverse spots deserving of brief visits, among them a remarkable antique car museum, archeological sites, and lakeside gardens. All are easily accessible by car, though most are much harder to reach by bus.

The Tallahassee Antique Car Museum

The **Tallahassee Antique Car Museum**, 3550 Mahan Drive (Mon–Fri 8am–5pm, Sat 10am–5pm, Sun noon–5pm; $16, children $7.50; ☎850/942-0137, ⓦwww.tacm.com), is well worth the three-mile drive east along Tennessee Street, which turns into Mahan Drive. The museum's owner, DeVoe Moore, began his career modestly by shoeing horses. But through quiet determination, which inspires admiration or distaste depending on whom you ask in Tallahassee, he is now one of the region's richest men: selling just one of his businesses in early 1998 netted $37.5 million. The biggest crowd-puller in the collection is the gleaming 21-foot-long Batmobile from the Tim Burton *Batman* movie, bought for $500,000 and complete with Batman's suits and gloves and a flame-thrower attachment. While the most valuable car in the collection is a $1.2 million 1931 Duesenberg Model J, the most intriguing specimen is an 1860-built horse-drawn hearse believed to have carried Abraham Lincoln to his final resting place.

The San Luis and de Soto archeological sites

Slowly being unearthed at the **Mission San Luis** site, 2021 W Mission Rd, about three miles west of downtown Tallahassee (bus #21), the village of San Luis de Talimali was a hub of the seventeenth-century Spanish mission system, second only to St Augustine. At its zenith in 1675, its population numbered 1400. Stop by the **Visitor Center** (Tues–Sun 10am–4pm; free; ☎850/487-3711) for a general explanation and to see some of the finds. Every day, period-attired individuals re-enact village life; it sounds tacky but can be fun.

The **de Soto State Archeological Site**, two miles east of downtown Tallahassee at the corner of Goodbody Lane and Lafayette Street (8am–sunset; $2; ☎850/922-6007), is where Spanish explorer Hernando de Soto is thought to have set up camp in 1539 and held the first Christmas celebration in North American history. All there is to actually see is a few holes in the ground and it's not an essential stop even when it's open. For more information on the de Soto expedition, which was the first European team to cross the Mississippi River, see Contexts, p.458.

Maclay State Gardens

For a lazy half-day, head four miles northeast of downtown Tallahassee to **Maclay State Gardens**, set in a lakeside park at 3540 Thomasville Rd, north of I-10, Exit 203 (park: daily 8am–sunset, cars $4, pedestrians and cyclists $1; garden: daily 9am–5pm; Jan–April $4, rest of year free; ☎850/487-4115, ⓦwww.florida stateparks.org). New York financier and amateur gardener Alfred B. Maclay bought this large piece of land in the 1920s and planted flowers and shrubs in order to create a blooming season from January to April. It worked: for four months each year the gardens are alive with the fragrances and fantastic colors of azaleas, camellias, pansies, and other flowers, framed by dogwood and redbud trees and towered over by huge oaks and pines. Guided tours of the gardens are conducted on weekends around Jan–April (for details and times, call ☎850/487-4556), but they're worth visiting at any time, if only to retire to the lakeside pavilion for a snooze as lizards and squirrels scurry around your feet. The admission fee to the gardens also gets you into the **Maclay House** (open Jan–April only), which is filled with the Maclays' furniture and countless books on horticulture. While you're here, take your time to explore the rest of the park and Lake Hall. A picnic area gives great views of the lake, as does the short **Lake Overstreet Trail**, which meanders through the wooded hillside overlooking it. There is also a swimming area close to the parking lot nearest the park's entrance.

North of Tallahassee

There's a wide range of roads snaking **north from Tallahassee** and many of them offer low-key but enjoyable forays. The Georgia border is only twenty miles away, and the most direct route is the Thomasville Road (Rte-319) to, unsurprisingly, **THOMASVILLE**, a sleepy little town just across the Georgia border that was a winter haven for wealthy northerners who built magnificent plantations on the Florida side of the border. Five miles south of Thomasville (and still in Georgia), the **Pebble Hill Plantation** (Tues–Sat 10am–5pm, Sun 1–5pm, with an hour-long guided tour of the house, last tour leaving at 3.45pm; $10, grounds only $5; ☎229/226-2344, ⊛www.pebblehill.com) remains from the time of cotton picking and slavery and shows how comfortable things were for the wealthy whites who ran the show. Much of the original Pebble Hill burned down in the 1930s and what you see now is a fairly faithful rebuilding of the sumptuous main house, complete with the extensive fine art, antique, crystal, and porcelain collections that belonged to the house's final owner, Elisabeth Ireland Poe, and which were rescued from the fire. Children under age 6 are not allowed in the house. Each April, the house comes back to life as people throng to a spring plantation ball.

If you're feeling hungry, take Centerville Road north from Tallahassee (Rte-151), which, after twelve miles, leads to **Bradley's 1927 Country Store** (Mon–Fri 8am–6pm, Sat 8am–5pm; ☎850/893-1647). For over eighty years, Bradley's has been peddling Southern-style food, specializing in smoked sausages and unusual delicacies like country-milled grits, hogshead cheese, and liver pudding.

Havana

Twelve miles northwest of Tallahassee along Monroe Street (Rte-27), tiny **HAVANA** (pronounced "Hey-vannah") is definitely worth time off the beaten track to explore. Providing an authentic taste of Americana, this historic little town takes a pride in its history and, although it has a number of shops catering to the tourist trade, this seems only to have strengthened the community's sense of identity. Havana's name came from its tobacco plantations, which once supplied cigar-making factories in Cuba. Following the embargo against Cuba in 1958, the town could no longer sell tobacco leaves to Havana and went into decline, only to be rejuvenated again in 1984 when the first antique center opened and the community discovered history can mean business.

The main body of shops and cafés huddles in the two blocks bordered by Second Street NW and N Main Street. For a sense of the town's history, walk by the **Havana Cannery** on East Eighth Avenue. The business packed seven million pounds of fruit during World War II but lost out to larger rivals and shifted to honey-packing before shutting down in 1994. It then housed a maze of antique and curio stores for a short time before once again becoming deserted.

The most you can do at the **McLauchlin House**, at the corner of Seventh Avenue and Second Street, is peer in the windows, but it's worth it. The 150-year-old farmhouse features a beautiful wraparound porch, sloping floors, and uneven doors. Nearby sits **The Planter's Exchange**, 204 NW Second St (☎850/539-6343; Wed–Sat 10am–5pm, Sun 12pm–5pm), a renovated former tobacco warehouse, now home to over 60 antique dealers. The charming *Tomato Café & Tea Room* 107 W 7th Ave (☎850/539-2285) serves afternoon tea, including scones and Devonshire cream, as well as soups and sandwiches. For other **eating options** in Havana, try the homey *Mocking Bird Café*, 211 NW First St (℡850/539-2212, ⓦwww.mockingbirdpottery.com/cafe), where you can dine alfresco on the lovely outdoor courtyard. Fill up on a Cuban sandwich served with a cup of black beans and rice. On Friday and Saturday nights, there's also live music. Unfortunately, there is no accommodation in Havana. The nearest places to stay are the motels along N Monroe Street in Tallahassee (see p.419) and the bed and breakfasts in Quincy twelve miles west (see p.431).

South of Tallahassee

On weekends, many Tallahassee residents head south to the Panhandle's beaches (see "The coastal Panhandle," p.434). If you're not eager to join them, make a slower trek **south** along routes 363 or 61 (which turns into US-319 outside of town), tracking down a few isolated pockets of historical or geological signifi-cance, or losing yourself in the biggest and best of Florida's forests.

One of the most enjoyable ways to explore is by **cycling** the sixteen-mile Tallahassee–St Marks Historic Railroad Trail, a flat and straight course through placid woodlands following the route of a long-abandoned railroad. You can rent bikes from the Great Bicycle Shop, 1909 Thomasville Rd (℡850/224-7461), in Tallahassee.

Leon Sinks Geological Area

Seven miles south of Tallahassee on Rte-319 is the **Leon Sinks Geological Area** (8am–8pm; $3), a fascinating karst (terrain altered by rain and ground water dissolving underlying limestone bedrock). It contains several prominent sinkholes, numerous depressions, a natural bridge, and a disappearing stream, all of which give a unique glimpse of the surrounding area before human interfer-ence. There are three manageable trails of between half a mile and three miles, described in a guide available from the ranger station at the entrance.

The Natural Bridge Battlefield State Historic Site and St Marks

Ten miles southeast of Tallahassee, a turn off Rte-363 at Woodville leads after six miles to the **Natural Bridge Battlefield State Historic Site** (daily 8am–sunset; free; ℡850/922-6007), where, on March 4, 1865, a motley band of Confederate soldiers saw off a much larger group of Union troops, preventing Tallahassee from falling into Yankee hands. Not that it made much difference – the war ended a couple of months later – but the victory is celebrated by a monument and an annual re-enactment on or close to the anniversary involving several hours of shouting, loud bangs, and smoke.

Twelve miles south of Woodville, Rte-363 expires at the hamlet of **St Marks**, where the **San Marcos de Apalache Historic State Park** (Thurs–Mon 9am–5pm; free, museum $1; ℡850/925-6216, ⓦwww .floridastateparks.org/sanmarcos) offers decent pickings for students of Florida history. Early explorers such as Pánfilo de Narváez and Hernando de Soto visited this sixteenth-century Spanish-built fort, which later became Andrew Jackson's headquarters when he waged war on the Seminole Indians. If you prefer wildlife to history, backtrack slightly along Rte-363 and turn east along US-98. Three miles on you'll find the main entrance to **St Marks National Wildlife Refuge** (daily 6am–9pm; cars $4, pedestrians and cyclists $1), which spreads out over the boggy outflow of the St Marks River. Bald eagles and a few black bears reside in the refuge, though from the various roadside lookout points and observation towers you're more likely to spot otters, white-tailed deer, raccoons, and a wealth of birdlife. Apart from the natural attractions, a drive to the end of the road will bring you to the picturesque St Marks Lighthouse, completed in 1831. Just inside the entrance, a **visitor center** doles out useful information (Mon–Fri 8am–4pm, Sat & Sun 10am–5pm; ☏850/925-6121, Ⓦwww.fws.gov/saintmarks).

Wakulla Springs

Fifteen miles south of Tallahassee, off Rte-61 on Rte-267, **Wakulla Springs State Park** (daily 8am–sunset; cars $4, pedestrians and cyclists $1; ☏850/926-0700, Ⓦwww.floridastateparks.org/wakullasprings) contains what is believed to be one of the biggest and deepest natural springs in the world, pumping up half a million gallons of crystal-clear pure water from the bowels of the earth every day – difficult to guess from the calm surface. The principal reason for visiting Wakulla Springs is to enjoy the scenery and to appreciate a part of Florida that remains pristine after hundreds of years.

It's refreshing to **swim** in the cool waters, but somewhat disconcerting to note the marked areas are just inches from those where swimming is prohibited due to alligators. To learn more about the spring, you should take the twenty-five-minute narrated **glass-bottomed boat tour** ($6; only operates when the water is clear enough) and peer down to the shoals of fish hovering around the 180-foot-deep cavern through which the water comes. Join the 45-minute **river cruise** ($6) for glimpses of some of the park's other inhabitants: deer, turkeys, turtles, herons, and egrets – and the inevitable alligators. If déjà vu strikes, it may be because a number of films have been shot here, including several of the early *Tarzan* movies and parts of *The Creature from the Black Lagoon*. To see the alligators and snakes at their most active, take the **moonlight** dinner cruise for $28; call for details.

▲ Wakulla Springs

You shouldn't leave without strolling through the 🏛 **Wakulla Lodge**, 550 Wakulla Park Drive (☎850/926-0700, check park website for more details; ❺), a hotel built beside the spring in 1937, which retains many of its original features: Moorish archways, stone fireplaces, and fabulous hand-painted Toltec and Aztec designs on the lobby's wooden ceiling. You can also pay your respects to the stuffed carcass of "Old Joe," one of the oldest and largest alligators ever known, who died in the 1950s, measuring eleven feet long and supposedly aged 200; he's in a glass case by the reception desk. The lodge and surrounding area have a relaxing ambience that can prove quite soothing. An added bonus is that once the day-trippers have departed, you'll have the springs and wildlife all to yourself.

Further south: the Apalachicola National Forest

With swamps, savannas, and springs dotted liberally about its half-million acres, the **Apalachicola National Forest** is the inland Panhandle at its natural best. Several roads enable you to drive through a good-sized chunk and multiple spots provide opportunities for a rest and a snack. But to see more of the forest than its picnic tables, you'll have to make an effort. Leave the periphery and delve into the pristine interior to explore at a leisurely pace, following hiking trails, taking a canoe on one of the rivers, or simply spending a night under the stars at one of the basic campgrounds.

Practicalities

The northeast corner of the forest almost touches Tallahassee's airport, fanning out from there to the edge of the Apalachicola River, about 35 miles west. Most of the northern edge is bordered by Hwy-20, the eastern side by US-319 and US-98, while to the south lies Tate's Hell Swamp (see p.431).

The main **entrances** are off Hwy-20 and US-319, and three minor roads – routes 267, 375, and 65 – form cross-forest links between the two highways. **Accommodation** is limited to camping; all the sites are free and have basic facilities – usually just toilets and drinking water. For more information, call ☎850/643-2282 or 850/926-3561. The only place to **rent a canoe or kayak** near the forest is TNT Hideaway (☎850/925-6412), at 6527 Coastal Hwy (US-98), two miles west of St Marks on the Wakulla River. Prices range from $25 to $35.

The edge of the forest: Lost Lake and Silver Lake

Lost Lake (daily: April–Oct 8am–8pm; Nov–March 8am–6pm), seven miles from Tallahassee along Rte-373 offers a few picnic tables beside a small lake, not really suitable for swimming, as well as a trailhead for the forest's motorcycle and horse trails. You can swim at **Silver Lake**, **Camel Lake**, **or Wright Lake**.

Apalachicola National Forest information

Always equip yourself with maps, know the weather forecast, and get advice from a ranger's office before setting off on a hike or canoe trip through the forest. The Ochlockonee River divides the forest into two administrative districts and the following offices are responsible for the west and east sides, respectively:

Apalachicola Ranger District Hwy-20, near Bristol ☎850/643-2282
Wakulla Ranger District 57 Taft Dr, near Crawfordville ☎850/926-3561

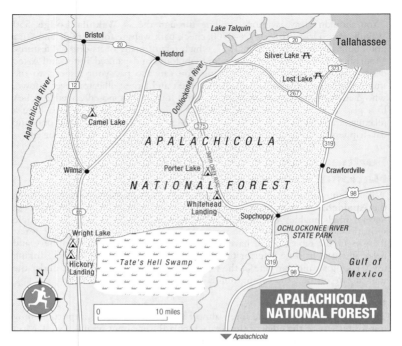

Apalachicola

Deeper into the forest: hiking and canoeing

Several short, clearly marked **nature walks** lie within the forest, but the major **hiking trail**, strictly for ardent and well-equipped backpackers, is the former **Apalachicola Trail**, now part of the state-wide 1400-mile **Florida National Scenic Trail** which begins close to Crawfordville, on US-319. Around 74 miles of the trail passes through the forest and includes a memorable (and sometimes difficult, depending on the weather conditions and water level) leg across an isolated swamp, the Bradwell Bay Wilderness. After this, the campground at Porter Lake, just to the west of the wilderness area, with its toilets and drinking water, seems the epitome of civilization.

The trail leads on to **Camel Lake**, whose campground has drinking water and toilets, and the less demanding nine-and-a-half-mile **Trail of Lakes**. By vehicle, you can get directly to Camel Lake by turning off Hwy-20 at Bristol and continuing south for twelve miles, watching for the signposted turn-off on the left.

Although there are numerous places to put in along its four rivers, **canoeists and kayakers** can paddle right into the forest from the western end of Lake Talquin (close to Hwy-20), and continue for a sixty-mile glide along the Ochlockonee River – the forest's major waterway – to the Ochlockonee River State Park, close to US-319. The length of trip means that to do it all you'll have to use the riverside **campgrounds** (info from the ranger's districts listed on p.429). Those with drinking water are at Porter Lake, Wright Lake, Whitehead Lake, and Hickory Landing; these are often concealed by dense foliage, so study your map carefully. There is no camping allowed in the park during deer hunting season from mid-November through mid-February, unless you're part of a deer hunting camp.

South of the forest: Tate's Hell Swamp

Driving through the forest on Rte-65 or Rte-67, or around it on US-319 (which merges with US-98 as it nears the coast), you'll eventually pass the large and forbidding area called **Tate's Hell Swamp**. According to legend, Tate was a farmer who pursued a panther into the swamp and was never seen again. It's a breeding ground for the deadly water moccasin snake; you're well advised to stay clear.

West of Tallahassee

To discover the social character of the inland Panhandle, take US-90 **west from Tallahassee**. This stretch is 180 miles of largely tedious rural landscapes and time-locked farming towns that have been down on their luck since the demise of the timber industry fifty or so years ago, but the compensations are the endless supply of rustic eating places, low-cost accommodation, several appealing natural areas – and a chance to see a part of Florida travel brochures rarely mention.

Quincy

Twenty miles west of Tallahassee on US-90 is **Quincy**, one of the first towns to strike it rich because of Coca-Cola. The Atlanta-based pharmacist who patented the fizzy drink sold company stock to friends in Quincy, who in turn, became rich and built grandiose villas throughout the town at the beginning of the twentieth century. Stop by the **Chamber of Commerce**, 208 N Adams St (Mon–Fri 9am–5pm; ☎850/627-9231), to pick up visitor information. From the square on **Madison Street**, observe the immaculate **Court House**, surrounded by topiaries, and a grand marble memorial to slain Confederate soldiers. Just opposite, on East Jefferson Street, the wall of Padgett's jewelry store is covered with the original Coke ad. Painted here in 1905, it espouses coke as "delicious and refreshing, five cents at fountains and bottles." Take time to explore the **Gadsden Arts Center**, 13 N Madison St (Tues–Sat 10am–5pm, Sun 1–5pm; ☎850/875-4866, ⓦwww.gadsdenarts.org). One of the finest art galleries in the area, it hosts major traveling exhibitions as well as the work of local and regional artists.

Wealthy Quincy, with its bungalow homes of delicate trellises and sweeping verandas, begins on East Washington Street. The most exquisite mansions, though, are between Love and King streets. The finest of all also happens to be the **bed and breakfast** *McFarlin House*, 305 E King St (☎850/875-2526, ⓦwww.mcfarlinhouse.com; ⑥), an exquisite, turreted mansion whose sumptuous interior and 42-pillar porch were created for John McFarlin, Quincy's richest tobacco planter, in 1895. Otherwise, try the *Allison House Inn*, 215 N Madison St (☎888/904-2511, ⓦwww.allisonhouseinn.com; ⑤), a lovely English-style bed and breakfast in another of the oldest houses in town.

Florida Caverns State Park

Florida Caverns State Park (daily 8am–sunset; cars $4, pedestrians and cyclists $1), 50 miles west of Quincy on Rte-166, has hourly **guided tours** (9am–4pm Thurs–Mon; $8) that venture through 65-foot-deep caverns filled with strangely shaped calcite formations. Far from being new discoveries, the caves were mentioned in colonial Spanish accounts of the area and used by

Seminole Indians to hide from Andrew Jackson's army in the early 1800s. Back in the sun, the park has a few other features to fill a day comfortably. From the **visitor center** (☏850/482-9598) by the caverns' entrance, a **nature trail** leads around the flood plain of the Chipola River, which dips underground for several hundred feet as it flows through the park. Rent a canoe (rental is $15 for four hours, $20 for eight hours) and bunk at its **campground** ($17 with electricity; reservations ☏1-800/326-352).

Chipley and Falling Waters State Park

Continuing west, the next community of any size is **CHIPLEY**, named for William D. Chipley, who put a railroad across the Panhandle in the mid-1800s to improve the timber trade. The town itself is, for the most part, unexciting and the Neoclassical bulk of the **Washington County Court House** on US-90 (also called Jackson Ave) seems very out of place. The only other building of interest is the large and elegant **First United Methodist Church**, built in 1910 and set on hand-hewn log foundations. If you can find someone to let you in, the interior is most unexpected. Towering over the vast, curved golden-oak pews are a huge pipe organ and semi-opaque stained glass that is especially radiant on a sunny day.

The Falling Waters State Park

Leave town along Rte-77 and head for **Falling Waters State Park** (daily 8am–sunset; cars $4, pedestrians and cyclists $1; ☏850/638-6130), three miles south and the home of Florida's only **waterfall**. The fall is in fact a 100-foot drop into a tube-like sinkhole topped by a viewing platform. A trail passes several other sinks (without waterfalls), and another leads to a decaying oil well – remaining from an unsuccessful attempt to strike black gold in 1919. The park has a **campground** (reservations ☏1-800/326-352; $15), but for more comfortable **accommodation**, head back to Chipley where there are a number of chain motels on US-90, including the *Comfort Inn & Suites*, 1140 Motel Drive (☏850/415-1111; ❹) which has comfortable rooms, free wi-fi and free continental breakfast. For tasty eats, try *Cancun's Mexican Grill*, at 1511 Main St (☏850/415-1655).

De Funiak Springs

A real jewel of the inland Panhandle, **De Funiak Springs**, forty miles west of Chipley on US-90, was founded as a fashionable stop on the newly completed Louisville–Nashville railroad in 1882. Drawn to the large, naturally circular lake, nineteenth-century socialites built fairy-tale villas to fringe the waters here. Three years later the Florida Chautauqua Alliance, a benevolent religious society espousing free culture and education for all, made the town its southern base. The alliance's headquarters was at the grandiose Hall of Brotherhood, which still stands on Circle Drive – an ideal cruising lane to view the splendid villas, painted in gingerbread-house style with white or wedding-cake blue trim. With the death of its founders and the coming of the Depression, the alliance faded away, and in 1975 their 4000-seat auditorium was demolished by Hurricane Eloise. There has been renewed interest in the Chautauqua ethos, however, and a **Chautauqua Assembly Revival** is now held here around the end of January or the beginning of February (call ℡850/892-7613 or check Ⓦwww.florida-chautauqua-center.org for details). In addition to holding workshops on whatever is the featured topic that year (for example, 2009 was 'Africa') and craft activities, the town also opens up its historic houses. If you miss that, the only building open to the public is the **Walton-De Funiak Library**, 3 Circle Drive (Mon & Wed–Fri 9am–5pm, Tues 9am–8pm, Sat 9am–5pm; free; ℡850/892-3624), which has been lending books since 1886 and has a small stash of medieval European weaponry on display.

Another unlikely find is the **Chautauqua Winery** (℡850/892-5887; Ⓦwww.chautauquawinery.com), at the junction of US-331 and I-10, whose diverse wines may not be the world's finest, but have picked up a few awards in their almost 30 years of existence (free tours and tastings daily 9am–5pm; last tour at 4pm). The actual vineyards are about twelve miles from the winery.

Stopping over in De Funiak Springs is a sound move if you're aiming for the more expensive coastal strip 25 miles south along US-331. The *Super 8*, 402 Hugh Adams Rd (℡850/892-1333; ❷), has good rates but is closer to I-10 than the town. The historical *Hotel de Funiak*, 400 E Nelson Ave (℡850/892-4383 ❹), is a charmingly restored hotel in the old business district. Alternatively, you can rent a log cabin at *Sunset King Lake Resort,* 366 Paradise Island Drive (℡850/892-7229 or 1-800/774-5454, Ⓦwww.sunsetking.com; ❹), where there's also an outdoor pool and boat rentals. *Bogey's Bar and Restaurant*, in the Hotel Defuniak (℡850/951-2233) serves breakfast, lunch and dinner, as well as a variety of specialty coffees and desserts. *McLains Family Steakhouse*, on US-331 (℡850/892-2402) offers a good selection of steaks, seafood, and salads, or head back to I-10 for the usual array of fast-food restaurants.

The Blackwater River State Forest

Between the sluggish towns of Crestview and Milton, thirty miles west of De Funiak Springs, the creeks and slow-flowing rivers of **Blackwater River State Forest** are jammed each weekend with waterborne families enjoying what's officially dubbed "the canoe capital of Florida." In spite of the crowds, the forest is by no means over-commercialized, being big enough to absorb the influx and still offer peace, isolation, and unruffled nature to anyone intrepid enough to hike through it. If you're not game for canoeing or hiking, but just want a few hours' break, the **Blackwater River State Park** (daily 8am–sunset; cars $3, pedestrians and cyclists $1), within the forest four miles north of Harold off US-90, has some easy walking trails.

From Milton, US-90 and I-10 both offer a mildly scenic fifteen-mile drive over Escambia Bay to the hotels and freeways on the northern fringes of Pensacola, the city marking Florida's western extremity (see p.446).

Accommodation in the forest

Adventures Unlimited at Tomahawk Landing, twelve miles north of Milton on Hwy-87 (℡850/623-6197 or 1-800/239-6864, Ⓦwww.adventuresunlimited .com), rents restored 1800s "cracker" **cabins**, runs the *Old School House Inn* with eight rooms, and offers camping; prices range from $20 for tent sites to $179 per night for a six-person cabin. State park accommodation is limited to **camping** (℡850/983-5363 for information, ℡1-800/326-3521 for reservations; $12). There are also five fully equipped campgrounds within the state forest (☎850/957-6140; $5–15), offering amenities including swimming, hiking trails, and boat ramps. Free basic sites intended for hikers are dotted along the main trails.

Hiking and canoeing

Hardened **hikers** carrying overnight gear can tackle the 21-mile **Jackson Trail**, named after Andrew Jackson, who led his invading army this way in 1818, seeking to wrest Florida from Spanish control. On the way, two very basic shelters have hand pumps for water. The trail runs between Karick Lake, off Hwy-189, fourteen miles north of US-90, and the Krul Recreation Area. The shorter **Sweetwater Trail** is a good substitute if your feet aren't up to the longer hike. An enjoyable four-and-a-half-mile walk, it leaves the Krul Recreation Area and crosses a swing bridge and the Bear Lake Dam before joining the Jackson Trail.

  Canoeing in the forest is offered by Adventures Unlimited (see p.433). You can also rent tubes and kayaks for around $16, $25, and $30 respectively per day.

The coastal Panhandle

Lacking the glamour and international renown of Florida's other beach strips, the **coastal Panhandle** is nonetheless no secret to residents of the Southern states who descend upon it by the thousands during the summer. Consequently, a few sections of the region's 180-mile-long coastline are nightmarishly overdeveloped: **Panama City Beach** revels in its "Redneck Riviera" nickname, and smaller **Destin** and **Fort Walton Beach** are only marginally more refined. By contrast, little **Apalachicola** and the **South Walton beaches**, both easily reached by car (they're inaccessible by bus) but out of the main tourist corridor, have much to recommend them as they have beautiful unspoiled sands and offshore islands where people are a rarer sight than wildlife.

Apalachicola and around

A few miles south of the Apalachicola National Forest (see p.429), and the first substantial part of the coast you'll hit on US-98 from central Florida, the **Apalachicola area** contains much of value. Mainland beaches may be few, but sand-seekers are compensated by the brilliant strands of three barrier islands, and the small fishing communities you'll pass through are untainted by the aggressive tourism scarring the coast fifty miles west in Panama City Beach.

Apalachicola

Now a tiny port with an income largely derived from harvesting oysters (ten per cent of the nation's oysters come from here), **Apalachicola** once rode high on the cotton industry, which kept its dock busy and its populace affluent during the early 1800s. A number of stately columned buildings attest to former wealth. Stop into the **Chamber of Commerce**, 122 Commerce St (Mon–Sat

10am–4pm; ☎850/653-9419, ⓦwww.apalachicolabay.org), to pick up an historic walking tour map to check them out.

To reach Apalachicola take US-98, which crosses the four-mile Gorrie Memorial Bridge, named for a physician held in high regard by Floridians. Arriving in the town in 1833, John Gorrie was seeking a way to keep malaria patients cool when he devised a machine to make ice (previously transported in large blocks from the north). He died, however, before the idea took off and became the basis of modern refrigerators and air conditioners. The **John Gorrie State Museum**, on the corner of Sixth Street and Avenue D (Thurs–Mon 9am–5pm; $1; ☎850/653-9347), remembers the man and his work, as well as the general history of Apalachicola, and includes a replica of the cumbersome ice-making device (the original is in the Smithsonian Institute in Washington DC).

Accommodation and eating

There isn't a lot to Apalachicola, but the town makes a good base for visiting the barrier islands (see below) and there's plenty of good **accommodation** to choose from. The rooms at the *Apalachicola River Inn*, 123 Water St (☎850/653-8139, ⓦwww.apalachicolariverinn.com; ❻), all have river views; the lovely *Coombs House Inn*, 80 Sixth St (☎850/653-9199, ⓦwww.coombshouseinn .com; ❻), is in a Victorian-style mansion filled with antiques and oriental carpets, and has bicycles available for guests' use; and the *Gibson Inn*, 57 Market St (☎850/653-2191, ⓦwww.gibsoninn.com; ❺), offers murder-mystery weekends and a full dinner menu in their own restaurant.

Good places to **eat** in town include the inexpensive *Apalachicola Seafood Grill and Steakhouse*, 100 Market St (☎850/653-9510), for a wide range of lunch and dinner specials; and the 🍴 *Boss Oyster Bar*, 123 Water St (☎850/653-9364), where you can tuck into fresh Apalachicola oysters. The motto of this place is "shut up and shuck," and it prepares its oysters in thirty-plus different ways: try the boss oyster combo for $15.95. *Tamara's Café Floridita,* 71 Market St (☎850/653-4111), serves delicious Venezuelan-style seafood dishes. For something lighter, pop into the same owner's *Café Con Leche Internet Café*, 32 Ave D (☎850/653-2233), where you can munch on tasty baked goods or surf the web.

The barrier islands: St George, Dog, and St Vincent

A few miles off the coast, framing the Apalachicola Bay and the broad, marshy outflow of the Apalachicola River, the three Apalachicola **barrier islands** are well endowed with beaches and creatures – including thousands of birds that use them as resting stops during migration – and two of them hold what must be among the most isolated communities in Florida. It's worth seeing one of the islands if you have the chance, but only the largest island, St George, is accessible by road – Rte-1A, which leaves US-98 at Eastpoint. Once here you can visit the rest with Journeys of St George's Island, 240 E Third St (☎850/927-3259, ⓦwww.sgislandjourneys.com; closed Jan–Feb), which provides a variety of instructional, guided canoe trips and hikes.

Twenty-seven miles of powdery white sands and Gulf vistas are not the only reason to come to **St George Island**, where shady live-oak hammocks and an abundance of osprey-inhabited pine trees add color to a day's lazy sunning. Occupying the island's central section are a few restaurants, beach shops, as well as the recently renovated *St George Inn*, 135 Franklin Blvd (☎850/927-2903, ⓦwww .stgeorgeinn.com; ❻), a beautiful wooden motel with a wraparound veranda. The *Buccaneer Inn*, 160 W Gorrie Drive (☎850/927-2585, ⓦwww.buccinn.com; ❺), has basic rooms and is near the island's restaurants and shops. The eastern sector is dominated by the raccoon-infested **St George Island State Park** (daily 8am–sunset; cars $5, pedestrians and cyclists $1; ☎850/927-2111), where a three-mile **hiking trail** leads to a very basic **campground** ($4; there's a better-equipped site at the start of the hike, $19; ☎1-800/326-3521).

A couple of miles east of St George, **Dog Island**, accessible only by boat – look for signs at the marina in Carrabelle on US-98 – has a small permanent population living in little cottages nestled among Florida's tallest sand dunes. Several footpaths lead around the windswept isle, which won't take more than a few hours to cover. The only **accommodation** is the *Pelican Inn* (☎1-800/451-5294, ⒲www.thepelicaninn.com; ❻), with its eight self-catering apartments (no maid service or restaurant) in a house on the beach. There is a minimum two-night stay, and you should bring all your food, as there is no grocery store on the island. Reservations are essential.

The freshwater lakes and saltwater swamps of the twelve-acre **St Vincent Island**, almost within a shell's throw of St George's western end, form a protected refuge for loggerhead turtles and bald eagles, among many other creatures. Trips to the island are available year-round with St Vincent Island Shuttle Services (☎850/229-1065, ⒲www.stvincentisland.com) from $10; they also organize bike rentals but you need to call in advance.

St Joseph Peninsula State Park and Port St Joe

For a final taste of virgin Florida coast before hitting heavily commercial Panama City Beach, take Rte-30 – eighteen miles from Apalachicola, off US-98 – to the **St Joseph Peninsula State Park** (daily 8am–sunset; cars $4, pedestrians and cyclists $1; ☎850/227-1327, ⒲www.floridastateparks.org/stjoseph). A long finger of sand with a short **nature trail** at one end and a spectacular nine-mile **hiking route** at the other, the park has rough **camping** with no facilities ($4) at its northern tip and better-equipped sites ($20 with electricity) and **cabins** ($90; ☎1-800/326-3521) about halfway along near Eagle Harbor.

The peninsula wraps a protective arm around **Port St Joe** on the mainland, another dot-on-the-map fishing port that has seen better days. One of these came in 1838 when a constitution calling for statehood (which Florida didn't acquire until seven years later) and liberal reforms was drawn up here – only to be deemed too radical by the legislators of the time. If you're feeling peckish, stop at the *Indian Pass Raw Bar*, 8391 County Road 30-A between Apalachicola and Port St Joe (☎850/227-1670), a local favorite renowned for its oysters. At the **Constitution Convention State Museum** (Thurs–Mon 9am–noon & 1–5pm; $1; ☎850/229-8029), signposted from US-98 as you enter the town, you'll find battery-powered mannequins that re-enact the deed. There are also more credible mementos of the town's colorful past, including an explanation of how its reputation for pirate pursuits earned it the title "Wickedest City in the Southeast" during its early years.

Panama City Beach

An orgy of motels, condos, go-kart tracks, mini-golf courses, and amusement parks, **PANAMA CITY BEACH** is entirely without pretensions, capitalizing as blatantly as possible on the appeal of its 27-mile-long beach. It's entirely

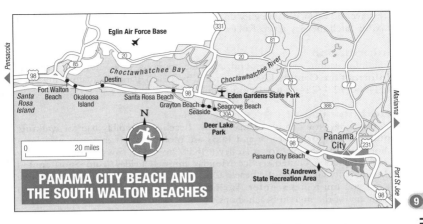

commercial, but with the shops, bars, and restaurants all trying to undercut one another, there are some great bargains to be found – from airbrushed T-shirts and cut-rate sunglasses to cheap buffet food. With everybody out to have a good time, there's some fine carousing to be done, too; not least during the Spring Break months of March and April when thousands of students arrive to drink and dance themselves into oblivion. Party town it may be, but Panama City Beach has zero drug tolerance and there are big signs along the beach to constantly remind you of this fact. As vulgar and crass as it often is, Panama City Beach cries out to be seen. Come here once, if only as a voyeuristic day-trip – you may well be tempted enough by its tacky charm to stay longer.

Seasons greatly affect the mood. Throughout the lively **summer** (the so-called "100 Magic Days"), accommodation costs are high and advance bookings essential. In **winter**, prices drop and visitors are fewer; most are Canadians and, increasingly, northern Europeans, who have no problems sunbathing and swimming in the relatively cool (typically around 65°F) temperatures.

What Panama City Beach doesn't have is any **history** worth mentioning. It began as an offshoot of **PANAMA CITY**, a dull place of docks and paper mills eight miles away over the Hathaway Bridge (which US-98 crosses). Today there's little love lost between the two communities that have nothing in common besides a name.

Arrival, information, and getting around

Since Panama City Beach is essentially a very long beach, **getting your bearings** could hardly be simpler, even if there are only two real, if rather similar landmarks (City Pier to the west, County Pier to the east). **Front Beach Road** (part of US-98A, which starts at the foot of the Hathaway Bridge) is the main track, a two-lane highway often called "the Strip" that's very much the place to prowl on weekends. When judging distances, count on having to go about a mile to get from, say, number 15,000 to 16,000 Front Beach Road. The speedier, four-lane **Hutchison Boulevard** loops off Front Beach Road for a few blocks around County Pier from the junction with **Thomas Drive** (which links the eastern extremity of the beach). If you don't want to see gaudy Panama City Beach at all, **Panama City Beach Parkway** (US-98) will take you straight through its anonymous residential quarter. Greyhound **buses** drop off passengers at the station in Panama City (917 Harrison Ave; ☎850/785-6111).

To travel between Panama City and Panama City Beach, you'll need to take a taxi or catch the Bay Town Trolley (see below).

Information

For information, magazines, and discount coupons, drop into the **Visitors' Information Center**, 17001 Panama City Beach Parkway (daily 8am–5pm; ☎1-800/722-3224, ⓦ www.visitpanamacitybeach.com).

Getting around

In terms of getting around, Panama City Beach is incredibly bad for **walking**; **public transport** is scarce and **taxis** are prohibitively expensive, even for a short journey. The Bay Town Trolley (☎850/769-0557, ⓦ www.baytowntrolley .org) provides a limited service Monday through Friday (6am–8pm) around Panama City and along the beach. One-way fares are $1.25. If you don't have a car, you can rent a **scooter** (around $45 per day; driver's license necessary) from any of the myriad beach shops.

Accommodation

Visitors to Panama City Beach outnumber residents, and though there are plenty of **places to stay**, these fill with amazing speed, especially on weekends. **Prices** are higher than you'll pay elsewhere in the Panhandle – $80–150 for a basic motel room in summer (March to Oct) – so if you're on a budget, stay inland and drive to the beach. In winter prices drop by 40–60 percent, with monthly rentals being even cheaper. **Campground** sites (three of which we mention below) are rarely more expensive than their equivalents elsewhere, though only a couple are good for tents. As a very general rule, **motels** at the eastern end of the beach are smarter and slightly pricier than those in the center, and places at the western end are quieter and older. That said, you're unlikely to find much to complain about at any place that takes your fancy.

Hotels and motels

Beachbreak By The Sea 15405 Front Beach Rd ☎1-800/346-4709, ⓦ www.bytheseareports.com. Many of the comfortable rooms in this four-story motel offer kitchenettes or full kitchens, and there's also a free airport shuttle. ⑤

Campers Inn 8800 Thomas Drive ☎1-866/872-2267, ⓦ www.campersinn.net. Offers proximity to the beach, as well as onsite amenities including fishing supplies, laundromat, and grocery stores. Suitable for RVs & tents, but also features cabin accommodation. Call for rates.

Scuba diving in Panama City Beach

While not as warm as the waters farther south, the Gulf of Mexico around Panama City Beach offers a greater variety of dive sites than is typically found elsewhere in Florida. Besides the natural reefs that lie a few miles offshore at depths of between eighty and a hundred feet, the coastal waters include some fifty artificial reefs created by the Panama City Marine Institute as an aid to marine research. Known as the "Wreck Capital of the South," Panama City Beach also offers divers the opportunity of poking around a number of sunken ships, including a 441-foot World War II Liberty ship, a 160-foot coastal freighter, and, most famously, the 465-foot **Empire Mica**, a large freighter that was torpedoed and sunk in World War II.

The best time for diving in Panama City Beach is from April to September, when water temperatures are at their warmest. Of the several **dive shops** along the beach, try Panama City Dive Center, 4823 Thomas Drive (☎850/235-3390, ⓦ www.pcdivecenter .com) for dive packages, courses, and equipment rental. The shop also has a second location at 1225 Airport Rd (☎850/215-3390) with a pool for certification classes.

Flamingo Motel and Tower 15525 Front Beach Rd ☎850/234-2232 or 1-800/828-0400, ⓦwww .flamingomotel.com. This large motel sits half a mile east of City Pier and features a tropical garden on the beach and kitchen-equipped rooms in the tower. The cheaper rooms are on the non-beach side of the road. ❹

Holiday Inn SunSpree 11127 Front Beach Rd ☎850/234-1111 or 1-800/633-0266, ⓦwww .hipcbeach.com. One of the most centrally located and comfortable hotels on the beach strip. All 340 rooms have balconies overlooking the palm-fringed pool – a useful aid to socializing for the young crowd that tends to congregate here. ❻

Legacy By The Sea 15325 Front Beach Rd ☎1-888/886-8917, ⓦwww.bythesearesorts.com. This sister property to the *Beachbreak* offers all-suite rooms, complete with full kitchens, as well as a free airport shuttle and complimentary continental breakfast. ❻

Marriott's Bay Point Resort Village 4200 Marriott Drive ☎850/236-6000 or 1-800/644-2650, ⓦwww.marriottbaypoint.com. Located on a 1100-acre wildlife sanctuary, this is one of the more upmarket accommodation options around. Every room has a view of either the sanctuary or the bay, and the resort offers four pools, whirlpools, an exercise room, and golf. ❻

Osprey 15801 Front Beach Rd ☎850/234-0303 or 1-800/338-2659, ⓦwww.ospreymotel.com. This family friendly, large beachfront motel offers heated pool, hot tub, and beach bar, and guests can also use the shuffleboard and volleyball facilities at the nearby *Driftwood Lodge*. All rooms have full kitchens. ❺

Racoon River Campground 12209 Hutchinson Blvd ☎850/234-0181, ⓦwww.raccoonriver.net. Caters mainly to RVs (check website for date and price ranges) but also offers primitive ($20) and electric ($25) tent sites.

Sandpiper Beacon 17403 Front Beach Rd ☎850/234-2154, ⓦwww.sandpiperbeacon.com. This large resort-style motel has an indoor pool with a lazy river ride, an outdoor pool with a waterslide, and a small grocery store on the ground floor. All rooms have a microwave and mini refrigerator. ❺

St Andrews State Recreation Area 4607 State Park Lane ☎850/233-5140 or 1-800/326-3521 for reservations, ⓦwww.floridastateparks.org /standrews. If you like camping right on the water, then this is the spot for you. The park also has three separate fishing piers if you're looking to catch your next meal – just make sure you have a license. Sites are $24 per night, year-round.

Sugar Sands 20723 Front Beach Rd ☎850/234-8802 or 1-800/367-9221, ⓦwww.sugarsands.com. Sitting in a peaceful spot on the western edge of the beach strip, this friendly, family-owned motel is ideal for those wanting a respite from the crowds further east. Rooms have been recently renovated, and facilities include shuffleboard, a heated pool, and hot tub, while on the shore there's volleyball and jet-skiing. ❻

Around the beach

Getting a tan, running yourself ragged at beach sports, and going wild at night are the main concerns in Panama City Beach – you'll get very strange looks indeed if you go around demanding history, art and culture. Other than the beach-based activities, you can try your hand at a variety of waterborne pastimes such as jet-skiing, parasailing, fishing, snorkeling and scuba diving (see box opposite), while go-kart rides and amusement parks are fodder for landlubbers. Panama City Beach's other main attractions are as follows.

Gulf World Marine Park
15412 Front Beach Rd. Daily 9am, closing times vary throughout the year; $24; ☎850/234-5271, ⓦwww.gulfworldmarinepark.com.

Allow about three hours to wander around this 20,000-square foot indoor tropical garden, where you can see dolphin, sea lion, and tropical bird shows, as well as view otters, alligators, penguins, and the like. Further attractions include the seasonal "Splash Magic" laser show and the chance to become a dolphin trainer for the day (all cost extra).

Museum of Man in the Sea
17314 W US-98. Daily 10am–4pm; $5; ☎850/235-4101, ⓦwww.maninthesea.org.

Though the exhibits are quite time-worn, there is a large collection of diving miscellany, including enormous eighteenth-century diving helmets, bulky air pumps, bodysuits, deep-sea cutting devices, and torpedo-like propulsion vehicles. A separate display documents *Sealab*, the US Navy's underwater research vessels, the first of which was fitted out in Panama City and now stands outside the museum.

Shell Island

Two three-hour cruises leave from Captain Anderson's Marina at the foot of Thomas Drive from Feb through Oct. Boat departures 9am and 1pm; return ticket $18. Alternatively, a 5min voyage from St Andrews State Recreation Area departs every 30min, 9am–5pm March–Aug.

This seven-mile strip of sand is a haven for shell collectors and sun worshippers alike. As there's little shade on the undeveloped island, however, sunglasses are essential; the glare off the sands can be blinding. There are numerous boat trips from Captain Anderson Marina, most of which include a brief stop at Shell Island. Prices vary wildly among tour operators, so shop around.

Shipwreck Island Waterpark

12201 Middle Beach Rd. Daily late April to early Sept 10.30am–5.30pm; $32; ☎850/234-3333, ⓦ www.shipwreckisland.com.

Gambling on the notion people would pay for the privilege of being tossed and turned in water (when they could get it for free in the Gulf of Mexico over the road), this water park built its reputation around a pool that produces three-foot waves roughly every ten minutes. So far at least, the venture appears to have paid off, and the wave pool, thrilling slides, and a play area for the kids make this a good break from a day on the beach.

St Andrews State Recreation Area

4607 State Park Lane. Daily 8am–sunset; cars $5, pedestrians and cyclists $1; ☎850/233-5140.

Get here early and you'll spot a variety of hopping, crawling, and slithering wildlife by following one of the nature trails around the pine forest and salt marshes within the park. By noon, however, the hordes will have arrived to swim, fish, and prepare picnics. If you're with kids, they'll enjoy splashing in the shallow lagoon sheltered by an artificial reef known as The Jetties. Clean enough that locals catch their dinner here, these crystal waters are ideal for swimming, snorkeling, diving, canoeing, and kayaking. Take advantage of the campground (see p.439) to enjoy the quietest times in this spot.

Zoo World

9008 Front Beach Rd. Daily 9am–6pm in summer and Mon–Sat 9:30am–5pm, Sun 11am–4pm in winter; last admission an hour before close; $16.95; ☎850/230-4839, ⓦ www.zooworldpcb.net.

If you're not opposed to animals being incarcerated, you'll enjoy this small collection of lions, tigers, orangutans, and other creatures, many of which prefer to sleep through the midday heat, so try to time your visit for early morning or late afternoon.

Eating

As you would expect on such a touristy stretch of coast, places **to eat** are plentiful. Many of these are as down-at-heel as their surroundings, and you can fill up on mediocre food – much of it presented in buffet style – without changing out of your swimsuit. You'll find more refined dining along Front Beach Road and Thomas Drive, with the more interesting choices concentrated at the eastern end of the beach strip. For upmarket options try the marinas off Thomas Drive.

Panama City Beach is known for its **seafood**, most of it fresh when cooked. Specialties include stuffed red snapper or grouper, seafood crêpes, and lobster thermidor.

Boatyard 5323 N Lagoon Dr ☎850/249-9273, ⓦwww.boatyardclub.com. Waterfront restaurant with a breezy, two-level open-air seating area and live music seven nights a week. Try the signature sweet potato fries. Most entrées around $25.

Capt. Anderson's 5551 N Lagoon Drive, in Captain Anderson's Marina ☎850/234-2225, ⓦwww.captandersons.com. One of the nicest restaurants in town, this stalwart offers mainly seafood dishes (around $25) including grilled bay shrimp, and a good enough selection of steaks to satisfy meat eaters. Dinner only. Closed Sun and mid-Nov to Feb.

Firefly 535 Beckrich Rd ☎850/249-3359, ⓦwww.fireflypcb.com. Panama City's best fine-dining restaurant offers an eclectic and well-executed menu with standouts like a dry-rubbed roasted pork tenderloin and redfish en papillote, as well as an extensive wine list. Entrées $35–40.

Mikato 7724 Front Beach Rd ☎850/235-1388. Watching the knife-throwing chefs is part of the show at this moderately priced sushi bar. Sushi rolls start at around $7.

Mike's Diner 17554 Front Beach Rd ☎850/234-1942. This place opens early, closes late, and offers good value all day. Has diner-style dishes ($8), and good home-made shakes and sundaes.

Pasta Grill 17840 Front Beach Rd, ☎850/236-6205; ⓦwww.pastagrill-pcb.com. Try the gnocchi Gorgonzola or veal Piccata at this great Italian joint, open for lunch and dinner. For dessert there's an authentic Italian bakery next door. Pastas start at around $13.

Schooners 5121 Gulf Drive ☎850/235-3555, ⓦwww.schooners.com. It may or may not be true to its billing as the "last local beach club," but it's lively enough and you can enjoy fresh seafood and listen to live music – plus they shoot off a cannon every night at sunset. Entrées are around $14.

Shuckum's Oyster Pub & Seafood Grill 15614 Front Beach Rd ☎850/235-3214, ⓦwww.shuckums.com. Cheap oysters in many styles, including delicious oyster PoBoy sandwiches ($13.95).

Sweet Basil's Bistro 11208 Front Beach Rd ☎850/234-2855, ⓦwww.sweet-basils.net. Classy Italian spot serving up traditional pasta dishes (from $9.75) and fresh seafood ($14–15).

The Treasure Ship 3605 Thomas Drive, in Treasure Island Marina ☎850/234-8881, ⓦwww.thetreasureship.com. A seafood restaurant built to resemble Sir Francis Drake's *Golden Hind*, with pirates hopping around the tables. Menu and prices subject to change. Closed Nov to mid-Feb.

Nightlife and entertainment

Even if you only stay a few minutes, you should visit one of the two beachside **nightlife** fleshpots, otherwise known as "superclubs": *Club La Vela*, 8813 Thomas Drive (☎850/235-1061, ⓦwww.lavela.com), or *Spinnaker*, at no. 875 on the same road 8795 (☎850/234-7882, ⓦwww.spinnakerbeachclub.com) – both open 10am to 4am, with cover charges varying nightly (generally $5–15). Each has dozens of bars, several discos, live bands, and a predominantly under-25 clientele eagerly awaiting the bikini and wet T-shirt contests and "hunk shows." Because competition between the two clubs is so intense, there will often be free beer in the early evening. During the day, the action is by the clubs' open-air pools, where you're overdressed if covering anything more than your bits.

Everywhere else is tranquil by comparison. Although they may also have live music, a number of **bars** are worth a call simply for a drink. *Schooners* (see above) is a popular place to hang out at night, or check out *Pineapple Willy's*, 9875 S Thomas Drive (☎850/235-1225), with a sports bar atmosphere.

West of Panama City Beach: the South Walton beaches

West of Panama City Beach, the motels eventually give way to the more rugged and less developed **beaches of South Walton County**: fifty miles of some of Florida's best-kept coastline. With some notable exceptions, accommodation here is in resort complexes with sky-high rates, but it's a gorgeous area to spend a few days. **Rte-30A** (far superior to US-98, which takes an inland route) is an eighteen-mile scenic road linking the region's small beach communities. For **general information** on the South Walton beaches and surrounding area, phone the South Walton Tourist Development Council (daily 8am–4.30pm;

☎ 1–800/822-6877, ⦿ www.beachesofsouthwalton.com), or visit their offices at the junction of Rte-331 and US-98, twenty miles west of Panama City Beach and ten miles east of San Destin. North of the tourist council on Rte-331 is the **Chamber of Commerce** at 63 South Centre Trail (daily 8:30am–5pm; ☎ 850/267-0683; ⦿ www.waltonareachamber.com).

Deer Lake State Park and Seagrove Beach

Deer Lake State Park, ten miles west of Panama City Beach on Rte-30A, is a dramatic stretch of creamy-white sand dunes on a coastline studded with smooth driftwood. The best beach of the South Walton bunch, it somehow goes almost without mention in the area's tourist brochures. The road signposted "Deer Lake Park" ends at a parking lot, and a five-minute walk through scrubland leads to the beach, a favorite hideout for nude sunbathing – officially, it's forbidden, but the rules are enforced infrequently.

A few miles west, **SEAGROVE BEACH** shares the same attractive shoreline as Deer Lake Park. If you wish to **stay**, the *Sugar Beach Inn Bed and Breakfast*, 3501 E Scenic 30A, at Seagrove Beach (☎ 850/231-1577, ⦿ www.sugarbeachinn .com; ❼), is a luxurious Victorian-style inn within walking distance of the sea. Among the places to **eat**, *Cocoons*, Hwy-30A (☎ 850/231-4544), is a great deli offering take-out sandwiches, barbecued ribs, and roast chicken for picnicking on the beach. You'll find more upmarket dining at the stylish *Café Thirty A*, 3899 East Scenic Hwy 30A (☎ 850/231-2166, ⦿ www.cafethirtya.com), with a brick oven and bar serving mainly fish and meat dishes in a casually stylish atmosphere. If you're keen to **cycle** or **paddle** around, Butterfly Bike & Kayak, 3657 Hwy-30A (☎ 850/231-2826), is a good place to start.

Inland: Eden Gardens State Park

Away from the coast road, only **Eden Gardens State Park** (daily 8am–sunset; $3), reached by Rte-395 from Seagrove Beach a mile east of Seaside, is worth a visit. The gardens, now disturbed only by the buzz of dragonflies, were once the base of the Wesley Lumber Company, which helped decimate Florida's forests during the 1890s timber boom. Impressed with the setting, the company's boss pinched some of the wood to build himself a grandiose two-story plantation-style home, the **Wesley House** (guided tours on the hour Thurs–Mon 10am–3pm; $3; ☎ 850/231-4214). After the death of the last Wesley, the house stood empty for ten years until Lois Maxon, a journalist with an interest in antiques, bought it in 1963 as a showcase for her collections, which include a Chippendale cabinet and a Louis XV mirror.

Seaside and Grayton Beach

An exception to the casual, unplanned appearance of most South Walton beach towns, **SEASIDE** (⦿ www.seasidefl.com), just west of Seagrove Beach, is an experiment in urban architecture begun in 1981 by a rich, idealistic developer named Robert Davies. The theory was that Seaside's pseudo-Victorian cottages, all in gleaming pastels and incredibly well kept, would foster village-like neighborliness and instill a sense of community. In reality, they did nothing of the sort, and it's basically a wealthy and sterile resort these days. Still, as elitist and economically discriminating as this place is, there's no escaping the unique appeal of the streets; you won't see houses like this anywhere else, and though you'll never feel like you belong, it's well worth stopping to explore. The shops are interesting and unusual, offering high-quality arts and crafts, gourmet food, and expensive clothing, and the beach is fantastic. Everything is expensive, though, starting with the **accommodation** at *Inn By the Sea*, *Vera Bradley*, 38 Seaside Ave (☎850/231-1940 or 1-800/848-1840, ⓦwww.cottagerentalagency.com; ❽), an almost impossibly twee inn, with decorating inspired by the flowery, calico and striped bags of the same name. Places to **eat** are equally pricey. *Bud and Alley's*, Rte-30A (☎850/231-5900, ⓦwww.budandalleys.com), offers a variety of great seafood dishes and sandwiches, while at lunchtime try *Pickle's Beachside Grill*, 2236 Rte-30A (☎850/231-5686), with delicious fried pickles and a mean cheeseburger. For luscious cakes and gourmet picnic supplies, head for Modica Market, 109 Central Square (☎850/231-1214), a well-stocked gourmet grocery store.

The antidote to Seaside's sterility is just a few miles further along Rte-30A at **GRAYTON BEACH**, whose secluded position (it's hemmed in by protected land) and ramshackle wooden dwellings have taken the fancy of a number of artists who now reside here. Check out some of their work at galleries such as The Studio Gallery (☎850/231-3331) and House of Art (☎850/231-9997), both on Logan Lane. **Accommodation** is a bit cheaper here than at Seaside and offers a more bohemian character. One unusual option is the ⚘ *Hibiscus Coffee and Guesthouse*, 85 De Funiak St (☎850/231-2733, ⓦwww.hibiscusflorida.com; ❻); they serve up a delicious (vegetarian) breakfast and also offer accommodation in nine eclectic and comfortable rooms – four in the coffeehouse building and five in a renovated 1904 house, as well as two standalone cottages. For **food**, meanwhile, *Another Broken Egg*, 51 Uptown Grayton Circle (☎850/231-7835), doles out tasty, moderately priced breakfasts. For a delicious Italian dinner, try *Borago*, 80 Hwy-30A (☎850/231-9167, ⓦwww.boragorestaurant.com), with a great antipasti menu including Parmesan-fried oysters and pan-seared scallops. If all the relaxing on the beach has you itching for a night out, pop by ⚘ *The Red Bar*, 70 Hotz Ave (☎850/231-1008, ⓦwww.theredbar.com, Wed–Sun). Open for breakfast, lunch and dinner, this funky restaurant serves a variety of fresh salads and entrées before morphing into a live music venue that stays hopping into the night.

Many who come to Grayton skip straight through to the **Grayton Beach State Recreation Area** (daily 8am–sunset; cars $4, pedestrians and cyclists $1; ☎850/231-4210, ⓦwww.floridastateparks.org/graytonbeach), just east of the village. The recreation area is walled by sand dunes and touches the banks of a large brackish lake. A night at the park's **campground** (☎1-800/326-3521; $19) leaves plenty of time for a slow exploration of the village and its natural surroundings. Continuing on to Destin (see p.444), Rte-30A rejoins US-98 seven miles west of Grayton.

Blue Mountain Beach and Santa Rosa Beach

Just west of Grayton Beach the relatively undiscovered **BLUE MOUNTAIN BEACH** is a welcome escape from the Spring Break crowds that zip past without a second glance. Don't make the same mistake; the quiet beach is an expanse of creamy white sand bordered by vacation homes. Wander into *For the Health of It*, no. 2217 on Scenic Route 30A (☎850/267-0558, ⓦwww .shopforthehealthofit.com), for a fresh smoothie and a huge selection of organic everything, as well as therapeutic massages.

A mile further west is **SANTA ROSA BEACH**. Slightly more developed than Blue Mountain, Santa Rosa has one of the best places to **stay** in the region: *A Highlands House Bed & Breakfast*, 4193 W Scenic 30A (☎850/267-0110, ⓦwww .ahighlandshouse.com; ❻), is housed in a converted, shabby-chic 1937 cottage with a perfect beachside setting and panoramic views. Right up the road is the ⚘ *Café Tango* (☎850/267-0054), serving some of the best food in the area including excellent pistachio-crusted grouper, which you can pair with any of eighty choices on the extensive wine list. The intimate dining room is in a little red and green cottage dating from 1945. *Smiling Fish Café*, Hwy-30A and Hwy-393 (☎850/622-3071), serves up a variety of healthy and flavorful salads and wraps.

Destin and around

Heading west from Panama City, six miles before you encounter **DESTIN**, you will pass through **San Destin**, its newer, more resort-like cousin. San Destin is an exclusive and somewhat soulless collection of high-rise resorts and is best given a wide berth. The real Destin, once a small fishing village and a cult name among anglers for the fat marlin and tuna lurking in an undersea canyon a few miles offshore now boasts towering condos, glimmering in the heat haze as you approach on US-98 and bear witness to more than two decades of unrestrained exploitation that have stripped away much of the town's character.

Accommodation

Most of the **accommodation** consists of rather monolithic hotels in central Destin, with a few notable exceptions. Just off Rte-2378, also known as Scenic US-98 or Beach Road, is the *Old Pier Motel*, 65 Pompano St (☎850/837-6442; ④), across the street from the Gulf but with beach access, offering comfortable rooms with full kitchens and outdoor barbecues. Another alternative is the centrally located *Hampton Inn*, 1625 US-98 E (☎850/654-2677 or 1-800/426-7866, ⓦwww.hamptoninn.com; ④), with standard rooms in a somewhat less soulless setting.

Camping options are limited to **Henderson Beach State Park**, just east of Destin, at 17000 Emerald Coast Parkway (☎850/837-7550 for information, ☎1-800/326-3521 for reservations, ⓦwww.floridastateparks.org/henderson beach; $21), and in central Destin, at the *Destin Campground*, 209 Beach Drive (☎850/837-6511; $40).

The town and beach

Evidence of Destin's sudden expansion can be found amid the fading photos in the **Old Destin Post Office**, **History and Fishing Museum** both at 108 Stahlman Ave (Tues–Sat 10am–4pm; $5), with mounted record-breaking catches and thousands of pictures of landed fish with their grinning captors, offering proof of Destin's high esteem among hook-and-line enthusiasts. Admission to the post office is by appointment only; ask for details at the Fishing Museum.

The enticing white sands just east of Destin provide an escape from the condo overkill. The **beach** here is family territory, but it offers relaxation, excellent swimming, and classic Gulf-coast sunsets. To reach it, take **Rte-2378**, which makes a coast-hugging loop off US-98, starting about four miles from Destin.

Eating and nightlife

On Old US-98, *The Back Porch*, at no. 1740 (☎850/837-2022), is Destin's oldest seafood and oyster house and one of the few places open late (until 11pm). At local favorite ⌁ *Dewey Destin Seafood*, 9 Calhoun Ave (☎850/837-7575, ⓦwww.destinseafood.com), you can sit on a weathered dock right on Choctawhatchee Bay. If you feel like sharing some of your terrific steamed shrimp or soft shell crabs, there are plenty of pelicans nearby to take leftovers off your hands. *Harbor Docks*, 538 US-98 (☎850/837-2506), offers top-notch made-from-scratch dishes, including Louisiana-style crawfish salad. Stop into the oceanfront *Beach Walk Cafe*, 2996 Scenic Hwy-98 East (☎850/650-7100, Ⓦwww.beachwalkcafe.com), winner of multiple best-of-Florida restaurant awards. Dinner dishes are a bit pricey, but there's a great, reasonably priced lunch menu with tasty options like Caribbean fish tacos.

Destin's **nightlife** has little vigor: a few of the beachside bars and restaurants offer nightly drinks specials – look for the signs – and live music. Dance the night away at *Nightown*, 140 Palmetto St (☎850/837-7625; open until 4am), two blocks east of the Destin Bridge (see below), where you can listen to live rock bands in one room or dance music in front of a video wall in another.

Okaloosa Island and Fort Walton Beach

US-98 leaves Destin by rising over the **Destin Bridge**, offering towering views of the two-tone ocean and intensely white sands, before hitting the crazy-golf courses and amusement parks of **OKALOOSA ISLAND**. The island's **beaches**, immediately west, are a better sight, kept in their unspoiled state by their owner – the US Air Force – and making a lively weekend playground for local youths and high-spirited beach bums.

A mile west, the neon motel signs greeting arrivals to **FORT WALTON BEACH** offer no indication this was the site of a major religious and social center during the Paleo-Indian period – so important were the finds made here that the place came to be associated with a rigid form of tribal society, the so-called "Fort Walton Culture" (see Contexts, p.458, for more). These days it's military culture that dominates, as the town is home to Eglin, the country's biggest Air Force base. Aside from a few crewcuts and topless bars, however, you'll see little evidence of the base close to US-98, and much of Fort Walton Beach has a more downbeat and homely feel – and slightly lower prices – than Destin. Stop by the local **visitors center**, 1540 Miracle Strip Parkway (Mon–Fri 8am–5pm, Sat & Sun 9am–4pm; ☎850/651-7131 or 1-800/322-3319, Ⓦwww.destin-fwb.com), for information on eating and accommodation.

The main attraction here is the world's oldest marine show aquarium: the **Gulfarium**, 1010 Miracle Strip Parkway (hours vary wildly, call for details; last admission two hours before closing time; $18.75; ☎850/244-5169, Ⓦwww .gulfarium.com). Opened in 1955, it's now one of the best aquariums in the area, with all kinds of sea life on show. Sharks, moray eels, and sea turtles are displayed in their natural habitat and other exhibits include penguins and alligators. A program of dolphin and sea lion shows, each lasting about twenty minutes, is scheduled throughout the day.

Accommodation

Accommodation in these parts is plentiful and much like the rest of the coastal Panhandle, with the exception of *Aunt Martha's Bed and Breakfast* at 315 Shell Ave SE (☎850/243-6702, Ⓦwww.auntmarthasbedandbreakfast.com; ❺), a little gem right off Hwy-98. Rooms are comfortable and the full, hot breakfasts are delicious. Most of the **motels** are along Miracle Strip Parkway (the local section of US-98). *Super 8*, at no. 333 SW (☎850/244-4999; ❸), is a very basic two-story motel with a small pool and some rooms with fridges and microwaves. *Quality Inn*, at no. 322 (☎850/275-0300 or 1-800/4CH-OICE; ❹), offers comfortable rooms with a pool and bayfront rooms.

The nearest **campground** is the RV-only *Playground RV Park*, four miles north on Hwy-189 (☎850/862-3513); campers with **tents** should make for

Navarre Beach Campground (☎850/939-2188, ⓦ www.navbeach.com), just outside Navarre, where a site costs $45 and cabins start at $59.

The Indian Temple Mound and Air Force Armament museums

If you were inspired by the sizeable temple mound standing incongruously beside the busy highway into Fort Walton Beach, then you might wish to inspect the small **Indian Temple Mound Museum** (Mon–Sat 10am–4:30pm; $5; ☎850/833-9595), at the junction of US–98 and Rte–85, which is crammed with over four thousand artifacts.

For an insight into more contemporary culture, the **Air Force Armament Museum**, 100 Museum Drive, Eglin (daily 9.30am–4.30pm; free; ☎850/651-1808), six miles north of Fort Walton Beach on Rte-85, has a large stock of what the local Air Force base is famous for – guns, missiles, and bombs, and the planes that carry them. The first guided missiles were put together here in the 1940s, and work on developing and testing (non-nuclear) airborne weaponry has continued unabated ever since.

Eating and nightlife

The area's better **restaurants** are considerably easier to reach with your own transport. *Old Bay Steamer*, 102 Santa Rosa Blvd (☎850/664-2795), serves fresh seafood and pasta dishes, while *Thai Saree*, 163 Eglin Parkway (☎850/244-4600), has excellent Thai food for lunch and dinner at reasonable prices. But best of all are the high-quality steak and seafood dinners at the *Coach-N-Four*, 1313 Lewis Turner Blvd (☎850/863-3443).

Fort Walton Beach **nightlife** amounts to little more than the usual **beachfront bars**, mostly on Okaloosa Island, with some good happy hours. The best are *Pandora's*, 1226 Santa Rosa Blvd (☎850/244-8669), which draws tourists and locals to its nightly specials; and *Fudpucker's On the Island*, 108 Santa Rosa Blvd (☎850/243-3833), which has live entertainment on "The Deck" during the summer season. *Pandora's* attracts a mature clientele, while the crowd at *Fudpucker's On the Island* is much younger.

West from Fort Walton

If you're driving, travel **west from Fort Walton** along Hwy-98. Rte-399, which branches off of Hwy-98, features sixty scenic miles along **Santa Rosa Island** to the Gulf Islands National Seashore, near Pensacola Beach (see "Pensacola and around," p.453), but was closed indefinitely at the time of writing. The parallel route, the continuation of Hwy-98, is much duller but is the one the thrice-daily Greyhound **bus** takes from the station at 101 SE Perry Ave (☎850/243-1940).

Pensacola and around

Tucked away at the western end of the Panhandle, **PENSACOLA** is built on the northern bank of the broad Pensacola Bay, five miles inland from the nearest beaches. Although its primary features are a naval aviation school and some busy dockyards, Pensacola is also of considerable historic interest. In 1559, Spanish soldiers and colonists established a settlement at Pensacola that lasted two years before being destroyed by a hurricane. A permanent settlement was not established

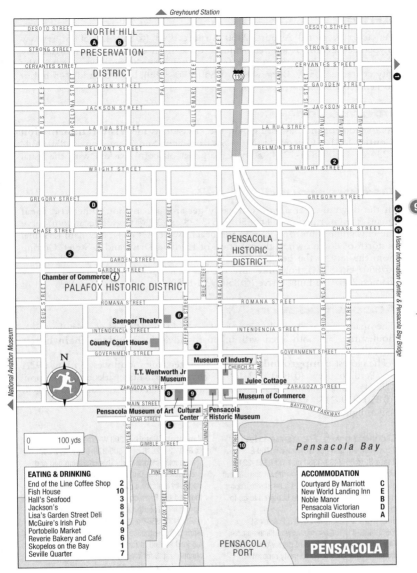

EATING & DRINKING

End of the Line Coffee Shop	2
Fish House	10
Hall's Seafood	3
Jackson's	8
Lisa's Garden Street Deli	5
McGuire's Irish Pub	4
Portobello Market	9
Reverie Bakery and Café	6
Skopelos on the Bay	1
Seville Quarter	7

ACCOMMODATION

Courtyard By Marriott	C
New World Landing Inn	E
Noble Manor	B
Pensacola Victorian	D
Springhill Guesthouse	A

here until 1698, when Fort San Carlos was built. The fort repeatedly changed hands between the Spanish, French, and British before becoming the venue where Florida was officially ceded by Spain to the US in 1821. The city has retained enough evidence of its mercurial history to warrant a short visit, but it also makes a good base for exploring one of the prettiest and least-spoiled parts of the coastal Panhandle. Just cross the Bay Bridge to the coast, and you'll find Pensacola Beach neighboring the wild, protected beaches of the Gulf Islands National Seashore.

Arrival

Pensacola Regional Airport, 2430 Airport Blvd (℡850/436-5005, @www .flypensacola.com), is a fifteen-minute drive from downtown. Unfortunately, the Greyhound **bus** station is far from central, being seven miles north of the city center at 505 W Burgess Rd (℡850/476-8199); bus #50 and #45 link it to Pensacola proper.

Information

At the foot of the Bay Bridge, on the city side, is the **Visitor Information Center**, 1401 E Gregory St (Mon–Sat 8am–5pm, Sun 11am–4pm; ℡850/434-1234 or 1-800/874-1234, @www.visitpensacola.com), packed with the usual worthwhile handouts.

Getting around

In the downtown area, you can easily get around on foot. Otherwise, **local buses** (for information call ℡850/595-3228 ext 30, @www.goecat.com) serve the city, while route #61 goes to the beach two times daily; the main terminal is north of downtown at the junction of Fairfield Drive and L Street. Getting from the city to the beach by **taxi** will cost roughly $25–30; try Yellow Cab (℡850/456-8294). For **bike** hire on the beach stop by Tiki Island Golf & Games, 2 Via De Luna Drive (℡850/932-1550).

Accommodation

The main approach roads from I-10 – N Davis Boulevard and Pensacola Boulevard – are both lined with billboards advertising **budget chain hotels** for $50–65 a night.

The closest **campgrounds** are *Big Lagoon*, ten miles southwest on Rte-292A on Perdido Key (℡850/492-1595, @www.floridastateparks.org/biglagoon; $17.84), and *Navarre Beach Campground*, 9201 Navarre Parkway US-98 (℡850/939-2188 @www.navbeach.com; $45), which also rents cabins from $59 a night.

Downtown Pensacola

Courtyard By Marriot Downtown 700 E Chase St ℡850/439-3330 or 1-800/321-2211, @www.courtyardpensacoladowntown.com. Brand new motel with comfortable, if a bit sterile, rooms and a nice pool if you can't be bothered to go to the beach. ➏

New World Landing Inn 600 S Palafox St ℡850/432-4111, @www.newworldlanding.com. This homey hotel, with lots of dark wood and plush carpeting, has comfortable, newly renovated rooms and a prime location at the south end of Palafox St. ➏

Noble Manor 110 W Strong St ℡850/434-9544, @www.noblemanor.com. This charming bed and breakfast sits in the peaceful North Hill District, with six cozy rooms. Breakfast is served in either the formal dining room or front porch and, unusually for a B&B, there is a pool, hot tubs, and koi pond. ➏

Pensacola Victorian 203 W Gregory St ℡850/434-2818 or 1-800/370-8354, @www .pensacolavictorian.com. This charming bed and breakfast is in a Queen Anne-style home that was originally built for a captain whose son also founded the Pensacola Symphony Orchestra. ➎

Springhill Guesthouse 903 N Spring St ℡850/438-6887 or 1-800/475-1956, @www .springhillguesthouse.com. The two suites feature a full kitchen and attractive fireplaces. They also offer cheaper rates for weekly stays and serve a continental breakfast. ➎

Pensacola Beach

Hilton Pensacola Beach 12 Via De Luna Drive ℡850/916-2999, @www.hilton.com. One of the beach's most luxurious properties, geared to business guests as much as to vacationing families. Here you'll find Pensacola's largest convention space, the city's only indoor heated

pool, and a "Kid's Club" with various activities to keep the youngsters entertained. ❽
Paradise Inn 21 Via De Luna Drive ☎850/932-2319 or 1-800/301-5925, ⓦwww.paradiseinn -pb.com. This casual hotel, across the street from the beach offers great value for the money; comfortable rooms, free continental breakfast and an onsite pool just sweeten the deal. ❺

Springhill Suites 24 Via De Luna Drive ☎850/932-6000 or 1-800/406-7885, ⓦwww .springhillsuites.com. All rooms are suites in this comfortable, Gulf-facing hotel, with refrigerators, microwaves, and coffeemakers. There are also three pools, one of them heated, and a complimentary buffet breakfast. ❼

The City

The city is grouped in three distinct, adjoining **districts**: the North Hill Preservation District in the northern section of the city, the south-central Palafox Historic District, and the Pensacola Historic District in the city's southeast quarter. The latter two are the most interesting because of their past – especially the Pensacola Historic District, the streets of which are lined with many houses and museums of interest. The only other attraction that might delay serious sunbathing at Pensacola Beach is the naval aviation museum.

The Palafox Historic District

Pensacola was already a booming port at the turn of the nineteenth century, and the opening of the Panama Canal was expected to further boost the city's fortunes. Sadly, the surge in wealth never came, but the optimism of the era is apparent in the delicate ornamentation and detail in the buildings around the **Palafox Historic District**. Take a look first at the **Escambia County Court House**, at the junction of Palafox and Government streets, which, besides its legal function, has also seen service as a customs house, a post office, and tax office. Opposite, the slender form and vertically aligned windows of the **Seville Tower** exaggerate the height of what, in 1909, was the tallest building in Florida. A block further north, at 118 S Palafox Place, the Spanish Baroque **Saenger Theatre** (see "Nightlife," p.452) was built in 1925, and is now the base of the Pensacola Symphony Orchestra.

North Hill Preservation District

Between 1870 and 1930, Pensacola's professional classes took a shine to the **North Hill Preservation District** area, just across Wright Street from the Palafox District, and commissioned elaborate homes in a plethora of fancy styles. Strewn across the tree-studded fifty-block area are pompous Neoclassical porches, cutesy Tudor Revival cottages, low-slung California-style bungalows, and rounded towers belonging to fine Queen Anne homes. These are private residences not open to the public, and the best way to see them is by walking or driving around Palafox, Spring, Strong, and Baylen streets.

The clamor to build houses in this fashionable neighborhood led to the dismantling of **Fort George**, which had once barracked two thousand British troops before falling to the Spanish at the Battle of Pensacola in 1781. Only an imitation cannon and a plaque at the corner of Palafox and La Rua streets commemorate the original location of the fort.

The Pensacola Historic District: Historic Pensacola Village

As a commercial center, Pensacola kicked into gear in the late 1700s with a cosmopolitan mix of Native Americans, early settlers, and seafaring traders gathering here to swap, sell, and barter on the waterfront of the **Pensacola Historic District**, just east of Palafox Street. Those who did well took up permanent residence, and many of their homes remain in fine states of repair, forming – together with several museums – the **Historic Pensacola Village** (Mon–Sat 10am–4pm; $6; T850/595-5985, W www.historicpensacola.org). Each ticket is valid for one week and allows access to all of the museums and former homes (and you should see them *all* – the effect of the whole is far greater than any of its parts) in an easily navigated four-block area. Start at the **Museum of Commerce**, next door to the gift shop, on the corner of Zaragoza and Tarragona streets; it's an entertaining indoor re-creation of Palafox Street in its turn-of-the-twentieth-century heyday, displaying many of the original storefronts and shop fittings. Much of the prosperity of Pensacola was based on the timber industry, a point celebrated by a noisy, working sawmill in the **Museum of Industry,** just across Zaragoza Street.

To catch up on earlier local history, cross Church Street from Historic Pensacola Village to the sedate **Colonial Archaeology Trail**, where bits of pottery and weapons suggest the lifestyles of the city's first Spanish inhabitants and a marked path leads around the site of the Government House, an outpost of the British Empire which collapsed in the 1820s. Virtually next door (opposite the gift shop), the 1809 **Julee Cottage** belonged to Julee Panton, a "freewoman of color" who had her own land, business, and even her own slave.

Other **restored homes** in the vicinity signify the mishmash of architectural styles, from Creole to Greek Revival, favored by wealthier Pensacolians in the late 1800s. Filled with period furnishings, they make for an enjoyable browse.

If you lack the energy or inclination to visit all the museums and old homes of the Historic Village, head instead to the **Pensacola Historical Museum**, 115 E Zaragoza St (Mon–Sat 10am–4.30pm; T850/433-1559, W www .pensacolahistory.org), operated by the Pensacola Historic Society and containing exhibits touching on pretty much every aspect of Pensacola's past.

The **T. T. Wentworth Jr Museum**, on Plaza Ferdinand (Mon–Sat 10am–4pm; free; T850/595-5985, W www.historicpensacola.org), contains the random, garage-sale-like collections that once belonged to a Mr Wentworth, who intended to create a museum of oddities. Thankfully, his ambitions were thwarted. The existing ephemera are briefly diverting, though it's the yellow-brick Renaissance building (constructed as the city hall in 1907) itself that is the real attraction. The upstairs has been converted to a museum of local history, which is comprehensive but not over-exciting. In the Plaza Ferdinand stands a statue to Andrew Jackson, the state's first governor, commemorating the spot where Florida was accepted into the US and, for the first time, an American flag was planted on US soil. If you want to learn more about the exhibits, join one of the tours running regularly throughout the day.

Museum of Art

Cleverly incorporated into the old jailhouse, Pensacola's **Museum of Art**, opposite the Cultural Center at 407 S Jefferson St (Tues–Fri 10am–5pm, Sat & Sun noon–5pm; $5, free Tues; T850/432-6247, W www.pensacolamuseum ofart.org), was built in 1906 on what was once the shoreline of Pensacola Bay (after ships started dumping their ballast stones, the shoreline was pushed out by half a mile). The art isn't of any particular distinction, but the building itself is worth exploring: old prison cells have been preserved as exhibition space, class-rooms for children now occupy the former women's incarceration area, and temporary exhibits fill the upstairs all-male cell block.

National Naval Aviation Museum and Fort Barrancas

You don't have to be a military fanatic to enjoy the ✈ **National Naval Aviation Museum** (daily 9am–5pm; free; T850/452-3604,

▲ National Naval Aviation Museum

ⓦ www.navalaviationmuseum.org), inside the US naval base on Navy Boulevard, about eight miles southwest of downtown Pensacola and accessible by bus #58 (no Sun service). If arriving by car, civilians must enter the base via the circuitous Gulf Beach Highway and Blue Angel Parkway. The highly enjoyable museum underscores Pensacola's role as the home base of US naval aviation, where thousands of new pilots are trained each year. Get a taste of that experience by climbing into many of the full-sized training cockpits and playing with the controls. The museum also displays an impressive collection of US naval aircraft, from the first flimsy seaplane acquired in 1911 to the Phantoms and Hornets of more recent times. Among them are a couple of oddities: a small Vietnamese plane, which carried a Vietnamese family onto a US carrier during the fall of Saigon, and the Command Module from the first Skylab mission in 1973, whose crew were naval pilots. The second floor features a Homefront exhibit that re-creates Palafox St during 1942, complete with a barbershop and dry goods store. There's also a seven-story-tall IMAX movie screen, on which a pilot's-eye view of flight makes for quite a visual sensation (tickets $8).

On the other side of the road lies the visitor center for **Fort Barrancas** (daily 9am–4pm; guided tours daily 2pm; free), part of the National Seashore area (see p.453). It's worth spending an hour or so at this well-preserved 1698 Spanish fort, whose design includes a fascinating system of connecting interior vaults.

Eating

The better **eating options** are in and around the downtown area. Many of the establishments here cater to office workers and are only open during the day, but you'll find some open for dinner. Along the beach, the dining options are more homogeneous but the views – over the bay and Gulf coast – are far superior.

Pensacola

End of the Line Coffee Shop 610 E Wright St ⓣ850/429-0336. Munch on snacks and sandwiches (from $8) in the 1970s-inspired interior, which is the frequent setting for poetry readings. Dinner is served on Thursday nights and there's also a Sunday brunch.
Fish House 600 S Barracks St ⓣ850/470-0003, ⓦ www.goodgrits.com. A good local restaurant

featuring sushi and steaks along with seafood (entrées from $18), which you can enjoy while sitting outside overlooking the bay. The signature dish is "Grits a Ya-Ya" (smoked Gouda cheese grits covered with grilled mushrooms and shrimp).
Hall's Seafood 920 E Gregory St, at the foot of the Pensacola Bay Bridge ⓣ850/438-9019, ⓦ www.hallsseafoodrestaurant.com. Come here

for all-you-can-eat fish dinners (from around $13) and stellar views over the bay. Given its distance from downtown, you'll need your own transport.

Jackson's 400 S Palafox St ☎850/469-9898, Ⓦwww.goodgrits.com. This elegant steakhouse occupies a restored 1860 building overlooking Plaza Ferdinand. The dinner menu includes wood-fired chicken ($28) or filet mignon with fried oysters ($33). Open for lunch and dinner; closed Sun.

Lisa's Garden St Deli 236 W Garden St ☎850/470-0305. For cheap specialty sandwiches ($8), try this deli, which serves excellent, inexpensive meals.

McGuire's Irish Pub 600 E Gregory St ☎850/433-6789, Ⓦwww.mcguiresirishpub.com. While the atmosphere here is very Irish (see opposite), the food menu is more mixed, ranging from down-to-earth corned beef and cabbage to excellent steaks. Entrées are $20–25. The restaurant also offers an impressive wine list, and if you've saved any room, finish off with the *brownie à la mode* for dessert.

Portobello Market 400 S Jefferson St (inside the Pensacola Little Theater) ☎850/439-6545. Inviting lunch spot with exposed brick walls, lots of light,

and tasty sandwiches, salads, and entrées (from $13) such as wasabi-crusted grouper.

Reverie Bakery and Café 101 S Jefferson St ☎850/432-6026. This bakery is a nice spot for lunch, offering soups, sandwiches (around $8), quiche, and good European-style breads, cakes and pastries. Closed Sun.

Skopelos on the Bay 670 Scenic Hwy ☎850/432-6565, Ⓦwww.myskopelos.com. This venerable fine-dining Pensacola restaurant serves great seafood – try the scampi Cervantes ($26) – in a lovely setting overlooking the water.

Pensacola Beach

Flounder's Chowder & Ale House 800 Quietwater Beach Rd ☎850/932-2003, Ⓦwww.flounders chowderhouse.com. This alehouse serves hearty seafood dinners such as shrimp salad, grouper, and, of course, flounder. Entrées start at around $20.

Peg Leg Pete's 1010 Fort Pickens Rd ☎850/932-4139, Ⓦwww.peglegpetes.com. Known for its Cajun food (entrées around $15) and excellent raw bar, where you can slurp down oysters with various tasty accompaniments. The outdoor playground in the sand makes this a good place to bring the kids.

Nightlife

Pick up a copy of *The Weekender*, a supplement published every Friday with the *News Journal* daily newspaper, for information on the entertainment and nightlife possibilities in Pensacola. The city boasts two good **theaters** showing plays, musicals, and dance performances, as well as more lowbrow entertainment such as body-building contests. The Pensacola Little Theatre, 400 S Jefferson St (box office Mon–Fri 10am–5.30pm and one hour before curtain; tickets from $15; ☎850/432-2042, Ⓦwww.pensacolalittletheatre.com), is housed in the Pensacola Cultural Center, and even if you don't see a production here, it's worth going inside just to look around. More architecturally impressive than the Little, the Saenger Theatre, 118 S Palafox Place (box office Mon–Fri 10am–5pm and two hours before curtain; ☎850/595-3880, Ⓦwww.pensacolasaenger.com), puts on plays and operas in a season running from October to April. At the time of writing, the theater was under complete renovation but scheduled to re-open in March 2009.

The Memorial Day party

Every year between the Friday and Monday of the last week of May, Pensacola is consumed by a **gay and lesbian party**, which began when a 20-year-old local, Dickie Carr, threw a party at the **San Carlos Hotel** (demolished to build the courts of law). Dickie's father, who managed the hotel in the Seventies, said he would foot the bill for any of the five hundred rooms that weren't taken. They all were. The party took place on Memorial Day and has become an annual event involving most of the town and drawing large numbers of outsiders. Despite a brief and quickly squashed homophobic reaction from local businesses in 1985, the party gets bigger every year, pulling Americans from every state. The daytime festivities are mainly at the beach, while at night the partying shifts to the Pensacola nightclubs.

For a city with a conservative reputation, there's also a lively gay scene and a wild gay Memorial Day celebration that annually envelops the city. A couple of prime venues are listed below.

Pensacola

Emerald City 406 E Wright St ℗ 850/433-9491, ⓦ www.emeraldcitypensacola.com. The biggest dance club for gays and lesbians features drag shows, wet boxer contests, and plenty of thumping dance music (dance floor closed Tues). It's also a popular venue for the Memorial Day party.

Jack & Ron's Piano and Video Bar 101 S Jefferson St ℗ 850/434-0291, ⓦ www.jackandrons.com. This lively downtown piano bar/pub (with a largely gay clientele) has one of the best happy hours in Pensacola and is a great spot for a martini.

McGuire's Irish Pub (See review oppposite for address and phone details). This lively pub brews its own ales and features nightly entertainment in each of its nine dining rooms. Beware: kissing the moosehead above the fireplace may be the price you pay for refusing to sing along to the Irish folk music.

Seville Quarter 130 E Government St ℗ 850/434-6211, ⓦ www.rosies.com. A local and tourist favorite, Seville offers eight venues decked out to reflect Pensacola's history. It's a bit more expensive than you might pay elsewhere, but it can be plenty of fun.

Pensacola Beach

Bamboo Willie's 400 Quietwater Boardwalk ℗ 850/916-9888, ⓦ www.bamboowillies.com.

This lively spot has a long bar lined with machines churning Technicolor frozen cocktails and enough space for a live band and the attendant dancing.

The Dock 4 Casino Beach Boardwalk, beside the pier ℗ 850/934-3314, ⓦ www.thedockpensacolabeach.com. Packed every Fri and Sat night when DJs set the mood, this club is also a venue for touring bands, local acts, and karaoke nights.

Flounder's Chowder & Ale House 800 Quietwater Beach Rd ℗ 850/932-2003. Possibly the most hyped place to drink, this bar draws as many drinkers as diners and has live beach bands about once a week. (See also review under "Eating," opposite).

Paddy O'Leary's Irish Pub 49 Via De Luna Drive ℗ 850/916-9808, ⓦ www.paddyolearysirishpub.com. Host of frequent Texas Hold 'Em poker tournaments, washed down with a pint of Guinness stout served the way it was intended.

Sandshaker Lounge 731 Pensacola Beach Blvd ℗ 850/932-2211, ⓦ www.sandshaker.com. The self-professed birthplace of the Bushwacker, an "adult milkshake" consisting of Kahlua, coconut, rum, and other ingredients – a popular tipple in these parts, and done very well at this bar.

Around Pensacola

On the other side of the bay from the city, the glistening quartz beaches of two **barrier islands** are ideal for sunbathing. Santa Rosa Island runs fifty miles from Fort Walton and contains Pensacola Beach, while Perdido Key sits to the west of Santa Rosa. The **Gulf Islands National Seashore**, a generic name for several parks, each with a specific point of natural or historical interest, stretches 150 miles along the coast from here to Mississippi and includes the Naval Live Oaks Reservation, the western section of Santa Rosa Island, Fort Barrancas, and the eastern section of Perdido Key.

Gulf Breeze and the Naval Live Oaks Reservation

En route to Santa Rosa Island, via the three-mile-long Pensacola Bay Bridge, you'll pass through the wealthy community of **Gulf Breeze**. Apart from a few supermarkets, the only reason to give it more than a passing thought is the **Naval Live Oaks Reservation** (daily 8am–sunset; free), about two miles east along US-98. In the 1820s, part of this live-oak forest was turned into a tree farm, intended to ensure a supply of shipbuilding material for years to come. Precise calculations were made as to how many trees would be needed for a particular ship, and the requisite number of acorns then planted – followed by a fifty-year wait. Problems were plentiful: the oak was too heavy for road transportation, wood rustlers cut down trees and sold them to foreign navies, and the final blow for the farm was the advent of iron-built ships.

The **visitor center** (daily 8.30am–4.30pm; ☎850/934-2600), near the entrance, has exhibits and explanatory texts on the intriguing forest, where fragments from Native American settlements from as far back as 1000 BC have been found. To escape the glare of the sun for an hour or so, take one of the short but shady **forest trails**, which include a two-mile section of what was, in the early 1800s, Florida's major roadway, linking Pensacola and St Augustine.

Pensacola Beach

From Gulf Breeze, another bridge ($1 toll) leads across a narrow waterway to Santa Rosa Island and the epitome of a Gulf Coast strand, **Pensacola Beach**. Featuring mile after mile of fine white sands, rental outlets for beach and water-sports equipment, a pier lined with fishermen, beachside bars, and snack stands, it's hard to beat for uncomplicated seaside recreation. With its sprinkling of motels and hotels (see p.448), Pensacola Beach also makes an alternative – if pricier – base to mainland Pensacola. The **Visitor Information Center** is opposite the pier at 735 Pensacola Beach Blvd (daily 9am–5pm; ☎850/932-1500 or 1-800/635-4803, ⓦwww.visitpensacolabeach.com).

Navarre Beach

Navarre Beach, unfortunately, is an explosion of unpleasant development, neither as pretty as Seaside nor as impersonally glamorous as San Destin. Yet just beyond where Rte-399 curves north to cross the Pensacola Sound is one of the loveliest stretches of reef dunes and sand on the coast. In some places along this stretch there are no lifeguards, so swim in the sea at your own risk. Hurricane Opal did its best to raze the dunes to nothing in 1995, but impressive conservation work has restored much of the coast. For the best and most popular food on the beach, you have to pay a visit to the *Sailor's Grill*, 1451 Navarre Beach Causeway (☎850/939-1092), where the breakfasts are scrumptious and the Key lime pie is legendary.

Perdido Key

Perdido Key, another barrier island to the west of Santa Rosa (Chamber of Commerce, 15500 Perdido Key Drive ☎850/492-4660 or 1-800/328-0107, ⓦwww.perdidochamber.com), offers more pristine beaches. Its eastern section, protected as part of the Gulf Islands National Seashore, provides five miles of island untouched by roads. A one-and-a-quarter-mile nature trail allows you to explore the area, and if you're smitten with the seclusion, stick around to swim or pitch your tent at one of the primitive **campgrounds** (see p.448). The remainder of Perdido Key is much like Santa Rosa Island, a hotbed of sport, drinking, and suntanning rituals.

Travel details

Buses

Panama City to: Fort Walton Beach (3 daily; 1hr 50min); Pensacola (3 daily; 3hr).
Pensacola to: Fort Walton Beach (3 daily; 1hr 10min); Mobile (3 daily; 1hr 5min); New Orleans (2 daily; 4hr or 10hr 25min); Panama City (3 daily; 2hr 40min); Tallahassee (4 daily; 5hr 40min).

Tallahassee to: Gainesville (4 daily; 2hr 30min); Jacksonville (4 daily; 2hr 55min); Miami (7 daily; 12–18hr); New Orleans (2 daily; 10–12hr); Orlando (5 daily; 6hr); Panama City (3 daily; 2hr 40min); Pensacola (3 daily; 5hr 15min); Tampa (4 daily; 6–9hr); Thomasville (2 daily; 40min).

Contexts

Contexts

The historical framework 457

Natural Florida 472

Florida on film 480

Books..487

The historical framework

Contrary to popular belief, Florida's history goes back far beyond Walt Disney World and motel-lined beaches. For thousands of years, its aboriginal inhabitants lived in organized social groupings with contacts across a large section of the Americas. During the height of European colonization, it became a Spanish possession and, for a time, was under British control. Only in the nineteenth century did Florida become part of the US: the beginning of a period of unrestrained exploitation and expansion and the start of many of the problems with which the state continues to grapple today.

Origins of the land

Over billions of years, rivers flowing through what's now **northern Florida** carried debris from the Appalachian mountains to the coast, and their deposits of fine-powdered rock formed the beaches and barrier islands of the Panhandle. Further south, the highest section of a sea-bed plateau – the **Florida peninsula** – altered in shape according to the world's ice covering. The exposed land sometimes measured twice its present size; during other periods, the coastline was far inland of its current position, with wave action carving out still-visible bluffs in the oolitic limestone base. In the **present era**, beginning about 75 million years ago, rotting vegetation mixed with rainfall to form acid that burned holes in the limestone, and natural freshwater springs emerged; the underground water accumulated from heavy rains that preceded each Ice Age. Inland forests of live oak and pine became inhabited 20,000 years ago by mastodons, mammoths, and saber-toothed tigers, thought to have traveled – over many generations – across the ice-covered Bering Strait from Siberia.

First human habitation

Two theories exist regarding the origins of Florida's **first human inhabitants**. It's commonly believed the earliest arrivals followed the same route as the animals from Siberia, crossing North America and arriving in northern Florida around 10,000 years ago. A minority of anthropologists take the alternative view that the first Floridians were the result of migration by aboriginal peoples in South and Central America. Either way, the **Paleo** (or "Early") **Indians** in Florida lived hunter-gatherer existences – the spear tips they used are widely found across the central and northern parts of the state.

Around 5000 BC, social patterns changed: settlements became semi-permanent and diet switched from meat to shellfish, snails, and mollusks, which were abundant along the rivers. Traveling was done by dugout canoe and, periodically, a community would move to a new site, probably to allow food supplies to replenish themselves. Discarded shells and other rubbish were piled onto the **midden mounds** still commonly seen in the state.

Though pottery began to appear around 2000 BC, not until 1000 BC was there a big change in lifestyle, as indicated by the discovery of **irrigation** canals, patches of land cleared for **cultivation**, and cooking utensils used to prepare grown food. From the time of the Christian era, the erection of **burial mounds** – elaborate tombs of prominent tribespeople, often with sacrificed kin and valuable objects also placed inside – became common. These suggest strong religious and trading links across an area stretching from Central America to the North American interior.

Spreading east from the Georgian coastal plain, the **Fort Walton Culture** became prevalent from around 200 AD, dividing society into a rigid caste system and forming villages planned around a central plaza. Throughout Florida at this time, approximately 100,000 inhabitants formed several distinct tribal groupings, most notably the **Timucua** across northern Florida, the **Calusa** around the southwest and Lake Okeechobee, the **Apalachee** in the Panhandle, and the **Tequesta** along the southeast coast.

European settlement

After Christopher Columbus located the "New World" in 1492, Europe's great sea powers were increasingly active around the Caribbean. One of them, Spain, had discovered and plundered the treasures of ancient civilizations in Central America, and all were eager to locate other riches across these and neighboring lands. The **first European sighting** of Florida is believed to have been made by the father and son team of John and Sebastian Cabot in 1498, when they set eyes on what is now called Cape Florida, on Key Biscayne in Miami.

Spaniard **Juan Ponce de León** made the **first European landing in 1513**. While searching for Bimini, Ponce de León sighted land during Pascua Florida, the Spanish Easter "Festival of the Flowers," and named what he saw **La Florida** – or "Land of Flowers." After landing somewhere between the mouth of the St Johns River and present-day St Augustine, Ponce de León sailed on around the Florida Keys, naming them Los Martires, for their supposed resemblance to the bones of martyred men, and Las Tortugas (now the Dry Tortugas), named for the turtles he saw around them.

Sent to deal with troublesome natives in the Lower Antilles, it was eight years before Ponce de León returned to Florida, this time with a mandate from the Spanish king to **conquer and colonize** the territory. Landing on the southwest coast, probably somewhere between Tampa Bay and Fort Myers, Ponce de León met a hostile reception from the Calusa Indians and was forced to withdraw, eventually dying from an arrow wound received in the battle.

Rumors of gold hidden in Apalachee, in the north of the region, stimulated several Spanish incursions into Florida, all which the aggression of the indigenes and the ferocity of the terrain and climate drove back. The most successful undertaking – even though it ended in death for its leader – was the **Hernando de Soto** expedition, a thousand-strong band of war-hardened knights and treasure seekers, which landed at Tampa Bay in May 1539. Recent excavations in Tallahassee have located the site of one of de Soto's camps, where the first Christmas celebration in North America is thought to have taken place, before the expedition continued north and eventually made the first European crossing of the Mississippi River – for a long time marking Florida's western boundary.

In time, news that Florida did not harbor stunning riches caused interest to wane. Treasure-laden Spanish ships sailing off the Florida coast between the

Americas and Europe proved attractive to pirate ships, however, many of them British and French vessels hoisting the Jolly Roger. The Spanish failure to colonize Florida made the area a prime base for attacks on their vessels, and a small group of **French Huguenots** landed in 1562, building Fort Caroline on the St Johns River.

The French presence forced the Spanish to make a more determined effort at settlement. Already commissioned to explore the Atlantic coast of North America, **Pedro Menéndez de Aviles** was promised the lion's share of whatever profits could be made from Florida. Landing south of the French fort on August 28, 1562, the day of the Spanish Festival of San August'n, Menéndez named the site **St Augustine** – founding what was to become the longest continuous site of European habitation on the continent. The French were quickly defeated, their leader **Jean Ribault** and his crew massacred after being driven ashore by a hurricane; the site of the killing is still known as Matanzas, or "Place of Slaughter."

The first Spanish period (1585–1763)

Only the enthusiasm of Menéndez held Florida together during the early decades of Spanish rule. A few small and insecure settlements were established, usually around **missions** founded by Jesuits or Franciscans bent on Christianizing the Indians. It was a far from harmonious setup: homesick Spanish soldiers frequently mutinied and fought with the Indians, who responded by burning St Augustine to the ground. Menéndez replaced St Augustine's wooden buildings with "tabby" (a cement-like mixture of seashells and limestone) structures with palm-thatched roofs, a style typical of early European Florida. While easily the largest settlement, even St Augustine was a lifeless outpost unless a ship happened to be in port. Despite sinking all his personal finances into the colony, Menéndez never lived to see Florida thrive, and he left in 1571, after the king ordered him to help plan the Spanish Armada's attack on Britain.

Fifteen years later, as war raged between the European powers, St Augustine was razed by a naval bombardment led by **Francis Drake**, a sign the **British** were beginning to establish their colonies along the Atlantic coast north of Florida. Aware the Indians would hold the balance of power in future colonial power struggles, the Spanish built a string of missions along the Panhandle from 1606; besides seeking to earn the loyalty of the natives, these were intended to provide a defensive shield against attacks from the north. By the 1700s the British were making forays into Florida, ostensibly to capture Indians to sell as slaves. One by one, the missions were destroyed, and only the timely arrival of Spanish reinforcements prevented the fall of St Augustine to the British in 1740.

With the French in Louisiana, the British in Georgia, and the Spanish clinging to Florida, the scene was set for a bloody confrontation for control of North America. Eventually, the **1763 Treaty of Paris**, concluding the Seven Years' War in Europe, settled the issue: the British had captured the crucial Spanish possession of Havana, and Spain willingly parted with Florida to get it back.

The British period (1763–83)

Despite their two centuries of occupation, the Spanish failed to make much impression on Florida. It was the British, already developing the colonies further north, who grafted a social infrastructure onto the region. They also divided Florida (then with only the northern section inhabited by whites) into separate colonies: **East Florida** governed from St Augustine, and **West Florida** governed from the growing Panhandle port of **Pensacola**.

By this time, aboriginal Floridians had largely died out through contact with European diseases, to which they had no immunity, and Florida's Indian population was becoming composed of disparate tribes arriving from the west, collectively known as the **Seminoles**. Like the Spanish, the British acknowledged the numerical importance of the Indians and sought good relations with them. In return for goods, the British took Indian land around ports and supply routes, but generally left the Seminoles undisturbed in the inland areas.

Despite attractive grants, few settlers arrived from Britain. Those with money to spare bought Florida land as an investment, never intending to develop or settle on it, and only large holdings – **plantations** growing corn, sugar, rice, and other crops – were profitable. Charleston, to the north, dominated sea trade in the area, though St Augustine was still a modestly important settlement and the gathering place of passing British aristocrats and intellectuals. West Florida, on the other hand, was driven by political factionalism and was also often the scene of skirmishes with the Seminoles, who received worse treatment than their counterparts in the east.

Being a new and sparsely populated region, Florida was barely affected by the discontent that fueled the **American War of Independence** in the 1770s, except for St Augustine, which served as a haven for British Royalists fleeing the war, many of whom moved on to the Bahamas or Jamaica. Pensacola, though, was attacked and briefly occupied in 1781 by the Spanish, who had been promised Florida in return for helping the American rebels defeat the British. As it turned out, diplomacy rather than gunfire signaled the end of British rule in Florida.

The second Spanish period (1783–1821)

The **1783 Treaty of Paris**, under which Britain recognized American independence, not only returned Florida to Spain but also gave it Louisiana and the prized port of New Orleans. Spanish holdings in North America were now larger than ever, but with Europe in turmoil and the Spanish colonies in Central America agitating for their own independence, the country was ill-equipped to capitalize on them. Moreover, the complexity of Florida's melting pot, comprising the British, smaller numbers of ethnically diverse European settlers, and the increasingly assertive Seminoles (now well established in fertile central Florida, and often joined by Africans escaping slavery further north), made it impossible for a declining colonial power to govern.

As fresh European migration slowed, Spain was forced to **sell land to US citizens**, who bought large tracts, confident that Florida would soon be under Washington's control. Indeed, in gaining Louisiana from France in 1800 (to whom it had been ceded by Spain), and moving the Georgia border south, it was clear the US had Florida in its sights. Fearful of losing the commercial toehold it still retained in Florida, and aligned with Spain through the Napoleonic wars, Britain landed troops at Pensacola in 1814. In response, a US general, **Andrew Jackson**, used the excuse of an Indian uprising in Alabama to march south, killing hundreds of Indians and pursuing them – unlawfully and without official sanction from Washington – into Pensacola, declaring no quarrel with the Spanish but insisting that the British depart. The British duly left, and Jackson and his men withdrew to Mobile (a Floridian town that became part of Alabama as the Americans inched the border eastwards), soon to participate in the Battle of New Orleans, which further strengthened the US position on the Florida border.

The First Seminole War (1817–18)

Jackson's actions in 1814 had triggered the **First Seminole War**. As international tensions heightened, Seminole raids (often as a result of baiting on the US side) were commonly used as excuses for US incursions into Florida. In 1818, Jackson finally received what he took to be presidential approval (the "Rhea Letter," thought to have been authorized by President Monroe) to march again into Florida on the pretext of subduing the Seminoles but with the actual intention of taking outright control.

While US public officials were uneasy with the dubious legality of these events, the American public was firmly on Jackson's side. The US government issued an ultimatum to Spain, demanding it either police Florida effectively or relinquish its ownership. With little alternative, Spain formally **ceded Florida to the US** in 1819, in return for the US assuming the $5 million owed by the Spanish government to American settlers in land grants (a sum never repaid). Nonetheless, it took the threat of an invasion of Cuba for the Spanish king to ratify the treaty in 1821; at the same time Andrew Jackson was sworn in as Florida's first American governor.

Territorial Florida

In territorial Florida it was soon evident the East and West divisions were unworkable, and a site midway between St Augustine and Pensacola was selected as the new administrative center: **Tallahassee**. The Indians living on the fertile soils of the area were rudely dispatched toward the coast – an act of callousness that was to typify relations between the new settlers and the incumbent Native Americans for decades to come.

Under Spanish and British rule, the Seminoles, notwithstanding some feuding among themselves, lived peaceably on the productive lands of northern central Florida. These, however, were precisely the agriculturally rich areas US settlers coveted. Under the **Treaty of Moultrie Creek** in 1823, most of the Seminole tribes signed a document agreeing to sell their present land and resettle in southwest Florida. Neither side was to honor this agreement: no time limit was imposed on the Seminole exodus, and those who did go found the new land to be unsuitable for farming. The US side, meanwhile, failed to provide promised resettlement funds.

Andrew Jackson spent only three months as territorial governor, though his influence on Florida continued from the White House when he became US president in 1829. In 1830 he approved the **Act of Indian Removal**, decreeing all Native Americans in the eastern US should be transferred to reservations in the open areas of the Midwest. Two years later, James Gadsden, the newly appointed Indian commissioner, called a meeting of the Seminole tribes at Payne's Landing on the Oklawaha River, near Silver Springs, urging them to cede their land to the US and move west. Amid much acrimony, a few did sign the **Treaty of Payne's Landing**, which provided for their complete removal within three years.

The Second Seminole War (1821–42)

A small number took what monies were offered and resettled in the west, but most Seminoles were determined to stay, and the **Second Seminole War** ensued, with the Indians repeatedly ambushing US militiamen who had arrived to enforce the law. The natives also ransacked the plantations of white settlers, many of whom fled and never returned. Trained for set-piece battles, the US troops were rarely able to deal effectively with the guerrilla tactics of the Seminoles. It was apparent the Seminoles were unlikely to be defeated by conventional means and in October 1837 their leader, **Osceola**, was lured to St Augustine with the promise of a truce – only to be arrested and imprisoned, eventually to die in jail. This treachery failed to break the spirit of the Seminoles, though a few continued to give themselves up and leave for the west, while others were captured and sold into slavery.

It became the policy of the US to drive the Seminoles steadily south, away from the fertile lands of central Florida and **into the Everglades**. There, the Seminoles linked up with the long-established Indians of south Florida, the "Spanish Indians," to raid the Cape Florida lighthouse and destroy the white colony on Indian Key in the Florida Keys. Even after bloodhounds were used to track the Indians, it was clear total US victory would never be achieved. With

▲ Seminole tribe members at the Big Cypress Seminole Reservation, circa 1917

the Seminoles confined to the Everglades, the US formally **ended the conflict** in 1842, when the Seminoles agreed to stay where they were – an area earlier described by an army surveyor as "fit only for Indian habitation."

The war crippled the Florida economy but stimulated the growth of a number of new towns around the army forts. Several of these, such as Fort Brooke (Tampa), Fort Lauderdale, Fort Myers, and Fort Pierce, have survived into modern times.

Statehood and secession (1842–61)

The Second Seminole War forestalled the possibility of Florida **attaining statehood** – which would have entitled it to full representation in Washington and to appoint its own administrators. Influence in Florida at this time was split between two camps. On one side were the wealthy slave-owning plantation farmers, concentrated in the "cotton counties" of the central section of the Panhandle, who enjoyed all the traditions of the upper rungs of Deep South society. They were eager to make sure the balance of power in Washington did not shift toward the non-slave-owning "free" states, which would inevitably bring a call for the abolition of slavery. Opposing statehood were the smallholders scattered about the rest of the territory – many of whom were Northerners, already ideologically against slavery and fearing the imposition of federal taxes.

One compromise mooted was a return to a divided Florida, with the West becoming a state while the East remained a territory. Eventually, based on a narrowly agreed upon **constitution** drawn up in Port St Joseph on the Panhandle coast (on the site of present-day Port St Joe), Florida **became a state** on March 3, 1845. The arrival of statehood coincided with a period of material prosperity: the first **railroads** began spidering across the Panhandle and central Florida; an organized school system became established; and Florida's population of 60,000 doubled within twenty years.

Nationally, the issue of slavery was to be the catalyst that led the US into civil war, though it was only a part of a great cultural divide between the rural Southern states – to which Florida was linked more through geography than history – and the modern industrial states of the North. As federal pressure intensified for the abolition of slavery, Florida formally **seceded from the Union** on January 10, 1861, aligning itself with the breakaway Confederate States in the run-up to the Civil War.

The Civil War (1861–65)

Inevitably, the **Civil War** had a great effect on Florida, although most Floridians conscripted into the Confederate army fought far away from home, and rarely were there more than minor confrontations within the state. The relatively small number of Union sympathizers generally kept a low profile, concentrating on protecting their families. At the start of the war, most of Florida's **coastal forts** were occupied by Union troops as part of the blockade on Confederate shipping. Lacking the strength to mount effective attacks on the forts, those Confederate soldiers who remained in Florida based themselves in the interior and watched for Union troop movements, swiftly destroying whatever bridge, road, or railroad that lay in the invaders' path – in effect creating a stalemate, which endured throughout the conflict.

Away from the coast, Florida's primary contribution to the war effort was the **provision of food** – chiefly beef and pork reared on the central Florida farms – and the transportation of it across the Panhandle toward Confederate strongholds further west. Union attempts to cut the supply route gave rise to the only major battle fought in the state, the **Battle of Olustee**, just outside Live Oak, in February 1864: 10,000 participated in an engagement that left nearly 3000 dead or injured and both sides claiming victory.

The most celebrated battle from a Floridian viewpoint, however, happened in March 1865 at **Natural Bridge**, when a youthful group of Confederates defeated the technically superior Union troops, preventing the fall of Tallahassee. As events transpired, it was a hollow victory: following the Confederate surrender, the war ended a few months later.

Reconstruction

Following the cessation of hostilities, Florida was caught in an uneasy hiatus. In the years after the war, the defeated states were subject to **Reconstruction**, a rearrangement of their internal affairs determined by, at first, the president, and later by a much harder-line Congress intent on ensuring the Southern states would never return to their old ways.

The Northern ideal of free-labor capitalism was an alien concept in the South, and there were enormous problems. Of paramount concern was the future of the **freed slaves**. With restrictions on their movements lifted, many emancipated slaves wandered the countryside, often unwittingly putting fear into all-white communities that had never before had a black face in their midst. Rubbing salt into the wounds, as far as the Southern whites were concerned, was the occupation of many towns by black Union troops. As a backlash, the white-supremacist **Ku Klux Klan** became active in Tennessee during 1866, and its race-hate, segregationist doctrine soon spread into Florida.

Against this background of uncertainty, Florida's **domestic politics** entered a period of unparalleled chicanery. Suddenly, not only were black men allowed to vote, but there were more black voters than white. The gullibility of the uneducated blacks and the power of their votes proved an irresistible combination to the unscrupulous and power-hungry. Double-dealing and vote-rigging were practiced by diverse factions united only in their desire to restore Florida's statehood and acquire even more power. Following a constitution written and approved in controversial circumstances, Florida was **readmitted to the Union** on July 21, 1868.

Eventually, in Florida as in the other Southern states, an all-white, **conservative Democrat government** emerged. Despite emancipation and the hopes for integration outlined by the Civil Rights Act passed by Congress in 1875, blacks in Florida were still denied many of the rights reasonably regarded as basic. In fact, all that distanced the new administration from the one that led Florida into secession was awareness of the power of the federal government and the need to at least appear to take outside views into account. It was also true that many of the former slave-owners were now the employers of freed blacks, who remained very much under their white masters' control.

A new Florida (1876–1914)

Florida's bonds with its neighboring states became increasingly tenuous in the years following Reconstruction. A fast-growing population began spreading south – part of a gradual diminishing of the importance of the Panhandle, where ties to the Deep South were strongest. Florida's identity was forged by a new **frontier spirit**. Besides smallholding farmers, loggers came to work the abundant forests, and a new breed of wealthy settler started putting down roots, among them Henry DeLand and Henry S. Sanford, who each bought large chunks of central Florida and founded the towns still bearing their names.

As northern speculators invested in Florida, they sought to publicize the region, and a host of articles extolling the virtues of the state's climate as a cure for all ills began to appear in the country's newspapers. These early efforts to promote **Florida as a tourist destination** brought the wintering rich along the new railroads to enjoy the sparkling rivers and springs, along with naturalists keen to explore the unique flora and fauna.

With a fortune made through his partnership in Standard Oil, **Henry Flagler** opened luxury resorts on Florida's northeast coast for his socialite friends, and gradually extended his Florida East Coast Railroad south, giving birth to communities such as **Palm Beach** and making the remote trading post of **Miami** an accessible, expanding town. Flagler's friendly rival **Henry Plant** connected his railroad to **Tampa**, turning a desolate hamlet into a thriving port city and a major base for cigar manufacturing. The **citrus industry** also revved into top gear: Florida's climate enabled oranges, grapefruits, lemons, and other citrus fruits to be grown during the winter and sold to an eager market in the cooler north. The **cattle farms** went from small to strong, with Florida becoming a major supplier of beef to the rest of the US: cows were rounded up with a special wooden whip that made a gunshot-like sound when used – hence the nickname "**cracker**" that was applied to rural settlers.

One group that didn't benefit from the boom years was the blacks. Many were imprisoned for no reason, and found themselves on chain gangs building the new roads and railroads; punishments for refusing to work included severe floggings and hanging by the thumbs. Few whites paid any attention, and those who were in a position to stop the abuses were usually too busy getting rich. There was, however, the founding of **Eatonville**, just north of Orlando, which was the first town in Florida – and possibly the US – to be founded, governed, and lived in by black people.

The Spanish–American War

By the 1890s, the US was a large and unified nation itching for a bigger role in the world, and as the drive in **Cuba** for independence from Spain gathered momentum, an opportunity to participate in international affairs presented itself. Florida already had long links with Cuba – the capital, Havana, was just ninety miles from Key West, and several thousand Cuban migrants were employed in the Tampa cigar factories. During 1898, tens of thousands of US troops, known as the Cuban Expeditionary Force, arrived in the state, and the **Spanish–American War** was declared on April 25. As it turned out, the fighting was comparatively minor. Spain withdrew, and on January 1, 1899, Cuba attained independence (and the US a big say in its future). But the war was also the first of several major conflicts that were to prove beneficial to Florida. Many of the soldiers would return as settlers or tourists, and improved railroads and strengthened harbors at the commercially significant ports of Key West, Tampa, and Pensacola did much to boost the economy.

The Broward era

The early years of the 1900s were dominated by the progressive policies of **Napoleon Bonaparte Broward**, who was elected state governor in 1905. Broward championed the little man against corporate interests, particularly the giant land-owning railroad companies. Among Broward's aims were an improved education system, a state-run commission to oversee new railroad construction, a tax on cars to finance road building, better salaries for teachers and the judiciary, a state-run life insurance scheme, and a ban on newspapers – few of which were well disposed toward Broward – knowingly publishing untruths. Broward also enacted the first **conservation laws**, protecting fish, oysters, game, and forests; but at the same time, in an attempt to create new land to rival the holdings of the rail barons, he conceived the drainage program that would cause untold damage to the Everglades.

By no means did all of Broward's policies become law, and he departed Tallahassee for a US Senate seat in 1910. Nonetheless, the forward-thinking plans of what became known as the **Broward era** were continued through subsequent administrations – a process that went some way toward bringing a rough-and-ready frontier land into the twentieth century.

World War I and after

World War I continued the tradition of the Spanish–American War by giving Florida an economic shot in the arm, as the military arrived to police the coastline and develop sea-warfare projects. Despite the influx of money and the reforms of the Broward years, there was little happening to improve the lot of Florida's blacks. The Ku Klux Klan was revived in Tallahassee in 1915, and the public outcry following the beating to death of a young black on a chain gang was answered only by the introduction of the sweatbox as punishment for prisoners considered unruly.

The coast so vigilantly protected from advancing Germans during the war was left wide open when **Prohibition** was introduced in 1919; the many secluded inlets became secure landing sites for shipments of spirits from the Caribbean. The illicit booze improved the atmosphere in the new resorts of **Miami Beach**, a picture-postcard piece of beach landscaping replacing what had been a barely habitable mangrove island just a few years before. Drink was not the only illegal pleasure pursued in the nightclubs: gambling and prostitution were also rife, and were soon to attract the attention of big-time **gangsters** such as Al Capone, initiating a climate of corruption that was to scar Florida politics for years.

The lightning-paced creation of Miami Beach was no isolated incident. Throughout Florida, and especially in the southeast, new communities appeared almost overnight. Self-proclaimed architectural genius **Addison Mizner** erected the "million-dollar cottages" of Palm Beach and began fashioning **Boca Raton** with the same mock-Mediterranean excesses, on the premise "get the big snob and the little snob will follow." Meanwhile, visionary **George Merrick** plotted the superlative **Coral Gables** – now absorbed by Miami – which became the nation's first preplanned city and one of the few schemes of the time to age with dignity.

In the rush of prosperity following the war, it seemed everyone in America wanted a piece of Florida, and chartered trains brought in thousands of eager buyers. The spending frenzy soon meant that for every genuine offer there were a hundred bogus ones: many people unknowingly bought acres of empty swampland. The period was satirized by the Marx Brothers in their first film, *The Cocoanuts*.

Although millions of dollars technically changed hands each week during the peak year of 1925, little hard cash actually moved. Most deals were paper transactions with buyers paying a small deposit into a bank. The inflation inherent in the system finally went out of control in 1926. With buyers failing to keep up payments, banks went **bust** and were quickly followed by everyone else. A **hurricane** devastated Miami the same year, and an even worse hurricane in 1928 caused Lake Okeechobee to burst its banks and flood surrounding communities.

With the Florida land boom well and truly over, the **Wall Street Crash** in 1929 proceeded to make paupers of the millionaires, such as Henry Flagler and Sarasota's **John Ringling**, whose considerable investments had helped to shape the state, and who would later found the **Ringling Brothers Barnum and Bailey Circus**.

The Depression and World War II

At the start of the 1930s, even the major railroads that had stimulated Florida's expansion were in receivership, and the state government only avoided bankruptcy with a constitutional escape clause. Due to the property crash, Florida had a few extra years to adjust to grinding poverty before the whole country experienced the Depression, and a number of recovery measures – making the state more active in citizens' welfare – pre-empted the national New Deal legislation of President Roosevelt.

No single place was harder hit than **Key West**, which was not only suffering the Depression but hadn't been favored by the property boom either. With a population of 12,000, Key West was an incredible $5 million in debt, and had even lost its link to the mainland when the Overseas Railroad – running across the Florida Keys between Key West and Miami – was destroyed by the 1935 Labor Day hurricane.

What saved Key West, and indeed brought financial stability to all of Florida, was **World War II**. Once again, thousands of troops arrived to guard the coastline – off which there was an immense amount of German U-boat activity – while the flat inland areas made a perfect training venue for pilots. Empty tourist hotels provided ready-made barracks, and the soldiers, and their visiting families, got a taste of Florida that would bring many of them back.

In the immediate **postwar period**, the inability of the state to plan and provide for increased growth was resoundingly apparent, with public services – particularly in the field of education – woefully inadequate. Because of the massive profits being made through illegal gambling, corruption became endemic in public life. State governor **Fuller Warren**, implicated with the Al Capone crime syndicate in 1950, was by no means the only state official suspected of being in cahoots with criminals. A wave of attacks against blacks and Jews in 1951 caused Warren to speak out against the Ku Klux Klan, but the discovery that he himself had once been a Klan member only confirmed there was poison flowing through the heart of Florida's political system.

A rare upbeat development was a continued commitment to the conservation measures introduced in the Broward era, with $2 million allocated to buying the land that, in 1947, became **Everglades National Park**.

The 1950s and 1960s

Cattle, citrus, and tourism continued to be the major components of Florida's economy as, in the ten years from 1950, the state soared from being the twentieth to the tenth most populous in the country, home to some five million people. While its increased size raised Florida's profile in the federal government, the demographic changes within the state – most dramatically the shift from rural life in the north to urban living in the south – went unacknowledged, and **reapportionment** of representation in state government became a critical issue. It was only resolved by the **1968 constitution**, which provided for automatic reapportionment in line with population changes.

The fervent desire for growth and the need to present a wholesome public image prevented the state's conservative-dominated assembly from fighting as hard as their counterparts in the other southern states against **desegregation**, following a ruling by the federal Supreme Court on the issue in 1956. Nonetheless, blacks continued to be banned from Miami Beach after dark and from swimming off the Palm Beach coast. In addition, they were subject to segregation in restaurants, buses, hotels, and schools – and barely represented at all in public office. As the **Civil Rights** movement gained strength during the early 1960s, bus boycotts and demonstrations took place in Tallahassee and Daytona Beach, and a march in St Augustine in 1964 resulted in the arrest of the movement's leader, Dr Martin Luther King Jr. The success of the Civil Rights movement in ending legalized discrimination did little to affect the deeply entrenched racist attitudes among much of Florida's longer-established population. Most of the state's blacks still lived and worked in conditions that would have been intolerable to whites: a fact that, in part, accounted for the **Liberty City riot** in August 1968, which was the first of several violent uprisings in Miami's depressed areas. The area would see its worst rioting over a decade later, on May 18, 1980, after an all-white jury acquitted four white police officers of the beating to death of a black citizen, Arthur MacDuffie. Eighteen people died, 400 were injured, and damage to property was estimated at over $200 million.

The ideological shift in Florida's near-neighbor, **Cuba** – declared a socialist state by its leader Fidel Castro in 1961 – came sharply into focus with the 1962 **missile crisis**, which triggered a tense game of cat and mouse between the US and the USSR over Soviet missile bases on the island. After world war was averted, Florida became the base of the US government's covert anti-Castro operations. Many engaged in these activities were among the 300,000 **Cuban immigrants** who had arrived following the Castro-led revolution. The Bay of Pigs fiasco in 1961 proved there was to be no quick return to the homeland, and while not all of the new arrivals stayed in Florida, many went no further than Miami, where they were to change completely the social character – and eventually the power balance – of the city.

Another factor in Florida's expansion was the basing of the new civilian space administration, **NASA**, at the military long-range missile-testing site at Cape Canaveral. The all-out drive to land a man on the moon brought an enormous influx of space industry personnel here in the early 1960s – quadrupling the population of the region soon to become known as the **Space Coast**.

The 1970s to 1990s

Florida's tourist boom truly began with the opening of **Walt Disney World** in 1971, which had actually been in development since the mid-1960s. The state government bent over backwards to help the Disney Corporation turn a sizeable slice of central Florida into the biggest theme park complex ever known, even though throughout its construction debate raged over the commercial and ecological effects of such a major undertaking on the rest of the region. Undeterred, smaller businesses rushed to the area, eager to capitalize on the anticipated tourist influx, and the sleepy cow-town of **Orlando** suddenly found itself the hub of one of the state's fastest-growing population centers – soon to become one of the world's best-known holiday destinations.

Around the same time, Florida's other multi-billion dollar business – the **drug trade** – also began taking off. Indeed, Florida's proximity to various Latin and South American countries with large drug production operations perfectly positioned the state as a gateway for drug smuggling and money-laundering; estimates suggest at least a quarter of the cocaine entering the US still arrives through the state. The inherent violence of the drug trade, along with lax Florida gun laws, helped Miami earn the unflattering designation "murder capital of the US" in the late 1980s, a label it has largely shaken off, though some incidents of **violence against tourists** in the early 1990s resullied its reputation.

Despite the social problems engendered, much money was being made by the US–Latin American trade – both legal and contraband – and poured into the coffers of a burgeoning **banking** industry, which set up shop in gleaming high towers just south of downtown Miami.

Time, plus Disney's success and Miami's rise to prominence, had only helped solidify Florida's place in the **international tourist market** by the 1990s. Directly or indirectly, one in five of the state's twelve million inhabitants was making a living from tourism. At the same time, the general swing from heavy to **hi-tech industries** had resulted in many American corporations forsaking their traditional northern bases in favor of Florida, bringing their white-collar workforces with them.

Increased protection of the state's **natural resources** was another positive feature of the 1990s. Impressive amounts of land were now under state control and, overall, wildlife was less threatened than at any time since white settlers first arrived. Most spectacular of all was the revival of the state's alligator population.

Behind the optimistic facade, however, lay many problems. For starters, much of southern Florida's resurgent landscape – and its dependent animals – could still be destroyed by south Florida's ever-increasing need for land and drinking water. And **nature** itself often posed a serious threat. In August 1992, **Hurricane Andrew** brought winds of 168mph tearing through the southern regions of Miami, blowing down the radar of the National Hurricane Center in the process and leaving an estimated $30 billion worth of damage in its wake. In the summer of 1999, another storm, **Hurricane Floyd**, came blowing through, leading to the evacuation of millions of residents all along the southeast US coast and causing considerable damage, though fortunately less than was feared.

The lack of state spending, due in part to low **taxes** intended to stimulate growth, reduced funding for public services, leaving the apparently booming state with appalling levels of adult illiteracy, infant mortality, and crime. Ironically, the switch in Florida's "war on drugs" from capturing dealers to clamping down on **money-laundering** began to threaten many of its financial institutions, built on – and it's an open secret – the drug trade.

The 2000 election and beyond

The political maneuvering by which **George W. Bush** became the 43rd president of the US in 2000 cast a shadow over the Sunshine State, as well as the entire country. The election itself was a virtual dead heat: **Al Gore**, the Democratic Party's nominee, won the country's **popular vote** by around half a million, but Bush led in the **electoral college** tally – with Florida too close to call. Bush's margin was so narrow – he led by less than 1000 votes out of a total of nearly six million cast – that a recount was called for. And although Bush's brother, **Governor Jeb Bush**, officially recused himself during the controversy, his Secretary of State – and Bush's campaign chairman for the state – **Katherine Harris**, didn't. Instead, she disallowed a full count, shutting down normal recount operations while her man was leading by only a few hundred votes and calling him the winner. Thousands of Floridians protested amid accusations of illegal police roadblocks that kept African-Americans – who overwhelmingly supported Al Gore – from even getting to the polls. Attempts by the **Florida Supreme Court** to overturn the Harris decision were summarily quashed by the right-leaning **US Supreme Court**, which allowed the peremptory decision to stand.

Four years later when Bush was re-elected, Florida remained newsworthy for other reasons. It has been pummeled by six major hurricanes since the start of the 2004 season: Jeanne, Katrina, and lumbering Frances battered the Atlantic

▲ Protestors in front of the Florida Supreme Court in Tallahassee following the presidential election of 2000

Barrier island A long, narrow island of the kind protecting much of Florida's mainland from coastal erosion, comprising sandy beach and mangrove forest – often blighted by condos.

Condo Short for "condominium," a tall and usually ugly block of (normally) expensive apartments.

Cracker Nickname given to Florida farmers from the 1800s, stemming from the sound made by the whip used in cattle round-ups (or possibly from the cracking of corn to make grits – a hot cereal). These days it's also a disparaging term for the state's conservative ruralites.

Crackerbox Colloquial architectural term for the simple wooden cottage early crackers lived in, ingeniously designed to allow the lightest breeze to cool the whole dwelling.

Florida ice Potentially hazardous mix of oil and water on a road surface following a thunderstorm.

Hammocks Not open-air sleeping places but patches of trees. In the south, and especially in the Everglades, hammocks often appear as "tree islands" above the flat wetlands. In the north, hammocks are larger and occur on elevations between wetlands and pinewoods. All hammocks make excellent wildlife habitats and those in the south are composed of tropical trees rarely seen elsewhere in the US.

Intracoastal Waterway To strengthen coastal defenses during World War II, the natural waterways dividing the mainland from the barrier islands were deepened and extended. The full length, along the east and southwest coasts, is termed the "Intracoastal Waterway."

Key Derived from the word "cay" – an island or bank composed of coral fragments.

No see'ums Tiny, mosquito-like insects; near-impossible to spot until they've already bitten you.

Snowbird Term applied to a visitor from the northern US or Canada coming to Florida during the winter to escape sub-zero temperatures – usually recognized by their sunburn.

Coast, Wilma powered through the Keys, and Charley and Ivan pummeled the Gulf Coast. As meteorologists predict twenty more years of such severe weather, it may be only a matter of time before Florida faces a similar challenge. For more on hurricanes, see box, p.478.

Florida's seems to be a mixed bag. With the NASA Space Shuttle program scheduled to shut down in 2010, the fallout for the Space Coast, in terms of tourism and jobs, remains to be seen. On a positive note, the state purchased 187,000 acres of land abutting the Everglades from the US Sugar Corporation in June 2008, ostensibly to help restore water flow to the imperiled ecosystem; whether it works remains to be seen.

Natural Florida

The biggest surprise for most people in Florida is the abundance of undeveloped, natural areas throughout the state and the extraordinary variety of wildlife and vegetation within them. From a rare hawk that eats only snails to a vine-like fig that strangles other trees, natural Florida possesses plenty you've probably never seen before, and which – due to drainage, pressures from the agricultural lobby, and the constant need for new housing – may not be on view for very much longer.

Background

Many factors contribute to the unusual diversity of **ecosystems** found in Florida, the most obvious being **latitude**: the north of the state has vegetation common to temperate regions, which is quite distinct from the subtropical flora of the south. Another crucial element is **elevation**: while much of Florida is flat and low-lying, a change of a few inches in elevation drastically affects what grows, due in part to the enormous variety of soils.

The role of fire

Florida has more thunderstorms than any other part of the US, and the resulting lightning frequently ignites **fires**. Many Florida plants have adapted to fire by developing thick bark or the ability to regenerate from stumps. Others, such as cabbage palmetto and sawgrass, protect their growth bud with a sheath of green leaves. Fire is necessary to keep a natural balance of plant species – human attempts to control naturally ignited fires have contributed to the changing composition of Florida's remaining wild lands.

Human intervention was desperately needed in July 1998, when Florida suffered one of its most severe summer droughts. In an instant, devastating wildfires roared out of control in Volusia County, and raged on a head-on course for downtown Daytona and the beaches. Over 140,000 acres of forested lands were destroyed – approximately ten percent of the land in Volusia County. The total loss attributed to the fires was estimated at $379 million. The positive aspect of this destruction was that the fire promoted a healthy rejuvenation of the forest floor.

Forests and woodlands

Forests and woodlands aren't the first thing people associate with Florida, but the state has an impressive assortment, ranging from the great tracts of upland pine common in the north to the mixed bag of tropical foliage found in the southern hammocks.

Pine flatwoods

Covering roughly half of Florida, **pine flatwoods** are most widespread on the southeastern coastal plain. These pine species – longleaf, slash, and pond – rise tall and straight like telephone poles. The Spanish once harvested products such as turpentine and rosin from Florida's flatwood pines, a practice that continued during US settlement, and some trees still bear the scars on their trunks. Pine flatwoods are airy and open, with abundant light filtering through the upper canopy of leaves, allowing thickets of shrubs such as saw palmetto, evergreen oaks, gallberry, and fetterbrush to grow. **Inhabitants** of the pine flatwoods include white-tailed deer, cotton rats, brown-headed nuthatches, pine warblers, eastern diamondback rattlesnakes, and oak toads. Many of these creatures also inhabit other Florida ecosystems, but the **fox squirrel** – a large and noisy character with a rusty tinge to its undercoat – is one of the few mammalian denizens more or less restricted to the pine flatwoods.

Upland pine forests

As the name suggests, **upland pine forests** – or high pinelands – are found on the rolling sand ridges and sandhills of northeastern Florida and the Panhandle, conditions that tend to keep upland pine forests drier and therefore even more open than the flatwoods. Upland pine forests have a groundcover of wiregrass and an overstory of (mostly) longleaf pine trees, which creates a park-like appearance. Redheaded woodpeckers, eastern bluebirds, Florida mice, pocket gophers (locally called "salamanders," a distortion of "sand mounder"), and gopher tortoises (amiable creatures often sharing their burrows with gopher frogs) all make the high pine country their home. The latter two, together with scarab beetles, keep the forest healthy by mixing and aerating the soil. The now-endangered red-cockaded woodpecker is symbolic of old-growth upland pine forest; logging and repression of the natural fire process have contributed to its decline.

Hammocks

Wildlife tends to be more abundant in hardwood **hammocks** than in the associated pine forests and prairies (see p.474). Hammocks consist of narrow bands of (non-pine) hardwoods growing transitionally between pinelands and lower, wetter vegetation. The make-up of hammocks varies across the state. In the south, they chiefly comprised tropical hardwoods (see "The south Florida rocklands," p.474); in the north, they contain an overstory of oaks, magnolia, and beech, along with a few smaller plants. Red-bellied woodpeckers, red-tailed and red-shouldered hawks, and barred owls nest in them, while down below you can also find eastern wood rats, striped skunks, and white-tailed deer.

Scrubs and prairies

Scrub ecosystems once spread to the southern Rocky Mountains and northern Mexico, but climatic changes reduced their distribution and remnant stands are now found only in northern and central Florida. Like the high pines, scrub occurs in dry, hilly areas. The vegetation, which forms an impenetrable mass, consists of varied combinations of drought-adapted evergreen oaks, saw palmetto, Florida rosemary, and/or sand pine. The **Florida bonamia**, a morning glory with pale blue funnel-shaped blossoms, is one of the most attractive plants of the scrub, which has more than a dozen plant species officially listed as endangered. Scrub also harbors some unique animals, including the Florida mouse, the Florida scrub lizard, the sand skink, and the Florida **scrub jay**. The scrub jay has an unusual social system: pairs nest in cooperation with offspring of previous seasons, who help carry food to their younger siblings. Although not unique to scrub habitat, other inhabitants include black bear, white-tailed deer, bobcats, and gopher tortoises.

Some of Florida's inland areas are covered by **prairie**, characterized by love grass, broomsedge, and wiregrass – the best examples surround Lake Okeechobee. Settlers destroyed the bison that roamed here some two hundred years ago, but herds are now being reintroduced to some state parks. A more diminutive prairie denizen is the **burrowing owl**: while most owls are active at night, burrowing owls feed during the day and, equally unusually, live in underground dens and bow nervously when approached, earning them the nickname the "howdy owl." Eastern spotted skunks, cotton rats, black vultures, eastern meadowlarks, and box turtles are a few other prairie inhabitants. Nine-banded **armadillos** are also found in prairie habitats and in any non-swampy terrain. Recent invaders from Texas, the armadillos usually forage at night, feeding on insects. As they have poor eyesight, they often fail to notice a human's approach until the last minute, when they will leap up and bound away noisily.

The south Florida rocklands

Elevated areas around the state's southern tip – in the Everglades and along the Florida Keys – support either pines or tropical hardwood hammocks on limestone outcrops collectively known as the **south Florida rocklands**. More jungle-like than the temperate hardwood forests found in northern Florida, the **tropical hardwood hammocks** of the south tend to occur as "tree islands" surrounded by the sparser vegetation of wet prairies or mangroves. Royal palm, pigeon plum, gumbo-limbo (one of the most beautiful of the tropical hammock trees, with a distinctive smooth red bark), and ferns form dense thickets within the hammock. The **pine forests** of the south Florida rocklands largely consist of scraggly-looking slash pine and are similarly surrounded by mangroves and wet prairies.

Epiphytic plants

Tropical hammocks contain various forms of **epiphytic plant**, which use other plants for physical support but don't depend on them for nutrients. In southern Florida, epiphytes include orchids, ferns, bromeliads (**Spanish moss** is one of the most widespread bromeliads, hanging from tree branches throughout the state and forming the "canopy roads" in Tallahassee; see "The Panhandle," p.415). Seemingly the most aggressive of epiphytes, **strangler figs**, after germinating in the canopy of trees such as palms, cut off their host tree from sunlight. They then send out aerial roots that eventually reach the soil and then tightly enlace the host, preventing growth of the trunk. Finally, the fig produces so many leaves that it chokes out the host's greenery and the host dies leaving only the fig.

Other plants and vertebrates

The south Florida rocklands support over forty plants and a dozen vertebrates found nowhere else in the state. These include the crenulate lead plant, the Key tree cactus, the Florida mastiff bat, the Key deer, and the Miami black-headed snake. More common residents include **butterflies and spiders** – the black and yellow yeliconia butterflies, with their long paddle-shaped wings and a distinctive gliding flight pattern, are particularly elegant. Butterflies need to practice careful navigation as hammocks are laced with the foot-long webs of the banana spider. Other wildlife species include sixty types of land snail, green tree frogs, green anoles, cardinals, opossums, raccoons, and white-tailed deer. Most of these are native to the southeastern US, but a few West Indian bird species, such as the mangrove cuckoo, gray kingbird, and white-crowned pigeon, have colonized the south Florida rocklands.

Swamps and marshes

Although about half have been destroyed due to logging, peat removal, draining, or sewage outflow, swamps are still found all over Florida. Trees growing around swamps include pines, palms, cedars, oaks, black gum, willows, and bald cypress. Particularly adapted to aquatic conditions, the bald cypress is ringed by knobby "knees" or modified roots, providing oxygen to the tree, which would otherwise suffocate in the wet soil. Epiphytic orchids and bromeliads are common on cypresses, especially in the southern part of the state. Florida's official state tree, the sabal palm, is another swamp/hammock plant: "heart of palm" is the gourmet's name for the vegetable cut from its insides and used in salads.

Florida swamps also have many species of **insectivorous plants**; sticky pads or liquid-filled funnels trap small insects, which are then digested by the nitrogen-hungry plant. The area around the Apalachicola National Forest has the highest diversity of carnivorous plants in the world, among them pitcher plants, bladderworts, and sundews. Other swamp-dwellers include dragonflies, snails, clams, fish, bird-voiced tree frogs, limpkins, ibis, wood ducks, beavers, raccoons, and Florida panthers.

Wetlands with relatively few trees, **freshwater marshes** range from shallow wet prairies to deep-water cattail marshes. **The Everglades** form Florida's largest marsh, most of which is sawgrass. On higher ground with good soils, sawgrass (actually a sedge) grows densely; at lower elevations it's sparser, and often an algae mat covers the soil between its plants. Water beetles, tiny crustaceans such as amphipods, mosquitoes, crayfish, killifish, sunfish, gar, catfish, bullfrogs, herons, egrets, ibis, water rats, white-tailed deer, and Florida panthers can all be found here. With luck, you might see a **snail kite**: a brown or black mottled hawk with a very specialized diet, entirely dependent on large apple snails. Snail and snail kite numbers have drastically fallen following the draining of marshes for agriculture and flood control, which so far has irreversibly drained over sixty percent of the Everglades.

Wetland denizens: alligators and wading birds

Alligators are one of the most widely known inhabitants of Florida's wetlands, lakes, and rivers. Look for them on sunny mornings when they bask on logs or banks. If you hear thunder rumbling on a clear day, it may in fact be the bellow of territorial males. Alligators can reach ten feet in length and primarily prey on fish, turtles, birds, crayfish, and crabs. Once overhunted for their hides and meat, alligators have made a strong comeback since protection was initiated in 1973; by 1987, Florida had up to half a million of them and another fifteen years later, the number was estimated to be 1.5 million. They are not usually dangerous – around twenty fatal attacks have been registered in the past 55-plus years. Most at risk are people who swim at dusk and small children playing unattended near water. To many creatures, however, alligators are a life-saver: during the summer, when the marshes dry up, they use their snouts, legs, and tails to enlarge existing pools, creating a refuge for themselves and for other aquatic species. In these "gator holes," garfish stack up like cordwood, snakes search for frogs, and otters and anhingas forage for fish.

Wading birds are conspicuous in the wetlands. Egrets, herons, and ibis, usually clad in white or gray feathers, stalk frogs, mice, and small fish. Plume-hunters in the early 1900s decimated these birds to make fanciful hats, and during the last few decades habitat destruction has caused a ninety-percent reduction in their numbers. Nonetheless, many are still visible in swamps, marshes, and mangroves. Cattle egrets, invaders from South America, are a common sight on pastures, where they forage on insects disturbed by grazing livestock. Pink waders – roseate spoonbills and, to a much lesser extent, flamingoes – can also be found in southern Florida's wetlands.

Lakes, springs, and rivers

Florida has almost 8000 freshwater **lakes**. Game fish such as bass and bluegill are common, but the waters are too warm to support trout. Some native fish species are threatened by the introduction of the **walking catfish**, which has a specially adapted gill system enabling it to leave the water and take the fish equivalent of cross-country hikes. A native of India and Burma, the walking catfish was released into southern Florida canals in the early 1960s and within twenty years had "walked" across twenty counties, disturbing the indigenous food chain. A freeze eliminated a number of these exotic fish, though enough remain to cause concern.

Most Florida **springs** release cold fresh water, but some springs are warm and others emit sulfur, chloride, or salt-laden waters. Homosassa Springs (see "Tampa Bay and the Northwest," p.396), for example, has a high level of chloride, making it attractive to both freshwater and marine species of fish.

Besides fish, Florida's extensive **river** system supports snails, freshwater mussels, and crayfish. Southern river-dwellers also include the lovable **manatee**, which inhabits bays and shallow coastal waters. The only totally aquatic herbivorous mammal, manatees sometimes weigh almost a ton but only eat aquatic plants. Unable to tolerate cold conditions, manatees are partial to the warm water discharged by power plants, taking some of them as far north as North Carolina. In Florida during the winter, the large springs at Crystal River (see "Tampa Bay and the Northwest," p.397) attract manatees, some of which have become tame enough to allow divers to scratch their bellies. Although they have few natural enemies, manatees are on the decline, often due to powerboat propellers injuring their backs or heads when they feed at the surface.

The coast

There's a lot more than sunbathing taking place around Florida's **coast**. The sandy beaches provide a habitat for many species, not least sea turtles. Where there isn't sand, you'll find the fascinating mangrove forests, or wildlife-filled salt marshes and estuaries. Offshore, coral reefs provide yet another exotic ecosystem, and one of the more pleasurable to explore by snorkeling or diving.

Sandy beaches

Waves bring many interesting creatures onto Florida's **sandy beaches**, such as sponges, horseshoe crabs, and the occasional sea horse. Florida's **shells** are justly famous; fig shells, moon snails, conches, whelks, olive shells, red and orange scallops, murex, cockles, and pen and turban shells are a few of the many varieties. As you beachcomb, beware of stepping barefoot on purplish fragments of **man-of-war** tentacles: these jellyfish have no means of locomotion, and their floating, sail-like bodies often cause them to be washed ashore – their tentacles, which sometimes reach to sixty feet in length, can deliver a painful sting. More innocuous beach inhabitants include wintering birds such as black-bellied plovers and sanderlings, and nesting black skimmers.

Of the seven species of **sea turtle**, five nest on Florida's sandy beaches: green, loggerhead, leatherback, hawksbill, and olive ridley. From February to August, the female turtles crawl ashore at night, excavate a beachside hole, and deposit a hundred-plus eggs inside. Not many of these will survive to adulthood; raccoons eat a lot of the eggs, and hatchlings are liable to be crushed by vehicles while attempting to cross the coastal highways. Programs to hatch the eggs artificially have helped offset some of the losses, however. The best time to view

Florida lobsters

Though the Maine coast may be the better-known source of **lobsters**, Florida boasts its share of these crustaceans, which differ from their northern counterparts by having a broad, flat tail, as opposed to the Maine variety's large, meaty claws. And while lobsters are prized as a delicacy, they're vital to the undersea ecosystem. As predators, lobsters are the custodians of the coral reefs: they gorge on the sea snails that aggressively graze the coral and keep the population in check. As prey, species like the spiny Florida lobster are a staple in the diet of many larger creatures – the jewfish, for example, feeds almost exclusively on them – and make a tasty treat for octopus, rays, and eels as well.

In recent years, **lobster fishing** has had a catastrophic effect on the underwater ecosystem around southern Florida, decimating the supplies of a key member of the food chain; at the same time, **pollution** has diminished the oxygen content of the sea to such an extent that even hardy crustaceans suffer. To stem the losses, fishermen have agreed to take part in a government program that would reduce the number of **traps** left out each year. In recreational fishing, too, there are now **strict regulations** on the lobster's size (the carapace or body must be at least three inches long), the length of the season (Aug 6–March 31), and the number that can be caught (six lobsters per person per day). Meanwhile, locals grumble that opportunistic tourists have less respect for supplies than fishermen who rely on the lobsters for their livelihood, especially during the two-day **Sport Lobster season** (starting at 12.01am on the last Wednesday in July), when you're most likely to hear amateurs bragging about their sizeable catches with little regard for the environmental consequences. Only time will tell whether the government's actions are enough to bolster the lobster supplies, or whether the crustacean's fate will mirror that of the conch – once so abundant in the Keys but now mainly farmed in the Caribbean.

sea turtles is during June – peak nesting time – with one of the park-ranger-led walks offered along the southern portion of the northeast coast (see "The Northeast," Chapter 7).

Mangroves

Found in brackish waters around the Florida Keys and the southwest coast, Florida has three species of **mangrove**. Unlike most plants, mangroves bear live young, as the "seeds" or propagules germinate while still on the tree; after dropping from the parent, the young propagule floats for weeks or months until it washes up on a suitable site, where its sprouted condition allows it to put out roots rapidly. Like bald cypress, mangroves have difficulty extracting oxygen from their muddy environs and solve this problem with extensive aerial roots,

Hurricanes

Florida has long taken a perverse pride in its ongoing battle with the weather but as tropical storms have grown more frequent and severe in recent years, that pride has proved rather misplaced. Weather forecasters say that in 2004, the Caribbean and its environs came out of a 25-year calm period; experts predict more frequent and more intense hurricanes in the next decade.

Florida's **storm season** officially spans from June to November, but most storms froth up in August or September, and last around ten days. The modern naming system, introduced in 1953, originally only used female names; it wasn't until 24 years later it began to alternate between men's and women's (the letters Q, U, X, Y, and Z are not used). Names are chosen from French, English, and Spanish to reflect the languages across the Caribbean. These days, to keep it manageable, the list repeats every six years; an exception is when a hurricane is especially deadly or causes major damage. In such cases – Jeanne, for example – the name is officially retired and replaced with a new one. If there are more than 21 storms in any season, as happened in the especially tumultuous 2005, Greek letters are used; the last storm to form, the harmless Epsilon, astonished weather-watchers when it swirled to life on December 30 (proving the idea of a hurricane season is at best a man-made guess).

Hurricanes all turn in a counter-clockwise direction around an eye – as a rule, the tighter the eye, the fiercer and more dangerous the storm – and because of this rotation pattern, the areas to the north and east of landfall are often most badly damaged by its leading edge. A hurricane's intensity is graded on what's known as the **Saffir-Sampson scale**: category 1 (sustained winds 74–95mph) will cause cosmetic problems like downed trees or broken windows while a category 5 (sustained winds 156mph and up) will level almost anything in its path, whether natural or man-made. Both Hurricane Charley, which killed 27 and caused $6.8 billion of damage to Florida's southwest coast in 2004, and Katrina, which hit New Orleans a year later, were only category 4 storms when they made landfall (winds 131–155mph). The sole category 5 to hit at full force since modern records began is Camille, which tore into Mississippi's Gulf Coast in 1969 and left destruction so severe observers likened it to an atomic bomb.

Florida's emergency management system has been tested, and taxed, by the onslaught of such severe storms; but although no one can predict when a devastating storm like Camille will whip up in the Atlantic again, advanced computer modeling to gauge its probable path – and so prepare people and property accordingly – is growing ever more sophisticated. For more information go to ⓦhurricanes.noaa.gov.

which either dangle finger-like from branches or twist outwards from the lower trunk. **Mangrove inhabitants** include various fish species that depend on mangroves as a nursery, such as the mangrove snapper, as well as frogs, crocodiles, brown pelicans, wood storks, roseate spoonbills, river otters, mink, and raccoons.

Salt marshes and estuaries

Like the mangrove ecosystem, the **salt marsh and estuary habitat** provides a nursery for many fish species, which in turn serve as fodder for larger fish, herons, egrets, and the occasional dolphin. **Crocodiles**, which have narrower and more pointed snouts than alligators, are seldom sighted and are confined to saltwater at the state's southernmost tip. In a few southern Florida salt marshes, you might find a **great white heron**, a rare and handsome form of the more common great blue heron. Around Florida Bay, great white herons have learned to beg for fish from local residents, with each of these massive birds "working" a particular neighborhood – striding from household to household demanding fish by rattling window blinds with their bills or issuing guttural croaks. A less appealing salt marsh inhabitant is the **mosquito**: unfortunately, the more damaging methods of mosquito control, such as impounding salt water or spraying DDT, have inflicted extensive harm on the fragile salt marshes and estuaries.

The coral reef

A long band of living **coral reef** frames Florida's southeastern corner. Living coral comes in many colors: star coral is green, elkhorn coral orange, and brain coral red. Each piece of coral is actually a colony of hundreds or thousands of small, soft animals called polyps, related to sea anemones and jellyfish. The **polyps** secrete limestone to form their hard outer skeletons, and at night extend their feathery tentacles to filter seawater for microscopic food. The filtering process, however, provides only a fraction of the coral's nutrition – most is produced via the photosynthesis of algae living within the polyps' cells. In recent years, influxes of warmer water, possibly associated with global warming, have killed off large numbers of the algae cells. The half-starved polyp then often succumbs to disease, a phenomenon known as "bleaching." Although this has been observed throughout the Pacific, the damage in Florida has so far been moderate; the impact of the tourist industry on the reef has been more pronounced, though reef destruction for souvenirs is now banned.

Coral reefs are home to a kaleidoscopic variety of brightly colored fish – beau gregories, porkfish, parrot fish, blennies, grunts, and wrasses – which swirl in dazzling schools or lurk between coral crevices. The **damselfish** is the farmer of the reef: after destroying a polyp patch, it feeds on the resultant algae growth, fiercely defending it from other fish. Thousands of other creatures live in the coral reef, among them sponges, feather-duster worms, sea fans, crabs, spiny lobsters, sea urchins, and conches.

Florida on film

The silver screen and the Sunshine State have one vital thing in common: escapism. Both on film and off, Florida has always represented the ultimate getaway. For nineteenth-century homesteaders, Cuban refugees, New York retirees, libido-laden college kids, or criminals on the lam, the state has always beckoned as some kind of paradise. Hollywood has also used Florida as an exotic backdrop for everything from light-hearted vacation flicks to black-hearted crime yarns, and the state has made the most of its movie-land charms. Henry Levin's phenomenally successful teen flick *Where the Boys Are* (1960), for instance, not only spawned a cinematic sub-genre, but also made Fort Lauderdale the country's top Spring Break resort. And Miami's rejuvenation in the 1980s can be attributed at least in part to the glamour imparted by filmmaker Michael Mann's TV series *Miami Vice*.

To immerse yourself in Florida's cinematic history, where images of palm trees, beaches, and luxury hotels predominate, is to take a virtual vacation. And though there are plenty of mediocre Florida flicks (most of them sun-addled Spring Break romps or Elvis Presley showcases), there are many conveying the unique and varied qualities of the state. Here are some of the best, of which those tagged with the ⚓ symbol are particularly recommended.

Drama and history

Any Given Sunday (Oliver Stone, 1999). Overblown football saga in which aging old-school coach Al Pacino wrestles with a cutthroat corporate owner played with surprising force by Cameron Diaz. They're battling for control of the fictional Miami Sharks, all while trying to win the big game with a cocky rookie quarterback ably played by Jamie Foxx.

Beneath the 12 Mile Reef (Robert Webb, 1953). In this beautiful travelogue, Greek sponge fishermen from Tarpon Springs venture south to fish the "Glades" and tangle with the Anglo "Conchs" of Key West. Robert Wagner plays a young Greek Romeo named Adonis, who dares to dive the "12 mile reef" for his sponge-worthy Juliet.

Distant Drums (Raoul Walsh, 1951). One of many movies that have focused on Florida's Seminole Indians (the first was made by Vitagraph in 1906), *Distant Drums*, set in the midst of the Seminole Wars

in 1840, stars Gary Cooper as a legendary Indian fighter who finds himself and his men trapped in the Everglades. Cooper and his band encounter snakes, alligators, and hordes of Seminole braves as they attempt to reach dry land.

In Her Shoes (Curtis Hanson, 2005). Above average, intelligent chick flick starring Cameron Diaz and Toni Colette as mismatched sisters who visit sassy, 70-something granny Shirley MacLaine at her amusingly thumbnailed retirement community in Florida.

Reap the Wild Wind (Cecil B. De Mille, 1942). A stirring account of skulduggery in the Florida Keys of the 1840s. Spunky Paulette Goddard vacillates between sea salt John Wayne and landlubber Ray Milland while trying to outwit pirates, gangs, and a giant squid off the deadly coral reefs.

Ruby in Paradise (Victor Nunez, 1993). Ashley Judd plays Ruby, who leaves her home in the Tennessee mountains and hitches a ride south to taste life in the Florida Panhandle. Settling in Panama City, Ruby finds work in a tourist shop selling tacky souvenirs. She fends off the boss's son and finds herself along the way. The film was sensitively directed by Florida's own Victor Nunez, a true regional independent who has been making movies in northern Florida since 1970.

Salesman (Albert and David Maysles, 1968). The second half of this brilliant and moving documentary follows four Bible salesmen to Opa-Locka on the outskirts of Miami. It's not a tale of beaches and luxury hotels, but rather low-rent apartments, cheap motels, and the quiet desperation of four men trying to sell overpriced illustrated Bibles door to door.

Seminole (Budd Boetticher, 1953). Set five years before *Distant Drums* (see opposite) and far more sympathetic to the Seminoles' plight, this Western stars Rock Hudson as a US dragoon and Anthony Quinn as his half-breed childhood friend who has become the Seminole chief Osceola. Attempting to claim even the swamps of Florida for white settlers, a power-hungry general sends a platoon into the Everglades to flush out the Seminole and drive them out west.

Stranger than Paradise (Jim Jarmusch, 1984). Jarmusch's austere indie masterpiece about two laconic hipsters and their Hungarian cousin. The trio travels from snow-bound Ohio to a lifeless, out-of-season Florida. The movie's Florida scenes consist of a cheap motel room and a deserted stretch of beach, proving the main characters' theory that everywhere starts to look the same after a while.

Sunshine State (John Sayles, 2002). Low-key but impressive ensemble piece featuring Edie Falco and Angela Bassett as two women facing disappointment over their unfulfilled dreams in small town Florida. Sayles highlights the power of real estate developers in the state, but doesn't neglect the quirky local details.

Ulee's Gold (Victor Nunez, 1997). Twenty-two years after *92 in the Shade*, Peter Fonda gave the best performance of his career as Florida beekeeper Ulee, a stoical Vietnam vet raising his granddaughters while his son is in jail. Local auteur Nunez (*Ruby in Paradise*) knows and captures northern Florida better than any filmmaker, and despite a strained plot about a couple of ne'er-do-wells and a stash of money, this meditative, measured movie is a triumph.

Vernon, Florida (Errol Morris, 1981). This documentary lovingly – if a little mockingly – captures every foible of the Florida eccentrics who fill the small town of Vernon in the Panhandle. Standout is the turkey hunter, memorable for his hushed and reverential attitude toward the birds he hunts and kills.

The Yearling (Clarence Brown, 1946). A classic about a family struggling to eke out a living in the scrub country of northern Florida (in the vicinity of Lake George and Volusia) in 1878. Oscar-winner Claude Jarman Jr plays the son of Gregory Peck and Jane Wyman who adopts a troublesome fawn. The movie was shot on location and based on Floridian Marjorie Kinnan Rawlings' Pulitzer Prize-winning novel of the same name.

Crime stories

Aileen Wuornos: The Selling of a Serial Killer (Nick Broomfield, 1993). British documentarian Broomfield stumbles into a swamp of avarice and exploitation in his search for the true story of Aileen Wuornos, America's first female serial killer. That a woman who was convicted of (and executed for) murdering seven men along a Florida Interstate comes across as more sympathetic than most of the people around her makes this portrait of backwoods Florida all the more chilling.

Bad Boys II (Michael Bay, 2003). Will Smith and Martin Lawrence return as a wisecracking, crime-busting duo in a movie packed with over-the-top action sequences. The plot – revolving around local drug dealers – may be skimpy, but the movie makes terrific use of locales in and around Miami, especially Coral Gables.

Black Sunday (John Frankenheimer, 1976). Palestinian terrorists, with the aid of disgruntled Vietnam vet Bruce Dern, plan to wipe out 80,000 football fans, including President Jimmy Carter, in the Orange Bowl on Super Bowl Sunday. Though the first half of the movie unfolds in Beirut and LA, the heart-stopping climax results in some fine aerial views of Miami.

Blood and Wine (Bob Rafelson, 1997). Jack Nicholson plays a dodgy Miami wine dealer with access to the cellars of southern Florida's rich and famous in this underrated thriller. He enlists a wheezy expat safe-breaker (Michael Caine) and a savvy Cuban nanny (Jennifer Lopez) in his scheme to snag a million-dollar necklace. When the jewels end up in the hands of his jilted wife (Judy Davis) and perpetually pissed-off stepson (Stephen Dorff) the action heads south to the Florida Keys.

Body Heat (Lawrence Kasdan, 1981). Filmed just south of Palm Beach in the small coastal town of Lake Worth, Kasdan's directorial debut makes the most of the sweaty potential of a southern Florida heat wave. Shady lawyer William Hurt falls for the charms of wealthy Kathleen Turner and plans to bump off her husband for the inheritance.

China Moon (John Bailey, 1994). Ed Harris plays a hard-boiled cop seduced into covering up a neglected wife's (Madeleine Stowe) murder of her philandering husband, only to find himself the prime suspect in this steamy, oddly satisfying B-movie.

Illtown (Nick Gomez, 1995). Depending on whom you ask, Nick Gomez's movie is either a stylish, strange, and ambitious achievement or a pretentious mess. Either way, it's hard to ignore Tony Danza as a gay mob boss, and a gaggle of familiar indie stars (including Michael Rapaport and Lili Taylor) playing an unlikely bunch of Miami drug dealers.

Key Largo (John Huston, 1948). Though shot entirely on Hollywood sets, Huston's tense crime melodrama about an army veteran (Humphrey Bogart) and a mob boss (Edward G. Robinson) barricaded in a Key Largo hotel during a major hurricane has the credible feel of a muggy summer in the Florida Keys.

Miami Blues (George Armitage, 1990). This quirky crime story about a home-loving psychopath (Alec Baldwin), the naive hooker he shacks up with (Jennifer Jason Leigh), and the burnt-out homicide detective who's on their trail (Fred Ward) is set in a seedy back-street Miami that glitters with terrific characters, gritty performances, and delicious offbeat details.

Miami Vice (Michael Mann, 2006). Glossy, big budget remake of the 1980s TV show that heralded South Beach's renaissance, this time starring Jamie Foxx and Colin Farrell as pastel-suited crimefighting duo Crockett and Tubbs.

Night Moves (Arthur Penn, 1975). In one of the great metaphysical thrillers of the post-Watergate era, Gene Hackman plays a weary LA private eye with marital problems who is hired to track down a young and underdressed Melanie Griffith in the Florida Keys.

Out of Sight (Steven Soderbergh, 1998). Flip-flopping between past and present and between a jazzy, sun-drenched Florida and a snow-peppered Detroit, Soderbergh's movie is a hugely satisfying adaptation of Elmore Leonard's novel of the same name. The action is set in motion when George Clooney's urbane bank-robber tunnels out of a Pensacola penitentiary and into the life of Federal Marshal Jennifer Lopez.

Out of Time (Carl Franklin, 2003). Denzel Washington stars as the police chief of fictional Banyan Key, caught up in a formulaic but fun Floridian noir thriller. There are enough satisfying twists and pantomime baddies to keep the story from getting too sluggish in the tropical heat.

Palmetto (Volker Schlondorff, 1998). Woody Harrelson returns from jail to the Sarasota beach town of Palmetto and becomes Florida's number one patsy when a bleach-blonde Elisabeth Shue walks into his life and proposes a little fake kidnapping. Perfectly exploiting Florida's sultry charms, *Palmetto* lapses into neo-noir cliché at times, but the twisty plot keeps things interesting.

Scarface (Brian De Palma, 1983). Small-time Cuban thug Tony Montana arrives in Miami during the 1980 Mariel boatlift and murders, bullies, and snorts his way to becoming the city's most powerful drug lord. One of the great Florida movies, De Palma's seductive and shocking paean to excess and the perversion of the American dream stars Al Pacino in a legendary, go-for-broke performance.

The Specialist (Luis Llosa, 1994). A priapic, glossy portrait of Miami props up this otherwise dismal thriller featuring one of Miami's high profile former residents, Sylvester Stallone, as an ex-CIA agent hired by vengeful Sharon Stone to execute the Mafiosi who wiped out her family.

Tony Rome (Gordon Douglas, 1967). Wise-cracking, hard-living private eye Frank Sinatra tangles with pushers, strippers, gold diggers, and self-made millionaires on the wild side of Miami The movie is a run-of-the-mill detective yarn, but Frank was entertaining enough to warrant a sequel: *Lady in Cement*.

True Lies (James Cameron, 1994). Pulsing with action and peppered with one-liners, this schlocky thriller is still great fun, with Arnold Schwarzenegger just about managing to convince as a CIA agent with a double life and Jamie Lee Curtis as his trusting wife. The explosive set piece features the destruction of a significant chunk of Henry Flagler's old bridge in the Florida Keys.

Wild Things (John McNaughton, 1997). A convoluted, noirish thriller about handsome high-school counselors, lubricious schoolgirls, and wealthy widows in a well-heeled community in the Everglades. Beautifully shot and played to the hilt by Matt Dillon, Kevin Bacon, Denise Richards, and Neve Campbell, the plot corkscrews with twists until the final frame.

Comic capers

92 in the Shade (Thomas McGuane, 1975). A nutty, laid-back comedy about rival fishing guides in Key West, starring a potpourri of Hollywood's greatest oddballs: Peter Fonda, Harry Dean Stanton, Warren Oates, Burgess Meredith, and William Hickey. Ripe with local color but somewhat lacking in effect, the movie was based on Thomas McGuane's acclaimed novel of the same name (see p.493).

Ace Ventura, Pet Detective (Tom Shadyac, 1994). The movie that launched Jim Carrey's thousand faces. He stars as a bequiffed investigator on a quest to recover Snowflake, the Miami Dolphins' kidnapped mascot, on the eve of the Super Bowl. The Miami Dolphins and their quarterback Dan Marino appear as themselves.

Adaptation (Spike Jonze, 2002). Susan Orlean's bestseller (see p.490) serves as the springboard for this entertaining, fictionalized version, in which the film's screenwriter (Nicholas Cage) struggles to adapt the book, undermined all the while by his twin brother (also played by Cage). Meryl Streep's Orlean pursues orchid-poacher Chris Cooper to the Loxahatchee National Wildlife Refuge.

The Bellboy (Jerry Lewis, 1960). This movie was shot almost entirely within Miami Beach's ultra-kitsch pleasure palace *The Fontainebleau* (the same hotel where James Bond is meant to be sunbathing at the beginning of 1964's *Goldfinger*). Jerry Lewis, in his debut as writer-director, plays Stanley, the bellhop from hell, and cameos as vacationing movie star Jerry Lewis in one of the most site-specific movies ever made.

The Birdcage (Mike Nichols, 1996). Nichols' Miami remake of *La Cage Aux Folles* makes lighthearted use of South Beach's burgeoning gay scene, portraying the rejuvenated Art Deco playground as a bright paradise of pecs, thongs, and drag queens – the opening scene plays as a love letter to Ocean Drive. Impresario Armand (Robin Williams) and reigning *Birdcage* diva Albert (Nathan Lane) are happily cohabiting in kitsch heaven until the day Armand's son brings his ultra-conservative future in-laws to dinner.

The Cocoanuts (Joseph Santley & Robert Florey, 1929). Set during Florida's real-estate boom, the Marx Brothers' first film stars Groucho as an impecunious hotel proprietor attempting to keep his business afloat by auctioning off land (with the usual interference from Chico and Harpo) in Cocoanut Grove, "the Palm Beach of tomorrow." Groucho expounds on Florida's climate while standing in what is really a sand-filled studio lot.

From Justin to Kelly (Robert Iscove, 2002). Witless, misguided attempt to resurrect the beach party movie genre of the 1960s, this cheesy musical – headlined by the winner and the runner up of the first season of talent contest *American Idol* – is most effective as an exhaustive showcase for every major Miami attraction, including an elaborate song and dance number in and around the Venetian Pool.

The Heartbreak Kid (Elaine May, 1972). An underrated comic masterpiece in which Charles Grodin marries a nice Jewish girl, and then, on the honeymoon drive down to Florida, starts to regret it. His doubts are compounded when goddess Cybill Shepherd starts flirting with him on the beach while his sunburnt bride lies in bed.

Heartbreakers (David Mirkin, 2001). Mindless but enjoyable romp with mother-and-daughter scam duo Sigourney Weaver and Jennifer Love Hewitt homing in on Palm Beach tobacco baron Gene Hackman as their latest victim.

A Hole in the Head (Frank Capra, 1959). Frank Sinatra plays an irresponsible Miami Beach hotel owner who has dreams of striking it rich by turning South Beach into "Disneyland." The breezy opening titles in this musical comedy are pulled on airborne banners across the Miami Beach skyline.

Miami Rhapsody (David Frankel, 1995). Sarah Jessica Parker kvetches like a female Woody Allen in this disappointingly uneven comedy. Parker weighs commitment against the marital dissatisfaction and compulsive infidelity of her extended family in an otherwise picture-perfect, upmarket Miami.

Moon Over Miami (Walter Lang, 1941). Gold-digging, Texas-hamburger-stand waitress Betty Grable takes her sister and aunt to Miami, where "rich men are as plentiful as grapefruit, and millionaires hang from every palm tree." Grable has little trouble snagging herself a couple of ripe ones in this colorful, sappy musical comedy. On-location shooting took place in Winter Haven and Ocala, a few hundred miles north of Miami.

The Palm Beach Story (Preston Sturges, 1942). In this madcap masterpiece, Claudette Colbert takes a train from Penn Station to Palm Beach ("the best place to get a divorce," a cabbie tells her) to free herself from her penniless dreamer of a husband and find herself a good millionaire to marry.

Pledge This! (Williams Heins, 2006). The latest *National Lampoon* installment centers on a sorority at fictional South Beach University and the attempts of a raft of freshmen to rush it. Notable mostly for giving Paris Hilton her first starring role.

Porky's (Bob Clark, 1981). The *Citizen Kane* of randy teen movies, this notorious film is set in fictional Angel Beach near Fort Lauderdale in the mid-1950s. A group of high-school guys with only one thing on their minds venture into Florida's backcountry in the hopes of getting laid at *Porky's*, a licentious redneck bar.

Some Like it Hot (Billy Wilder, 1959). Wilder's classic farce sees jazz musicians Tony Curtis and Jack Lemmon escape retribution for witnessing the 1929 Chicago St Valentine's Day massacre by disguising themselves as women and joining an all-girl jazz band on a train to Miami. Though *Some Like it Hot* could be a candidate for the best movie ever set in Miami, it was actually shot at the *Hotel del Coronado* in San Diego.

There's Something About Mary (Peter and Bobby Farrelly, 1998). Years after a heinous pre-prom disaster (involving an unruly zipper), Rhode Island geek Ben Stiller tracks down Mary, the eponymous object of his affection, to her new home in Miami. Once there he finds he's not the only one suffering from obsessive tendencies. The Farrelly brothers have created a hysterical, gross-out masterpiece.

Fantasy lands

Cocoon (Ron Howard, 1985). Even extraterrestrials vacation in Florida. This charming fantasy centers on residents of a Florida retirement community who discover a local swimming pool with alien powers of rejuvenation. Nearly half a century after appearing in *Moon Over Miami*, Don Ameche won a Best Supporting Actor Oscar for this film.

Dumbo (Ben Sharpsteen, 1941). In the opening sequence of this Disney animated classic there is a wonderful stork's-eye view of the entire state of Florida, where the circus has hunkered down for the winter. Though the show eventually goes on the road, this eyeful of Florida seems prescient considering Disney's role in the state some quarter of a century later.

Revenge of the Creature (Jack Arnold, 1955). Transported comatose from the Upper Amazon, the Creature from the Black Lagoon is brought to Marinelands oceanarium to create the "greatest scientific stir since the explosion of the atomic bomb." He creates an even bigger stir when he cuts loose and heads for the beach, crashing a swing party at a seafront oyster house.

The Truman Show (Peter Weir, 1998). The picture-perfect, picket-fence community of Seahaven that Jim Carrey's Truman Burbank calls home turns out to be nothing more than a giant television studio, where Truman is watched every minute of the day in the world's longest-running soap opera. The false paradise of Seahaven is actually the real, but equally artificial, Florida Gulf Coast town of Seaside.

Books

F lorida's perennial state of social and political flux has always promised rich material for historians and journalists eager to pin the place down. Rarely have they managed this, though the picture of the region's unpredictable evolution that emerges can make for compulsive reading. Many established fiction writers spend their winters in Florida, but few have convincingly portrayed its characters, climate, and scenery. Those who have succeeded, however, have produced some of the most remarkable and gripping literature to emerge from any part of the US. Books tagged with the 🦎 symbol are particularly recommended. Publishers are listed after the title, and o/p denotes out of print.

History

Edward N. Akin *Flagler: Rockefeller Partner and Florida Baron* (Florida Atlantic University). Solid biography of the man whose Standard Oil fortune helped build Florida's first hotels and railroads.

Willie Drye *Storm of the Century* (National Geographic Society). Astonishing account of the Labor Day Hurricane in 1935, which tore across – and decimated – the Upper Keys. Provides a chilling foreshadowing of the potential dangers from current extreme weather patterns.

Charles R. Ewen and John H. Hann *Hernando de Soto Among the Apalachee* (University Press of Florida). A history and description of the archeological site (located in downtown Tallahassee) believed to be a campsite used by Spanish explorer Hernando de Soto in the sixteenth century.

John T. Foster and Sarah Whitmer Foster *Beechers, Stowes, and Yankee Strangers* (University Press of Florida). An entertaining and relatively brief account about a group of Yankee reformers who lived in Florida at the end of the Civil War – including Harriet Beecher Stowe, author of *Uncle Tom's Cabin* – and their designs on a postwar Florida.

John J. Guthrie Jr, Philip Charels Lucas, and Gary Monroe *Cassadaga: The South's Oldest Spiritual Community* (University Press of Florida). A look at the history, people, and religious beliefs of the "metaphysical mecca" of Cassadaga, a small town between Orlando and Daytona Beach established more than a hundred years ago on the principle of continuous life.

🦎 **Carl Hiaasen** *Team Rodent* (Ballantine). A native of Florida, Hiaasen has been a firsthand witness to Disney's domination of Orlando, and this book is a scathing attack on the entertainment conglomerate, exposing Disney for what Hiaasen thinks it is: evil. "Disney is so good at being good that it manifests an evil," he writes, "so uniformly courteous, so dependably clean and conscientious, so unfailingly entertaining that it's unreal, and therefore is an agent of pure wickedness." Like Hiaasen's fiction work (see p.492), the prose is a mix of sharp wit, informed research, and a lot of humor.

Stetson Kennedy *The Klan Unmasked* (Florida Atlantic University/University Press of Florida). A riveting history of the Klan's activity in the post-World War II era, including specific references to Florida.

Robert Kerstein *Politics and Growth in Twentieth Century Tampa* (University Press of Florida). A history of the politics and growth in Tampa from the coming of the railroads and cigar industry to the mid-1990s.

Howard Kleinberg *Miami: The Way We Were* (SeaSide Publications US). Oversized overview of Miami's history; colorful archival photos accompany text by a former editor-in-chief of the now defunct newspaper, *The Miami News*.

Stuart B. McIver *Dreamers, Schemers, and Scalawags* (Pineapple Press). An intriguing mix of biography and storytelling that tells Florida's history through its mobsters and millionaires. This is volume one of a continuing series.

Jerald T. Milanich *Florida's Indians, from Ancient Times to the Present* (University Press of Florida). A comprehensive history spanning 12,000 years of Indian life in Florida.

Gary R. Mormino and George E. Pozzetta *The Immigrant World of Ybor City* (University Press of Florida). Flavorful accounts of the Cuban, Italian, and Spanish immigrants who built their lives around Ybor City's cigar industry at the turn of the twentieth century.

Helen Muir *Miami, USA* (University Press of Florida). An insider's account of how Miami's first developers gave the place shape during the land boom of the 1920s; a little toothless, but a fair overview.

John Rothchild *Up for Grabs: A Trip Through Time and Space in the Sunshine State* (University Press of Florida). An irreverent look at Florida's checkered career as a vacation spa, tourist trap, and haven for scheming ne'er-do-wells.

Les Standiford *Last Train to Paradise* (Crown). Miami-based novelist Standiford turns his storytelling eye to the twisty tale of Flagler's railroad; it's a rollicking narrative, but Standiford's tendency to digress into minutiae does drag it down somewhat.

Charlton W. Tebeau *A History of Florida* (University of Miami Press). The definitive academic tome, but not for casual reading.

Victor Andres Triay *Fleeing Castro* (University Press of Florida). An emotional account of the plight of Cuba's children during the missile crisis. With their parents unable to obtain visas, 14,048 children were smuggled from the island; many never saw their families again.

Garcilaso de la Vega *The Florida of the Inca* (University of Texas Press). Comprehensive account of the sixteenth-century expedition led by Hernando de Soto through Florida's prairies, swamps, and aboriginal settlements. Extremely turgid in parts, but overall an excellent insight into the period.

David C. Weeks *Ringling* (University Press of Florida). An in-depth work chronicling the time spent in Florida by circus guru John Ringling.

Patsy West *The Enduring Seminoles* (University Press of Florida). A history of Florida's Seminole Indians, who, by embracing tourism, found a means to keep their vibrant cultural identity alive.

Lawrence E. Will *Swamp to Sugarbowl: Pioneer Days in Belle Glade* (Great Outdoors Publications o/p). A "cracker" account of early times in the state, written in first-person redneck vernacular. Variously oafish and offensive but never dull.

Natural history

Holly Ambrose *30 Eco-Trips in Florida* (University Press of Florida). Exhaustively researched handbook for off-road trips across the state from the Everglades to the Panhandle. Ideal for anyone keen to spend extended periods exploring Florida's vanishing ecosystem.

Mark Derr *Some Kind of Paradise* (University Press of Florida). A cautionary history of Florida's penchant for mishandling its environmental assets, from spongers off the reefs to Miami's ruthless hotel contractors.

🚶 **Marjory Stoneman Douglas** *The Everglades: River of Grass* (Pineapple Press/Florida Classics). Concerned conservationist literature by one of the state's most respected historians (who died in 1998 at the age of 108), describing the nature and beauty of the Everglades from their beginnings. A superb work that contributed to the founding of the Everglades National Park.

David McCally *The Everglades: An Environmental History* (University Press of Florida). For both general readers and environmentalists, this book examines the formation, development, and history of the Everglades – believed to be the most endangered ecosystem in North America.

National Geographic Society *Field Guide to the Birds of North America* (4th ed) (National Geographic). The best country-wide guide, with plenty on Florida, and excellent illustrations throughout.

Bill Pranty *A Birder's Guide to Florida* (American Birding Association). Detailed accounts of when and where to find Florida's birds, including maps and charts. Aimed at the expert but excellent value for the novice birdwatcher.

Joe Schafer and George Tanner *Landscaping for Florida's Wildlife* (University Press of Florida). Step-by-step advice on how to replicate a sliver of Florida's wildlife in your own garden.

Glen Simmons with Laura Ogden *Gladesmen* (University Press of Florida). Entertaining accounts of the "swamp rats": rugged men and women who made a living wrestling alligators and trekking the "Glades."

Travel impressions

🚶 **William Bartram** *Travels* (University of Virginia Press/Peregrine Smith). The lively diary of an eighteenth-century naturalist rambling through the Deep South and on into Florida during the period of British rule. Outstanding accounts of the indigenous people and all kinds of wildlife.

Edna Buchanan *The Corpse Had a Familiar Face* (Diamond/Berkley Pub Group). Sometimes sharp, often sensationalist account of the author's years spent pounding the crime beat for the Miami Herald: five thousand corpses and gore galore. The subsequent *Vice* is more of the same.

Joan Didion *Miami* (Vintage). Didion's bony prose is hard going but it's worth persevering, at least in the early chapters, to understand the complex relationship between Cuban expats and the US government. Midway, though, she's derailed into musings on the minutiae of Washington politics, and the book rapidly loses focus.

Lynn Geldof *Cubans* (St Martins Press). Passionate and rambling interviews with Cubans in Cuba and Miami, which confirm the tight bond between them.

Herbert Hiller *Highway A1A* (University Press of Florida). Hiller uses a trip along the road that rims the length of Florida's Atlantic coast as a framework to look at the emergence of tourism, development, and the myth of sunny, worry-free Florida. An insightful, offbeat read.

Henry James *The American Scene* (Penguin). Interesting waffle from the celebrated novelist, including written portraits of St Augustine and Palm Beach as they thronged with wintering socialites at the turn of the twentieth century.

Norman Mailer *Miami and the Siege of Chicago* (New American Library/Penguin). A rabid study of the American political conventions of 1968, the first part frothing over the Republican Party's shenanigans at Miami Beach when Nixon beat Reagan for the presidential ticket.

Kevin McCarthy *Alligator Tales* (Pineapple Press). This intriguing collection of both actual and slightly overblown encounters with alligators is illustrated with the photographs of John Moran.

Michele McPhee *Mob Over Miami* (Onyx Books). Gripping, exhaustively researched true crime tale, focusing on Staten Island mobster turned South Beach nightlife mogul Chris Paciello.

Susan Orlean *The Orchid Thief* (Ballantine). *New Yorker* staff writer Orlean immerses herself in the orchid-fancying subculture of South Florida, following an eccentric gardener on his illegal gathering trips in the wild. The basis for Spike Jonze's film *Adaptation* (see p.484).

Roxanne Pulitzer *The Prize Pulitzer: The Scandal that Rocked Palm Beach* (Ballantine). A small-town girl who married into the jet-set lifestyle of Palm Beach describes the mud-slinging in Florida's most moneyed community when she seeks a divorce.

Alexander Stuart *Life on Mars* (Black Swan). "Paradise with a lobotomy" is how a friend of the author described Florida. This is an often-amusing series of vignettes about the empty lives led by the beautiful people of South Beach and the redneck "white trash" of upstate.

John Williams *Into the Badlands: A Journey through the American Dream* (HarperCollins/Flamingo). The author's trek across the US to interview the country's best crime writers begins in Miami, "the city that coke built,"; its compelling strangeness is all too briefly reveled in.

Architecture

Barbara Baer Capitman *Deco Delights* (E.P. Dutton/Penguin). A tour of Miami Beach's Art Deco buildings by the woman who championed their preservation, with definitive photography.

Laura Cerwinske *Miami: Hot & Cool* (Three Rivers Press/Random House). Coffee-table tome with text on high-style south Florida living and glowing, color photos of Miami's beautiful homes and gardens. By the same author, *Tropical Deco: The Architecture & Design of Old Miami Beach* delivers a wealth of architectural detail.

Donald W. Curl *Mizner's Florida: American Resort Architecture* (MIT

Press). An assessment of the life, career, and designs of Addison Mizner, the self-taught architect responsible for the "Bastard Spanish Moorish Romanesque Renaissance Bull Market Damn the Expense Style" structures of Palm Beach and Boca Raton.

Hap Hatton *Tropical Splendor: An Architectural History of Florida*

(Knopf/Random House). A readable, informative, and well-illustrated account of the wild, weird, and wonderful buildings that have graced and disgraced the state over the years.

Nicholas N. Patricios *Building Marvelous Miami* (University Press of Florida). The architectural development of Florida's favorite city documented by 250 photos.

Art and photography

Todd Bertolaet *Crescent Rivers* (University Press of Florida). Ansel Adams-style photos of the dark, blackwater rivers that wind through Florida's Big Bend.

Anne Jeffrey and Aletta Dreller *Art Lover's Guide to Florida* (Pineapple Press). A comprehensive guidebook featuring 86 of the most dynamic and exciting art galleries in Florida, including museums and art centers.

Gary Monroe *Life in South Beach* (Forest and Trees US). A slim volume of black-and-white photos showing Miami Beach's South Beach before the restoration of the Art Deco district and the arrival of globetrotting trendies.

Tom Shroder and John Barry *Seeing the Light Wilderness and Salvation: A Photographer's Tale* (Random House). An attractive

book describing the story of photographer Clyde Butcher's long connection with the Everglades and showcasing his wonderful pictures of the area.

Woody Walters *Visions of Florida* (University of Florida Press). Black-and-white photos, but ones that convey the richness and beauty of Florida's terrain, from misty mornings in Tallahassee to bolts of lightning over the Everglades.

William Weber *Florida Nature Photography* (University of Florida Press US). A glossy, pictorial look at Florida's many state parks, recreation areas, and nature preserves.

Millard Wells *Florida Key Impressions* (Pineapple Press US). An illustrated journal describing a journey through the Florida Keys, highlighted by the author's original watercolor paintings.

Fiction and poetry

Pat Booth *Miami* (Ballantine UK). Miami's South Beach is used as a backdrop for this pot-boiling tale of seduction and desire.

Liza Cody *Backhand* (Doubleday/Bantam). London's finest female private investigator, Anna Lee, follows the clues from Kensington to the west coast of Florida – highly entertaining.

Harry Crews *Florida Frenzy* (University Press of Florida). A collection of tales relating macho outdoor pursuits like 'gator poaching and cockfighting.

Kate Di Camillo *Because of Winn-Dixie* (Candlewick Press). When a stray dog appears in the midst of the produce section of the Winn-Dixie grocery store, it leads 10-year-old

India Opal Buloni from one new friend to the next in a small Florida town. The stories India gathers in this award-winning children's book help her to piece together a new definition of family.

Tim Dorsey *Triggerfish Twist* (HarperTorch). The standout novel in Dorsey's ongoing saga of psycho Florida eccentric Serge A. Storms takes in homicidal Little League parents, predatory real estate agents, and a mild-mannered corporate cog. Try also his newest novel, *Torpedo Juice*, where Serge – in his own crackpot way – decides to find himself a wife.

Edward Falco *Winter in Florida* (Soho Press/Bellow Pub Co). Flawed but compulsive story of a cosseted New York boy seeking thrills on a central Florida horse farm.

Connie May Fowler *Before Women Had Wings* (Ivy Books). Set in and around Tampa in the 1960s, this powerful novel tells the story of the youngest daughter of a family crippled by poverty and the effects of alcohol, violence, and broken dreams.

James Hall *Under Cover of Daylight; Squall Line; Hard Aground* (W.W. Norton). Taut thrillers with a cast of crazies that make the most of the edge-of-the-world landscapes of the Florida Keys.

Ernest Hemingway *To Have and Have Not* (Scribner/Arrow). Hemingway lived and drank in Key West for years but set only this moderate tale in the town, describing the woes of fishermen brutalized by the Depression.

Carl Hiaasen *Double Whammy* (Warner). Ferociously funny fishing thriller that brings together a classic collection of warped but believable Florida characters, among them a hermit-like ex-state governor, a cynical Cuban cop, and a corrupt TV preacher. By the same author, *Skin Tight* explores the perils of unskilled plastic surgery in a Miami crawling with mutant hitmen, bought politicians, and police on gangsters' payrolls, and *Native Tongue* delves into the murky goings-on behind the scenes at a Florida theme park. Anyone with a passing interest in Florida should read at least one of these.

Carl Hiaasen (ed) *Naked Came the Manatee* (Ballantine/Fawcett). Thirteen of Miami's best-known novelists teamed up to pen this caper, which centers on the discovery of Fidel Castro's dismembered head. Full of in-jokes, this broad satire is good, if uneven, fun.

Zora Neale Hurston *Their Eyes Were Watching God* (Perennial/Virago Press). Florida-born Hurston became one of the bright lights of the Harlem Renaissance in the 1920s. This novel describes the founding of Eatonville – her home town and the state's first all-black town – and the laborer's lot in Belle Glade at the time of the 1928 hurricane. Equally hard to put down are *Jonah's Gourd Vine* and the autobiography *Dust Tracks on a Road*.

Elmore Leonard *Stick* (HarperTorch); *La Brava* (HarperTorch/Avon); *Gold Coast* (HarperTorch/Penguin). The pick of this highly recommended author's Florida-set thrillers, respectively detailing the rise of an opportunist ex-con through the money, sex, and drugs of Latino Miami; lowlife on the seedy South Beach before the preservation of the Art Deco district; and the tribulations of a wealthy gangster-widow alone in a Fort Lauderdale mansion.

Peter Matthiessen *Killing Mister Watson* (Vintage). The first in a thoroughly researched trilogy on the early days of white settlement in the Everglades. Slow-paced but a strong insight into the Florida frontier mentality.

Thomas McGuane *Ninety-Two in the Shade* (Vintage). A strange, hallucinatory search for identity by a young man of shifting mental states who aspires to become a Key West fishing guide – and whose family and friends are equally warped. McGuane directed the film version; see p.484 for review.

Theodore Pratt *The Barefoot Mailman* (Florida Classics). A 1940s account of the long-distance postman who kept the far-flung settlements of pioneer-period Florida in mail by hiking the many miles of beach between them.

Marjorie Kinnan Rawlings *Short Stories* (University Press of Florida). A collection of 23 of Rawlings' most acclaimed short pieces, which draw heavily on Florida's natural surroundings for inspiration.

John Sayles *Los Gusanos* (Harper Perennial Library/HarperCollins). Absorbing if long-winded novel set around the lives of Cuban exiles in Miami at the time of the Mariel boatlift – written by the indie movie director.

Edmund Skellings *Collected Poems: 1958–1998* (University Press of Florida US). A "best of" collection of work by Florida's poet laureate.

Patrick D. Smith *A Land Remembered* (Pineapple Press US). This historical novel is an epic portrayal of the lives of an American pioneering family, set against the rich and rugged history of Florida.

Randy Wayne White *Sanibel Flats* (St Martins Press). First in a series of Doc Ford detective novels, this book tells the story of a murder committed on a deserted mangrove island on Florida's west coast.

Charles Willeford *Miami Blues* (Ballantine). Thanks to an uninspired movie, the best-known but not the best of a highly recommended crime fiction series starring Hoke Mosely, a cool and calculating, but very human, Miami cop. Superior titles in the series are *The Way We Die Now*, *Kiss Your Ass Goodbye*, and *Sideswipe*.

Cooking

Linda Gassenheimer *Keys Cuisine* (Atlantic Monthly Press/Avalon Travel Publications). A collection of recipes that captures the flavor of the Florida Keys.

Sue Mullin *Nuevo Cubano Cooking* (Book Sales). Easy-to-follow instructions and mouthwatering photographs of recipes fusing traditional Cuban cooking with nouvelle cuisine.

Dawn O'Brien and Becky Roper *Florida's Historic Restaurants and Their Recipes* (J.F. Blair US). Featuring a variety of cuisines, this book contains fifty recipes from Florida's best-known restaurants.

Ferdie Pacheco and Luisita Sevilla Pacheco *The Christmas Eve Cookbook* (University Press of Florida). A collection of over 200 holiday recipes and stories that illustrates the melting pot of immigrants that settled in Ybor City.

Travel store

UK & Ireland
Britain
Devon & Cornwall
Dublin **D**
Edinburgh **D**
England
Ireland
The Lake District
London
London **D**
London Mini Guide
Scotland
Scottish Highlands
  & Islands
Wales

Europe
Algarve **D**
Amsterdam
Amsterdam **D**
Andalucía
Athens **D**
Austria
Baltic States
Barcelona
Barcelona **D**
Belgium &
  Luxembourg
Berlin
Brittany & Normandy
Bruges **D**
Brussels
Budapest
Bulgaria
Copenhagen
Corsica
Crete
Croatia
Cyprus
Czech & Slovak
  Republics
Denmark
Dodecanese & East
  Aegean Islands
Dordogne & The Lot
Europe on a Budget
Florence & Siena
Florence **D**
France
Germany
Gran Canaria **D**
Greece
Greek Islands
Hungary

Ibiza & Formentera **D**
Iceland
Ionian Islands
Italy
The Italian Lakes
Languedoc &
  Roussillon
Lanzarote &
  Fuerteventura **D**
Lisbon **D**
The Loire Valley
Madeira **D**
Madrid **D**
Mallorca **D**
Mallorca & Menorca
Malta & Gozo **D**
Moscow
The Netherlands
Norway
Paris
Paris **D**
Paris Mini Guide
Poland
Portugal
Prague
Prague **D**
Provence
  & the Côte D'Azur
Pyrenees
Romania
Rome
Rome **D**
Sardinia
Scandinavia
Sicily
Slovenia
Spain
St Petersburg
Sweden
Switzerland
Tenerife &
  La Gomera **D**
Turkey
Tuscany & Umbria
Venice & The Veneto
Venice **D**
Vienna

Asia
Bali & Lombok
Bangkok
Beijing
Cambodia
China

Goa
Hong Kong & Macau
Hong Kong
  & Macau **D**
India
Indonesia
Japan
Kerala
Korea
Laos
Malaysia, Singapore
  & Brunei
Nepal
The Philippines
Rajasthan, Dehli
  & Agra
Shanghai
Singapore
Singapore **D**
South India
Southeast Asia on a
  Budget
Sri Lanka
Taiwan
Thailand
Thailand's Beaches
  & Islands
Tokyo
Vietnam

Australasia
Australia
East Coast Australia
Fiji
Melbourne
New Zealand
Sydney
Tasmania

North America
Alaska
Baja California
Boston
California
Canada
Chicago
Colorado
Florida
The Grand Canyon
Hawaii
Honolulu **D**
Las Vegas **D**
Los Angeles &
  Southern California
Maui **D**

Miami & South Florida
Montréal
New England
New York City
New York City **D**
New York City Mini
Orlando & Walt
  Disney World® **D**
Oregon &
  Washington
San Francisco
San Francisco **D**
Seattle
Southwest USA
Toronto
USA
Vancouver
Washington DC
Yellowstone & The
  Grand Tetons
Yosemite

Caribbean
& Latin America
Antigua & Barbuda **D**
Argentina
Bahamas
Barbados **D**
Belize
Bolivia
Brazil
Buenos Aires
Cancùn & Cozumel **D**
Caribbean
Central America on a
  Budget
Chile
Costa Rica
Cuba
Dominican Republic
Ecuador
Guatemala
Jamaica
Mexico
Peru
Puerto Rico
St Lucia **D**
South America on a
  Budget
Trinidad & Tobago
Yucatán

D: Rough Guide
DIRECTIONS for
short breaks

Available from all good bookstores

Africa & Middle East

Cape Town &
 the Garden Route
Dubai **D**
Egypt
Gambia
Jordan
Kenya
Marrakesh **D**
Morocco
South Africa, Lesotho
 & Swaziland
Tanzania
Tunisia
West Africa
Zanzibar

Travel Specials

First-Time Africa
First-Time Around
 the World
First-Time Asia
First-Time Europe
First-Time Latin
 America
Make the Most of
 Your Time on Earth
Travel with Babies &
 Young Children
Travel Online
Travel Survival
Ultimate Adventures
Walks in London
 & SE England
World Party

Maps

Algarve
Amsterdam
Andalucia
 & Costa del Sol
Argentina
Athens
Australia
Barcelona
Berlin
Boston & Cambridge
Brittany
Brussels
California
Chicago
Chile
Corsica
Costa Rica
 & Panama
Crete

Croatia
Cuba
Cyprus
Czech Republic
Dominican Republic
Dubai & UAE
Dublin
Egypt
Florence & Siena
Florida
France
Frankfurt
Germany
Greece
Guatemala & Belize
Iceland
India
Ireland
Italy
Kenya & Northern
 Tanzania
Lisbon
London
Los Angeles
Madrid
Malaysia
Mallorca
Marrakesh
Mexico
Miami & Key West
Morocco
New England
New York City
New Zealand
Northern Spain
Paris
Peru
Portugal
Prague
Pyrenees & Andorra
Rome
San Francisco
Sicily
South Africa
South India
Spain & Portugal
Sri Lanka
Tenerife
Thailand
Toronto
Trinidad & Tobago
Tunisia
Turkey
Tuscany

Venice
Vietnam, Laos
 & Cambodia
Washington DC
Yucatán Peninsula

Phrasebooks

Croatian
Czech
Dutch
Egyptian Arabic
French
German
Greek
Hindi & Urdu
Italian
Japanese
Latin American
 Spanish
Mandarin Chinese
Mexican Spanish
Polish
Portuguese
Russian
Spanish
Swahili
Thai
Turkish
Vietnamese

Computers

Blogging
eBay
FWD this link
iPhone
iPods, iTunes
 & music online
The Internet
Macs & OS X
MySpace
PlayStation Portable
Website Directory

Film & TV

American
 Independent Film
British Cult Comedy
Chick Flicks
Comedy Movies
Cult Movies
Film
Film Musicals
Film Noir
Gangster Movies
Horror Movies

Sci-Fi Movies
Westerns

Lifestyle

Babies
Ethical Living
Pregnancy & Birth
Running

Music Guides

The Beatles
The Best Music
 You've Never Heard
Blues
Bob Dylan
Book of Playlists
Classical Music
Elvis
Frank Sinatra
Heavy Metal
Hip-Hop
Led Zeppelin
Opera
Pink Floyd
Punk
Reggae
The Rolling Stones
Soul and R&B
Velvet Underground
World Music

Popular Culture

Classic Novels
Conspiracy Theories
Crime Fiction
Cult Fiction
The Da Vinci Code
Graphic Novels
His Dark Materials
Poker
Shakespeare
Superheroes
Tutankhamun
Unexplained
 Phenomena
Videogames

Science

The Brain
Climate Change
The Earth
Genes & Cloning
The Universe
Weather

ROUGH GUIDES

Small print and

Index

A Rough Guide to Rough Guides

Published in 1982, the first Rough Guide – to Greece – was a student scheme that became a publishing phenomenon. Mark Ellingham, a recent graduate in English from Bristol University, had been travelling in Greece the previous summer and couldn't find the right guidebook. With a small group of friends he wrote his own guide, combining a highly contemporary, journalistic style with a thoroughly practical approach to travelers' needs.

The immediate success of the book spawned a series that rapidly covered dozens of destinations. And, in addition to impecunious backpackers, Rough Guides soon acquired a much broader and older readership that relished the guides' wit and inquisitiveness as much as their enthusiastic, critical approach and value-for-money ethos.

These days, Rough Guides include recommendations from shoestring to luxury and cover more than 200 destinations around the globe, including almost every country in the Americas and Europe, more than half of Africa and most of Asia and Australasia. Our ever-growing team of authors and photographers is spread all over the world, particularly in Europe, the USA and Australia.

In the early 1990s, Rough Guides branched out of travel, with the publication of Rough Guides to World Music, Classical Music and the Internet. All three have become benchmark titles in their fields, spearheading the publication of a wide range of books under the Rough Guide name.

Including the travel series, Rough Guides now number more than 350 titles, covering: phrasebooks, waterproof maps, music guides from Opera to Heavy Metal, reference works as diverse as Conspiracy Theories and Shakespeare, and popular culture books from iPods to Poker. Rough Guides also produce a series of more than 120 World Music CDs in partnership with World Music Network.

Visit www.roughguides.com to see our latest publications.

Rough Guide travel images are available for commercial licensing at www.roughguidespictures.com

Rough Guide credits

Text editor: Harry Wilson
Layout: Anita Singh
Cartography: Maxine Repath, Rajesh Chhibber, Deshpal Dabas
Picture editor: Emily Taylor
Production: Rebecca Short
Proofreader: Elaine Pollard
Cover design: Chloë Roberts
Photographer: Anthony Pidgeon, Angus Oborn, Dan Bannister
Editorial: Ruth Blackmore, Andy Turner, Keith Drew, Edward Aves, Alice Park, Lucy White, Jo Kirby, James Smart, Natasha Foges, Róisín Cameron, Emma Traynor, Emma Gibbs, Kathryn Lane, Christina Valhouli, Monica Woods, Mani Ramaswamy, Lucy Cowie, Helen Ochyra, Amanda Howard, Lara Kavanagh, Alison Roberts, Joe Staines, Peter Buckley, Matthew Milton, Tracy Hopkins, Ruth Tidball; **Delhi** Madhavi Singh, Karen D'Souza, Lubna Shaheen
Design & Pictures: **London** Scott Stickland, Dan May, Diana Jarvis, Mark Thomas, Chloë Roberts, Nicole Newman, Sarah Cummins; **Delhi** Umesh Aggarwal, Ajay Verma, Jessica Subramanian, Ankur Guha, Pradeep Thapliyal, Sachin Tanwar, Nikhil Agarwal, Sachin Gupta

Production: Vicky Baldwin
Cartography: **London** Ed Wright, Katie Lloyd-Jones; **Delhi** Ashutosh Bharti, Rajesh Mishra, Animesh Pathak, Jasbir Sandhu, Karobi Gogoi, Alakananda Bhattacharya, Swati Handoo
Online: **London** George Atwell, Faye Hellon, Jeanette Angell, Fergus Day, Justine Bright, Clare Bryson, Aine Fearon, Adrian Low, Ezgi Celebi, Amber Bloomfield; **Delhi** Amit Verma, Rahul Kumar, Narender Kumar, Ravi Yadav, Debojit Borah, Rakesh Kumar, Ganesh Sharma, Shisir Basumatari
Marketing & Publicity: **London** Liz Statham, Niki Hanmer, Louise Maher, Jess Carter, Vanessa Godden, Vivienne Watton, Anna Paynton, Rachel Sprackett, Libby Jellie, Laura Vipond, Vanessa McDonald; **New York** Katy Ball, Judi Powers, Nancy Lambert; **Delhi** Ragini Govind
Manager India: Punita Singh
Reference Director: Andrew Lockett
Operations Manager: Helen Phillips
PA to Publishing Director: Nicola Henderson
Publishing Director: Martin Dunford
Commercial Manager: Gino Magnotta
Managing Director: John Duhigg

SMALL PRINT

Publishing information

This eighth edition published August 2009 by
Rough Guides Ltd,
80 Strand, London WC2R 0RL
14 Local Shopping Centre, Panchsheel Park, New Delhi 110017, India
Distributed by the Penguin Group
Penguin Books Ltd,
80 Strand, London WC2R 0RL
Penguin Group (USA)
375 Hudson Street, NY 10014, USA
Penguin Group (Australia)
250 Camberwell Road, Camberwell, Victoria 3124, Australia
Penguin Group (Canada)
195 Harry Walker Parkway N, Newmarket, ON, L3Y 7B3 Canada
Penguin Group (NZ)
67 Apollo Drive, Mairangi Bay, Auckland 1310, New Zealand
Cover concept by Peter Dyer.

Typeset in Bembo and Helvetica to an original design by Henry Iles.

Printed and bound in Singapore by SNP Security Printing Pte Ltd

© Rough Guide 2009

512pp includes index

A catalogue record for this book is available from the British Library

ISBN: 978-1-84836-174-4

Help us update

We've gone to a lot of effort to ensure that the eighth edition of **The Rough Guide to Florida** is accurate and up-to-date. However, things change – places get "discovered", opening hours are notoriously fickle, restaurants and rooms raise prices or lower standards. If you feel we've got it wrong or left something out, we'd like to know, and if you can remember the address, the price, the hours, the phone number, so much the better.

Please send your comments with the subject line "Rough Guide Florida Update" to ℮mail@roughguides.com. We'll credit all contributions and send a copy of the next edition (or any other Rough Guide if you prefer) for the very best emails.

Have your questions answered and tell others about your trip at ℗community.roughguides.com

Acknowledgements

Stephen Keeling: A big thank you to Kathye Susnjer, Reina Rojas Gonzalez and Robert Stoney in Key Biscayne, as well as the numerous chambers of commerce, local tipsters and Key lime pie makers that helped make researching this guide such a pleasure. Thanks also to Steve Horak and Andrew Rosenberg in New York, the judicious editing of Harry Wilson in London, and finally Tiffany Wu, whose love and support, as always, made this possible.

Rebecca Strauss: Thanks to the tourism boards of Daytona Beach, St Augustine, Jacksonville, Pensacola and Panama City. Thanks also to Andrea Farmer, Jay Humphries, Tangela Boyd and Tom Bartosek. As always, without the guidance and persistence of the editorial team at Rough Guides, with special thanks to Harry Wilson, this project would never have been completed.

Ross Velton: Thanks to editor Harry Wilson for his enthusiastic approach to the new edition of this guide.

The editor thanks the authors for their diligent, hard work and attention to detail; Anita Singh and the Delhi team for their excellent typesetting; Emily Taylor for her superb picture research and editing; Maxine Repath in London and Rajesh Chhibber in Delhi for their collective mapmaking skills; Elaine Pollard for her insightful proofreading; and Mani Ramaswamy, Andy Turner and all other Rough Guides editors and colleagues for their overall guidance.

Readers' letters

Thanks to all the readers who have taken the time to write in with comments and suggestions (and apologies if we've inadvertently omitted or misspelt anyone's name):

Barbara Bothwell, Amanda Briffa, V Harwood, Brian Heffernan, Bob Iles, Ita Kelly, Selene Murtagh, Roger Newman, Adrian Penn, Jerry van Beers

SMALL PRINT

Photo credits

All photos © Rough Guides except the following:

Introduction
Causeway, Biscayne Bay © Tim Kiusalaas/Corbis
Lifeguard tower, Miami © Axiom
Hawksbill sea turtle © Michael Patrick O'Neill/
  Alamy
Shark, Key West © Axiom
Big Pine Key © Visit Florida

Things not to miss
01 Kennedy Space Center © Kordcom Kordcom/
  Photolibrary
03 Captain Tony's Saloon, Key West © Richard
  Klune/Corbis
05 Manatee © Brandon Cole/Marine
  Photography/Alamy
06 Sanibel Island © Gabriel J. Jimenez/Estock
  Travel
07 Sunshine Skyway Bridge © Cameron
  Davidson/Jupiter Images
10 Amazing Adventures of Spider-Man ride
  © Courtesy of Universal Studios
11 Canoeing, the Everglades © Axiom
12 Expedition Everest Mountain ride © Courtesy
  of Orlando CVB
13 Stilt shack, Cedar Key © Paul Franklin/Alamy
14 Castillo de San Marcos, St Augustine
  © VisitFlorida.com
15 Apalachicola Trail © VisitFlorida.com

Coastal Florida color section
Caladesi Island State Park © St Petersburg/
  Clearwater Area CVB
Nightlife, South Beach © Visit Florida
Siesta Key © Tom Mackie/Alamy
Wild dolphins, Panama City © Visual&Written
  SL/Alamy
Elkhorn coral © Stephen Frink/Corbis

Unexpected Florida color section
Sankey's Rodeo School, Homestead © Gerrit De
  Heus/Alamy
Fountain, Celebration © Mark Peterson/Corbis
Plantation house © Andre Jenny/Alamy
Fantasy Fest © Getty Images
Salvador Dalí Museum, St Petersburg © David
  Lyons/Alamy
Horse racing, Hallandale Beach © EPA/Corbis
Paradise Lakes nudist camp © Karen Davis/Rex
  Features

Black and whites
p.126 Christ of the Deep © Michael Friedel/Rex
  Features
p.157 Hemingway Home and Museum © Sylvain
  Grandadam/Photolibrary

p.168 Big Cypress National Preserve © Stephen
  Frink Collection/Alamy
p.173 Anhinga Trail, the Everglades © Marvin
  Newman/Tips Images
p.177 Airboat driver and passengers, the
  Everglades © VisitFlorida.com
p.184 Boca Raton beach © Axiom
p.206 Morikami Museum and Japanese Gardens
  © Nick Greaves/Alamy
p.211 Palm Beach condominiums © Alan Schein
  Photography/Corbis
p.219 Spring training © The Star-Ledger/Corbis
p.232 Ringling Brothers and Barnum & Bailey
  poster © Bettman/Corbis
p.254 Edison and Ford Winter Estates Botanic
  Research Lab © Ilene MacDonald/Alamy
p.261 Blind Pass, Sanibel & Captiva Islands
  © World Stock Travel Image/PCL
p.267 Tin City, Naples © Ilene MacDonald/Alamy
p.303 The Simpsons, Universal Orlando Resort
  © Courtesy of Universal Studios
p.307 Killer whale, Seaworld © Courtesy of
  VisitFlorida.com
p.320 Aerial view of Jacksonville © Think Stock/
  Alamy
p.327 Nine-banded armadillo, Merritt Island
  National Wildlife Refuge © Martin Rugner/
  Photolibrary
p.345 Flagler College, St Augustine © Visitflorida
  .com
p.357 Dunes and bikes, Amelia Island © Bill
  Heinsohn/Alamy
p.362 Sponges, Tarpon Springs © Dennis
  Macdonald/Photolibrary
p.377 St Petersburg Pier © J Lightfoot/Jupiter
p.386 Don Cesar Hotel, St Petersburg © Jon
  Arnold Images Ltd/Alamy
p.388 Clearwater Beach © John Coletti/
  Photolibrary
p.397 Manatees, Crystal River © Andre Seale/
  Photolibrary
p.405 Ocala National Forest © Bruce Heinemann
  /Photolibrary
p.414 Seaside © M. Timothy O'Keefe/Alamy
p.420 Canopy Road, Tallahassee © Douglas
  Peebles/Photolibrary
p.428 Walluka Springs © Franz-Marc Frei/Corbis
p.451 National Naval Aviation Museum,
  Pensacola © Jim Schwabel/Photolibrary
p.462 Seminole women and children
  © Underwood & Underwood/Corbis
p.470 Protesters, Florida Supreme Court,
  Tallahassee © Reuters/Corbis

**ROUGH
GUIDES**

SMALL PRINT

Selected images from our guidebooks are available for licensing from:

ROUGHGUIDESPICTURES.COM

Index

Map entries are in colour.

A

accommodation...... 27–29
agents............................ 22
Ah-Tah-Thi-Ki Museum
.... 181
Air Force Armament
Museum..................... 446
air passes 22
airboat tours 176, 178,
310
airlines 22
alligators 12, 43, 169,
173, 339, 475,
Coastal Florida color
section
Amelia Island 356–360
Amtrak 26
Amtrak rail pass 22
Anastasia Island 339
Anheuser–Busch Brewery
.... 354
Animal Kingdom 296
Anna Maria Island........ 246
Antique Car Museum ... 425
Apalachee Indians 417,
458
Apalachicola 434
**Apalachicola National
Forest**.......... 16, 429–431
Apalachicola National
Forest 430
Appleton Museum of Art
.... 402
Art Deco 12, 67, 69, 72
ATMs.............................. 46
Avon Park 230

B

Bahia Honda State Park
.... 138, *Coastal Florida*
color section
Bailey-Matthews Shell
Museum..................... 259
banks.............................. 46
Barberville.................... 318
baseball 34
Atlanta Braves................. 35
Baltimore Orioles 190
Boston Red Sox........ 35, 252
Detroit Tigers 35
Florida Marlins 34, 218
Minnesota Twins 252
NY Mets 35, 218
NY Yankees........................ 35
spring training 35
St Louis Cardinals............ 218
Tampa Bay Rays........ 35, 379
basketball 35
Battle of Olustee........... 464
Bay of Pigs 87, 140,
468
beaches 67,
Coastal Florida color
section
bed and breakfast 28
beer 32
Bethune, Mary McLeod
.... 336, 421
Big Bend............. 395–401
Big Cypress National
Preserve............ 177, 207
Big Cypress Seminole
Reservation............... 180
Big Pine Key....... 138–140
Big Talbot Island........... 356
Biketoberfest and Bike
Week............... 332, 337
Billie Swamp Safari 181
birdlife....... 38, 476, *Coastal
Florida* color section
birdwatching.................. 38
Biscayne National Park
.... 101
Blackwater River State
Park 433
Blue Mountain Beach
.... 443
Blue Spring State Park
.... 318
Boca Raton 199–204
Boca Raton 200
Bok, Edward......... 314, 392
booking online 21
books 487–493
Bradenton........... 244–247
Bradenton 245
Brickell, William 55, 82
Brighton Seminole Indian
Reservation............... 228
Broward, Napoleon
Bonaparte 466
Bulow Plantation Ruins
.... 338
Busch Gardens............. 371
buses........................ 21, 25

C

Cabbage Key................ 263
Caladesi Island............. 389
Calusa, the 134, 270,
458
camping.................... 28, 37
Canaveral National
Seashore................... 327
canoeing.......... 15, 37, 101,
126, 174, 373, 430, 434
Captain Tony's Saloon... 12,
160
Captiva Island.............. 261
cars........................... 21, 23
Cassadaga 316,
Unexpected Florida color
section
Castro, Fidel 80, 87,
88, 468
Cedar Key...... 13, 399–401
Celebration 311,
Unexpected Florida color
section
Chalet Suzanne 392
children, traveling with ... 38
Chipley 432
Chokoloskee Island...... 180
cigars....................... 8, 370
Civil Rights movement
.... 468
Clearwater Beach........ 387,
388
Clearwater Marine
Aquarium 388
Clewiston..................... 229
climate 9
Cocoa.......................... 329
Cocoa Beach................ 328
Collier County Museum
.... 268
Collier, Barron...... 179, 264,
268
Conch Republic, The.... 144
coral reef 126, 479,
Coastal Florida color
section
Corkscrew Swamp
Sanctuary 264
cowboy culture.... 198, 227,
Unexpected Florida color
section
Crane Point 134

crime.................................40
Cross Creek..................406
CROW 259
Crystal River 13, 397
Cuban heritage..........8, 86, 150, 370
Cuban question, the.......87
Cummer Museum of Art and Gardens..............353
cycling 26, 61, 95, 117

D

Dalí, Salvador 381
Dania 188
Davie.............................198
Daytona 500 ....332, 337
Daytona Beach
..........................332–339, *Coastal Florida* color section
Daytona Beach 333
Daytona International Speedway..................337
De Funiak Springs........432
De Soto National Memorial 245
De Soto State Archeological Site......425
Deer Lake State Park 442
Deering, Charles.......94, 98
Deering, James 94
DeLand 317
Delray Beach 204
Destin 444
Devil's Millhopper 410
disabled travelers 49
Discovery Cove 307
Disney, Walt..................285
Disney's Hollywood Studios 295
diving.............36, 101, 126, 127, 130, 134, 149, 199, 214, 221, 438
Dog Island ....436, *Coastal Florida* color section
Dolphin Cove................128
Dolphin Research Center 123
dolphins..........96, 123, 128, 131, *Coastal Florida* color section
Dolphins Plus 127
Don Cesar Hotel..........384, 386

Don Garlits Museum of Drag Racing...............402
drinking...........................32
driving............................24
drug trade.....................469
Dry Tortugas National Park 164
Dudley Farm 410

E

eating 29–32
Eatonville 313
Eden Gardens State Park 442
Edison and Ford Winter Estates.......................253
Edison, Thomas............253
electricity 41
entry requirements 41
EPCOT 292–295
Everglades City 179
Everglades, the
..........................169–181, *Coastal Florida* color section
Everglades 170
Expedition Everest... 15, 296

F

Fakahatchee Strand Preserve State Park... 178
Falling Waters State Park 432
Fantasy Fest................162, *Unexpected Florida* color section
Fantasy of Flight...........391
Fernandina Beach
..........................357–360
festivals 34, 161
film, Florida on.... 480–486
Fisher, Carl 57, 71, 128
fishing 36, 127, 130, 134, 227, 229
Flagler Beach 339
Flagler College 345
Flagler Museum............210
Flagler, Henry 57, 80, 123, 136, 207, 210, 227, 345, 369, 465
Flamingo.......................174
flights..............................19
Florida Aquarium 368

Florida Canoe Trails System 37, 174
Florida Caverns State Park 431
Florida Holocaust Museum 380
Florida Keys History of Diving Museum..........130
Florida Keys Wild Bird Center.........................129
Florida Keys, the
.... 121–166
Florida Keys, the 122
Florida National Scenic Trail 37, 177, 430
Florida Panther National Wildlife Reserve.........178
Florida State University 421
food and drink 29–32
football............................35
Ford, Henry...........254, 332
Fort Barrancas..............451
Fort Caroline National Memorial....................349
Fort Clinch State Park 358
Fort de Soto Park........387, *Coastal Florida* color section
Fort Jefferson 164
FORT LAUDERDALE
.... 188–197
Fort Lauderdale 189
  accommodation 191
  airport................................. 190
  arrival 190
  bars 196
  beach 194
  boat tours.......................... 194
  gay and lesbian................ 197
  information 190
  Las Olas Boulevard.......... 193
  Museum of Art 192
  Museum of Discovery & Science........................... 193
  Nightlife............................. 196
  Restaurants....................... 195
  Riverwalk Arts and Entertainment District... 193
  Stranahan House 192
Fort Myers 250–256
Fort Myers....................251
Fort Myers Beach.........255
Fort Pierce 221–224
Fort Pierce 222
Fort Walton Beach........445
Fort Walton Culture 445, 458
Fountain of Youth 346
Frost, Robert 153

G

Gainesville 406–410
Gainesville..................... 407
Gamble Plantation........ 247
Gamble Rogers Memorial
State Recreation Area
.... 339
Gatorland..................... 309,
Unexpected Florida color
section
gay and lesbian travelers
.... 42
Gold Coast 186–216
Grayton Beach 443
Great Florida Birding Trail
.... 38
Greyhound Discovery Pass
.... 22
Gulf World Marine Park
.... 439
Gulfport 382

H

hammocks.................... 473
Harry Harris Park.......... 129
Havana 426
health........................... 43
Hemingway, Ernest 152,
156, 162
High Springs................. 411
hiking 36, 227, 405,
430, 434
Historic Bok Sanctuary
.... 392
history................. 457–471
hitching.......................... 26
Hohauser, Henry....... 69, 70
Hollywood..................... 187
Hollywood Seminole
Reservation................ 198
Homestead 100
Homosassa Springs 396
Honeymoon Island 389
Hontoon Island State Park
.... 318
horse country .... see
Unexpected Florida color
section
horseback riding...310, 403
hostels 28
hurricanes............. 469, 478
Hurston, Zora Neale....314,
421
Hutchinson Island........ 221

I

ice hockey 36, 190
immigration.................... 41
Indian Key..................... 131
Indian Temple Mound
Museum..................... 446
insurance....................... 43
internet 44
Islamorada 129–133
Islands of Adventure 303

J

J.N. "Ding" Darling National
Wildlife Refuge 260
Jackson Trail................. 434
Jacksonville 350–355
Jacksonville 351
Jacksonville beaches
.... 348–350
Jacksonville Jaguars 354
Jacksonville Zoo........... 354
John Pennekamp Coral
Reef State Park...125–127
Jonathan Dickinson State
Park 219
Juno Beach 217
Jupiter 217

K

Kanapaha Botanical
Gardens 410
kayaking 80, 101,
126, 138, 174, 225, 262,
373, 430, 434
Kennedy Space Center
.... 11, 323–326
Key Biscayne................. 96
Key deer 138
Key Largo 124–128
Key lime pie......... 128, 136,
159, 206
Key Marco Cat 270
KEY WEST 142–164
Key West...................... 143
accommodation 146–148
airport............................... 145
arrival............................... 145
Audubon House 152
Bahama Village 157
bars 160
bike rentals...................... 145
buses 145

Butterfly Conservatory 150
Conch Tour Train.............. 145
Customs House 152
Curry Mansion................. 153
Ernest Hemingway Home and
Museum....................... 156
Fantasy Fest 162,
Unexpected Florida color
section
festivals 161
Florida Keys Eco-Discovery
Center 154
Fort East Martello Museum
and Gardens................. 158
Fort Zachary Taylor Historic
State Park..................... 155
gay and lesbian............... 162
Heritage House Museum
.... 153
Historic Seaport 153
information 145
internet 163
Key lime pie 159
Key West Aquarium 151
Key West Cemetery 155
Lighthouse Museum 157
Little White House Museum
.... 154
Mallory Square................ 150
Mel Fisher Maritime Heritage
Society Museum 151
nightlife........................... 160
restaurants 158–160
San Carlos Institute 149
Secret Garden................. 156
Shipwreck Historeum....... 151
Sloppy Joe's 161
tours 145
Truman Annex 154
Wrecker's Museum 149
Kingsley Plantation....... 355
Kissimmee........... 309–311
Koreshan State Historic
Site 263
Ku Klux Klan................. 464,
466, 467

L

Lake Okeechobee 226
Lake Wales 391
Lake Woodruff National
Wildlife Refuge 317
Lake Worth 206
Lakeland....................... 390
Lantana......................... 206
Lapidus, Morris 72, 75
Lauderdale-By-The-Sea
.... 199
laundry............................ 44
Lee County Manatee Park
.... 256

Leon Sinks Geological Area 427
Liberty City riots 468
Lido Key 241
Lignumvitae Key 132
Lion Country Safari 216
Little Talbot Island State Park 356
living in Florida 44
lobsters 477
Long Key State Park 132
Looe Key Marine Sanctuary 140
Lovers Key State Park 255
Lower Suwannee National Wildlife Refuge 400
Loxahatchee National Wildlife Refuge 203

M

Maclay State Gardens 425
Magic Kingdom 291
mail 45
Maitland 314
manatees .... 13, 180, 223, 245, 256, 396, 476, *Coastal Florida* color section
maps 45
Marathon 134–136
Marco Island 269
Mariel boatlift 87
Marineland 339
Marjorie Kinnan Rawlings Home 406
media 33
Menéndez de Aviles, Pedro 459
Merrick, George 57, 88, 89, 90–92, 466
Merritt Island National Wildlife Refuge .... 326, *Coastal Florida* color section
MIAMI 54–118
Miami 56
Coral Gables 89
Downtown Miami 77
South Beach 68
accommodation 62–66
Adrienne Arsht Center for the Performing Arts 80
airport 57
arrival 57
ArtCenter/South Florida 72

Art Deco 67, 69, 72
Art Deco District 67
Art Deco Walking Tour 62
Bal Harbour 75
Barnacle Historic State Park 93
bars 107–109
Bass Museum of Art 73
Bayside Marketplace 79
beaches 67
bike rental 117
Bill Baggs Cape Florida State Recreation Area 97
Biltmore Hotel 92
Biscayne Bay 80
Biscayne Corridor 82–86
Biscayne National Park 101
boat rental 117
boat tours 80, 101
Boca Chita Key 101
Brickell 82
Britto Central 72
buses 60
Calle Ocho 86
car rental 59, 117
Casa Casuarina 69
Central Miami Beach 74
Children's Museum 76
Coconut Grove 93–95
Coral Castle 100
Coral Gables 88–93
Coral House 71
cycling 61, 95, 117
Davie 198
De Soto Boulevard 91
Design District 84
Downtown Miami 76–82
driving 59
Elliott Key 101
Ermita de la Caridad 95
Española Way 71
Fairchild Tropical Garden ... 98
festivals 112, 113
film 112
Flagler Memorial Island 80
Flagler Street 77
Fontainebleau 75
Freedom Tower 80
Fruit and Spice Park 99
gay and lesbian 114
Golden Beach 76
Haulover Beach Park .... 75, *Coastal Florida* color section
Historical Museum of Southern Florida 78
Holocaust Memorial 73
Homestead 100
Ichimura Miami-Japan Garden 76
information 59
Jackie Gleason Theater 73
Jungle Island 76
Kampong Garden 94
Key Biscayne 96
Lincoln Road Mall 71
Little Haiti 85

Little Havana 86–88
live music 110
Lowe Art Museum 93
Metro-Dade Cultural Center 78
Metromover 61
Metrorail 60
Metrozoo 99
Miami Art Museum 14, 78
Miami Beach 67–76
Miami Beach Post Office 71
Miami Circle 78, 81
Miami Dolphins 35, 190
Miami Heat 35
Miami River 81
Miami Science Museum 95
Miami Seaquarium 96
MiMo 72, 75
Miracle Mile 90
Monkey Jungle 100
Museum of Contemporary Art 86
Museum Park 79
nightlife 109
Normandy Isle 75
North Beach 75
Ocean Drive .... 67, *Coastal Florida* color section
Overtown 81
Park West 80, 109
restaurants 102–107
shopping 115
South Beach ....67–74, *Coastal Florida* color section
South Miami 98–100
South Pointe 74
Stiltsville 97
Sunny Isles Beach 76
SuperShuttle 58
Surfside 75
taxis 61
theater 112
Torch of Friendship 79
tours 61
trains 58
Venetian Pool 91
Virginia Key 96
Vizcaya Museum and Gardens 94
Watson Island 76
Wolfsonian-FIU 71
World Erotic Art Museum 71
Wynwood Art District 83
Ziff Jewish Museum of Florida 74
Micanopy 406
Miccosukee Indian Village 175
MiMo 72, 75
Mission San Luis 425
Mizner, Addison 201, 207, 210, 215, 466
money 46
Morikami Museum 205

Mount Dora 316
Museum of Man in the Sea
.... 439
Museum of the Arts and
Sciences (Daytona).... 337
Myakka River State Park
.... 247

N

Naples................. 264–269
Naples 265
NASA 326, 468
national and state parks
Apalachicola National Forest
.... 16, 429–431
Apalachicola National Forest
.... 430
Bahia Honda State Park
.... 138, Coastal Florida
color section
Big Cypress National Preserve
.... 177
Biscayne National Park
.... 101
Blue Spring State Park 318
Canaveral National Seashore
.... 327
Dry Tortugas National Park
.... 164
Eden Gardens State Park
.... 442
Everglades National Park
.... 169–181
Fakahatchee Strand Preserve
State Park 178
Florida Caverns State Park
.... 431
Florida National Scenic Trail
.... 37
Florida Panther National
Wildlife Reserve 178
Fort Clinch State Park 358
Hontoon Island State Park
.... 318
Indian Key 131
J.N. "Ding" Darling National
Wildlife Refuge.............. 260
John Pennekamp Coral Reef
State Park 125–127
Jonathan Dickinson State
Park 219
Lake Woodruff National
Wildlife Refuge.............. 317
Lignumvitae Key 132
Little Talbot Island State Park
.... 356
Long Key State Park........ 132
Looe Key Marine Sanctuary
.... 140
Lovers Key State Park 255
Lower Suwannee National
Wildlife Refuge.............. 400

Loxahatchee National Wildlife
Refuge 203
Merritt Island National Refuge
.... 326, Coastal Florida
color section
Myakka River State Park
.... 247
Naples Museum of Art 268
National Key Deer Refuge
.... 139
Ocala National Forest 404
Ocala National Forest 404
Rainbow Springs State Park
.... 402
Sebastian Inlet State Park
.... 225
St Joseph Peninsula State
Park 436
St Marks National Wildlife
Refuge 427
Tomoka State Park........... 338
Weeki Wachee Springs State
Park 395
National Key Deer Refuge
.... 139
National Naval Aviation
Museum...................... 450
Natural Bridge Battlefield
State Historic Site 427
Natural Florida 472–479
Naval Live Oaks
Reservation................ 453
Navarre Beach................ 454
New Smyrna Beach 331
newspapers 33
No Name Pub....... 139, 142
North Hutchinson Island
.... 224
Northeast Florida
.... 321–360
Northeast Florida......... 322
Northwest Florida
.... 363–412
Northwest Florida........ 364
nudist resorts......... 76, 376,
Unexpected Florida color
section

O

Ocala.................... 401–403
Ocala Hiking Trail 405
Ocala National Forest
.... 404
Ocala National Forest 404
Okaloosa Island............ 445
Okeechobee town 227
ORLANDO 273–284
Orlando 274

Downtown Orlando 280
Greater Orlando........... 277
Orlando's northern
suburbs 313
accommodation 277–279
airport................... 273, 275
Aquatica 308
arrival............................. 273
bars 284
CityWalk 305
Discovery Cove............... 307
Downtown Orlando ...279–281
Harry P. Leu Gardens....... 281
Holy Land Experience...... 308
information 275
International Drive........... 281
Islands of Adventure 303
Loch Haven Park 281
nightlife.......................... 284
Orlando Magic 35
Orlando Museum of Art ... 281
Orlando Science Center
.... 281
Pirate's Cove Adventure Golf
.... 308
restaurants 282–284
SeaWorld Orlando.....305–307
SkyVenture 308
transportation.................. 276
Universal Orlando 301–305
Walt Disney World....284–301,
409
Wet 'n' Wild..................... 309
Wonderworks 309
Osceola 462
Overseas Highway (US-1)
.... 123, 136

P

Palm Beach......... 207–213
Palm Beach 208
Panama City Beach
.... 436–441,
Coastal Florida color
section
Panama City Beach..... 437
Panhandle, the
.... 415–454
Panhandle, the............. 416
Paradise Lakes............376,
Unexpected Florida
color section
parking............................ 24
Paynes Prairie 406
Peanut Island................ 211
Pebble Hill Plantation
.... 426
Pensacola............ 446–453
Pensacola 447
Pensacola Beach 454

Pensacola Historic District
....................................449
Perdido Key...................454
Perky's Bat Tower.........140
phones...........................47
pick-your-own fruit 229
Pigeon Key 137
Pinellas Trail..................384
poisonwood tree 37
Ponce de León, Juan ...458
Ponte Vedra Beach 348
Port St Joe 436
public holidays 46
Punta Gorda 249

Q

Quincy 431

R

radio stations.................33
Rainbow Springs State
    Park 402
Rawlings, Marjorie Kinnan
   406
Reptile World Serpentarium
   310,
    Unexpected Florida color
    section
Ringling Brothers...238, 467
Ringling Museum of Art
   237

S

sales tax 39
Salvador Dalí Museum
    .... 381, Unexpected
    Florida color section
St Andrews State
    Recreation Area.........440
St Augustine.................16,
    340–348, 459
St Augustine: The old
    town 341
St Augustine Alligator Farm
   339
St George's Island........435
St Joseph Peninsula State
    Park 436
St Marks National Wildlife
    Refuge 427

St Petersburg......376–382
St Petersburg...............378
St Petersburg beaches
   383–390
St Vincent Island 436
Sanford 315
Sanibel Island 15,
    257–261, Coastal Florida
    color section
Sanibel Island 259
Sanibel-Captiva
    Conservation Foundation
   259
Santa Rosa Beach........443
Santería 85
SARASOTA 233–244
Sarasota.......................236
Sarasota, Downtown...238
    accommodation 235
    airport...............................234
    arrival................................234
    Asolo Theater...................240
    bars 243
    beaches............................240
    bike rental 235
    bookstores 237
    buses 235
    FSU Center for the Performing
        Arts 240
    gay nightlife......................244
    information 235
    Lido Key 241
    nightlife.............................243
    restaurants 242
    Ringling Museum of Art
       237
    Sarasota Classic Car Museum
       240
    Siesta Key 241
    theater..............................244
Seagrove Beach 442
Seaside........................442,
    Unexpected Florida color
    section
SeaWorld Orlando
   305–307
Sebastian Inlet State Park
   225
Sebring 230
Seminole Indians and
    Seminole Wars 176,
    180, 198, 228, 460,
    461–462
senior travelers 48
Seven Mile Bridge 136
Shark Valley..................175
Shell Island 440
shells 260, 477
Siesta Key 241
Silver Springs 402
Singer Island.................217
snakes 43, 310

snorkeling 36, 101, 125,
    127, 130, 134, 137, 138,
    149
Sombrero Beach 134
Soto, Hernando de........91,
    245, 425, 458
South Florida Museum
   244
South Walton beaches
   441
Southeast Florida
   185–230
Southeast Florida 186
Southwest Florida
   233–270
Southwest Florida 234
Southwest Florida Museum
    of History 253
Space Coast, the
   323–331
Space Coast, the.........324
Space Mountain 291
sponge docks...............394
sports......................34–38
Spring Break..........34, 189,
    332, 437
springs, warm–water 404
Stephen Foster Folk
    Culture Center 411
Stetson University 317
Stuart............................220
student discounts...........46
study programs 45
Suncoast Seabird
    Sanctuary 387
Sunken Gardens...........381
Sunshine Skyway Bridge
    ....14, 383

T

Talbot Islands 356
TALLAHASSEE.... 417–424
Tallahassee 418
    accommodation 419
    Antique Car Museum.......425
    arrival................................417
    bars 424
    Black Archives Research
        Center and Museum.....421
    downtown 420
    Florida State University....421
    information 419
    Knott House Museum......422
    Mary Brogan Museum of Art
        and Science.................421
    Museum of Florida History
       421
    nightlife.............................424

Old City Cemetery 422
plantations 422
restaurants 423
transportation................. 419
Tampa Bay.......... 365–395
Tampa Bay and the
    Northwest................ 364
Tampa Bay area.......... 366
TAMPA 365–376
Downtown Tampa........ 369
Ybor City 369
    accommodation 367
    airport............................ 365
    arrival............................ 365
    bars............................... 375
    Busch Gardens 371
    Downtown...................... 368
    Florida Aquarium............ 368
    gay and lesbian.............. 375
    Henry B. Plant Museum
    370
    Hillsborough River State Park
    373
    Hyde Park 370
    information 365
    Lowry Park Zoo............... 372
    Museum of Science and
        Industry..................... 373
    nightlife......................... 374
    restaurants 374
    Tampa Bay Hotel............. 369
    Tampa Museum of Art 368
    Tampa Theatre 368, 375
    transportation................. 367
    Ybor City 370
Tarpon Springs.... 393–395
Tarpon Springs 395
Tavernier 129
Telegraph Cypress Swamp
    249
telephones.................... 47
temperatures, average ... 10
Ten Thousand Islands
    179
Tequesta, the.... 55, 82, 458
The Villages .... see
    Unexpected Florida color
    section
Theater of the Sea........ 131
theme parks 9
    Animal Kingdom............. 296

Blizzard Beach 297
Busch Gardens 371
Discovery Cove............... 307
EPCOT 292–295
Islands of Adventure 303
Magic Kingdom............... 291
SeaWorld Orlando.....305–307
Space Mountain.............. 291
Typhoon Lagoon 298
Universal Orlando 14,
    301–305
Walt Disney World....284–301,
    469
Walt Disney World.......... 286
Wet 'n' Wild.................... 309
Thomasville 426
time zone....................... 48
tipping 40
Titusville.......................330
Tomoka State Park.......338
tourist information 48
trains.........................21, 26
travelers' checks 46
Treasure Coast.... 216–225
Tri-Rail 26
Truman, Harry S 154
Turtle Hospital 135
turtles..............135, *Coastal*
    Florida color section
TV 33

Universal Orlando........ 14,
    301–305
University of Florida 408
Upper Matecumbe Key
    130

Venice 248
Vero Beach 224
visas 41

Wakulla Springs............ 428
Walt Disney World
    .... 284–301, 469
Walt Disney World 286
    accommodation 287–289
    Animal Kingdom............. 296
    Blizzard Beach 297
    cruise line...................... 299
    Disney Institute 299
    Disney's Hollywood Studios
    295
    Downtown Disney............ 298
    EPCOT 292–295
    FastPass 290
    Magic Kingdom............... 291
    restaurants 300
    Richard Petty Driving
        Experience.................. 299
    Space Mountain.............. 291
    tickets............................ 291
    transportation................. 287
    Typhoon Lagoon 298
    Wide World of Sports....... 299
watersports..................... 36
Weeki Wachee Springs
    State Park.................. 395
West Palm Beach
    213–216
West Palm Beach 208
Wilderness Waterway... 174
Williams, Tennessee 153,
    155
wine 32
Winter Park................... 312
working in Florida........... 44
Wright, Frank Lloyd 390

Yankeetown 398

Map symbols

maps are listed in the full index using colored text

– – –	Chapter boundary	⟋⟍	Marsh
—··—	State boundary	⟍⟋⟍	Spring/spa
▬⟨95⟩▬	Interstate	⟟	Lighthouse
=⟨2⟩=	U.S. highway	@	Internet
=⟨27⟩=	State highway	ⓘ	Information office
=⟨33⟩=	Secondary state highway	★	Bus stop
——	Unpaved	✈	International airport
- - - -	Walking path/bicycle trail	✈	Air Force base
——	River	🅿	Parking
— —	Ferry route	) (	Bridge
▬●▬	Railway	⊠	Gate
——	Wall	⊞	Hospital
🏛	Stately home	⊠	Post office
⟟	Garden	♦	Point of interest
♥	Museum	⊙	Statue
▮	Tower	⚠	Campground
♯	Castle	◉	Accommodation
Ⓜ	Metro	+—	Church
⏚	Observatory		Building
⼤	Picnic area	⊞	Cemetery
⚓	River boat		Park
ⱦ	Monastery		Beach
⚔	Battlefield	⧄	Indian reservation